IF HITLER HAD WON

THE PLANS HE MADE
THE PLANS HE CARRIED OUT
THE PLANS HE HOPED TO ACHIEVE

by

Richard E. Osborne

Riebel-Roque Publishing Company, Inc.

Indianapolis, Indiana

ISBN 0-9628324-6-4
Date of Publication 2004

Published and printed in the U.S.A.
Book design and production by **Steve Miller**

Editorial advice and assistance provided by
Sara Streeter

The author is grateful for the technical
advice on military matters provided by
Major General Richard D. Chegar, AUS(ret)

RIEBEL-ROQUE PUBLISHING COMPANY, INC.
6027 Castlebar Circle
Indianapolis, Indiana 46220

Other books by author:

WORLD WAR II SITES IN THE UNITED STATES
CASABLANCA COMPANION
WORLD WAR II IN COLONIAL AFRICA
TOUR BOOK FOR ANTIQUE CAR BUFFS

TABLE OF CONTENTS

INTRODUCTION

If Hitler, along with his depraved and murderous cohorts, had won World War II, the world would not have looked or functioned as it did in the last half of the twentieth century. Germany would have become a police state dominating most of Europe and controlling the lives of hundreds of millions of people. This criminal state would have become a super power, equipped with atomic weapons, and every bit as strong and impregnable as any other super power of its day. Any attempt to rid the world of this evil force by military means would have been unthinkable. The only hope would have been that it disintegrated on its own accord as had been the fate of past dictatorial empires. But that took time — lots of time.

Germany's major ally, Italy, controlled by the pompous dictator, Benito Mussolini, would also have become a super power and a police state, and, very likely, would have acquired atomic weapons. It too would have controlled the lives of hundreds of millions of people.

This book examines the historical records of the plans the Axis leaders made for that glorious day when they would have attained victory. Those plans are interpreted and projected into a scenario of what might have happened if Hitler had won.

The plans that Hitler and his cohorts made were extensive and surprisingly detailed. They included everything from the geopolitical and economic restructuring of Europe to the selection of music that was to be played from the bell tower of Hitler's crypt.

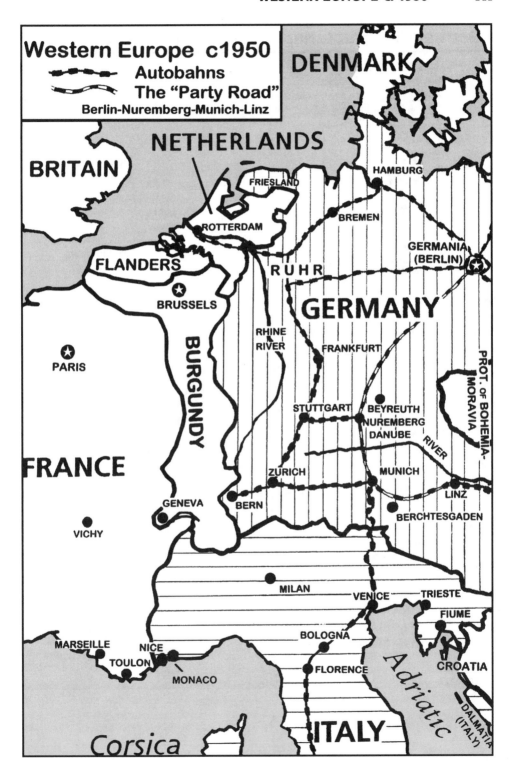

Western Europe c1950
Autobahns
The "Party Road"
Berlin-Nuremberg-Munich-Linz

Germany's Structuring of European Russia — 1918

FINLAND

Lake Ladoga

Lake Onega

Gulf of Finland

Petrograd

N

Volga R.

Gulf of Riga

Kurland Pen.

RUSSIA (Civil war)

Riga

KURLAND (to be annexed by Germany)

Moscow

GERMANY

Minsk

BELORUSSIA (WHITE RUSSIA) (Independent)

Warsaw

Brest-Litovsk

Don R.

POLAND (Independent)

Kiev

UKRAINE (Independent)

Dnieper R.

AUSTRIA-HUNGARY

Sea of Azov

CAUCASUS (Future undetermined)

ROMANIA

CRIMEA (Ukraine)

SERBIA

Bucharest

Danube R.

Eastern Europe c1950

Autobahns

□ **New all-German cities**

▦ **Administered from Germania**

◉◉ **German settlements, Hitler's "Strings of Pearls."**

The Armed Frontier
c1950

Armed Frontier

Autobahns

Admin. from Germania

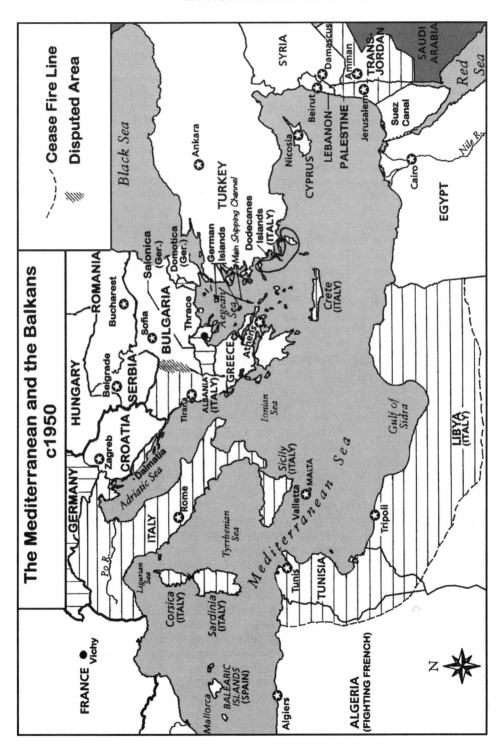

The Mediterranean and the Balkans
c1950

Cease Fire Line

Disputed Area

FRANCE ● Vichy

GERMANY

HUNGARY

ROMANIA

Bucharest

Belgrade

CROATIA

SERBIA

Zagreb

Tiranë

ALBANIA (ITALY)

BULGARIA

Sofia

Salonica (Ger.)

Domotica (Ger.)

Thrace

GREECE

Athens

Aegean Sea

German Islands

Main Shipping Channel

Dodecanes Islands (ITALY)

TURKEY

Ankara

Black Sea

Crete (ITALY)

Ionian Sea

Dalmatia

Adriatic Sea

ITALY

Rome

Po R.

Ligurian Sea

Tyrrhenian Sea

Corsica (ITALY)

Sardinia (ITALY)

Mallorca

BALEARIC ISLANDS (SPAIN)

Algiers

ALGERIA (FIGHTING FRENCH)

Tunis

TUNISIA

Sicily (ITALY)

MALTA

Valletta

Mediterranean Sea

Tripoli

Gulf of Sidra

LIBYA (ITALY)

EGYPT

Nile R.

Cairo

Suez Canal

Jerusalem

PALESTINE

LEBANON

Beirut

Nicosia

CYPRUS

SYRIA

Damascus

Amman

TRANS-JORDAN

SAUDI ARABIA

Red Sea

N

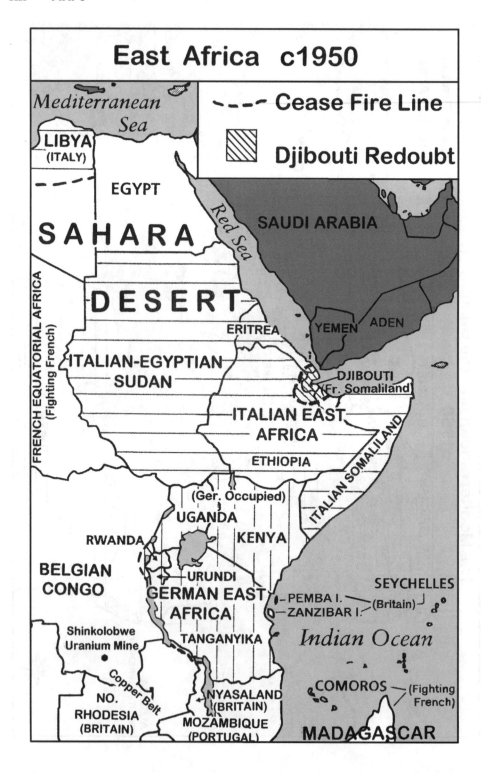

East Africa c1950

- - - Cease Fire Line

Djibouti Redoubt

CHAPTER 1

🔊 LINKUP AT THE SVIR RIVER

November 13, 1941: This was a day of great rejoicing at Hitler's headquarters in East Prussia because word had just been received that German and Finnish forces had made contact with each other at the Svir River 90 miles east-northeast of Leningrad. This action severed the last Soviet supply route into Leningrad. The city was surrounded and it would now be only a matter of time until the Soviet forces there would be starved into submission. ☑️

READER'S NOTE

It is at this point in the war that we deviate from the true history of World War II and begin our interpretive account of what might have happened if Hitler had won.

The action described above never happened. The Germans and Finns tried to link up at the Svir River but failed. This allowed the Soviets to retain a supply corridor to Leningrad that remained open throughout the siege. This, in turn, forced the Germans to keep a large number of forces engaged in the north.

That supply corridor ran from the town of Tikhvin, 115 miles east of Leningrad, to Lake Ladoga, across the lake by boat in summer, and across the ice by truck in winter, to the environs of Leningrad.

Reinforcements and supplies sent by this route, though meager at times, were sufficient to enable the troops and citizens of Leningrad to withstand their heroic 880-day siege.

In our scenario, however, that supply route was cut by the linkup of the Germans and Finns at the Svir River, and Leningrad eventually surrendered. This, then, released a large part of the German Army to disengage at Leningrad and march on Moscow. *(continued)*

The next interpretive event occurred in September 1942, when the Axis troops, trapped at Stalingrad, were rescued and that city was then besieged and eventually surrendered.

THE OSBORNE-MILLER METHOD FOR THE DIFFERENTIATION OF HISTORICAL EVENTS

Since this book is a blend of historical and interpretive events, the author has devised the following method, utilizing icons, to enable the reader to differentiate between the two:

> The text of this book is to be considered factual history until the symbol 🔒 **and bolder type** are encountered. At that point the text that follows is the author's interpretation and projection of historical events.

> When the ☑ symbol is encountered, the text returns to factual history until the next 🔒 symbol is encountered.

EXAMPLE:

> World War II in Europe began on September 1, 1939. 🔒 **It ended on July 4, 1945. Soon afterwards, Hitler went into retirement.** ☑ On August 6, 1945, the Americans dropped the first atomic bomb on Japan. In early September, Japan surrendered unconditionally to the Allies.

CHAPTER 2

"REICH"

Reich! This is a word that the Germans have used for centuries to describe the times when Germany was a dominant military and political power in central Europe. Always accompanying these periods of strength were wars and German territorial expansion.

The First Reich was the Holy Roman Empire that lasted from 962 to 1806. It stretched from the Baltic Sea to the Mediterranean, and from the borders of France deep into the present-day countries of Poland and Hungary. In its latter years the Holy Roman Empire disintegrated into a few large, and many small, independent states. This unstable condition lasted until 1864 when Otto von Bismarck, Prime Minister and Secretary of Foreign Affairs of Prussia, the largest of the fragmented German states, began a program of reuniting Germany. Bismarck used the threat of force, as well as force itself, to bring about a united German state under the King of Prussia, Wilhelm I. Bismarck's activities perpetrated several wars, the last and most costly being the Franco-Prussian War of 1870–71, which the Prussians won. This victory was the final act in bringing about a revitalized and powerful Germany which, in turn, became the Second German Reich. Bismarck's Germany was not formally known as the Second German Reich although Bismarck was given the title of Reichschancellor. King Wilhelm, now having a large and united country, took unto himself the title "Kaiser" (German for Caesar), a title used by several of the emperors of the Holy Roman Empire.

With the defeat of France in 1871, German expansionism ended mainly because Bismarck believed that it was more important to consolidate Germany's gains than risk further wars to acquire more territory. Others in Germany did not share Bismarck's belief and the dream of expanding German territory lingered on among various segments of the German population.

In the late 1800s, Germany joined the race for overseas colonies along with the other major European powers. She gained several major colonies in Africa, several island groups in the Pacific and a large concession in China. In Africa, Germany's plans to build a huge colonial empire had been extravagant. She had hoped to colonize virtually all of central Africa, generally referred to by the Germans as "Mittel Afrika." That dream was shattered by the actions of the other European nations but Germany, nevertheless, managed to gain several large and valuable colonies. This did not satisfy the pan-Germanists who felt they had been cheated by the other European powers.

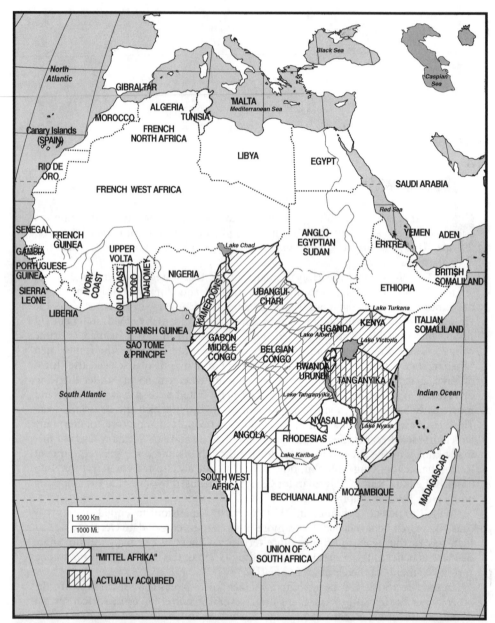

Germany's hope and Germany's reality. Germany hoped to build a huge colonial empire in the heart of Africa that spread from the Atlantic Ocean to the Indian Ocean. They called it "Mittel Afrika." What Germany got was considerably less.

DREAMS FOR GERMAN EXPANSION IN EUROPE

In 1894, the "All Deutscher Verband" (Pan-German League) was formed in Germany to promote German expansion, primarily in Europe. It gained strong popular support and grew rapidly. The League was also racist, openly criticizing the Kaiser's government for Germany's alliance with non-German nations such as the Austro-Hungarian Empire, the Ottoman Empire and Bulgaria.

During the 1910s, a young Austrian named Adolf Hitler was one of the many who supported the League and its programs although he never became a formal member.

There were other organizations during these years that also supported German expansionism: "The Society for the Eastern Marches," "The Colonial Society," "The Defense League," and "The Navy League." Another form of German expansionism was expressed by the Kaiser's much-publicized scheme to build a Berlin-to-Baghdad railroad. This would extend German influence throughout the Balkans and deep into the Middle East.

THE IMPRESSIONABLE FUTURE FUEHRER

In September 1907, 18-year-old Adolf Hitler, a high school dropout, left his home in Linz, Austria for what he hoped would be a better life in Vienna. Vienna was the capital of the Austro-Hungarian Empire, which was a vast multi-cultural empire with twelve major ethnic groups. It bordered Germany on the north, Russia on the east, Italy on the south and sprawled across central Europe and into the Balkans.

Hitler, an aspiring artist, hoped to enroll in the prestigious Academy of Fine Arts and make painting his life's career. However, he failed to meet the entrance qualifications because the paintings he submitted did not meet the admissions board's standards. His art work regarding architecture was quite good, but he was weak when it came to painting the human figure. His rejection notice stated curtly, "Sample drawings inadequate, few heads."

Hitler then tried to enroll in an architectural school in Vienna but was denied admission because he did not have a high school diploma. Following these rejections, the now-embittered young man fell on hard times but was able to survive on his own by selling hand-painted postcards and an occasional painting. At times, he worked as a decorative painter on construction and renovation projects, and as a common laborer.

Hitler's bitterness turned him against the city of Vienna and its citizens who comprised a very visible assortment of the nationalities and races from throughout the Austro-Hungarian Empire. With time on his hands, young Hitler became an avid reader of newspapers, periodicals and books, many of them politically oriented. It was at this time, and due to these influences, that he drifted to the far right in his political thinking. And, as a part of this orientation, Hitler fell in with the Austrian pan-Germanist who had long called for the German-speaking province of Austria to detach itself from the polyglot Austro-Hungarian Empire and unite with Germany.

Hitler was impressed by several right-wing political writers of the day. One such man was Lanz von Liebenfels who used the swastika as his symbol and was greatly concerned about syphilis, cancer and castration. Another writer, named List, advocated ridding all of Europe of the "dark ones" and "undermen" (untermenschen) and creating a large German state headed by a strong and dictatorial leader ("fuehrer"). List further recommended that political districts, called Gaus, be created and headed by Gauleiters (Gau leaders) who were absolutely loyal to the national leader and independent of all local political controls.

Another writer and pamphleteer, Adolf Harpf, used the word "Aryan" to describe the Germanic people of Europe, and advocated an Aryan crusade be undertaken to conquer the territories and slavic peoples of the east. Once accomplished, those vast and productive lands would be turned into Aryan-dominated colonies and the indigenous peoples relegated to the status of colonial subjects.

Another piece of grey literature circulating Europe at this time was a book entitled "Protocols of the Elders of Zion" which claimed to have uncovered a plot perpetrated by the leaders of international Jewry to take over the world by economic means. It is generally believed that the book is a

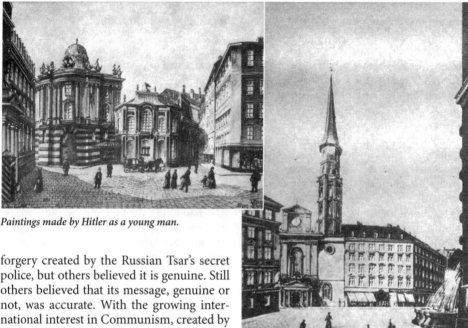

Paintings made by Hitler as a young man.

forgery created by the Russian Tsar's secret police, but others believed it is genuine. Still others believed that its message, genuine or not, was accurate. With the growing international interest in Communism, created by the Jew, Karl Marx, it was easy for many to believe that the book's prophecies were coming true. It is not known if Hitler read the Protocols book, but it is almost certain that he knew of its existence and its message.

Hitler flatly rejected the tenants of Communism. But being an impoverished artist, and believing that governments could do more for the people, he was drawn toward the political philosophy of the socialist. Most of the socialist organizations of the times, however, supported international socialism which preached that all peoples should be treated equally and united into a world-wide socialist society. Hitler opposed this form of internationalism in favor of a socialist program that would be tailored exclusively for the German people.

In addition to studying politics, Hitler became an ardent lover of the theater and opera, and found time to attend those events, always sitting in the cheapest seats or standing in the gallery. He also found time to dabble in writing plays and even tried writing an opera. During this time, Hitler discovered motion pictures and became an ardent fan of that form of entertainment. There was one form of stage entertainment, however, that Hitler rejected. That was the cabarets. He considered them decadent and unworthy of the German people.

In December 1907, just before Christmas, Hitler's mother died of breast cancer. Hitler's father had died four years earlier in 1903. His father was 19 years older than his mother. With the passing of his mother, Hitler was now an orphan. He acquired a small inheritance from his mother's estate and a small, state-provided, orphan's pension which he would receive until he was 24. This money enabled him to continue living in Vienna as a struggling artist.

As if 1907 were not bad enough for young Adolf, an event on the political scene gave the young Austrian another cause for concern. During that year, Britain, France and Russia signed the "Triple Entente", a political and military pact designed to surround and contain Germany and Germany's ally, Austro-Hungary. Hitler was now able to direct much of his anger outward toward Britain, France and Russia.

But at this point in Hitler's life, it was not Britain, France or Russia that were his main concern. At the top of Hitler's hate list were the Jews. They comprised about 9% of Vienna's population and thousands more were steadily streaming into the city from the east. To Hitler, the Jews seemed to be everywhere. Furthermore, the district of Vienna where Hitler rented his one-room apartment was slowly becoming a Jewish ghetto. The next year, 1908, Hitler decided to take action against the Jews. He joined his first political organization, the "Anti-Semitic Union."

In the years that followed, Hitler's political beliefs hardened. He had become more of a German than an Austro-Hungarian and believed that if the German race was to survive, and Germany remain the strongest power in central Europe, its people must be kept racially pure and must acquire for themselves more living space — "liebensraum." He also came to believe that the Germanic population of Europe should increase substantially and that the governments of Germany and Austria should support this.

THE JEWS AND PLANS TO MOVE THEM OUT OF EUROPE

The Jews had been disliked in Europe for centuries and during the latter decades of the 1800s various proposals had been offered, primarily by anti-Semitic groups, stating that a homeland for Europe's Jews might be found at some distant location — far away from Europe. The Ottoman Empire and Russia were mentioned as were various parts of the British and French colonial empires. One popular notion suggested that Europe's Jews might emigrate to the large French-owned island-colony of Madagascar off the east coast of Africa. This was an idea Hitler that liked. He would refer to it frequently in later years.

HITLER: 1911 TO 1914

During the summer of July 1911, Hitler took a vacation and returned to his home town of Linz. It was on this trip that he developed a stomach ailment that would plague him for the rest of his life. The doctors could do little for him, so he began a regimen of self-medication centered around his diet. He ate very little meat and subsisted mainly on fruits and vegetables. He became convinced that this helped his condition. There was one thing, however, that he did not purge from his diet — pastry sweets. Hitler loved them with a passion.

By early 1913, Hitler was out of money, and facing the possibility of being drafted into the Austro-Hungarian Army. Therefore, in late May he moved to Munich, Germany where he hoped to enroll in an architectural school. Before he could accomplish this, the Great War (later to be known as World War I) broke out. It was August 1914. Germany's war aims called for Germany to become the undisputed master of central Europe and for the acquisition of territory at the expense of Germany's enemies. In other words, the expansion and enhancement of the Second Reich. For Adolf Hitler, these were goals worth fighting for. So, a few days after hostilities began, Hitler volunteered for service in the German Army. By October, private Hitler was at the front in France where he would stay for the next four years.

GERMANY IN THE GREAT WAR

Germany's specific territorial aims during the Great War called for the annexation of Luxembourg, Belgium, and possibly some French territory in northeastern France. It was also a German goal to permanently weaken France both politically and militarily.

In the east, the Germans hoped to conquer all of the Russian-controlled parts of Poland, parts of Belorussia (also known as

The territory of Kurland was to be annexed by Germany after World War I.

Berlin's racial qualms ended at the recruiting office. The German armed forces accepted almost anyone who was willing to fight for Germany, even Jews. In Africa, the colonial administrators in the German colonies trained and armed large contingents of black men to fight for Germany.

As the war progressed, the western front became bogged down in bloody trench warfare and remained that way for most of the war.

In the east, however, the fronts were more fluid and see-sawed back and forth.

By late 1916, the Germans and their ally, the Austro-Hungarians, were gaining the upper hand in the east. German forces had reached the Pripet Marshes northwest of Kiev, and advanced to within a short distance of Riga, Latvia. On the southern part of the line the Austro-Hungarians had not done as well, but were holding their own.

Then, during the winter of 1916-17, the Russian armed forces began to collapse. Lacking food, ammunition, clothing, medical supplies and many other things, troop morale plummeted and desertions became rampant. By March 1917, the Tsar's government had lost control of the situation and the Tsar was forced to abdicate. A provisional government came into being and vowed to continue the war and convert Russia into a democratic state.

The next month, Lenin arrived at Petrograd (St. Petersburg), the capital of Russia,

White Russia), and the Baltic states of Lithuania, Latvia and Estonia. Those states, and parts of Belorussia would be called "Kurland" and combined into an area under German economic and political control. This was an area which contained a large number of Germanic people and, after a sufficient period of Germanization, would be annexed to Germany.

German war aims further called for an area around Warsaw to become a resurrected Polish state which would become a vassal state to Germany. Furthermore, the Germans sought to detach the Ukraine, the Crimea, and the Caucasus region from Russian control and turn those areas into German satellites. As with France, the German leaders hoped to render Russia permanently weak.

To accomplish these goals, Germany needed a mighty Army. Because of this, with the help of the Germans, and took control of the powerful Bolshevik political faction there. He demanded an end to the war and gained much popular support because of this. During the next seven months political and military chaos reigned in Russia and centered around Petrograd. The Germans and Austro-Hungarians held back militarily, realizing that they might now attain their war aims with a minimum of military action.

During this time the Ukrainians, Finns, Latvians, and Estonians detached themselves from Russia and proclaimed their independence. In November 1917 (October by the Russian calendar), the Bolsheviks carried out a successful coup in Petrograd and took control of the government. Immediately, they sued for peace with Germany and Austria-Hungary and an armistice was signed in December 1917. By this time, however, a gigantic civil war raged throughout Russia in which the Bolsheviks ("Reds") were pitted against a weak coalition of anti-Bolsheviks ("Whites").

The Bolsheviks, who controlled the government in Petrograd along with most of northern and central European Russia, met with the Germans at the Polish city of Brest-Litovsk in March 1918 to conclude a peace treaty. Heading the Bolshevik delegation was Leon Trotsky, a Jew and the second most powerful man in the Bolshevik regime after Lenin. Agreement was quickly reached because the Bolsheviks granted the Germans most of their demands, including their designs on Kurland. With this, Germany gained a huge colony in the East.

In the south, the Germans advanced deep into the Ukraine and Belorussia which were areas the Bolsheviks did not control.

In the weeks that followed, German troops occupied the Ukraine, the Crimea and parts of the Caucasus. Under German tutelage, the Ukraine, Belorussia and several small states in the Caucasus declared their independence. Now, Germany had a cluster of vassal states in the East.

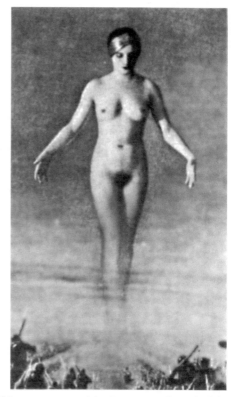

This poster appeared in Germany at the end of the war. Mother Germany is seen, stripped naked and with nothing to offer, greeting her returning soldiers. Some of these soldiers, upon being mustered out of the army, attended classes intended to help them make the transition to civilian life. One such class was given by Corporal Hitler.

From the German government's point of view, Germany had won the war in the east and thousands of German troops could now be released to fight in the west.

But the German victory in the east was short-lived. Things were not good in Germany. The people had grown war-weary and demoralized by the terrible loss of lives and the recent military setbacks on the western front at the hands of the Americans. Four years of war had put a very heavy strain on the German economy and there were shortages of all kinds. Several anti-government factions had evolved and openly called for an end to the war. These factions united and, suddenly, on November 9, 1918, took control of the government in Berlin. The Kaiser fled to neutral Holland as a new democratically-oriented provisional government took control of Berlin. Immediately, that government asked the Western Allies for an armistice. The Western Allies agreed and an armistice was signed two days later, on November 11. The war was over, and Germany was defeated. On November 28, the Provisional Government in Berlin declared Germany a republic and the various factions organized themselves into political parties and began making their bids for power. Germany, which had always been ruled by a strong monarch, now it embarked on a strange new form of government — democracy.

During these days, 29-year-old Adolf Hitler was in a military hospital recuperating from temporary blindness caused by a poison gas attack. It was his second war-wound. Hitler, now a corporal and holder of the Iron Cross First Class (one of Germany's highest medals), was devastated by the military collapse of Germany. He would later admit that it was one of the few times in his life that he cried. All of his hopes for Germany had been dashed. The Second Reich had ended and Germany was humiliated.

Hitler could take solace in one event of the moment, however. On November 12, the day after the German armistice was signed, his native Austria declared itself independent from the decrepit Austro-Hungarian Empire. Hitler was now a citizen of an independent all-German state — Austria.

CHAPTER 3

GERMANY IN DEFEAT

1919 was a year when much of the world was turned upside down, and Germany was in the center of the turmoil. For Corporal Hitler, who was about to be discharged from the Army and who faced an uncertain future as a civilian, it was a bitter time.

In Germany, the new democratic government was now being called the "Weimar Republic." It soon acquired another name, the "unloved republic," because numerous political parties and factions had emerged and the political wrangling throughout Germany kept the country in a near-constant state of political turmoil. It was a troubled beginning for German democracy.

When elections were held, no one party was able to garner a majority of the votes which would allow it to form a government on its own. Therefore, the governments formed were always weak coalitions which soon proved to be incapable of addressing Germany's major problems. These coalition governments fell apart with alarming regularity and the people were obliged to go to the polls once again and vote. It was a far cry from the paternalistic and orderly days of the Kaiser.

The year 1919 began with a revolution underway in Berlin. It was started by the communist "Sparticus League" which had made an attempt to take over the fledgling government during the last weeks of 1918. This period of turmoil was not resolved until January 1919, when American troops entered the city and restored order. These were the first Allied troops to set foot in Berlin.

The leaders of the Sparticus League, Rosa Luxemburg and Karl Liebknecht, both Jews, were killed by the German reactionaries and quickly became martyrs of the political left. The fact that the Sparticus leaders were Jews, gave the political right powerful ammunition to press home their claim that communism was an international Jewish conspiracy as had been predicted by the hate literature that circulated through Germany before the war.

The Jews were further linked to the political left because a significant number of the leader of the Social Democrat Party were Jews. This party was, at the time, Germany's largest, and espoused many liberal and internationalist views.

One of those who viewed Germany's political situation with considerable alarm was Corporal Adolf Hitler.

VERSAILLES PEACE TREATY

The peace treaty that ended the Great War between Germany and the Western Allies was negotiated and concluded at the French Palace of Versailles just outside Paris. It was signed on June 28, 1919. That treaty relegated Germany to one of the weakest nations in Europe and stripped her of much of her European territory and all of her overseas colonies. These actions placed some 3 million Germans outside Germany's new borders. Also, Germany was saddled with huge, open-ended, reparation payments.

Her armed forces were reduced to little more than a self-defense force. Under the terms of the Versailles Treaty, the German Army was to be no larger than 100,000 men and was not allowed to have airplanes, tanks, heavy artillery, zeppelins or poison gas. The German Navy was stripped of most of its capital ships and was not allowed to have submarines or newly-constructed warships over 10,000 tons (about the size of a large cruiser). This left the German Navy in a condition whereby it could do little more than patrol Germany's coastal waters. Furthermore, and one of the deepest cuts of all, especially for individuals like Adolf Hitler, article #231 of the Versailles Treaty specifically blamed Germany for having started the war — the most costly war ever.

Another insult thrust upon the German people was a clause in the Versailles Treaty that turned the German Rhineland into a demilitarized zone. This was the land between the Rhine River and the French border. It was intended to be a permanent buffer zone between Germany and France. The Germans were not allowed to place any of their armed forces in the area, but French armed forces could enter at will.

It could have been worse. At Versailles, the French wanted to divide Germany into several small republics, and the Rhineland would have been one of them. But the other Allied nations vetoed the idea in favor of the demilitarization plan.

The French were greatly dissatisfied with this and other features of the peace treaty. After its signing, Marshal Ferdinand Foch, French's top military commander during the war lamented, "This is not a peace, it is an Armistice for 20 years." He was right. War between France and Germany resumed in September 1939, 21 years and 2 months after he made the statement.

Another device to keep Germany weak was a clause in the Versailles Treaty that specifically prohibited Germany from seeking union with Austria. For a pan-Germanist like Hitler, this was totally unacceptable. He would never accept that foreigners should dictate to the German people that his native Austria and Germany could never become one.

GERMANY'S ALLIES PUNISHED, NEW STATES CREATED

During 1919 and 1920, Germany's wartime allies were also punished. The Treaties of St. Germain (September 10, 1919) and the Treaty of Trianon (June 4, 1920) with Austria-Hungary, tore that nation apart. Austria and Hungary were separated and became two independent countries while their former empire was parceled out to others and used to create new states. Territory was given to Poland, Italy, and Romania, and two new states, Czechoslovakia and Yugoslavia were created.

The state of Czechoslovakia gave Germany a new neighbor on its southeastern border and included within its borders were many ethnic Germans. Most of them lived in the westernmost end of Czechoslovakia in a crescent-shaped area long known to the Germans as the "Sudetenland" ("Southeastern land"). This was an area, along with Austria, that pan-Germanists coveted.

In Russia, the lands that Germany had conquered were taken from her and subdivided. Finland and the three Baltic states of Lithuania, Latvia and Estonia emerged as independent countries. Large slices of Belorussia and the Ukraine were given to Poland and another large piece of the Ukraine, Bessarabia, was given to Romania, one of the Allied nations.

The Treaty of Neuilly, November 27, 1919, transferred land from Bulgaria, a German ally, to Greece and Romania, which were Allied nations, and to Yugoslavia.

On August 10, 1920, the Treaty of Sevres, established peace between the Allies and the Ottoman Empire, and stripped the latter of its Middle Eastern empire. Lebanon and Syria were mandated to France by the newly-formed League of Nations; Palestine, Trans-Jordan and Iraq, were mandated to Britain. The British were also able to obtain strong influential positions in Iran and the desert lands of the Arabian Peninsula.

What was left of the Ottoman Empire was eventually renamed Turkey and a democratic government emerged in its new capital, Ankara.

These treaties left in their wake a tremendous amount of resentment in the loser nations and a false sense of victory and security in the victor nations. To monitor and maintain the new peace in Europe, the Allies had created the League of Nations. That body, located at Geneva, Switzerland, began to function in January 1920. It was widely believed that, with the decisive victory over Germany and her Allies and the creation of the League of Nations, the Great War would be the world's last great conflict. The war was now being referred to as the "war to end all wars."

Within two generations, however, history would show that the peace settlements of 1919-1920 were political illusions and would only set the stage for a second, and much greater, world war.

THE "RED SCARE"

Despite the end of the Great War in Western Europe, a terrible war still raged in the former Russian Empire between the Bolsheviks, the "Reds", and their various opponents, the "Whites." The Allied nations attempted to intervene, beginning in 1918, but without success. The war spread and during 1919, the Bolsheviks became embroiled in a war with Poland which would go on for more than a year. In the north, Finland had broken away from the Russian Empire and the Bolsheviks were also embroiled in a military conflict there.

The Russian civil war raged on until 1921 and ended with a Bolshevik victory. During the intervening years, however, tensions in the rest of Europe were extremely high because it appeared that a new and powerful Russian state might re-emerge in the East with a very radical political philosophy which it intended to export. Not surprisingly, the Reds had their imitators in Europe and elsewhere in the world, who supported the concept of revolution to bring about this new political order. The eventual Bolshevik victory, and the onset of communism in the Soviet Union, only served to spark the enthusiasm and dedication of the mass of foreign admirers.

In 1919, Lenin established an organization in Moscow called "The Communist Internationale" ("Comintern"), to promote the spread of communism world-wide and by any means. This frightened many people, and to add to these fears, the international socialist formed the "Socialist Internationale" to compete with the Comintern for the minds, hearts, and votes of the working classes. The menace of these two political forces which now threatened the world's political order were given a name: "The Red Scare."

In Germany, the Bolsheviks and international socialists attracted large numbers of people and the prospect of a revolution in Germany was on everyone's mind.

JEWISH-COMMUNISM

Many of communism's opponents, and especially individuals of right wing political persuasion, vigorously pointed out that the communists and world Jewry seemed to be cooperating with each other hand-in-glove. After all, the communist political philosophy was the invention of a Jew, Karl Marx, and many of the communist leaders in the Soviet Union were Jews. This lent some credibility to the long-standing fears, as outlined in the Protocols of the Elders of Zion and other publications, that the Jews were making their move to take over the world by economic means. Furthermore, as communism spread through Europe, many Jews became leaders in the various communist organizations that evolved. The belief that communism was a Jewish conspiracy was all but confirmed for many by the unsuccessful revolution which had started in Germany in late 1918 by the Jewish-led Sparticus League and, in March 1919, by another communist revolution in Hungary led by another Jew, Bela Kuhn. Kuhn's revolution succeeded in taking over the Hungarian government and lasted until August when it was ousted by the Hungarian military.

For many people in Europe, communism was no longer just communism, it was now Jewish-communism.

FASCISM BEGINS IN ITALY

On March 23, 1919, the "Fascist Party" was formed in Milan by Benito Mussolini, a wounded war veteran and a man of some political note for having been an editor of a well-known socialist newspaper before the war. Mussolini had abandoned his former socialist beliefs because of its internationalism, and he became a nationalist favoring a form of socialism suited specifically for the Italian people. Mussolini was vehemently anti-communist and was not a supporter of the democratic form of government. He was not necessarily an anti-Semite except in cases where the interests of the Jews clashed with those of the Italian people.

Mussolini was an accomplished public speaker, an admirer of the Roman Empire, an expansionist and, above all, a showman. At Mussolini's insistence, his followers draped themselves in the trappings of the Roman Empire including the out-stretched arm salute. Even the name of the organization was taken from an old Roman symbol, the fasces, an ax bundled in reeds. The ax represented a man of great power and the reeds represented his loyal advisors.

In late 1918 and 1919, Italy was another nation in turmoil. Although one of the Al-lied victors in the war, the Italian economy was in shambles, the democratic process was not working well, there were bitter strikes and high unemployment and the communists and international socialists threatened revolution. Many believed that civil war was inevitable.

To complicate matters even more, most of the Italian people, including Mussolini, had turned against their former allies because it had become evident that promises made to Italy early in the war by Britain and France for significant territorial expansion in the Balkans would not be honored by the majority of the delegates then gathered at Versailles.

The Fascist Party's program challenged this problem head-on by calling for the territorial expansion of Italy, with or without the approval of Italy's former allies. The Fascists took a determined anti-communist and anti-international socialist stance, and called for a strong military with a strong dose of Italian nationalism in regards to internal and foreign policies. The Party also advocated a single-party all-Fascist government led by a head of state who served at the behest of the Fascist Party's Grand Council and was not elected by the general public. To help justify this anti-democratic position, the Fascists pointed out that the electoral system they proposed was not unlike that used in the Vatican to appoint a Pope.

As conditions in Italy deteriorated, Fascism began to grow, but at the same time, the communists and socialists also grew. The political scene in Italy was polarizing to the right and to the left.

In Germany, Corporal Hitler knew nothing of Fascism and would not learn of it or Mussolini until 1921. In the meantime, Hitler unknowingly subscribed to many of Mussolini's political beliefs.

HITLER ENTERS POLITICS

Hitler was released from the military hospital in early 1919 but was still in the

Army. Ever mindful of his health, Corporal Hitler sometimes referred to himself as "the blind cripple", a reference to the two war wounds he had received, a shrapnel splinter in the leg and temporary blindness by poison gas.

Hitler's superiors had discovered, though, that he was intelligent and could speak well, so he was given the job of speaking before groups of soon-to-be-discharged fellow soldiers to help prepare them for civilian life. It was during this time that Hitler, too, realized that he had a natural ability as a public speaker.

In the fall of 1919 Hitler, still in the army, discovered the fledgling political party known as "The German Worker's Party" (DAP). The DAP was a very small party that was vehemently anti-Semitic and proposed the formation of non-democratic government that carried out a program of national socialism for the benefits of the German people. The party also called for the abrogation of the Versailles Treaty, a strong military, the return of Germany's lost territory in Europe and overseas, and territorial expansion in the east as had been accomplished during the war and after the defeat of Russia. These beliefs paralleled Hitler's own and he began attending the DAP's meetings. The DAP's political meetings, held in a Munich beer hall, were open to the public and were rather raucous affairs in that anyone who desired could address the gathering from the speakers podium. Hitler, a fairly accomplished barracks orator, took advantage of this and spoke on several occasions. The party's founder, Anton Drexler, a toolmaker by trade, pressured Hitler to join the party. Hitler was reluctant at first but eventually joined. This was in October, 1919. He was party member number 55, but years later he had the party's books adjusted to show that he was party member number 7.

Upon joining the party, Drexler gave Hitler the chairmanship of the party's leadership committee which also was responsible for disseminating party propaganda. This thrust the young corporal into the position of being the party's leading spokesman, a position he came to love and cherish.

Hitler was soon discharged from the army and decided to devote his efforts, full time, to the Party. But, Hitler never lost his love for the Army. It was in the Army that he found a meaning to his life. He also carried with him the concept that Army life would be good for others, as it had been for him. As a high school drop-out, the Army was the nearest thing he had to an alma mater. With his natural gift for oratory, Hitler quickly became the Party's main speaker at their public meetings and drew ever increasing audiences, including many women supporters. At this time, the German people were living under this new, and somewhat strange, political system called democracy, and attending political meetings offered a certain fascination they had not experienced before. Besides, the meetings were free and provided a night's entertainment. One of the most entertaining was the DAP.

By January 1920, Drexler, seeing that the party was progressing well under Hitler's direction, stepped aside and let Hitler take over much of the activities of the party. Drexler, though, remained party chairman.

Within a year, the party, under Hitler's direction, acquired its own newspaper, the "Volkischer Beobachter," and adapted the swastika as its symbol. Hitler changed the name of the party from the "German Worker's Party" to the "National Socialist German Worker's Party" (NSDAP) to better reflect the party's emphasis on its social programs specifically designed for the German people. Since Hitler could not be called chairman, party members began calling him "leader" (fuehrer — small f). He was 30 years old. In later years, he would point out that Christ was also 30 when he began his mission.

War heros such as General Erich Ludendorf, air ace Hermann Goering and Major Ernst Roehm, a much-wounded army hero,

Communist workers in revolt in the Ruhr in April 1920.

joined the party and gave it a new measure of prestige.

GERMANY IN TURMOIL

In Germany there was unemployment, inflation, shortages of food and electricity, and general despair. From neighboring Poland came another blow to German pride. The new pro-Allied regime in Warsaw ordered that all Germans living in the lands newly-acquired from Germany change their last names to the Polish versions.

There were big troubles in Bavaria in late 1919 and early 1920. King Ludwig of Bavaria had abdicated and a radical socialist government had come to power under Kurt Eisner, a former theatrical critic and a Jew. Eisner was unpopular and was assassinated a few weeks later. A socialist school teacher, Johannes Hoffmann, then became President of Bavaria, but was overthrown in March 1920 by the communist "Sparticusbund" which then formed a proletarian republic and began a radical political program of nationalizing businesses and industry and carrying out land reform. Here, in Hitler's home province, was a communist regime top-heavy with Jews; five out of the top seven leaders. The Sparticusbund government, however, was soon ousted by a "Free Corps", a paramilitary force organized by the central government in Berlin and consisting mostly of war veterans. A new regime loyal to Berlin was then installed in Munich.

Hitler was in Munich during this time and personally witnessed these events.

The next month, April 1920, communist workers revolted in the Ruhr, the heart of German industry. This event led to the eventual French military occupation of the Ruhr which lasted several years.

36.7%

The year 1919 ended on a dismal note for Germany. And there was another tragic statistic yet to come. No one knew it at the time, but 36.7% of the male babies born in Germany in 1919 would perish in World War II.

CHAPTER 4

THE EARLY 1920s AND "MEIN KAMPF"

The first years of the 1920s brought no relief for the suffering German people, and the new democratic process was working very poorly. Between March 1920 and June 1922, the country had six governments, four chancellors, and yet another attempted coup in Berlin known as the "Kapp Putsch".

This period also marked the beginning of several years of decline in the German birth rate because there were so few men of marriageable age. Young women outnumbered young men four to one. From the shadows of society came suggestions that polygamy might be the answer. It had been implemented in Germany once before — after the Thirty Years' War. But now it was unthinkable.

During April 1921, reparations that Germany owed the Allied victor nations of the war were set at 132 billion gold marks — a staggering sum destined to keep Germany a debtor nations for years to come. In July, 1921, Anton Drexler retired from politics and Hitler became chairman of the National Socialist German Workers' Party which by now had acquired the nickname "Nazi Party." The word nazi was a Bavarian word that meant peasant, worker, or country bumpkin. Hitler and party members seized upon this word exclaiming in the party propaganda, that yes, they were nazis — the hard-working, honorable, grass-roots people of Germany.

During 1921, the German economy stabilized to some degree due to the influx of huge foreign loans. But, during the summer of 1922, the economy began a sharp decline. Inflation soared, taxes went uncollected and Germany was unable to make its reparation payments. In January 1923, French and Belgian troops occupied the German Ruhr, the heartland of German industry, in an attempt to glean reparation money out of the German economy. Also at this time, France tried again to fulfill its hopes dashed at Versailles in 1919 to detach the Rhineland from Germany and turn it into a buffer state between France and Germany. The effort failed for lack of international support, just as it had in 1919.

HITLER AND THE NAZIS ON THE RISE

During February 1920, the Nazi Party formalized their demands by producing a 25-point program. It put down in writing all that the Nazis were saying verbally. Within the 25 points were demands to unify all Germans into one Great German Reich, repudiate the Versailles Treaty, rearm Germany, do away with the democratic process, recover lost territories, and drive the Jews out of Germany. Point number three hinted of war. It stated in part, "…we demand territory and land… ." This could only be accomplished at the expense of Germany's neighbors, most of whom had alliances with the major Allied powers which would enable them to resist such demands by military means.

HITLER GAINS NOTORIETY

By the end of 1920, thirty-one year old Adolf Hitler was making a name for himself in German politics as the leader of a growing, but still small, political party. His followers now called him Fuehrer (leader — capital F) as opposed to "chairman" which Drexler had used. His fame brought him a measure of financial success and he had acquired a nice apartment in Munich, the city which was his power base.

The Nazi Party had adapted the swastika as its symbol, red as its color and made generous use of flags, banners, posters and other accoutrements to draw attention to itself.

ITALY GETS A "LEADER"

During November 1921, Benito Mussolini decreed that, as head of the Fascist Party, he should henceforth be referred to as "Duce" (leader). With both Hitler and Mussolini taking the title "leader", this set a pattern that would be followed in years to come by other emerging fascist-like parties whose top man would be called leader or something akin to leader. This was a deliberate move to avoid using the words "president" or "chairman" which were used by organizations promoting democracy and/or communism.

A THIRD REICH

Creeping into the Nazi's political rhetoric now were references to a third Reich, a time when Germany would, once again, be a large and powerful nation. Ironically, in Italy, the followers of Mussolini's Fascist Party were speaking of creating the "Third Rome". The First Rome, the Fascists claimed, was the original Roman Empire, the Second was the decadent period of 1500 years that lasted until the present time, and the Third Rome was beginning now with the coming of the Fascist Party.

Nazi public meetings had become more frequent, drew larger crowds and were, at times, raucous. The latter was due to the fact that opponent political parties took to raiding and disrupting each other's meetings. To protect his followers and preserve order at the meetings, Hitler created the "Sturmarbeitlungen" (SA), a private security force. These men wore surplus military-style brown shirts, army caps, across-the-chest leather belts, boots, all acquired at bargain prices. They also wore swastika arm bands and, on command, gave the Nazi out-stretched arm salute accompanied by a hardy "Heil Hitler." They acquired a military bearing and paraded ceremoniously at party meetings and at any public function in which they could appear. The Sturmarbeitlungen acquired three names, "SA", "Brown Shirts" and "Storm Troopers," the latter being a name applied to elite German forces during the Great War.

Oratory at the meetings regularly emphasized Germany's future and how wonderful it could be if only the obstacles standing in the way could be eliminated.

When party meetings ended and the audience filed out, each individual would be greeted by a smiling and courteous SA man who would thank them for coming and ask them to come again. The antics of the SA were a marvelous attention-getting device and made attending Nazi Party meetings ever more exciting.

Other political organizations also had their para-military organizations. Three of the most prominent were the German Communist Party's "Red-Front Fighters League," the Social Democrat's "Reichsbanner," and the German National People's Party's (Nationalists — DNVP) "Stahlhelm" (Steel Helmets). They too, attempted to dazzle the crowds.

With the overall showiness of the Nazi Party, and Hitler's magnificent oratory, the Nazi Party's message was getting through to the people. Membership in the Party grew significantly, from approximately 3,000 in 1921 to 55,287 by 1923.

HITLER'S FIRST PUBLIC REMARK
ON INCARCERATING AND KILLING JEWS

For the first two years of its existence, the Nazi Party had put forth no definitive program for dealing with the Jews to back up its hate-filled rhetoric. This changed in 1921. In an article written by Hitler for the March 13, 1921 issue of the "Volkischer Beobachter," the Nazi newspaper, Hitler stated, "One has to prevent the Jewish subversion of our people, if necessary by securing its instigating virus in concentration camps." The phrase "concentration camp" was relatively new. It had first been used to describe the camps built by the British to hold Boer civilians during the Boer War (1988-1902) in South Africa. The Boer civilians were incarcerated because the British believed that they were materially aiding their menfolk who were the combatants in the field.

Then, in 1922, Hitler was interviewed in Munich by Josef Hell, a German journalist, who asked Hitler the direct question as to what his plans were for the Jews. According to Hell, Hitler hesitated, stared into space, and then said, "Once I really am in power, my first and foremost task will be the annihilation of the Jews. As soon as I have power to do so, I will have gallows built in rows — at the Marienplatz in Munich, for example — as many as traffic allows. Then the Jews will be hanged indiscriminately, and they will remain hanging until they stink... As soon as they have been untied, the next batch will be strung up, and so on down the line, until the last Jew in Munich has been exterminated. Other cities will follow suit... until Germany has been completely cleansed of Jews."

COMMUNIST THREAT INCREASES

During 1921, the Bolsheviks emerged victorious in the Russian civil war and began consolidating their power. Now, communism loomed over the eastern horizon and provided a great stimulus to the many communists groups in Europe who wished to emulate the Bolshevik's success.

The right-wing organizations of Europe were universally opposed to communism, but had nothing to compete with the fact that a communist state had emerged in the East and was now the supporter and benefactor of communist organizations in other lands. Many members and supporters of the political right came to believe that their movement was now in great jeopardy.

This was especially true in Italy, and there Mussolini and his followers took action. In late October 1922, they carried out an extremely bold move by "marching" (via train) from Milan to Rome with a large body of armed Fascists and with the express purpose of taking over the government. The Italian military and most of the Italian police forces in the country, fearing a communist-inspired revolution, stood by and let it happen. Mussolini's bold move paid off. The Duce established himself in Rome as the new Italian head of state. In Germany, the Fuehrer was very impressed.

Meanwhile, in Germany, the rise in communism caused great concern among the political moderates. Those who leaned toward the political left began supporting left-wing extremist while those with politically right aspirations began supporting the right. This showed up in the German elections in which both political extremes gained votes. It was one of the reasons for the rapid growth of the Nazis. Unfortunately though, the German electorate was becoming polarized, a dangerous situation that could lead to revolt and even civil war.

Revolution was definitely in the air with the Nazis becoming the most visible and vocal political party on the right. During January 1923, the Nazis held their first nation-wide congress with lots of flags, banners, swastikas, marching SA men and anti-communist and anti-democratic rhetoric. It was well-attended and gained considerable nation-wide attention. Then on "May Day", May 1, the communist-inspired day of celebration for workers and peasants, the Nazis temporarily seized a number of military barracks throughout Germany as a protest to the May Day celebrations. No action was taken against them. They got away with it. During August, the leftists struck back, flooding Germany with leaflets calling for a soviet government in Germany. In Berlin, the coalition government of Wilhelm Cuno fell and was replaced by another coalition government headed by Gustav Stresemann, who was known to be sympathetic to the left.

In September, there were political riots in Dusseldorf. Then it got worse. On October 3, 1923, Stresemann's cabinet announced that it could no longer work together and resigned. Stresemann was forced to form a new cabinet. Ten days later, Stresemann asked for, and was given, temporary dictatorial powers by the Reichstag to deal with the growing crisis. On the 20th, the provincial government of Bavaria broke relations with Berlin and threatened to secede from the German federation. The next day communist-led separatists in the Rhineland proclaimed their province an independent country. In Saxony and Thuringia, the provincial governments had gone communist. Germany was coming apart at the seams.

At this point inflation went off the scale. The German mark, which had a value of 12 billion to the U.S. dollar, plunged to 4 trillion to the dollar.

On October 24, 1923, a communist uprising broke out in Hamburg. Stresemann, using his dictatorial powers, sent German Army troops to put it down by force. Three days later Stresemann ordered the communist governments in Saxony and Thuringia to step down under threat of force. He also threatened to invade Bavaria to prevent its secession. At that point French troops invaded the German Rhineland and occupied the cities of Wiesbaden and Bonn out of concern for the turmoil developing on their border.

In early November, Kaiser Wilhelm's oldest son, the Crown Prince, attempted unsuccessfully to enter Germany from his family's exile in Holland to reestablish the monarchy.

By November 6, 1923, a loaf of bread in Germany cost 140 billion marks.

THE "PUTSCH"

As conditions worsened in Germany, Hitler and his advisers became more convinced than ever that Germany was heading for civil war and that it was their duty to try to save the nation. They were also watching developments in Italy. There, Mussolini and the Fascists were consolidating their authority after their takeover in late October, 1922. Mussolini gained control over the Italian parliament which, in November, granted him dictatorial powers to take control of the Italian economy which, as in Germany, had been ravaged by inflation. In December, Mussolini imposed censorship on the media and in February, 1923 arrested several hundred troublesome socialists and communists. In April, he replaced May Day with a holiday celebrating the founding of Rome. And in July, he dissolved all political parties except his own. All the while, the other elements of power in the Italian state, the King, the Army, and the police, stood idly by allowing Mussolini to have his way.

In Germany, Hitler and his supporters came to believe that they could emulate the success of the Fascists in Italy. Accordingly, they planned a "Putsch" (political take-over) that would have some of the aspects of Mussolini's march on Rome in October 1922. The Nazi plan called for the uprising to begin in Munich, where they would oust the separatist Bavarian government, proclaim Bavaria's loyalty to the Germany federation and then march on Berlin and take control of the central government. The Nazis also came to believe that the Germany Army and the local police forces would not interfere as had been the case in Italy. As for the Army, the Nazis guessed right, but as for the local Bavarian police, the Nazis guessed wrong. This would be their undoing.

The Putsch began on the evening of November 8 when Hitler and a group of armed SA men interrupted, at gun point, a meeting of the local Bavarian leaders being held in a beer hall and placed those at the meeting under house arrest. Hitler took over the meeting and proclaimed himself Chancellor of Germany and that the "National Revolution" had begun.

The next morning, November 9, 1923, Hitler gathered his forces in the streets of Munich and began to march in the direction of the army headquarters. He and his followers never made it. They were confronted by a strong force of armed policemen. A shot rang out and a brief but deadly fire-fight ensued. Sixteen Nazis and policemen were killed or lay mortally wounded in the street. The Nazis scattered and fled in all directions. Hitler was later arrested, unhurt, found hiding in the home of a local supporter some 40 miles outside Munich.

The German nation, and most of the world, saw the failed Nazi Putsch as just another indicator that the German state was disintegrating. On November 23, the Stresemann government in Berlin fell and the value of the German mark plunged again. For all intents and purposes, the German economy had collapsed.

In the weeks that followed, Hitler was charged, tried and convicted of treason and, on April 1, 1924, given a sentence of five years in Landsberg Prison. The decision of the court was reported world-wide. But Hitler was not a beaten man. Rather, he was now internationally known and more determined than every to pursue his political ambitions. In the interim, he decided to write a book spelling out in great detail his plans for Germany. He named the book "Mein Kampf" (My Struggle).

"MEIN KAMPF"

While in Landsberg Prison Hitler spent hours dictating his book to a friend, Emil Maurice, and then to his fellow prisoner, Rudolf Hess. At times, Hitler expounded on his thoughts to the music of Wagner played in the background on a gramophone. As the weeks and months passed Hitler developed a slight tremor in his left arm and leg. He thought little of it and pressed on.

In his typical rambling oratorical style, Hitler put into print most of the words he had been speaking publicly for five years.

Three main themes ran through the book repeatedly: Germany must become a major political and military power, its people must acquire new living space in the East, and it must rid itself of the Jews.

After an early release from prison, Hitler continued to add to Mein Kampf in what he called "Volume Two." When completed the book was nearly 700 pages in length and it became the manifesto of the National Socialist German Workers' Party.

Here are some of the Fuehrer's words:

On German expansion: *"Common blood must belong to a common Reich." This was on page one of Mein Kampf. "If our hearts are set upon establishing our Great German Reich, we must, above all things, force out and exterminate the slavonic nations — the Russians, Poles, Czechs, Slovaks, Bulgarians, Ukrainians, Belorussians. There is no reason why this should not be done." "If land was desired in Europe (for Germany), it could be obtained, by and large, only at the expense of Russia... " "And if we speak of land in Europe today, we primarily have in mind Russia and her vassal border states." "The way to do this is... not to leave the settlement of newly acquired territories to chance, but to subject it to special norms. Specially constituted racial commissions must issue settlement certificates to individuals... It will thus gradually become possible to found border colonies whose inhabitants are exclusively bearers of the highest racial purity... "*

On Jews: *"The Jew of all times has lived in the states of other peoples, and there formed his own state, which, to be sure, habitually sailed under the disguise of 'religious community'..." "To what an extent the whole existence of this people is based on a continuous lie is shown incomparably by the 'Protocols of the Wise Men of Zion'..." "...Marxism itself* systematically plans to hand the world over to the Jews." "Systematically these black parasites (Jews) of the nation defile our inexperienced young blond girls and thereby destroy something which can no longer be replaced in this world." "By defending myself against the Jews, I am fighting for the work of the Lord... there can be no making pacts with Jews; there can only be the hard: either-or."

Mein Kampf is filled with many more derogatory references to the Jews. Hitler took great pains to define the Nazi's concept of the "Jewish question", but made no definitive suggestions as to how it should be resolved. This was not the time or place to discuss the expulsion of people to the east or extermination camps. The final solution to the Jewish question would be defined later and not in the public arena.

On democracy: Hitler often used the word `bourgeois' to define those who believed in the democratic sources. "...we must make no mistake about all of this: our present bourgeoisie has become worthless for every exalted task of mankind... those political clubs which carry on under the collective concept of `bourgeois parties' have long ceased to be anything else but associations representing the interests of certain professional groups and classes..." "Our enemies love the German Republic (Weimar Republic) and let it live because they could not find a better ally for the enslavement of our people." "The concern of the National Socialist movement (should be): pushing aside all philistinism, to gather and to organize from the ranks of our nation those forces capable of becoming the vanguard fighter for a new philosophy of life." "Therefore it is really necessary to confront the master bookkeepers of the present material republic by faith in an ideal Reich." "It must itself be an embodiment of the endeavor (of the state) to place thinking individuals above the masses, thus subordinating the latter to the former."

On euthanasia: "It is a half measure to let incurably sick people steadily contaminate the remaining healthy ones... The demand that defective people be prevented from propagating equally defective offsprings is a demand of the clearest reason and if systematically executed represent the most humane act of mankind." "It (the state) must declare unfit for propagation all who are in any way visibly sick or who have inherited a disease and can therefore pass it on..."

On negroes: "One hears from time-to-time that a negro has become a lawyer, teacher, tenor or the like. This is a sin against all reason; it is criminal lunacy to train a born semi-ape to become a lawyer. It is a sin against the Eternal Creator to train Hottentots and Kaffirs to intellectual professions." Hitler repeats later in the book, "From time-to-time illustrated papers bring to the attention of the German petty-bourgeois that some place or other a Negro has for the first time become a lawyer, teacher, even a pastor, in fact a heroic tenor, or something of the sort... it is criminal lunacy to keep on drilling a born half-ape until people think they have made a lawyer out of him... it is a sin against the will of the Eternal Creator if His most gifted beings... are allowed to degenerate in the present proletarian morass, while Hottentots and Zulu Kaffirs are trained for intellectual professions."

On colonies: Hitler wrote very little on colonial issues and seemed, at this time, to have very little interest in regaining Germany's lost colonies. "For Germany, consequently, the only possibility for carrying out a healthy territorial policy lay in the acquisition of new land in Europe itself. Colonies cannot serve this purpose unless they seem in large part suited for settlement my Europeans." "(We must) See to it that the strength of our nation is founded not on colonies, but on the soil of our European homeland."

On Mussolini and Italy: "*I admit it openly... I conceived the most profound admiration for that great man south of the Alps who, full of ordered love for his people, would not deal with the internal enemies of Italy, but pushed their annihilation in every way and by all means.*" "*The struggle that Fascist Italy is waging... The prohibition of Masonic secret societies, the persecution of the supranational press, as well as the continuous demolition of international Marxism, and, conversely, the steady reinforcement of the Fascist state conception, will in the course of the years cause the Italian government to serve the interests of the Italian people more and more...*" "*What will rank Mussolini among the great men of this earth is his determination not to share Italy with the Marxists, but to destroy internationalism and save the fatherland from it.*"

On prostitution and syphilis: Hitler devoted ten pages of his book to these subjects. He said, in general, that both were a scourge on the German people and must be wiped out. One solution he offered was "early marriages" as a means to defeat syphilis.

On Great Britain: Hitler stated repeatedly that Great Britain, along with Italy, was Germany's "natural" ally, and that Britain would cooperate with Nazi Germany if, "*...Germany refrains from threatening the British Empire and from building a large navy.*" "*How hard it is to best England, we Germans have sufficiently learned.*"

On the United States: Hitler writes very little about the United States, but does say, "*The former colonial country (USA), child of the great mother (Britain), seems to be growing into a new master of the world. It is understandable that England today re-examines her old alliances with anxious concern and British statesmen gaze with trepidation toward a period in*

which it will no longer be said: `Britannia rules the waves!' But instead `The seas for the Union!'*" "*It is Jews who govern the stock exchange forces of the American Union... only a single man, (Henry) Ford, to their fury, still maintains full independence.*" In the second edition of Mein Kampf, the phrase "only a single man, Ford" was replaced by "only very few".

On his struggling years in Vienna: "*To me Vienna... represents, I am sorry to day, merely the loving memory of the saddest period of my life. Even today, this city can arouse in me nothing but the most dismal thoughts.*" "*This was the time of the greatest spiritual upheaval I have ever had to go through. I had ceased to be a weak-kneed cosmopolitan and became a fanatical anti-Semite.*"

On German youth: "*...self confidence (of the German people) must be cultivated in the younger members of the nation from childhood onwards. Their whole education and training must be directed towards giving them a conviction that they are superior to others.*" "*...It must be considered reprehensible... to withhold healthy children from the nation.*" "*No boy and no girl must leave school without having been led to an ultimate realization of the necessity and essence of blood purity.*" "*...Education... must find its ultimate completion in military service.*" "*The `folkish state' (Nazi rhetoric for the people's state) divides its inhabitants into three classes: citizens, subjects, and foreigners... the status of subject is acquired by birth... the foreigner is distinguished from the subject only by the fact that he is a subject of a foreign state... after completion of his military duty, the right of citizenship is solemnly bestowed on the irreproachable, healthy young man. It is the most precious document for his whole life on earth... It must be a greater honor to be a street-cleaner of this Reich than a king in a foreign state.*"

On women and increasing and improving the Germanic race: *"...the German girl is a subject and only becomes a citizen when she marries. But the right of citizenship can also be granted to female German subjects active in economic life."* *"...it (the State) must take care that the fertility of the healthy woman is not limited by the financial irresponsibility of a state regime which turns the blessing of children into a curse for the parents... Its (the State's) concern belongs more to the child than to the adult." "...(we must) put an end to the constant and continuous original sin of racial poisoning, and... give the Almighty Creator beings such as He Himself created... By mating again and again with other races, we may raise these races from their previous cultural level to a higher stage, but we will descend forever from our own high level."*

On war in general: *"...victory lies eternally and exclusively in attack... he who rests, rusts." "True, they (the people of the East) will not willingly do this (give up their land). But then the law of self-preservation goes into effect; and what is refused to amicable methods, it is up to the fist to take." "The soil on which some day German generations of peasants can beget powerful sons will sanction the investment of the sons of today..." "...this aim (of territorial expansion) could be achieved only by struggle, and consequently face to the contest of arms with calm and composure." "...oppressed territories are led back to the bosom of a common Reich, not by flaming protests, but by a mighty sword. To forge this sword is the task of a country's internal political leadership..." "If... we harbor the conviction that the German future... demands the supreme sacrifice... we must set up an aim worthy of this sacrifice and fight for it." (With regard to war with France), "I emphasize the fact, and I am firmly convinced of it, that this second eventuality (war with France) must and will some day occur, whatever happens."*

"Almighty God, bless our arms when the time comes; be just as thou hast always been; judge now whether we be deserving of freedom, Lord, bless our battle!"

On war with Russia: *"Since the days of September 1914, when for the first time the endless hoards of Russian prisoners from the battle of Tannenberg began moving into Germany... this stream was almost without end — but for every defeated and destroyed (Russian) army a new one arose. Inexhaustibly the gigantic empire gave the Tsar more and more soldiers... How long could Germany keep up this race? Would not the day eventually come when the Germans would win their last victory and still the Russian armies would not be marching to their last battle? And what then?" "We take up where we broke off six hundred years ago. We stop the endless German movement (emigration) to the south and west, and turn our gaze toward the land in the east... we can primarily have in mind only Russia and her vassal border states."* Hitler argues against any alliance with Russia, *"And so the very fact of the conclusion of an alliance with Russia embodies a plan for the next war. Its outcome would be the end of Germany." "Germany is today the next great war aim of Bolshevism. It requires all the force of a young missionary idea to raise our people up again, to free them from the snares of this international serpent..."*

On submarine warfare: In discussing a possible war with Britain, Hitler wrote, *"...her trade lanes are exposed to the effects of submarine warfare. A submarine campaign, based on the long Atlantic coast (of Britain)... would be devastating in effect."*

On a German-dominated Europe: *"The political testament of the German nation... should and must be... (to) never suffer the rise of two continental powers in Europe... any attempt to organize a second military power on the German frontiers... (must be seen) as an attack on Germany." "The right of personal freedom recedes before the duty to preserve the race." "The German Reich as a state must embrace all Germans and has the task... of assembling and preserving the most valuable stocks of basic racial elements... and... raising them to a dominant position." "This (National Socialist) foreign policy will be acknowledged as correct only if, after scarcely a hundred years, there are 250 million Germans on this continent, and not living penned in as factory coolies for the rest of the world, but: as peasants and workers, who guarantee each other's livelihood by their labor."*

THE GRAND PLAN

Here it was then: Hitler's grand plan for the rebuilding of Germany. Lengthy, rambling, adjective-laden, hard-to-read and, according to one literary critic, containing some 164,000 grammatical and syntax errors. Nevertheless, Mein Kampf spelled out the foundation of the Nazi Party's political platform in great detail. Hitler was seen as an anti-Semitic, pariah-like public figure with a radical political program that promised immediate solutions, hell-bent-for-leather action and the creation of a mighty, powerful and respected third German Reich.

The message that Mein Kampf carried to the German people struck a receptive cord in the hearts and mind of thousands. At this time in postwar Germany the people had three alternatives with regards to politics: 1) to continue with the political system they had in place, the democratic Weimar Republic, which was having more failures than successes; 2) turn to the political left and risk becoming a vassal state to Moscow, or; 3) to support a home-grown plan of action, such as Mein Kampf offered, tailor-made by Germans, for Germans.

Mein Kampf was published in July 1925 and began to sell very well. For the thousands of Germans who bought it and labored through it, they received a first-hand account of what the Nazi Party was all about. And thousands more, who did not buy the book, but learned of its basic content, also learned of the Nazi's message.

From this point on, anyone who voted for the Nazi Party knew they were voting for a group of people who were promoting very radical ideas. They knew that if the Nazis came to power, democracy would die and a dictatorial police state would evolve. In a best-case scenario, Germany would revive peacefully and become the great nation it once was, or, in a worst-case scenario, Germany would be plunged into a second Great War. There was little prospect for anything in between.

CHAPTER 5

FROM MEIN KAMPF TO CHANCELLOR

Hitler was released from Landsberg Prison on parole on December 20, 1924. The Germany he reentered was very different from the Germany he tried to take over thirteen months earlier. While Hitler was in prison, the democratic leaders in Berlin were able to generate enough unity to address and rectify Germany's economic crisis. Laws and decrees were passed, massive loans were acquired from foreign sources, and new money was printed. By the end of the year, runaway inflation had ended and the economy, while still not robust, was fairly stable and growing slowly.

As conditions of his parole, Hitler was restricted from making public speeches until February 1927, and he could not resume his office as head of the Nazi Party. The latter condition was resolved by his appointing one of his closest aides, Joseph Goebbels, to be Party chief. Goebbels did not take the title Fuehrer and did nothing without Hitler's approval. Hitler also had to promise, as a condition of his parole, to work legally within the political system or face re-arrest or possible deportation to his native Austria. Hitler was still a citizen of Austria.

THE REVIVAL OF THE NAZI PARTY

Hitler went back to Munich to rebuild the Nazi Party. In February 1925, the official ban on Nazi Party activities was lifted and a Nazi Party congress was held that month at Ramberg to re-launch the Party back into the political arena. The ban on the SA was still in effect, however. That July, Mein Kampf was published which gave Hitler more notoriety as well as money from royalties. By the end of 1925, 9473 copies had been sold. During 1926, sales dropped to 6913 copies and the growth of the Nazi Party was disappointingly slow. What had happened? It was the German economy. It had improved and the German people showed less interest in radical politics.

The first edition of Mein Kampf, published in July 1925.

Hitler, nevertheless, still had high hopes. So high were his hopes, that later in the year he made his first architectural sketches for a gigantic triumphal arch he would someday build in Berlin to commemorate the creation of the Third Reich.

Hitler also sketched other structures including baroque public buildings, ornate domed halls and theatrical sets for Wagner Operas. He recorded his ideas in a sketchbook which he always kept close at hand. Over pastries one day he told a friend, Walter Stennes, leader of a free corps, "…after the final victory, we'll build a Victory Boulevard from the Doberitz to the Brandenburg Gate sixty meters wide and lined on the right and left by trophies and war booty."

Berlin's triumphal arch-to-be sketched by Hitler in 1925.

In later years, Hitler commissioned a scale mockup of the Victory Boulevard he envisioned in Berlin. Hitler's 1925 triumphal arch was to be incorporated as the centerpiece

Along with his architectural schemes, Hitler began putting together plans for a German national art museum and compiled a list of artists whose works would be displayed.

During the year, the Nazi Party was able to purchase a magnificent mansion in Munich with funds provided by a wealthy supporter. It was to be the new party headquarters. Hitler named it the "Brown House", hired an architect, and worked closely with him to remodel the interior. Hitler was in his glory. He designed furniture, doors, inlaid wood floors and walls, a grand staircase, his office and a large conference room. In the basement was a canteen which contained a vacant chair, the "Fuehrer seat", which no one used except Hitler. The Fuehrer spent many happy hours in the Brown House, sipping coffee or tea and chatting with Party workers.

During April 1925, Hitler travelled to Austria to file papers formally renouncing his Austrian citizenship. This would complicate any attempt by the German government to deport him. Hitler did not take out German citizenship and for the next few years was a man without a country.

In November 1925, with the ban on his SA still in effect, Hitler created another security unit called the Schutzstaffel (SS) which, like the SA before it, was charged with keeping order at the Party's functions and protecting the Party leaders.

In 1926, Hitler formed two youth groups for the Nazi Party called the "Hitler Youth" for boys, and "The League of German Girls" for girls. Political youth groups were not uncommon in Germany at this time and several political parties had them. In the Nazi youth organizations, boys could join an entry-level group called the "Jungvolk" at 13 while the girls, aged 13, joined "Jungmadel". The intent of both groups was to drill into the children of party members and supporters the tenets of Nazi ideology and prepare the young people for leadership roles in the Party and in public service. For the boys, preparations for military service were emphasized, and for the girls the importance of family, children and race purity were stressed.

Also organized by the Nazis was a school for public speakers. Hitler was still under a speaking ban so the school's graduates filled in at rallies and other functions.

On March 5, 1927, the government lifted the speaking ban on Hitler in return for his promise that he would, henceforth, obey the law. The Nazi schools for public speakers continued to operate.

About this time, Hitler met sixteen-year-old Mitzi Reiter, a shop girl and, according to various reports, appeared to be madly in love. Hitler was twenty years older than Mitzi, but the difference in their ages made little difference to him because his father had been 23 years older than his mother.

Hitler and Mitzi's relationship started off hot and heavy, but waned with time and would end in near disaster when Mitzi tried, unsuccessfully, to hang herself.

MUSSOLINI LEADS THE WAY

In Italy, Mussolini had by now become the undisputed dictator of that country and had begun to do things in Italy that Hitler longed to do in Germany.

The Duce repeatedly preached territorial expansion for Italy. "Expand or explode," he proclaimed. In this respect, Italy had long-standing territorial claims in both Europe and Africa. In Europe, Italy claimed areas in southeastern France, the Dalmatian coast of Yugoslavia, the French-owned island of Corsica, the British-controlled island of Malta, and the Italian part of Switzerland. In Africa there were claims on Tunisia, Ethiopia, French Somaliland and British Somaliland. No hard demands had, as yet, been made with regard to these areas from Rome, but Italy's Fascist propaganda machine kept the Italian claims alive and in the public's eye. In areas where there existed viable pro-Italian organizations, the Italian government secretly subsidized them with money and agents. In Corsica there was a separatist organization that called for independence for Corsica and eventual union with Italy. In Tunisia, where some 100,000 Italians lived, there was a grass-roots union-with-Italy movement known as the "Italianita." On the

island of Malta, a pro-Italian organization existed but was less effective than those in either Corsica or Tunisia. The great majority of the Maltese people had no interest in closer ties with Italy.

In the Italian enclaves in Switzerland, there was virtually no support at all for union with Italy due in part to the fact that the Swiss government freely allowed Italian cultural activities to flourish, thereby giving the Italian-Swiss little incentive to look to Italy for support.

In the Middle East, Italy had aspirations for becoming a dominant power there. This emanated, mainly, from the peace settlements of 1919 when Italy had hoped to acquire mandate powers over some parts of the defeated Ottoman Empire. Instead, all of the mandates for that area were assigned, by the League of Nations, to France and Britain. Italy was shut out altogether, and this became one more reason why the Italian people felt betrayed by their allies of the Great War.

All the while, Mussolini was rattling the sword, preparing his people for the possibility of war. This caused great concern among Italy's neighbors. The Italian people were told that, ever since Roman days, they were great warriors and were destined, once again, to be the dominant power in the Mediterranean basin. As for the prowess of the Italian military, the fact that during the Great War over a half million Italian troops deserted was never mentioned.

During April 1926, Mussolini decreed a number of socialist-like programs for Italy whereby major parts of the Italian economy would be formed into government-controlled corporations and controlled from Rome. This gave fruition to the Fascist Party's long-standing plan to create some major socialist programs designed specifically for Italy. In Italy, this undertaking was labeled as the beginning of "The Corporate State."

In October 1926, Mussolini abolished all political parties except for his own, and elevated the Fascist Party to an official branch of the Italian government. This was the final step in guaranteeing that Mussolini could rule in Italy by decree. Later in the month, he escaped an assassination attempt and the Pope extended his blessing over the Duce by saying, "This is a sign that Mussolini had God's full protection."

In December 1926, Mussolini decreed a law taxing bachelors aged 26 to 65. This, of course, was to encourage the increasing of Italy's population and to solve the problem of Italy having too many women as a result of the losses of the Great War.

Another program to increase Italy's population was introduced to induce Italians living abroad to return home. Italian embassies abroad were ordered to take a secret biennial censuses of the Italians living in their respective countries and undertake measures to induce them to return to Italy. This effort yielded very disappointing results, and its secrecy was soon revealed to the world which created diplomatic problems for Italy's Foreign Ministry — which Mussolini himself, headed.

1927 AND "BLACK FRIDAY"

The year 1927 would prove to be a turnaround year for the Nazis. The year began with the renewed prosperity of the German economy still in place, and the growth of the Nazi Party minute. In March, the ban on Hitler's public speaking was lifted. On May 1, the symbolic May Day workers' holiday, the Nazi Party held its first big rally in Berlin. This symbolized that the Nazi Party was back in action and that it, too, was the friend of the workers.

Then on May 13, 1927, the German economy suffered a sudden and serious economic reversal. They called it "Black Friday." Germany's three-year economic bubble had burst. Once again unemployment began to rise, factories closed, banks failed and the leftist-controlled labor unions renewed their aggressive stance. And once again, the democratic process, capitalism, and political parties of the center were heaped with blame. All this provided a bonanza for the Nazis. People began to listen to them once again.

A PRELIMINARY PLAN FOR THE "EAST"

As the Nazis loudly preached their doctrines in public, Hitler was quietly working behind the scenes planning for the day when he would fulfill his most important dream, the conquest of the "East." The Nazi Party's program for German expansion to the East had, up to now, been discussed only in generalities. Hitler decided, at this time, that that doctrine should be more accurately formulated and assigned the task to one of his closest aides, Alfred Rosenberg. Rosenberg was a German Balt, born in Tallinn, Estonia, educated at the University of Moscow, emigrated to Germany in 1918 and settled in Munich where he studied architecture. He spoke Estonian, Russian and German. In Munich, he discovered the Nazi Party and became one of its earliest adherents. He also participated in the 1923 Putsch. Rosenberg gained Hitler's notice and rose to become editor of the Nazi's newspaper, *Volkischer Beobachter*. Rosenberg was extremely anti-Semitic and anti-communist. He had gained some notoriety in Germany by writing a book entitled, *"The Myths of the Twentieth Century"* which was filled with right-wing political rhetoric.

At Hitler's behest, Rosenberg went to work formulating a plan for the East. It was based on the experiences and successes of Germany in 1917-18 when, after the Brest-Litovsk peace settlement with the Russians, Germany gained control of two of the three Baltic states, Lithuania and Latvia, leaving Estonia (Rosenberg's birth place) to the Russians. Germany also created the state of Poland as a buffer zone between Germany and the slavic world, and allowed the Ukraine, Belorussia and the national groups in the Caucasus to proclaim their independence under German protection.

Rosenberg's proposal called for a revival of the goals attained at that time, but with several modifications. Germany would take control over all three of the Baltic states with an aim of eventually integrating them into the German Reich. As for Poland, it was to be eliminated as a state, and a common German/Ukrainian border established. The Ukraine would, once again, be allowed to proclaim its independence under German protection. Rosenberg went on to write that the Ukrainians were the natural enemies of the Russians and that the Ukrainian capital, Kiev, had once been a center of nordic culture. Because of this, Rosenberg claimed that the Ukrainians were of "good blood." Rosenberg also envisioned the Ukraine having control of the Crimea and extending the eastern boundary of the Ukraine to the Volga River at the expense of the Russia.

Rosenberg down-played the importance of overseas colonies in favor of Germany colonial expansion to the East.

The plan did not impress Hitler. The Fuehrer could not bring himself to accept the independence of the Ukraine nor to believe that the Ukrainian people were of good blood. In his thinking, they were slavs through-and-through. Also he did not like the idea of eliminating Poland. This brought up the question of what to do with the Polish people. For this, there was no easy answer. Furthermore, Hitler wanted to extend German control over the Crimea. Because of its mild climate, he had visions of turning it into a German Riviera. And finally, the Caucasus area was now a major producer of oil, a condition that did not exist in 1917-18, and he wanted that oil.

Rosenberg's plan, therefore, was filed and forgotten, and the geopolitical structure of the proposed German colonial empire in the East still remained an open question.

THE FORTUNES OF THE NAZIS RISE

By late 1927 to early 1928, the adverse effects of Black Friday had plunged the German economy, once again, into full recession. The economic downturn not only affected the working classes, but now the middle classes were in distress. Hitler and the Nazis saw this and began to redirect their political propaganda toward the middle class while maintaining their strong influence on Germany's workers. This paid off in that an increasing number of middle class people joined the Party. But, Nazi political rhetoric did not change. The programs and demands, and the condemnations of the socialist and communist left, outlined in Mein Kampf were preached over and over again. These themes found fertile ground among Germany's middle classes who, not surprisingly, began to demonstrate a loss of faith in the democratic process. These events all contributed in tipping the political scales toward the Nazi Party.

During 1928, Party membership rose to 96,918, up from 55,287 in 1923 at the time of the Putsch. In the national elections of May 20, 1928, the Nazis garnered 2.6% of the national vote and acquired twelve seats in the Reichstag. It was a modest number, but an encouragement to Hitler because it gave them a voice in the government.

HITLER'S SECOND, BUT UNPUBLISHED, BOOK

During 1927–28, one of the burning issues in Germany, Austria and Italy was the controversy over an area in the Alps known as South Tyrol. This area had a mixed population of Austrians and Italians, and had been detached from Austria-Hungary after the Great War and awarded to Italy. Now, Austria wanted it back and most of the people of Germany supported the Austrian position. This issue strained diplomatic relations between Germany and Italy.

Hitler was one of the few voices in Germany that supported the Italian position, mainly because he wanted Italy as a future ally. He felt that this was much more important to the future of Germany than the question over a few thousand Germans living in northern Italy. His general argument was that there were millions of Germans living elsewhere under foreign rule, and that making an issue over South Tyrol was insignificant. It was a fact of life, he proclaimed, that the Germans would have to accept in order to maintain friendly relations with Italy.

Since his book, Mein Kampf, had been so successful, he decided to write a second book outlining his position on South Tyrol and other issues. However, before he could complete the book, the South Tyrol issue was resolved in favor of Italy and the book became irrelevant. Therefore, it was not published nor was it even titled. The content of the book, however, survived and gives a very good picture of the issues the Nazi Party was pursuing at this time.

As was the case with Mein Kampf, Hitler wrote in his rambling and wordy way. He rehashed all of the themes he had laid down in Mein Kampf and wrote that Italy was "...the first possible ally of Germany." He expounded on how Germany and Italy, along with other cooperative nations, could form a strong alliance that would dominate all of continental Europe.

On one of the newer issues of the day, that being the emergence of the United States as a great economic power, he wrote that the German/Italian alliance could also stand up against the "American Union." Hitler put little faith in American isolationism and believed that one day the United States would shake off isolationism and emerge as a world power to become a threat to the interests of Germany. He also wrote that the United States role in world affairs was beginning to surpass that of Britain: "For it seems to me that the existence of English world rule inflicts less hardships on present-day nations than the emergence of an American world rule." Yet, he wrote in admiration of America's living standard and that it should be copied in the Greater German Reich of the future: "A model living standard is (to be) created here which is primarily determined by a knowledge of conditions and of life in the American Union." After all, in America they called it the "roaring twenties."

In this book, Hitler expanded his list of undesirable peoples which, in Mein Kampf, had been limited to Jews, slavs and Poles. In his rambling and un-grammatical style

he wrote of racial deterioration elsewhere: "...all of southeastern Europe, especially the still older cultures of Asia Minor and Persia, as well as those of the Mesopotamian lowlands provide classroom examples of the course of this process."

Hitler wrote that he fully supported Italy's territorial claims, and reiterated Germany's need to expand to the East. In this light, Hitler wrote now of a reduced role for the German Navy which had not even been mentioned in Mein Kampf, "Since this territory (of expansion) can be only in the East, the obligation to be a naval power also recedes into the background." He further justified territorial expansion in religious terms: "...this earth is not allotted to anyone, nor is it presented to anyone as a gift. It is awarded by Providence to people who in their hearts have the courage to take possession of it, the strength to preserve it, and the industry to put it to the plough."

And, as in Mein Kampf, Hitler wrote of the relative success German submarines had against England in the Great War. The implication was that it could be repeated: "Nothing had made the fight against German submarine warfare easier than the spatially conditioned restrictions of its (England's) port areas."

Yet, Hitler wrote, as before, on Germany and England being natural allies. And in his book he expressed an admiration for England's colonial troops — one of the very rare examples of Hitler ever saying anything positive about non-Aryans, "...the English mercenary army never acquired the bad characteristics of other mercenary troops. It was a fighting military body of wonderful individual training with excellent weapons and a conception of service which viewed it (war) as a sport."

Another new facet of Nazi policy revealed in the book, was that Hitler did not favor the exporting of German capital and expertise. He wrote that in his Germany there would be "...no interest... (in) a German factory opening... in Shanghai which builds ships for China with Chinese workers and foreign steel… (resulting in) orders lost to German shipyards…"

And, on Germanizing other peoples, Hitler wrote, "It (Nazi policy) will never see in the subjugated so-called Germanized Czechs or Poles a national… strengthening, but only the racial weakening of our people." On this issue, Hitler would reverse himself completely during World War II. Plans were adopted at that time to Germanize virtually all of the Czechs and a large number of Poles.

With regard to the many different nationalities that existed in Europe, Hitler stated that each racial group in Europe should have its own territory, that is, after Germany took what it wanted.

HITLER SPEAKS OF EUTHANASIA

At the Nazi Party rally in Nuremberg during September 1929, Hitler spoke again on two controversial issues in the Party's political agenda, birth and death. He extolled the virtues of the German people dramatically increasing their birth rate and, at the same time, recommended a program of euthanasia for the useless members of society. When the Nazis came to power, they put both programs into effect.

HITLER AND GOD

In preaching euthanasia, Hitler was, in effect, playing God. But it must be understood that Hitler was a man who believed that all religions had been created by man to meet the needs of the people. It followed then, that he too, could create religious concepts for the needs of National Socialism.

In a Christmas speech during December 1929, he compared himself to Christ. He said that when he came to power he would "…translate the ideals of Christ into deeds" and that it was he who would complete "…the work that Christ had begun, but could not finish."

In the coming years, Hitler would exercise this self-proclaimed right to make more religious statements that benefitted National Socialism or himself.

He would, as in the speech above, occasionally use the word "Christ." More often though, he used the words "Providence," "Fate," and occasionally "the Almighty" and "the Lord." Seldom if ever did he uses the word "Jesus."

ONE EYE ON ITALY

As the Nazis struggled for political power in Germany, Hitler kept one eye on Italy where Mussolini was doing revolutionary things. By watching events in Italy, Hitler learned from Mussolini's successes and failures.

In March 1928, Mussolini dissolved all non-Fascist youth movements leaving the Fascist youth movement, the "Young Fascists", as the only one remaining.

During May, Mussolini reduced the Italian electorate from twelve million people to three million. Those purged from the voting rolls were, of course, individuals who had voted against the Fascists or whose loyalty to the regime was questionable.

During October 1930 Mussolini began a propaganda campaign demanding significant changes in the Versailles Treaty.

On September 2, 1931, Mussolini's government signed a concordant with the Vatican guaranteeing freedom of religion in Italy so long as the Church remained out of politics. Also during the year, he outlawed homosexuality and passed a regulation encouraging civil servants to have large families as an incentive for promotion. Both of these measures were pleasing to the Vatican and to the supporters of Fascism.

CRASH! HERE COME THE NAZIS

In far-away America, on October 24, 1929, stock prices on the New York Stock Exchange suddenly plummeted — then plummeted again, and yet again in the following days. The roaring twenties had come to a sudden end. Since the United States was, by now, such a financial giant in the world economy, the adverse effects of the crash soon spread abroad.

Life bust of Geli Raubal, Hitler's niece.

If there was one country in the world that did not need more bad economic news, it was Germany. When the effects of the crash reached Germany, the German economy began a rapid downward spiral that seemed to have no end. Stock prices in Germany plummeted, industrial production fell by half, foreign trade dropped by two-thirds, corporations went into bankruptcy, banks failed, and once again, unemployment soared. The German political scene exploded. Now, vast numbers of the German electorate lost all faith in the political moderates and wanted quick and decisive solutions. They found what they wanted in the preaching of the extremist parties on both ends of the political spectrum.

On the political right, it was the showy and gregarious Nazi Party that benefitted the most. In January 1930, local elections were held in Thuringia and the local Nazi leader there, Wilhelm Frick, became provincial Minister of the Interior. This was the first high office acquired by the Nazis.

During March 1930, the national government in Berlin — the seventeenth in ten years — fell and on the 30th of the month a new right-of-center government was formed. The Nazis were not a part of it, but the trend of the German political scene was clearly moving in their direction.

Also during March 1930, the Nazis introduced a land reform program that would make modest-sized parcels of land available for the peasant farmers. The program also included the promise of government subsidies.

In September 1930, national elections were held and the fortunes of the Nazis surged. They won 103 seats in the Riechstag making them the strongest right-wing political faction in the assembly. The prospects of a dictatorship were in the air. On September 30, President Hindenburg asked the Reichstag for temporary dictatorial powers to deal with the economic crisis. This was not granted, but the concept of a dictatorship in Germany was now on the political table, and from the highest voice in the land.

At this point, all eyes were on the Nazis. In late November 1930, local elections were held in Bremen and the Nazis scored another victory at the polls.

By the end of 1930, Nazi Party membership had risen to 129,563, up from 96,918 in 1928.

During the summer of 1931, with the Nazi Party having become a force to be reckoned with, Hitler was given the honor of a meeting with President Hindenburg. The meeting was more symbolic than substantive. About this time, too, the Party became financially self-supporting from Party dues and small contributions from Party members and supporters. Because of this, the Nazi Party, and Hitler were beholden to no one except their own constituents.

THE SUICIDE OF HITLER'S NIECE, GELI RAUBAL

On the evening of September 18, 1931, Hitler, while on Party business in Munich, received a dreadful phone call. His twenty-two-year-old niece, Geli Raubal, had committed suicide in his apartment. Geli and her mother Angela Hitler Raubal, Hitler's half sister, lived with Hitler in his spacious apartment in Munich. He had engaged An-

Hitler shown with his half-sister, Angela Rabual.

gela in 1930 to serve as his hostess for the social functions he frequently held in his apartment. Along with Angela, came Geli. Hitler then became the father-figure in that relationship and, by most accounts, was a firm taskmaster when it came to Geli's activities.

Details of Geli's death are sketchy, but it appears that Hitler and Geli had a violent argument on that morning over her wanting to go to Vienna to study singing. Hitler angrily refused to consider it and then left for his appointments. Geli retired to her bedroom and, sometime during the day, shot herself through the heart. This tragedy was to haunt Hitler the rest of his life. He kept her bedroom as it was when she died, making it something of a shrine to Geli's memory.

NAZIS WIN AGAIN

In November 1931, the Nazis won the local election in the province of Hesse and, in January 1932, national elections were held again and the Nazis won 37.4% of the vote, the strongest showing of any party. This gave the Nazis 229 seats in the Reichstag. Yet, President Hindenburg, who knew

that Hitler would try to destroy the democratic process in Germany, was reluctant to allow Hitler to form a government and gave the honor to another right-winger, Heinrich Bruening. Bruening had promised to uphold the democratic process.

During this time, another election campaign was underway for the election of Germany's Presidency itself. The vote was scheduled for March 13, 1932. In February, Hitler felt politically strong enough to run for that office, but he had to become a German citizen in order to meet constitutional requirements. Hitler applied for German citizenship and it was granted on February 25, just in time for the election.

Hitler's main opponents were Hindenburg, who was running for reelection, and a strong communist candidate. When the elections of March 13, and a subsequent runoff of April 10, were held, Hindenburg won with a vote count of eighteen million, but Hitler made a strong showing by coming in second with a vote count of eleven million. The communist candidate received five million.

In July, yet another election was held and the Nazis did very well again, so well in fact, that Hermann Goering, sometimes called

"The Number Two Nazi," was elected President of the Reichstag.

EVA BRAUN

In 1929, Hitler met another teenage girl, 17-year-old Eva Braun, who was an assistant to his photographer friend Heinrich Hoffmann. Hitler was 40. With time, a relationship developed and by 1932 she was his mistress. But she was a very unhappy mistress. Hitler would make arrangements for them to be together and invariably cancel at the last minute due

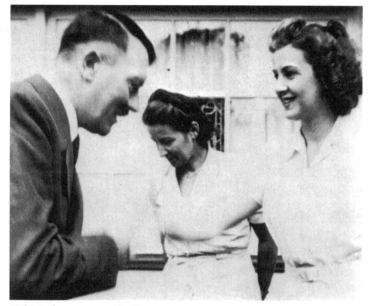
Hitler and a very young Eva Braun.

to his tortuous schedule. On September 1, 1932, out of desperation and despair, she attempted suicide, shooting herself in the neck with a gun. The wound was not fatal, she recovered, and the incident was hushed up. But it was a wake-up call for Hitler. In the days that followed, he lavished her with gifts and devoted as much time as he possibly could to be with her. For Hitler, the aspiring politician, this was one more burden on his shoulders, albeit a pleasant one.

Angela, Hitler's half-sister, who was still serving as his formal hostess in his Munich apartment, did not like Eva. A few months after Angela's daughter, Geli, committed suicide, Angela and Hitler had a falling out over Eva and Angela moved out of the apartment. From then on, the relationship between Hitler and Angela was strained.

HITLER AND HIS HEALTH

Hitler had a life-long concern about his health. He mentioned his health in Mein Kampf several times and claimed that he had a bad lung disease in 1905 that he thought was tuberculosis. By this time in his life, he believed he could control many of his health problems with a vegetarian diet. He also believed that eating meat paved the way for smoking and excessive drinking.

Hitler had smoked quite heavily during his Vienna days — 20 to 40 cigarettes a day, but by now he had come to detest smoking and did not like for others to smoke in his presence. He had given up all hard liquor and drank wine and beer only occasionally. As for beer, he commented that one, just before bedtime, helped him sleep. The future Fuehrer had an enemy with which he had to do constant battle — germs. When his schedule permitted, he bathed frequently, washed his hair every day, washed his hands repeatedly, brushed his teeth after every meal, shaved twice a day and changed clothes two to three times a day. On one occasion, he told his dentist that he had a "noxious bacteria" infection in his colon that could only be controlled by a special diet.

When he travelled, he always carried a suitcase full of medicines.

In 1928, he wrote to an associate saying, "...even at best... (I have) barely twenty years available." This implied that he believed he would die around the age of sixty.

During the summer of 1932, he had come to believe that he might have colon cancer. Hitler said to an aide, "I have no time to wait. I must have power soon in order to solve the colossal tasks in the time remaining to me. I must! I must!" Hitler was 43. His mother had died of breast cancer at age 47.

NAZIS COME TO POWER

The political turmoil continued in Germany until January 1933, when yet another national election was held. In this election the Nazis scored bigger yet, winning 43.9% of the vote, again, the most of any party.

Because of this sizeable vote, which was something of a popular mandate in German politics, Hindenburg could no longer deny Hitler the opportunity to form a government. In the negotiating that followed, the Nazis concluded an agreement with their closest rival, The Germany National People's Party (DNVP — "Nationalists") to form a coalition government with Hitler as Chancellor. Hindenburg accepted the arrangement and on January 30, 1933, Hitler became Chancellor of Germany. His Vice-Chancellor was the highly respected leader of the Nationalist Party and former Chancellor, Fritz von Papen.

The Nazis had arrived — but at what cost to Germany?

CHAPTER 6

THE EMERGENCE OF NAZI GERMANY—1933

Hitler's elevation to the position of Chancellor, on January 30, 1933, was a necessary first step in the Nazi plan to gain complete control of Germany. Becoming Chancellor did not yet mean that Hitler could rule indiscriminately. He still had to gain the support of his coalition partners, the Nationalists, satisfy the Reichstag, and retain the support of President Hindenburg. Of the three, the Reichstag, being dominated by Nazis and Nationalists and with Hermann Goering serving as its President, would be the easiest to win over. The other two would be more difficult and would have to be attained through negotiations.

The toughest obstacles of all facing Chancellor Hitler, given the history of past Chancellorships, was to somehow survive in office long enough to make a difference.

In a move to gain popular support, Hitler immediately waived his salary as Chancellor. By now, he was living quite well off of the royalties from Mein Kampf.

THE POLITICAL LEFT THREATENS

The rise of the right-wing parties to power in Germany posed a condition that the extreme political left could never accept. The Nazis and Nationalist were the arch-enemies of the communists and socialists and co-existence was next to impossible.

The violence that everyone realized might happen began immediately on the morning of January 31. It was the Nazis who struck first. All over Germany, SA men took to the streets, roughing up communists and socialists. They surged into public buildings and unceremoniously forced leftist mayors and other high officials out of their offices. Private homes of some of the opposition leaders were also entered and damaged. The communist reaction was to call for a general strike—which was only partially successful. In some places, there were leftist counter-demonstrations, but the Hitler government and the Nazi Party were prepared. And they had the upper hand. Hitler, as Chancellor, could command the loyal support of most of the police forces throughout Germany and, of course, could count on his own, well-seasoned, SA Brown Shirts. In the arena of demonstrations, the Nazis, with their uniformed and disciplined SA men could, in most instances, out-demonstrate the forces of the left. In the realm of riots and street battles, Hitler here again had the upper hand, by using the German police to make arrests and the SA to bash heads.

Still, the violence from the left was so intense and threatening that the prospect of revolution, and/or civil war, loomed. With nine million unemployed, there were plenty of angry and desperate men available to make a revolution.

Hitler was fully aware of these dangers and would say years later, "…we were on the verge of catastrophe."

…WITH A VENGEANCE

In the days after becoming Chancellor, Hitler began to implement his plan to become the dictator of Germany but his powers were limited by the German constitution. Under the constitution, only President Hindenburg, in cooperation with the Reichstag, could give a Chancellor dictatorial powers, and for a limited time only. To bring this about, there had to be a national emergency. With the German political scene so polarized and revolution in the air, a national emergency was a very likely possibility.

Until that time occurred, Hitler's plan was to do whatever it took to firm up his position and to carry out whatever social and economic reforms he could manage to gain the confidence of both the people and Hindenburg.

On February 1, 1933, he dissolved the Reichstag in order to silence whatever opposition he had there until the next election. Furthermore, under the constitution, the President could authorize the Chancellor to rule by decree until a new Reichstag was elected. Hindenburg reluctantly gave Hitler this authority.

Shortly thereafter, the election for a new Reichstag was set for March 5. So, once again, the Nazis and the other political parties began election campaigning. A new Nazi slogan was coined for this election and set the tone of the Nazi campaign; it was "Attack against Marxism." It was Hitler's hope that the German electorate would now vote the Nazis back into office with a majority vote, 50% or more, allowing him to rule on his own without his Nationalist coalition partner.

On February 2, Hitler issued orders putting curbs on the leftists on the grounds that they were disturbing the peace and threatening criminal activities. This gave the Nazis control of the streets. On the 6th, he imposed censorship on the German press.

In Prussia, the largest province in Germany with Berlin as its capital, Hermann Goering was Provincial Minister of the Interior and, as such, head of the Prussian police. He began, at once, a campaign to rid the streets of Prussia of prostitutes. The main reason given was to stem the tide of venereal disease, especially syphilis. Ridding Germany of syphilis had been a long-standing goal of the Nazi Party and that goal was well-known to the public. It will also be remembered that Hitler devoted ten pages to the subject in Mein Kampf.

Here now, in Prussia, the Nazis were demonstrating that they intended to carry out their promises. The next day, Goering issued another decree closing down short-term hotels and other places frequented by prostitutes and homosexuals. These clamp downs were the first Nazi programs bestowed on the German people. There would be many more to come, and the German people were told of that, time and again, by the spokesmen of the Hitler government.

Working behind the scenes, Hitler confirmed his campaign promises to the German military leaders that he would begin conscription as soon as possible as well as commence the rebuilding of Germany's armed forces.

On February 6, Hindenburg, at Hitler's request, issued an edict entitled "For the Restoration of Regulated Governmental Conditions in Prussia." This closed down the elected government in Prussia and, at Hindenburg's insistence, turned the affairs of the province over to Vice Chancellor von Papen, whom he trusted and who, for the moment at least, was cooperating with Hitler. The end result was that democracy in Prussia was dead. It had long been the announced goal of both the Nazis and Nationalists to end democracy in all parts of Germany and this was an imposing and precedent-setting first step.

On the 10th, Hitler addressed the German voters via radio regarding the upcoming elections. His message was, "Give us four years, then judge us."

On the 15th, Interior Minister Goering appointed thirteen loyal Nazis to the posts of police chief in the major cities in Prussia, including Berlin.

During these days, Hitler's SA boys were very active and given a virtual free hand by the German police. SA men raided communist headquarters, disrupted their meetings and sacked several of their printing offices. The communists did not take this lying down. They fought back with the same tactics. Confrontations in Prussia and elsewhere were commonplace.

On February 20, 1933, Hitler met with German industrialists at the "Industry Club" in Dusseldorf, to assure them that he could carry out his promises to stimulate the German economy, to build up a military arsenal, and to guarantee that they would retain control and ownership of their industrial assets. Furthermore, he asked them to support him in ridding Germany of the communist menace, an issue that was dear to their hearts. For this he needed money. The Party coffers were low and money was needed to do the necessary campaigning for the March election. The industrialists embraced Hitler and his program with enthusiasm. Gustav Krupp, head of the gigantic Krupp industrial empire, stood up at the meeting and pledged one million marks to the Nazi Party. This opened a flood gate. Georg von Schnitzler, head of I. G. Farben, followed with a pledge of 400,000 marks. Others followed with their pledges. By the conclusion of the meeting, Hitler had his money and the support of the industrialists.

The day after Hitler met with the industrialists, one of the largest communist organizations in the country, "The Union of Red Fighters", urged its members, and German workers in general, to disarm the SA. Hitler saw this as an opportunity more than a threat. He would let the Reds strike first and then use that as an excuse to launch a massive counter-strike. If a civil war was to start, it would be the Reds who started it.

In the midst of this turmoil, Hitler issued a series of decrees designed to curry favor with the German people as well as to carry out some of the party's previous campaign promises. On February 23, Hitler issued a decree that banned all forms of pornography and closed down the "League of Human Rights" which had been outspoken on the rights of homosexuals. With regards to homosexuals, the Nazis' wrath was directed primarily against male homosexuals. Female homosexuals were not overly harassed because they were seen, despite their sexual orientation, as producers of much-wanted German babies.

Then, incredibly, on February 27, as everyone waited in a state of extreme tension to see if the Union of Red Fighters would carry out its threat, a momentous event occurred. The Reichstag building was destroyed by fire—and a communist extremist was caught in the act.

THE REICHSTAG FIRE

It was just past 9 p.m. on the night of February 27, 1933, when a passing pedestrian noticed smoke coming from a second-story window of the Reichstag building. He also saw the shadow of a man behind the window carrying a flaming torch. The pedestrian immediately called authorities and, by the time the first firemen arrived, at 9:20, the main chamber was completely engulfed in flames. Minutes later, a policeman grabbed a young man inside the building who was stripped to the waist and running down the hall of the burning building shouting communist slogans. On the way to the station, the man was laughing and gibbering senselessly. He had no identification on him.

At about 10:00 p.m., Prussian Interior Minister Goering, arrived, then, minutes later, Hitler and Goebbels arrived. Hitler sensed the importance of the moment and summoned up all of his theatrical skills. He posed dramatically for several minutes, in silence, staring at the burning building for the benefit of the photographers. He then turned to the gathered reporters and in a most dramatic voice shouted, " Now we will show them! Anyone who stands in our way will be mowed down! Every communist official must be shot! All communists deputies must be hanged this very night!"

Such vile pronouncements from the Chancellor of Germany would have been unthinkable under normal circumstances—but this was far from normal. The Nazis went into action. Goering ordered his Prussian police to arrest every known communist in Prussia. Goebbels ordered all of his people at the Minister of Enlightenment and Propaganda to report to work—in the middle of the night. By midnight his ministry was whipping out one report after another on the fire and its implications. Many came to believe that this was the action the Union of Red Fighters had threatened.

Meanwhile, at the police station the suspected arsonist was identified as 24 year-old Marinus van der Lube, a Dutch citizen, who confessed to setting the fire in the hopes of starting a communist revolution in Germany. Van der Lubbe's claim that he had acted alone was withheld from the public. The Nazis wanted the public to think that the burning of the Reichstag was a dastardly communist conspiracy.

The next morning, February 28, Hitler called an emergency meeting of his Cabinet. It was unanimously agreed that the Chancellor should issue a decree entitled "Decree for the Protection of the People and the State" that would suspend Article 48 of the German constitution, the German equivalent to the American "Bill of Rights."

The Nazis were quick to point out, as a precedent, that similar action was taken against them in November 1923 at the time of their Putsch.

President Hindenburg signed the decree, and by nightfall Goering's police had some 500 communists and other political opponents in custody. Berlin's jail were overflowing.

In the days that followed, the government claimed to have discovered evidence revealing that the communist uprising was to have begun at 4:00 a.m. on the morning of February 28, just hours after the fire was started. These reports were widely believed.

Van der Lubbe was tried, found guilty, and executed.

THE GRAB FOR POWER

With the election only nine days away, the Nazis drove home their claim that the nation was on the verge of a revolution and that their quick actions had saved the day.

As the campaign progressed, the leaders of the German Army remained silent. Hitler took that as a very good omen—that the Army was with him.

Prussian Interior Minister Goering saw the need to increase his police force in the wake of the pending communist revolution, so he began to deputize members of the SA as auxiliary policemen. Since it had always been the duty of the GESTAPO, an acronym for the Prussian secret state police, to monitor the activities of subversives, these new men were placed in that department. In the weeks that followed, some 4,000 SA men became Prussian Gestapomen. Furthermore, with the jails of Prussia overflowing, Goering ordered the building of a temporary prison camp at Oranienburg to hold many of those detained. It would soon be referred to as a concentration camp.

Also in the weeks following the Reichstag fire, the Hitler government found cause to suppress the Social Democrat Party, the strongest left-of-center party in the country. These efforts destroyed the party as a political force.

THE MARCH 5 ELECTIONS: A RUDE AWAKENING

During the last days of February and the first days of March 1933, the Nazis campaigned with great vigor. As he had done in previous campaigns, Hitler flew from place to place in an airplane demonstrating that he was a "modern man" and that he had great faith in Germany's aircraft industry. Upon landing, he would often emerge from the airplane wearing an aviator's helmet for the benefit of the photographers.

On March 3, Goering, in an effort to gather in more votes, issued another decree in Prussia putting strict controls on nudism, a health fad that had blossomed in Germany during the 1920s, but was an aberration to most Germans.

On March 5, 90% of Germany's registered voters went to the polls. But the results were a great disappointment for the Nazis. Hitler did not get the majority he had hoped for. Actually, this vote was little different than that in January. The Nazis acquired slightly more than 44% of the vote, up from 43.9% in January. Thus, they still needed the Nationalists as a coalition partner. The newly elected Reichstag came together, now, in Berlin's Kroll Opera House. Hitler had lost his power to rule by decree, but he began taking steps to see that this was Germany's last national election.

The Nazis hid their disappointment and claimed that this election was yet another mandate from the people as had been the election in January.

A cartoon at the time critical of the Nazi takeover of the Reichsbank. Monday June 19, 1933 (note the sign), was the first day of the bank's operation under Nazi control.

THE NAZIFICATION OF GERMANY; THE ALL-IMPORTANT "ENABLING ACT"

Despite the Nazi disappointment at the polls, President Hindenburg appeared to be pleased with the actions the Hitler government had taken and showed it by calling Hitler to meet with him without Vice Chancellor Papen being present. This was a significant display of respect toward Hitler. Years later, Hitler would write of this meeting, "The old gentleman... had progressed so far that his attitude towards me became affectionate and paternal..."

And it was time for the Nazis to pay off political debts. In this, and other recent elections, the German upper class had become relatively strong supporters of, and contributors to, the Nazi Party. To show his appreciation and maintain their further support, Hitler now began to make the rounds of upper class parties and social events. He wore a tuxedo, kissed ladies' hands, sipped champagne and tried not to monopolize the conversation. At these endeavors, Hitler was noticeably awkward and uncomfortable, but the members of the German aristocracy loved the attention.

At the other end of the social spectrum, Reichstag President Goering began a bold program of threats and intimidation to bring the non-Nazis of the Reichstag into line. It was the Nazi's plan to introduce into the Reichstag an "Enabling Act" which would allow Chancellor Hitler to rule, once again, by decree, but for an unlimited period of time. To obtain this, Goering needed the approval of two-thirds of the Reichstag, an additional 43 votes over those that he controlled. Goering made no secret of his intentions to secure them. He stated publicly, "...my measures will not be crippled by any legislative hesitation. Here, I don't have to give justice, here I have only to destroy and exterminate, nothing more..." This was a threat to use force against those who opposed the Enabling Act, and Goering had the muscle to carry out this threat in the form of the SA.

Meanwhile, the Nazification of Germany continued. On March 12, President

Hindenburg, at Hitler's request, decreed that the swastika flag of the Nazi Party could be flown throughout Germany, with equal status, alongside the regular tri-color flag of Germany. More than a year later, in September 1934, a month after Hindenburg died, Hitler decreed that the Nazi flag was Germany's only national flag.

On March 16, 1933, Hitler maneuvered one of his most loyal followers, Hjalmar Horace Greeley Schacht, into the presidency of the Reichsbank, Germany's central bank. Now the Nazis controlled Germany's money supply and banking system. Hitler knew that Schacht would cooperate with him when it came time to rearm Germany.

During the third week of March, a second concentration camp was opened in an abandoned powder factory near Dachau. Other camps were being constructed or being planned.

On March 23, Hitler's supporters introduced the Enabling Act into the Reichstag. It was officially titled "Law to Remove the Distress of the People and the State." Hitler then spoke to the assembly telling them of the great need for the legislation. He spoke in glowing terms of the bright future for Germany and that Germany's Third Reich, which he would give them, would last for a thousand years. Uniformed and armed SA and SS men patrolled the opera house's lobby and corridors as the action in the assembly was taking place. The next day the Reichstag passed the Enabling Act 441 to 94. Hindenburg then signed it into law.

Goering had done his job well. Buried deep in the fine print of the act was the most important clause in the bill. It allowed the Chancellor to "...deviate from the Reich Constitution..." The law also authorized Chancellor Hitler to rule by decree until April 1, 1937—an unprecedented length of time.

The practice of using positive-sounding titles and including important clauses in fine print in legislation would become a Nazi trademark.

GERMAN EXPANSIONISM RAISES ITS UGLY HEAD

In his speech to the Reichstag on March 23, Hitler made a remark that caused considerable concern among Germany's neighbors. Hitler declared that his government would use "...all means at its disposal" to protect Germans living in foreign lands. In countries such as Austria, Poland and Switzerland, which had large German-speaking populations, Hitler's remark was viewed as an intrusion into their internal affairs.

Behind closed doors, Hitler did, indeed, intend to interfere with the internal affairs of other countries and his ambitions stretched well beyond his immediate neighbors. He told a small gathering of his closest associates that Germany should, in addition to seeking an alliance with Italy, work toward seeking an alliance of sorts with "...the Ukraine, the Volga basin, Georgia. An alliance, but not of equal partners; it will be an alliance of vassal states with no army, no separate policy, no separate economy." This was very similar to the arrangement Germany had enjoyed briefly in 1918 after the signing of the Brest-Litovsk Peace Treaty with the Bolsheviks. This brief accomplishment was viewed by every German as a major German victory of the Great War. Reviving it was a dream the Nazis knew they could easily sell to the German people—when the time came.

But, this was not the time to act. Hitler was not yet Germany's all-powerful dictator and could do virtually nothing toward expanding Germany's "liebensraum" (living space), a word used generously in Nazi propaganda. He was restrained from pursuing this goal any further because of his lack of military means and because of the constitutional powers accredited to President Hindenburg. At this point in time, Hitler dared not jeopardize his delicate relationship with the President.

HITLER TAKES CONTROL OF HIS CABINET

By now, the Nazis had proven that they would not hesitate using any means necessary to have their way. This fact was duly

A poster publicizing the first Nazi-controlled May Day celebration.

The first order of business was to take control of all of the departments of the national government and many of Germany's major institutions. From the Chancellor's office came a steady stream of decrees to make these things happen. Hindenburg was usually consulted beforehand to make sure he would not object. Many of these things appealed to Hindenburg's monarchist sympathies, so he went along.

Wilhelm Frick, Minister of the Interior in Hitler's Cabinet and a Nazi, was given the task of physically taking over the offices of government. Goebbels took control of all radio stations in Germany and put them under his control at the newly-formed Ministry of Enlightenment and Propaganda. The takeover of Germany's press was begun by Goebbels and would be implemented step-by-step over a period of months.

On April 1, 1933, the Nazi Party called for a one-day boycott of all Jewish businesses. Many Germans ignored the boycott and it was not very successful. That same day, the German government seized the personal assets of physicist Albert Einstein, one of Germany's most famous Jewish expatriates.

Also that day, Hitler met with industrialist Alfred Krupp at the Chancellory, and the two gentlemen struck a deal. Hitler asked Krupp to head a new program for the Party's solicitation of funds from industry. That program would be known as "The Adolf Hitler Fund." If Krupp accepted, it would be the only solicitation the Nazi Party would make on industry. Along with the chairmanship of the Fund, Krupp would be given the official title "Fuehrer" of German industry. Krupp accepted and an arrangement was worked out whereby one-half of one percent of the workers' wages and salaries would be deducted from their paychecks and passed on to the Party. This program worked very well and, in time, became the Party's largest source of revenue.

On April 7, "The Law for the Reestablishment of the Professional Civil Service" was enacted. This law purged from civil

noted by Hitler's Nationalist Cabinet members who, by now, had no effective countermeasures. Alfred Hugenburg, one of the most powerful members of the Nationalist Party serving as Economics Minister, was then forced out of office as a warning to the others. The remaining Nationalist members, knowing that they too could be forced out, became completely subservient to Hitler. This also applied to Vice Chancellor Papen.

A DELUGE OF DECREES

The Nazis wasted no time in forcing National Socialism on the German people, whether they wanted it or not. But it must be remembered that it was the people of Germany who voted the Nazis, and their cohorts, the Nationalists, into office knowing full well that they intended to destroy the democratic process.

service all communists, Jews and political opponents of the Nazis. It also incorporated all recognized news journalists into the civil service thus making them servants of the state.

On April 20, Goering replaced von Papen as the Prime Minister of Prussia. Goering, as Prussia's Interior Minister had, heretofore, ruled the roost in Prussia with Papen's tacit approval. Now, the arrangement was simply formalized. Six days later, the Gestapo department of the Prussian police was elevated, by the Hitler government, to a nation-wide organization.

On the 25th, another law was enacted entitled "Law Against Overcrowding in German Schools." This law set a quota of 1% on the enrollment of Jews in Germany's universities, their proportion in the general population of Germany. Since the enrollment of Jews in the universities was currently 10%, nine out of ten Jewish students had to leave school.

On May 1, the huge annual workers'-oriented May Day celebration was conducted all over Germany. Heretofore, this event was leftist oriented, but now it was an all-Nazi event complete with Nazi trappings and Nazi rhetoric. Even its name was Nazified. It was officially renamed "The National Festival of the German People." The event had been organized by Goebbels and would continue as an annual affair under the auspices of his Ministry.

Also on May 1, a somewhat negative decree was issued and purposely downplayed under the hoopla of the National Festival celebrations. It was that new membership in the Nazi party was to be temporarily suspended. In the last year or so, Party membership had soared to the point where the Party was becoming unmanageable. At this time, Party membership was nearly 850,000.

On May 2, all of Germany's 216 trade unions were closed down and their assets confiscated by the government and 88 labor leaders, with doubtful loyalty to the Hitler government, were arrested. On the 10th, Germany's workers became members of one nation-wide, government-approved trade union, the "Deutsche Arbeiter Front" (German Labor Front—DAF). Its leader was Robert Ley, a Hitler loyalist. Jews were denied membership in the DAF and employment for German workers in many of Germany's trades was now dependent on approval by the union.

The emergence of the DAF was to have a negative effect in Germany over the next few years. The decree establishing the DAF also froze wages and required each worker, union or not, to pay union dues to the DAF through a payroll deduction. Also, in every factory a government-appointed "Labor Front Leader" was appointed for every 20 workers. These measures were resented by most of the workers and their work incentive declined. This was reflected in a decline in the quality and quantity of goods produced. Also, a black market was created. But, the view from the Chancellory was more positive because the Nazi Party now had control over the principal breeding-ground for leftist political activities.

Later in the month, another decree ended collective bargaining and replaced it with a system whereby disputes were settled by a board of "labor trustees", whose members were appointed by the government. German industrial leaders were delighted. The workers, many of whom had supported the communists and socialists, now dared not to speak out against the Nazis or the company managers. All knew that their jobs were at stake.

To win over the workers, Ley soon introduced a new vacation program called "Strength-Through-Joy." This program provided conducted tours and cruises at rates the average worker could afford. Among the first excursions offered was a trip to Italy costing only $62.00.

On May 10, Goebbels, as Gauleiter of Berlin, organized a massive book burning ceremony in the Franz Joseph Platz in Berlin. As the books burned, Goebbels went on radio to explain to the German people that the burning was a symbolic gesture that decadent printed material within the Reich would be purged and that "…the evil spirits of the past… (and) the age of intellectualism…" were over.

On the 15th, the "Reich Hereditary Farm Law" was passed. This law prevented the family farms of Germany from being further splintered into ever smaller parcels by declaring that such farms must be passed on, in their entirety, to one heir.

Another event that happened in Nazi Germany during May was the appearance, in the market place, of cheap radios. This was a subsidized government program to enable the German people to more easily receive the propaganda and messages the government wanted them to receive. During 1933, Hitler would take full advantage of this development and address the German people 50 times—almost once a week. Goebbels' Ministry also set up a world-wide broadcasting system to disseminate Nazi propaganda abroad and tout the upcoming 1936 Olympics which were to be held in Berlin.

On June 1, the "Law for the Reduction of Unemployment" was decreed. This was a make-work program known as the "Reinhardt Program". Unemployment was a major problem in Germany and the Nazis had promised to correct it. In many areas of the country the unemployment rate was 15% or more, and in a few areas it was as high as 75%. The program showed success and in the next few years more make-work programs were instigated.

During June 1933, another law appeared to help further alleviate unemployment as well as stimulate marriages. This law allowed any newly-married couple to take out a loan of 1000 marks provided the woman agreed to remain out of the work place to make a job available for another. Also, for each child born, 250 marks of the loan was forgiven.

GERMAN FOREIGN POLICY DETERIORATED

Almost without exception, Germany's European neighbors were greatly concerned about the events occurring in Germany.

Hitler's radical ideas and plans for territorial expansion were no longer the mere rhetoric of an aggressive political party, but were now a part of Germany's foreign policy.

Hitler was fully aware of the fears he had created in Europe. To allay these fears as much as possible, he made several public conciliatory comments toward his neighbors and claimed that he wanted only peace. In fact, however, he was only trying to buy time. He needed to consolidate his control in Germany and build up Germany's military strength before venturing into the rough and tumble arena of international politics.

MORE NAZIFICATION FOR GERMANY

Meanwhile, the Nazis tightened their grip on Germany.

On June 18, Hitler made a confidential speech to members of the SA in which he threatened to take away the children of those parents who opposed him and raise the children in Nazi-approved foster homes or in state institutions. Word of this soon reached the public which showed a measure of alarm for such a cruel program. But there was no disclaimer or apology forthcoming from the Chancellery.

On June 22, the Social Democrat Party, whose leaders were in jail, and the Nationalist Party, whose leaders were in the Cabinet, were dissolved by a decree from the Chancellory. There were no organized protests.

GERMAN REARMAMENT BEGINS—SECRETLY

By the end of June, the top Nazi leaders had formulated their plans to rebuild Germany's armed forces. The first undertaking would be to establish an air force. This could be done, in part, under the guise of commercial aviation. Furthermore, some military efforts to build up a German air force had already been conducted secretly by the Weimar governments in, of all places, the Soviet Union. Under the Nazi plan, Goering, who was to head the new air force, issued secret orders on June 29 to the necessary military and industrial leaders for the creation of 32 squadrons of military aircraft (about 320 planes). The target date for their activation was set for October 1934.

Another part of the rearmament plan was to increase the number of German border guards as well as the number of reservists for the SA. These new recruits were given military training in preparation for the time when they would become soldiers in the Army.

AND MORE DECREES

On July 14, Hitler's government enacted another law entitled, "Law to Prevent the Spread of Hereditary Diseases." This was a law that allowed certain individuals, who might pass on hereditary deceases to the offsprings, to be sterilized. For adults it was a voluntary program and for children the consent of their parents or guardian was required. In time, the program would become mandatory.

That same day, July 14, Goebbels' Ministry took control of Germany's movie industry.

On July 20, Germany's Minister of the Interior, Frick, announced that the Nazi's out-stretched arm salute, accompanied by the verbal salute, "Heil Hitler", was now to be used as the primary formal greeting for all Germans.

PEACE WITH THE VATICAN

Also on the 20th, the German government signed a concordat with the Vatican. Here, Hitler followed Mussolini's lead in making peace with the Catholic Church—another action that improved Germany's international image. The Concordat guaranteed that the Catholic Church could continue its operations in Germany without interference from the government so long as it stayed out of politics. Signing for the Vatican was Cardinal Eugenio Pacelli who would become the next Pope. Vice Chancellor von Papen, a practicing Catholic, signed for Germany.

It was about this time that the government began an effort to replace the word "Christmas" with "Yuletide."

NAZIFICATION OF GERMANY CONTINUES

Hitler's government designated August 12 as Mothers' Day in Germany. This was Hitler's Mother's birthday. In time, an official decoration in the form of "Mother's Crosses" was created and awarded to the most deserving mothers in the land—women who had from four to eight children. For four children, the woman would receive the Bronze Mother's Cross, for six children, the Silver Mother's Cross, and for eight or more the Gold Mother's Cross. Furthermore, recipients of Mother's Crosses would be given some financial aid from the government and hailed by members of the Nazi Party with the Nazi salute. It was not long after their inception that the Mother's Cross acquired another name, "The Order of the Rabbit."

The creation of a Mothers' Day was only a part of the government's overall, and ongoing, program to reverse the trend toward the emancipation of women which had occurred during the 1920s. In Nazi ideology, the woman's place was in the home. The Nazi leaders frequently made use of an old German saying, called the three-Ks, which spelled out the idyllic role for a woman, "Kuche, Kinder, Kirche" (Kitchen, Children, Church).

Abortion was seen by the Nazis as a plague upon the German people. Under the Weimar Republic the fine for an abortion was a mere forty marks. The Nazis greatly increased the fine and issued a decree giving doctors who performed abortion prison sentences of from six to fifteen year.

With regards to the Jewish question, Hitler's government, during August 1933, arrived at an understanding with Jewish leaders in Germany that German Jews could leave the country and take with them their assets so long as they left voluntarily. This was known as the "Haavara Agreement" (Transfer Agreement). One of the main features of the agreement was that the government would help the German Jews emigrate to Palestine. This agreement was doomed to failure. The Arab world rose up as one voice bitterly opposing the influx of Jews into Palestine and the British, who controlled Palestine under a League of Nations mandate, rejected the idea out of hand. Most other countries of the world let it be know that they, too, would not welcome any large number of German Jews. With these barriers facing them, the majority of German Jews remained in Germany.

At this point, the situation took a turn for the worst in that the government began arresting Jews, usually on trumped up charges, and casting them into the rapidly expanding system of concentration camps.

On September 1, 1933, Hitler, speaking at the annual Nazi Party Day at Nuremberg, blessed the German people with yet another social improvement. This was in the field of art, one of his most beloved subjects. He told the people that, in Germany, all facets of the art world, henceforth, would be kept on a strictly "Nordic basis." Hitler, a traditionalist with regard to art and a self-styled art expert, now outlawed all forms of modern art and other art that he deemed to be decadent. During the month, Hitler laid the corner stone of a new art museum in Munich to be called the "House of German Art." At the same time, he designated Munich as the art center of Germany. Munich had been the home base for the Nazi Party since the Party's inception. In the Nazi view of things, this was a pay-back for the consistent support the people of Munich had demonstrated in supporting Hitler's rise to power. It was also a factor in Hitler's personal planning. If the time ever came when he would leave politics, it was his plan to resume his life as an artist and spend more time in Munich.

Another government program introduced in September was a program called the "Reichsnahrstand" (German Food Estate). This extended government controls over all aspects of German agriculture; growing, processing and the distribution of food, forestry, fishing, hunting, bakeries, breweries, and more.

Also during September, it was announced with great fanfare, that the promised program to build "Autobahns" (super highways) all over Germany had begun. The first Autobahn would be built between Frankfurt and Heidelberg and others would soon follow. In a much-publicized ground-breaking ceremony, Hitler turned the first spade-full of earth.

Then, there were the street people. It had long been a Nazi goal to remove these people from Germany's cities. September 18 through 25 was designated by the government as "Beggars Week." More than 100,000 beggars and homeless people all over Germany were taken off the streets and detained by the police. But within a few days, most of them were released because the police had no facilities in which to keep them. These individuals were, however, now required to carry with them at all time a "Vagrant's Registration Book" and log in the book all of their overnight stays in shelters. This way, the government could keep track of most of them.

Back in April 1933, the Hitler government had nationalized the nation's journalist. Now it was the editors' turn. In October, a decree was issued requiring all editors to obtain licenses from the Ministry of Propaganda and, in the future, abide by standards prescribed by that Ministry for their profession.

On October 14, Germany withdrew from the League of Nations, claiming that that body was grossly unfair to Germany.

On November 1, 1933, another new governmental program known as the "Chamber of Culture" was announced. This organization, controlled by Goebbels, brought together all theatrical people, artists, poets, authors, musicians, etc. under one organization. Membership was mandatory in order to work in Germany. Jews were prohibited from membership.

On December 1, the "Law to Secure Unity of the Party and the State" was enacted that merged the Nazi Party with the government of Germany. This law made many Party workers civil servants who would now be paid from state funds rather than from the Party coffers. It also opened the door for Party members to more easily acquire government jobs, and for those in high places to participate more effectively in the traditional spoils system that had long existed in German politics. Furthermore, the Party gained another measure of protection because an attack on the Party was now viewed as an attack on the government, and such attacks were punishable by the laws of the state. To further strengthen the laws of the state, and to silence the few critics that remained in Germany, another law was passed, with the comical title, "Decree Combating Griping and Defeatism." This law was enacted in early 1934 to further punish those who dared to speak out against the Party or the government.

Also, during December 1933, the Hitler government contracted with the huge chemical firm, I. G. Farben, to manufacture synthetic gasoline from coal. This was another step toward rearming Germany. Synthetic gasoline was not competitive in the marketplace with petroleum-based gasoline, which was readily available from many sources. Its only practical use would be for military needs in the event Germany's oil imports were cut off by international boycott or by war. The government guaranteed to subsidize Farben and provide a market for the gasoline at a price whereby Farben could make a profit. This venture was another action taken to reduce unemployment.

As the industrial moguls cashed in on the Nazi phenomenon, the smaller entrepreneurs of Germany, who still had a measure of economic freedom, also saw business opportunities. During the year, many products appeared on the market bearing Hitler's picture, swastikas or both. Hitler's picture appeared on ties, hand mirrors, handkerchiefs, etc. while swastikas appeared on beer mugs, ash trays and other items. There was even a brand of canned herring introduced called "Good Adolf." This trend did not last, however. The Nazis thought such products were undignified and put an end to their production.

At various times during 1933, the Nazis took steps to revamp the German educational system from primary school through college. This process of Nazifying German schools would go on for years. Reeducating teachers, purging unreliable ones, training new ones, changing curriculum and the like would take time.

"...EVERY NEED OF EVERY INDIVIDUAL..."

By the end of the year Hitler had ample reason to be proud of his accomplishments. Germany was well on its way to becoming an ideal National Socialist state, and there were more controls to come. He commented at this time, "We must develop organizations in which an individual's entire life can take place. Then every activity and every need of every individual will be regulated by the collectivity represented by the Party. There is no longer any arbitrary will, there are no longer any free realms in which the individual belongs to himself... The time for personal happiness is over."

As 1933 ended, reliable sources estimated that there were some 27,000 people in German concentration camps.

CHAPTER 7

BUILDING THE NAZI DREAM: YEARS TWO, THREE AND FOUR, 1934–35–36

January 1934 marked the first anniversary of the Nazi's rise to power, and their programs for the Nazification of Germany continued at a brisk pace. Plans for rearming Germany were also being implemented.

On January 1, the German Navy launched its second new battleship since the end of the Great War, the "Graf Spee." Hitler was in attendance. The first battleship was the "Deutschland" launched in 1931 by a pre-Nazi regime.

On January 14, the "Law for the Organization of National labor" was enacted to provide tighter governmental control over labor. This was touted as another step in reducing unemployment. And, as a secondary benefit, such controls allowed the government to conscript labor, as needed, to improve the economy and, most importantly, to provide adequate manpower for the forthcoming rearmament program.

Also during January, Hitler assigned a group of economic planners to explore the Danubian area as a region for German economic expansion. Hitler, who grew up on the banks of the

Danube River at Linz, Austria, had long planned for that river to become Germany's exclusive waterway to the East. There were times in German history when this was the case.

The Danube empties into the Black Sea which would provide German ships easy access to the Crimea, the southern Ukraine, the Caucasus, Romania, Bulgaria, Turkey and the Turkish Straits. Hitler's overall intentions were to take complete economic and political control of the Danubian area. Economic matters would suffice for now, though. Political matters would be addressed later. Hitler meant every word he said. With regard to the "political matters", Hitler told a colleague, "...to make us independent of every possible political grouping and alliance...we must have the mastery as far as the Caucasus... In the west we need the French coast. We need Flanders and Holland. Above all we need Sweden."

January 30, 1934, was the first anniversary of Hitler's appointment as Chancellor, and the day was declared a national holiday. As part of the celebration, Hitler addressed the Reichstag and, despite all of the proclamations during 1933 that Germany wanted peace, the old Nazi rhetoric came to the fore. In his usual dramatic way, Hitler told the assembly and the nation, once again, what they had all heard all too often before including the prediction that Germany would expand its territory. Hitler said that the boundaries of Germany, "...will not halt at the border posts of a land which is German not only in its people, but in its history as well, and which was for many centuries, an integral part of the German Empire."

It is surprising that Hitler would make such a controversial statement as this when he was obviously trying hard to mollify his frightened neighbors. It was now becoming clear that Hitler was a man who talked out of both sides of his mouth. How could such a man be trusted?

During February, Rudolph Hess, considered by many to be the number two man in the Nazi Party, created a Party organization known as the "Auslandsorganization" (Foreign Organization—AO). Its mission was to take care of all foreign policy matters of interest to the Party. This broad mandate, in effect, created a second foreign ministry, much to the dismay of Constantin von Neurath, the government's Foreign Minister. But this kind of Party activity was not new. The Party had long had organizations to deal with foreign matters, but none had approached the size and importance of this new entity. Those older organizations were, for the most part, left in place. This overlap of responsibilities, understandably, generated in-fighting among Hitler's subordinates, confusion in decision-making, and added expense. But for Chancellor Hitler it was a plus. It gave him the opportunity to draw on several sources of information and, more importantly, to play one organization against the other so that everyone involved worked to their utmost to gain his favor.

On February 27, 1934, another new law came into being authorizing the Minister of Economics to create government-sponsored associations for the various facets of German industry. This accumulation of associations was to be known as the "Reich Economic Chamber." It replaced all such existing associations, and membership in one of the Chamber associations was mandatory for all small and large businesses.

In an effort to keep the German public well-informed of all the new developments underway, the Hitler government instigated a program of subsidizing the manufacture

and distribution of radios. This made radios so inexpensive that virtually anyone could afford them. The public responded enthusiastically and radio sales were brisk.

HITLER PREDICTS AN EARLY DEATH

Hitler, as ever, was worried about his health. During February he told an associate, "I do not have long enough to live...I must lay the foundations on which others can build after me. I will not live long enough to see it completed."

AN OMINOUS MEETING IN BERLIN

In late February, 1934, Hitler called his top military people to a secret meeting in Berlin to tell them of his plans for the future—plans for war. He instructed his generals and admirals to be ready to fight a defense war by 1939 and an offensive war by 1942. They would, he promised, be given the wherewithal to accomplish these objectives. Their jobs, he told them, was to take the men and equipment that would soon be flowing into their hands and mold them into the most powerful military force in Europe. He further told these soldiers of the Reich that he would strike first in the West, and then in the East just as he had outlined in Mein Kampf. The military men were generally elated to hear of Hitler's plans. To the man, all in attendance were enthusiastic. They all sought revenge for the humiliation of 1918.

MUSSOLINI RATTLES THE SABRE, TOO

By an interesting coincidence, Mussolini also spoke of war at this time, but in public. On March 19, he addressed the Italian Parliament and outlined what he believed would be the future of Italy. He told his listeners, "The historic objectives of Italy have two names, Asia and Africa...The South and the East are the principle areas which must absorb the interests and the aims of the Italians."

Foreign reactions to this speech was immediate, especially from Greece and Turkey. Both countries made it perfectly clear through their news media and their diplomatic channels, that Italian aggression in their areas of interest would be strongly resisted and might, very possibly, lead to war. The Turks went so far as to recall their ambassador to Rome, and a short while later carried out military maneuvers in the Aegean Sea. Most other nations of the world also registered their concerns about Mussolini's aggressive intentions. Mussolini might well have avoided all of these unpleasantries by keeping his plans secret as Hitler was doing.

MORE NAZI PLANS FOR THE PEOPLE—AND FOR WAR

In late March 1934, another new program, called "The Domestic Service Years," was introduced for German teenage girls. It provided for the girls to leave school and take government-assigned jobs for a year in the domestic field in order to prepare them for marriage and motherhood. The girls would be assigned to appropriate jobs in both the general economy and with families, especially families with many children. They would not be paid, but their expenses would be offset by tax concessions for them or their parents or guardians. Participation was voluntary, but pressures were put on all Party members to lead the way by enrolling their daughters in the program. The first year, some 625,000 young women participated.

Also during March, the Army secretly ordered the first 100 tanks from German industry. This was a direct violation of the Versailles Treaty because the German Army was forbidden to have tanks.

ANOTHER DEAL WITH THE ARMY

Hitler was well aware of the Army's concern for the Party's large and aggressive SA organization, so he formulated a plan.

He invited the top Army leaders to take a cruise with him on the battleship "Deutschland" for another very secret meeting. No SA leaders were invited.

In Hitler's eyes, the SA had evolved into a potential threat to both the Army and his own leadership. This was due, in part, to the fact that the top commanders of the SA were doing the unthinkable. Ernst Roehm, com-

mander of the SA and others, were boasting openly that it was they, the SA, that was responsible for bringing Hitler to power. The implication was, of course, that they could also bring Hitler down and take control of Germany themselves. To Hitler's ear, this was treason. Furthermore, Roehm was a closet homosexual, but many people knew it.

Then there was President Hindenburg. His health was noticeably deteriorating and his death appeared to be imminent.

So, here was Hitler's secret proposal to his Generals and Admirals. He would cut the strength of the SA by two-thirds if the Army would back him for the Presidency when Hindenburg died. He further assured the Army leaders that the SA would never become a rival to the Army.

All were aware that if Hitler became President he would then become the absolute dictator of Germany.

This was a deal the military gentlemen could not refuse and it was sealed with a handshake. There was to be nothing in writing.

Now, Hitler had an ugly task facing him—the suppression of his own SA.

A BREATHING SPELL

During April, May and June 1934, the German people were given a respite from the torrent of new legislation pouring forth from Berlin. From a practical point of view, the Nazis had enacted so many new programs that they needed time now to get them underway. Also, Hitler had a very important matter on his mind—the task of ridding himself of Roehm and the SA.

HITLER AND MUSSOLINI MEET FOR FIRST TIME

During June 14-16, 1934, Hitler visited Mussolini in Italy. Hitler, who had openly admired Mussolini, had long looked forward to this moment, but it was to turn into a disaster. First of all, Hitler arrived wearing a business suit while Mussolini appeared in full uniform—a slip-up in protocol.

Hanging like a cloud over the meeting were the concerns of both men with regards to Austria. Hitler, an Austrian by birth, had long spoken of Austria being united with Germany. Mussolini, on the other hand, wanted to keep Italy's northern neighbor free and thereby maintain Italy's considerable influence and commercial interests there. This issue noticeably chilled relations between the two dictators.

It was Mussolini who displayed hostility toward Hitler rather than the other way around. Mussolini gave a speech in German knowing full well that Hitler could not reciprocate by giving a speech in Italian. On the way to Venice, they got into a very heated discussion over Austria. On Friday the 16th, Hitler's last day in Italy, Mussolini's Black Shirts paraded for Hitler and were noticeably unshaven and wearing sloppy uniforms. At the last dinner that evening, Mussolini abruptly left the dining hall without bidding Hitler farewell. When Hitler left for Germany, he was in a bad mood.

As might be expected, though, the state-controlled medias of both countries reported that the meeting had been friendly and constructive. But the true nature of the meeting was soon leaked to the foreign media and the whole world knew.

THE SUPPRESSION OF THE SA

By late June, Hitler had his plans completed for the suppression of the SA. He had struck a deal with Heinrich Himmler, commander of the SS, his personal bodyguard unit, to carry out this dirty job. Himmler, who was technically subordinate to Roehm, would conduct a surprise attack on the SA leadership and eliminate them in one stroke. His reward would be that the SS would be elevated to a much more important organization, under Himmler of course, and would take over many of the assets and responsibilities of the SA. Furthermore, Himmler would have the everlasting gratitude of Adolf Hitler.

In the early morning hours of Saturday, June 30, 1934, Himmler struck. The leaders of the SA were in their beds at a lakeside resort hotel at Weissee, Germany after having a raucous party the night before. Some say it was an orgy. The SS men stormed into the hotel and murdered the SA leaders in their beds or as they tried to flee. Roehm was captured, sent to Stadelheim Prison in Munich and later summarily executed. The official explanation given to the public was that the SA and its leaders were involved in a treasonable conspiracy against the State. Details of the event reported to the public were necessarily sketchy.

Hitler carried out his promise to Himmler. From this point on, the SS replaced the SA as the Party's enforcers. The rank and file of the SA was greatly reduced in numbers and new commanders, totally loyal to Hitler, were placed at its head. The SA was now relegated to doing administrative tasks such as training newly recruited Party members. It also became subject to a supervisory board whose members were appointed by Himmler.

Following the Roehm affair, Hitler complained again about his health. Apparently, the stress of events had taken a toll. He told his closest associates, at various times, that he was suffering from gas, eczema on his left calf, dizziness and a metallic ringing in his ears.

INTRIGUE CONTINUES

On July 3, 1934, von Papen, under strong pressure from the Nazis, resigned his post of Vice Chancellor in Hitler's Cabinet. Hitler then deviated from the constitution and eliminated the position. This resolved the problem of someone not selected by Hitler, succeeding him as Chancellor.

On July 25, 1934, Austrian Nazis attempted to take over the Austrian government by force. The attempt failed, but in the process the Austrian Premier, Englebert Dollfuss, was murdered. Considerable blame fell, of course, on the German Nazis but the Hitler government completely disavowed itself from the events in Austria. This fooled no one and relations soured between Germany and Austria, and Germany and Italy. Furthermore, Mussolini's personal attitude toward Hitler turned very negative. This was a major setback for Hitler who had, all along, hoped to gain Italy as an ally. Mussolini's negative attitude toward his fellow dictator would last for several years.

HINDENBURG DIES

About 9:00 a.m. August 2, 1934, President Hindenburg died at the age of 87. Within hours, Hitler's Cabinet voted that Hitler should assume the vacated post. This was a direct violation of the German constitution that stipulated that the President was to be elected by popular vote. But Hitler deviated again from the constitution and assumed the post. The Nazi Party cheered; the Army, true to its deal with Hitler, remained silent, and the people of Germany acquired an absolute dictator who could not be removed by any legal means.

To provide the appearance of legitimacy, a plebiscite was held on August 19 whereby the people of Germany could affirm or reject Hitler as President. This was a plebiscite in which the Nazis made the rules, controlled the polling places and counted the votes. The election officials subsequently reported that almost 90% of Germany's voters gave their approval.

Hitler refused to take the title of President, feeling that it was a term associated with the democracies. Instead, he decreed that he should be known, henceforth, as the "Fuehrer of Germany" and referred to as "The Head of State." He retained the posts of Fuehrer of the Nazi Party and Chancellor of Germany. As Head of State, he also became the titular head of Germany's armed forces.

HIS LEFT ARM

Some of the people that knew Hitler well noted that he was using his left arm less and less. Nothing was said, of course. Then, in September 1934, Hitler became the central figure in the annual Nazi rally at Nuremberg, at which his every public appearance was filmed. Years later, two American physicians, Dr. John K. Lattimer, doing research for a book on Hitler, and Dr. Abraham Li-

eberman, Medical Director of the National Parkinson's Foundation, working independently, viewed the 1934 films and noticed what others had noticed at the time with regards to Hitler's left arm. Knowing that later in life, Hitler developed symptoms typical of Parkinson's Disease, both physicians came to the same conclusion, that in 1934, Hitler was beginning to show stage one symptoms of the disease. Lattimer's assumption was also based on reports that Hitler suffered, at this time, from constipation, excess sweating, gas, and an erratic sleep pattern. According to Lattimer, these are symptoms of post-encephalitis Parkinson's Disease as opposed to idiopathic (old age) Parkinson's disease.

In any case, Hitler's problems with his left arm, and later his left leg, would progress very slowly and would not be noticeable to the untrained eye until the 1940s.

NAZI GERMANY—YEAR THREE—1935

During the latter part of 1934, membership in the Nazi Party was opened again, and by January 1, 1935, it had 1,017,000 dues-paying members.

By now the Nazification of Germany's schools was well underway, and in elementary schools, the children were being taught a new prayer, "Fuehrer, my Fuehrer, bequeathed to me by the Lord, protect and preserve me as long as I live." The government also had established recommended rituals for baptisms, weddings and burials. On March 1, 1935, a League of Nations-sponsored election was held in the Saar region of Germany. This was a coal mining region, bordering France, which was detached from Germany after the Great War and administered by the League of Nations. The people of the Saar were now asked if they wanted to return to Germany. The vote was 90.3% in favor and Hitler had another triumph to his credit.

By this time, Hitler felt confident to admit to the world that Germany was rearming. On March 16, 1935, his government officially announced this fact in direct defiance of the now sixteen year old Versailles Treaty.

It was also announced that Germany would begin military conscription. International reaction was, again, limited to protests only. Hitler took this as a sign that the creators of the Treaty had lost their zeal with regard to enforcing it and that he was free to further abrogate the Treaty as he wished.

During May 1935, another new governmental office was created—the "Wehrwirtschaft" (Military Oriented Industry). This was a government office designed to coordinate and control military contracts, subsidies and other activities within Germany's industrial complex. Hjalmar Horace Greeley Schacht was appointed head of the new office.

Also during May, Eva Braun attempted suicide. Hitler was still neglecting her. To cheer her up, he gave her a new Mercedes automobile and a chauffeur whose duty was to drive her about and keep an eye on her. The next year, Hitler brought her to live with him at the newly remodeled Berghof where she served as his hostess for the few insiders who knew of their relationship. This seemed to give her a purpose in life and she became a much happier person. When others visited the Berghof who were not aware of their relationship, she stayed out of sight or was identified as part of the help.

With Eva's attempt at suicide, the attempted suicide of Mitzi Reiter, the successful suicide of his niece, Geli Raubal, his falling out with his half-sister Angela, and stories of unsuccessful love affairs during his Vienna days, it is easy to make the case that Hitler had a big problem with women.

About this time, Hitler had yet another personal problem. He was experiencing bouts of hoarseness and feared that he might have throat cancer. On May 21, he had a secret operation during which a small laryngeal polyp, known as a "singer's node," was removed. To Hitler's great relief, it was benign.

A GERMAN COUP

On June 18, 1935, Germany signed an agreement with Britain known as the "London Naval Treaty." This treaty stipulated that Germany could built up its naval strength to 35%, in tonnage, of that of the British Navy, then the world's largest navy. This was a unilateral action taken by Britain and something of a slap-in-the-face to Britain's Allies, especially France. The British justified the treaty by claiming that this was the naval ratio they wanted to establish at the time of the Versailles Treaty in 1919, but were prevented in doing so by the other Allied nations. The German explanation was simply that it was a fair and equitable treaty. But, in Berlin it was seen as much more than that. Firstly, it represented a major crack in the solidarity of the Great War Alliance and, secondly, it abrogated, with London's approval, the conditions in the Versailles Treaty which had imposed much lower tonnage limits on the German Navy. Hitler also interpreted the event as indicating that Britain would not greatly interfere with Germany's rearmament. He was also pleased by the symbolism of the treaty being signed on June 18, the 120th anniversary of the British and Prussian victory over France at Waterloo. Hitler told his closest associates, "This is the happiest day of my life" and, in keeping with his love-hate relationship with Britain, began talking of the possibility of an alliance with Britain against France.

Negotiating the treaty for Germany had been the task of Joachim von Ribbentrop, a well-educated and well-travelled aristocrat, and Hitler's Ambassador-at-large. In Hitler's eyes, von Ribbentrop's effort was a stroke of genius, and in the summer of 1935 appointed him Ambassador to Britain. Three years later, Hitler would elevate him to the post of Foreign Minister, a post he would keep until the end of World War II.

Confident now that the British government was neutralized with regard to naval affairs, the German government announced on July 8, 1935, that Germany would build two more battleships and 28 submarines now permitted under the London Naval Agreement.

MORE ANTI-JEWISH LEGISLATION – "A FINAL SOLUTION"

Hitler used the annual Nazi rally at Nuremberg in September 1935 to announce another series of decrees against the Jews. The official reason given was that they were yet another attempt to get the Jews to voluntarily leave Germany.

The degrees stripped the Jews of German citizenship, thus relegating them to German subjects. As such, they could not vote or take part in politics. Another decree made it a crime for Jews to marry, or to have extra-marital relations with a German citizen. They were also forbidden from flying the German flag. Yet another decree forbad German women, under the age of 45, from working in a Jewish household. This very unusual decree had its roots in Hitler's past. Hitler's grandmother, Maria Schickelgruber, had worked as a domestic servant in a Jewish household in Vienna in the 1830s and, while there, became pregnant. Speculation was then, and continued to be, that the father of Maria's baby was the young son of the household. This would make Hitler one-fourth Jewish. Neither Maria nor the Jewish family ever revealed the father's identity which, fortunately for Hitler, gave him the opportunity to deny the ugly rumors that he had Jewish blood in his veins. Stories were circulated that the father of Maria's baby was one of her suitors who was fully German.

And the anti-Jewish legislation continued. A few days after the rally, the government announced that all Jewish-owner firms would be bought out. And, in December, all Jewish doctors were forced to resign from private hospitals.

Hitler had some apprehensions that the anti-Jewish programs might not work. He lamented to his associates, "...the German people...may find a tolerable relation toward the Jewish people...", and if that happened, the problem "...must be handed over by law to the National Socialists Party for a final solution."

ITALY INVADES ETHIOPIA

For months, Mussolini had made an all-to-obvious effort to pick a fight with the independent East African nation of Ethiopia. Ethiopia was wedged between two Italian colonies, Eritrea and Italian Somaliland. By conquering Ethiopia Italy could unite the three territories into one large colonial holding in East Africa. Italy had tried before to conquer Ethiopia in the 1880s, but had suffered a humiliating defeat at the hands of the Ethiopians. Mussolini, and many others in Italy, sought revenge.

On October 3, 1935, Italian forces launched an invasion of Ethiopia from the neighboring Italian colonies. It was a most unequal contest—a modern European army doing battle with a primitive African army.

Italy's actions enraged the world community and the League of Nations branded the Fascist State an aggressor and called for economic sanctions against Italy.

In Berlin, Hitler was one of the few world leaders who did not condemn the Italian aggression. Quite the opposite, he saw in it significant opportunities for Germany.

When it was clear that France, Britain and other nations would implement the sanctions against Italy, Hitler informed Mussolini that Germany would not go along with the sanctions but, instead, would provide Italy with arms, munitions, coal, food and other supplies.

It took the Italians the better part of a year to subdue the Ethiopians and, in the end, the Italian people were generally pleased with the Duce's actions, despite the sanctions and the world-wide criticism heaped upon Italy. Mussolini could now boast that he had promised his people territorial expansion, and now he had delivered on that promise. Hitler was also pleased, and moreover, Mussolini was grateful for Hitler's support. The two dictators now became much closer although the question of Austria continued to be a major problem in their relationship.

Grossdeutschland (Greater Germany) according to Nazi propaganda in the mid-1930s.

EVENTS IN GERMANY

On November 28, 1935, the Hitler government took another step toward rearmament by decreeing that all German men 18 through 45 years of age not subject to conscription were, nevertheless, liable for service in the military reserves. By the end of 1935, the actual size of the German Army was 350,000 men. This number, of course, were kept secret. The French, though, becoming ever more paranoid with regard to Germany, estimated that the German Army was 700,000 strong.

As far as the German economy was concerned, it was better than it had been since the end of the Great War. Unemployment had been greatly reduced and the nation was producing both consumer goods and military hardware. Some called it a "cannon and margarine" economy or, at times, a "guns and butter" economy.

During the year, an alarming map had circulated around Europe showing what

the territorial limits of "Greater Germany" would be if the German propagandists were taken seriously. The map showed Germany taking complete control of the countries of The Netherlands, Belgium, Luxembourg and Austria as well as major parts of Switzerland, northern Italy, Czechoslovakia, and Poland. It also showed Germany acquiring parts of France, Yugoslavia, Lithuania and Denmark. Needless to say, it was yet another cause for alarm for Germany's neighbors.

The Fuehrer, however, was still experiencing health problems. At various times he complained of stomach pains, gas, constipation, belching and pains in the area of the heart. He blamed these maladies on the food he ate, and one by one cut items from his diet. He told Albert Speer, at the time, that he was on a starvation diet and hardly ate anything. This was probably an exaggeration because he did not lose weight and continued to indulge in the rich pastries he so loved. Others observed, and at time commented privately, that it was Hitler's eating habits that were at fault. He ate fast, did not chew his food well, and often talked while eating which caused a condition known as aerophagia, the swallowing of air. In addition, Hitler had bad teeth and was a frequent visitor to the dentist's chair—an experience which he detested.

NAZI GERMANY—YEAR FOUR—1936

The year 1936 opened on a positive note for Germany because she was host to the 1936 Winter Olympics with the Summer Olympics to follow. The Hitler government had seen to it that Nazi Germany was a bright and shiny place with new buildings, clean streets, modern hotels, good restaurants, and an overall aura of prosperity. Nazi trappings were to be seen, but were not gaudy. The mysterious SS, SA and Gestapo men were out of sight, and the Jews were treated with a measure of respect. Since all eyes were on Germany, Hitler wanted the image to be positive, especially since the Olympics were televised for the first time ever.

Hitler appeared regularly at the Olympic events and when there, personally handed out the gold medals. By the end of the Olympics, German athletes had won 33 gold medals, one of the highest medal counts of all the participants—and another triumph for National Socialism.

With the televising of the Olympics, the Nazis were quick to realize the great value of the new medium. Plans progressed after the Olympics to further develop the television industry in Germany and eventually hand out some 10,000 free TV sets to selected individuals in the general public to generate public enthusiasm.

On January 17, 1936, Goebbels made a fiery speech in which he demanded the return of Germany's colonies. This issue had run hot and cold with the Nazis over the years; now it was heating up again.

In late February, Switzerland, which had long been concerned about developments in Germany and with a sizeable and troublesome Nazi party of its own, closed the bor-

This poster reads, "You must save five marks a week if you want to drive your own car."

der to any known German Nazis. This was seen in Berlin as a very unfriendly act and greatly strained German-Swiss relations.

February 26 was a day of triumph for National Socialism. On that day, the Volkswagen automobile was introduced to the German people. Ceremonies were held in which Hitler took a short ride in a convertible prototype of the car. Photos and reports of the event were flashed around the world. At the ceremony, it was announced that a huge factory would be built at Fallersleben, Saxony to build the car and would employ thousands of workers. The price of the car, it was stated, would be approximately 1000 marks ($140) and do 60 miles-per-hour. Here, again, was another Nazi promise being fulfilled.

GERMAN TROOPS MARCH INTO THE RHINELAND

The Rhineland area of Germany, bordering France and Belgium, had been demilitarized by the Versailles Treaty in 1919 which meant that no German military forces, whatsoever, could be stationed there. For several years thereafter, the area was physically occupied by French and Belgian troops, and in October 1923 the French attempted to detach the area from Germany altogether and establish an independent Rhineland Republic. There was no support for this action among the Allies and the effort collapsed in January 1924.

By now, the Allied troops were gone but the area was still off-limits to the German military. The Hitler govern-

The Nazis also had a campaign against women smoking. Signs were posted in most restaurants such as this one which reads, "The German Woman Does Not Smoke." SS troopers would sometimes enforce this ban by snatching cigarettes from a woman's mouth and giving her a verbal reprimand.

ment, and a large percentage of the German people, saw this as an insult to Germany and a situation that should be rectified

On March 7, 1936, it was rectified. On that day, 30,000 German soldiers and 15,000 armed border guards crossed the Rhine River and entered the Rhineland. This was another grievous violation of the Versailles Treaty and created a situation whereby Allied troops, under the terms of the Treaty, could legally re-enter the area and oust the Germans by force. But no action was taken by the Allied nations except for the stream of angry protests which came from many sources. The resolve of the enforcers of the Versailles Treaty was found to be wanting. Hitler got away with this daring move and was now a greater hero to the German people than before.

And Hitler was elated with his own success. He told his associates, "Am I glad! Good Lord, am I glad it's gone so smoothly. Sure enough, the world belongs to the brave man. He's the one God helps."

To drive home their success in the Rhineland, another Nazi-controlled plebiscite was held in Germany on March 29 concerning the actions taken by the Nazi government. It was reported that 99% of the German people supported the Rhineland action.

NAZI GERMANY LAYS LOW

For the next few months Nazi Germany laid low in the arena of international politics in order to let the dust settle from the Rhineland affair.

In early May 1936, the war ended in Ethiopia with an Italian victory and Mussolini became as popular in Italy as Hitler was now in Germany.

But no measure of popularity was enough to cure the Fuehrer's health problems. During May, Hitler engaged a new physician, Dr. Theodor Morell, who promised the Fuehrer he could cure his gastronomical problems within a year with a treatment called the "Mutaflor Cure." Morell had come highly recommended, so Hitler put his health problems into the hands of the good doctor.

During June, the Nazis went back to work. A new decree was issued banning women from serving as judges, prosecutors or administrators. This was another attempt to keep women in the home. About this time another government-sponsored slogan appeared to emphasize the new decree: "The German woman is knitting again."

The Hitler government also considered banning women from the practice of medicine, but this effort failed because it would have created a shortage of doctors.

THE SPANISH CIVIL WAR

On July 17, 1936, the catastrophe that everyone feared might happen in Spain, happened. The Spanish Army, assisted by right-wing political elements, began a rebellion against the legally-elected leftist government in Madrid. Democracy had failed in Spain and this was the result. Both Hitler and Mussolini were quick to point out, through their respective propaganda organizations, that it was exactly this sort of tragedy that could have happened in their respective countries if they had not acted when they did. It was an argument that was hard to refute.

Not only was there polarization in Spain, much of the world now polarized over the Spanish war. The right-wing dictatorships of the world, including Germany and Italy, showed strong support for the rebels, while the Soviet Union, France (which had a liberal government at the time), and other moderate and left-leaning nations openly sided with the Madrid government. The

United States, deeply immersed in isolationism, tried to remain neutral, but could not. The vast majority of Americans sympathized with the Loyalists and the Roosevelt government could not ignore this huge wave of sentiment.

Intense international diplomatic efforts commence to end the fighting in Spain and/or prevent third parties from entering the fray. Committees were formed, resolutions were passed by the League of Nations, and various nations pledged non-intervention, but nothing worked. The fighting continued and others intervened.

The Germans and Italians were the first foreigners, with the exception of the Portuguese, to intervene. Both Germany and Italy began sending war supplies to the rebels and later, men. The Soviet Union, hoping to keep the leftist government in Madrid alive, responded by sending supplies and so-called volunteers to fight for the Loyalists.

In the initial stages of the rebellion, the rebels succeeded in taking control of only parts of Spain, leaving other parts in the hands of the Loyalists. Militarily, both sides were about equal. This made for a long and bloody war which would last until 1939. Years later, with the advantage of hindsight, many people saw the war in Spain as a prelude to World War II.

For Hitler's Germany, it was just that. It gave the Germans an opportunity to test their newest military equipment, especially aircraft, and gave their "volunteers" who went to Spain valuable war experience. Likewise, Mussolini and Stalin saw the same advantages in testing their respective military prowess in the Spanish arena.

HITLER CHOOSES JAPAN

With conflict in the air, Hitler made a decision he had long been contemplating. In the Far East, Japan and Nationalist China had been at odds with each other for decades and war there was very possible. The German governments, even before Hitler, had retained relatively strong ties with both nations. But the Germans could not escape the realization that one day they would have to choose between one or the other. During July 1936, with all eyes on Spain, and after weighing the prospects of supporting either Japan or China, Hitler chose Japan. From this point on, German aid and foreign policy would favor Japan. That country, like Germany, had a determined policy of territorial expansion—expansion which could only come at the expense to China, possibly the Soviet Union, and the colonies in the region which belonged to Britain, France, The Netherlands and the United States.

DEVELOPMENTS IN GERMANY

By mid-August, the Olympics had ended in Berlin and the Hitler government could revert to its true self. It did not take long. On August 24, 1936, Hitler extended compulsory military service from one year to two. One of the reasons announced for this was that France already had compulsory military service of two years. Another reason given was that the armed forces of the Soviet Union were rapidly expanding and all of Europe was at risk.

During September, with Hitler's full approval, Heinrich Himmler, Head of the SS, established a new, and very unique, program in Germany for his SS men. It consisted of a number of SS-run maternity homes where pregnant mistresses of SS men could go to have their babies in safety and seclusion, and at government expense. Since SS men were among the most elite members of the Nazi Party they had been encouraged to propagate the race. The taking of mistresses, even for married men, was encouraged and the babies thus produced were seen as a precious addition to the German race. These homes were know as "Lebensborn Homes" (Fount of Life Homes).

If the unwed mother chose to keep her offspring she would receive a small stipend from the government. If she chose to give up the child, it would be given to approved foster or adoptive parents or raised in state-run childrens' homes. And, all of the mothers could return as often as they wished. Some of the first residents of the homes would be young women who were, at this time, planning to attend the September Party rally at Nuremberg. Read on.

The homes gave first choice to women of the SS, but if space was available, any German women of good blood carrying a child of equally good blood, could be admitted.

THE FOUR-YEAR PLAN

On September 9, 1936, the annual Nazi Party Nuremberg rally began once again. In his main speech, made on the 12th, Hitler proudly announced a gigantic new program designed to make the German nation self-sufficient in virtually every aspect of life. It was call the "Four-Year Plan." Now, with government controls over industry, labor, agriculture, the economy and other aspects of German life, those entities would be harnessed under one leadership to better coordinate their respective activities for the benefit of the German people. And, although it was not announced, the Four-Year Plan was created to make Germany blockade-free in the event of war. To the Nazi planners, this was very important because the allied blockade of Germany during the Great War had caused many difficulties for the Germans.

Hermann Goering was chosen to head the Plan with the new title "Plenipotentiary for the Four-Year Plan." This would make Goering Germany's economic Czar. And, in the process, Goering would become fabulously wealthy.

To account for some of the products that Germany could not produce, such as natural rubber and imported fibers, government financed programs were begun, under the Plan, to develop substitutes. A program to produce synthetic oil was already under way and would now be incorporated into the Plan. Another thing that was not mentioned at Nuremberg was that Hitler had given secret orders to the armed forces and government agencies to begin stockpiling military-

Hitler made sketches of the buildings and other structures he wanted built in Germany and gave them to architect Albert Speer (right) to formalize.

now, young ladies in this predicament had a place to go; the newly-established Lebensborn Homes.

Yet another incursion into the sexual life of the German people occurred in October. The Hitler government established a governmental agency called "The Reich Office for Combating Homosexuality and Abortion." Laws against homosexuality and abortion were already on the books, but now the government established a special department to deal with these specific issues.

Also during October, Jazz music was banned from all German radio stations. Hitler hated Jazz.

BERLIN—MAGNIFICENT BERLIN

During the year, Hitler had been working very closely with architect Albert Speer on the reconstruction of the nation's capital, Berlin. It had long been Hitler's dream to build Berlin into one of the most magnificent cities in the world. This was a project in which Hitler took great personal enjoyment because now he could pursue his architectural ambitions to no end. When working with Speer, Hitler would often make sketches of what he wanted in the way of government buildings, monuments, triumphal arches, parks, etc., and give them to Speer to formalize. Even when Speer was not present, Hitler made sketches. He kept a sketch pad and pencils nearby and put down his ideas on paper when an inspiration hit him. Speer kept all of these sketches on file for the time when they could be carried out.

Berlin would, according to Hitler's plans, have many broad avenues which would be wide enough to accommodate large formations of marching soldiers. There would be a huge triumphal arch, which Hitler had first sketched in 1925, that would be 49 times larger than the Arch de Triumphe in Paris. A Great Hall capable of seating 150,000 people would dominate the Berlin skyline with a dome 825 feet in diameter, larger than that of St. Peter's in Rome. A giant stadium would be built to seat 450,000 people and there

related imports that Germany needed. But Hitler's long-range plans went well beyond the Four Year Plan. Many of the items Germany needed were available in the East.

In his speech of the 12th, Hitler spoke of many things. He expounded at length on the bright future the German people had ahead of them under National Socialism and the fact that it was his regime that preserved Germany from the horrors that were now engulfing Spain. He called, once again, for the return of Germany's overseas colonies, and for the maintenance of world peace. In a more provocative and expansionist tone, he boasted that if the German people controlled the Ukraine, they would "swim in plenty."

Another noteworthy event that took place at the rally was that some 900 young women, mostly members of the "League of German Maidens", the female branch of the Hitler Youth, became pregnant. In only about half of the cases were the fathers known. But

Wooden model of the proposed 400,000-seat Nuremberg Stadium designed by Albert Speer.

would be a statue honoring German women which would be 46 feet higher than the Statue of Liberty in New York. Also, Hitler would build a personal palace-like residence in Berlin of some 22 million square feet.

Over the years, scale models would be built of most of these projects and kept in the Chancellory where Hitler would spend hours going over them in detail.

Grandiose plans were also made for Nuremberg. There, a large Reviewing Stand and parade ground, which doubled as a Zeppelin landing field, had already been built. This was the place where the annual Nazi Party rallies were held. After the war, though, a much larger parade ground, five times the size of the existing one, would be built along with a 400,000-seat stadium where future Olympics would be held. And there would be a large meeting hall to be called "Congress Hall." Beginning in 1933, concentration camp inmates were employed in a nearby stone quarry to provide stone for these magnificent structures. Their work would continue until the fall of 1939, when work on the Nuremberg complex ended due to the onset of war.

THE BIRTH OF THE "AXIS"

Ever since the Ethiopian affair, German and Italian diplomats had been talking about the possibility of an alliance between their two countries. And, with the advent of civil war in Spain, they found themselves on the same side fighting the forces of both communism and the democracies.

These talks came to fruition and on October 20, 1936, the foreign ministers of the two nations signed a treaty of political alliance in Berlin. The most important aspect of the alliance was that Germany and Italy would work together to draw the other nations of Europe into their political orbits and detach them from their ties with Britain and France.

As for Austria, the Germans claimed that they were currently satisfied with the political situation there and had no designs on annexing the country. The Italians accepted this explanation which, it turned out, was a bold-faced lie. This would not be the last time Hitler would lie in order to get what he wanted.

On November 1, 1936. Mussolini made a speech in Milan explaining the alliance to the Italian people. In the speech he said, "This agreement...this vertical line joining Rome and Berlin...(is) an axis round which all those European States which are animated by a desire for collaboration and peace may work together." The world media immediately picked up on the word "axis" and began using it, with a capital "A," to describe the new alliance. One of the reasons the word "Axis" came into wide use was that it was short, descriptive and fit easily into newspaper headlines.

ENTER CLARETTA

During 1936, Mussolini met a beautiful young woman named Claretta Petacci and, by all contemporary accounts, fell madly in love with her. Il Duce pursued her and she soon became his mistress. Now he had another thing in common with Hitler—they both had young mistresses. There was a difference in age between Claretta and Mussolini of nineteen years, and between Eva Bruan and Hitler of twenty-three years.

"ADOLF HITLER SCHOOLS"

During 1936, a new level of schooling was introduced in Germany called "Adolf Hitler Schools." These schools would take only the most talented of students and provide them with special education in political subjects and physical education. The mission of the schools was to provide future leaders for the Nazi Party. The initial selection of students numbered only about 600.

There were now, in the German educational system, 14 levels of schools to train students for the various needs of the nation.

JAPAN

For some time, the Germans had been courting the Japanese because they saw in Japan another potential ally for the German/Italian Axis. This effort took a great leap forward when, on November 23, 1936, the two nations signed a pact designed to combat world communism. It became known as "The Anti-Comintern Pact" (Comintern being the acronym for the Soviet Union's "Communist Internationale", an organization designed to promote world communism.) The pact identified the Comintern as a threat to world peace and obligated the two parties to coordinate their efforts to combat it. In a secret protocol the pact provided that if either of the signatories went to war against the Soviet Union, or any other communist nation, the other could remain neutral, but would be supportive of the other.

The public portion of the pact was carefully written so as not to appear to be a threat against the Soviet Union, but only against the Comintern. This thin veneer fooled no one, least of all Moscow.

Upon announcing the new pact, both Germany and Japan called upon other nations to join it.

NOW IT'S THE CRITICS' TURN

In the recent past, the Hitler government had put strict controls on the activities of German journalist and editors. Now it was the critics' turn. On November 27, 1936, Goebbels' Ministry of Propaganda issued a decree dissolving the profession of professional criticism and prohibiting anyone in the media from making negative comments in the fields of art, sculpture, drama, literary works and movies. Justification for this action was that the people of Germany were to be free to make their own judgements in such matters.

CHAPTER 8

GERMANY BECOMES A MAJOR POWER AND EXPANDS ITS TERRITORY

On January 26, 1937, Hitler issued his first decree of the year which dealt with the operations of the German civil service. Hitler had a life-long dislike for bureaucracy. When he made decisions the bureaucrats were often slow to implement them and, at times, put obstacles in the way. The decree of the 26th laid down some guidelines to correct these problems, but Hitler soon discovered that the problems still existed. The Fuehrer would have to struggle on with his obstinate bureaucrats.

CRITICISM FROM THE VATICAN

During March, the Pope issued an encyclical condemning racial policies that were inconsistent with Christianity. In the document, Nazi Germany's treatment of minorities was specifically mentioned.

From Hitler's point of view, this was a violation of the concordant signed in 1933 in which the Catholic Church agreed to stay out of German politics. Hitler let this insult pass, because he had other problems to deal with and did not want to start troubles, at this time, with the Catholic Church. But, he would remember it, and the day would come when he would settle accounts with the Vatican.

MUSSOLINI COURTS THE ISLAMIC WORLD

It had long been the ambition of Italian leaders, even before Mussolini, to extend Italian influence over the Arab countries in North Africa and the Middle East which were, at this time, under British and French mandates. Mussolini's predecessors, at the Versailles Treaty negotiations in 1919, had sought League of Nations' mandates over major territories taken from the Ottoman Empire during the war, but their efforts were thwarted by the other Allied nations. This remained a sore spot in Italy's foreign relations with her former Great War allies. But now, with the Axis on the ascendancy and the old Allies in apparent decline, Mussolini saw opportunities in the Arab world.

During the middle of March 1937, Mussolini travelled to Libya, a North African Islamic nation that had been an Italian colony since before the Great War. Being in Libya, he would have the attention of the Islamic world and it was very likely that his message to the Arabs would be heard. In Libya, he made several speeches claiming that

Italy was the friend of the Arab nations and that it was Italy's intention to help the Arabs throw off their colonial oppressors and advance and prosper. It was during this time that Mussolini made one of the most audacious claim of his career, that being that he, personally, was "The Protector of Islam." He claimed that that title had been bestowed on the leader of Italy after Italy's conquest of Libya during the Italian-Turkish War of 1911–12.

This claim got him headlines in newspapers around the world. In Italy, and the controlled Arabic language press of Libya, there was nothing but praise for the new Protector. But, in foreign nations there was criticism and wonderment which contributed to the long-held beliefs, in some circles, that Mussolini was something of a buffoon. However, Mussolini was dead serious. He pointed to the progress made by Italy in Libya since 1933 in improving schools, medical facilities, water resources and other necessities of life. The Italians had also made efforts to reduce tribal conflicts, and to induce the Bedouins to give up their nomadic way of life. What was not said was that the Bedouins were looked upon as a future source of cheap labor. Also not emphasized was the fact that the Italian settlers already in Libya had acquired the best land, often with government help, and that Mussolini had banned mixed marriages.

To support his claims with regard to the Islamic world, Mussolini, at this time, sent Italy's first diplomatic envoy to Saudi Arabia, an independent Arab nation, and in the world of Islam, a holy land, because within its borders were the holy cities of Mecca and Medina. British influence had been strong in Saudi Arabia ever since the end of the Great War because it was they who, during the last years of the war, helped the Saudis expel the Turks and establish their vast desert kingdom. But now, from the Saudi point of view, British influence had become overbearing and the Saudis sought counterweights to that influence. This had been recently demonstrated by the fact that the Saudis had awarded their valuable oil concessions to the Americans rather than to any of the other European bidders, including Britain.

Then too, the Saudis had made a gesture of friendship toward Rome by befriending Italy during the Ethiopian war. They did this by ignoring the League of Nations sanctions against Italy and supplying Italy with food and raw materials. This relationship now blossomed into a full-scale friendship between Saudi Arabia and Italy.

A short time later, the Saudis and Italians struck a deal whereby the Saudis would acquire Italian arms. This included an arrangement whereby Italian military missions would be sent to Saudi Arabia to train Saudis in the use of those weapons.

From the political point of view, these undertakings, with one of Islam's most important nations, gave some credibility to Mussolini's claim that he was, in fact, the Protector of Islam.

A year later, Saudi/Italian friendship would further strengthen when Saudi Arabia would be the first Islamic nation to politically recognize Italy's conquest of Ethiopia.

And there was more. Mussolini's claims toward the Islamic would be strengthened further during March, 1937, when Italy signed a treaty of friendship and trade with Yugoslavia, a nation with a sizeable Islamic minority.

POTPOURRI OF ACTIVITIES IN GERMANY

During the spring, summer and fall of 1937 there was a flurry of diversified activities in Germany. The German economy was smoothly humming along building both machines of war and consumer goods. Employment had, by now, been greatly reduced and the German people were supportive of Hitler's regime. There was virtually no political opposition to the Nazis except for an occasional, and often veiled, pronouncement from various churchmen.

Both German and Italian diplomats were scurrying about Europe seeking support, and hopefully new members, for their newly-formed Axis alliance. Jews were trickling out of Germany, and a few Germans from overseas were returning.

Despite the outward successes of the German nation, the man behind it all was suffering. This time it was his nerves. In April 1937, Hitler commented, "I must restore my nerves...That is self-evident. Worries, worries, worries, insane worries; it truly is a tremendous burden of worries."

On May 6, 1937, Germany suffered a setback with regard to its much-touted, show case, trans-Atlantic Zeppelin air service when the Zeppelin, "Hindenburg," burst into flames and crashed as it tried to land at Lakehurst, New Jersey. Hours earlier it had flown over New York City low enough so that everyone on the ground could see the huge swastikas painted on its tail. And it was well remembered that the Germans had bombed London with Zeppelins during the Great War.

During the summer of 1937, the AO, Germany's organization for overseas Germans, held a huge rally in Germany to attract more German people back to the Fatherland permanently or, at least, for visits. The theme of the rally was, "Blood is Stronger Than Passports." The AO claimed to have over three million members, worldwide.

In Paris, at the 1937 World's Fair, the Germany pavilion, designed by Albert Speer, was an outstanding attraction. It was huge and was surrounded by hundreds of searchlights pointed straight up into the air. This "cathedral of light" had been used at Nuremberg rallies and, at night, could be seen by virtually everyone in Paris. One of the major displays at the German pavilion was a plan to build a two-and-a-half mile long vacation resort complex on Rugen Island in the Baltic as part of the Strength-Through-Joy Program. The complex would have its own subway and house tens of thousands of vacationers. The display won the fair's grand prix for its category.

While the Nazis were showing off in Paris, they were sterilizing children in the Rhineland. These victims were the mulatto "Rhineland Bastards" which had been fathered by black African troops serving in the French Army during the years of the French occupation of the Rhineland. Now, with the children about to reach puberty, the Hitler government decreed that they should all be sterilized to preserve the purity of the German race.

At Keil, Germany, the keel for Germany's first aircraft carrier was laid. It was another military development that Germany's adversaries were obliged to watch. The aircraft carrier, however, was never completed.

In Spain, the Nationalists were slowly gaining the upper hand but their progress was painfully slow. This required both Germany and Italy to continue sending men and war materials to Spain that could otherwise have contributed to their respective overall military buildups.

On July 7, 1937 (triple seven), the Japanese started a new war with China that had every indication of being long and bloody. Japan, with its modern army, clearly had the military advantage. In Berlin, Hitler congratulated himself for having recently chosen to support Japan rather than China. He had another laurel to his credit.

Later in the month, the German government opened another concentration camp near Wiemar—Buchenwald.

In early September, the largest Nazi rally yet was held at Nuremberg and Hitler spoke glowingly of the future. He told the assembled throngs, "Because we believe in the eternity of this Reich, its works must also be eternal ones, that is...not conceived for the year 1940 and for the year 2000; rather they must tower like the cathedrals of our past into the millennia of the future...This country must not be a power without culture and must not have strength without beauty."

On September 25, 1937, Mussolini arrived in Munich for a meeting with Hitler. It was their first fact-to-face meeting since the very stressful initial encounter in June 1934. Despite the fact that they now had an alliance, both men were on the defensive with respect to each other. The meeting, reception and dinner were cordial but not warm. Hitler was seen biting his fingernails. Then, Mussolini was taken on a tour of Germany to see for himself the progress made in rearmament as well as some of the industrial plants producing weapons. Mussolini was very impressed. The two dictators then met again, and Mussolini was noticeably warmer toward Hitler than before.

During October, Hitler revealed to a group of propaganda chiefs in a meeting at the Chancellory that he had finally come to grips with his religious beliefs. Raised as a Roman Catholic in Austria, Hitler had always been rebellious to the teachings of the Church, but doubts had always lingered in his mind. Now, at the age of 48, he felt free. As one of the propaganda chiefs recorded, "After grave inner struggles, he had freed himself from what remained of his childhood religious notions." The author went on to note that Hitler said, "I now feel fresh as a colt in pasture."

On October 20, 1937, Hitler ordered his military planners to prepare a contingency plan to occupy the Portuguese-owned island of the Azores in the Atlantic. The purpose was to provide a base from which North America could be bombed in the event of war.

On October 22, ex-King Edward VIII of England, now the Duke of Windsor, and his new bride, the Duchess, visited Hitler at the Berghof. This was a visit that would plague the Duke for the rest of his life while, at the same time, offer encouragement to Hitler. The Fuehrer's impression that the Duke was sympathetic toward National Socialism was confirmed by the visit and, it was clear, that if the Duke was ever able to regain his crown, he would be a great asset to Germany as King of England.

During October, a lengthy debate took place in the British Parliament over whether or not to return to Germany all or some of her lost colonies. The idea was rejected, but Hitler was, nevertheless, encouraged because, at least, the subject had been raised in the innermost chambers of the British government.

On the 28th, Mussolini, gave the Germans support in this respect by saying that Italy fully supported the return of Germany's colonies. Three days later, Germany and Italy signed another pact in which they pledged mutual support if attacked. A week later, Italy signed the German/Japanese Anti-Comintern Pact.

And during November, Germany and Japan signed yet another agreement, a military and political pact. Italy would later join this pact too.

THE HOSSBACK MEMO

On November 5, 1937, Hitler met again in secret with his top military leaders in the Chancellory. The proceedings were recorded by Colonel Friedrich Hossback, one of Hitler's adjutants, and have gone down in the history books under Hossback's name.

In his preliminary comments to the generals and admirals, Hitler explained that the German people were in need of land, food, oil and raw materials but, due to the costs of rearmament and the other programs, the government was running deep into debt. The only solution, he told them, was to conquer the territories Germany had long sought so that their assets could provide for all the things that were needed now and in the future. This, he admitted, would mean war. Thus, the purpose of the meeting was to instruct Germany's military leaders to begin making plans for that contingency. He told them that he wanted to be ready for war by 1943, or 1945 at the latest, and it was their duty to see that the German armed forces were ready. He pointed out that Austria and Czechoslovakia would be the first targets, and then Poland. He predicted that the Western Allies, France and Britain, would not go to war over these states.

Once these lands were secured, Hitler continued, some thirteen million Jews would be expelled from Austria and Czechoslovakia, and even more from Poland, thus providing additional land, food and other resources for the German people. Furthermore, the German Army could raise another dozen or more divisions from the Germans thus incorporated into the Reich. He went on, saying that the initial German attacks against these countries must be "blitzkrieg schnell" (lightening-like) so as to deter any of their allies coming to their aid in time to make a difference. Hitler also foresaw a grand world-wide alliance headed by Germany which would include Italy, Japan, Spain, and several other states.

Hitler even predicted the course of the war. At the opening of hostilities, he said, Germany would be stronger than any of her enemies and would strike first and be successful in every endeavor. Then, in all likelihood, Germany would attack in the East. With the prospect of communism erased from the face of the earth, he predicted that neither France nor Britain would actively interfere with this effort. But, to make sure of this, both nations would have to be neutralized beforehand.

With time though, Hitler admitted, Germany's enemies would grow stronger, and at a faster rate than Germany, until a balance of military power resulted. At that time, the war should be ended.

Hitler spoke constantly for four and a half hours.

Then, at last, the others had a chance to speak. Field Marshal von Blomberg, General Fritsch, Admiral Raeder and Foreign Minister von Neurath all raised lengthy questions about Hitler's proposal. In trying to defend his position, Hitler became enraged and the meeting turned into a shouting match. It ended in discord. After cooling down and reflecting on the meeting, Hitler came to the conclusion that these people had to go. The others began to think that Hitler had to go, and von Neurath had a mild heart attack. It would be Hitler who would prevail. Within months, Blomberg, Fritsch and von Neurath would be gone. Raeder would retain his post for several years but would, eventually, be dismissed.

THE "SUDETENLAND" AND A DEAL: ANGOLA AND THE CONGO FOR TANGANYIKA

On November 17, 1937, Lord Edward F. L. W. Halifax, the soon-to-be British Foreign Minister, visited Hitler. Halifax was a close confidant of Neville Chamberlain, who had become Prime Minister in May, and both men were known to be strong proponents for the appeasement of Germany and Italy. It was their belief, and the belief of others of the same ilk, that Hitler's and Mussolini's ambitions could be contained by offering concessions.

One of the main purposes for Halifax's visit was to seek a way to negotiate the recently escalated territorial dispute on Germany's eastern border with regard to the "Sudetenland" (South Eastern Land). This was a crescent-shaped area within the western border of Czechoslovakia which, prior to the Great War, had been part of Austria-Hungary. When the victorious Allies created the State of Czechoslovakia, the Sudetenland was attached to it. The population of the Sudetenland was a mix of Germans and Czechs in which Germans out-numbered Czechs four to one. For this reason, the Nazis had long called for the Sudetenland to be detached from Czechoslovakia and added to Germany. In recent months, German propagandists had raised the issue to a new level. Halifax was not empowered to make any deals with regard to the Sudetenland—only to discuss the issues.

Halifax did, however, bring with him a secret proposal with regard to Africa, which was completely irrelevant to the Sudetenland question. This was that Britain would arrange for Germany to acquire the colonies of Portuguese Angola and the Belgian Congo in exchange for Germany's commitment that Tanganyika, a German colony in East Africa conquered by British forces in the Great War, would remain British.

Hitler was non-committal on both the Sudetenland and African issues and the two gentlemen parted company amiably. Halifax came home with nothing while Hitler came

This poster appeared in Germany in 1936 to remind the German people of the loss of Mt. Kilimanjaro in Tanganyika, the old German Empire's only snow-capped mountain.

to the realization that he was dealing with a weak and wimpish government in London.

Emboldened by Halifax's offer, Hitler made another speech on November 21, demanding the return of Germany's colonies.

On November 30, the Chamberlain government backed away from the Halifax proposal by declaring that the question of German colonies was an issue that had to be agreed to by several countries and that the British government would take a neutral position on the issue until that happened.

When Portugal and Belgium eventually learned that the British had tried to bargain away their colonies, their relationships with the Chamberlain government soured. This dished up yet another political victory for the Fuehrer.

With regards to Tanganyika, the Hitler government had its own plan for regaining that colony. Volunteers were sought who were willing to go to Tanganyika as settlers even though the colony was controlled by the British under a mandate given them by the League of Nations. The volunteers were trained and financed for the undertaking and sent off to East Africa, usually with passage paid. They were instructed to settle in the northern part of the colony, where most of the older German settlers were, and imbue the older settlers with admiration for Nazi Germany. Just how Tanganyika would be brought back into the German fold was unclear, but the presence of a strong German majority in the colony would certainly be advantageous when the time came.

Behind closed doors in various offices of the Berlin bureaucracy, German planners were producing comprehensive long-range German policies for Africa. Such plans were needed in the event that Germany regained one or more of its former colonies. Along with the recovery of the German colonies the planners saw the prospect of acquiring the resource-rich Belgian Congo. This huge expanse of geography in central Africa had been claimed by Germany in the 1880s, but due to an international conspiracy against Germany—so the German scenario went—the territory was awarded to Belgium.

OFF TO THE CAMPS

During December, two more laws were added to the books: "The Law for the Protection of Hereditarily Diseased Offspring" and "The Marriage Health Law." These laws authorized the arrest and incarceration in the concentration camps of all beggars, tramps, Gypsies, and other asocial individuals. Prostitutes and alcoholics with contagious diseases were also arrested. Upon their arrival at the concentration camps they were to be employed as laborers for the State.

LIFE IS GOOD

By the end of 1937, life for the Fuehrer was about as good as it had ever been. He was the absolute dictator of Germany, he had restructured the country to his liking, his

Architect's model of the 300 flat "Dr. Joseph Goebbels Settlement" in Berlin for Nazi patriots and their families.

military strength was rapidly growing, his health was relatively good—thanks, he said, to Dr. Morell—and he had time for some relaxation. When circumstances permitted, he would often go back to his comfortable nine-room apartment in Munich, which took up the entire second floor of the building, to get away from the responsibilities and bureaucracy of the Chancellory. In Munich he could relax even better than he could at the Berghof. One of his favorite activities in Munich was to attend the Opera. There were no operas at the Berghof. When the Fuehrer attended an opera, there was usually a party planned for him after the performance, at the Kunsterhaus (Artist House), so Hitler could meet the cast. The pretty girls of the cast were always there. The parties usually lasted late, until around 3:00 a.m., and Hitler was one of the last to leave. All knew that Hitler loved discussing opera and enjoyed being with the people of the opera.

Also while in Munich, Hitler devoted attention to the new House of German Art which he had built to be Germany's premier art museum. But a problem had developed in late 1937. To fill the museum, Hitler had organized a board of art critics to select, and purchase art wherever it could be found. Unfortunately, Hitler did not like most of the art work they found, so he fired them. He then engaged his personal photographer and friend, Heinrich Hoffmann, to gather photographs of art works available and present them to him. Hitler, then, made all the selections himself.

The next year, 1938, Hitler became a Munich landlord. He purchased the building in which he had his apartment. This was not so much an investment for the Fuehrer as it was a security measure. Now Hitler could choose his neighbors. Furthermore, all of the tenants on the first floor were moved out and his SS bodyguards moved in.

ALSO BY THE END OF 1937...

In Berlin, new building construction was underway all around the Chancellory. Whole blocks of older buildings had been torn down to make way for the new ones. This was Hitler's doing, and Speer was in charge. Hitler wanted his various ministries close at hand, and in new and modern buildings that would reflect the importance of the Third Reich. Hitler had sketched some of the buildings himself, and was working closely with Speer and the architects. He often visited the construction sites. The whole undertaking was touted throughout Germany as yet another Nazi achievement. Nothing was said about the fact that much of the stone used in the buildings was being quarried by concentration camp inmates.

On January 11, 1938, Hitler commissioned Speer to begin work on the "New Chancellory" which, in reality, was a major expansion of the existing chancellory. The New Chancellory would be huge and elaborate, and Hitler would have the largest private office of any national leader in Europe. It was to be an appropriate status symbol of his power and importance. Target date for completion was January 1939.

Also in Berlin, the construction of a huge apartment complex to be known as the "Dr. Joseph Goebbels Settlement" was underway. This was to be an upscale subsidized housing project for individuals deemed to be heros of the nation.

Hitler said of Berlin at this time, "The whole world will come to Berlin to see our buildings." Berlin would also take on a new name—"Germania." On February 12, 1938, Hitler told visiting Austrian Chancellor Schuschnigg that he planned to build skyscrapers in Berlin taller than those in America.

During 1937, another law concerning the morals of the German people had appeared. This law provided for the forced castration of repeat sex offenders. Pedophiles where the most frequent victims. By the end of the year, 189 sex offenders had been castrated.

At this time, Hitler was immensely popular. Many German homes had "Hitler Corners" which consisted of a picture of the Fuehrer, a copy of Mein Kampf, and the various awards the family had won from participating in Nazi programs. Virtually every adult in Germany remembered the difficult days of the 1920s and early 1930s and appreciated the good economic times that now prevailed.

Beyond Germany's borders, Hitler was not a hero. Slowly, but very perceptively, Europe was becoming a powder keg and Hitler was seen as the culprit. Because Germany was rearming, everyone else felt the need to do likewise. It was obvious that a point would be reached where all the powder keg needed to explode would be a spark. And the continuing and threatening Nazi propaganda made the situation even more frightening. Then too, at the end of 1937, there were a total of 52 boundary disputes in Europe, any one of which might provide that spark.

30,000 ITALIANS

By the end of 1937, unemployment in Germany had all but disappeared and there was now a labor shortage. To help resolve this, Hitler turned to his friend, Mussolini, and it was agreed that, beginning in January 1938, some 30,000 Italians would be sent to work in Germany. In Italy there were still large numbers of unemployed.

OUT WITH THE OLD

On February 4, 1938, Hitler held what was to be his last Cabinet meeting. With Hitler's dictatorial power, his Cabinet had, for some time, been superfluous. This meeting had a very important purpose. Hitler confirmed that Blomberg and Fritsch had resigned and that he, personally, would now assume their responsibilities. He would, also, eliminate the post of Minister of War. In its place a new organization was to be formed to unify the top commands of every branch of Germany's military services under his leadership. The new organization was to be called the "Oberkommando der Wehrmacht" (OKW). By this move, Hitler was now in a position to direct Germany's military future with much less opposition from Germany's professional officer corps and the bureaucrats.

Also at the meeting, Hitler announced that General Wilhelm Keitel, a former aide to Blomberg and a loyal Nazi, would become OKW's Chief of Staff and serve directly under Hitler. Keitel was well-known in military circles as the perfect "yes" man, and it was not long before Keitel acquired a couple of less-than-complimentary nicknames. The first being "Lakeitel", a play on the German word for lackey, and the second being "Nikesel" after a popular toy of the day which was a donkey that, when wound-up, bobbed its head up and down.

Also at this time, Hitler confirmed that the Foreign Minister's position, formerly held by von Neurath, was to be filled by Joachim von Ribbentrop, a long-time Hitler loyalist and a man who, so Hitler believed, had strong ties to Britain.

The shake-up of Germany's military command reverberated down the line. In the days that followed, sixteen high-ranking generals were relieved of their commands and forty four others were transferred.

It was well-known that Hermann Goering had hoped to become head of OKW, but Hitler rejected the idea because Hitler believed that Goering had enough responsibilities already. To sooth Goering's ruffled feathers, the Fuehrer promoted him to Field Marshal.

AND NOW FOR AUSTRIA

As the absolute commander of Germany's armed forces, Hitler wasted no time in wielding his new power. Within days after the fateful Cabinet meeting, Hitler dispatched his faithful and respected non-Nazi, Fritz von Papen to Vienna with a message for Austria's dictator, Kurt von Schuschnigg. The message was that Hitler wanted to meet personally with Schuschnigg, and he insisted upon it.

Schuschnigg knew what the message was before von Papen arrived. It was that Hitler

wanted to fulfill his life-long dream of uniting his Austrian homeland with Germany. And, if Schuschnigg refused, it would be done by force. This was the tactic Bismarck had used successfully in the 1800s when he forced the many German mini-states to join Prussia in a united Germany.

Schuschnigg was all but defenseless. His army was no match for Germany's and he could not count on his two traditional allies, Italy and Hungary. Mussolini had previously announced that he would not interfere in German/Austrian relations. Hungary, whose armed forces were, like Austria's, no match for the Germans, also backed away from a military confrontation with Germany.

As for the major European powers, France was all but neutralized because of its unstable internal political turmoil, and London showed no indication that it would go to the aid of Austria. Instead, the British tried to dissuade Hitler by making him a secret offer—one that they had made before—a redistribution, in Germany's favor, of colonial territories in Africa in the region below 5 degrees south latitude and the Zambezi River. This would included parts of the Belgian Congo and Portuguese Angola. Hitler rejected this offer out of hand.

Schuschnigg tried various political maneuvers to fend off the Nazis, but nothing worked. Hitler was ready to strike.

On March 11, 1938, Hitler, as Commander-in-Chief of OKW, issues his first "Directive," entitled Directive Number One, to the armed forces. A Directive from Hitler was something less than an order, but more than a set of guide-lines. It was expected that the general conditions in the Directive would be carried out, but most of the details on how to do so were left to the discretion of those named to carry it out. The Directive was entitled, "For the Occupation of Austria."

The next day, Hitler issued Directive Number Two entitled, "For the Bloodless Occupation of Austria." This was the order to occupy Austria. German troops entered Austria that day. There was no resistance. It was then announced from Berlin that Germany and Austria were now one. Those who had long favored the union of Germany and Austria had a word for this day, "Anschluss." Now it had come, and Adolf Hitler had brought it about.

During the next few days, Hitler made a triumphant tour of Austria visiting many cities including Vienna and his home town of Linz. In a highly publicized event to show that Hitler was, after all, an Austrian, he placed flowers on the graves of his parents at Linz. Also while in Linz, he signed the decree entitled, "Law Concerning the Reunion of Austria with the German Reich." One observer recorded that as he signed the document, tears ran down his cheeks.

In Vienna, he made speeches and visited the Kunsthistorisches Art Museum, a place he knew well. As a struggling artist in Vienna before the Great World War, he had spend many happy hours here. He had also been engaged by the museum, at times, to do some decorative painting.

Upon returning to Berlin, Hitler spoke to the cheering multitudes from the Chancellory balcony. Below him was a huge banner that portended his next move. The banner read "Fuehrer, Your Sudetenland is also waiting for you." In London, Prime Minister Chamberlain did not see the banner, but he knew what was coming next. In a personal letter to his sister on March 20 he wrote that there was "...nothing that France or we could possibly do to save (the Sudetenland of) Czechoslovakia from being overrun by the Germans..."

From France came an ominous report that smacked of war. The massive Maginot Line protecting France's border with Germany, had been completed and would be fully manned and armed for the foreseeable future. The German counterpart, the much-touted Siegfried Line, had hardly been started.

ONWARD GERMANY!

While the Austrian situation was being addressed, Hitler plowed on. He went before his favorite captive audience, the Reichstag, to explain his actions with regard to Austria and other subjects. It was Sunday, February 20, and throughout Germany, citizens were listening in on their new cheap radios. In his typical rambling way, Hitler touched on many subjects, one of which was Germany's lost colonies. Again, he demanded their return. This put that issue, once again, on the front burner. Hitler also announced that Germany would recognize the nation of Manchukuo, a puppet state set up by the Japanese after their conquest of Manchuria in 1932. This, of course, was a move to strengthen Germany's ties with Japan. Germany was only the third nation—in six years—to recognize the puppet state. The other two were El Salvador and the Vatican.

Soon after Hitler finished his speech, he received word that Britain's hawkish Foreign Secretary, Anthony Eden, had resigned and would be replaced by Lord Halifax, a supporter of Chamberlain's appeasement policies. Hitler smiled when he read the report.

A few days after the Anschluss, Hitler sent a telegram to Mussolini thanking him profusely for not interfering with the takeover of Austria. In the telegram, Hitler said that he would "never forget" the Duce's support in this matter, and as history would show, Hitler never did.

In the months following the Anschluss, Austria was Nazified at a very rapid rate. All the Nazi laws that had been introduced in Germany over a period of six years were now imposed on the Austrian people in a matter of months. It was a difficult period for the Austrian people. Their daily lives were turned upside-down. Many Jews fled the country along with a significant number of Austrians.

In Vienna, the Lebensborn organization took over a Jewish-owner sanitarium and a Jewish-run children's home and converted them into maternity homes. These homes would perform the same function they had in Germany, but with one addition. Since it was well-known that the Austrians were the darkest of the German people, fair-haired and blue-eyed mothers-to-be from northern Germany would be sent to the Vienna homes so that their offspring who would remain in Austria and contribute to the lightening of the southern Germans.

After the Anschluss, Speer came forward with a proposal to memorialize all of the locations in Austria which were significant to Hitler and his family. Hitler was luke-warm to the idea. He was not very proud of certain members of his family and feared that this dirty laundry could hardly be ignored if the places where they lived were glorified. For example, his older brother, Alois, Jr., who was now a prosperous inn-keeper in Germany had, in his youth, been a petty criminal and served time in jail. He had abandoned Germany and emigrated to England. There, he married an English woman and produced a son, Patrick Hitler. Then he abandoned them and returned to Germany when brother Adolf became a celebrity. Young Patrick now lived in Paris and was a favorite interviewee of the French media because he was openly critical about his uncle Adolf.

And there was Hitler's father, Alois Hitler, Sr. Alois, a bastard and rumored to be half-Jewish, had been raised in the Austrian town of Spital. The thought of Spital made Hitler very uneasy so Spital, most definitely, was not to be glorified. Then there was Dollersheim, the town in which his father was born, his grandmother was buried, and the local birth records were kept in the parish archives. Hitler had plans for Dollersheim which were already underway. The citizens of the town and surrounding area were being relocated, and the parish records confiscated and the area turned into an artillery range. The empty buildings of Dollersheim would become primary targets for the gunners. In time, the town was obliterated as was its cemetery.

The only towns in Austria that Hitler wanted commemorated were his boyhood town of Linz, for which he had grandiose plans, and Braunau, his birthplace. In both places, Jews were already being removed.

There was one exception, however. In Linz, Dr. Eduard Block, who had attended Hitler's mother in the last years of her life, and who had been so kind to young Adolf at the time of her death, was allowed to remain in Linz along with his family. The Blocks were given SS protection.

During the year, the Mauthhausen Concentration Camp was established near Linz. This would ensure the availability of plenty of slave laborers when it came time to re-structure the city to Hitler's plans.

On April 2, another dose of appeasement arrived from London. Chamberlain's government had formally recognized the German takeover of Austria. Four days later, the United States followed suit. In Hitler's mind, it was all too easy. In the United States, though, there was a mounting wellspring of popular resentment toward Germany. Because of this, the German government thought it prudent to announce, on April 26, that Germany would withdraw from the forthcoming 1939 World's Fair in New York City—a city with a large Jewish minority. By now, Hitler had changed his mind about America. Before he was elected, he praised the vigor and ingenuity of the Americans and suggested that their's was a model others might emulate. But now, due mainly to the American-generated Depression and the anti-Nazi attitude which had developed, he saw America as a reservoir of racial mongrels whose politics and economy were controlled by Jews.

Not surprisingly, there had been world-wide criticism of Germany's takeover of Austria. To allay this criticism, Berlin announced that a plebescite would be taken to obtain the true feelings of the Austrian people. That plebescite, Nazi-controlled of course, was held on April 10, and soon afterwards it was announced that 97% of the Austrian people approved of the Anschluss. Independent observers, at the time, estimated that only about 40% of the Austrian population really favored the Anschluss and the remainder favored the status quo or even a leftist government.

CANCER FEAR AGAIN AND A
GLITTERING DISAPPOINTMENT IN ITALY

In late April, Hitler suffered another bout of hoarseness and, like before, believed he might have throat cancer. He was so concerned that he made out a will dated May 2, 1938. The principal heir was to be his faithful mistress, Eva Braun. He also directed that each of his sisters, Angela and Paula, should receive an annual income of 12,000 marks per year, which was a sizeable income at the time. To his brother, Alois, Jr., of whom he was never very fond, Hitler left a lump sum of 60,000 marks. He left an additional 30,000 marks to various other relatives in Austria.

Also, during this month, Hitler issued secret documents declaring that, after his death, Goering was to be his successor with Hess the next in line. This was a sequence of events that would not happen.

A subsequent operation found another polyp on his vocal cords which was removed and tested benign. Much relieved, Hitler was able to keep his appointment to meet with Mussolini in Italy. In Italy, Hitler hoped to lay the groundwork for a military alliance to augment their political alliance that had now become known as the Axis. But the Italians had other ideas. With Hitler coming to Rome, it was a golden opportunity for Italy to show off before the world.

Hitler, still recovering from his throat operation, was met at the Rome station by Mussolini and a large entourage, and,with cameras rolling, was escorted on foot into an adjoining square which had just recently been renamed "Piazza Adolf Hitler." Then they rode in a six-horse royal carriage, past thousands of cheering spectators to the King's palace where Hitler was to stay. It was a place where he knew he would not feel welcome. The streets were lined with thousands of Italian and German flags; there were several hundred hanging from the Coliseum along with a huge banner proclaiming "Viva il Fuehrer." He had a painful meeting with the King and other Italian nobility, then he witnessed Italian Army maneuvers, a pass-by of ninety Italian submarines, and a demonstration by the Italian Air Force. In Florence, Hitler was given four hours in the magnificent Ufizzi Art Gallery.

When Hitler and Ribbentrop finally got a chance to talk business with Mussolini and Foreign Minister Galeazzo Ciano, Mussolini's son-in-law, the Germans discovered that the Italians had no interest, at all, in a military alliance.

There was yet another disappointment. Hitler had hoped to be received by the Pope, but the Pope declined. It was a diplomatic snub due to Germany's rough treatment of the Austrian Catholics. Also, the magnificent Vatican Art Museum, which Hitler had hoped to see, was temporarily closed to all, including the Fuehrer.

Hitler, nevertheless, kept up appearances. At the final dinner he proclaimed, "Mussolini is not only my friend, but my master, my chief."

Hitler had hoped, too, to take a short private vacation in Italy after the formalities were over. But it did not work out. Hitler returned to Germany feeling disappointed and that he had been used.

THE SUDETENLAND

By mid-May the German-made Sudetenland crisis had reached a crisis state. Hitler's plan was to threaten Czechoslovakia as he had Austria; cede Sudetenland to Germany or risk having it taken by force. But Czechoslovakia was no Austria. It was a state with very strong allies, Britain, France and the Soviet Union. A German military attack on Czechoslovakia could touch off another world war. But there was an Achilles Heel to this arrangement. None of Czechoslovakia's allies had a common border with her and it was the feeling in both Paris and London that it would be next-to-impossible to send her significant reinforcements and supplies. If war started, the most likely scenario would be that Germany would quickly overrun Czechoslovakia and the British and French would be faced, with fighting a lengthy war on the Western Front while the Soviet Union would hold back, offering only token support. Stalin's game would be to avoid creating a second front, thus forcing the Nazis and democracies to fight out a long hard war. Then, at the end, he would move in and gather up the pieces.

In London, and to some degree in Paris, this situation was seen as another job for appeasement—and Hitler knew it, so he pressed on. On May 30, The Fuehrer, as OKW chief, issued another Directive to his armed forces entitled, "Fall Grun" (Case Green), the military occupation of the Sudentenland and, if possible, all of Czechoslovakia. A deadline was set for October 1, 1938.

OTHER DEVELOPMENTS IN GERMANY

One of the most pressing problems in Germany now was the shortage of labor. To resolve this, another law was passed to force the lazy and under-employed to work harder. The law was called, "Reich Campaign Against the Workshy." Those who were caught up in its net were told that they had to become useful workers, or be sent off to a concentration camp and used as forced laborers.

Also, to use labor efficiently and coordinate the many government construction projects planned and underway, a new super-construction agency was formed under Fritz Todt. Todt was a general in the Luftwaffe and a very capable engineer. The first task of the "Todt Organizations," as it was called, was to speed up the construction of the Siegfried Line in western Germany opposite the French Maginot Line. Todt's agency quickly proved itself to be very capable and was soon enlarged and given additional projects.

During July, "The Law for Compulsory Labor Service" was decreed which greatly increased the government's control over the working lives of many German citizens. This was yet another move to make Germany's labor force more efficient and productive.

One of Hitler's aims, with regard to Austria, was to reduce the influence the Catholic Church had in that country. On July 12,

1938, he canceled Austria's concordat with the Vatican in favor of Germany's concordat which was much more restrictive on Church activities. Two weeks later, he issued a decree legalizing divorce in Austria. Later, all government sanctioned religious holidays were eliminated.

Despite the on-going problems, the summer of 1938 was one of the happiest times for the German people since before the Great War. There was prosperity, full employment, a low crime rate—most of the criminal elements of German society were in the concentration camps—and there was world respect once again for Germany. To substantiate the latter, delegations from all over the world came to Germany to study Germany's economic recovery, labor system, Autobahns, workers' housing, athletic fields, etc. Still another reason for this feeling of well-being was because the Labor Front's Strength-Through-Joy program was now up and running. Many ordinary working people in Germany were able to take vacations and excursions they could only have dreamed of before the Nazi era. Another facet of the Strength-Through-Joy program was that there were many paid holidays for workers. A government agency had been established for this purpose; "The Bureau for the Organization of Festivals, Leisure and Celebrations." Other than New Year's Day, the year's holiday calendar began with a holiday on January 30, commemorating the day Hitler became Chancellor. Most of the holidays that followed had political overtones. The holiday season ended with the traditional Christmas/News Year's festivities. The word "Christmas," however, was dropped from the official language and replaced by the word "Yuletide."

By August 1938, the ranks of the SS had grown to the point where Hitler had enough men to organize a division-sized military unit that would be under Himmler, and his direct control, independent of the Army. To calm the fears of the Army leaders, Hitler promised that this unit would be put under their command in the event of war. In peacetime, though, it would do the work of the Party that the police and the armed forces could not be expected to do. The new unit, called the "Leibstandarte-SS, Adolf Hitler," consisted of three motorized infantry regiments: one each motorcycle, engineer and communications battalion and a medical unit. The SS acquired its own training camp and received basically the same military training and equipment provided by the Army. With time, this unit would grow into the "Waffen-SS" (Armed-SS) and consist of some 30 divisions with over 600,000 men.

MUNICH

The Nazis used their annual Party rally at Nuremberg as a platform to rail against the Czechs threatening to resolve the Sudetenland issue by force. The atmosphere in Europe was turning ugly and war-jitters spread throughout the continent. The British began building bomb shelters and distributing gas masks, and the British Fleet was mobilized. On the German/Czech border, German troops positioned themselves for an attack. To the west, the French sent 65 divisions to the French/German border. From far-away Moscow came pronouncements that the Soviet Union would honor its alliance with Czechoslovakia if France would do the same. In Switzerland, German citizens were harassed on the streets and German-owned businesses were boycotted. The Swiss Army, fearing that the Germans might move through Switzerland to attack France and circumvent the Maginot Line, began mining important bridges and tunnels. Swiss cities also practiced blackouts.

Hitler knew he was playing with fire, but justified his actions by telling his associates, "I would rather have war when I am fifty rather than fifty-five or sixty."

In the Czech part of Czechoslovakia, that country's armed forces were fully mobilized and ready to fight. But this was not necessarily so in Slovakia. A large percentage of the Slovak people saw this as a Czech problem and argued that the Slovaks would stay out of it. The people of Czechoslovakia were divided.

Then, on September 13, Chamberlain took a bold step. He wired Hitler saying, "I propose to come over at once to see you with a view of trying to find a peaceful solution." This was the break Hitler had been hoping for because it was almost certain that Chamberlain was ready to capitulate and seek a face-saving way out of this dilemma. Hitler could smell another Bismarckian victory.

Two days later Chamberlain arrived at the Berghof. French Premier Edouard Daladier was invited, as was Mussolini who spoke German, French and English and would serve as a moderator. Conspicuously absent were the Czechs and the Soviets. The talks over the Sudetenland continued, on and off, for the next two weeks. Finally, a solution was reached. The British and French were willing to back out of their alliance commitments to Czechoslovakia for a piece of paper. Written on the piece of paper was a promise from Hitler that the Sudentenland would be his last territorial demand in Europe. Hitler signed the piece of paper around midnight on September 30, only hours before the German troops were due to march.

While Chamberlain was on his way home, Hitler, in a jovial mood made a joke of it all. He told his associates, "Well, he (Chamberlain) seemed like such a nice old gentleman, I though I would give him my autograph as a souvenir."

On the morning of October 1, Chamberlain arrived in England by plane. He waved the piece of paper before the crowds at the airport, and proclaimed that there would be "peace in our time." Churchill, ever the hawk, countered a short time later saying to Chamberlain, "You were given the choice between war and dishonor. You chose dishonor and you will have war."

Daladier flew home to a much more subdued welcome. The French people were still as politically divided as ever.

In Prague, Czech crowds gathered in the streets to denounce Hitler and Chamberlain alike.

The world's media became fascinated with Mussolini's role in the settlement and proclaimed him a peace-maker. This pleased the Duce to no end.

From Moscow came the quiet announcement that the Soviet Union would not go to war with Germany, alone, over the issue of the Sudetenland.

Czechoslovakia, now without allies, was a wounded wildebeest surrounded by hungry wolves. Both Hungary and Poland had territorial claims against Czechoslovakia and now pressed their demands. And from Slovakia came strong calls for secession from the Czechoslovak union. Many Slovaks believed that it would now be better to go it alone rather than be bound in a union in which the central government was discredited and, for the moment, very unstable. Even Ruthenia, the eastern-most province of the Czechoslovak union, a land peopled mainly by Ukrainians, announced that it would secede from the union.

On October 3, 1938, German troops marched into the Sudetenland. Hitler followed a few hours later making a triumphal entry.

For about two weeks, there was a honeymoon atmosphere in Europe. War had been averted and Hitler contained—so most people thought. Then Hitler revealed his true nature. He began making demands on Poland to return to Germany the lands taken from her after the Great War. The most important piece of land was known as the "Polish corridor", a narrow stretch of land that gave Poland access to the Baltic Sea, but split Germany into two parts, Germany proper and East Prussia. Another of Hitler's demands was the return of the Baltic seaport of Danzig at the northern end of the Polish Corridor. Danzig was a centuries-old German city but had been taken from Germany by the Versailles Treaty and established as an independent City State.

By the end of October 1938, tensions in Europe were right back where they were before Munich, but now, Hitler was unmasked. Only a fool would now take Hitler at his word.

On November 2, 1938, at a conference in Vienna, Germany mediated the territorial dispute between Hungary and Czechoslova-

kia. The Hungarians were given virtually all they demanded including control of Ruthenia. Czechoslovakia lost 29% of its remaining territory and 34% of its population. This was called the "Vienna Award" and as a result, Hungary was now a stronger friend of Germany than before. As for Czechoslovakia, she had been raped for a second time.

On November 20, the German and Czech governments reached an agreement on the transfer of populations. About 379,000 ethnic Germans were uprooted from all over Czechoslovakia and transferred to Germany, while all of the Czech citizens in the Sudetenland were transferred to Czechoslovakia. This was another laurel for Hitler because, as he had so often promised, he had, once again, delivered another large group of Germans into the arms of the Reich while, at the same time, removing a large number of slavs from German territory.

POLAND

As for Poland, the German demands were much the same as those with regard to the Sudetenland; give us the land we demand or we will take it by force. And, like Czechoslovakia, Poland had military alliance treaties with France and Britain, although not with the Soviet Union. But now, from both Paris and London, came strong pronouncements that the treaties with Poland would be honored if Germany attacked. There would not be a second "Munich," they vowed. Hitler, though, was not so sure—and seemed willing, once again, to gamble.

On October 29, Hitler kept the pot boiling by again demanding the return of Germany's colonies.

"KRISTALLNACHT"

In late October, the Nazis took the first actions with regard to their new policy of forcing Jews to leave Germany. Some 17,000 Jews were rounded up and forced across the border into Poland. The Poles deeply resented this action and were very slow to go to the aid of the Jews. In the meantime, the Jews starved and suffered in this man-made limbo.

A week later, a Jewish youth, seventeen-year-old Herschel Grynszpan, living in Paris, learned that his parents were among those deported. In a fit a anger, he charged into the German embassy in Paris and gunned down the first diplomat he encountered, Ernst von Rath, the embassy's third secretary. Von Rath died on the tenth which signaled nationwide, Nazi-prompted riots throughout Germany against the Jews. The riots, augmented by the SS, concentrated on Jewish-owned properties to such a degree that, in many cities, the broken glass from the shop windows glistened like crystals in the street. Thus, this terrible night became known as "Kristallnacht" (Crystal Night). And it went on for days because Hitler saw this as a grand opportunity to rid Germany of more Jews. Jews were murdered in incredible numbers and some 30,000 more were arrested and thrown into the concentration camps.

As part of the horror, the government levied a collective fine on the entire German Jewish community which amounted to some $8,000 for each man, woman and child. This outrageous sum gave the German state an ersatz legal reason to confiscate the Jews' property.

To justify these actions before the world, the Germans claimed that the Jews were arming themselves and planning a revolution. To further justify this claim, another law was promulgated, several days later, entitled, "Regulations Against Jewish Possession of Weapons."

With an excuse now to incarcerate large numbers of Jews in concentration camps, and because of problems with the Warsaw government, the dumping of Jews into Poland ended. Of the approximately 17,000 Jews dumped into Poland, almost all found refuge in a squalid refugee camp at Zbaszyn, Poland.

MORE SABRE RATTLING FROM BOTH GERMANY AND ITALY

On November 8, SS Chief Himmler made a speech in which he made a blood-curdling statement, "I really intend to take German blood from wherever it is to be found in the world, to rob and steal it wherever I can." This was a statement justifying kidnapping. A few years later, Himmler would put these words into action when he introduced a program to forcibly take racially acceptable children from their parents in some of the conquered territories and raise the children in German foster homes or German institutions.

Also at this time, Mussolini again pressed Italy's demands in colonial Africa and the Mediterranean. Specifically, he targeted French-controlled Tunisia, the French Island of Corsica, the British-controlled Suez Canal, and French Somaliland in East Africa.

JEWS TO AFRICA AND SOUTH AMERICA

In the wake of Kristallnacht, France, The Netherlands and Britain came forward with new offers to open some of their colonial territories to Jews. France offered areas in their African colonies and The Netherlands offered areas in the Dutch East Indies. Britain offered up to 40,000 square miles in their South American colony of British Guiana, and some 50,000 square miles in their African mandate of Tanganyika. All of the areas offered were, for the most part, undeveloped lands with native populations and very little modern infrastructure. Some of them were tropical jungles. In the case of Tanganyika, which was perhaps the best offer made, the British appeared to have an ulterior motive: if Tanganyika was heavily populated with Jews, it might lessen the Nazi's desire to recover it.

All of the offers made by the European nations satisfied no one and it all came to naught.

THE ATOM

On December 17, 1938, two German scientists, Otto Hahn and Fritz Strassmann, working in their laboratory at the Kaiser Wilhelm Institute of Chemistry just outside Berlin, made a great scientific discovery. When atoms of the element uranium are bombarded by neutrons, the atoms split into two or more pieces. Every scientist knew, from basic atomic theory, that if an atom could be split (fission), a tremendous amount of energy would be suddenly released. Here was an all-new source of energy previously unknown to mankind. News of the discover spread throughout the world scientific community and experiments by others confirmed Hahn's and Strassmann's findings. Reports of the finding also circulated up the German governmental bureaucracy, but virtually no one, including Hitler, understood their significance.

NAZI GERMANY'S FIRST OVERSEAS COLONY

In December 1938, the Germans acquired an overseas colony. A German scientific expedition was sent to Antarctica, and its members trekked around a portion of the continent dropping little Nazi flags as they went. From Berlin, the world was informed of Nazi Germany's new acquisition. This claim, however, was open to dispute, because others had claims to the same territory. In Germany, however, it made good reading in the newspapers and gave the German people pride. Also, macabre jokes circulated that this might be a place to send Germany's Jews.

THE STATUE OF FASCISM

In Rome, the thinking was that if Germany could have a new colony, then Italy could have a world-class statue—something on the order of the Statue of Liberty in America. Il Duce studied several designs that would be representative of Fascism, but the venture was eventually shelved. Italy had higher priorities than a statue.

MERRY CHRISTMAS

In Britain the illusion that peace had been assured at the Munich conference was not totally dead. Prime Minister Chamberlain's Christmas card for 1938 pictured an airplane and the phrase, "Munich, September 1938."

DIVORCE

Under Nazi law, the fact that a wife was unwilling or unable to bear children provided grounds for divorce. Since there were more women than men in Germany, and since it was something of a patriotic duty to have children, men found it relatively easy to discard their old wife and find another. By the end of 1938, German statistics recorded over 62,000 divorces, up from 42,000 in the pre-Nazi and depression year of 1932.

On the other side of the coin, marriage was now to be the goal of virtually every young German man and woman; so much so that mass weddings were encouraged and fairly common.

CHAPTER 9

PRELUDE TO WAR–
JANUARY-SEPTEMBER, 1939

By 1939, the Nazification of Germany had reached a state of development that allowed Hitler to do virtually anything he wanted, with the confidence that the German people would follow. The Nazis had strict controls over the population and nearly every citizen was a member of one or more Nazi organization. The streets of Germany were filled with men, women and children wearing uniforms. The education system was firmly in the hands of the Nazis; every child had a structured environment which would guide him through his educational years from kindergarten to service in the armed forces. There were now 41 training camps for government-approved "educators," and some 215,000 had been trained. Because of all the demands on German youth by the government, there were fewer young people in the colleges and universities. By 1939 enrollment had dropped 57% from 1933.

The German media, arts, theater and sports were, likewise, controlled from above. Over seventy percent of German households had radios to insure that everyone received every message of importance from the government. Also, a system of some 6,000 loud speakers had been placed in public places all over Germany. Furthermore, German-language radio stations broadcasted to the "Volksdeutsch" (ethnic Germans living abroad). These efforts paid off. By 1939, some 4,000 Germans per month were returning to the Fatherland from abroad.

Unemployment was a thing of the past and overtime was available to many. Foreign workers were becoming numerous. Also, about one-third of the non-industrial jobs in Germany were now filled by women, especially on the farms. These women were known as "land-girls." The increase in the employment of women was due to the fact that a law called the "Compulsory Labor Decree of February 1939" had been passed requiring every able-bodied woman under the age of twenty-five to donate twelve months of service to the German economy. In addition to office and farm work, many young women were employed as domestics and nannies in households with large numbers of children.

With regard to agriculture, farming methods had improved to the point where Germany was rapidly approaching the point of self-sufficiency in the foodstuffs that its climate and soil were capable of producing.

By 1939, 3077 miles of new autobahns had been completed and the construction of more milage was underway. Government reports claimed that the production of synthetic petroleum had reached about three-fourths of Germany's peacetime needs. It was a much smaller fraction, however, of wartime needs.

Fewer and fewer Jews were seen on the streets and in public places. Both the incarceration of Jews and Jewish emigration from Germany continued. Since the Nazis came to power in 1933, more than one-half of Germany's Jews had emigrated. As for those who remained, various governmental sources made frequent comments that the time was approaching when Germany's remaining Jews would be resettled in some unidentified location in the east. This was reinforced by the decree of January 1, 1939, entitled "The Measure for the Elimination of Jews from the German Economy" which banned Jews from working virtually anywhere in Germany.

With the expansion of the Germany military, there also came a significant expansion in the SS. That organization counted more than 250,000 members and had secured a monopoly on the security apparatus inside the Third Reich. In addition, all of Germany's police now worked for the SS. The SS had also made inroads into the economy to help finance its operations and personnel. By 1939, the SS owned companies producing such diverse items as mineral water and jam.

On January 8, 1939, Hitler brought up the question of Germany's lost colonies once again in a speech in Munich saying, "We want absolutely nothing more from these countries (Britain and France) except the restoration of the colonies which have been unjustly taken from us..." The phrase "nothing more" implied another Hitler promise, a promise that only the foolhardy would now believe.

The next day, January 9, Hitler was back in Berlin for the grand opening of the New Chancellory which had been completed precisely on schedule by its architect and builder, Albert Speer. A grand ceremony took place, attended by representatives of fifty-two nations, and Hitler heaped praise on Speer and predicted glorious things for the Third Reich that the glory of this magnificent edifice portended.

This magnificent edifice, however, was not quite grand enough for the Fuehrer. He had told some of his closest associates, "...we will build a totally new Reichschancellory sometime after 1950 which will provide a new artistic and professional bench mark for the genial architect and builder, Albert Speer."

On January 30, the sixth anniversary of his coming to power, Hitler again raised the colonial issue in a speech before the Reichstag. This speech was more threatening than that on the 9th. Hitler accused the leaders of the democracies, especially the Americans, of being "warmongers." And, as he had done before, he blamed international Jewry for fomenting war by saying, "If international Jewish finance...should succeed in plunging nations into another world war, the result would not be a victory for Jewry, but the eradication of the Jewish race in Europe."

On February 6, Hitler spoke to the Reichstag again and once more brought up the colonies issue. By now, political analysts around the world had to question Hitler's motives on this issue. Did he really mean what he said or was he raising the colonies issue as a smoke screen for some other action he planned to take; or was he creating a bargaining chip that could be used in some future negotiations? As a result, war jitters continued to mount throughout the world.

At the end of February 1939, another scheme materialized with regard to sending Jews to Africa. This was brokered between an American, George Rublee, Chairman of the "International Committee for Refugees," and German negotiators. Under this agreement, German Jews, who, heretofore, were not allowed to leave Germany with cash or other assets, would be allowed to buy and take with them German-made machinery, farm equipment, clothes, etc., plus one-way tickets to British East Africa (Kenya, Uganda and Tanganyika). There, they would settle and begin new lives. This scheme centered on the British mandated colony of Tanganyika which had been a German colony before the Great War and still had a sizeable German population. The program would function over a five year period during which time the Jews would be allowed to work in Germany to earn the necessary money. This scheme, however, like all the others, failed to materialize.

FUEHRER, COME RESCUE US

From the Belgian Congo, in the heart of central Africa, came a rather unusual request from one Simon Mpadi, the leader of a Christian/Pagan religious sect. Mpadi had come into conflict with the Belgian colonial administrators and sent a letter to Hitler asking him to come and rescue him and his people from the Belgian oppressors. No response was forthcoming from the Chancellory.

SWITZERLAND: FRIENDSHIP WITH— AND FEAR OF—GERMANY

Over the years, Switzerland and Germany had developed very close ties. A large minority of the population was, as it is now, of German heritage, spoke German, and maintained much of their German culture. The two neighbors had a long history of favorable trade relations and Germans accounted for a large portion of Switzerland's tourist trade. By the late 1930s, with the German economy on the upswing, German trade and tourism were very profitable for the Swiss. Many Germans also made use of Switzerland's secretive banking system much to the dismay of the Nazi leaders in Germany who believed that German citizens were spiriting money out of Germany and/or avoiding German taxes.

But ever since the Nazis came to power in 1933, fears of Germany mounted among the Swiss people. The democratic Swiss had a problem unique in Western Europe in that they had an exceptionally large proportion of German-speaking people; 2.9 million out of a total of 4.2 million citizens. Switzerland also had a fairly large Swiss-Nazi party. Therefore, the Swiss watched with apprehension as democracy died in Germany and

was replaced by an aggressive dictatorship which preached both expansionism and pan-Germanism. Furthermore, the Swiss saw what had happened to Austria and the Sudetenland, and could not help but harbor fears that it might happen to them. As a measure against internal dissention, the Swiss-Nazi party was actively suppressed by the Swiss government and diplomatic relations between the two nations cooled considerably. This, however, had little effect on trade and tourism.

Then too, German propaganda was vicious and threatening against Switzerland's neighbor to the west, France, and the possibility of another war between Germany and France was a great concern. With the French having built the Maginot Line along the French-German border, military logic dictated that a German attack on France would, almost certainly, go around one end or the other of that Line. If the Germans chose to go around the southern end of the Line, they would have to march through Switzerland.

What is more, Switzerland was suffering from another Nazi-created burden; the heavy flow of refugees fleeing Germany, a large percentage of whom were German Jews. And it was apparent to the Swiss that the flow of refugees was not likely to diminish any time soon. Consequently, the Swiss Government took steps to slow its progress which took the form of passport controls agreed to by Germany.

Freedom of speech still reigned in Switzerland, though, and there were many influential people who spoke out against the Nazis and Germany. Out of necessity, the Swiss armed forces had been increased. The Nazi government responded to these unfriendly acts by discouraging German tourism to Switzerland and making the ownership of Swiss bank accounts illegal for German citizens. To enforce this, the Germans sent spies into Switzerland to try to catch German wrong-doers. The Swiss, of course, learned of this and resented the intrusion into their internal affairs. Also, the Germans regularly intercepted mail, and they monitored phone calls, to and from Switzerland which further strained relations between the two nations.

At times, this battle of words and wits became somewhat ridiculous. In Germany, Hitler banned the popular Swiss play, "William Tell" on the grounds that Tell, the play's hero, was a revolutionary who opposed a dictatorial regime. In Switzerland, it was common for audiences in movie theaters to boo and hiss at newsreels from Germany showing people heiling Hitler. In an attempt to quell this irritant to Berlin, the Swiss government ordered that the movies be edited to remove as much heiling as possible.

Beginning in January 1939, the verbal battle heated up when the German press began a campaign accusing the Swiss of harboring fugitives from German justice and displaying an overall anti-Swiss attitude.

This claim was, in fact, quite accurate and caused another escalation of the confrontation. The Swiss parliament granted special war powers to the executive branch of the government in case of a national emergency. To drive this point home to the Germans, the announcement of this decision was made by the Swiss government on January 30, just hours before Hitler was due to give his annual anniversary speech to the Reichstag. The Swiss had been forewarned that the speech would have an anti-Swiss tone.

During the first months of 1939, diplomatic relations between Germany and Switzerland were at a low ebb.

MUSSOLINI EXPANDS HIS TERRITORIAL DEMANDS

During February, Mussolini made a speech in which he reiterated Italy's territorial demands and this time he included British-controlled Gibraltar. This was, no doubt, related to the situation in Spain in which the Nationalist forces of Generalissimo Francisco Franco were on the verge of victory. Once a fascist regime emerged in Spain, it seemed undeniable to Mussolini that that regime would work hand-in-glove with Italy's program of expansion out of appreciation for the massive military aid that Italy had supplied the Nationalists during the three-year-long civil war. Because of this, Mussolini felt justified in adding Gibraltar to his list of future acquisitions.

Behind the scenes, however, Mussolini was not so confident. He told his generals that Italy was not yet ready for war and needed several more years to build up its armed forces. Such a build-up, he claimed, would include the creation of a huge black army in Italian East Africa. Efforts so far, in that respect, had been less than impressive due to the lack of interest in Italy's military circles and the reluctance of the blacks to serve in their master's army.

MARCH 1939—A MONTH OF DYNAMIC EVENTS

During the month of March 1938, several world-shaking events occurred. On the second day of the month, a new Pope, Pope Pius XII, was elected to replace the late Pius XI who had died on February 10. Pius XII, as a Cardinal and the Vatican's State Secretary before his election, had been a strong opponent of Fascism and National Socialism, but it was not yet clear what attitude he would take toward the fascist states with regards to the Vatican's foreign policy.

Also in March, Germany signed a trade agreement with Romania, Europe's largest oil producer. This gave Germany access to Romania's oil in the event of war.

Another action taken by the German government during the month was the issuing of a decree that made membership in the Hitler Youth mandatory for German boys and young men, aged ten to eighteen. These youngsters would now receive a solid dose of Nazi indoctrination and pre-military training.

During three days in mid-March, the political situation in Czecho-Slovakia (the new post-Munich spelling for the name of the country) disintegrated and the country was on the verge of civil war. This gave Hitler an excuse to consider sending the German Army into the country to prevent a civil war from erupting on Germany's eastern border. The turmoil stemmed from the Slovaks' threat to secede from the union and the Czech's determination to prevent that from happening by force of arms.

Hitler was able, through strong diplomatic pressures, to coerce Czecho-Slovakia's President, Emil Hacha, to "invite" German forces into the country in order to keep the peace. Hacha complied and German troops peacefully occupied the Czech provinces of Bohemia and Moravia. They did not occupy Slovak territory.

Back at Hitler's headquarters, the Fuehrer was ecstatic. In a burst of enthusiasm he said to his female secretaries, "Give me a kiss girls! This is the greatest day in my life. I shall be known as the greatest German in history."

The Hungarian government, now a strong German ally, took advantage of the situation and sent its army into the southern part of Slovakia to occupy territories long-claimed by Budapest. The remainder of Slovakia was allowed to declare its independence. Slovakia became a one-party, fascist-like, dictatorship with a Catholic priest, Monsignor Josef Tiso, as its leader.

In the Czech half of the country, the Germans proclaimed the areas they had occupied as a protectorate naming it "The Protectorate of Bohemia-Moravia."

The western Allies complained bitterly about Germany's and Hungary's actions, but did nothing. Berlin claimed that the occupation and the splitting up of Czecho-Slovakia was not a violation of the Munich Agreement because German troops had been invited into the country and that the country, as a protectorate, could not be considered an integral part of the Third Reich. It must be remembered that this was the age of colonialism and, Berlin rightfully point out, that the western powers, themselves, had protectorates all around the globe and that some of them had acquired under similar circumstances.

Throughout Germany, Hitler was now more popular than ever and he reveled in it. He made several speeches reminding the German people that he was keeping his promises to them to expand German living space, protect Germany's borders and make Germany the principle political and military power in Central Europe. He also claimed with pride that, by acquiring Bohemia-Moravia, he had brought another 378,000 ethnic Germans, living in the protectorate, back to the fold of the Reich. A decree soon followed granting those people full German citizenship and naming them the guardians of Nazi ideology in the protectorate. The Czech people were relegated to the status of colonial subjects.

A short time later, Berlin announced that since Bohemia-Moravia was bordered on the north and west by Germany, and by German-controlled Austria on the south, a new autobahn would be built across the protectorate connecting the German borderland on the north with Austria on the south. Also, a canal would be built across Bohemia-Moravia connecting the Oder River with the Danube.

As for Hitler, himself, he acquired yet another title, the "Aggrandizer of the Reich."

On March 22, Hitler aggrandized the Reich even further by sending German troops to seize the port-city of Memel from Lithuania. Memel was just across the eastern border of East Prussia and had been a German city up to the end of the Great War when it was awarded, by the victorious Allies, to the newly-created state of Lithuania. The Nazis, forthwith, declared Memel an integral part of the German Reich.

This act, however, was an undeniable violation of Hitler's promise given at Munich that he would not seek territorial expansion for Germany in Europe. The occupation of Memel could not be explained away as a measure to preserve the peace as had been the case with Bohemia-Moravia. Therefore, by this action, the Munich Agreement had become null and void and Hitler's political promises were proven to be worthless.

Since Memel had a large ethnic German population, some 70,000, Hitler could once again boast to the German people that he had brought another large number of Germans back to the Reich.

Then it was Poland's turn. Riding the crest of expansionism, German Foreign Minister, Joachim von Ribbentrop, summoned Poland's ambassador to the German Foreign Office in Berlin. The ambassador was told that the German government demanded an immediate settlement on Germany's demands that Polish territory, taken from Germany after the Great War, be returned. This would amount to about one-fourth of Poland's territory.

This demand, not surprisingly, was rejected by Warsaw and from London and Paris came pronouncements that if Germany tried to take the territory by force, the Allies would come to Poland's defense. This would mean war. This reply was not unexpected in Berlin. But Hitler could see three options, all of them favorable to Germany. Option one would be that Britain and France would abandon Poland as they had abandoned Czechoslovakia; option two, that Britain and France would mount a token war to save face and then negotiate a settlement; and option three, that a longer war would ensue that Germany could win because of its now-superior military might.

In this respect, Hitler knew he had a formidable new and secret weapon which was soon to be at his command—long range rockets. During March, Hitler visited the new rocket-building complex at Peenemunde, on the Baltic coast of Germany, and was very impressed with the progress being made there under its director, Wernher von Braun. These were weapons that Hitler knew the Western Powers could not match and against which had little defense.

Another factor that strengthened Hitler's military hand at this time was the completion of the Siegfried Line, the principal element in Germany's western defenses. It stretched from the Swiss border to Holland and was designed to deter any invasion of Germany from the west.

In Rome, Mussolini stirred the pot even more. Seeing how easy it was for Hitler to gain territory, he decided to try his hand at it. Italy had had a long-running dispute with Albania, a small independent country on the eastern shore of the Adriatic Sea across from southern Italy. On March 25, Italy made demands on the Albanian government of King Zog that would make Albania an Italian protectorate, much on the order that Bohemia-Moravia had become a German protectorate.

The next day, Mussolini upped the ante by demanding a meeting with the French to discuss Italian claims against Tunisia and French Somaliland. The Duce would eventually have his way with Albania, but the French would prove to be too tough a nut to crack.

On March 29, the last battle of the three-year-long Spanish Civil War was fought and won by the Spanish Nationalists. Generalissimo Franco, the Nationalist leader, was now Spain's absolute dictator. Because of the significant military aid given his cause during the civil war, Franco was deeply indebted to Hitler and Mussolini. In a show of allegiance with Germany and Italy, Franco's regime joined the Axis-sponsored Anti-Comintern Pact and assumed many fascist-like trappings and programs. As the Fuehrer and the Duce had done, Franco assumed a personal political title for himself. He was now to be known as the "Caudillo" (Protector) of Spain.

Not to be outdone by their European counterparts, the Japanese, on March 31, invaded and seized the Spratly Island, a small group of islands in the South China Sea, claimed by France. Possession of the islands put the powerful Japanese fleet within striking distance of many vital points in Southeast Asia.

Needless to say, a large number of Europeans were greatly concerned with the turn of events in Europe. This was reflected in the fact that, on March 31, some 60 million dollars worth of European gold arrived in New

York City aboard the ocean liner "Manhattan" for safe-keeping in America.

ALBANIA

On April 7, 1939, Italian troops, many of them veterans of the conflict in Spain, invaded Albania and conquered the small nation within a few days. Mussolini then proclaimed Albania to be an Italian protectorate. King Zog fled to Britain and guerrilla bands began to form in the mountains. The Albanian people would not accept their new situation as peacefully as had the Czechs.

The British and French protested Italy's action and warned Rome against any further incursion into the Balkans, especially against Greece, a strong British ally. Mussolini took this as so much hot air.

Since Albania had a substantial Muslim population, Mussolini could, once again, flaunt his claim that he was the true Protector of Islam. Many Muslims thought otherwise because there were many anti-Italian demonstrations throughout the Islamic world over the invasion of Albania.

HAPPY BIRTHDAY, MEIN FUEHRER

On April 20, 1939, Adolf Hitler turned fifty. A huge parade, displaying much of Germany's military might, was held in Berlin, and the entire nation seemed to be in a festive mood.

In Munich, a brewery announced that it had created a special brew to celebrate the occasion. It contained only 1% alcohol. Hitler, a teetotaller, liked the beer and ordered it regularly thereafter. Gastronomically speaking, however, Hitler's stomach ailments had returned and, once again, he feared he might have cancer.

In London, rumors were received that Goering's Luftwaffe would present Hitler with another birthday gift, an airborne invasion of the former German African colony of Tanganyika. The British took this seriously and mobilized their military units in Tanganyika, which consisted mainly of native units known collectively as the "Kings African Rifles" (KAR). Defensive measures were taken including the blocking, around the clock, of airfield and other possible landing sites. The invasion failed to materialize.

RAVENSBRUCK

On May 15, 1939, the Nazi government opened another concentration camp, Ravensbruck. This camp was different from all the rest in that it was for women only.

THE "PACT OF STEEL"

On May 22, 1939, Germany and Italy consummated their relationship to the maximum by signing a ten-year pact typing the two countries together economically, politically and militarily. It was appropriately called the "Pack of Steel." The world wasnow put on notice that war with one meant war with both.

Secretly, however, the Pact was not as ominous as it appeared. In a secret document generated by Field Marshal Count Ugo Cavallero, on May 30, the Italians spelled out their position with regard to the Pact. Fundamentally, the Cavallero Memorandum stated that Italy would not be ready for war until 1942 because the Italians needed time to change their economy to a war footing and the Italian armed forces needed time to replace its antiquated artillery and build a large black army in Italian East Africa. Politically, Italy needed time to foster pro-Italian movements in several British and French colonies, the Arab world and, surprisingly, Cavallero noted, in countries such as Ireland, India and the Brittany region in France.

It was also mentioned in the Memorandum that it was Rome's understanding that Italy's sphere of interest included all of the Balkans south of the Danube. This implied that Yugoslavia, Greece, European Turkey, Bulgaria and most of Romania, with its valuable oil fields, were within Italy's realm. The Germans, of course, could not agree with the Memorandum in its entirely, but made no objection at this time. Time and circumstances would dictate who would control what, more so than a piece of paper. As for Italy's reluctance to join in any war before 1942, Hitler informed Mussolini that he accepted this.

It was understood in Rome and Berlin that both countries would have interests in each other's spheres of influence which were to be addressed as the needs arose. One such German interest was agreed to on July 13, 1939, when the Italians assigned a portion of the harbor at Trieste to the Germans on a ten-year lease. This gave the German Navy a window on the Mediterranean Sea and a port from which German warships and submarines could operate. It was also a port through which German troops could be transported to all of the lands bordering the Mediterranean.

Another German threat to the Mediterranean arose when Germany and Spain signed an agreement that allowed German supply ships to lay at anchor in Spanish ports in order to resupply German warships and submarines operating in the area.

LINZ, HITLER'S HOMETOWN

Hitler had a life-long love for his hometown, Linz, Austria. It was there that he spent the happiest years of his life and grew to manhood. One of the major goals was to enrich the city and make it one of the great art centers of the world. After attaining his final goals for Germany, Hitler planned to build a magnificent art museum in Linz that would include works by all the great masters and, not surprising, a small collection of his own paintings done during his youthful years in Vienna. To this end, Hitler, on June 26, 1939, commissioned the highly respected Art Director of the Dresden Art Gallery, Dr. Hans Posse, to begin acquiring art for the future Linz museum.

Later, other art professionals would also be commissioned to acquire art objects for Linz and Hitler's friend and renowned architect, Albert Speer, would be commissioned to design a complete makeover of the city. Hitler told Speer that after the war he intended to retire to Linz and devote the remainder of his life to art, architecture, music and the special needs of Germany. He told Speer that he would retire completely from politics so as not embarrass his successor, and predicted that in his old age he would be nearly forgotten, left in peace and able to visit occasionally with his old cronies.

Furthermore, Linz would have access to a new Autobahn, then under construction, to be known as the "Party Road." This superhighway would connect the four main cities important to National Socialism; Berlin-Nuremberg-Munich-Linz.

As for the Autobahns, by August 1939, 3077 Km of the planned 14,000 Km had been completed. The target date for completion was 1950.

AUGUST 1939, THE LAST MONTH OF PEACE

By the beginning of August 1939 all Europe was on the edge of an abyss. Political negotiations between Germany and Poland to return the lands taken from Germany had reached an impasse. The Poles, backed by their allies, Britain and France, stood their ground. War with Germany loomed on the horizon. All three nations were rapidly arming, as were Switzerland, Belgium and The Netherlands. South of the Alps, the Italians had built up their military strength along their border with France. There were no indications coming from London and Paris that the western allies would back down from their promises to defend Poland. Likewise, Hitler would not back down, and an armed conflict seemed inevitable. Many world leader predicted the outbreak of a second world war—and soon.

From Germany, the signs were plentiful and ominous. German forces were gathering along the Polish border in Germany and in Slovakia, Germany's ally which bordered Poland on the south. For several months Germany's civilian population had been practicing blackouts and air raid defenses. Air raid shelters were being built all over

Germany and food, medical supplies, gas masks and other necessities were being stock-piled. German propaganda, along with denouncing Poland's and the western Allies' positions, spoke repeatedly of the need for lebensraum in the east and the return of Germany's overseas colonies.

By now, Hitler was meeting twice a day with his generals and admirals. Meetings were held at noon and midnight—a practice Hitler would continue throughout the war.

On August 8, another decree was issued by the German government requiring every able-bodied individual in Germany, male and female, from age five through seventy, to register for possible wartime assignments.

By mid-August, all of Europe was an armed camp with some ten million men under arms. Germany had the most with 2.5 million, the Soviet Union had 1.8 million, and France and Poland had about one million each.

On August 23, 1939, simultaneous announcements from Berlin and Moscow startled the world by announcing that Germany and the Soviet Union had signed a non-aggression pact. This was a military agreement, with secret clauses, whereby the Soviet Union promised it would not ally itself with the Western Powers in the event of war. This was a guarantee to Hitler that he would not have to fight a two-front war. In return, Berlin agreed to not interfere with efforts taken by the Soviet Union in Eastern Europe to regain territory lost to its various neighbors as a result of the Bolshevik Revolution and the Great War. In short, the devil in Berlin had made an agreement with the devil in Moscow and Europe took a giant leap closer to war. Hitler confirmed as much to British Ambassador Neville Henderson when the two met at the Berghof soon afterwards. After the meeting, Henderson reported to London, "He was, he said, 50 years old; he preferred war now to when he would be 55 or 60." Hitler, according to Henderson, went on to place all of the blame for the current crisis on Britain and France.

In the secret clauses of the German-Soviet pact were further agreements to divide other parts of the world. Germany, looking out for its ally, Italy, secured the Soviet's guarantee that Italy would have dominance in the Mediterranean, North Africa and East Africa. Germany would, in return have dominance over the Central Africa—a renewal of Imperial Germany's lost colonial dream of acquiring Mittel Afrika. The Soviet's, in return, were guaranteed that Germany would not interfere if Moscow attempted to expand its interests southward into Afghanistan, India and the Indian Ocean. On August 24, the day after the announcement of the German/Soviet pact, Poland, Britain and France began mobilizing their armed forces, and the French government advised that as many people as possible leave Paris. Hitler returned to Berlin from the Berghof on the 24th and went into all-day conferences with his military aides. President Roosevelt called upon King Victor Emmanuel of Italy to mediate an agreement between Germany and Poland, and the Pope went on Vatican radio pleading for peace.

The next day British Ambassador Henderson visited Hitler again and was told by the Fuehrer that after the Polish matter was settled he would begin to wind down his political activities. According to Henderson, Hitler said that he wanted to, "end his life as an artist and not a war monger."

On the 26th, food rationing was begun throughout Germany and the annual September Nazi Party rally at Nuremberg was canceled.

Over the next five days, the world prepared for war. Merchant ships and passenger liners at sea were called home by their respective governments and warships sailed out from their home ports to secret locations at sea. Diplomats scurried back and forth hoping for a last-minute reprieve, and influential people all over the globe called for peace. Throughout Europe, troops of various nations rushed to their respective borders which were in the process of being closed to civilian and commercial traffic. In England, the evacuation of civilians from London began.

Mussolini, fearful that Italy might be dragged into the war because of its alliance with Germany, ordered food rationing throughout Italy and nightly blackouts in Rome.

On the back pages of only a few newspapers around the world a brief article, drowned out by the reports of pending war, appeared stating that the Germans had announced that they had successfully test-flown an airplane with a new type of power source called a jet engine.

THE GREAT WAR RESUMES

During the early morning hours of September 1, 1939, the tragedy that no one wanted, began. German armed forces attacked Poland from three directions; East Prussia in the north, Germany proper in the west and from Slovakia in the south.

As the German forces drove into Poland defeating the inadequately prepared Polish Army at every turn, all eyes were on London and Paris. Would the British and French honor their promises to come to Poland's aid and declare war on Germany, or would they back down? After 72 hours of desperate last-minute political maneuvering, all of which failed, the British and French made good their respective pledges and declared war on Germany. Not only did Britain and France go to war, but so did their vast colonial empires.

The second Great War had begun, but it was not called that now. It was promptly named the Second World War and the Great War of 1914–18 was renamed the First World War.

CHAPTER 10

VICTORY IN EAST, VICTORY IN THE NORTH, VICTORY IN THE WEST

With Britain at war with Germany, the various members of the British Commonwealth, who controlled their own foreign policies, soon followed suit. On September 3, India, New Zealand and Australia declared war on Germany. On the 5th, the Union of South Africa declared war, followed by Canada on the 10th. Ireland, technically a Commonwealth nation, did not declare war because of the on-going issues over Northern Ireland. Truly, though, it was a world-wide war from the start.

The Germans were aware that some hard times lie ahead, so on September 4, a broad rationing program was put in place throughout Germany, and the production of many consumer goods was halted.

Hitler remained confident, though, that the war would be brief and that Germany would prevail. He said at this time, and repeated often in the months that followed, that the war would be over in two years—by the end of 1941.

It was at this time that Hitler restructured his daily activities around the two situation conference he held with his military leaders each day at noon and at midnight. For the remainder of the war his daily routine would be to rise in the morning about 10:00 am, eat a late breakfast, attend the noon situation conference, have tea at 5:00 pm, attend the second situation conference at midnight and retire about 3 or 4:00 a.m. Those who worked closely with the Fuehrer were obliged to follow suit. This routine, though, had one shortcoming. Since most enemy military operations were launched in the early morning hours, Hitler and his closest associates would be asleep at that time.

POLAND SMASHED BY THE "BLITZKRIEG"

The war in Poland lasted only 27 days. By September 9, German troops had reached and surrounded Warsaw. On the 16th, the Soviet Union invaded Poland from the east and stopped at a line, east of Warsaw, previously agreed to between Berlin and Moscow under their pact signed in late August. Much of the territory occupied by the Soviets had been part of Czarist Russia before World War I.

On the 27th, Warsaw fell to the Germans and the Polish Government fled into exile.

Political and military leaders around the world were astonished at the speed with which the Polish Army was defeated, but the reason was clear. The German Army had invented, developed and perfected a new kind of offensive attack called "Blitzkrieg" (Lightening War). This new military tactic was built around large formations of tanks, aircraft and motorized infantry. This is how it worked: After an intensive artillery and aerial bombardment on a rather short segment of the enemy line, massed tank formations smashed into that segment, forced their way through, then circle about to the right and left to get behind the defender's line. This trapped large numbers of enemy troops in pockets. Motorized infantry units followed closely behind the tanks and set up siege lines around the trapped troops. All this effort was facilitated by large formations of German aircraft which gave the tanks and ground troops close support. In Poland, it work perfectly. The trapped Polish troops were soon annihilated or forced to surrender and their front collapsed. German tanks and troops then drove deep into Poland's heartland.

Nothing like the Blitzkrieg tactic had ever been used before in modern warfare and it was extremely successful. Most ominous of all, none of the major armies of the world had the know-how, nor the means, nor the training, to stop it. Prior to the attack on Poland, military leaders outside Germany believed that a renewed European war would be a trench war much like that of World War I. The application of Blitzkrieg proved that they were gravely mistaken.

DIVIDING POLAND

Following the military collapse of Poland, the country was divided into three entities by the Germans and the Soviets. In the west, the German lands taken by Poland after World War I were reunited with Greater Germany. This included the city-state of Danzig.

Central and southern Poland, including the Warsaw area—the traditional land of the Poles—was structured by the Germans as a separate political entity known as the "General Government." The General Government included the major cities of Warsaw, Krakow, Lublin and Lodz. This, many believed, would be the future state of Poland, but the Germans made no commitment in that regard.

Eastern Poland, conquered by the Soviets, was incorporated into the Soviet Union. The northern portion going to the Soviet Republic of Belorussia and the southern portion to the Soviet Republic of the Ukraine.

In the areas annexed by Germany, ethnic Germans were given full German citizenship while the Poles were relegated to the status of German subjects. Hundreds of thousands of people, though, could not be sharply defined as being pure Germans or pure Poles. Since it was a Nazi goal to gather in all people of good blood, a program was established, under the SS, to examine these people. It centered around what became known as "The German People's List." Those who believed they were of good blood could sign the list and be examined. In some cases, individuals were forced to sign the list. The examinations consisted of a review of what was known about the individual's ancestry and his physical appearance. Judgements were quite liberal and many people were declared Aryans. This was done over the objection of some of the SS hard-liners, but Germany needed workers and soldiers so the liberal view prevailed.

Through a series of Fuehrer decrees, the Jews in the annexed areas were made subject to the anti-Jewish legislation that already existed in Germany, and were to be moved into the General Government as soon as practicable.

THE GENERAL GOVERNMENT

The General Government was a very unique entity within the German political system. It was to be the condensed homeland of the Poles, but not a protectorate (as was the case with the Czechs), nor was it an occupied territory, nor was it to be incorporated into the Greater German Reich—at least not all of it. Its geographical area matched very closely, but was smaller than, the Polish state created by the Imperial German government of 1916. At that time, the land assigned to the new Polish state had been won from Czarist Russia and the new state was to serve as both a homeland for the

Polish people and as a buffer state between Imperial Germany and the eastern slavs.

In 1939, the Nazi government of Germany followed the same general thinking, but without the commitment that the area, or any part of it, would become a reconstituted Polish state. Also, unlike the thinking of 1916, the Nazi government named Krakow as the capital of the General Government rather than Warsaw. Furthermore, the Nazis looked upon the area as a dumping ground for both the Poles and Jews who had been swept up in the conquest of Poland and Danzig. As a result, a massive relocation of Poles and Jews began to flow into the General Government. All of this was planned and carried out by Himmler's SS. The Poles relocated were fewer in number compared to the number of Jews because, in many cases, the labor and services of the Poles were needed where they resided due to the overall manpower shortage in Germany.

The Jews, though, were treated very badly and forced into the existing ghettos in the larger cities. This resulted in over-crowding and deplorable living conditions.

The creation of an additional and larger reservation for Jews was begun in the Lublin area and was completed by the end of the year, at which time, the Germans began filling it with Jews.

Extensive war-damage had been done in Poland which needed to be repaired along with general improvements to the infrastructure which, in many respects, was below German standards. The roads and railroads in the former Polish state needed considerable attention because they were inadequate for handling heavy military traffic which one day might be of great importance now that Germany shared a common border with the Soviet Union. The intense labor shortage in Germany made it nearly impossible to obtain German workers to perform these tasks, so the Poles and Jews had to be used.

As the Poles and Jews began to flow into the General Government, the Nazi propaganda machine went into action reminding the German people that Nazi promises were continuing to be fulfilled: that only people of good blood would reside in Greater Germany, and that the Jews would be resettled in the east.

On October 3, 1939, Hans Frank who had been appointed Governor-General of the General Government, drew up a memo that outlined the future of his new realm. Frank wrote, "Poland shall be treated as a colony; the Poles shall be the slaves of the Greater German World Empire...Poland will be reduced to its proper position as an agrarian country which will have to depend on Germany for importation of industrial products."

Since Germany needed the food already being produced in the General Government, strict rationing was imposed on those who resided therein so that a maximum amount of food could be sent to Germany. Germans living within the General Government were allotted 2600 calories per day of rationed items, Poles 670 and Jews 184. There were, however, several food items not rationed such as potatoes, barley and sauerkraut.

As for the priests in deeply Catholic Poland, Frank said in private, "The priest will be paid by us and will, in return, preach what we wish him to preach. If any priest acts differently, we shall make short work of him. The task of the priest is to keep the Poles quiet, stupid and dull-witted."

Furthermore, another, and very sinister, use was to be made of the General Government. Since the area was such an inhospitable place and off limits to almost all foreigners, it was an ideal place to build new concentration camps. One such camp, converted from an old Polish army base 30 miles west of Krakow, would become infamous—Auschwitz.

EUTHANASIA

On September 1, 1939, the day German troops invaded Poland, Hitler set another program into motion that he had promised the German people. That was the elimination of Germany's "useless eaters", people who were mentally or physically handicapped beyond recovery. With the advent of war, it was the Nazi's belief that emotions would hardened and that the program would, for the most part, be accepted. Furthermore, Nazi propaganda had long prepared the German people for such an eventuality ever since the publication of Mein Kampf.

The program, called "Akton T-4," was placed under the direction of the SS and extended to include the General Government. Very little of substance was reported about Akton T-4 and what was reported was glossed over in general and sanitized terms.

Over the next few months, patients from sanitoriums and various medical facilities began to disappear. They were taken to designated killing centers, disposed of by medical procedures and their bodies cremated. Their relatives were informed of their deaths but, in all cases, the cause of death was falsified and disguised in medical terms. When a medical facility was cleared of patients, it was closed down or used for some other purpose and its medical personnel reassigned. These things, of course, were the benefits realized by the program. A few medical facilities were left open to hold border-line patients, receive new patients, and give the impression that the Nazi government was still a caring entity. The euthanasia program was on-going and as more useless eaters appeared, they too were euthanized.

The truth about the program, of course, spread to the world's media and a torrent of criticism came down upon the Nazi government from many sources, especially from religious organizations. The end result was that the image of Nazi Germany was severely damaged even among Germany's friends and allies.

The total number of people euthanized is much in dispute. Estimates range from 50,000 to 250,000. Some hard facts are known, however, such as the estimates put together by diligent bureaucrats on the food that would be saved by the program. One of their calculations predicted that by 1951,

5,902,920 kilos of marmalade would be saved.

In Germany an unexpected development evolved among Germany's older citizens. Many of them feared that they might be the next to be euthanized and therefore refused to go to state-controlled hospitals. People living near the death centers soon learned the awful truth and their children made up riddles and sayings to describe what was going on. One such example was that the busses which arrived full of people and departed empty were called "death boxes."

The first stages of the euthanasia program ran its course, but Hitler had learned a lesson. Any future mass extermination programs had to be carried out in utmost secrecy. In this regard, it was eventually decided that only verbal orders on such matters were to be used in the future. From this point on, virtually no written records were generated by the Nazi leadership referring to mass exterminations. It appears that Hitler would tell his chief executioner, Himmler, verbally what he wanted and Himmler would carry it out with an absolute minimum of written documentation.

HAVE MORE BABIES, BUT NO MORE DANCING

The advent of war gave the Nazis another reason to promote their program of increasing the German population. A wave of public statements, pamphlets and other forms of propaganda came down upon the women of Germany urging them to have more babies. The theme was that since men would now be sacrificed on the field of battle, it was the German woman's duty to replace those lost lives with new ones. Unmarried women were encouraged to have children also, especially by soldiers who had gone off to war. This, according to the Nazi propagandists, would be very satisfying to the men by knowing that they had left behind something of themselves.

The day hostilities began, the German government ordered a ban on all forms of dancing with the apparent purpose of curtailing social activities and keeping the German families at home where they could produce more babies. This ban soon proved to be very unpopular and, by month's end, was lifted, but with the governmental warning that dancing to the decadent "swing" music, so popular in the West, would be prohibited.

With the dancing issue resolved, the Nazi government now addressed prostitution. On September 9, a decree was issued nationalizing brothels for the benefit of the men in the armed services. Pimps and uncooperative ladies were sent to the concentration camps. There were brothels for both officers and enlisted men. The Nazi reasoning for nationalizing the brothels was simple. Servicemen, when on leave, seek out prostitutes and a certain percentage of them get venereal diseases thereby becoming "casualties" of war. By controlling the brothels, venereal diseases could be controlled. All this was very much in keeping with Hitler's personal paranoia concerning syphilis.

"I HAVE AGAIN PUT ON MY COAT..."

Soon after hostilities began, Hitler addressed the Reichstag and claimed that he was now nothing but a soldier. He said, "I want to be no more than the first soldier of the German Reich...I have again put on my coat (military uniform), which was sacred to me as a volunteer in the World War. I will take off this coat only after victory, or I will not live to see the end." Since even a soldier like Hitler puts his life at risk, the Fuehrer took this opportunity to remind the Reichstag as to who would be his successors. This was a decision that had been made several years earlier. Hitler said, "If anything should happen to me, my successor will be Hermann Goering, and if anything shall happen to him, his successor shall be Rudolf Hess...Shall anything happen to Rudolf Hess, I have nominated a senate who will choose the most worthy, namely the bravest, as successor." The concept of a senate choosing the next head of state would carry through to the postwar years.

From this point on, Hitler was always in uniform when seen in public or in the media.

IN THE WEST, A "PHONEY WAR"

Within a few days after hostilities began in Poland, Hitler began carrying out the next phases of his war plan. This consisted of making peace overtures toward France and Britain. On September 3, he issued the secret Directive #2 which put the initiation of hostilities in the west squarely in the hands of the French and British. The Directive read in part, "The opening of (ground) hostilities in the west will be left to the enemy... Offensive (ground) action against France will only be permitted if the enemy has first opened hostilities... Offensive action (by the Luftwaffe) against France will only be undertaken after French attacks on German territory."

It was Hitler's hope that the Western Powers, after a brief period on low-level conflict, would opt for peace, and he was encouraged. The lack of hostile actions by the Western Allies during the first weeks of the war seemed to indicate that the Western Powers would comply with this thinking. By mid-September, two new names for the war appeared, "The Phoney War" and "The Sitzkrieg."

The only significant military action happened at sea. Predictably, the Western Powers, with their powerful navies, immediately declared and implemented a naval blockade of Germany as they had done in World War I. To counter this, Hitler announced a German naval blockade of Britain. That blockade was to be conducted primarily by German submarines which, the Germans hoped, would sink enough of Britain's commercial shipping in order to starve the British into submission.

The German submarines had been dispatched to British waters before the onset of hostilities and began at once attacking Allied commercial shipping in British waters. The new German battleship Graf Spee had also been dispatched and began raiding Allied shipping lanes in both the North and South

Atlantic. The Graf Spee, however, met a disastrous end when it was cornered by Allied ships in South American waters and eventually scuttled off the port of Montevideo, Uruguay.

GERMANY'S PEACE OFFER

Hitler had made comments throughout the political crisis with Poland that he wanted nothing from the Western Powers. At the time, Hitler's words meant little in the West because his credibility was completely shattered. Now, with the Polish issue being resolved in Germany's favor, Hitler's peace initiative got under way. Goering, was one of the first Nazi leaders to speak out. As early as September 9, he made a speech calling for peace and Hitler and others followed suit. But these efforts failed completely. Only negative responses were forthcoming from both Paris and London.

THE SOVIETS SETTLE OLD SCORES IN THE EAST.

In 1918, when the Bolshevik leaders of Russia made peace with Imperial Germany, they paid a high price in lost territory. At the time, a full-scale civil war was evolving and the Bolsheviks needed all of their resources to defend what they had already attained. The Germans, by dealing with the Bolsheviks, acknowledged that they, the Bolsheviks, controlled Russia, but Russia only. This allowed the Ukraine, Belorussia and other parts of the former Czarist empire, to declare their respective independence with Germany's acquiescence.

When Germany was defeated in November 1918 by the Western Allies, the victors did not restore the lost territories to the Bolsheviks. Instead, they gave the land away to others. Poland, Romania and Finland were all given slices of former Russian territory, and three new independent states were created out of Russian land along the Baltic coasts; Estonia, Latvia and Lithuania.

By 1922, the Bolsheviks had won the civil war, reconquered the Ukraine, Belorussia and virtually all of the remaining parts of the Czar's former empire. The Bolsheviks then granted all of these states their "independence" and they "voluntarily" united into a federation known as Union of Soviet Socialist Republics (USSR) with Moscow as its capital. It then became Moscow's goal to recover all of the territories that had been lost in the aftermath of World War I, as well as to entice other nations to accept communism, if they chose, and move into Moscow's sphere of influence.

Now, thanks to the secret clauses in the German-Soviet pact of August 1939, the Soviets had their chance to expand westward into northern and central Europe.

The Soviets wasted no time in pursuing their goal. The conquest of the eastern part of Poland had been the first target. In the months that followed, the Soviets were able to recover territory from Romania and absorb the three Baltic states into the Soviet Union. Finland, however, was a different matter. The Finns fought for the land that they felt was rightfully theirs and this sparked a brief war between Finland and the Soviet Union which lasted from November 1939 to March 1940. It was known as "The Winter War." The powerful Soviet Red Army eventually won back the disputed territory, but only after a very difficult struggle against the greatly outnumbered Finns. The poor showing exhibited by the Red Army astounded many foreign observers and made the Red Army appear to be a weak giant. This observation was of great interest to Hitler and his generals, and would influence their thinking with regard to the Soviet Union in the months to come.

VOLKSDEUTSCH RESETTLED IN GENERAL GOVERNMENT

As part of the German-Soviet agreement of August 1939, Volksdeutsch living in the areas to be reclaimed by the Soviets were allowed to leave and return to Germany. Many of them did so which, in turn, gave Goebbels' propagandist another victory. Absorbing the sudden influx of these people, however, caused a problem as to what to do with them. It was finally decided that since most of the Volksdeutsch coming in from the East were peasant farmers and accustomed to living among Slavs that they would be resettled in the southern part of the General Government.

To ease the burden of resettling, the German government gave the Volksdeutsch land and German citizenship along with housing comparable to what they had had before. They were also guaranteed full compensation for the land and property they left behind. This plan was compatible with the German's aim to make the General Government into an agrarian state. Those Volksdeutsch with industrial skills or trades were given well-paying jobs in Germany and resettled wherever they were needed. The elderly and infirm were resettled in Germany wherever accommodations could be found for them.

All this required the Germans to carry out a major land-reform program in the General Government. Land was taken from the Jews and Poles and new farms were created from 50 to 300 acres. To qualify for a new homestead, the Volksdeutsch applicants had to pass a battery of tests to prove that they were physically, politically and racially acceptable. Those deemed to be the most politically reliable were given the larger parcels of land, which meant that they would prosper better than their neighbor. It was the hope of the Nazis that, with time, this would produce a group of country squires who would become the leaders of the local peasantry and loyal to the Nazi Party.

On the other side of the coin, those Volksdeutsch who were judged to be less politically reliable or less racially pure were given smaller parcels of land. Those who failed the battery of tests altogether were held in detention until their individual cases could be reviewed.

Upon arriving at their new homesite, the Volksdeutsch were given seed, fertilizer, machinery, livestock, and other necessities, much of which had been confiscated from the Jews and Poles. The newcomers were also given advice on what to grow and promised a guaranteed market for their produce. Many of the dispossessed Poles were retained in the area to work as farm hands.

One major problem soon arose, however. Since most of the Volksdeutsch had lived for generations among the Slavs many of them had taken on the ways of the Slavs. This meant that they were, in the opinion of the Nazi overseers, more lackadaisical in their work habits and, in many cases, satisfied with a lesser standard of living than their peasant counterparts in Germany. The German planners soon concluded that this was a problem that would have to be addressed in the future.

There was yet another problem that was just beginning to materialize. Polish guerilla bands were forming in the mountains and forests in the southern-most part of the General Government. When Poland collapsed, a sizeable number of former Polish soldiers, along with many civilians and Jews, fled to this area to continue the fight. In time, they would become stronger and, from time-to-time, would carry out raids on the Volksdeutsch.

COAL, ITALY AND SWITZERLAND

In the last months of 1939 another problem developed for the Germans regarding coal. Italy had, for years, imported large amounts of coal from Germany which was usually shipped by sea. Now, the Allied naval blockade made that impossible so the coal had to be shipped to Italy by rail through Switzerland. This caused a tense political situation with Switzerland as well as tying up a considerable amount of Germany's rolling stock. This arrangement, though, put the Swiss in an advantageous political and military position because they could cut off Italy's coal supply virtually any time they wanted. It was well known that the Swiss military had mined the important railroad bridges and tunnels in question as a part of their overall national defense program.

Therefore, it was now important to both Germany and Italy that relations with the Swiss remain good. This, in turn, gave the Swiss an added measure of security.

WAFFEN SS FORMED

During November 1939, Hitler authorized the SS to form large division-sized military units patterned after those of the German Army. These units would be known collectively as the "Waffen SS" (armed SS) and become, in reality, a Nazi Party army. The creation of the Waffen SS now blurred the strict division of responsibilities between the SS and the German Army that had been agreed to and maintained ever since the neutering of the SA in 1934. To prevent a possible conflict of interests between the Waffen SS and the Army, a new understanding was reached between Hitler and his Army commanders under which the Waffen SS units would, when operating in the field against a foreign enemy, serve under Army command. A precedent for this had been set in 1938 and 1939 when smaller armed SS units had participated in the occupation of Austria and Czechoslovakia and had, on those occasions, served under Army command.

It would also be the mission of the Waffen SS to combat guerilla and terrorist activities within occupied areas during and after the war. This would leave the Army free to concentrate on national defense.

The Waffen SS was to be an elite military force, made up mostly of Party members and others loyal to the Party, and its members were to be well-trained and well-equipped.

With time, the Waffen SS grew considerably, manned in a large part by young Volksdeutsch who volunteered their services. They came from all over Europe where Germany's military conscription laws did not apply.

This arrangement satisfied all concerned.

MISSED

On November 8, 1939, Hitler gave his annual speech in Munich commemorating the unsuccessful Nazi Putsch of 1923. The event was held in the beer hall where the

Nazis had gathered at the time. Minutes after Hitler left the hall, a bomb went off near where he had been speaking and killed several people. It was obviously an assassination attempt against Hitler. The individual accused of the deed, a German citizen named Georg Elser, was apprehended as he tried to cross into Switzerland. The fact that Elser felt he could find sanctuary in Switzerland sent the Nazi media into a renewed flurry of condemnation of the Swiss government. The main theme, this time, was that Switzerland was a haven for criminals. The Swiss government was genuinely fearful that the Germans might retaliate in some manner, but nothing happened. Elser was eventually convicted and executed in Germany.

About this time, knowing that his person was in more danger than before, Hitler began cutting back considerably on his public appearances and his movements were kept secret from the public. This situation continued throughout the war.

AN EVENTFUL FORTNIGHT

By late October 1939, it was clear that the Phoney War was ending and the real war was heating up. Artillery duels had erupted on the western front along with small-scale incursions by ground forces. The Germans had, by now, completed a comprehensive plan to attack France, called "Case Yellow," which called for the initial attacks to begin against France in mid-November. But Hitler had doubts about the plan and had not yet given up hope on making peace with the West. On November 13, he postponed Case Yellow.

On the 18th, the air war escalated when the British carried out one of the first large air raids of the war by bombing Wilhelmshaven.

That same day, the Nazi government decreed a ten-hour work day as standard because of the manpower shortage. Also another decree followed ordering the boys and girls of the Hitler Youth to spend the coming summer doing "Land Service," which primarily meant helping out on farms. Hitler Youth members were also assigned the task of delivering "call up notices" to those being drafted.

On the 23rd, Hitler ordered his military planners to consider military options other than an immediate attack on France. Areas to be considered were Scandinavia, the Balkans and the Middle East.

Clearly, Hitler was ready to act to end the Phoney War.

HITLER STRIKES NORTH

By spring, 1940, the war at sea had become intense between the Allied navies and Germany's submarines. In the air, the Germans had attacked British shipping and the British had bombed targets in Germany. But, on the ground, there were virtually no major activities.

Then, on April 9, 1940, Germany stunned the world by suddenly attacking Denmark and Norway without warning. Berlin reported that the actions were taken in order to "forestall" an invasion of those countries by the Allies. Denmark was overrun in a few hours—before its government could even declare war. But the Norwegians declared war and with the aid of both the British and French, fought on for several weeks.

The Danish government remained in place in Copenhagen with a promise from Berlin that it, and the Danish monarchy, could continue to function, and that Danish independence would be restored at the end of the war. It was Hitler's dearest hope that the intelligent Aryan people of Denmark would, by then, see the great benefits of National Socialism, embrace it and become a close ally of Germany.

The Norwegian government of King Haakon, however, fled to England to set up a government-in-exile. The Germans then installed a puppet Norwegian government under Vidkun Quisling, the leader of Norway's minuscule Nazi party. Quisling had virtually no public support and his name soon became synonymous with "traitor" since he was the first so-called head of state to serve as a Nazi stooge.

In Norway, the Germans were unable to use their Blitzkrieg tactic because the German Navy was incapable of getting large numbers of tanks across the North Sea in a short time. This was one reason why the war dragged out for weeks. Also, the German Navy lost a considerable number of ships during the operation, especially destroyers, due to encounters with the British Navy. What is more, it took almost the entire German submarine fleet to support the invasion.

The Germans eventually won a military victory in Norway, but that was only half the conquest. Hitler and the other German leaders could see that maintaining communications with occupied Norway across the North Sea would be difficult and risky. This problem would become a major factor in late 1940 when the Germans gave serious consideration to crossing the English Channel to invade Britain.

Because of the problem of maintaining communications with Norway, the Germans put strong pressure on Sweden to allow the passage of German troops and supplies across Swedish territory to Norway. The route of passage would be from Copenhagen, Denmark, up the west coast of Sweden into Norway, a distance of some 300 miles. The Swedes gave in partially and agreed to allow only German Red Cross units and other humanitarian groups to pass through Swedish territory. The Germans agreed, but soon began to violate the understanding by sending combat troops and military supplies disguised under the Red Cross banner.

With their foot in the door, the Germans kept up the pressure on Stockholm to allow more German forces to cross Sweden. In July 1940, after the defeat of France, the Swedes acquiesced with the promise from Berlin that German troops would not be armed while on Swedish soil. From then on, virtually all military traffic between Germany and Norway used this route and the Germans honored the agreement by keeping their troops unarmed.

At this time, also, Germany and Sweden signed a new trade agreement making more items from Sweden available to the Germans.

As for Norway, Hitler hoped to win the hearts and minds of the Norwegian people. In an effort to do this, he ordered, on May 9, that all captured Norwegian soldiers be released, and he personally praised them for their courage.

VICTORY IN THE WEST

With his northern flank secured, Hitler ordered the long-planned invasion of France. The German Army had grown substantially since the invasion of Poland. At that time it had 78 divisions with 15 more in reserve. Now it had 157 divisions with 26 in reserve. In numbers, though, the Germany Army was a fairly even match with the Allies. The British, French and Belgians had a total of 170 divisions and more tanks than the Germans, but the German tanks were superior. And the Germans had the Blitzkrieg—the unstoppable Blitzkrieg.

The invasion of France began on May 10, 1940, through Holland and Belgium in order to outflank the Maginot Line. As had happened in Poland, the Western Allies had no way to stop the Blitzkrieg. The Germans broke through the Allied lines in the Ardennes area, also known as the Burgundian Gap, where the French, Belgian, Luxembourg and German borders meet. Within a matter of hours, all Allied resistance in that area collapsed and the German forces, led by a powerful tank force, headed due west virtually unopposed. It was their intention to reach the English Channel and split the Allied forces in the north from those in France to the south.

As the German Blitzkrieg thundered on, Hitler wasted no time in reclaiming lost German lands. On May 18, he issued a decree annexing three small areas of Belgium; Malmedy, Eupen and Moresnet, that had been taken from Germany after World War I and awarded to Belgium. Once again, Hitler was bringing more Volksdeutsch back to the Reich. On the 20th, the German tanks reach the Channel. To the north, the British undertook a massive evacuation at the small port of Dunkirk, France in which they were able to save most of their troops, but lost most of their equipment. The British Army retreated to Britain and was now an army without guns.

The Allied war effort in the north collapsed and the Germans overran all of Holland, Belgium and northern France. Now, the French Army stood alone. This was an army that was equipped for, and had practiced for, trench warfare—and it was doomed.

ADDING MORE TERRITORY AND A BUFFER STATE TO THE GREATER REICH

The very day his tanks reached the coast, Hitler began speaking, once again, of making peace with the West. It was almost a certainty now that France would be militarily defeated and seek peace, and that Britain would likely follow suit. But the British would have to pay a price. Hitler said to his colleagues, this day that the British, "…can have their peace as soon as they return our colonies to us."

And, for good measure, Hitler gave the order to occupy the undefended British-owned Channel Islands of Guernsey and Jersey. It was Hitler's plan that these islands were to be permanently occupied by Germany and would become the first English-speaking territory within the German Reich.

On May 22, 1940, Hitler spoke again to his colleagues on the future of the now-conquered Benelux countries. It was a certainty that Luxembourg would be annexed to the Reich, but Belgium and Holland would be treated differently. They would be restructured to become German border dependencies with Nazi-style governments such as was now the case in Norway. There was also considerable discussion within the German leadership that a new buffer state be created between Germany and France. The new state would be formed out of French territory and would extend from Switzerland to the English Channel. It would be French-speaking, but with a Nazi-style government.

The idea of a buffer state was not new. In centuries past, the state of Burgundy had filled that role. In more modern times, Bismarck, in 1871, considered creating such a state after the Germans had won the Franco-Prussian War. Then, after the German defeat of 1918, the French had pressured their fellow Allies to turn the German Rhineland into a buffer state. France's Allies vehemently opposed the idea and a compromise was reached in which the Rhineland would remain German but be permanently demilitarized.

JEWS TO AFRICA AND GERMANY'S COLONIAL CLAIMS

On May 25, Himmler and Hitler met to discuss the fate of the Jews which had now come under German control with the conquest of the Benelux countries. Since the General Government was already overcrowded with Jews, Himmler suggested that a place for them be found in Africa. Hitler's response is unknown, but Himmler knew well that Hitler had spoken in the past of sending the Jews to the French-owned island colony of Madagascar off the east coast of Africa. And now, with France on the verge of defeat, such an arrangement might be possible. Therefore, a decision on what to do with the Benelux Jews was temporarily postponed.

Also regarding Africa, the Germans felt that, since they had defeated Belgium, they were entitled to claim Belgium's overseas colonies. Belgium had three colonies in Africa, the huge mineral-rich Belgian Congo in central Africa and, on the eastern border of the Belgian Congo, two small, former German colonies, of Rwanda and Urundi. The latter two colonies had been mandated to Belgium by the League of Nations after World War I. The Nazis had, all along, disputed Belgium's control over Rwanda and Urundi and included them as parts of the former German colonial empire that Hitler wanted returned. Furthermore, all three colonial entities were parts of the huge Mittel Afrika that Germany tried, unsuccessfully, to acquire for itself in the 1880s.

Germany's claims against Belgium were, of course, meaningless to the Allies since a Belgian Government-in-Exile existed in Britain and was firmly in control of the Belgian colonies. Furthermore, the Allies needed the Congo's minerals for their military needs. And, unbeknownst to almost everyone at the time, except for a handful of nuclear scientists, the Belgian Congo was the world's primary source for a strange and, as yet, little-used metal called uranium.

In conquering The Netherlands, the Germans had the opportunity to lay claim to the huge and sprawling Dutch East Indies in southeast Asia, but declined. This was an area of primary importance to Germany's ally, Japan, and the Germans did not want to interfere with Japanese aspirations there. Neither did Germany lay claim to the Dutch colonies in the Western Hemisphere; Dutch Guiana in South America, the islands of Aruba, Curacao and several other small islands in the Caribbean area. These colonies were important to the United States and, at this point in the war, Hitler did not want to further aggravate the Americans.

JEWS TO ALASKA

In America, the U.S. Congress was debating a measure called the "King-Havenner Bill," It had been introduced on June 17, at the time the French Army was collapsing in Europe, and proposed that the U.S. territory of Alaska be opened for the settlement of Europe's Jews. Roosevelt supported the bill, but the American public did not. Opposition was so strong that the proposal was quickly abandoned. After all, it was an election year.

A BRITISH VICTORY

While Hitler was discussing the future of the Benelux countries, the British, on May 22, scored a silent but significant victory totally unbeknownst to the Germans. The victory was in the field of intelligence. British code-breakers at a government-owned country estate outside London known as Bletchley Park, successfully broke one of

Germans' most-used secret codes, the Luftwaffe's "Red" code. Aided by a huge, primitive, but very effective computer, the British could now read most of the Luftwaffe's secret wireless messages. The crew at Bletchley Park would go on to break additional German codes and create one of the most powerful weapons in the Allied arsenal. The undertaking was given the name "Ultra."

FRANCE DEFEATED

Following the defeat of the Allied forces in the Netherlands, Belgium and northern France, the German army remained very strong with 136 divisions still battle-ready. The badly mauled French Army had only 37 and a lull developed as both sides reorganized their forces. On June 5, the Germans renewed their attack and began to drive deep into France.

Mussolini, realizing that France was doomed and thinking, as did Hitler, that the war would be short, wanted to get in on the spoils. Italy had long-standing territorial claims in southern France and in France's colonial empire. Therefore, on June 10, 1940, Italy declared war on France and Britain. The Italians then invaded southeastern France, but their attack was weak and they managed to advance only a few miles into southeastern France and capture several small villages.

By Italy's entering the war, a tense situation developed in North and East Africa where British, French and Italian colonies shared common borders.

Meanwhile, the German advance into the heart of France progressed rapidly. On June 14, Paris fell and the French government fled into southern France. That evening, Hitler ordered a three-day holiday in Germany to celebrate the fall of the French capital.

The same day, Spain took advantage of the disaster that was befalling the Western Allies and occupied the international city of Tangier on the southern shore of the Strait of Gibraltar. Tangier, which adjoined the Spanish protectorate of Spanish Morocco, had long been claimed by the Spaniards who, in the past, had been forced into sharing power there with others, primarily the French and the British. Two days later, the Spanish dictator, Franco, informed Hitler that Spain was ready to attack and recover the British-controlled bastion of Gibraltar and asked for German help. Hitler promptly replied that that help would be made available.

At midnight, June 16-17, the French government of Paul Reynaud resigned and 84-year-old Marshal Henri Petain, a hero of World War I, became France's premier. Hours later, Petain sent word to the Germans and Italians that he was ready to end hostilities. Hitler promptly agreed to an armistice and Mussolini followed suit. Hours later, an announcement came from London stating that Britain would fight on.

June 18 was a day of decisive events. Hitler and Mussolini met in Munich to discuss the political settlement they would impose on France. From London came a radio announcement from a little-known French general named Charles de Gaulle that he would carry on the fight for France and asked Frenchmen all over the world to join him.

Also in London that day, the newly-appointed British Prime Minister, Winston Churchill, addressed Parliament and uttered the now famous words, "...if the British Empire and its Commonwealth last for a thousand years, men will say, `This was their finest hour.'"

Events progressed rapidly over the next few days. The German-French armistice was signed on June 22, the French government moved into the famous spa town of Vichy where large, and nearly vacant, hotels were available to house the government and the hundreds of people associated with it. From this moment on, the government of Marshal Petain was known as the "Vichy Government."

On June 24 the French-Italian armistice was signed in an old villa outside Rome.

Under the armistices, all of northern France, including Paris, and the Atlantic coast of France were occupied by the Germans. Several small enclaves in the southeast were occupied by the Italians. The Vichy government retained control over about one-third of French territory in the south and southeast and the vast French colonial empire. The Vichy government was allowed considerable freedom of action, but the French armed forces were greatly reduced, and any major military actions by the French had to be approved by both the German and Italian Armistice Commissions. Hitler and Mussolini had agreed that it would be best that a relatively strong French government should remain in France to prevent a government-in-exile from emerging, and that that government should be strong enough to defend itself and its empire. The acquisition of the French Atlantic coast was important in two ways. It provided a number of sea ports from which Axis warships, primarily submarines, could come and go into the Atlantic. Secondly, the Germans now had land contact with friendly Spain.

FRANCE BECOMES A DICTATORSHIP

At Vichy, the mood of the Petain government was one of deep despair. Much of the blame for France's defeat was now placed on France's democratic form of government which had never been strong due to the ever-present squabbling between France's numerous political parties. The coalition governments formed in Paris, many of them very short-lived, had fostered an atmosphere of both political and military weakness. It was now the consensus among the French leaders that France needed a strong government and that the old political system had to be scrapped. Therefore, the French Assembly voted itself and French democracy out of existence and assigned all powers of the state to Marshal Petain. With a stroke of the pen, Petain became the absolute dictator of France acquiring the new title, "Head of State." The post of premier remained but was renamed "Chef du Gouvernment," and whoever held that post was answerable, in all respects, to the Head of State. Considering the pressures Petain was under, it was very likely that this new government of France would develop along the lines of Fascism.

✓

CHAPTER 11

DIVIDING THE SPOILS IN THE WEST AND PLANNING FOR THE FUTURE

Before the last shot was fired in France, the Germans and Italians began carving up western Europe and the huge French and British colonial holdings in Africa. Such plans had long been in the making; now, the time had come to act.

THE ITALIANS GET GREEDY

On June 7, 1940, three days before Italy entered the war, Italy's Foreign Minister, Count Galeazzo Ciano, met with Hitler to spell out Italy's latest territorial demands in return for Italy's participation in the war. Most of the demands were not new. The Italian government had already made demands on parts of southern France, the French island of Corsica, the British-controlled island of Malta, French-controlled Tunisia, parts of eastern Algeria, French and British Somaliland in East Africa, French Morocco, the Greek island of Corfu at the southern end of the Adriatic Sea, and the mainland province of Northern Epirus which adjoined Italian-controlled Albania.

As for Egypt, it was the Italian plan, in most respects, to simply step into Britain's shoes and take control of the Suez Canal and the Anglo-Egyptian Sudan. Egypt's nominal independence would be maintained, but under strict Italian controls.

Ciano reminded Hitler of Italian interests in the Middle East and especially in the Persian Gulf oil fields.

To his grocery list, Ciano added demands for the British-controlled colony of Aden on the southern tip of the Arabian Peninsula along with the strategic British-controlled islands of Perim, at the southern entrance to the Red Sea, and to Socotra in the Gulf of Aden. This was in keeping with Mussolini's dream to extend Italian influence deep into the Indian Ocean. To pursue this dream, Mussolini had taken unto himself the post of Minister of Colonies.

Ciano said that Italy also wanted the northern third of French Equatorial Africa as far south as Lake Chad. This territory would be added to Italian-controlled Libya. The Foreign Minister made the further suggestion that the British-controlled island of Cyprus, in the eastern Mediterranean and which had a large Greek population, might be given to Greece to compensate her for territory lost to Italy.

Ciano was willing to give a little. He renounced Italy's claim to French Morocco because Spain had ambitions there as did Hitler who had said that he wanted to build German military bases on the Atlantic coast of Africa.

The Hitler-Ciano meeting was amiable, but its interpretation was blurred. Ciano reported to Mussolini that Hitler agreed with him on every count, while the German report of the meeting stated that Hitler was noncommittal.

On June 10, Italy entered the war; on the 14th the Germans entered Paris and on the 17th the French sued for peace. On the 18th and 19th Hitler and Mussolini met in Munich to further discuss the division of the spoils. Hitler acknowledged Italy's territorial demands but spoke of them only in generalities, making no definite commitments. It was obvious to Hitler, and it should have been obvious to Mussolini, that all of Italy's demands could not be won at the peace table and that some of them would have to be won by force of arms. In this regard, Hitler reminded Mussolini that they should go easy on the Petain government lest it flee to Algeria and rejoin the Allies. The French still had considerable military potential especially in their fleet which was the fourth largest in the world. If France re-entered the war, Hitler said, it would be very disadvantageous for both Germany and Italy because it would encourage the British to fight on and might even provide cause for the United States to enter the war.

Also on colonial matters, Hitler pressed the point with Mussolini, as he had done before, that if and when Britain surrenders, the major part of her empire should remain intact and under Britain's control. Hitler also stressed that if a negotiated peace could be made with Britain, some of Italy's expansionist dreams might have to be sacrificed. Mussolini did not fully agree with this point of view, but let the comments pass without dispute. Mussolini also held his tongue on another matter, his hopes to recover all Italian works of art currently in Paris museums. Mussolini was aware of Hitler's deep interest in art and apparently concluded that this was not the time, nor the place, to discuss such an issue.

Hitler agreed that Italy was right to renounce her claim to French Morocco and that that colony, along with parts of western Algeria, including the Oran area, and, of course, Gibraltar should go to Spain if she entered the war. It was further agreed that Germany and Italy would have separate armistice agreements with France but that they would be every similar in nature.

Now, with France defeated, the two dictators saw themselves as the masters of Europe and agreed that that role should be actively pursued and coordinated between Berlin and Rome.

The subject of sending Europe's Jews to Madagascar came up in discussions between Ciano and German Foreign Minister, von Ribbentrop. Von Ribbentrop stated that Germany still harbored the hope that the huge French-owned island might be acquired for use as a Jewish homeland. Ciano indicated that Italy had no objection to this.

THE LIRA BLOC

In Italy, Mussolini's territorial claims were widely publicized and a number of new themes were added. Once the Axis Powers had become victorious, the Italian propagandists declared, it would be Italy's plan to set up a powerful economic consortium called the "Lira Bloc" which would include all of the nations bordering on the Mediterranean. The Bloc would exclude France, but include Portugal, Bulgaria, and parts of the Middle East. Italy, of course, would be the dominant partner.

With Italian expansionism in the air, other reports flowed from Rome suggesting that Italy might gain control of the large French naval base at Toulon as well as much of the French fleet. In addition, Italian publications called for the return from France of Italian works of art—the subject Mussolini hesitated to raise in person with Hitler. Still more expansionist rhetoric suggested that Italy might gain control of the British colonies of Kenya and Uganda in East Africa, and Nigeria in West Africa, and that an Italian-controlled trans-African rail system be built connecting Nigeria with Italian North and East Africa.

The feeding frenzy went on. It was further suggested that Italy should take control of the famous British-owned Cape Town to Cairo Railroad and bring the British Commonwealth nation of the Union of South Africa into Italy's and Germany's economic and political spheres. What is more, it was suggested that Switzerland be dismantled and its Italian-speaking section be annexed by Italy. In their efforts to outdo one another, some Italian newspapers suggested that territorial concessions along the eastern shore of the Adriatic Sea might be gained from Yugoslavia and that Italy might gain control of all, or parts, of the Romanian oil fields. Also, the old claims of the House of Savoy (Italy's royal family) might be resurrected which laid claim to the thrones of Cyprus and Jerusalem. With regard to the latter, it was suggested that the Holy Land of Palestine be administered jointly by Italy and the Vatican.

To allay fears of Italian expansion among the Moslem populations of the Middle East, the Italian government announced on July 7 that the nations of the Middle East, which were independent, would retain their independence, and those that were not, would gain their independence after the final Axis victory. What was not said was that they would become vassal states closely allied with Italy. Rome's pronouncement on Arab independence was an appropriate statement for the Italian government to make at this time in light of the fact that Mussolini was the Protector of Islam. Furthermore, there were millions of Muslims in the French colonial empire whose support both Rome and Berlin hoped to gain.

And there was more. The dreamers in the Italian media suggested that Italy might aid Mahatma Gandhi and his Indian nationalist in their quest to free India from British rule. And, they suggested, Australia and New Zealand might also be "liberated."

Finally, with such world-wide interests, Italy would need a mighty navy and a gigantic merchant fleet that would propel the nation into becoming one of the world's great merchant states.

What a wonderful dream it was! Mussolini let it run on without interruption because such things were worth fighting for. It fit well with his overall plans to make Italy into a nation of warriors.

And run on it did. As late as October 9, 1940, an article appeared in an Italian newspaper, that often spoke for the government, suggesting that if the United States cooperated with the Axis New Order, she would receive Canada, Newfoundland, the Bahamas, Bermuda, Jamaica and possibly Australia and New Zealand.

SPAIN THREATENS

Like Mussolini, Generalissimo Franco in Madrid saw opportunities for Spain in the defeat of France. On June 14, as previously mentioned, Spain occupied the international city of Tangier. But Franco wanted more. As the battles in France played out, and with Britain badly weakened, the Spanish government spoke openly of entering the war in order to settle long-standing territorial disputes with both Britain and France. The main dispute with Britain was, of course, Gibraltar. With France, Spain's main concern centered in North Africa. Immediately south of Spain, and along the southern shore of the Strait of Gibraltar, was the protectorate of Spanish Morocco which encompassed about fifteen percent of Morocco. The remainder consisted of the protectorate of French Morocco. It was Madrid's hope to one day gain protectorate status over all of Morocco. Also, Spain claimed territories adjacent to, and east of Spanish Morocco in French-controlled Algeria. Furthermore, Spain hoped to grab parts of British and French colonies in sub-Saharan Africa and add them to the Spanish colonies in the area.

Finally, there were small areas in the Pyrenees Mountain border between France and Spain which were claimed by Spain but were currently under French control.

Spain was still recovering from the devastating Spanish Civil War (1936-39) and was militarily and economically weak. But Hitler had offered military aid, especially with regard to Gibraltar. Franco had concluded that his best move would be to enter the war just before Britain's surrender, call in German aid, take Gibraltar, gain a seat at the peace table and acquire his goals in Africa through negotiations.

Hitler was receptive to Franco's intentions and, more than once, confirmed his offer of military aid. But everything depended on the defeat of Britain. Therefore, in both Madrid and Berlin the national leaders undertook the policy of watchful waiting.

FRANCE AND THE BENELUX COUNTRIES

The future of the Netherlands, Belgium, Luxembourg and the greater part of France was exclusively a German matter and there was no need for the Germans to consult with Rome. Therefore, in the weeks following the armistice with France, the Germans proceeded to implement the plans they had made for these nations.

The Netherlands was totally occupied by German forces and its future was to be decided at a later date. In all probability, it would become a vassal state with a Nazi-style government closely allied with Germany. In the mean time, it was to be ruled by a German civil administration with no puppet Dutch government being formed. The Germans planned on having a permanent presence in The Netherlands at Rotterdam at the mouth of the Rhine River. This port city was slated to be the largest seaport in postwar Germanic Europe.

By converting the Netherlands into a close ally, it might be possible for Germany to gain concessions in the Dutch colonial possessions in the Western Hemisphere and, if Japan failed to act, in the Dutch East Indies.

Belgium was also totally occupied and its future was also to be determined later. Belgium remained under German military administration with the reason given that it was a military staging area for the coming invasion of England. Behind the scenes, however, the Germans planned to dismantle Belgium. Flanders, in the northern and western parts of the country, with its Germanic

Flemish population, was likely to become a separate political entity closely allied with Germany. Eastern Belgium, with its French-speaking Walloon population, was likely to become a part of the often-discussed buffer state that was to be created between Germany and France. The idea of dismantling Belgium was not new in Berlin. It had been a part of the German postwar planning during World War I.

Luxembourg was to be annexed to Greater Germany and its people Germanized.

As for France, it would be carved up in such a way that a united France could never again become a threat to Germany. It was a forgone conclusion that the provinces of Alsace and Lorraine, with their mix of German-speaking and French-speaking people would, once again, become Germany territory. This was to be the third time those much-disputed provinces changed hands between France and Germany since the 1870s.

A narrow strip of land along the northern border of France, ranging from 75 to 100 miles wide, was placed under German military control and administered from Belgium. It, like Belgium, was designated as a part of the staging area for the invasion of England. But, in all likelihood, it would be included in the proposed buffer state between Germany and France.

The occupied areas of northern and western France were to remain under the military control of the German armed forces. Civil control of both occupied and unoccupied France remained, theoretically, under the control of the French government at Vichy which had a standing invitation by the Germans to return to Paris. Petain, however, had no intention of leaving Vichy.

All of the principle ports along the Atlantic coast were taken over by the German Navy to serve, primarily, as operating bases for German submarines. France's industry within the occupied areas, which was extensive, was taken over by German interests to produce now for Germany.

The southern, unoccupied, part of France was to remain under both the civil and military control of Vichy. The overall future makeup of France was to be determined later.

In the southeast, the small enclaves occupied by Italy were to remain under Italian control.

Another political entity that might emerge in postwar France would be an autonomous or, perhaps, independent state of Brittany. This had often been discussed by the German leaders. Justification for this was in keeping with the Nazi's overall plans to weaken France, and to gather under German control all European people of good blood. In Nazi theory, the people of Brittany were not French, but rather Celts related to the English and, therefore, of good blood. This was substantiated by the fact that the culture of the people of Brittany was different from that of France and that the local language showed a relationship to Welsh.

Soon after the conquest of France, a German People's List was authorized in France for those who volunteered to be tested for acceptable Aryan blood. It was widely publicized in Brittany.

To win over the Bretons, the German occupation authorities there projected their image as liberators of the long-suppressed Breton nationality. Also, Bretons taken as POWs were sent to camps in Brittany where they were well-treated and allowed visits by family members. The Bretons, though, proved to be surprisingly loyal to France. This was due, in part, to the fact that it was no secret that the Germans wanted to make Brest, Brittany's major city, into a permanent military base. This idea was most unwelcome in Brittany.

For the moment, however, and because of its close proximity to England, Brittany would remain under German military control. In the meantime, Nazi political agents were sent into the area to work with local Nazi sympathizers in order to build up a pro-German political base for the future. Another purpose for taking these political actions in Brittany was to keep the Vichy government in line.

A LITTLE VACATION

On June 28, Hitler took a little vacation—to Paris. He had never been there. His tour lasted only four hours, from 5 am to 9 a.m. During that time the citizens of Paris were ordered to remain in their homes. Along with Hitler and his generals came Albert Speer and a contingent of Speer's architects and artists. They had instructions from Hitler to take special note of the city's magnificent architecture and art treasures so that such information might be of use in rebuilding Germany. During his tour, Hitler spend a considerable amount of time at the Arc de Triomphe and studied it intensely.

Later, after leaving Paris, Hitler told Speer, "It was the dream of my life to be permitted to see Paris."

While still in France, Hitler toured several sites in northern France where he had fought in World War I. He also inspected the Maginot Line and subsequently ordered that it be dismantled and its guns, furnishing, and other items of value be confiscated for use by the German armed forces. He further ordered that its extensive acreage be turned into farmland.

Hitler then returned to Berlin to make a triumphal entrance into the city amid the cheers and adulation of the German people.

Over at the Foreign Ministry, von Ribbentrop and his people began drafting a proposed peace treaty for Britain.

ITALY STRIKES IN EAST AFRICA

In their East African colonial empire, the Italians had a military force of some 350,000 men while the British forces in the surrounding colonies totalled only about 25,000. In both cases, about three-fourth of the troops were natives. The French forces in East Africa, mainly in the French colonies of Madagascar and French Somaliland (also known as Djibouti after its main city and seaport), remained loyal to Vichy and had been ordered to stand down to a defensive posture. This neutralized the French colonies, but the British colonies were still enemy territory.

War was slow in coming to East Africa. Several minor ground skirmishes and air raids had occurred between the Italians and the Allies, but no decisive action had been taken by either side.

Then, on July 4, 1940, the Italians struck by invading the Anglo-Egyptian Sudan. This was a large desert colony south of Egypt, north of Italian East Africa, transversed north and south by the Nile River and administered jointly by Britain and Egypt.

The Italian attacks centered on two border towns, Kassala and Gallabat on Sudan's southern border. Both towns were occupied, after which the Italian offensive stopped. Then, on July 13-15, the Italians invaded the British colony of Kenya, to the southeast, and occupied the border town of Moyale. And once again, the Italian advance stopped. This was the third time, so far in the war, that Italy had launched such short-lived "invasions." Needless to say, this pattern of Italian offensive action was not well-admired in Berlin.

In Italy, though, the banners waved, the soldiers paraded and the politicians spoke brazenly of Italy's military prowess.

"THE MEDITERRANEAN PLAN"

With Italy's entrance into the war, Admiral Raeder, Commander-in-Chief of the German Navy, saw great potentials for Germany. Italy had a formidable navy, at least on paper, which appeared to be a valuable asset to the Axis cause.

Based primarily on this belief, Raeder and his staff worked up a long-range comprehensive plan that would extend German influence, with Italian help, into the Mediterranean and the waters beyond. It was called, "The Mediterranean Plan." The Admiral personally presented the plan to Hitler in late June 1940.

As Raeder saw it, by utilizing the combined strength of the German and Italian Navies, and operating from bases in Italy,

Sicily and Libya, they could dominate the central area of the Mediterranean Sea thereby forcing the British to split their Mediterranean fleet into two weaker segments. One segment could be destroyed and then the other. This would open the way for the Axis Powers to pursue their goals with regard to Gibraltar and the Suez Canal. All this would be facilitated further if the Vichy government could be induced into joining the Axis Powers and contribute its powerful fleet to the Axis cause.

It then followed, in Raeder's thinking, that if the Mediterranean could be cleared of the British, there would be no more need to station large numbers of German and Italian warships there. Hence, the combined Axis navies could, with the adequate protection provided by land-based aircraft, strike out into the Atlantic as well as the Indian Ocean. In the Atlantic, they could cut Britain's lifelines to the south, dominate the west coasts of North Africa and the Iberian Peninsula and possibly gain control of the Canary Island group, or the Azores, or both. If this was achieved, the combined naval and air forces, operating from the Atlantic islands, could reach even further west to threaten the Western Hemisphere. Such bases would also act as way stations for German actions to be carried out further south to reclaim her African colonies in central and southern Africa as well as acquiring the Belgian Congo.

Raeder's plan went on to suggest that, in the eastern Mediterranean area, Axis troops might advance southward from Vichy-controlled Lebanon and Syria, take Palestine and the Suez Canal and force the British out of Egypt.

Once these things were accomplished, Axis forces could then advance on land and sea down the Red Sea, re-establish connections with Italian East Africa and move out into the western Indian Ocean. From bases in the area, Axis forces would be able to close off the entrance to the Persian Gulf and thereby stop the flow of Persian Gulf oil to the Allies.

To help accomplish these goals, the German Army and Navy were already working jointly on a giant, long-range seaplane with a range of 8,000 Km range and a bomb-carrying capacity of 4,000 Kg. Such a plane could reach parts of the Western Hemisphere from western Europe and western Africa, and reach eastern India and Burma from eastern Africa.

When, in late July 1940, it became clear that Britain would not seek peace but, in all likelihood have to be defeated militarily, Reader presented Hitler with an expanded Mediterranean Plan containing demands that might be made at a future peace conference after the military defeat of Britain.

The expanded plan proposed that once Germany had established itself in the Indian Ocean, the strategic British-owned island groups of Mauritius and the Seychelles along with the Vichy-controlled Comoros Islands in the Western Indian Ocean might be acquired. Madagascar, too, might be acquired from Vichy and the plan to send Europe's Jews there could then be implemented. Also, the British colonies of Kenya and Uganda in East Africa might be acquired along with the lost German colonies of Tanganyika, Rwanda and Urundi. From these conquests, the Belgian Congo would be accessible to the Germans from the east.

Furthermore, with a strong presence in the Western Indian Ocean, German sea and air routes to the Far East, and especially to Japan, could be opened.

If all of this could be accomplished, Raeder went on, all of the Balkans, the countries of the Middle East, and Turkey would be cut off from the outside world and would be forced to make accommodations with the Axis Powers. With Turkey receptive to Axis demands, Axis ships and planes could pass through the Dardanelles and penetrate the Black Sea area, thereby flanking the Soviet Union on the south. To mollify the Soviets, Moscow could be offered concessions in Iran, Afghanistan and India.

Raeder's Mediterranean Plan represented a monumental undertaking for Germany with a considerable degree of cooperation from Germany's allies and friends. Such cooperation was an unknown factor, however, and a very large part of Germany's overall military strength would have be committed to this venture. For these reasons, Hitler was not enthusiastic about the plan. He felt he had a better use for Germany's great military resources to acquire a huge colonial enterprise directly adjacent to Germany in the East.

Hitler, though, instructed Raeder to continue working on the plan because it might be useful later. Hitler did have some good news for Raeder. He confirmed his intentions, which Raeder had heard before, to build a string of strong naval bases in the west that would extend from Trondheim, in Norway, to the Belgian Congo.

HITLER'S PRELIMINARY THOUGHTS ON HOW TO DIVIDE THE EAST

Much had been said in Germany about acquiring Liebensraum in the East, but little details as to the makeup of that gigantic colonial empire had been given. It was generally believed that the division of the East would follow the lines established by Imperial Germany in 1918. On July 31, 1940, Hitler commented on how he saw the East being divided. In a conversation with his aides on the subject he said, "Ukraine, Belorussia, Baltic States to us, Finland extended to the White Sea." This statement coincided in some ways with the plans of Imperial Germany but differed in others. Under Imperial Germany, the Ukraine and Belorussia were given their independence, and the Baltic States were to be annexed by Germany and organized into a territory called "Kurland." Finland was not considered because, in 1918, it had not yet established its independence from Russia. Furthermore, Hitler did not mention what the future of the Russian heartland or the Caucasus areas would be. And, there was no indication as to how Germany's potential allies, such as Italy, Romania, Hungary and possibly Turkey, would share in the spoils. Clearly, much planning had to be done before Germany's eastern colonial empire could become a reality.

THE SCOREBOARD

By late summer 1940, Germany had conquered ten of its neighbors and snatched territory from two others. The German occupation policies for these newly-acquired lands were, however, anything but consistent. The only consistency was that certain areas were absorbed totally into the German Reich. The others were administered in a variety of different ways. The German scoreboard of conquests to date looked like this:

Austria: Absorbed totally into the German Reich.

Czechoslovakia: Divided into five parts: 1) The Sudetenland was annexed to the Reich and the Czech population expelled, 2) the Czech provinces of Bohemia and Moravia were formed into a German protectorate, 3) a disputed strip of land in southern Slovakia was annexed by Hungary, 4) a small enclave on the northern border of Slovakia was taken by Poland, and 5) the remainder of Slovakia was set up as an independent state. In a decision taken in the fall of 1940, the Czechs were to be Germanized after the war and the protectorate eventually absorbed into the Reich.

Lithuania: By threats of force, German troops had, in 1939, taken control of the city of Memel, a former German city awarded to Lithuania after World War I. The rest of Lithuania was not occupied and remained independent.

Poland: Divided into three parts: 1) The western areas, which had formerly belonged to Germany, were annexed by the Reich, 2) the eastern areas which had formerly belonged to Czarist Russia were annexed by the Soviet Union, and 3) the Polish heartland was turned into the Nazi-controlled political entity known as the General Government. It was administered by German civil authorities and policed by the SS. The northern part of the General Government became a dumping ground for Poles and Jews, while the southern part was to be opened for German settlers.

Danzig: A German city before World War I, was conquered at the same time as Poland was conquered and added to the Reich.

Denmark: Occupied by German military forces to protect against an Allied invasion. The Danish King and the elected government continued to function in Copenhagen and the fiction was put forth that Denmark was still an independent country.

Norway: Occupied by German military forces to protect against an Allied invasion, but administered by a Norwegian puppet government under the Norwegian Nazi, Vidkun Quisling, who answered to the German Reich Commissioner, Josef Terboven. A rival Norwegian Government-in-Exile existed in Britain. Norway was to be Nazified from the inside and eventually become a German vassal state.

The Netherlands: Placed under German civil administration with no Dutch civil administration created such as that in Norway. A Dutch Government-in-Exile existed in Britain.

Belgium: Divided into two entities: 1) Three small enclaves on the eastern border were annexed to the Reich, 2) the rest of the country remained under German military control. A Belgian Government-in-Exile existed in Britain, but the Belgian King remained in Belgium, theoretically, as a prisoner of war.

Luxembourg: Added to the Reich with its people slated for Germanization.

France: Divided into five entities: 1) The northeastern provinces of Alsace and Lorraine were annexed directly to the Reich, 2) a strip of French territory along the northern border was placed under German military rule and administrated by the German Army command in Belgium, 3) Northern and western France were occupied by German forces but, theoretically, still under the civil administration of the French government in Vichy, 4) the southern third of the country was not occupied by Axis forces and remained under the military and civil control of Vichy, 5) several small enclaves in the southeast were occupied by Italian forces.

Britain: The Germans occupied the Channel Islands: Guernsey, Jersey and a number of smaller islands, off the coast of Brittany. These were an integral part of Britain itself.

ITALY ADDS ONE TO THE SCOREBOARD

During August 1940, the Italians in East Africa added another Axis conquest to the scoreboard by conquering the neighboring colony of British Somaliland. The colony was taken in just sixteen days by a force that was seven times that of the British.

A ROAD TO THE MIDDLE EAST

On August 4, 1940 the German news media announced another triumph. The German-sponsored Berlin-to-Baghdad Railroad had been completed. This project, begun in the 1930s, had taken years to complete. But now, at this very opportune time, it provided the Germans with a direct land route to the Middle East. The railroad ran from the southern Balkans, through Turkey, and into the oil-rich nation of Iraq. When the time came for Germany to press its interests in the Middle East, the railroad would be a valuable asset.

THE SS ORDERED TO KEEP THE "NATIVES" IN CHECK

In early August, Hitler authorized Himmler and his SS organization to take control of internal security matters in all conquered territories. This had been the assignment of the SS inside Germany for several years and had worked well for the Nazis. In the conquered territories, however, there was one major difference. Himmler would have a para-military force, the Waffen SS, which was to be used against any organized resistance that might occur. This arrangement was intended to be permanent and continue after the war. It was also suggested that in peace time the name of the Waffen SS might be changed to the more peace-oriented name of The Armed State Police.

It must be remembered that this was the era of colonialism and that in acquiring colonies all of the colonial powers had faced some form or other of organized resistance from the "natives." There were still areas in the colonial world, even at this time, that had not been totally pacified by their colonial masters.

Himmler realized that this new role would, eventually, result in a greatly expanded SS—especially after the conquests of the East. And since the war would likely be over soon, as Hitler had predicted, planning for that time was begun at once. In order to fill the ranks of the expanded SS, Himmler saw that he had to turn to the Volksdeutsch and foreigners of good blood because Germany's conscription laws favored the German Army, Navy and Luftwaffe. In the near term, recruits could be found in the conquered lands and in nations friendly to Germany. Longer term, however, and after peace returned, recruiting for the SS would be world wide. Recruits would be sought even in the United States and the British Empire. A target date for the beginning of this world-wide recruitment program was estimated to be by 1953.

It was further planned by the SS leaders that men who had served their time in the SS would be offered generous incentives to become settlers in the East. There, it was anticipated that native resistance would be the most intense and probably last the longest. Therefore, it followed, that these SS veterans could be used as a reserve force for the SS units in the field at that time.

In keeping with his new assignment, Himmler sent a top-secret, six-page memorandum to Hitler on August 15 entitled, "Some Thoughts on the Treatment of Foreign Populations in the East." The memo was something of a summation of the Nazi philosophy that had developed over the last two decades regarding treatment of the untermenschen (people of lesser culture). The memo began with the suggestion that every possible small racial group in the East be recognized and set apart, one from the other. As examples, Himmler mentioned the Gorales, Lemkens and Kashhubs. The purpose of this would be to destroy all remnants of the Russian union by encouraging individual nationalism. He also suggested that those groups that were most cooperative might be used as police officials and burgomasters, and that racially valuable individuals among them might be sent to Germany for assimilation.

As for the Jews of the East, Himmler wrote, "I hope to see... a great emigration of all Jews to Africa or some colony elsewhere."

With regard to the non-German children of the East, he wrote that this was a question of "... screening and sifting of the young. For the non-German population... there must be no schooling higher than the fourth elementary grade. The object of this elementary schooling must be merely... (to teach the children) ...simple addition up to 500 at the most, how to write their name, and instruct them that it is a divine commandment to obey the Germans and be honest, industrious and upright. I do not think reading is necessary." Children that are racially "perfect," Himmler suggested, might be taken from their parents with a promise that they were to be sent to schools in Germany for further education but, in reality, remain in Germany permanently. The parents of such children would be encouraged to have more children.

Regarding the General Government, Himmler suggested that it should become a huge reservation for untermenschen laborers. He wrote, "In the course of the next ten years, the population of the General Government will consist of a permanently inferior population... This population will be available as a leaderless race of laborers and will provide Germany yearly with migrant workers and workers on special projects (road building, quarrying, construction work); they will have more to eat and will lead a better life than under Polish rule, and with their lack of culture, and under strict, consistent and just leadership of the German people will be called on to co-operate in the latter's everlasting cultural achievements..."

These things were music to Hitler's ears and he agreed that such thinking was leading Germany in the right direction.

BUT NOW, TO DEFEAT BRITAIN

After the British government rejected Hitler's peace proposals, the German propagandists began to speak with great conviction that Britain would be invaded and conquered. In preparation for this invasion, which the Germans dubbed "Operation Sea Lion," large-scale, and very visible, military operations, were undertaken by the Germans in western Europe and along the Channel coast.

Before an invasion was undertaken, however, the Luftwaffe was given the chance to bring Britain to the negotiating table by air power alone. Goering had promised Hitler that this could be done. Therefore, a massive aerial bombardment was launched against Britain beginning during the first week in August, 1940. It became known as the "Blitz,"—but it failed. It proved to be very costly for the Luftwaffe because the Royal Air Force (RAF) proved to be much more of a challenge than the Germans had anticipated.

With the failure of the Blitz, the only military alternative left was an invasion. But Hitler's heart was not in it. Winter had arrived and foul weather could make such an undertaking very difficult. Also, in order to get, and sustain, an invasion force on the other side of the Channel, in any weather, the German Navy would have to gain and maintain control of the English Channel. Considering the superior size of the British Navy, this too, would be difficult.

Getting troops and tanks ashore would be, perhaps, the greatest challenge. The Germans had no large landing craft that could land large numbers of soldiers and tanks and other heavy equipment onto a beach. The only alternative was to capture one or more serviceable seaports during the first hours of the attack and then rush in freighters and unload tanks, trucks, artillery pieces, etc. in the conventional manner.

The Germans had been able to do this when they invaded Norway by sneaking German troops into Norwegian harbors in coal barges, a common sight in Norwegian harbors, because the Norwegians imported German coal. There would be no such opportunities, though, with regard to Britain. It was logical to predict that the British would doggedly defend their seaports and if a port could not be held, they would most likely destroy the port's piers, cranes and other off-loading facilities and block the port's channels with mines and sunken ships.

If the invasion of Britain failed, the results would be catastrophic for Germany because such a victory would embolden the British government and its people to the point were they would never negotiate a peace settlement favorable to Germany.

Hitler was greatly perplexed by these problems and began to explore other options.

RUSSIA

The Soviet Union, known as "Russia" by most people in Germany, had long dominated Hitler's thinking. The conquest of the East was, in many ways, his ultimate goal as he had amply pointed out in Mein Kampf. But there was a problem—should it be attempted before Britain was defeated? Hitler pondered this question at length and finally concluded that it should. He concluded that the British Army would not be strong enough to undertake an invasion of the continent for more than a year, and in that time the conquest of Russia could be accomplished. Then the bulk of the German armed forces could be withdrawn from Russia and placed along the western coast of Europe to thwart any invasion. And with the riches of the East then available, Germany would be self-sufficient enough to exist indefinitely, even without a formal peace settlement.

Hitler discussed the invasion of Russia at length with his military commanders, but it was not until December 1940 that he gave the order to proceed. Russia would be invaded while Britain was held at bay.

WAR SPREADS TO NORTH AFRICA

After months of sabre rattling and much rhetoric, the Italians, on September 13, 1940, launched their anticipated invasion of Egypt from Libya. Italian troops advanced a few miles into Egypt and, as they had done in France and East Africa, stopped.

Once again, the Germans were not impressed. Admiral Raeder, however, saw opportunities in the invasion of Egypt and talked with Hitler twice in September on the subject. He suggested that the Italian attack be exploited, with German help, with the objective to drive through Egypt, take the Suez Canal, drive on through Palestine and Trans-Jordan into Iraq and Iran to take the Persian Gulf oil fields. By taking the Suez Canal, Raeder argued, the British Navy would be eliminated in the eastern Mediterranean; the German and Italian Navies could then concentrate all their efforts on driving the British Navy out of the western Mediterranean. This was, in a way, a modification of his Mediterranean Plan.

Neither Hitler nor the majority of army generals, who would have had to carry out the ground operations, had any interest in such a venture. Their feelings were that North Africa was a side show and that Germany had much more to gain by marching eastward.

A few days later, a group of Army generals, including Generals Halder, Heusinger, Paulus and Gehlen, proposed another venture into the Arab world. They suggested that German forces march from Turkey, through Syria, Lebanon, Palestine and into Egypt to take the Suez Canal from the east. Hitler rejected this idea, at least for the time being, and remained focused on Russia.

MORE VOLKSDEUTSCH

During September and October, Germany and the Soviet Union signed several agreements which allowed the Volksdeutsch, who lived in the areas of the east newly acquired by the Soviet Union, to voluntarily emigrate to Germany. Several hundred thousand people agreed to do this. This sparked another propaganda campaign by Goebbels praising the gathering-in of lost Germans. Furthermore, the influx of these people into Germany helped the manpower shortage to some degree and gave Himmler's SS recruiters more prospects for the SS and the Waffen SS.

A MESSAGE FROM TOKYO

With the Italian invasion of Egypt, and indications mounting that the European Axis Powers had ambitions in the East, the leaders in Japan felt obligated to set forth and define their interests in the East so that Japan and the European Axis Powers did not come into conflict. On September 9, 1940, the Japanese ambassador to Berlin presented a note to the German government stating that Eastern India, Burma, Australia and New Zealand were in the Japanese sphere of influence and that Tokyo would oppose any moves by the European Axis Powers to foster their interests in those areas. Hitler and Mussolini, despite the bombastic territorial claims recently reported by their respective medias, had little interest in these areas and gave Japan assurances that they would not interfere.

A LOT HAPPENED IN SEPTEMBER AND OCTOBER, 1940

On September 14, the Italian offensive in Egypt came alive again and Italian troops inched their way forward. By the 18th, they had reached the coastal town of Sidi Marrani. There they stopped again. They were now 60 miles inside Egypt but still 350 miles from Cairo.

On the 16th, Hitler concluded that the air Blitz against Britain was not going to bring the British to the peace table so he ordered a halt to all daylight bombings—the most costly form of bombing. There was no mention in the German media, of course, that the Blitz was over.

Additionally, the German Navy's submarine offensive against Britain had failed to starve them into submission, as had been hoped. While the submarines sank an impressive number of Allied ships, the British, who had gone to the convoy system, were able to get enough food, raw materials and supplies through to keep the British people adequately fed and British industry humming.

On the 17th, Hitler postponed the invasion of Britain once again.

Also at this time, Hitler discussed with Rosenberg and others how religion would be handled in the postwar Reich. Rosenberg recorded in his diary that night, "The Fuehrer took up the subject (of religion) in greater detail. Every Catholic state must elect its own Pope... the more the better." This was in keeping with Hitler's overall plan to break the power of all organized religions.

During September, Hitler and Foreign Minister von Ribbentrop met with Spanish dignitaries to prepare a meeting between Hitler and Franco to discuss, among other things, Spain's entry into the war. In conversation with the Spanish dignitaries, Hitler said that he wanted to reestablish the German colonies in central Africa, an area where Spain also had colonies. Hitler said that the German colonies would not be for the settlment of German people but for the acquisition of raw materials and food. Hitler confirmed to the Spaniards that he was still receptive to Spain's colonial ambitions in Africa.

On September 27, 1940, one of the great documents of World War II came into being, the "Tripartite Pact." This was the document that expanded and defined the Axis. It came about as a result of the talks opened earlier between Japan, Germany and Italy. Article three of the Pact contained the meat of the subject; it read, "They (Germany, Italy and Japan) further undertake to assist one another with all political, economic and military means when one of the three Contracting Parties is attacked by a power at present not involved in the European war..." This was a diplomatic coup for the Japanese who, unbeknownst to the Germans and Italians, were planning an attack on the United States. By signing this pact, Germany and

Italy obligated themselves to declare war on the United States if that country and Japan went to war.

This concession by Germany, however, had a price. In a secret addendum to the pact, Tokyo agreed to return to Germany her colonies in the South Pacific mandated to Japan by the League of Nations after World War I. This was to come about "... upon conclusion of peace ending the present European War." But, in the same addendum, it was agreed that after the war, Germany and Japan would enter into negotiations concerning the possibility of Japan buying back the colonies for an agreed-to "compensation" to Germany.

On October 9, 1940, an article appeared in an Italian newspaper which rehashed Italy's rather strange view of the world situation. The article suggested that if the United States remained neutral while the Axis Powers established their new orders in Europe and the Far East, the Americans might be rewarded by being given all of Canada, Newfoundland, the Bahamas, Bermuda, Jamaica and possibly New Zealand and Australia. Not surprisingly, this proposal went nowhere and quickly died.

During October, Hitler travelled to the Spanish border to meet Franco, and then to Vichy France to meet Petain. His intention was to feel out the Spaniards and French with regard to their entering the war after the Soviet Union had been defeated.

The results of the meetings were that Franco was receptive to the idea, but Petain was evasive. Furthermore, Hitler and Franco took an instant dislike for each other which dampened the prospects for future cooperation. On the other hand, Hitler and Petain developed feelings of mutual respect which encouraged Hitler in his hopes that Petain would cooperate with him when the time came to solidify the new European order.

Hitler then journeyed to Italy to meet with Mussolini on October 28. Upon his arrival in Italy, the Fuehrer received one of the most unwelcome surprises of his political career. Just a few hours earlier Italian troops had invaded Greece from Italian-controlled Albania. Hitler had not been informed of this beforehand and was furious. The meeting was tense but Hitler held his temper because there was serious business to conduct. Mussolini was boastful of his actions and confident of a quick victory. Hitler was not so sure. His great concern was that, since Greece was a British ally, British forces would now come to Greece and be in a position to disrupt his plans to attack Russia—which Mussolini knew nothing about. Hitler certainly remembered how, during World War I, the Allies brought stong forces into Salonika, Greece and, from there, invaded deep into the Balkans threatening Central Powers' front in Russia.

Hitler's immediate concern was that British planes, based in Greece, would be within range of the all-important Romanian oil fields upon which the German armed forces would be totally dependent until they could capture the oil fields of the Caucasus. The agreed-to purpose of the meeting was for Hitler to inform Mussolini of Franco's and Petain's attitudes toward postwar developments. Mussolini repeated Italy's territorial and economic demands and Hitler confirmed, as he had before, that Germany would support Italy's endeavors. Hitler then repeated his postwar demands as best he could without disclosing the forthcoming attack on the Soviet Union. Hitler concentrated on matters in Europe and in Africa. Hitler told Mussolini that, despite his personal dislike for Franco, he still had hopes of bringing Spain into the war, at the appropriate time and, with German help, assist Spain in taking Gibraltar from the British. Gibraltar would then be turned over to Spain with the understanding that the western Mediterranean would be closed to the British.

Also, Hitler said that Germany wanted to establish permanent military bases on the west coast of Africa and possibly in one or more of the Atlantic island groups. On these, and other matters, Mussolini reciprocated by promising that Italy would aid and support Germany in attaining these goals.

The two dictators parted company with Mussolini exuding confidence in his adventure in Greece, but Hitler was in a state of high anxiety over the new threats to his plans to attack Russia.

On October 30, as Hitler had feared, British Marines landed in Greece and the British Navy began to prepare several Greek harbors for the arrival of additional British forces.

By the end of November, the Italian invasion was in serious trouble. British and Greek forces had taken the offensive and pushed the Italians back into Albania. A daring British air raid had also destroyed important elements of the Italian Navy in an attack on the Italian naval base at Taranto in the heel of Italy. The surviving ships abandoned Taranto and the central Mediterranean and sought refuge further north at Naples. In Berlin, Hitler knew now that he had to intercede in the Balkans.

And from Spain came indications that Franco, becoming ever more concerned about Britain's endurance, was backing away from his commitment to enter the war.

THE BIELFELD PLAN FOR AFRICA

While Hitler contemplated his moves in the Balkans, his bureaucrats were busy concocting a plan for Germany's future in Africa. A Foreign Ministry team, headed by H. Bielfeld, formulated such a plan which was presented to Hitler on November 6, 1940. Fundamentally, the Bielfeld Plan called for Germany to acquire its long-sought goal of Mittel Afrika and more. The plan called for the following African colonies to come under direct German control: Togo, Dahomey, Gold Coast, Nigeria, southern Niger, southern Chad up to 15 degrees north latitude, the Cameroons, French Equatorial Africa, Belgian Congo, Rwanda, Urundi, Tanganyika, Uganda, Kenya, Northern Rhodesia, Southern Rhodesia, Nyasaland, and South West Africa.

The plan also called for German naval and air bases to be established all around the coast of Africa on both the Atlantic and Indian Oceans. Additional German bases would be established off shore in the islands surrounding the continent. Much of this could be accomplished before the end of hostilities by German advances through the Spanish and Vichy-controlled colonies in Africa. The remainder would be acquired at the peace table. The plan suggested that the resources and markets of a German-dominated Africa be shared with all of Germany's allies through German-controlled monopolies.

The black people of Africa would become permanent colonial subjects and laborers and live in preserves near large cities. The cities would be primarily for whites with the blacks commuting back and forth between the cities and the preserves. Black laborers would be moved about from preserve to preserve as needs arose. Every black male, 16 years and older, would be required to work and carry on their person, at all times, a work record-book (arbeitsbuch). This was already done by many foreign workers in Germany.

Sexual relations between blacks and whites would be strictly forbidden with harsh punishments, even death, metered out to black offenders and heavy fines and possible relocation imposed on whites.

The Arab peoples of the German colonies, who were considered whites, would fall into social and economic categories well above the blacks, but below the Europeans. And, of course, there would be no Jews in any of Germany's colonies.

Parcels of African territory would be offered to Spain to induce that nation to cooperate more fully with Germany and possibly enter the war on the side of the Axis.

Germany's military and industrial leaders, along with the SS leaders, would be consulted on how best to economically exploit the African territories.

Finally, Bielfeld suggested that a slogan be adapted to express the ultimate aim of

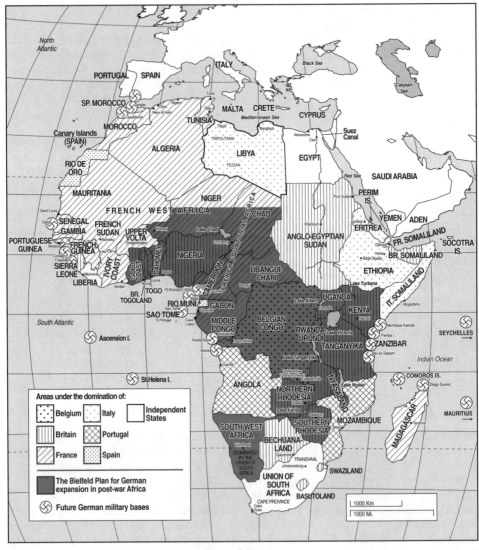

The Bielfeld Plan for German expansion in postwar Africa.

this great scheme: "Eurafrica for the Europeans."

Certain steps for German expansion into Africa had already been taken. Two training schools for future colonial police administrators were already in operation at Vienna and Oranienburg. Graduates were being sent for field training to Rome and Italian North Africa to work with Italian police who had considerable experience in colonial police work.

THE AXIS GROWS

Between November 20-25, the leaders of Hungary, Romania and Slovakia formally allied themselves with Germany, Italy and Japan by signing the Tripartite Pact. The Axis Alliance was now six strong.

GERMAN BASES IN IRELAND

On December 3, 1940, Hitler and Admiral Raeder discussed the Navy's Mediterranean Plan again. Hitler confirmed his interest in establishing German bases on the Atlantic coast and in the Atlantic Islands. He also brought up another possibility that after the defeat of Britain, Germany might obtain bases in Ireland.

A few days later, a major obstacle was laid in the path of the Mediterranean Plan when Hitler concluded that Gibraltar, a corner stone of the Plan, would not be taken due to the increasing lack of cooperation from Spain.

"BARBAROSSA" AND THE A-A LINE

Hitler's Directive #21, issued on December 18, ordered planning for the invasion of the Soviet Union to be begun in detail. The directive was entitled, "Case Barbarossa" thus giving a name to the undertaking. The directive defined, among other things, what the limits of Axis penetration into the Soviet Union would be. This was described as a line, 1250 miles long, running from the Arctic port of Archangel to Astrakhan at the mouth of the Volga River on the Caspian Sea. It became known as the "A-A Line." Heretofore, the eastern boundary of the Third Reich was generally considered the Ural Mountains, which was the dividing line between Europe and Asia. But these mountains would make a poor military boundary if the Soviets withdrew into Siberia and continued the struggle indefinitely—which was expected to be the case. It then followed that the eastern frontier of the Reich would have to be west of the Urals on flat lands upon which the very mobile German Army could operate effectively. The A-A Line would also be permanently manned as in ancient times when the civilized nations of Europe had to maintain permanently-armed frontiers against the barbarians of the east. This was also within the thinking of General Erich von Falkenhayn, German Chief of Staff during the Great War, who believed that a solid and permanent peace in the East would not be attainable.

The A-A line was to consist of permanent defenses and military settlements where the German soldiers would live with their families. In the postwar years, every German soldier would be expected to spend time posted on the eastern frontier.

LIFE IN GERMANY DURING THE LAST MONTHS OF 1940

Hitler's concerns about Russia were kept secret while, at the same time, all the world was invited to witness the military buildup for the invasion of Britain. The German media covered the coming invasion in depth, government spokesmen mentioned it frequently and a popular song appeared in Germany with the title, "We Are Sailing Against England."

But, there were problems. In Germany there was still a critical manpower shortage, and more foreign workers and slave workers were being imported. Food was scarce as were many consumer good. Meat was in such short supply that, on November 14, the government authorized the use of dog meat for human consumption.

Unbeknownst to the German people, but painfully evident to the Nazi leaders, was the fact that the German economy would soon be pressed even harder with the beginning of Barbarossa.

The British air raids over Europe had intensified. Because of unacceptable losses in daylight raids, the RAF had switched to night time bombing which contributed to the indiscriminate bombing of German cites and much suffering to the German civilian population. This was intentional and designed to demoralize the German civilians by destroying their houses. "Dehousing", it was called in Britain. With the advent of night time bombing, virtually all of Germany's cities were now blacked out all night long and thousands of people spent valuable time huddled in air raid shelters trying to sleep and otherwise manage.

The blackouts also extended to Switzerland. Since the lighted Swiss cities could serve as points of reference for Allies night-bombers, the Swiss government was prevailed upon to black out their cities, too.

Furthermore, thousands of German children were evacuated from Germany's cities and sent to safer places in the countryside.

Then, during November 1940, there was trouble in Denmark. The Danish Nazis attempted to gain public support for a coup to oust the elected Danish government in Copenhagen. The coup failed miserably. From this example, and others, the German government, as well as the German people, were now forced to recognize that most of the peoples of Europe were not as receptive to National Socialism as the people of Germany had been in January 1933 when they voted the Nazis into power.

During December, the German armed forces acquired their first sizeable military unit comprised of foreigners. This was the 4th SS Wiking (Viking) Division of the Waffen SS. It was comprised mostly of Scandinavians, and would be the first of many such units of foreigners formed by the Germans in the coming years.

On December 10, 1940, a new decree ordered that Poles, living in the annexed areas of Germany, were to be treated as "Protected Persons." Also a "Racial Register" was created whereby Polish individuals were to be listed according the degree of Polish or German blood. This represented a new, and more lenient, policy by Germany toward the Poles who were now badly needed in the labor-short German economy.

On December 31, 1940, Hitler addressed the German people over the radio. He boasted of the great achievements made so far by his government and went on to tell his listeners that the war would be over by the end of 1941.

CHAPTER 12

OH, HOW WONDERFUL IT WILL BE

With the coming of the new year, the handful of top Nazi leaders who knew of Barbarossa showed renewed vigor because this was the year that the Nazis would attain their long-sought goal of gaining liebensraum in the East, as well as eliminating, forever, Jewish Communism. Oh, how wonderful it will be when these things are accomplished!

MILITARY PLANNING

Military planning for the conquest of the East took precedence over everything else. The size of the areas to be conquered was staggering and consisted of about 40% of Europe's total land mass. To accomplish this gigantic task, virtually the entire German Army and Luftwaffe had to be committed.

The military offensive was to consist of two phases and would be carried out by three German Army groups (North, Center and South). Incorporated into these army groups would be military units supplied by Germany's allies. The three Army groups would simultaneously attack the Soviet Union on the first day of the offensive. Army Group North would drive northward, out of East Prussia, occupy the three Baltic states, take Leningrad and link up with the Finns at the Svir River east of Leningrad. Leningrad would be surrounded and starved and bombarded into submission. Hitler, and most of his generals, wanted to avoid invading the city which would result in bloody house-to-house fighting which always favors the defenders.

Army Group Center would advance directly toward Moscow out of the General Government. Army Group South would advance out of Romania and take the Ukraine, the Crimea, the industrialized Donets Basin area, and then Rostov, which was the gateway to the Caucasus.

Once these tasks were accomplished, the second phase would begin. Army Group North would turn south, Army Group South would turn north and they would link up at a point east of Moscow. Meanwhile, Army Group Center would advance to the western environs of Moscow and set up a siege line around the western part of the city. Once Army Groups North and South had linked up, Moscow would be surrounded by the bulk of the German forces. Siege lines would be established and the city starved and bombarded into submission in the same manner as Leningrad.

While German forces carried out the two-phase operation in the central part of European Russia, the Finns would attack and support the German advance on its northern flank while the Romanians would do the same on its southern flank. Other allied forces would be utilized as needed.

Hitler was optimistic that Barbarossa could be completed by the end of 1941, or the spring of 1942 at the latest. He based his judgment on the Red Army's poor showing against Finland during the Winter War of 1939/1940, and the general belief that the people of the Soviet Union would not actively support the communist government. He told Field Marshal von Rundstedt, "You have only to kick in the door, and the whole rotten structure will come crashing down."

Once Moscow surrendered, or reached a point where it was no longer a viable military threat, it would be considered that Barbarossa was completed. Then, between 50 to 60 army divisions would be retained in the East to man the A-A Line, mop up pockets of resistance and assist the SS in eliminating any guerilla activities that might appear. The remainder of the Axis forces, which would then consist of approximately 150 divisions, would be sent elsewhere. A large part of this force would be sent to protect the west coast of Europe against a possible British invasion, while another sizeable force would advance into the Caucasus and, at the appropriate time, into the Middle East. A German force would be dispatched to North Africa to march across the Vichy-controlled territories of Algeria and French Morocco to the Atlantic coast. Help would also be given to the Italians in taking Egypt and the Suez Canal.

It was anticipated that the surviving Soviet forces would withdraw into Siberia, east of the Urals, where a large industrial complex had been developed. It was not intended that Axis forces would cross the Urals to occupy these areas at this time. Rather, Hitler and others believed that, due to the fact that the region east of the Urals would be virtually cut off from the rest of the world and would be without the oil from the Caucasus, it could be neutralized by air power alone. A similar situation had already existed for three years in China where the Japanese had driven the forces of the Chinese Nationalists into the mountains and sparsely-settled areas of western China with their only lifeline to the outside being the Burma Road.

Once the objectives in the Middle East and North Africa were completed, German forces would march down the Atlantic coast of Africa to retake their lost colonies of Togo, the Cameroons and South West Africa. They would also take the western part of the Belgian Congo and whatever British and French colonies deemed of value.

At the same time, German and Italian forces would march down the Nile Valley in East Africa to recapture Italian East Africa, the British colonies of Kenya and Uganda and the lost German colonies of Tanganyika, Urundi and Rwanda. From the recaptured German colonies, German forces would march into the Belgian Congo from the east and link up with the German forces advancing from the west. At this time, the long-sought goal of creating Mittel Afrika would be met.

After the Axis Powers had gained all of their objectives, they would offer peace. If the enemy rejected the peace efforts, the Axis Powers would go forward without a peace treaty because, at this point, the Axis Powers would be self-sufficient and could withstand a state of international confrontation indefinitely.

PLANNING THE NEW COLONIES IN THE EAST

The conquered lands in the East would be divided into three very large German-controlled colonies, called commissariats. Other sizeable areas would be awarded to Romania, Hungary and Finland.

The three German commissariats would be known as "Ostland" (Eastland), the Ukraine, and "Muscovy," the latter being the land traditionally known as Russia. The word "Russia" would disappear.

All three commissariats would be ruled by a civilian leader called a Riechscommissar, an old, pre-Nazi title denoting one who had extraordinary powers in a time of crisis.

The Commissariat of Ostland would consist of the three Baltic states, Lithuania, Latvia, Estonia and parts of Belorussia. Ostland would extend northward from East Prussia to the Finnish border, eastward to a point approximately 150 miles west of Moscow, southward to a line running eastward from the general area of Warsaw. This would be the favored colony and one that would eventually be incorporated into the Greater German Reich. The reason for this was that it was heavily populated by Estonians, Latvians and Lithuanians who were, for the most part, people of good blood. These people, it was believed, could be quickly and easily Germanized. The people of Belorussia were slavs but, under Nazi racial theory, were of better blood than their neighbors, the Ukrainians and Russians. Therefore, it followed that a significant number of them could be Germanized also.

The identity of Lithuania, Latvia and Estonia would be preserved as provinces, called general commissariats, and a fourth general commissariat, south of Lithuania, would be formed primarily from Belorussian land. It would be named "Weissrussland" (White Russia—another name for Belorussia). The headquarters of the Ostland Reichscommissar would be in Riga, Latvia.

While the people of good blood in Ostland were being Germanized, the undesirable elements would be banished. The Ostland would be incorporated into the Reich in phases as each area was deemed ready for incorporation. Statements by Hitler suggested that the Estonians would be the first to be incorporated into the Reich, followed by the Lithuanians, then the Latvians, and finally the Belorussians. The possibility was left open, that Ostland might become a German protectorate during its time of preparation for incorporation.

During the war, little effort would be devoted to Germanizing the Ostlanders, as would generally be the case throughout the conquered territories. The needs of the war came first. However, during the war, the Volksdeutsch and others of good blood in Ostland would be favored by the laws and regulations that would be imposed. The untermenschen would be maintained at a lower standard of living which would include lower food rations, lower wages,

monitoring by the SS, and the stern justice of a court system established exclusively for them.

The people of good blood in the respective general commissariats would be allowed to establish advisory councils, which would have no real power, but would be able to express the feelings of their own kind in the region.

Private property seized by the communists after the annexation of the three Baltic states into the Soviet Union in 1939 would remain under German control until its distribution could be determined at a later date. An effort would also be made to distribute the private property seized by the Soviets in Belorussia at the time of the Russian Revolution (1917–1922).

The Commissariat of the Ukraine would encompass the traditional area of the Ukraine, less the Crimean Peninsula and the adjacent area to the north. It would be bordered on the north by Ostland and Muscovy, on the east by Turkestan, on the south by the Caucasus, the Crimea, and the Black Sea, and on the west by Romanian territory and the General Government. The overall size of this commissariat would be about as large as Greater Germany itself.

The Ukraine would have a civil administration under a Reichscommissar and would be divided into six general commissariats. The SS would maintain order while the army provided external security.

A large percentage of Ukrainian land in collective farms would be retained, as is, until after the war. At that time, it was anticipated that some collectives would be broken up to provide land for settlers while others would simply be taken over by German commercial interests. Land would not be given or sold to the local people but they would be assigned small plots to raise vegetables and live stock.

The Commissariat of Muscovy would be bounded on the north by the Arctic Ocean, the White Sea and Finland, on the west by Ostland, and on the south by The Ukraine. The eastern boundary of Muscovy would extend, initially to the A-A Line, and beyond if possible. Muscovy would be almost twice as large as Greater Germany and would be completely isolated from the outside world.

Most importantly, Muscovy would become the dumping ground for Jews, slavs and other undesirables from the occupied East and from other parts of Europe. Also, the bulk of the Russian people would live there. Muscovy's future population, after all of the undesirables had been transferred there, was estimated to become approximately 60 million people. No German settlements would be established in Muscovy for the foreseeable future. The territory would be closed to foreigners and there would be little reported about it in the media. When questions arose as to what happened to the Jews and others, one of the answers would be that they have been resettled in Muscovy.

To justify their actions in Muscovy, the Germans would point to the precedent established by other colonial powers who had established penal colonies. The prime examples would be those of Australia, which was established by Britain, and French Guiana in South America (Devil's Island) by France.

Rosenberg suggested that since the Russians and Belorussians had long had friendly relations with each other, a large number of Poles be settled in eastern Muscovy as a buffer between the two nationalities. The Poles hated both the Russians and Belorussians and their presence, Rosenberg believed, would tend to break down the Russian-Belorussian affinity for each other.

Hitler rejected this idea. He had already made up his mind about the Poles. In January 1941 he had issued a decree making the inhabitants of the General Government stateless persons. This meant that there would no longer be a Poland, and the Poles would become colonial subjects.

Like Ostland and the Ukraine, Muscovy would have a German civil administration, but with a much stronger SS presence. The army would also operate in Muscovy in considerable strength guarding the northern sector of the A-A Line and maintaining its military facilities and lines of communication.

Valuable resources such as mines, forests, hydroelectric power facilities, etc., which could not be moved, would be under strict German control with the understanding that, at some time in the future, they might be turned over to German industrial interests who would operate them under trusteeships.

Living conditions for the non-German residents of Muscovy would purposely be kept low so that the life expectancy of the inhabitants would be short. Also, efforts would be taken to keep the birth rate low. There was talk that, after several decades, the undesirable population of Muscovy might be reduced to the point where significant amounts of land could be made available for German settlers. Rosenberg held another view of this, arguing that the Russian people were a hardy race and almost certainly would not disappear in the foreseeable future. That being the case, he argued that Russian nationalism within Muscovy would always be a problem of concern.

The fates of Moscow and Leningrad were something of a question mark. Hitler said rather frequently that he would erase those cities from the map. He also spoke of destroying Kiev in the Ukraine. It appears that Hitler said these things out of anger and under tension, and that it made him feel good to say them. No one challenged him on these issues, but it is safe to assume that there were those in his entourage that realized that such undertakings would be counterproductive and difficult to carry out.

The oil-rich Caucasus would not become a Commissariat, but the northern part would come under absolute German control. Its political structure would be determined at a later date.

In the south, the ancient countries of Georgia, Azerbaijan, and Armenia would be able to reclaim their independence, as the Germans had allowed them to do in 1918. These counties, however, would become vassal states to Germany.

Finland would recover all of the territory lost to the Soviet Union as a result of the Winter War (1939/1940) and would acquire new land from Russia as far east as the White Sea. This would include the nickel-rich Kola Peninsula, the port of Murmansk and all of Karelia which bordered Finland on the east and south. This is the land of the Karelian people, who are racially related to the Finns.

Romania would recover Romanian-speaking Bessarabia, which had been lost to the Soviet Union in 1940. Land beyond the Dniester River, which was known as "Transnistria," might also be given to Romania depending on military and political developments. Transnistria would include the large seaport of Odessa.

POLITICAL PLANNING

The Reichscommissars, who would answer directly to Hitler, would be responsible for implementing the decrees from Berlin and would manage the day-to-day affairs in their respective realms. Their staff would be comprised of Germans in all positions except for the lowest ranks in which local people would be used.

The SS would be responsible for the security of the respective commissariats and work closely with the Reichscommissars. Local people would be recruited for a police force which would operate under the SS. All matters of race would be the exclusive area of the SS as would be the acquisition of land and other properties for future settlers. Neither the Reichscommissars nor the German Army commanders were to interfere with the SS in these matters.

External security would be in the hands of the German Army which would also be responsible for maintaining and guarding its own military facilities and lines of supply throughout the commissariats.

On April 2, 1941, Alfred Rosenberg, the Nazi Party's racial theorist, was authorized to create a new government agency to be known as "The Political Bureau of the East." This was the first step in the creation of a Cabinet-level colonial office similar to those that all the other colonial powers had at the time.

ECONOMIC PLANNING

Economic development of the East would take place in three time frames: 1) while hostilities were still continuing in the East and for a period of occupation up to three years, minimal effort would be devoted to economic matters, 2) for the duration of the war against Britain and the other Allies, there would be an increase in economic developments as conditions permit, 3) after the conclusion of peace, long term planning would be implemented.

During the first stage of economic development, the needs of the German armed forces would be paramount. The Army Group commanders were authorized to take virtually anything they needed in the occupied areas to complete the military missions assigned to them. It was expected that the German Army would, for the most part, feed itself off the land and make use of a wide variety of captured military and civilian equipment and machinery.

As for industrial equipment, raw materials, finished goods, etc. that had no immediate military value, they would be evaluated by representatives from Goering's Four Year Plan who would follow in the wake of the advancing armies. Those assets found useful would be either shipped to Germany or secured in the East for future use. Factories, mills, mines, industrial lands and other assets that could not be moved would be secured by Goering's representatives for later use. The needs of the local people would be given very low priority.

The tasks assigned to Goering's representatives were not new. They had been performed in 1939 after the conquest of Poland.

Stage two would come into effect as the bulk of the German forces began evacuating the eastern territories. Surplus items and materials no longer of value to the military would be evaluated and sent to Germany or left in place. Food, especially Ukrainian grain, no longer needed by the military in the East, would be gathered and shipped to Germany. Again, the needs of the local people would be virtually ignored with the exception of those individuals who collaborated with the German authorities.

During stages one and two, the Soviet economic system would, for the most part, be preserved. Collective farms and industrial enterprises would remain intact and, for the most part, continue to operate as they had before the invasion. At Goering's insistence, captured farm machinery would remain in the East for future use.

After the final Axis victory, phase three would begin. Only generalities could be given at this time with details to be worked out. Generally, the economy of the East would be one of supplying Germany and western Europe with food, raw materials and cheap labor. Only limited industrialization of the East was contemplated. Local technicians and skilled laborers who were willing to cooperate with the Germans would be sent to the west if needed, while the others would remain in the East and be utilized there. Technical schools would be established to train local people in traditional skills such as carpentry, masonry, plumbing, etc.

Germany's economic plans were to be kept secret from the local peoples of the East. With regard to the future, the local people would be told virtually anything that would keep them quiescent for the short term. Most importantly, they would be told that the hated collective farms would be abolished and the land redistributed to those who farmed it. This was an outright lie. The Germans planned to take control of all of the land in the East which would either be doled out to settlers or kept in reserve for future exploitation. The local people would be allowed to farm small parcels for their own need, but they would never be allowed to own land.

The Soviet money in the East would be replaced by script called "Reichskreditkas-senscheine" (RK) which had been used in other occupied areas. It would remain in use until a new monetary policy for the East could be established. The rate of exchange would be fixed so that it favored the Germans giving them stronger purchasing power with RKs than with Reichsmarks. Also rigid price controls would be imposed to keep the monetary system stable. The existing Soviet wage scale was to be maintained throughout the war and adjusted later to favor Germany's economic interests.

THE NATIVES

Hitler had said, "Our colonizing penetration must be constantly progressive, until it reaches the stage where our own colonists far outnumber the local inhabitants." This was the edict followed by the Nazi planners during the first half of 1941.

Inherent in the German planning was the need to drastically reduce the size of the population in the East to make way for the influx of settlers. Several ways were devised to do this. The methods included deportation, executions, starvation, disease, neglect, shortening of life span, and birth control. For the mentally ill and disabled a euthanasia program, similar to that in Germany, would be applied in the East.

Those able-bodied individuals who would be eliminated first would be the Jews, Gypsies, communist hierarchy, jail inmates and anyone who forcefully resisted the occupation. For these tasks, killing squads called "Einsatzgruppen" (Action Groups), were formed by the SS to summarily murder those people wherever they were found. Killings were to be done by several means; shooting, drowning, burning, and by an ingenious invention called "gas vans." Gas vans were air-tight mobile vans that could be towed to a given location by a motorized vehicle. The vans would be filled with people and exhaust fumes from the vehicle would be piped into the vans to suffocate those inside.

The Einsatzgruppen were to kill quickly. Time was not to be wasted on slower techniques such as starvation or disease. The bodies were to be disposed of by mass burial or cremation.

While the conquest of the East was in progress, the fate of the Jews in the rest of Europe would be on hold.

The fate of the great majority of the local people in the East would be on hold until the military conquests were completed. Then, under the direction of the SS, they would be sorted out to find Volksdeutsch and other people of good blood. For this, the German People's List would be used. People who qualified as Aryan, but who had lost the German language and culture, would be sent to training centers in Germany for "reGermanization." Many of these people, especially those who eagerly accepted Nazi ideology, would then be returned to their home areas where they would serve as liaison personnel between the German administrators and the local people. These liaison people would be fluent in the local language and be familiar with the local conditions and customs.

People of good blood in the East who refused to be reGermanized would have their children taken from them and turned over to the Lebensborn organization to be raised as loyal Germans. The children would be given German names and false birth certificates, and they would be raised in foster homes or state institutions in Germany.

Non-Germans of value would also be sought out. This would include able-bodied workers and others who might be of use during and after the war. Large numbers of willing helpers (hilfswillinger or "hiwis") were expected to come forward to work with the German armed forces during hostilities. Furthermore, entire groups of people, who were known as anti-communist or anti-Russian, would be approached and evaluated for possible use in military or para-military roles, or as political and economic collaborators after the conquest. The Cossacks of the southern steppes were one of the groups that interested the planners because of their recognized military prowess and the long history of resistance to Russian domination. Thought was given to the possibility of using the Cossacks to help man the A-A Line.

Another group of people of interest to the planners were the Volga Germans who had been settled, over a hundred years earlier along the Volga River, by the Czarist government. This was a tightly-knit community to which the Soviets had granted a local political status known as the "Volga-German Autonomous Republic." These people were still thought to be very German although little was known of them and negative rumors circulated that they were, by now, heavily assimilated with the slavs. There was some discussion on possibly using the Volga-Germans as a part of the protective force that would man the A-A Line. Other thoughts were that they might be moved westward.

At this stage of the planning, though, no firm decisions were made concerning the Volga Germans until more was known about them.

In both the Ostland and the Ukraine, a relatively small number of local people would be selected to become permanent workers and servants for the Germans. As for the great masses of people, they would be left to fend for themselves and provide a ready labor pool as needs arose. These people would be managed in such a way that the feeling of nationalism would no longer exist among them. To do this, old ethic, religious and regional rivalries would be encouraged and even managed.

Religion would be used as a tool of the conquerors. Since religion was still a sore point between the communists and much of the population, the Germans would enter the East waving the banner of religious freedom. Hitler had said that it was better for the people to believe rather than not to believe. There would be no attempt to eliminate religion but, later on, there would be determined effort to regulate it. Basically, all organized religious bodies would be eliminated and each town or village would have its own cluster of churches which would

Ostland, an area inhabited for the most part by racially acceptable people, would eventually be annexed by Germany after a sufficiant period on Germanization.

operate independently from the churches in neighboring communities. Existing religious differences were to be exploited in an effort to drive the various religious groups apart. The church leaders would be stripped of their role in education and no effort would be made by the Germans to physically maintain churches or religious shrines, etc.

As for the official language to be used in the East, it would, of course, be German. The local people would be taught just enough German to take orders and respond to questioning. German administrators would be discouraged from learning the local languages.

In the Ostland, where many people were already Germanized or partially Germanized, they would be taught to be fluent in German. Racially acceptable elements in Belorussia would also become fluent in German. In the Ukraine, the use of Russian, which was widespread, would be discouraged and only the top Ukrainian officials would be taught German. In Muscovy, no at-

tempt would be made to introduce German over and above the ability to take orders.

The Cyrillic alphabet would be replaced with the Latin alphabet throughout the East.

Converting the East to the German language would be a gigantic undertaking. Books in libraries and schools would have to be changed as would newspapers, magazine, road signs, etc. Therefore, this program would not be undertaken to any large degree until after the war.

PLANNING FOR THE SETTLERS

"A string of pearls," Hitler called it. The string referred to the new transportation corridors that would be built in the East, and the pearls referred to the new all-German cities that would be built along the corridors at approximately every 100 kilometers or so. Each city would be the hub of an agricultural community some 60 to 80 Km in diameter where the Aryan settlers would live and work. The cities would provide all of the urban services necessary to support the settlers and would be the headquarters of the local governmental and SS administrators. It was seen that it might be necessary to fortify some of the cities as places of refuge for the settlers in areas that were not fully pacified. Also, in this respect, it would be necessary to give the settlers military training and personal arms so that they could serve as reserves for the official peacekeeping units in the area.

Some compared these communities to the frontier towns of the old American Wild West. This was a part of history in which Hitler took a personal interest. He occasionally spoke admiringly of how the Indians of the American west were defeated and sent off to reservations and the land acquired by white men.

Branching out from each of the new cities would be a system of good roads to reach the farms and villages that would spring up in the area. There might also be large corporate farms in the area which, for the most part, would be carry-overs from the Soviet collective farm system.

With time, the cities would grow and the limits of the surrounding communities pushed outward. Overcrowding of any area was to be avoided. A figure for the ideal population density considered at this time was 140 people per square kilometer.

And how would the skilled trades and other non-agricultural tasks be managed? In this regard, Hitler had made some specific suggestions. He said that the veterans who had acquired technical skills while in the armed forces should be retrained to become the skilled workers in the East: plumbers, carpenters, electricians, etc. He further proposed that former non-commissioned officers would make ideal managers for the gas stations along the Autobahns.

Preliminary plans, in this respect, were made under which servicemen, while still on active duty, would begin their retraining. That training would begin about two years before their discharge.

Non-German workers would live in designated areas within the agricultural

Design and floor plan for a settlement farm house. There was to be a master bedroom on the main floor and a loft for additional bedrooms. The house had a high-pitched roof to prevent snow buildup and an attached hen house, pig sty and shed, which was a common practice in Europe. Garden plots and orchards surround the house.

communities and their movement and other activities would be strictly controlled. There would be no social interaction between the settlers and the non-German workers. Frequent rotation of the workers might be employed to insure this.

The first strings of pearls to be built would be in the Ukraine because it was here that the all-important transportation corridor between Germany and the Crimea would be built. That corridor would consist of an Autobahn, a multi-track rail line, phone and telegram lines and, perhaps, an oil pipeline bringing oil from the Caucasus to Germany. While this corridor was being built, the resort areas along the southern coast of the Crimea would be improved in anticipation of a large and steady influx of vacationers from Europe.

Another transportation corridor to be built in the Ukraine would connect Germa-

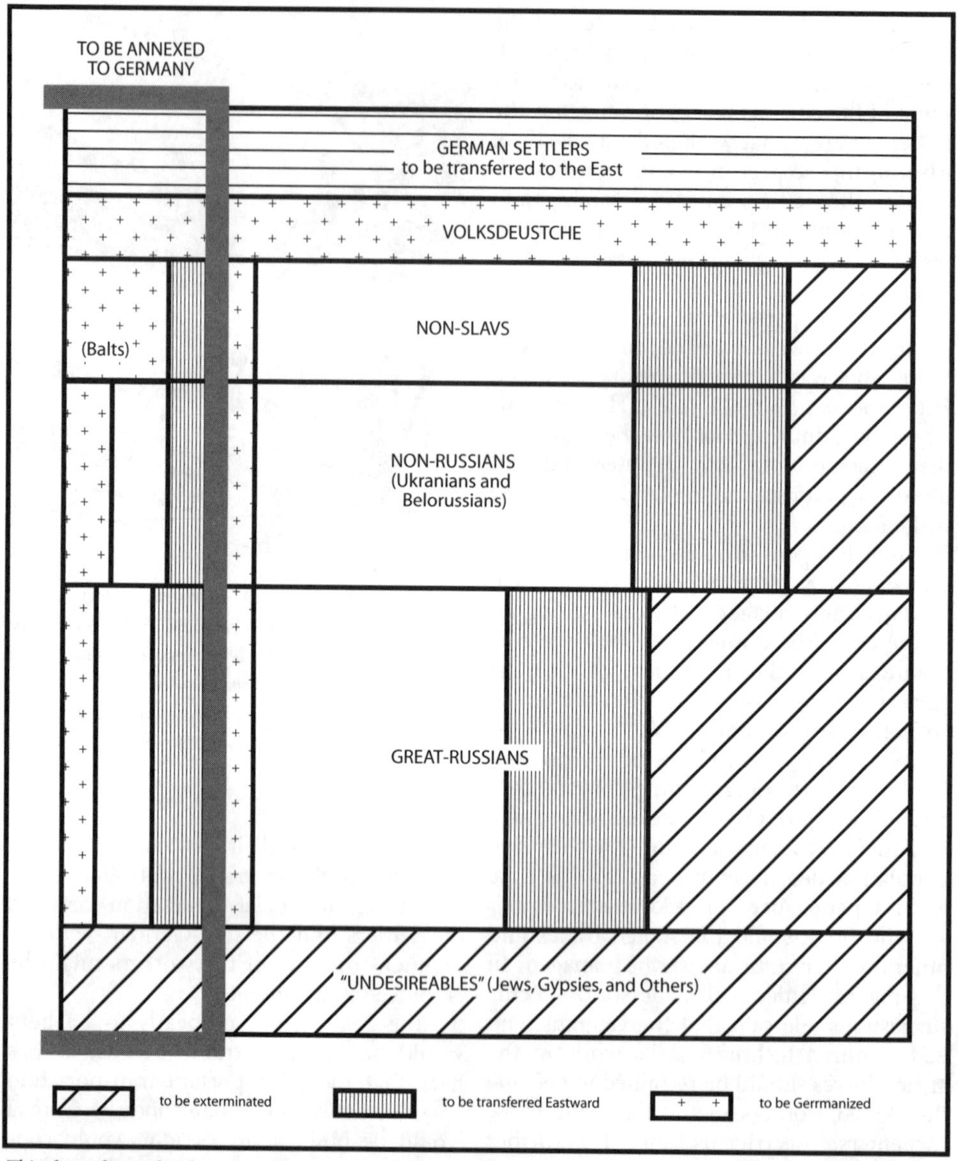

TO BE ANNEXED
TO GERMANY

GERMAN SETTLERS
to be transferred to the East

VOLKSDEUSTCHE

(Balts)

NON-SLAVS

NON-RUSSIANS
(Ukranians and
Belorussians)

GREAT-RUSSIANS

"UNDESIREABLES" (Jews, Gypsies, and Others)

| to be exterminated | to be transferred Eastward | + + to be Gerrmanized |

This chart shows the class strata that was expected to evolve in the East and the fates of those who would be displaced. Adapted from Alexander Dallin, *"German Rule in Russia 1941-45: A Study In Occupation Policies"*; 1981.

ny with the coal-rich and food-rich Donets Basin and the Caucasus.

These corridors were one of Hitler's pet projects. He visualized three-lane-per-side Autobahns and heavy-duty high-speed rail lines where trains would travel up to 125 mph, rushing food and other commodities to Germany.

Other transportation corridors were planned for the East in the Ostland and Muscovy. All of these corridors would be built with considerable attention being given to the future needs of the German military in maintaining the defenses along the A-A Line.

The existing major cities in the Ukraine and Muscovy would be connected to the transportation corridors but inhabited, almost exclusively, by the local people. In this manner, the cities would serve as preserves for laborers who could be transported quickly and easily along the corridors. The maintenance and cleanliness of these older cities would be left, for the most part, to the local population.

In the Ostland, it would be considerably different. Most of the existing cities were already populated by racially acceptable people and they would be maintained in a conventional manner. Fewer new cities would be built and there would be no sharply defined pattern of settlements.

Throughout the East, the names of cities and other geographic sites would be given Germanic names. Some of those names would glorify German history, German heros and Nazi ideology.

In Ostland and the Ukraine, a multi-class society would eventually develop. At the top would be the German settlers, then would come the Volksdeutsch. The next four categories dealt with the non-Aryans who, in varying degrees, would be Germanized, transferred to the East or exterminated.

NUMBERS

The exact number of untermenschen in the East to be disposed of was never really known with any accuracy. But, it was generally estimated to be well over 45 million people. Some estimates stated that as many as 100 million people had to be displaced while one estimate claimed 180 million.

The settlers would remain a minority in the East for many years to come. The SS Race and Resettlement Office (RSHA) produced a report stating that, at the end of hostilities in the East, only about five million people would be available as settlers, and that their numbers would grow slowly. This seemed to have no impact on the planners. They pro-

ceeded with their devilish plans to displace and exterminate millions.

THE CRIMEA

Considerable planning was devoted to the Crimea because this was another area in which Hitler took a personal interest. Hitler referred frequently to the Crimea as "Germany's Riviera" and as a future "German Gibraltar" in the Black Sea.

The Crimean Peninsula and land to the north along the Black Sea coast would be annexed directly to Germany. This general area had, in the 1300s, been known as the Khanate of the Crimea. Its balmy climate would provide Germany with citrus fruits and winter vegetables.

The name of the Crimea would be changed to "Taurida," an ancient Greek name for the area derived from Taurus.

Germany's claims to the strategic peninsula, as if they were needed, were based on the fact that the area had long contained a rather large number of German settlers. Also, centuries earlier the Germanic Goths had ruled in the Crimea.

In populating the Crimea after the war, the local Volksdeutsch and other people of good blood would be allowed to remain, while the rest would be removed. A small number of non-Germanic people would be retained to become workers and servants. Under an agreement with Romania, the Volksdeutsch from the Soviet areas to be acquired by that country would be transferred to the Crimea. This would constitute the first influx of settlers. Their numbers were estimated to be 140,000 people. Other settlers, of course, would follow.

A place would be found within the Crimean social and economic structure for the Crimean Tartars who are racially related to the Turks. This was seen as a political necessity to appease Turkey.

The Crimea would have its own civil administration with security provided by the SS. A permanent military presence was also anticipated and the Crimea would be the home base of the future German Black Sea Fleet. Consideration was also given to building a new capital city for the Crimea somewhere along the southern coast.

THE CAUCASUS

As already mentioned, the Caucasus was not to become a German commissariat, but the Germans would, in some manner, take permanent control of the area's oil resources. They would also take permanent control of Batum in the southern Caucasus and at the easternmost end of the Black Sea. This area, which borders Turkey, would have a permanent German military base.

The three countries in the southern part of the Caucasus, Georgia, Armenia, and Azerbaijan, would be allowed to declare their independence but would be vassal states to Germany. The Georgians would be the most favored people in this area because they were well-respected in Germany for their culture and their long history of opposition to the Russians. The Armenians would be at the bottom because they were looked upon by many Germans as pushy traders akin to the Jews. The Azerbaijanies would fall in between. Another factor that was considered for this area was that Armenia, which bordered Turkey, might be used as a buffer state between that country and the German interests in the Caucasus. Turkey had territorial claims in the area and had long tried to increase its economic interests there. Here was an opportunity for the future to improve relations with Turkey at Armenia's expense.

From the military point of view, the German occupation of the Caucasus was essential in denying its oil to the Soviets. It was known that the Caucasus supplied 86% of the Soviet Union's oil, although new fields were being developed by the Soviets beyond the Urals. Control of the Caucasus was also important in maintaining the southern end of the A-A Line.

In Nazi racial theory, the people of the Caucasus were non-slavs and, therefore, of better blood. Some Nazi theorists held that they were actually lost Aryans. Unfortunately, however, they had a long history of feuding with one another. This could not be tolerated and was another reason why the Germans felt that they had to control this all-important region. No effort would be made to Germanize the people of the Caucasus and they would be allowed to maintain their own traditional cultures and religions. Also, no plans were made to open the Caucasus to German settlers.

To further secure this important region, the good will of the Caucasian people was to be sought through humane treatment as well as positive political and economic policies. A slogan was devised for use in the Caucasus to express this goal; "Long live the free Caucasians in alliance with, and under the protection of, the Greater German Empire and Adolf Hitler."

BEYOND THE A-A LINE

Beyond the A-A Line lay Asia. At the northern end of the A-A Line is the emptiness of Siberia. At the southern end is the emptiness of the Turkestan deserts. The area in between was well-populated on both sides of the Ural Mountains. On the eastern side of the mountains, the Soviets had built a rather large and modern industrialized community around the city of Sverdlovsk. The Germans had no immediate plans to invade any of these areas. It was obvious, however, that after the defeat of the Soviets in European Russia, the Sverdlovsk region would become the last stronghold of the Soviet regime. As such, it would be an ongoing threat but, the planners concluded, a manageable threat. It was concluded that this area could be neutralized by cutting off its communications with the outside world and its oil supply from the Caucasus and by attacking it frequently from the air. The only modern transportation link the Soviets would have to the outside world would be the 4000-mile-long Trans-Siberian Railroad which terminated at the port of Vladivostok on the Pacific Ocean. It was possible that Japan, if she became militarily active—and it appeared that she would—might conquer Vladivostok and other parts of eastern Siberia. This was even more likely if the Soviet Union was militarily weakened after having suffered massive losses in Europe. The only remaining outlets to the world for the Soviets would be the primitive roads and caravan trails across the Gobi Desert into China, the deserts of Turkestan and Afghanistan, and the tenuous sea route along the northern coast of Siberia which was operative for only a few months during the summer.

The northern portion of the A-A Line would be the most difficult to manage. Here, the terrain is flat and heavily forested making it very favorable for guerrilla activities—which were expected. The region is frigid, very sparsely settled, and with only one major road and railroad that run from the town of Vorkuta, at the northern end of the Urals, in a southwesterly direction toward Moscow. The region's commercial value consisted of forest products, fur and some undeveloped coal deposits. The German planners were undecided as to the benefits of conquering this region, but could not rule out the fact that it had to be neutralized or pacified in some manner.

Opposite the southern part of the A-A Line was the huge desert region of Turkestan, also known as the Kirghiz Steppe. This was another very sparsely settled area which was arid and hot and had only primitive roads that criss-crossed the region. Here, the Soviets had formed three of their republics: the Kazakh Soviet Socialist Republic, the Uzbek Soviet Socialist Republic, and the Turkmen Soviet Socialist Republic.

Here again, the German planners, saw an area not worth conquering at this time. Furthermore, it formed an effective natural barrier between their soon-to-be colonial empire and the yellow hoards of the East.

There was, however, one area of Turkestan on the eastern shore of the Caspian Sea, near the port of Sevcenko, that was rich in oil. If this area were not conquered, its oil would be available to the Soviets. Conquering it, though, posed a problem. There was a road around the northern end of the Caspian Sea from Astrakhan to Sevcenko, but it was some 700 miles long. This road could be used by a military force to capture the Sevcenko oil fields, but then it would have to be defended and would, thereby, considerably increase the length of the A-A Line. Or, as another option, the Sevcenko area could be taken from the sea once the Germans had had time to build a naval force to operate in the Caspian Sea, which is a land-locked body of water. In that case, a much shorter permanent defensive perimeter could be established around Sevcenko and its oil fields. A final decision on this matter was left for the future.

Another factor that favored the Germans along this southern portion of the A-A Line was the fact that the people of the Kirghiz Steppe were mostly Muslims and might easily be separated from the influence of the Soviets because of the great cultural and religious differences between them and communism.

THE MIDDLE EAST

Some attention was given to the Middle East at this time, but no military action was contemplated there until after the conquest of the Soviet Union. Also, it had been agreed between Hitler and Mussolini that the Middle East would, after the war, come within the Italian sphere of influence. The Germans realized, however, that the Italians were incapable of conquering the region alone and that considerable German help would be needed.

Germany would gain little in the Middle East except that the region would be removed from the influence of the British and French and its most valuable asset, oil, would be acquired by Italy. This would provide Italy with its own source of oil and would leave the Romanian oil and the Caucasus oil for Germany's use.

What little planning that was done called for an Axis invasion of the Middle East, possibly in 1942, in a two-pronged attack; one from the Caucasus and the other from North Africa. Along with occupying the Middle East, Hitler spoke occasionally for occupying Afghanistan which would be used as a base of operations against the British in India. No formal planning was done with regard to Afghanistan, but it remained an item to be addressed in the future.

THE EUROPE OF THE FUTURE

While the secret planning for Barbarossa was underway, Goebbels' propaganda machine began an extensive campaign to tell the people of Europe what their future would hold. Goebbels' theme ran thusly: Germany, and to a lesser degree, Italy, would become the sole industrial giants of Europe with their immediate allies having a smaller industrial base, but these being coordinated with those of Germany and Italy. Everyone else would be Germany's suppliers and customers. Industrial enterprises, now outside of Germany and her allies, would be moved to Germany or shut down. Some exceptions would be permitted if they fit into the overall plan for Europe's New Order. These areas might have a mix of industry and agriculture.

Certain countries would have specific roles to fill in the New Order. Denmark, for example, would serve as Europe's dairyland; France, the Balkans, and the East would produce a wide variety of foodstuffs for all of Europe and would become food exporters. Mineral wealth would be exploited where it was found, and huge German-controlled cartels would control all of the major facets of the economy throughout Europe. Germany would write long-term trade agreements with other nations to guarantee world-wide markets for European goods and products. Prices and wages would be controlled, currency stabilized, customs barriers reduced, and inflation eliminated. Labor would be organized under government controls and workers treated fairly and provided with virtually all of the necessities of life, including generous retirements.

Africa, which would be controlled by Germany, Italy, Spain, Portugal and possibly France and Britain, would be incorporated into the European order to become a supplier of food and raw materials and a marketplace for European goods. And lastly, favorable economic arrangements would be worked out with Japan and her vassal states in the Far East.

The propagandists pointed out that some of these projects had already begun. Denmark's dairy industry was working at full capacity and exporting dairy products to various parts of Europe, raw materials from Norway and some industrial products from Sweden were flowing to Europe, and, in France, Marshal Petain had recently decreed a "Back to the Land" program to increase French agricultural production.

"I HOPE I LIVE LONG ENOUGH"

As planning for the great dream was underway, Hitler, as ever, was concerned about his personal health. On several occasions, he commented to his aides that he hoped to live long enough to see the New Order in Europe come into being.

CHAPTER 13

THE WAR GOES ON, BARBAROSSA BEGINS

While the German planners were studying their maps and generating their secret reports, the war in Europe, Africa and at sea went on. In both the Balkans and North Africa, the Italians were still in trouble. In the Balkans, winter had set in and the front in Albania was stagnant. In North Africa, the British had counterattacked and driven the Italians back into Libya.

In January, Hitler agreed to send military aid to Italy for both fronts. To get troops to the war zones in the Balkans, however, he needed permission from Bulgaria and Yugoslavia to allow their troops to pass through those countries. Diplomatic efforts were begun in this regard.

With regard to North Africa, Hitler had already sent a large contingent of the Luftwaffe to operate out of Italian bases in Sicily, and now, in February, he sent panzer units to Libya and one of his best generals, Erwin Rommel.

These concessions to Italy had a price, however. Mussolini agreed to send an additional 20,000 Italian workers to Germany to add to the 112,000 Italian workers already there. Mussolini further agreed to allow some of Italy's industrial plants to begin producing war materials for Germany.

EAST AFRICA

On January 19, 1941, the war in East Africa flared anew. British forces launched an attack from the Sudan, recovered the border towns taken by the Italians earlier, and penetrated deep into the northern part of the Italian colony of Eritrea. On the 29th, the British launched a second invasion from Kenya in the south driving into Italian Somaliland.

This was a completely different kind of war from that in Europe and North Africa. Here, it was black soldiers fighting black soldiers with white officers commanding on both sides. There were no large tank battles and the battles in the air were fought, for the most part, with outdated aircraft. The Italians were cut off from all supplies and reinforcements from Italy which made their prospects of victory look bleak, indeed. The British, on the other hand, had adequate resources from the various parts of their empire.

The British attacks in Italian East Africa progressed rapidly as the demoralized Italian troops gave way at nearly every encounter. Here was an area of Italy's realm that Hitler could not save.

THE AIR WAR IN EUROPE

During the first months of 1941, British air raids increased in number and intensity over Axis-controlled Europe, and the RAF was rapidly growing in strength. At the same time, German air raids over England diminished as more and more Luftwaffe units went off to the Balkans and the Mediterranean. Germany's skies were becoming British territory.

On March 16, 1941, Hitler admitted the severity of the bombing attacks in public. In a speech at the Berlin Arsenal he said that the home front will have to suffer heavier casualties than before, and it would be not only the men who suffer but "...above all, the women."

SPRING – THE TIME OF THE GENERALS

Every military leader knows that spring, in the northern hemisphere, is the best time of the year to launch major military offensives because of the long period of good weather ahead. The planners working on Barbarossa had hoped to invade Russia in the spring, but now, Germany's armed forces had to be used to rescue the Italians. Most of those forces would be committed to the Balkans and Greece. *a factor in delay*

On March 1, the Bulgarian government of *was the Russian wish* King Boris gave its permission to allow German troops to march through their territory to attack Greece. On March 25, the Yugoslav government of Prince Paul, Regent for young King Peter, did likewise. Then, the next day the situation in Yugoslavia suddenly took a dramatic turn. A clique of Yugoslav generals in Belgrade overthrew Prince Paul's government while the Prince was still in Germany. They proclaimed Peter as King and declared that Yugoslavia would continue its policy of neutrality and that German troops would not be permitted to pass.

Hitler went into a rage. Within minutes, he made the decision to erase Yugoslavia from the face of the map. Within hours, many of the German planners working on Barbarossa were ordered to shelve their

work and concentrate on the elimination of Yugoslavia. Now, Hitler had another war on his hands and the clock of spring was running out.

Knowing that all of Yugoslavia's neighbors, except for Greece, had territorial claims against Yugoslavia, they were secretly contacted and asked to join in the conquest. None refused.

On April 6, German troops invaded Yugoslavia from the north, and within days, the other members of the coalition joined in. Also, German and Bulgarian forces invaded the eastern panhandle of Greece (Thrace) from Bulgaria. Having been attacked from all sides, the Yugoslav position was hopeless and the country surrendered on April 14. The Greeks followed suit and surrendered on the 23rd and the British forces withdrew to Egypt.

Yugoslavia was dismembered and its component parts were divided into two small independent nations, Croatia and Serbia, while the remaining territory was doled out to the members of the coalition; Italy, Hungary, Romania, Bulgaria and Germany.

Croatia was taken over by local Croatian fascists under the leadership of Ante Pavelic. Pavelic soon brought Croatia into the Axis alliance and took for himself a fascist title, "Pogrovnic" (leader). Serbia, the heart of Yugoslav nationalism, became an occupied country with a puppet government under General Milan Nedic, a Petain-like figure.

Germany's reward for the conquest of Yugoslavia was the acquisition of half of Slovenia, the northernmost province of Yugoslavia bordering Austria. Italy took the other half. The Slovenes were westernized slavs, much like the Czechs, and the decision was eventually made in Berlin that they were suitable for Germanization. The Italians took a similar view and made plans to Italianize their Slovenes.

Greece did not disappear from the map as had been the case with Yugoslavia. Its national territory, though, was reduced to about half its pre-war size. Most of the new

Germany intended to have a permanent outlet to the Mediterranean via the Aegean Sea and a measure of control over the Turkish Straits.

Greece was occupied by the Italians with the exception of the following areas, which were occupied by the Germans; Athens, the Salonica area, part of eastern Thrace bordering Turkey known as Domotika, and several Aegean island; Thasos, Samothrace, Lemkos, Lesbos and Khios in the Aegean Sea. A puppet government was installed in Athens under General Zolakoglou, another Petain-like figure. The Italians annexed an area of northwestern Greece and several islands in the Adriatic Sea adding them to Albania. Bulgaria annexed the remainder of Thrace giving that county an outlet to the Aegean Sea.

Hitler intended that the German occupation of Salonica be permanent, giving Germany a window on the Mediterranean. Domotika and the Aegean islands near the entrance to the Straits were another matter. These areas had been ceded to Greece by Turkey after World War I and might be held permanently, or they might be used as bargaining chips in future negotiations with Turkey.

Athens would eventually be returned to the Greeks.

BACK TO BARBAROSSA

Most of the German troops were withdrawn from Greece and the German planners went back to work on Barbarossa. At this point, it might seem that Hitler's problems in the Balkans were over, but this was not the case. The large Greek island of Crete, approximately 100 miles off the southern tip of mainland Greece, was still in Allied hands. Like Greece, Crete was within bomber range of the Romanian oil fields. Since an amphibious invasion of Crete was out of the question because of the inadequacies of the Italian Navy, Hitler ordered that the island be taken in an air assault by German paratrooper and glider forces. These were well-trained elite forces that were to take part in Barbarossa, but now they would not be available for the opening of that campaign. *Heavy casualties*

WOMEN TO THE FACTORIES

Because of the increasing need for more soldiers and more materials of war, the labor shortage in Germany was getting worse. It was at this point that Hitler had to compromise on one of Nazism's most sacred tenants — that the woman's place was in the home. During May, Hitler authorized German industry to begin recruiting German women.

IRAQ, SYRIA, LEBANON

While preparations were being made for the air assault on Crete, still another problem developed for the Germans and Italians. This time, it was in the Middle Eastern country of Iraq. Iraq was an independent country which had very strong military ties to Britain, and a sizeable British military presence existed within its borders.

Several months earlier, a nationalistic clique of Iraqi Army officers gained control of the government and installed one of their own, Rashid Ali el-Gailani, as Premier, who soon demanded that the British leave. London refused, citing agreements with previous Iraqi governments.

Matters deteriorated and, on May 2, 1941, the Iraqi Army rebelled against the British and the Gailani government declared war on Britain. Gailani asked for help from Germany and Italy; both agreed, and sent small contingents of German and Italian-piloted aircraft to Iraq. Additional aid was to be supplied to Iraq via German and Italian air lifts. The German and Italian military aid was too little, however, to tip the balance in Iraq and the British were able to suppress the rebellion, oust the Gailani government and install one favorable to Britain.

But all this, in turn, caused yet another problem for the Axis and drew Vichy into the conflict as well. In order to get their aircraft to Iraq, the Germans and Italians had to land in Vichy-controlled Syria to refuel since their aircraft did not have the range to reach Iraq from the Axis-controlled air fields in the Balkans. Also, the Vichy French, under pressures from Germany and Italy, sent some war supplies of their own to the Iraqis and allowed volunteers from Syria and Lebanon to go to Iraq.

These acts were blatant violations of Vichy's self-proclaimed neutrality. Subsequently, the British used these unfriendly activities as justification to invade Syria and Lebanon. That invasion began on June 8 from Palestine with a contingent of de Gaulle's Free French as part of the invading force. The Vichy-controlled French forces resisted, but were eventually defeated, and by mid-July, the British and Free French had taken complete control of Syria and Lebanon.

During this Iraqi interlude, Fritz von Papen, Germany's ambassador to Turkey, began negotiating an agreement with the Turkish government for the passage of Axis troops through Turkey to the Middle East. The Turks did not want this, but dared not to refuse Germany's request, especially in light of what had happened in Yugoslavia. As a result, the Turks stalled. During these negotiations Hitler, through Papen, offered a treaty of friendship under which Germany would guarantee Turkey's integrity and reward her with some territorial "adjustments" along the Bulgarian border — obviously Domotika — and one or more of the Aegean islands. The rapid collapse of the Iraqi rebellion made further negotiations on the passage of German troops meaningless, but negotiations continued on the treaty of friendship. Agreement was reached on this, but with no provisions for the passage of German troops through Turkey and no territorial adjustments. The treaty of friendship, signed on June 18, dealt mostly with trade and commerce. Turkey, however, had been drawn closer to the Axis.

The Iraqi affair had both pros and cons for the Axis Powers. On the plus side, Hitler and Mussolini, the latter being the Protector of Islam, had demonstrated that they were willing to militarily support an Arab uprising against the British. This was a valuable tool in their respective propaganda campaigns directed toward the Arab world. In addition, Germany now had a treaty of some value with Turkey.

On the minus side, the British, having moved into Syria, were on the southern border of Turkey and were in a better position now to influence events in that country. Also, the Free French had two more parts of the French colonial empire under their control and new recruiting grounds for their armed forces as well as added tax revenues to support their war effort.

Perhaps, most detrimental of all to the Axis Powers, was the fact that when, in the near future, the Axis Powers made their move to take over the Middle East, three countries, Iraq, Syria, and Lebanon, which otherwise would have been cooperative, were now under Allied control. The cost of the future conquest of the Middle East had risen. Hitler, however, did not seem too concerned about this. On June 8, he told Ribbentrop that after Barbarossa, German troops would march through Turkey and retake Syria and also bring Iraq back into the Axis fold.

BACK TO BARBAROSSA — AGAIN

As a result of his involvement in the Balkans and the Middle East, Hitler was obliged to advance the launch date for Barbarossa to June 22, 1941, the second day of summer. Barbarossa would no longer be a spring offensive. *Grave delay, rather*

Nevertheless, Hitler was confident that the conquest of European Russia might still be concluded in 1941 or, at the latest, by spring 1942.

But the troubles in the Balkans simply would not go away. In Yugoslavia, two guerilla organizations had emerged and were growing rapidly. One organization, the "Chetniks", was loyal to King Peter and the royal government, now in exile, and the other, known as the "Partisans," was led by a mysterious communist figure named "Tito." So here again, Hitler and Mussolini were obliged to commit more of their armed forces to contain this new menace. What is more, several additional guerilla organizations were emerging in Greece. Also, fearing an Allied invasion of the Iberian Peninsula while Germany was engaged in Russia, Hitler, on May 8, ordered that a plan be created for German troops to occupy the Atlantic coasts of both Spain and Portugal in case the British might try to invade those countries. The plan was called "Operation Isabella." Here again, more German forces would have to be held in reserve and would not be available for Barbarossa.

Finally, on May 20, the invasion of Crete got underway. It was successful and brief, but costly, and an experience Hitler did not want to repeat.

During that offensive, however, the Luftwaffe and Axis subs took a heavy toll on the British Navy, sinking an aircraft carrier, three cruisers and six destroyers and damaging three British battleships, six cruisers and seven destroyers. Accordingly, Hitler was very impressed with the ability of his aircraft to sink warships.

The victory in Crete caused Hitler to rethink his ability to conquer islands, so he turned his attention, once again, to the Portuguese Azores in the North Atlantic.

One of Hitler's fears was that while the bulk of Germany's forces were in the East, the United States might enter the war on Britain's side. If this came about, he wanted a way to attack America. This could be accomplished by positioning submarines closer to the North American continent and by using the new long range ME-264 "Amerika Bomber," which was currently under development. With this in mind, Hitler summoned Admiral Raeder for a meeting on May 22 to discuss once again, the possibility of Germany occupying the Azores.

Raeder discouraged an attack on the Azores claiming that, once occupied, they could not be supplied in the face of the British Navy. And, he argued, if the American Navy joined in, the task would be even more difficult. Hitler was not convinced. It was his opinion that German submarines could keep the lackadaisical American tied up in their home waters and that the Luftwaffe, flying out of both the Azores and Europe, could protect the German supply ships.

The German ME-264 "Amerika Bomber," designed to bomb the American east coast from Europe. This bomber shows a strong resemblance to the Boeing B-29 long-range bomber then under development in the United States.

No decision was made with regard to the Azores, but Hitler considered it a viable option for the near future.

The Americans could see the German threat to the Azores and, by an interesting coincidence, on the day after Hitler and Raeder talked, President Roosevelt ordered the American Army and Navy to prepare a plan to send 25,000 American soldiers to the Azores in case they became threatened. Thus, the stage was set for an armed clash between American and German forces far out in the North Atlantic. Such action would, undoubtedly, bring the United States into the war on the side of Britain. As for what Portugal would do, that was undetermined.

On May 27, Raeder's words rang true as reports reached Hitler that the battleship "Bismarck" had been chased down and sunk by the British Navy off the coast of France. It would be these very waters that the Germans would have to control in order to keep their sea lanes open to the Azores. Not surprisingly, Hitler said little about attacking the Azores thereafter.

Raeder, however, kept up the facade that the German Navy could control most of the eastern Atlantic and parts of the Indian Ocean. On June 20, he sent Hitler a report suggesting that, in addition to the bases already agreed upon along the European Atlantic coast, Germany should establish additional Atlantic naval bases in Iceland (a recent development in planning); the Canary Islands; the Cape Verde Islands; Casablanca, French Morocco; Dakar, French West Africa; Duala, Cameroons; and Point Noire, French Equatorial Africa. In the Indian Ocean, Raeder suggested that bases be established on the island of Madagascar, and in some of the island groups to the east.

As for the Canary Islands, Raeder suggested that an entire island might be ceded to Germany by Spain in exchange for French Morocco, less, of course, Casablanca.

And there was more. At various times Raeder put forth suggestions that yet another base be established at Bathurst, Gambia (British), which was south of Dakar, and that South West Africa, on the southwestern corner of Africa, be exchanged with Britain for the British colony of Kenya in East Africa. South West Africa had been a German colony before World War I and was given to the Union of South Africa, a British Commonwealth Nation, to control under a mandate from the League of Nations. Under this scenario, Germany would simply relinquish its claim to South West Africa and take over Kenya.

The Navy also recommended that at the peace conference, a new naval tonnage ratio might be established between Germany, Italy, Britain and France of 4-2-2-1, but with the British and French not being allowed to have submarines. This report went on to predict that it was reasonable to expect that, in the years that followed, the British and French Navies would cooperate with the Axis Navies, especially if their colonial empires were threatened by a third party such as the United States.

BARBAROSSA NEARS – PLANNING BEGINS FOR THE POST-BARBAROSSA PERIOD

With the military planning for Barbarossa nearing completion, Hitler turned his attention to the period immediately following Barbarossa. This became the basis for his Directive Number 32 issued on June 11, 1941 — eleven days before the launch date of Barbarossa. Directive 32 acknowledged that, as already planned, about 60 army divisions were to be left in the East to pacify the conquered areas and man the A-A Line. A relatively strong Luftwaffe force, consisting of one Air Fleet, would also remain and continue to attack the Soviets east of the Ural Mountains.

The bulk of the German forces would be returned to Germany and the armed forces restructured. In the words of the Directive, it was stated, "The defense of this area (conquered Europe), and foreseeable future offensive action, will require considerably smaller military forces than have been needed hitherto."

Once accomplished, the new Wehrmacht, in conjunction with Italian forces, would then conquer the Middle East and parts of Africa. It could be expected that Iraq, Iran, Turkey, Spain and Vichy France would join the Axis and participate in the final battles against Britain. The various Arab liberation movements in the region would also be helpful and were to be aided.

The cooperation of France would be crucial with regard to North and West Africa. The Directive stated, "Closer cooperation between Germany and France ... will eliminate the threat from the rear in the North African theater of war, will further restrict the movements of the British Fleet in the Western Mediterranean and will protect the southwestern flank of the European theate... from Anglo-Saxon attack."

As for the Middle East and Egypt, the Directive went on to say that the struggle against the British positions in the Mediterranean and in the Middle East will be continued by converging attacks launched from Libya through Egypt, from Bulgaria through Turkey, and from the Caucasus as well. The Directive stated further that the German operation from Bulgaria through Turkey will be planned, with the aim of capturing the Suez Canal from the East. A target date for the beginning of the attack from Libya was set for November 1941.

Paragraph 2d of the Directive was entitled, "Exploitation of the Arab Freedom Movement." It stated that the situation of the English in the Middle East will be weakened if more British forces are tied down by civil commotion of revolt. All military, political, and propaganda measures to this end were to be closely coordinated.

Paragraph 3 dealt in detail with Gibraltar, West Africa and Central Africa. It stated that preparations for 'Undertaking Felix' (the march through Spain to take Gibraltar — already planned), would be resumed even during the course of operations in the East. After the capture of Gibraltar, it was stated, only such forces will be moved into Spanish Morocco as are needed to control the Strait of Gibraltar.

The Directive further stated that the defense of the seaboard of North and West Africa, the elimination of English possession in West Africa, and the recovery of the areas controlled by de Gaulle, (the colony of French Equatorial Africa) would be the responsibility of the French, who will be granted such reinforcements as the situation required. The directive went on to state that the use of West African bases by the German Navy and Air Force, and possibly also the occupation of the Atlantic Islands, will be facilitated by Germany and Spain controlling the Strait of Gibraltar.

It was foreseen that one or more modern transportation corridors would have to be built across the Sahara Desert into central Africa so that the army there could be adequately supplied. A sea route along the west coast of Africa might be secured with the help of the French Navy and German bases at strategic locations along the coast. Spain could be expected to cooperate in this endeavor and allow transit across her West African colony of Rio de Oro and the use of the Canary Islands off the coast of Africa.

Once these routes were secured, German forces, accompanied by French troops, would cross the Sahara and sweep along the west coast of Africa, conquering the British colonies of Gambia, Sierra Leone, Gold Coast and Nigeria. These colonies would then be given to France as her reward for joining the Axis as well as compensation for French territorial losses in Europe.

Parts of the British colonies of Gold Coast and Nigeria, along with some French colonial territory, would have to be given to Germany so that the lost German colonies of Togo and Cameroons could be reestablished. Additionally, territorial concessions would have to be made to Spain for her cooperation. But the area in question was huge and there would be plenty for all.

From occupied Nigeria, the French would move into the central and southern parts of French Equatorial Africa liberating that colony from the Free French. It was to be expected that the northern part of the colony, adjoining Libya, would be invaded by the Italians to secure territorial claims that Rome had in that region.

Once French Equatorial Africa was secured, Axis forces would be on the northern bank of the Congo River with the Belgian Congo, and its capital, Leopoldville, on the other side. Here, German forces would take the offensive. They would secure Leopoldville along with the western part of the Belgian Congo, and using the natural transportation route of the Congo River, move deep into the interior to take the northern part of the colony and the colony's third largest city, Stanleyville.

Securing the mineral-rich "Copper Belt" region in the extreme southern part of the Belgian Congo, along with Elizabethville, the colony's second largest city, would be a difficult undertaking. Between the Congo River, in the north, and the Copper Belt lay about 700 miles of very primitive landscape with only light-duty and intermittent rail, road and water routes available. For this reason, the German planners could see that it might be easier to conquer the Copper Belt region by an advance down the east coast of Africa.

These were weighty decisions that had to be left to the future.

Directive 32 went on to cover other matters after the conclusion of Barbarossa. Article 4 stated that the siege of England was to be resumed with the utmost intensity by the Navy and Air force, and that visible preparations for the invasion of England along the Channel coast would serve the double purpose of tying down English forces at home and eventually bringing about a final English collapse through a landing in England.

The Directive concluded by stating that the operations planned in the Mediterranean and the Near East might best be achieved by a simultaneous attack on Gibraltar, Egypt and Palestine.

Off the record, Hitler also discussed with his associates the possibility of establishing a land route to Japan.

LAST MINUTE DEVELOPMENTS BEFORE BARBAROSSA

The massive buildup of German forces along the German/Soviet border did not go unnoticed by the Soviets. A large part of the Red Army had been stationed on the border and was on high alert.

On June 8, German troops began arriving in Finland. They moved on to the northernmost part of the country where they were to assist the Finns in an advance along the coast of the Arctic Ocean to take the Soviet seaport of Murmansk.

Beginning in mid-June, the Soviets suddenly began deporting Lithuanians, Latvians and Estonians to Siberia. They were people of good blood who would never serve the Germans.

As late as June 20, Rosenberg was still out of sync with Hitler and other top Nazis on the future political developments in the East. In speaking to a group of his closest associates, he told them that once the Ukraine was conquered, it would be set up as an independent country. Hitler was determined that this would never happen.

On June 21, Hitler wrote a letter to Mussolini, telling him of Germany's plans to invade the Soviet Union. The next morning, he phoned Mussolini, at 3:00 a.m., to tell him that the invasion had begun.

BARBAROSSA LAUNCHED

During the early morning hours of June 22, all three German Army Groups, consisting of a total of 227 divisions, surged across the Soviet border using their Blitzkrieg tactics. Within hours, the unstoppable attacks had broken through the Soviet lines at several places. The Soviets were no better at stopping the Blitzkrieg than had been the Poles, British, or the French. Surprise attacks by the Luftwaffe caught and destroyed some 500 Soviet planes parked on the Russian airfields.

German motorized infantry poured through the holes created by the Blitzkrieg attacks, circled about and surrounded hundreds of thousands of Soviet troops. The tank columns then surged on to the east against very light Soviet opposition. In Germany, after most of the German citizens had awakened, Hitler went on the radio to announce the invasion and its goals. He ended his speech by asking God to aid the German effort.

The next day, June 23, Hungary declared war on the Soviet Union and began mobilizing its army for action in the East. By nightfall on the 23rd, German tanks had completely traversed Lithuania and entered Latvia.

By the 24th, some 2,000 Soviet planes had been lost and the Luftwaffe held mastery in the air. On the 25th, Finland declared war on the Soviet Union and ordered its army to join in the assault. On the 28th, Minsk, the capital of Belorussia and the first major Russian city in the invader's path, was surrounded by German forces. It was besieged and fell on July 9.

On June 27, Lvov and Brest-Litovsk fell. That same day, Stalin had the Soviet commander in the west executed. On July 1, Riga, the capital of Latvia, fell.

The Einsatzgruppen followed the advancing German troops, as planned, and began their gruesome work. As expected, they found many willing collaborators to assist them in their mission. By July 2, some 7,000 people had been executed, mostly Jews.

Romania, too, had its killing squads, the "Escalon Special," which added more victims to the tally. During July and August, the Romanian squads killed some 150,000 Jews in Bessarabia.

On July 3, Stalin ordered that the "scorched earth" policy be applied — a sign that the Soviet leadership expected the retreat to continue. At this point, it appeared that Hitler was right, the door to the Soviet Union had been kicked in and the evil regime was crashing down.

Throughout July, the Axis advance continued and the Red Army soldiers sur-

rendered in droves along with much of their equipment. And the other German enemy was not forgotten. On July 27, after a ten-week hiatus, the Luftwaffe renewed air attacks on London.

SURPRISES AND HARD KNOCKS

Not everything was going the Germans' way, however. The British air offensive over Germany was as intense as ever. The German city of Munster was bombed three nights in a row and one-forth of it destroyed. On July 8, the British bombed Wilhelmshaven using, for the first time, American-built B-17 "Flying Fortresses." The RAF now had a new, and very proficient, source for warplanes — America.

On the Eastern Front, the Germans had discovered that the nice red lines on the Russian maps did not necessarily depict paved roads. In many places the red lines were roads of gravel and in some places, dirt. Only time would tell what they would be like when the fall rains came. The Soviet railroads were wanting, too, and of a different gage, but this was foreseen. In July, the Germans began a major overhaul of the Soviet railroads so that the German forces could be adequately supplied as they moved eastward. Many hiwis were used as laborers.

Also on the Eastern Front, the Russians had introduced two new weapons that the Germans knew nothing about. The first was the heavily-armored "KV" tank which the Germans found almost unstoppable. And there were large numbers of them.

The second new Soviet weapon consisted of a truck-mounted cluster of rocket launchers known as "Katyushas." The Germans had such cluster rockets, but did not expect the Soviets to have them. These rockets, fired in rapid succession, could devastate an area of enemy terrain within a few seconds killing or wounding nearly everyone in that area who was not totally protected.

Then, there was a surprise at Moscow. As the German forces advanced and Moscow became within range of German aircraft, the Luftwaffe began bombing the city. But the Germans discovered on the very first raid that the Soviet anti-aircraft defenses were extremely intense and effective. Aircraft losses were higher than expected. The Luftwaffe continued the raids, but they took heavy losses.

As the German ground forces sped eastward, pockets of Red Army troops were bypassed and German troops had to be left behind to keep them contained. By now, many Soviet soldiers, and some entire units, had escaped encirclement and melted into the forests, swamps and other remote places with sizeable quantities of their arms and equipment. There, they formed into Partisan units and continued to resist. The German planners had anticipated this, but expected it to be a minor problem as had been the case during World War I. The German plans were that the guerrillas would be contained during the conquest and eliminated later.

During July, the Russians began one of the greatest human endeavors of the war — the relocation of their industrial plants from the Donets Basis and elsewhere to new locations east of the Ural Mountains. This undertaking continued night and day for five months, relocating over 1,500 factories and hundreds of thousands of workers. These plants would continue to produce for the Soviet war effort so long as they could get fuel and raw materials.

In a way, the relocation of the Soviet industrial plants and hundreds of thousands of people fed into the German's overall plan to vacate the land for future German settlers. But it was a tradeoff that mostly benefitted the Soviets.

On August 2, the United States and the Soviet Union signed an agreement whereby the Soviet Union would receive massive amounts of war materials from America. This was an extension of America's "Lend-Lease" program, enacted in March 1941, through which those nations fighting the Axis Powers would receive American-made equipment now and return it later.

LAND FOR ALL

In accordance with the pre-invasion planning, the Russian people were subjected to an intense propaganda campaign designed to enlist their support. The overall theme was that the Germans had come as liberators and would create a new order of freedom and social justice for the peoples of the East. One of the main themes was that the hated and compulsory collective farming system would be eliminated in favor of privately owned farms and voluntary collectives. The German propaganda made clear that those who actively supported the German war effort now would be favored when the time came to redistribute the land. To placate the Russian peasants even more, the Germans gave those who worked on collective farms wage increases or, in some cases, allowed them to enlarge their private garden plots up to two hectares.

Another promise put forward at this time was that the Germans would bring back religious freedom. Details, however, were not spelled out.

These efforts paid off handsomely for the Germans because thousands of local people came forward to offer their services.

The Soviet leaders were well aware of what was happening so they made it a policy to evacuate those individuals who had skills that might be helpful to the German war effort. As a result, most of the hiwis employed by the Germans were unskilled laborers.

A MODERN-DAY CRUSADE

For years, the fear of communism had been wide-spread throughout Europe. So, it was not surprising that when the defeat of communism appeared to be at hand, many Europeans wanted to aid in that effort. The Germans had anticipated this and had propaganda programs in place to encourage this support and create a crusade-like atmosphere throughout Europe. The governments of Denmark, Norway, Spain, Vichy, Croatia and Slovakia all offered volunteer combat forces and service units for use in the East.

In leaderless occupied countries such as the Netherlands and Belgium, individuals were encouraged to step forward and offer their services. Neutral countries, such as Switzerland and Sweden, offered no formal help but many of their citizens found ways to offer their services to the Germans. Then too, the Vatican made it known that it would welcome the demise of atheistic communism.

All of this represented a new and large source of manpower for the German armed forces. The decision, therefore, had to be made on how best to use these people. By the end of June, Hitler made that decision. Generally, volunteers of military age and of good blood would be utilized by the Waffen SS while the others would be utilized by the Army. The offer of services from Czechs and Russians would be rejected, but Ukrainians, Cossacks and others would be accepted.

The foreigner would first be formed into legions and, as their numbers grew, into larger units up to division size.

Since the men assigned to the Waffen SS were of good blood, they were given extensive training and equipped with the best weapons. Thus, they were considered to be elite units and were often thrust into the most critical parts of the front.

As rewards for their services, they were promised that they would receive the same postwar benefits as German soldiers and would be given priority treatment if they chose to become settlers in the East.

COME NOW THE ADMINISTRATORS

As the front moved eastward, the German civil administrators moved in to begin the process of setting up their respective administrations. As this happened, the propaganda campaign directed toward the local peoples escalated. Posters were put up everywhere informing the people as to how they were to act. Pictures of Hitler, with the inscription "Hitler the Liberator," were handed out by the thousands.

But the German administration of the East was starting off on bad footing. Being an administrator in the East had little glamour and few sought out the new posts. Furthermore, the best administrators were already assigned to posts in other parts of Europe. Therefore, administrators of lesser capabilities were sent to the east. At times, coercion had to be used to fill positions. Also, administrative supervisors took this opportunity to rid themselves of incompetent individuals and trouble-makers. The practice was so widespread that these people gained the nickname "Ostniete" (East failures). The territories given to the new administrators were usually very large due to the on-going German manpower shortage and to Hitler's belief that if the British could rule India with a skeleton force of administrators, the Germans could do likewise in the East.

As the administrators went into the smaller towns, they sought out the village elders to see who would, and would not, cooperate with them. Local mayors and police chiefs were appointed and police organizations formed. Also, able-bodied men were recruited to form para-military units to help the Germans keep order and guard against Partisan activities. These para-military forces were usually equipped with captured Soviet arms and equipment.

HE DID IT AGAIN

In Germany and the other Axis nations, the mood of the people was ecstatic. Hitler had brought them another great victory — this time over communism. As the German armies moved ever eastward and photos of tens of thousands of Russian prisoners of war appeared in the newspapers and newsreels, responsible individuals spoke out in public and in private saying that the war was won.

At Hitler's headquarters optimism reigned. Halder predicted the Russians would last only two more weeks. Hitler estimated six.

This type of thinking reached across the ocean and into the highest political offices in America. On June 23, while the German

Blitzkrieg was still in the process of bursting through the Soviet lines, Secretary of the Navy, Frank Knox, told Roosevelt, "...the best opinion I can get is that it will take anywhere from six weeks to two months for Hitler to clean up on Russia."

FOR POSTERITY

Because of the new world order unfolding in Europe, it was deemed appropriate that the private conversations of the man who was bringing it all about should be recorded for posterity. This began on July 5, 1941. A stenographer was engaged to be in the room and record the conversations when Hitler and his closest associates dined together, which was the norm at the Fuehrer's headquarters. It was at this time the great man talked openly and freely with his dinner companions.

Hitler dined with the same people most of the time, although guests were often included. Also, the "regulars" were not always present. Hitler's dinner table normally had six places. To his right sat Otto Dietrich, Reich Press Chief and Goebbels' representative; then came Luftwaffe General Karl Bodenschatz, Goering's representative; then, directly opposite Hitler was Field Marshal Wilhelm Keitel, Chief of the High Command of the Armed Forces (OKW); then Martin Bormann, Nazi Party Secretary and, to Hitler's left, General Alfred Jodl, OKW Chief of Operations. The mid-day meal began about 2:00 p.m., then tea was at 5:00 p.m. and supper was between 7:30 and 8:00 p.m.

Hitler, the vegetarian with the nervous gut, was a light eater and had his own special diet. Usually he finished first, at which time he launched into his monologues. When Hitler spoke, no one dared to interrupt. And he spoke and spoke and spoke. Two hours of Fuehrer dialogue was common.

The stenographer's transcripts were edited by both Hitler and Bormann and many passages were deleted. Then, two copies were made. One set was sent to the German archives office in Munich, and the second

was given to Eva Braun who kept and filed that set for her's and Hitler's use.

Hitler's table talk was often interesting, frequently repetitive, sometimes vindictive and heavily focused on the future. Here, in the pleasant atmosphere of dining, Hitler expressed his loves and hatreds. He loved the German people, the New Order he was bringing about, art, architecture, music and a host of grand schemes for the future. He hated the Jews, the Russians, Churchill, royalty, organized religions, judges and lawyers.

Excerpts from the first two transcripts at lunch and dinner on Saturday, July 5, 1941, give an example of the wide range of topics discussed. Hitler said that the Fascist movement was a spontaneous return to the honorable traditions of ancient Rome and that the Italians were as diligent as an ant. As for the Russian, Hitler said that the principle support for their civilization was vodka and it was doubtful as to whether anything can be done in Russia without the help of the Orthodox priest. It were the priest, Hitler continued, who had reconciled the Russian to the fatal necessity of work by promising him more happiness in another world. Hitler went on saying that he thought there was petroleum in "thousands of places. Mankind, Hitler declared, was the most dangerous "microbe" imaginable. As for the Crimea, he said, we shall make it accessible by means of an autobahn and that it will be Germany's Riviera. Croatia too, he said was a tourists' paradise.

Hitler's ramblings continued. He said that he expected that after the war there would be a great upsurge of rejoicing. And on still another subject he said that to those people who ask whether it will be enough to utilize the Ural Mountains as an eastern frontier, he would reply "...that for the present it is enough... "

After supper, there was almost always a movie shown with servants, cooks, secretaries, guards and others invited. Hitler always selected the movie. Then, after the movie, Hitler would sit with various individuals by the fireplace, talk, drink tea, maybe a little champaign, sometimes eat cake or sandwiches, and await the midnight situation conference.

A MILITARY STAND DOWN

On July 8, Hitler ordered the army to begin making plans for the billeting of German troops in the East over the winter. On July 14, he issued Directive 32a, a supplement to his Directive 32 of June 11, ordering that the emphasis on German armaments production now be shifted from the needs of the Army to the needs of the Luftwaffe and Navy. The panzer divisions would continue to be maintained, however, and would be built up from twenty divisions to thirty-six by May 1942. These measures were to be taken in preparation for the renewal of hostilities against Britain and for the coming highly-mobile battles in the Middle East and Africa.

Directive 32a further stated that all industrial contracts for military armaments to be delivered beyond "…six months ahead…" be canceled. Exceptions to this were the armaments intended for those units that were to operate in "the tropics."

A GERMAN COLONIAL OFFICE — THE FUTURE GERMAN EMPIRE

With Directive 32 and 32a fresh in his mind, and victory in the East a certainty, Hitler gathered his top associates together at his headquarters on July 16 to create a new cabinet-level ministry, and to make further plans for the development of the East, the Middle East and Africa.

The new ministry was to be called the "Ostministeriam" (East Ministry) and would serve as a colonial office such as those in the governments of the other great colonial powers. Alfred Rosenberg was assigned to be its head. At this point, however, the East Ministry had very little power so long as hostilities were in progress.

The next day, July 17, Hitler issued a decree establishing the Reichscommissariat

(RK) of the Ukraine with the city of Rovno as its capital. Kiev, the traditional capital of the Ukraine, was purposely bypassed to prevent any vestige of Ukrainian nationalism from coming to the fore. The Crimea was to be a temporary part of the RK Ukraine until it could be reorganized and annexed directly to Germany. With the creation of the RK Ukraine, Germany now had its first colony in the East.

To the southeast of RK Ukraine lay the oil-rich Caucasus. Here, the German goal remained the same — that that area would be occupied, long-term, by Germany, and that the three Caucasus states at the southern end of the region would be granted their independence. As for Azerbaijan, however, Hitler had recently added another condition regarding that state. He said that the oil fields around the Caspian Sea port of Baku, the capital of Azerbaijan, should be tightly controlled by Germany because it would not be wise to allow the Azerbaijanis, alone, to control such a valuable asset.

In discussing the future of the Caucasus, Hitler suggested, and it was generally agreed, that the cities of Rostov and Astrakhan should be included in the German-controlled area and not the RK Ukraine. Furthermore, the traditional rivalries between the peoples of the Caucasus should be encouraged in order to stymie any attempt by the Caucasian peoples to establish a unified political agenda.

Germany's allies, Finland and Romania, were also discussed. Hitler said that, one day, Finland might be incorporated into Greater Germany. But for now, it would remain independent. He added that plans must be made to insure that Germany gained control of the extensive nickel deposits on the Kola Peninsula, an area which would probably be given to the Finns. It was also agreed that the Leningrad area would be offered to the Finns after the city had been razed and that the Neva River would become the new boundary between Finland and Ostland. Finns found living in the occupied areas of

Hungary's reward for participating in the conquest of the East would be the expansion of its eastern border to the Dniester River.

the East and among the Soviet POWs would be returned to Finland.

Since the Romanians were fighting well in the southern Ukraine, Hitler said that they should receive Transniestria, the territory they sought east of the Dniester River. This was dependent, of course, on Romania's continuing military successes and political cooperation.

Hungary would be rewarded for its participation in the war by acquiring the ancient principality of Halicz and some land on both sides of the Carpathian Mountains extending eastward to the Dniester River. Most of this territory would be detached from the General Government and awarded to Hungary.

With regard to the Middle East, Hitler said, massive ground operations, such as those employed in the Soviet Union, would not be needed, but increased air power and fast and mobile armored tank formations would. Hitler ordered that the military planners begin a study, called "Plan Orient," for the conquest of the Middle East with an attack from the Caucasus into Iran, and from Turkey into Syria and Iraq. Hitler estimated that ten German Army divisions, half of

them panzers, would be sufficient for the attack through Turkey.

In Libya and Egypt, Hitler said, the German and Italian forces would go on the defensive and be reinforced. And then, there was another problem in North Africa that had to be addressed. Ever since early 1941, reports had reached Berlin from both Axis and neutral sources that the Allies were planning to invade French North Africa. This had to be factored into Germany's planning in North Africa.

After Syria, Iraq and Iran had been conquered; the forces in the Middle East would move into Palestine and attack the British in Egypt from the east. At that time, the forces in Libya would advance on Cairo from the west.

With regard to the East in general, Hitler ordered that no more tanks be sent there. He believed that those already committed would be sufficient to complete the conquest. Also, Hitler ordered that those units remaining in the East should be equipped with second-line, and captured, arms and equipment.

When asked where the remnants of the Russian armed forces might go, Hitler replied that they would very likely go behind the Urals, or beyond, and that German forces would not follow them.

Once the Red Army was forced out of the future RK Muscovy, Hitler said, the city of Moscow would be liquidated. And he had a plan. A dam would be built on the Moskva River and the city flooded under a giant reservoir to extinguish its memory forever.

JEWS TO SIBERIA?

During the summer of 1941, it had been decided in Berlin that holding Europe's Jews in ghettos in the East was proving to be unworkable. It was too expensive and took too much manpower. The question now arose among the top German leaders as to what to do with the Jews.

During July, Hitler gave a hint of his thinking at this time with regard to the Jews. He met with the Foreign Minister of Croatia and in the discussions Hitler suggested that Europe's Jews might be sent to Siberia. Just how this would be accomplished was not clear. But, Hitler's reasoning was supported by the fact that there already existed in Siberia, along the Siberian/Chinese border, a political entity known as the "Jewish Autonomous Republic" (JAR). This was one of the Soviet Republics created by the communists in the 1920s at a time when Soviet thinking was that each nationality within the Soviet Union should have its own, well-defined, homeland. For the Jews, their homeland would be the JAR. The scheme, however, failed miserably. Very few Jews went there voluntarily and the communists, fearing an internal upheaval among the Jews and international complications, did not force the issue. But, the communist leaders could not admit to the world that the scheme had been a failure, so the JAR remained on the map.

Hitler, of course, knew this and, judging from his statement to the Croatian Foreign Minister, was very possibly considering the JAR as a Jewish homeland.

But there were other alternatives. On July 31, Goering ordered SS General Reinhard Heydrich to propose a plan to be about "the final solution" to the Jewish question.

BARBAROSSA SURGES ON

By the middle of July, the Germans had some 600,000 Soviet prisoners of war on their hands and another 70,000 deserters. Furthermore, thousands of POWs and deserters offered to serve the Germans as Hiwis and even as combatants. German losses, so far, were set at 8,886 casualties.

The German Army began sorting through the Eastern volunteers for reliable hiwis but none of them would be used, at this time, as combatants. Furthermore, some of the POWS, mostly Ukrainians, who proved to be sufficiently anti-Soviet, were released. Such numbers and attitudes helped to spark an optimistic atmosphere in Germany. Emboldened by these successes, Hitler began, at this time, speaking of advancing some 200 miles beyond the Urals.

But here, in the second month of the war in the East, perhaps Hitler would have done well to heed his own words that he put down in Mein Kampf, concerning the second month of World War I. In 1924, he wrote, "Since the days of September 1914, when for the first time the endless hoards of Russian prisoners ... began moving into Germany ... the stream was almost without end — but for every defeated and destroyed army a new one arose. Inexhaustibly the gigantic Empire gave the Tsar more and more new soldiers ... How long could Germany keep up the pace?"

On July 11, Himmler gave the order to begin kidnapping children of good blood. The first children taken were sent to existing children's homes in cities in eastern Europe such as Riga and Libau, both in Latvia. It was the Germans' plan to keep these children permanently in the East to strengthen the overall Aryan blood line there. These homes quickly filled, however, and children were then "provisionally entrusted" to politically reliable families for their care.

That evening, Hitler told his dinner companions that the time would come when it would no longer be possible to conceive of a form of life different from that in Germany.

"INEXHAUSTIBLY THE GIGANTIC EMPIRE GAVE THE TSAR MORE AND MORE SOLDIERS..."

By the third week in July, Field Marshal Franz Halder, Chief of Staff of the German Army, came to realize that his people had badly underestimated the strength of the Red Army. At the time Barbarossa was launched, the Army leaders estimated that the Russians had between 164 and 200 divisions. Then, on July 8, Halder told Hitler that the Red Army had been so badly mauled that it had only 46 combat ready divisions left. But now, with new information having been received, Halder learned that there had been 360 divisions and that 93 of them were still in the field. He had the unpleasant duty of telling this to Hitler.

Hitler, though, was unperturbed and still confident of victory. Furthermore, he could see a better life for himself in the future. That evening, he told his dinner companions that he was looking forward to the time when his burden of conducting the war would be lifted. He said that his "dearest wish" would be to wander about Italy as an unknown painter.

And he expressed another of his hopes saying, as he had done so often before, that the end of the war would bring about a lasting friendship with Britain. Later, he commented that Britain and America would one day have a war and that one of them would disappear.

GERMANY'S SECOND COLONY

On July 25, 1941, the German Army relinquished control of much of Lithuania, Latvia and parts of Belorussia and turned those areas over to the German civil administrators. The German colony of RK Ostland was born.

On the 27th, Hitler discussed the East at dinner saying that it was his belief that Germany could control their eastern empire with 250,000 men plus a cadre of good administrators. Let's learn from the English, he said, who govern 400 million Indians with only 250,000 administrators and 50,000 soldiers.

He also spoke of the soldier-turned-farmer settlers. Hitler implied that sons of peasant farmers would be preferred as settlers in the East and that Germany would provide them with a completely equipped farm, including a house.

But, Hitler was concerned as to how to keep the new settlers down on the farms so that they would not be tempted to migrate to the cities. Here, he had a unique solution; "One single condition will be imposed on him: that he may not marry a townswoman, but a countrywoman..."

CHAPTER 14

EUPHORIA TURNS TO CONCERN

During the last days of July and the first days of August 1941, Hitler became quite ill. He complained of stomach pains, nausea, dizziness and diarrhea. He also had chills, a high fever and swelling in the legs. His aides said he looked bad, and he missed several situation conferences. Dr. Morell found his blood pressure to be high and diagnosed the illness as a slight case of apoplexy. He prescribed some pills for the symptoms and leeches for the high blood pressure. It took the Fuehrer about two weeks to recover, and even then some of the symptom lingered on throughout the month. All this was during a time when a number of crucial decisions had to be made on the Eastern Front. Hitler ordered that his illness be kept secret.

THE EUPHORIA CONTINUES

On the evening of August 1, it was an ailing, but still enthusiastic Hitler, who talked to his dinner guests once again about his plans for the East. He said that in ten years the settlers in the East would become a German elite class and a race of rulers. He added that such a thing would not happen in the West.

At the next afternoon meal, Hitler lambasted lawyers and the penal system. He said that lawyers take care of the criminals and the unsavory members of society. When it came to punishing young offenders, he said he favored corporal punishment over prison terms. He said that while in prison these youths were at too good a school. There, the hardened criminals teach them that they were stupid to get caught, and should try to do better the next time.

That evening he spoke again about Germany's future. He said that visitors to Germany must be well-treated and be cured of their prejudices against Germany. He repeated what he had said before that he did not want to force National Socialism on anybody. If some countries wanted to remain democratic, he said, they must be allowed to do so.

Then he rambled on about farming, increasing the numbers of livestock, rubber production, energy and other matters. As for rubber, he said that some 100,000 acres in the Crimean region would be devoted to its cultivation. And concerning electrical energy, he predicted that coal would disappear one day, and that the world would be forced to rely more upon water power. He added that dams upon dams could be built on "the slightest slopes." He further predicted that Norway would become the electrical center of Northern Europe and that the winds, the tides and hydrogen would be utilized to generate power.

In table conversations recorded on August 8 through 10, Hitler dreamed on. On colonizing the East, he said that the German colonist should live on handsome and spacious farms, and that the governors should live in palaces. What exists beyond the German settlements, he added, would be "another world," where the local people would live as they pleased. To impress the eastern people of Germany's power, he said that troops of "Kirghizes" should be brought to Berlin from time-to-time in order to show them the size and greatness of its monuments and great buildings. Hitler continued by saying that Germans should no longer be allowed to emigrate to America and that Norwegians, Swedes, Danes and Dutch people, who might otherwise emigrate to the west, should be induced to settle in the Eastern territories. As for the Swiss — the democratic Swiss for whom he had little respect Hitler said, "we can use them...as hotel keepers."

And he spoke again of the huge marsh lands of Russia, saying that there was no need to drain them for farm land because there was adequate farm land already. Instead, they would be incorporated into a gigantic area for military maneuvers some three hundred and fifty by four hundred kilometers in size.

Hitler said that he would not live long enough to see the day when Britain and Germany would march together against America, but that he rejoiced just in the thought of it.

Hitler then switched his attention to the Middle East saying that one very important person there, the Shah of Iran, was "praying" for the moment when the Germans would arrive. "As soon as we drop in on him," Hitler said, he will abandon Britain and become a friend of ours.

Then Hitler — the vegetarian — jumped to the subject of generating commercial gas for the production of vegetables. He spoke of recovering the vapors produced by the manufacture of gas and using them to generate electricity which could warm greenhouses and thereby provide the German cities with fresh fruits and vegetables all winter long. "Nothing is lovelier than horticulture," he said.

MORE SURPRISES IN THE EAST

As more reports flowed into the Fuehrer's headquarters on military conditions in the East, the more ominous the task of conquering this huge land became. By now, the Germans knew that the Soviets had more of virtually everything than that which pre-Barbarossa intelligence information had indicated. On August 8, Goebbels noted in his dairy, "The number of enemy tanks was originally estimated at 10,000, but is now assumed to be 20,000."

As the Luftwaffe acquired airfields in the East, their reconnaissance planes could penetrate further into the interior of Russia and this produced another surprise, that being that the extent of the Soviet industrial complexes east of the Urals was much larger than expected. The Germans could console themselves, however, in the belief that Soviet industry had to have an army to utilize the war materials being produced and that that army was rapidly being decimated.

Another serious problem existed in that thousands of Soviet troops were now wandering behind the German lines, some still resisting, some joining the Partisans, some robbing and looting. German supply columns were one of their favorite targets.

And the propaganda war was heating up. Radio Moscow was broadcasting reports of the horrible treatment being meted out on POWs, Jews and Communist Party members. This was designed to strengthen the resolve of the Soviet soldiers to fight harder, and it had a noticeable effect.

In late August, Stalin ordered that the Volga Germans, living along the Volga River, be forcibly relocated to Siberia. Here were thousands more people of good blood that could no longer be counted on by the Germans to fill the colonial settlements in the East.

MILITARY PLANNING FOR
THE POST-BARBAROSSA PERIOD

In the German Army planning offices back in Berlin, the timetable for defeating the Soviet Union, as laid down in Directive #32, was still being adhered to — at least on paper. And the time had now come to work out details for Plan Orient, the invasion of the Middle East.

Orient called for German forces to be available to invade the Middle East by early 1942. The decision had been made that the invasion of the Middle East would be through both the Caucasus and neutral Turkey. If Turkey resisted, the Axis partners would force their way through.

The German Navy drew up a similar plan calling for German troops to march through Turkey, into Syria, Lebanon, Palestine and on to Suez. Quite understandably, the Navy had more interest in the Suez Canal than did the Army. The Navy plan estimated that this undertaking would take 85 days if Turkey cooperated or 145 days if she did not.

Navy planners were also busy at Raeder's headquarters, determining what the future German Navy would look like after the war. It was estimated that there would be twenty-five battleships, eight aircraft carriers, fifty cruisers, 400 submarines plus numerous smaller vessels. The planners used the phrase, "Atlantic capabilities," to denote that the ships would be designed specifically to operate in, and dominate, the Atlantic Ocean. This implied that both the British and American Navies would be defeated and that the German Navy would have the capability of transporting an amphibious force to the Western Hemisphere and keep it supplied.

The Navy's plans also went forward on future naval bases. One of the most important bases was to be at Trondheim, Norway and this project was to be given top priority. Hitler agreed, and had already authorized in June 1940, that the first of several large wharfs, capable of handling the Navy's largest ships, be built at Trondheim. This was only the beginning. It was estimated that it would take twelve to fifteen years to actually complete all the facilities planned for Trondheim. A part of that planning called for Trondheim to become a major shipbuilding center.

For the near future, however, plans were proceeding for reinforcing the Axis troops in North Africa and the capture of Gibraltar.

"EVERY FIFTEEN OR TWENTY YEARS"

On the evening of August 19, Hitler told his dinner guests that Germany should have a war "every fifteen or twenty years," otherwise the German people will get soft. He also foresaw a significant increase in the German population so that within ten years there would be another ten to fifteen million Germans in the world. Hitler spoke at length, praising those German parents who had large families.

He then expounded on the Ukraine and the Volga Basin, saying that they would become the future granaries of Europe and that the conquered East would provide Germany with many other commodities. He gave the example that if, some time in the future, Sweden refused to sell iron ore to Germany, "We'll get it from Russia."

And as for the Ukrainian people, he added it was alright with him if they lived in their churches.

IRAN

On August 25, 1941, British and Soviet troops invaded the Middle Eastern country of Iran from the south and north respectively. This came as a very unwelcome surprise to the Germans. The government of Reza Shah Pahlevi in Teheran had been cooperating to some degree with the Axis Powers by allowing their agents operate freely within the country. This was an intolerable situation for the Allies — and especially for the United States — who needed a secure route to get Lend-Lease supplies to Russia. Iran had proven to be the best route. For Hitler, the Allied invasion of Iran served as a precedent that might be useful to justify an Axis invasion of Turkey if Turkey refused to cooperate. The leaders in Ankara also saw the parallels.

The Iranian Army resisted but was no match for the Allied forces, and in a few days the country was in Allied hands. Reza Shah was forced to abdicate in favor of his son, Mohammed, who was willing to cooperate with the Allies.

HITLER HAD DOUBTS

On August 28, 1941, Hitler sent a secret memorandum to a very few of his top aides, telling them that Barbarossa was falling behind schedule and that the military goals in the East might not be met by the end of the year. He also stated that it was very unlikely that Japan would attack the Soviet Union via Siberia, as some German leaders had hoped, but would strike toward the south. The memorandum also stated that Turkey and Spain could not be counted upon to become combatants on the Axis side.

ON THE EASTERN FRONT

During the last days of August, German forces began the siege of Leningrad. The German plan was to starve the city into submission rather than to enter it and become engaged in costly house-to-house fighting. The Finns were manning the northern part of the siege line but were not expected to attack the city.

Leningrad, though, was not yet completely surrounded. The Russians had one remaining lifeline from the east which ran across Lake Ladoga. Now, with warm weather, supplies were being ferried to Leningrad by boat. When winter came, trucks could be driven across the ice. For a period in the fall, as well as in the spring when the ice was forming or melting, neither mode of transportation could be used and the city was, during those brief periods, truly isolated.

During the first days of September, Hitler was given the figures on losses in the East. They were considerably higher than expected.

To help compensate for these losses, and to be a part of the great victory that would certainly follow, Italy had sent its first Expeditionary Corps. But, due to transportation problems, they were slow in arriving. Also, the all-volunteer Spanish "Blue Division" had arrived. Most of the men of this unit were veterans of the Spanish Civil War and the Germans had high hopes that the unit would perform well in the East. They would not be disappointed.

The Nazi leaders now had to back down from one of their earlier decisions not to allow local collaborators to bear arms. The Partisan menace had also become greater than expected, so local volunteers were formed into paramilitary units for the purpose of fighting the Partisans and guarding transportation routes and supply dumps. The Partisan menace was especially bad in the Bryansk area.

Local people were badly needed, too, to work on construction projects, especially roads and railroads. Since the invasion, some 2,000 new road bridges and over 400 railroad bridges had been built, along with some 18,000 miles of new rail lines, and another 10,000 miles of rail lines were converted to German gage.

Then too, the Germans allowed the reopening of certain trade schools in the conquered areas to train local people as carpenters, mechanics, electricians, etc. because these services were badly needed by the Wehrmacht.

HITLER PEERS INTO THE FUTURE AGAIN

Hitler's table conversation of September 17 was, once again, on Germany's future. After the final German victory, Hitler said, he foresaw that the Western capitalists would view Germany as a huge new market opening up to them and that this would be good for Germany. He said that it would "...incline the most liberal of the western democrats" to cooperate with their former enemies.

The Fuehrer reminded his listeners that he had little desire to chase the British out of

India, saying that if the English were driven out of India, India would perish.

On educating the "natives" in Germany's new empire, Hitler repeated what he had often said before, that it would be a mistake to educate them beyond a certain point. If they were given a certain level of "half-knowledge," he said that it might be just what's needed for them to conduct a revolution. Hitler added that it was better not to teach them to read, or to give them a locomotive to drive, and that it would be complete "stupidity" to give them land. He said that those best suited for tilling the land would be sought out, given employment and well-treated. Payments to the natives could be made with "...scarves, glass beads and everything that colonial peoples like."

On other subjects, Hitler stated that Germany would one day get citrus fruit, cotton and rubber from the Crimea, and reeds from the Pripet Marshes.

He said that he foresaw the East becoming a popular destination for German tourist. "We'll take them on trips to the Crimea and the Caucasus..," he said, adding that new roads would open up a whole new world for them.

And then there were dinner parties, which were common in European political circles. Hitler hated them. On the 22nd, he said he would do away with them because "One is afflicted the whole evening with the same female neighbor..." He said that cold buffets would be much better.

On the 23rd, Hitler indicated that the Ural Mountains might not be the final eastern frontier of the Reich. He stated that the real frontier was the one that separated the Germanic world from the Slav world and that the Germans had the right to place it where they wanted it to be.

Hitler turned again to religion. He stated that the Church holds out the bait of a better world, but it should be the mission of National Socialism to preach that mankind should live "worthily" here on earth. In the long run, he said that National Socialism will triumph over religion. During this conversation, Hitler made one of his rare comments indicating that he believed in God by saying "God...suddenly hurls the masses of humanity onto the earth, and He leaves it to each one to work out his own salvation."

On September 25, Hitler contradicted, somewhat, the statement he made on the 17th — that the Western democracies would hasten to do business with their former enemies. Now he said that it would be a wise policy for Europe, abandon the idea of exporting its goods to the whole world because whatever is produced in Europe should be retained in Europe in order to give the people the highest possible standard of living. This comment was directed against the United States. Hitler predicted that some time in the future Germany, with all its conquests, would be a big country with tremendous assets and would have twice the population of the United States. This implied that there would be little need to trade with the United States.

Other comments on the future were that, "in twenty years' time," the people of Europe would no longer be emigrating to America but to the East. Hitler was quite redundant on this subject. And he added that the Black Sea would provide an inexhaustible supply of sea food. Thanks to the cultivation of the soy bean, he said that Germany would be able to increase its numbers of livestock, and for the next centuries, have an unequalled field of action. Oh, what a beautiful future awaited Germany!

THE WAR

While Hitler talked of the glories of the future, his servicemen were living and dying in the agonies of the present. In the East, the German juggernaut still advanced, but now more slowly, and at a frightful cost. On September 19, the German Army High Command admitted publicly to suffering 402,865 casualties on the eastern front in seventy-one days of fighting. That translated to 5,674 casualties per day. Two weeks later, the Soviet government put German casualties at three million. And the Soviets still had enough strength to launch occasional, and sometimes very effective, counterattacks. In all likelihood, the high German casualty rate would continue.

Also on September 19, there was good news; Kiev had fallen. When Hitler heard of the fall of Kiev, he was elated. At the time, he was having lunch with Dr. Fritz Todt, the Minister of Armaments and Munitions and Germany's chief builder. This news motivated Hitler to expound again on the future and talk of some projects in considerable detail. For example, Hitler told Todt that the houses to be built for the German people at the port-city of Trondheim, Norway, must be rebuilt facing south in order to receive the full strength of the sun all day long. He also told Todt that autobahns would stretch from Trondheim to the Crimea. And Hitler went on to predict that after the war every German citizen would have the opportunity of "taking his Volkswagen" and personally visiting the conquered territories.

MORE TALK OF THE FUTURE

In dinner conversations from September 27 through early October Hitler talked repeatedly of the future. With regard to Germany's "gifted adolescents," he said that they would be educated at the state's expense and that no door would be closed to them. And, as for the workers, they would have many holidays and would be able to go on a sea-cruise at least "once or twice" in their lifetimes.

On farming in the Ukraine, Hitler said that there should not concentrate too heavily on growing grain but that they should leave room for pasturing. And on the Russian marshes — Hitler seemed to have a fascination with the Russian marshes — they should be left as is, not only so they could be used for military training purposes, but also because they affect the "local climatological conditions."

In his love-hate relationship with the city of Vienna, Hitler said that that city should "declare war on bugs and dirt." The city had to be cleaned up and once that was done, he added that the city will become one of the "loveliest" cities in the world.

Hitler, the self-appointed expert on everything, even delved into the preservation of news reels. He said that the news reels of the war must be preserved for posterity and suggested that they be printed on strips of metal for that purpose.

ON THE GERMAN HOME FRONT

On the first day of September 1941, the initial phase of the euthanasia program — the killing of useless eaters — formally came to an end. But it would continue on an as-needed basis and out of sight from the public

Within about seven months, another and much more horrible program of extermination would begin — against the Jews. That same day, September 1, the Jews of Germany were ordered to begin wearing a yellow star on their outer garments so they could be easily identified. On the 3rd, the first of several gassing experiments were carried out at Auschwitz on small groups of camp inmates to make sure that the newly-installed killing equipment worked properly.

British air raids continued to plague the citizens of Germany. Berlin was bombed several times during September and October.

The labor shortage was as acute as ever, and during September the German government had to reverse a policy it made in July. Then, when it looked as if the war would be won within weeks, the decision was made not to use Soviet POWs as workers in Germany. Now, that was reversed and the Germans began transporting thousands of Soviet POWs to Germany to work. Some 10,000 Soviet POWs, alone, would be sent to the giant Hermann Goering Werks. And this was only the beginning. Tens of thousands more POWs would follow as Germany's need for laborers increased. At this point in time, the Germans had over two million Soviet POWs from whom they could choose.

Already in Germany there were some 3.7 million foreign workers, or about five percent of the population. A steady stream of Ukrainian workers, which were favored by many employers, were coming to Germany, most of them voluntarily. It was soon announced that another 1.6 millions Ukrainians would be brought to Germany.

One of the reasons German industry needed so many workers was that it was more labor-intensive compared to that in the West. This was due to the fact that Hitler and the other decision-makers believed that the war would be short and that mass-production methods would not be needed. Now, the Germans were in a catch-22. To retool German industry for automated mass production would be terribly expensive, and, create considerable downtime while factories were updated. The best course of action, it appeared, was to forego automation and simply bring in more foreign workers.

Increased efforts then had to be taken to minimize their fraternization with the German public. The foreigners were not, and never would be, the social equal to Germans.

Young Ukrainian women with Aryan features were given special attention, however. They were sought out by the authorities to work in the households of German families. If their work was satisfactory, they were promised that they could become German citizens after the war, which implied the possibility of acquiring a German husband.

Food continued in short supply throughout Germany as well as in the occupied territories. During September, the rationing of potatoes began — a staple in the German diet. Sugar had all but disappeared, but artificial sweeteners were available. Cosmetics were not available and dancing — considered a waste of valuable time — was discouraged.

In an effort to persuade the German people to endure these inconveniences, Hitler announced from Berlin, on October 3, that the Soviet Union was on the verge of defeat and that the rebuilding of Europe was about to begin. Hitler was fully aware that this was not likely to happen.

The next day, Hitler slipped back into his dream world. He told his luncheon guests that in fifty years there would be millions of German farmers in the East providing Germany with all of the food it needed. Concerning the food that could not be grown in the East, he said that just one colony, such as the Belgian Congo, would be needed to provide Germany with such things as tea and coffee. The conversation, that afternoon, also included discussions on sources for oysters, crabs and caviar.

Despite the optimistic talk at the Fuehrer's table, the streets of Germany gave a different view. Taxis had disappeared and there were very few private cars to be seen. Public transportation was still running, but people had to walk more so now than ever.

Most cities had a 9:00 p.m. curfew which was strictly enforced, and some streets were covered over with camouflage netting.

ON THE ITALIAN HOME FRONT

The Italian people were not suffering as many air raids as the Germans, but they suffered in kind when it came to food and other necessities of life. For the coming winter, the civilian ration of heating fuel had been cut to less than fifty percent of the previous winter and there was now rationing of clothes and bread. The bread ration was fixed at seven ounces per person per day. Rationing, of course, created a black market, and the Italian police, not being as ruthless or efficient as their SS-controlled German counterpart, had trouble coping with this. As a result, the black markets in Italy were rampant compared to those in Germany.

THE FINNS PLAN THEIR TERRITORIAL EXPANSION

The leaders of Finland were greatly emboldened by their own military successes against the Soviets, and the country's President, Risto Ryti, told a German delegation on September 11 what he foresaw as the future territorial limits of Finland. He stated that the all-important southern border would consist of the Neva River (after Leningrad had been levelled); the western, northern and eastern shores of Lake Ladoga; the Svir River; the western, northern and eastern shores of Lake Onega, and the Dvina River, which led from the lake, to the White Sea. Opposite this border, he presumed, would be German-controlled territory. Finland's eastern border would become the White Sea, giving Finland all of Karelia and the Kola Peninsula. Finland's northern border would be the coast of the Arctic Ocean which would include the ice-free port of Murmansk, a city the Finns tried to capture during the Russion Revolution. To the west would be Norway and Sweden.

MORE PLANS FOR GERMANY'S FUTURE

Heinrich Himmler, head of the SS and Germany's resettlement program in the East, saw the same things that Hitler saw. On October 4, he spoke to his associates, saying that perhaps some one and a half billion people would surge Eastward toward the Urals and beyond. He said that because of this, the SS would have a gigantic task, in the future, of relocating these people and securing their living space.

On October 13, Hitler spoke to his dinner companions about the other nations that would work with Germany to settle the East. He said that they should have a share of the natural riches and find an outlet there for their industrial production. America, Hitler went on, could never become a partner for these countries because America can be paid "only in gold...(a) policy born in the smokey brain of a Jewish thinker."

Hitler than changed the subject to rivers. The most important river in postwar Europe, he said, will be the Danube; "We'll connect it to the Dnieper and the Don by the Black Sea." With that, he predicted that the petroleum and grain of the East would come "flowing towards us." He went on to say that wide canals would be built in central Europe connecting the Danube with the Main and Oder Rivers and that the new European canal system would become an economic circuit of unheard-of dimensions.

Then, back to the subject of Europe versus America and another contradiction of what he had said previously. Hitler now said that Europe, and no longer America, would be the area of boundless possibilities. He went on to say that if the Americans are intelligent they would realize how much it would be to their interest to take part in this work.

Hitler went on to talk of the many assets that are to be found in the Ukraine; iron, nickel, coal, manganese, molybdenum, vegetable oils and hevea (rubber trees). The side that wins this war would have to concern itself only with "economic juggleries."

Hitler spoke of creating a customs union for Europe which would include Denmark, Norway, Holland, Belgium, Sweden and Finland. Once the business leaders in these areas realized the great advantages that awaited them in the East they will "...come over into our camp with banners waving."

Hitler revealed to his table companions how he concocted all of these plans for the future by saying that although he spent about ten hours a day thinking about military matters, before going to bed, he spent some time on matters for the future and on architecture.

TIKVIN

On October 13, Hitler issued a field order to the 16th Army, which was fighting at the northern end of the eastern front, to advance and occupy the town of Tikvin, east of Leningrad. The attack was to begin on the 16th. Once Tikvin was taken, the order stated, the next advance would be to the Svir River and a linkup with the Finns.

RELIGION AND THE WEATHER

Back at the Fuehrer headquarters, Hitler was pontificating once again on religion. Himmler was his guest. Hitler spoke at length about how he had kept religion out of National Socialist ideology in order to keep his supporters from "knocking each other out with the Bible and the sprinkler." The Fuehrer said that he would continue this policy in the future and predicted, because of the advance of science, religion would weaken. He said that the best course of action for the National Socialists to take was to let Christianity die a natural death. Hitler went on to ask a question and then answer it. He posed the question that might not the belief in God disappear with the demise of Christianity? Hitler's answer was that that would not to desirable, saying, "Why should we destroy this wonderful power they (the believers) have." Hitler then said that he envisaged a future in which each man followed his own private beliefs. He added sarcastically, "Superstition must not lose its rights."

The next night, Hitler told his table companions how he would reorganize Germany's meteorological services which were currently controlled by the Army. He said that what Germany needed was a civilian organization staffed by men gifted with a "sixth sense" and who live in nature and with nature — whether or not they understood anything about "isotherms and isobars." The Fuehrer went on to describe a weather organization that would rely on hundreds of "human barometers" all around Europe. He described these people as individuals who had skills passed down from father to son, who understood what the flight of midges and swallows meant and who could feel the wind and were familiar with the movements of the sky. Hitler said that these weather informants would be supplied with a free telephone and paid a nominal monthly fee to report periodically to a central control office and describe the weather conditions in their areas. The central office would then compile that information and issue a forecast.

GOOD NEWS FROM THE ROMANIAN FRONT

On October 16, Romanian troops occupied the Black Sea port of Odessa after a 73-day siege. Two days later, Romanian Prime Minister, Ion Antonescu, proclaimed the region of Transnistria a Romanian province, and on November 8, a great victory parade was held in Bucharest. Field Marshal Keitel attended.

There were those around Antonescu that advised him to order a halt to any further advance by Romanian troops into the Soviet Union. But Antonescu ignored that advice and ordered his troops to march on. One major factor was that Romania's acquisition of Transnistria still had to be ratified by Hitler.

AGAIN — THE GLORIES-TO-BE IN THE EAST — PER A.H.

On October 17, 18 and 19, Hitler spoke once again of the wonderful things that were in store for Germany in the East. He repeated his comments on how roads would be built and German cities and farming communities should be established and foreigners of good blood moved in. He also said again that the Russian cities would be left to decay. In a roundabout way, Hitler told his dinner guests that he did not expect to live to be 72. Hitler, then 52, said, "I shall no longer be here to see all that, but in twenty years the Ukraine will already be a home for twenty million inhabitants besides the natives."

On the subject of Ukrainian wheat, Hitler gave more insight on how that vital commodity should be processed in the East. He believed that it would be folly to install electrically powered flour mills in the Ukraine. Instead, windmills should be built "all over the place."

Turning to Dr. Todt, his master builder, who was again a guest at the table, Hitler told him that he would have to extend his programs for the East, but that that should not be done until the road and rail networks were completed. Then the Fuehrer reflected, "What a task awaits us!" The German people, he continued, would have a hundred years of great satisfaction in restructuring the East.

That same day, Hitler praised the efforts of his soldiers fighting in the East and said that the monuments he would erect in Berlin would continue to proclaim their glory for a thousand years. They would include, he said, the Arc de

Triomphe, the Pantheon of the Army, and the Pantheon of the German people.

On October 18, Hitler spoke of some of the wartime restrictions in Germany that would be retained during the days immediately following the end of the war. He said that the working day, currently exceeding eight hours, could have to continue for some time and that the rationing of meat and fats would be continued until it was certain that the peoples' needs were adequately met. Talking further about food, Hitler said that the production of both tobacco and soy beans, currently produced in Europe in only limited quantities, would be increased and that soy beans would provide generous supplies of vegetable oil and animal fodder.

And then he spoke of colonies saying that for a colonial policy to make sense, one had to first dominate Europe. He went on to reveal that his demands for overseas colonies might be surprisingly modest. He said, "The only colony I'd like to have back would be our Cameroons — nothing else."

On the 19th, the Fuehrer expounded on the virtues of the family saying, as he had often said before, that it was essential that the German people have lots of children. Parents should be persuaded that a family's well-being is secure only when it has four or more children.

Hitler then delved into the details of private home construction. The components of new homes must be "standardized," he said. This included such things as wash-basins, window and doors. He added that in the next year or two, the practice of producing non-standard items of this sort should be stopped. On electrical current, which differed in some parts of Germany, Hitler said that it too had to be standardized. And he went on to say that the people should have a cheap radio and a typewriter and suggested that lessons in typewriting might be given in primary school instead of religious instruction.

JESUS OF GALILEE

On October 21, Hitler enlightened his table companions on some popular misconceptions about Jesus Christ. Hitler said that Jesus was not a Jew but a Galilean who labored against Jewry. He added that many Jews regarded Christ as the son of a Philistine whore and a Roman soldier and because He preached against "Jewish capitalism," Hitler declared, the Jews liquidated Him. Hitler went on to explain how St. Paul corrupted Jesus's origin for his own purposes and made Him out to be a Jew.

FESTIVE OCCASIONS – BERLIN – JEWS – RE-WRITING HISTORY – THE BIG BOOK

On October 21, after setting the record straight about Jesus, Hitler lectured his dinner companions on how Germany should greatly enhance and upgrade its public ceremonies. In this regard, he reminded his fellow diners of the colorful ceremonies the English conducted, and he said that it was important to him to develop such customs in his lifetime rather than leave it to a successor. As an example, Hitler suggested that, in the future, the German Chancellor should have at his disposal, for ceremonial purposes, two hundred of Germany's finest motor cars and that the chauffeurs should act as footmen.

Hitler spoke of rebuilding Berlin saying that there would be nothing too good for the beautification of the nation's capital. He said that the city should be built on such a grand scale that St. Peter's in Rome would seem like a toy by comparison. Hitler favored using granite in the public buildings because it would last forever. Hitler went on to say that he would install his best architect in Berlin and predicted, for the umpteenth time, that Berlin would one day become the capital of the world.

At the noontime meal on October 25, Hitler reminded his dinner companions that he had prophesied from the rostrum of the Reichstag that the Jews of Europe would disappear. He then confirmed, what had finally become Nazi doctrine on this matter, that he would "park them in the marshy parts of Russia." This was almost certainly a reference to Muscovy.

And, on writing the history of the future, Hitler said that the reflections of the Roman Emperor Julian (331-363) should be circulated in the millions. In Hitler's mind, Julian was an able military and political leader who substantially improved the Roman Empire, and was loved by his people. He also tried to restore paganism. Hitler went on to say that the Party should see to it that history is rewritten from a racial point of view.

At the evening meal that day, Hitler again launched into a tirade against the churches and repeated, as he had often done before, a litany of offenses committed by the clergy against the people. During his discourse, Hitler said that he had numerous accounts to settle with the churches and that he had been writing them down. The time would come "to bring out the big book."

AT THE FRONT – AT ARMY HEADQUARTERS – AT THE FOREIGN OFFICE

At the front, it was raining heavily, but the German Army was still advancing, but now more slowly than before. Red Army resistance had stiffened, attrition was taking its toll on the Axis forces, and getting supplies through was an increasing problem as the Army's supply lines lengthened. Hitler was concerned. He told Ciano, who was a dinner guest, that if he had known the strength of the Red Army, he might not have acted as he did.

By the end of October, the Luftwaffe reported that it had carried out 251 air attacks on Leningrad in the last three months — almost three a day. It was commitments like this in the East that prevented the Luftwaffe from defending the skies over Germany.

At Army headquarters in Berlin, planners were working on the next conquest — the Middle East. The invasion of the Middle East from the Caucasus would be launched from the Caucasus into Iran and Iraq only after the German Army controlled the west bank of the lower Volga River to guard against a Soviet flank attack. And, in order to gain control of the river's west bank, the cities of Stalingrad and Astrakhan would have to be taken.

German plans called for Italian forces and the Arab formations within the German Army to be included in the attack into the Middle East. British resistance, which was expected to be offered by a mix of Indian and other empire formations, was expected to be light. It was anticipated that the British would have to withdraw forces from North Africa in order to protect the Middle East which would make Rommel's advance into Egypt easier. The beginning date for the invasion of the Middle East was to be spring 1942.

It was further foreseen that once Axis troops were deep into the Middle East, Turkey might join the Axis or, at the least, become a friendly neutral.

The German planners foresaw that by the end of the summer of 1942, Axis troops would have reached the Persian Gulf and secured the area's oil fields. With this, the invasion of Iran and Iraq would be complete. It was expected that there would be no significant threat to the Axis's eastern frontier in the Middle East from neutral Afghanistan or India. With regard to the latter, it was generally understood that India was within the political sphere of Japan and, in fact, neither Germany nor Italy had any great interest in conquering India.

Down at the Foreign Office, von Ribbentrop's bureaucrats were busy working on their draft peace treaty with Britain. Ernst von Weizacker, the Chief State Secretary, summed up these efforts in a diary entry of October 21; "The peace compromise with Britain which we are ready to accept consists of this: the British Empire remains intact (woe, if India fell into other hand or chaos); in Europe, of course, Britain must stand back. Britain — which would shortly be ruled by Beaverbrook — will come to realize that Germany's mission is to organize Europe against the Mongol flood from the east and that Germany and Britain would eventually have to stand side-by-side against the USA."

BACK AT THE TABLE

"I wish today we had thirty million sheep," Hitler said in a discussion about wool production. In Germany, before the war, wool production had declined drastically because of cheap imports from Australian. In the future, Hitler predicted that this would change.

Hitler jumped from subject to subject as usual, then spoke again of the Ukraine saying that to properly exploit the Ukraine the only thing that was needed was peace in the West. But as for peace in the East, Hitler said that he did not expect a formal end to the war. The frontier police would provide the security needed to protect the conquered territories.

Hitler switched then to Britain and the United States. He said that if the British were really clever they would drop out of the war and instigate a policy of putting their principle competitor — the United States — "out of the game...for thirty years." He predicted that if that happened, the United States would suffer internal upheavals because it would be enormously in debt and that unemployment would rise to gigantic proportions. Hitler then predicted that Germany would control the European continent and thereby would have a dominant position over all the nations of the world, including Britain and the United States.

Speaking of his own death, Hitler said that when he died, he would leave behind the most powerful army in the world and a Party that would be the "most voracious animal" in history.

On the 29th, Hitler spoke again of marshes, rehashing his plans to build a giant maneuver area in the East using the Pripet Marshes. Then, out of the blue, he suggested that the Croatians — Hitler liked the Croatians — might be employed to police that area.

During this same two-hour-plus monologue, Hitler spoke of education, saying that it made no sense to educate teachers in upper schools so that they could teach peasant children, for the next thirty five years, that B-A spells `ba'. To provide the teachers needed in rural areas, Hitler suggested that discharged Army sergeants might be employed as teachers in village schools. He added that those old soldiers would also make excellent gymnastics instructors.

Additionally, Hitler wanted to reform the German diplomatic service. He had long been displeased with the lack of elan his diplomats had shown when it came to collecting information from foreigners. He said that postwar German legation should include about half a dozen young attaches who would busy themselves fraternizing with influential women because that was an excellent way of keeping informed. Hitler then gave an example, saying that it was a grievous error that no one in all the German Foreign Ministry could get their "clutches" on the daughter of the former American ambassador, William E. Dodd. That was their job, he said, and it should have been done.

On the evening of November 1, Hitler addressed the problem of conflicts of interest with regard to public servants. He said that the future public servants should not be allowed to own stocks or other interests in private firms and must not be involved, in any way, in financial speculations. It would be alright if they put their money into real estate and government securities. Hitler went on to chastise one of his favorite villains — bureaucrats. He said that Germany's civil service had become "...a blind machine" and that a massive restructuring and decentralization program was needed. He explained that the bureaucratic structure created by the old Reich would not be applicable for such newly-acquired areas such as the Crimea.

While on this same theme, Hitler lashed out at another of his favorite whipping boys — judges. Hitler had long thought them to be too lenient and hamstrung by very narrow interpretations of the law. It was his goal to simplify the laws of the land

and give the judges much broader powers. Instead of municipal magistrates and juries they will set up courts with a single judge, who will be well paid, and who would be authorized to exercise broad interpretations of the law.

On the 2nd, Hitler spoke again of Europe a hundred years hence, predicting that German would be the universal language. And, in the Eastern territories, he said that he would replace the Slav geographical titles by German names. The Crimea, for example, might be called "Gotenland." The planners over at Rosenberg's Eastern Ministry, however, were planning on calling it Taurida.

On November 5, Hitler spoke again of how he would change the German penal system and described certain types of criminals upon whom society should have no mercy. He said that the only remedy for such criminals was to impose the death penalty — and without hesitation. Hitler went on to say, one more time, that Germany's penal system was "a mess," and that young offenders should not be required to live with hardened criminals. He said he believed in the restoration of corporal punishment; "A good hiding does no harm to a young man of seventeen, and often it would be enough."

5,008 CASUALTIES PER DAY

November 6 and 7 were gloomy days at Hitler's headquarters. On the sixth, a report came in from OKW stating that the Wehrmacht had suffered 686,108 casualties on the eastern front from June 22 to the present — 5,008 per day.

The same day, Hitler received a letter from Mussolini telling him that Italian industry was working at only sixty percent capacity due to lack of fuel.

At the situation conference on the 7th it was clear that Barbarossa was well behind schedule due to a combination of continuing Soviet resistance and bad weather. That day, Hitler postponed the planned invasion of the Middle East without giving a new date.

It was also a bad day for the Russian workers in Germany. On the 7th Goering reduced their food rations.

On November 8, Hitler journeyed from his headquarters in East Prussia to Munich to participate in the annual celebration of his abortive 1923 Putsch. The city was blacked out and the streets nearly deserted for fear of air raids. Among the people seen on the streets were many women in black and a noticeable number of young men with missing arms, legs and eyes.

On the afternoon of the 9th, there was good news. A report came in from the eastern front that the town of Tikvin, 100 miles east of Leningrad, had been taken by German troops. To the north, sixty miles away, was the Svir River where the Germans would linkup with the Finns. That evening, German radio programming was interrupted to tell the German people the good news.

DINING WITH THE FUEHRER

On November 11, Hitler gave his captive audience of five another dose of the vindictive side of his personality — this time he lashed out at royalty. Hitler hated royalty; he called them obsolete and useless, yet they fascinated him and he felt that lessons might be learned from them. He commented that it might be worthwhile to study these princely families to see how they maintained themselves in power.

Hitler then, once again, lambasted organized religion and then jumped to the subject of diet. As usual, he was critical of eating meat and he made a prediction that eventually "the world of the future will be vegetarian."

CHAPTER 15

🔒LINKUP AT THE SVIR RIVER

November 12, 1941: It was a day of great joy at Hitler's headquarters in East Prussia, and also at the Helsinki headquarters of Field Marshal Carl von Mannerheim, commander of Finland's armed forces. Word had just been received at both headquarters that German and Finnish forces had made contact with each other at the Svir River 90 miles east-northeast of Leningrad. This action cut the last Soviet supply route into the Leningrad area. Leningrad was surrounded. Now, it would be only a matter of time until the Soviet forces there would be starved into submission. 🖍

Linking up with the Finns had been one of Germany's primary military objectives. 🔒 **It would be the only one met in 1941.** 🖍

The advances of both Army Groups Center and South had been slowed by increased Soviet resistance, bad weather and supply problems. Barbarossa was badly behind schedule.

AT HITLER'S TABLE

At the noon meal on November 12, Hitler, once again, spoke optimistically of the future. With regard to the East, he repeated some of what he had said before; that the natives would be adequately fed and given plenty of "rot-gut" alcohol, and if they refused to work, they would be deprived of alcohol or put into concentration camps. With German know-how and cheap native labor, he went on, we can grow anything in the East from "the orange to cotton."

At the evening meal, Hitler offered a dialogue on the future economy in Germany. He said that Germany would become a financially solid State "without an once of gold behind it." Wages and prices would be controlled and offenders would be sent off to concentration camps.

Hitler spoke again of how the new Germany must be self-sufficient in every necessity of life and not dependent on imports of any kind. He stressed that the land and the workers of the East would insure these things. As a gesture of Nazi kindness toward those workers, Hitler said that they would be given household utensils in order for them to properly feed themselves.

Then, on the subject of feeding the German people, Hitler told his dinner companions that the alluvial deposits on the shores of the North Sea made the best manure in the world. Collecting this treasure would be the work of foreign workers and concentration camp laborers.

The conversation then switched to the German economy and he blamed the current problems within the economy on capitalist thinking and college professors. In order to fully convert that thinking into National Socialist ideology, he said that it would take ten years.

THE WAR ON HOMOSEXUALS

Ever since Hitler came to power in 1933, he waged a war against homosexuality. Yet, it still persisted, even in the SS. Heretofore, homosexuals discovered within the SS were expelled from the organization and sent to concentration camps. But it still existed within the SS and Hitler concluded that stiffer penalties were needed. Therefore, on November 15, 1941, he issued a decree stating that any homosexual found within the ranks of the SS was to be executed. Furthermore, on the subject of homosexuality, Hitler told his associates that after the war, a concentrated program would be enacted to eliminate this scourge from all of German society. Now, however, was not the time for such an undertaking.

BUREAUCRATS AND LAWYERS

At the noon meal on November 16, Hitler lashed out at bureaucrats and lawyers again. He reminded his listeners that the British ruled the multitudes of India with only 145,000 men, whereas the Germans currently needed millions to govern their conquered peoples. For this sorry state of affairs, Hitler blamed government lawyers. He said that after the war, the first thing to do would be to chase the lawyers out of all of the government Ministries. They can be given subordinate jobs, he said, and serve only as advisers. He continued that it would be wise to discourage young people from becoming lawyers. He added that Frederick the Great had similar ideas.

As for bureaucrats, Hitler said that we can get rid of two-thirds of them.

That evening, Hitler lashed out again at lawyers and judges for the way they coddled criminals. "Why not wipe out the criminals at once," he asked his companions, saying that it was senseless to arrest an offender, lock him up, let him go, watch over him, and then arrest him again. Here, in Hitler's mind, was another problem to be dealt with in the future.

THE CRIMEA IS OURS — ALMOST

On November 17, 1941, Axis forces in the Crimea, which consisted mostly of German and Romanian units, captured the city of Kerch in the eastern end of Crimea. With this, Germany's future Riviera was now in Axis hands except for the heavily-fortified port-city of Sevastopol on the peninsula's southwestern coast. Sevastopol was surrounded on the landward side by Axis forces, but it was still receiving supplies and reinforcements by sea because the Soviet's Black Sea Fleet was still dominant in that body of water. The siege of Sevastopol would last for almost eight more months before the Germans could claim title to the vital peninsula. During that time, Kerch would be retaken by the Soviets and then taken again by the Axis forces. Hundreds of thousands of Axis troops were thus engaged in the Crimea for a considerable length of time and casualties were high. The citrus fruits and suntans that Hitler hoped for were coming at very high price.

Two hundred and fifty miles to the east, Army Group South was stopped by strong Soviet resistance at the city of Rostov, the gateway to the Caucasus. Losses were such that Army Group South would not be able to recover until spring. The southern arm of Barbarossa was stalled.

On November 29, Hitler heard another disturbing report on the East. This time it was from the lips of one of his most trusted aides, Fritz Todt, Minister of Armaments and Munitions. Todt had just toured the Eastern front and had seen, first hand, the terrible losses suffered by the German forces there. He told Hitler that, in his opinion, Germany could not win the war militarily because of those losses and that German industry could not keep pace with the industrial supremacy of the Western Powers. Todt was one of the very few people within the German hierarchy that could speak so bluntly to the Fuehrer. Hitler was visibly annoyed and replied, "How am I supposed to end it then?" Todt did not have a solution.

A TRAUMATIC WEEK, DECEMBER 1-7, 1941

On December 1, Hitler received a report that the sinking of Allied shipping by German submarines during November was the lowest so far in the war. Also, the RAF had, by now, gained air superiority over the Bay of Biscay, the route that German submarines had to take in and out of their bases on the coast of France to reach the Atlantic. Clearly, the Allies were getting better at defending against submarines.

One of the losers here was Hermann Goering, head of the Luftwaffe. This was another example of his failure. In addition, Goering was being blamed for the failure of his Four Year Plan to provide adequate food and consumer goods for the German people. The result of all this was that Goering's influence in high places was steadily declining. As the war progressed, the decline would continue.

On December 3, German troops west of Moscow began to fall back in the face of strong Soviet counterattacks and extremely cold weather. Some units reported that forty percent of the men were suffering from frostbite.

That same day, Hitler issued the "Rationalization Decree" reversing all of the relaxations made previously within the German economy and placing it on an intense wartime footing.

On December 5, Hitler ordered a halt to the advance on Moscow. It was a belated gesture. His troops there had already halted and some were in retreat.

On the 6th, the Soviet forces in front of Moscow, reinforced by three new armies from Siberia, launched a major counterattack against Army Group Center. The Germans began to fall back all along the line.

That same day, in a show of solidarity with the Soviet Union, Britain, Australia, Canada, New Zealand and South Africa declared war on three members of the Axis coalition that had invaded Russia: Finland, Hungary and Romania

On December 7, word came to the Fuehrer's headquarters early in the day that German troops were in general retreat from Moscow.

Then came the big surprise. Japanese naval forces had attacked the huge American naval base at Pearl Harbor, Hawaii. It was now a certainty that Japan and the United States would go to war. This was seen as good news in Germany because now the United States would be forced to direct its attention toward the Pacific and away from Europe.

That same fateful day, Hitler issued another, but secret, decree in support of his Rationalization Decree called the "Night and Fog Decree." This decree authorized the SS, through their police organizations, to arrest and summarily execute anyone suspected of jeopardizing national security. The decree was so-named because now individuals would simply disappear into the night and fog and would never be heard from again.

12 MORE ENEMIES

With the Japanese attack on Pearl Harbor, the entire complexion of World War II changed. During December 1941, twelve more nations declared war on Germany: USA, China, Costa Rica, Cuba, Czechoslovakia, Dominican Republic, El Salvador, Guatemala, Haiti, Honduras, Nicaragua, and Panama. That made a total of twenty-nine nations at war with Germany by the end of 1941. On the Axis side, four nations entered the war on Germany's side: Japan, Croatia, Manchukuo (in December) and Thailand (in January). That put the Axis count at twelve. In the final analysis, about two-thirds of the world's population was now Germany's enemy.

The leaders in Berlin and Rome seemed to be unperturbed by this increase in enemies. The Italian propagandists went so far as to predict that, with the USA now in the war, one bombardment of New York City would be enough to bring the Americans to their knees.

German propagandists, likewise, minimized the new developments. About this time, though, Dr. Morell took Hitler's blood pressure and found it to be 200 systolic.

A HARD WINTER IN THE EAST AND AT HOME

In the East, German forces were in retreat at several locations. On December 8, Hitler issued Directive 39 which ordered those troops being forced to retreat to destroy everything of human value as they withdrew. It was called "scorched earth."

Directive 39 also ordered the armed forces to go on the defensive for the winter, and called for more service personnel stationed at home and in the occupied areas to be sent to the Eastern front. Furthermore, the directive called for more Soviet POWs to be brought to Germany as workers.

On the German home front, conditions were harsh due to the rationing on fuel, food, transportation and other necessities. And there was no letup in the British air raids.

OURS AND YOURS

On December 11, 1941, Germany, Italy and Japan divided the world between them. In an appendix to the Tripartite Pact of September 1940, Germany and Italy on the one hand, and Japan on the other, stipulated that the dividing lines between their respective spheres of interest would be the Seventieth Meridian East. This line on the map ran through the Indian Ocean and was roughly parallel to the west coast of India. The appendix granted to Germany and Italy, "the waters west of approximately 70 degrees eastern longitude to the east coast of the American continent, as well as the continents and islands...which are located

in these waters." This included all of Europe, including the European part of the Soviet Union, the Middle East, the Mediterranean, all of Africa and the Atlantic Ocean.

The appendix gave Japan, "the waters east of approximately 70 degrees eastern longitude to the west coast of the American continent, as well as the continents and islands which are located in these waters." This gave Japan all of East Asia, Southeast Asia, Australia, New Zealand and the Pacific Ocean. Neither the western Axis nor Japan claimed jurisdiction over the North and South American continents. It was generally believed in Berlin, Rome and Tokyo that, once the Axis Powers were victorious, the United States would withdraw to its North American redoubt and, protected by two oceans, very possibly return to a policy of isolationism. *This is what had happened in the United States after World War I when the American people had become appalled at the terrible loss of lives in the war and were disgusted with the never-ending squabbles among the European nations. The Axis leaders hoped that history would repeat itself.

The appendix provided that each party's armed forces could operate in the other's areas as the needs arose and that an "open sea connection and sea transport across the Indian Ocean" and a "military air link" would be established when conditions permitted.

The German's interpretation of the dividing line was that, at the point where the Seventieth Meridian East reached land, the line then followed the western border of India, the western and northern borders of Afghanistan, the western border to China, the northern border of Mongolia to a point near Lake Uvs Nuur, and then northward along the Yenisei River to the Arctic Ocean and on to the North Pole. This divided Soviet Siberia approximately in half.

TABLE TALK, DECEMBER 13, 1941

At the midday meal on December 13, Hitler had five special guests; Ribbentrop, Rosenberg, Goebbels, Terboven and

Reichsleiter Philipp Bouhler who was head of the Chancellory. The main topic this day was religion. Hitler said that the war would be over one day and that his final task would be to smash organized religion.

Hitler repeated himself saying that the SS had uncovered evidence that Christ was an Aryan and that St. Paul corrupted Christ's messages for his own purposes. He then expounded on his own beliefs saying that Christianity is an invention of sick minds. The Japanese religion, he explained, was superior because it put mankind into contact with nature. Hitler said that there was no heaven as the Christians claimed, but that life goes on in other ways. It is our duty to encourage that thinking.

Hitler explained how Mussolini was now plagued with religious problems because he had compromised with the Catholic Church. Hitler said that if he were in Mussolini's place, he would take over the Vatican and throw everyone out and apologize later.

With regard to the United States entering the war, Hitler said that Germany would have to hold out against her until the end. This was something of an admission that Hitler believed he could not militarily defeat the Americans.

DRASTIC MEASURES

The setbacks in the East called for Hitler to take more drastic measures. On December 19, he fired General Walter von Brauchitsch, Commander-in-Chief of the German Army, and assumed the post himself. This put him on a par with Raeder of the Navy and Goering of the Luftwaffe. Under this curious arrangement, Hitler, as head of the Army, was now subordinate to Keitel, Chief of OKW. But of course, Keitel took his orders from the German Chancellor — Adolf Hitler.

That same day, Rosenberg, the Minister of the Eastern Territories who was trying to build his influence in the matters of the East, decreed that all residents of the occupied Eastern Territories would be subject to compulsory labor if so ordered. The downside of this was that more Soviet citizens,

when faced with this possibility, fled to the Partisans.

The next day, Goebbels went on national radio appealing to the German population to donate fur coats and other warm clothing for use by the troops in the East. This was a gross admission that the German Army had not been adequately prepared for the Russian winter.

Hitler's dinner conversations of December 23-31 reveal little of the grave situation in the East. Whatever he said on that subject was most likely purged from the stenographer's notes. Since these were records for posterity, it would not do to reveal how deeply stressed the Fuehrer was at this time. Instead, the record shows that he spoke on subjects he liked. He talked at length about art and how grand the Linz Art Museum would be and that it could "bear comparison with no-matter-which museum in New York." He darted from subject to subject, speaking on the wonders of vegetarianism, the new observatory he would one day build in Linz, the memoirs he might write, and the gigantic economy Germany would enjoy after the war which would be fueled by cheap eastern labor. Because of this labor source, Hitler told his dinner guests that the factories of the future Germany would be run on double shifts to save the cost of building additional ones. And, with Japan having achieved its goals in the Far East, Germany would have wonderful markets for her products throughout Asia.

In one of his meetings with Mussolini at this time, Hitler told the Duce that, after the war, he would take a long vacation in Italy and he wanted especially to visit Florence.

If Hitler would not speak out publicly on conditions in the East, Goebbels would. On December 25, Goebbels broadcast a so-called "Yuletide message" (the word "Christmas" had been dropped from official use) to the German people. It was, in fact, another plea for clothing for the troops in the East. He told his listeners that such things as overshoes, stockings, woolen underwear, blankets, gloves, earmuffs, etc., would make excellent Yuletide gifts for the troops in the East.

HITLER'S DINNER COMPANIONS ENDURE

Hitler's recorded dinner conversations during the first days of January, 1942 were devoid of most military matters, but generously laced with more of his plans for the future.

It had been suggested to Hitler that, in place of religious instructions in the German schools, some sort of Nazi-oriented philosophy be taught. Hitler's response was that he would work out the formula when he had time.

On other matters, Hitler said that couples should get married in group weddings. It would be more efficient that way.

When peace comes, he said, the SS would regain its independence from the Army and would become an elite police force capable of crushing any adversary.

In ten years, he said that the title "Fuehrer" would no longer be used and would be replaced by "Reichs Chancellor."

He stated that in discussions on how industrial advances were given to the world through the current patent process, Hitler said that after the war new patents would be permitted only under the authorization of a government office established for that purpose. And with regard to recent new developments in armor-piercing artillery, Hitler predicted that, by the end of the war, tanks will have become obsolete. This, of course, would nullify the German Army's main offensive weapon, the Blitzkrieg. By these words, Hitler was predicting that Germany was in a race against time to win the war.

With regards to one of the persistent devils in his closet, government bureaucracies, Hitler offered a solution. He explained how the current bureaucratic system paralyses all initiative and that an arrangement must be worked out whereby a third party can intervene to make decisions.

Speaking on another of his favorite themes, that being the day when Germany and Britain would work together against the Americans, Hitler said that one of the first undertaking would be for a joint German-British army to chase the Americans out of Iceland. This would give the Germans and British control of a large part of the North Atlantic and force the Americans back to the North American continent.

On the evening of January 9, Hitler told a bold-faced lie about himself that, certainly, no one at the table believed — nor challenged. He said that he had never been sick since he was sixteen but admitted that he feared illness because if a strong illness attacked, it might have a "violent effect on me."

Then, on the Autobahns of the East, Hitler said that they would have to be different from those in Germany. He went on to explain that driving across the endless Russian steppes was boring and that the routes in the East must be made as scenic as possible for the enjoyment of the travellers. Those Autobahnen, he went on, would have to be built on ridges, so that the wind would continually sweep them of snow in the winter.

Then, on the subject of whale oil (Hitler seemed to be somewhat behind the times on this subject), he said that, since humanity depended so much on whale oil for its fats, vegetable oil from the East would be a better substitute.

On January 12, engineer Hitler expounded on the future of automobiles and locomotives, saying that the water-cooled automobile engine would disappear completely in favor of air cooled engines. The Volkswagen had an air-cooled engine and Hitler considered it adequate for most automotive needs.

On the subject of locomotives, numerous reports had been received that the cold Russian winter had caused unexpected problems with the operation of German-made locomotives. Hitler said that would be rectified by building locomotives especially designed for local conditions.

TIME TO MOVE

Part of the Nazi's plans for the future Germany was to move people about for political, racial and economic purposes. This process was now begun. About 100,000 ethnic Germans living in the annexed French provinces of Alsace and Lorraine who were deemed to be politically unreliable were sent to settle in the East. Some were resettled in the General Government and others were held temporarily at various locations, ready to be sent to the new settlements in the East when they became available. To fill the void created in Alsace and Lorraine, some 80,000 politically reliable Germans from the Saar and Westphalia were moved in.

In the area of Zhitomir, Ukraine, eighty miles west of Kiev, the first all-German settlements began to take shape. Zhitomir was in the heart of "Galicia," the western part of the Ukraine where the people had been fairly well westernized and who, over the decades, had been friendly toward the Germans.

The first Germans to move into the Zhitomir region were Volksdeutsch who had been found scattered throughout the general area living amongst the Ukrainians. This was deemed to be an unhealthy arrangement by the SS population experts, so it was decreed that the area's Volksdeutsch would be brought together into one settlement. It was also ordered that Volksdeutsch from elsewhere in the occupied East would be relocated to the Zhitomir area when conditions permitted. Since these people were fluent in Russian and/or Ukrainian and had adapted to much of the local cultures, it was expected that some assimilation had taken place and the ethnic Germans would have to be re-Germanized. As that process began, provisions were made for some of the Galicians to be Germanized also.

For the near future, the relocated Volksdeutsch were given land to till, but not to own. Hitler had issued a general decree that the determination of land ownership in the East would not begin until such time that the war veterans could participate.

In creating the Zhitomir settlements, some entire villages were cleared of their occupants and the Volksdeutsch moved into the existing homes and farms. Once this was accomplished, some of the young men were drafted into the German armed forces.

Those who now lived in the new settlements had to struggle for their existence because the retreating Russians had destroyed many buildings and removed most equipment. This greatly reduced the productivity of the area and it was recognized that the Zhitomir settlements would not be significant producers of food until after the war.

The next all-German settlements established were set up in Belorussia and conditions there were much the same as at Zhitomir.

Others to be "moved" were, of course, the Jews. This ugly process took another step forward during December after the gassing experiments had been successfully completed at Chelmno and Auschwitz. Gassing facilities were being installed at Belzec and Sobibor Concentration Camps, and later at Treblinka, Majdanek and others. Many of the extermination camps were in the General Government, an area closed to foreigners now and in the future.

RESTRUCTURING THE EAST – THE BEGINNING

During the latter part of 1941, the Germans began restructuring those portions of the East that could be put under German civil administration. One step that was quick and easy to take was to close all of the schools above the fourth grade. This was done in all of the occupied areas except in Ostland. Ostland was eventually to become a part of Germany and the educational programs there were to be brought up to German standards.

In the areas where the schools were closed, the ten- and eleven-year-old children were expected to go to work. The Soviet propagandists picked up on this and soon made it one of their main themes in an attempt to convince the Soviet population that the Nazis had come to enslave the people and not to liberate them.

Another project undertaken in the East was the reconstruction of the Ukrainian railroads. These railroads were in shambles but, nevertheless, were badly needed to support the German Army's supply system. Fritz Todt and Albert Speer worked together to convince Hitler that the railroads should be rebuilt as soon as possible in order to get vitally needed supplies to the troops and bring vitally needed food and other goods back to Germany. To do this, Todt and Speer asked that some 30,000 laborers, currently at work in Germany on non-military and postwar projects, be sent to the Ukraine to work on the railroads. Hitler agreed, and in January 1942, that undertaking began.

THE "OTHER" WAR IN THE EAST AND SS ESTATES

Even before the conquest of the East began, several of the top Nazi leaders engaged in a power struggle to carve out for themselves personal niches in the forthcoming new empire. By now that struggle was well-defined. There was Goering, agitating for control of most of the East's resources to support his Four Year Plan and the German war economy for which he was primarily responsible; there was Rosenberg, the newly-appointed, and often ignored, Minister of the Eastern Territories, trying to establish his authority wherever he could; then came Rosenberg's subordinates, the Reichscommissars of Ostland and the Ukraine, who had ruled their domains before Rosenberg came onto the scene and wanted to retain their powers; and von Ribbentrop, of the Foreign Ministry, picking up what political crumbs he could in the East. Stepping into this fray, the leaders of the Army constantly preached that all activity in the East must be secondary to their war needs. And, lastly, there was Himmler, who had an upper hand over everyone else. Since the SS was responsible for internal security and questions of race and the resettlement, Himmler saw in the East the makings of his own personal empire. For the moment, Himmler had one overriding responsibility that took priority over everything else — suppressing the Partisans. These feisty guerrilla fighters had

become more of a problem than had been expected. In some regions, the Partisans controlled enough territory to build air fields, so that the Soviet Air Force was able to keep them supplied with small arms, food, medical supplies, communications equipments, anti-tank weapons, small artillery pieces, mortars and many other things that could be transported in an airplane. These activities made for good Soviet propaganda and almost all of the various Partisan units remained loyal to Moscow.

The Nazi leaders had not been so naive as to believe that, once conquered, the people of the East would roll over and play dead. Given the history of colonialism over the past hundred years, they knew that the suppression of those who refused to be conquered would take a long time. It was a given that the SS would be engaged in the East for decades to come. This was Himmler's strong suit and during January he played one of his first cards. It had already been agreed that the SS would establish "strong points" throughout the East as their bases of operation. Now, the question came up as to what was to be the nature of these strong points. In Berlin, the SS and several governmental economic agencies reached an agreement which would allow the SS to establish its own agricultural enterprises within the strong points to produce food for those stationed there. These enterprises would take on the nature of huge agricultural estates ruled by the strong hand of the SS and worked by large numbers of low-paid, and if necessary, conscripted laborers. In some respects, it was a return to the old feudal system of the Tsarist days.

THOSE TROUBLESOME PARTISANS

In October 1941, the German Army issued its first directive to deal with the mounting Partisan threat. Called "The Directive for Anti-Partisan Warfare," it authorized field commanders to assign regular army troops, when they could be spared from the front, to work in cooperation with the various SS units in containing this troublesome enemy. The main tactic to be used against the Partisans was that of "encirclement and annihilation" or "surround and sweep." This tactic took lots of foot-soldiers. Tanks, artillery, aircraft and other highly developed weapons of war were of minimal value. Generally, Partisans operated from heavily-forested areas and marshes where they could easily hide, hit, run, and then hide again.

Given the nature of the Russian landscape, Partisan activities were more numerous in the northern forested areas than in the vast open and treeless steppes of the south.

Experience soon showed that the encirclement operations were effective, but the limiting factor, other than weather, was manpower. Therefore, as Partisan activities increased so did the SS's need for men. And, as the number of SS men increased, so did Himmler's importance.

Combatting the Partisans was a very ugly type of war. Since the Partisans had no facilities for POWs, they usually killed those who surrendered. Accordingly, the SS did likewise as well as meting out communal punishments by executing hostages, burning villages, and deporting those thought to be supportive of the Partisans.

During November 1941, Army Group Center formed six battalions of POWs and former Soviet citizens who were willing to fight against the Partisans. They were called "Osttruppen" and wore German Army uniforms and ranks. Since the anti-Partisan units were formed by the Army, race was not a primary factor except, of course, with regard to Jews.

The Osttruppen units soon proved their worth and more such units were authorized by the Army's High Command. Many people in the East hated the communists, so Osttruppen units were relatively easy to form.

Railroads were favorite targets of the Partisans and this activity contributed measurably to the German Army's supply problems. Generally, the Partisans would strike at night and the Germans would make repairs during the day. Similarly, many of the roads in the East were controlled by the Partisans at night, and by the Germans by day. In some places, the only way the Germans could travel a railroad or road was in convoys.

Many roads and railway bridges had to be permanently guarded, and on some stretches of roads sentries were stationed at intervals of one hundred or two hundred yards. Similarly, some villages and small towns had to be fortified. Here again were needs for more men.

Before the month was out, the decision was made by Himmler that he had to do what the Army had done in November — employ within the ranks of the SS non-Aryans who were willing to fight the Partisans. With this decision, the SS's emphasis on the racial purity of its members went out the window.

THE UNITED NATIONS VS THE EUROPEAN CHARTER

In Washington, DC, twenty-six of the nations at war with the Axis Powers met to sign a document in which they formally designated themselves as the "United Nations." It was fully understood that these nations, and others who adhered to the Allied cause, would form a new international organization after the war to replace the discredited League of Nations. It would be a democratic organization designed to maintain world peace.

The Axis Powers responded in kind a while later, declaring that they would form an international organization with the same general goals as the United Nations. Their organization would be known as the "European Charter." There was no great fanfare associated with this announcement and very little media attention given to it because any such organization would, unquestionably, be dominated by Germany, relegating all of other members to secondary roles. Given the planned political makeup of a future Europe dominated by the Axis Powers, it was very likely that this was a propaganda gesture for the moment and that the creation of the European Charter would come to pass only if a United Nations organization was formed. On the other hand, if the European Charter became a reality it would only be a political continuation of the Axis alliance. This, in turn, would create a situation whereby the world would be divided into two camps for the indefinite future. Under such circumstances, world peace would be extremely difficult to attain.

INDIA AND KHAN HITLER

At the dinner table on the evening of January 10, 1942, the subject of India came up again. Hitler had never been enthusiastic about adventures in India and was even less so now because of the recent agreement with Japan which placed India within their sphere of influence. On India, Hitler said that if the Axis Powers were to take India, the Indians would certainly not be enthusiastic and might even look longingly toward the good old days of British rule.

On January 12, Bormann commented at the table that Hitler was a very religious person. The Fuehrer confirmed this assessment, and responded by saying that, after the war, "I will become clerical (kirchlich)." He said that he would be looked upon as the chief of the Tartars and be called "Khan." The Arabs and Moroccans, he said, offer prayers to him today. But then, in one of his rare jovial moods, he said he would refuse to eat their mutton and prefer to "stick to the harem."

REFINING THE PLANS FOR AFRICA

In Berlin and Rome the future plans for Africa had, by early 1942, been fairly well defined and agreed to by both parties. But refinements were still being made. It was realized that, as Axis forces moved deeper into Africa, the interests of the Union of South Africa (South Africa) had to be addressed. This called for a revision of the Bielfeld Plan.

South Africa was a self-governing member of the British Commonwealth and something of a political anomaly. Some two million whites ruled over about eight million black inhabitants who had, ever since the inception of the country, been economically and socially oppressed and disenfranchised. Of the two million whites, more than half were Afrikaners (formerly known as Boers), descendants of early Dutch settlers of the 1800s. These people spoke their own Dutch dialect called "Afrikaans" and had strong ties to the Germanic people of Europe. The balance of the white population were English-speaking descendants of British settlers. Ever since the Boer War of 1899-1902, a war the Afrikaners lost, the Afrikaner population had been resentful of, and often at odds with, the English speakers. However, the English speakers, supported by a sizeable minority of moderate Afrikaners, had managed to rule the country most of the time since 1902. Such was the situation in South Africa in 1942. Even the country's prime minister was an Afrikaner, General Jan Christiaan Smuts, a hero of the Boer War, who had fought against the British.

With the advent of World War II, the country was divided. Most of the Afrikaner population wanted the country to remain neutral, but the English-speakers, together with their moderate Afrikaner supporters, held a small majority in the parliament, and managed to bring the country into the conflict on the side of Britain. South Africa then raised an army of whites, both Afrikaners and English-speakers, which took the field against the Italians and Germans in both East Africa and North Africa. But the political situation at home remained fragile.

The German Foreign Ministry took note of South Africa's political situation and predicted that, when German troops approached their borders, the political attitude in South Africa would swing favorably toward the Axis Powers. They foresaw that the Smuts government would fall and the all-Afrikaner National Party, headed by the Reverend Daniel Malan, would come to power. Malan had taken unto himself the title "Volkileier" (leader — but whose meaning was more paternalistic than was Fuehrer or Duce).

With Malan in power, the Berlin planners believed that South Africa would drop out of the war if incentives from Germany were sufficient. It was suggested that those incentives might be to recognize South Africa's suzerainty over the former German colony of South West Africa, which was mandated to South Africa by the League of Nations after World War I. In exchange, South Africa would be expected to recognize German territorial gains in Mittel Afrika.

There were no plans by the Axis Powers to invade South Africa because it was well known that both the Afrikaners and English-speakers would unite to resist such a move. From Berlin's perspective, the best course of action would be to convert South Africa into a friendly neutral. Another move afoot was to support the effort of some Afrikaners to drop out of the British commonwealth and form, in their words, an independent "Christian-National Republic."

As for the black population of South Africa, both the English-speakers and the Afrikaners had long agreed that they should, together, continue their stewardship as guardians of the natives and that there should be permanent separation of the races. The Nationalists, however, called for even more stringent measures with regard to separation than those which currently existed. They had a name for it; "apartheid" (separateness).

The Nazi leaders also admired another trait of the South African whites in that they were staunchly anti-Semitic. Very few Jewish refugees from Europe had been allowed into the country since the expulsion of German Jews began in the early 1930s.

Other changes in the Bielfeld Plan suggested that Germany might give up its claim to the French half of the former German colony of Togo, in West Africa, and allow it to remain French as compensation for French territorial losses elsewhere and especially in Europe. The Germans would reclaim the British half of Togo, though, along with the British colonies of Gambia and Sierra Leone. The West African colonies of Gold Coast and Nigeria could remain British in exchange for British concessions elsewhere.

The modified Bielfeld Plan also called for Germany to acquire Spanish Guinea and Rio Muni, both in West Africa, and give Spain compensation elsewhere.

MORE ON THE FUTURE

At the dinner table, on the evening of January 15, one of the subjects of conversation was that of providing medical care for the lesser peoples of the world. Hitler took the negative view and criticized those German doctors who advocated giving the same levels of medical care to those people as was given to the whites. And as for the whites who refused to be vaccinated, Hitler's response was simple; "Let 'em croak."

The subject of natural resources also came up and Hitler said that he believed that the world's supply of iron ore and coal would soon run out. But the Fuehrer had a magical solution. He said that we will replace them with "air and water."

On the subject of museums, Hitler had a new motto for his future museum in Linz; "To the German people, that which belongs to it." And at Konigsberg, a rather dingy city on the Baltic, Hitler said that he would build a large museum to display many of the things found in Russia. He also said that he would build a magnificent opera house and a library in Konigsberg.

With regards to the many museums that currently existed in Nuremberg, Hitler said he would combine them all into one large Germanic Museum which would result in the creation of a magnificent and wonderful collection.

On the evening of the 18th, Hitler expressed his gratitude toward Fritz von Papen who was currently the Ambassador to Turkey and the highest ranking non-Nazi in Hitler's government. Hitler said of Papen, "We owe a debt of gratitude to Papen" for it was he who, in March 1933, helped lead the fight to modify the German constitution and bring about the Enabling Act which gave Hitler dictatorial powers.

On January 19, the subject was duelling and Hitler spoke out strongly against it. But he made an exception, saying, "I'd be inclined to permit duelling between priests and lawyers."

THE WANNSEE MEETING

On January 20, 1942, fifteen of the top SS leaders held a secret meeting at an elegant villa on the shore of a lake known as The Wannsee. The purpose of the meeting was to finalize the ways and means of carrying out the final solution to the Jewish question. It had already been determined that the Jews of Europe were to be exterminated in the gas chambers and crematoriums at certain concentration camps equipped for that purpose. This meeting was one of logistics — how to go about carrying out the exterminations, how to keep the victims unaware of their fate, and how to keep the whole program secret from the world.

In typical German efficiency, those people who were to be exterminated had already been listed. They totalled eleven million. Among the questions settled at Wannsee were how to transport the victims, how to feed and house them, who would be spared for laborers and other purposes. It was decided that the Jews from the General Government would be taken first, and next, the Jews from Western Europe. The Jews in the East were being taken care of, on the spot, by the Einsatzgruppen. It was also confirmed that the program had to be completed before the end of the war because, at that time, Germany would, necessarily, be more open to foreigners and other probing eyes.

The planners at Wannsee were following a principle laid down by Hitler in Mein Kampf, "The most cruel weapons are humane if they lead to a quicker victory."

The meeting lasted only ninety minutes. That night, Himmler dined with Hitler. Nothing was recorded as having been said about the Wannsee meeting.

STALEMATE IN THE EAST, BUT STILL MORE TALK OF THE FUTURE

In the East, Barbarossa was in shambles. The Soviets were using the winter weather to their advantage to launch counterattacks and win back some of their lost territory. The Germans and their allies were hanging on as best they could, trying to survive both the Soviet onslaughts and the weather.

At Hitler's table there was occasional talk of events in the East, but always in the tone that the setbacks were temporary.

And as always, Hitler spoke of the future. On January 22, 1942, he peered far into the future and saw the possibility of a unified Europe. He told his associates that it would be possible within two hundred years of German rule and Germanization to solve the problem of nationalities. He said that this had been accomplished for a brief period during the Thirty Years' War and it could be accomplished again with the German people in control. He added that the SS would be the "nursery" for those who ruled Europe.

On the 23rd, the Fuehrer talked at length about the Czechs, who were in the beginning stages of being Germanized. In so many words, he confirmed that this was the right course of action because the Czechs were a large foreign body of people in the midst of the German community and one or the other had to "give way."

He also launched into one of frequent diatribes against the Jews saying, as he had many times before, that they must get out of Europe. This time, however, he predicted their return — in three or four hundred years. He said they would return first as "commercial travellers" and then gradually begin settling here. Hitler went on to predict that they would prosper and become philanthropists and endow foundations and that the "poor Aryan boobies" would think kindly of them.

On the 24th, Hitler predicted one scenario as to how the war might end. It would come with a change of government in London and the decision by a majority of the British leaders to abandon Europe. He said that they would keep Churchill in power for appearance sake but only as long as it would take for their will to continue the struggle lasted. Hitler predicted that a chain reaction would follow the departure of Churchill which would destroy the western alliance and precipitate a collapse of the American economy, and the personal collapse of Roosevelt.

Then Hitler spoke of taxes. He said that he would change, and greatly simplify, the tax codes in Germany by using only four forms of taxation: a tax on luxury goods, a stamp tax (a form of national sales tax), a tax on private means, and a tax on commercial profits. He predicted that this change alone would reduce the bureaucracy by a third. And with regard to bureaucracies, he added that they must not be allowed to grow but, on the other hand, he favored installing them in majestic buildings on the condition that no enlargement would take place.

And back on taxes, he said that it might be best to allow peasants to pay their taxes "in produce" and that in Russia it would be absolutely necessary to do such things.

Hitler spoke of parades and how tiring they were as the long lines of soldiers passed by. He said that after the war he wanted to shorten the time it took for parades by having the soldiers march past sixteen deep as opposed to twelve deep which was the current practice.

On the evening of January 25, 1942, Hitler launched into a dissertation on the trials and tribulations of being a national leader and that, one day, he would like to give it all up. He said that the finest day of his life would be the day he left politics behind with all of its "grief and torments." When the war ended, and he had the sense of accomplishing his duties, he said, he would retire.

On the 27th, Hitler spoke again of the Jews and seemingly offered another solution to solving the Jewish question other than the gas chambers. He said, "The Jews must pack up, disappear from Europe. Let them go to Russia." This statement, however, since it was recorded for posterity and would eventually become known to the world, might well have been an intentional coverup for the exterminations which were now beginning.

On February 2, Hitler spoke admiringly of America's ability to mass-produce material things. He said that it was reading Henry Ford's books "that opened my eyes to these matters." He continued by saying that Germany, too, must adapt the principle of mass-production and encourage and develop the manufacture of machine tools.

On the evening of the 4th, Hitler spoke of the superior abilities of the southern Germans (like himself) to appreciate art and architecture. He said that he would make use of these men from the South in restructuring the North and the East. He continued saying that if he relied on Prussian architects to beautify Berlin he would do better to "abandon the project."

The next day, Hitler ranted again against the priests and referred, again, to this big book. "It's all written down in my big book," he said.

Talking about himself and his successors, he said that he was not of the opinion that the Fuehrer of Germany should be appointed for life. At the end of a certain time the Head of State must give way to a successor.

ON THE FRONTS AND AT HOME

The realities of the day for the German people were considerably different than the pictures painted of their future at Hitler's dinner table. In the East, millions of men were suffering and dying at the hands of a determined enemy and the terrible cold. In North Africa, Germans were dying too, but there they had something to show for it. Rommel's forces, in conjunction with the Italians, were pushing the British back into Egypt and it appeared that they would charge on to take Cairo and the Suez Canal. And, Hitler said again that, after the war, Egypt and the Suez Canal should belong to Italy.

In the Far East, the Japanese were beating back the Allies on every front, sustaining German hopes for a world-wide Axis victory.

On the German home front, though, there were no victories. The German people were living under the ever increasing Allied air attacks, and now had to make another sacrifice. During February, some 100,000 restaurants and places of amusement were closed in order to provide more manpower for the military and the war industry.

NOT SO BRIGHT A FUTURE FOR ITALY

As Hitler saw it, the future of Germany was very bright, but admitted that it might not be so for Italy. At the noon meal on February 17, he discussed Italy's future at length. Hitler said that the Duce would never be fully in charge in Italy until he got rid of the royal family and the Mafia. Furthermore, there was ample evidence that the Italian people were tiring of the war, which was substantiated by the poor showing of the Italian military forces in the East and in North Africa.

HUNGARY, RUSSIANS, NEGROES AND FUTURE PROJECTS

That evening, Hitler made remarks that modified, somewhat, his dislike for Europe's aristocracy. He told his associates that the great and beautiful estates of Hungary should be preserved and retained under the control of those who owned them. This was, he explained, because they were "centers of culture." Hitler sometimes used the word "culture" as a euphemism for any political entity that supported a dictatorial system similar to Germany's — which was the case in Hungary.

On the 19th, Hitler again spoke of the future he had planned for the Russians. "No vaccinations for the Russians," he said, "and no soap to get the dirt off."

Hitler then went on to utter one of his rare comments about Negroes. He said that dirt showed on black people only when the missionaries obliged them to wear clothes. In the state of nature, he added, Negroes are very clean but they have a horror of water. A couple of days later, Hitler made the comment that on the day when Germans had firmly reorganized Europe, they would be able to "look towards Africa."

Then Hitler turned to two of his favorite subjects, Trondheim and art. With regard to the future German bastion in Norway, he said that we must not forget to set up a museum of German masters at Trondheim.

And, with regard to the current practice of soliciting money from the rich to fund art museums, Hitler said that that was not good and should be changed.

Then on another favorite subject, he spoke of the observatory he would have built at Linz. He went on to tell how it would take on a religious significance and that people would come "every Sunday" to visit it. He said it would reveal to them "the greatness of the universe...but without the priests." He even had a spiritually appropriate motto ready for the observatory; "The heavens proclaim the glory of the everlasting."

THE SPRING OFFENSIVE

Virtually nothing is recorded in Hitler's conversations with regard to the coming spring offensive in the East, the offensive that Hitler and his associates hoped would finally defeat the Soviets. But on the evening of February 22 he gave a hint. In discussing the virtue of the Volkswagen and how it would become the car of the future and continually be improved, he admitted that there would still be the problem of petrol, but that that will be solved.

Hitler's dinner companions knew what he meant. Soon, the advance in the East would resume and the oil-rich Caucasus would be conquered. Then the Volkswagen drivers would have plenty of petrol.

CHAPTER 16

ON TO THE CAUCASUS!
ON TO CAIRO!

In the spring of 1942, the Germans would try again to conquer the European portion of the Soviet Union. The grand strategy called for the major effort to be exerted in the south with the goals there to invade and secure the Caucasus as well as to reach the southern portion of the Volga River.

It was anticipated that Leningrad would soon fall, freeing Army Group North which would then march on Moscow. Army Group Center would attack Moscow from the west and the city would eventually be surrounded and besieged until it surrendered. Any Soviet forces remaining west of the Urals would be destroyed or forced to retreat into Siberia.

Once European Russia was conquered, an advance into the Middle East would be undertaken. By then, Rommel would very likely have taken Cairo and the Suez Canal, and the Middle East could be invaded from both the north and the west.

As the Russian territories came under German control, a number of cartels would emerge to control such things as mineral resources, oil, chemicals, agriculture, fur and hides, tobacco, etc. Responsibility for organizing, and then managing, these commercial enterprises would be doled out to German concerns such as Krupp, Siemens, The Hermann Goering works, etc. Resources from the East would be utilized, as soon as possible, in support of the continuing war effort.

OPTIMISM AT THE TABLE AND THE RISE OF SPEER

With the prospects of victory close at hand, Hitler was noticeably up-beat. On the night of February 26, 1942, he told his dinner companions that Sunday will be the first of March, implying that good weather would follow and the advance to the east could be resumed. "Boys," he said, "you can't imagine what that means to me." Buoyed by such thoughts, Hitler again spoke of his personal future plans. When peace returns, he said he would spend three months without doing anything; "I'll immediately resign the command of the Wehrmacht... (and) send for Speer again." Speer? Why Speer? Is the Fuehrer saying here — and for the historical record — that Speer would be his replacement? What about Goering who, in the late 1930s, had been officially designated as Hitler's successor? In the next few sentences, Hitler confirmed that Goering's star had fallen and that, indeed, Speer was now his choice. Hitler went on to say that he would reduce the wartime administrative services to the bare necessity. Even the Four Year Plan (one of

Goering's power bases) would be reduced to a more modest operation and it would be passed over to the Ministry of Economics (and out of Goering's hands). Hitler went on to say that the postwar work of the government must be properly organized and for that it was necessary to find (speaking in English) "the right man in the right place." He continued by saying that a "new youth" was waiting and eager to carry on. Apparently, that new youth was Speer, who was thirty-eight. Goering was forty-nine.

Whether or not this came as a surprise to Goering is not recorded. Most likely, it did not. Goering could see the handwriting on the wall.

On the 28th, Hitler went into great detail describing the future private homes he planned to build for the German people. He said that when war was over, a million dwellings a year would be built for five consecutive years. The Fuehrer continued by saying that a modern home could be built in three months and that it must have all the latest labor-saving devices so that the hausfrau would be freed from her minor chores to make better use of her time. The children will have "play-gardens" near the homes so that the mothers can watch them from the house. And each household would have a domestic servant — presumably a woman servant from the East. Hitler went on saying that the hausfrau need only "press a button" for the woman to appear. Then, in the morning, an electrical timer will automatically turn on the stove to boil water for coffee or tea. To accomplish all these things, Hitler said he had already picked his man, Robert Ley, leader of the National Labor Front; "A nod from me, and he'll set everything humming." And there was more. Hitler said that as he had before, that building components for the homes must be standardized and that every home must have an inexpensive garage for the Volkswagen. Infatuated by his own rhetoric, the Fuehrer concluded by saying, "Let's begin at once!"

On March 8, German newspapers announced yet another postwar scheme; that

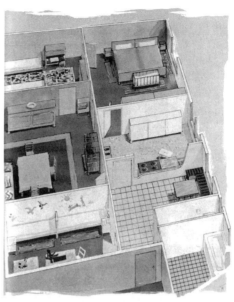

Plan of a medium-sized apartment for a worker's family of up to four children. Placement of furniture is included and the utility room would double as a children's play room. Over 1.4 million such units had been built before the war and construction continued during the war at a reduced pace. Full-scale construction was to resume after the war.

of building a dam and a series of locks across the Strait of Gibraltar to utilize the powerful tides there to generate electricity.

ON THE BATTLE FRONTS

In the East, there had been stalemate all winter at Leningrad and Sevastopol, but the good news was that the Soviet winter offensive seemed to be running out of steam. The Red Army, nevertheless, managed to make some gains in the Ukraine north of the Sea of Azov and push elements of Army Group Center back across the border into Belorussia. The German lines gave way but remained unbroken.

Optimism was high at Army headquarters that 1942 would bring the collapse of the Soviet Union and that, by the end of the year, Axis forces could begin their invasion of the Middle East. Some new plans had been created for that invasion, and old plans were revised.

Within the new proposals were contingency plans for the invasion of Afghanistan and India. This reflected the new optimism that had swept over the German High Command. Also, plans were being made for re-equipping German forces for operations in the tropical climates of sub-Saharan Africa.

With regard to North Africa, a study was underway to send Rommel a second armored corps to hasten his advance on Cairo. The units would come from the East as soon as Russia was defeated.

Behind the scenes, Hitler's health was still an issue. Goebbels recorded in his diary at the end of February that Hitler complained of bouts of dizziness and had said that the sight of snow gave him "physical pain." About this time, Ribbentrop recorded that Hitler suffered a brief fainting spell.

There was a mix of bad news and good news coming from the fronts. On March 16, a very depressing report was received at the Fuehrer's headquarters, stating that German casualties in the East now exceeded one million. Since June 22, 1941, that averaged out to be 3,968 men per day.

Also on the Eastern Front, the Russians had surrounded the entire II Corps of the German 16th Army in the Staraya area. Losses were extremely heavy as the Corps tried to free itself, and other German forces attempted to break through the Russian ring.

At sea, the German submarines were still sinking Allied shipping at a steady rate, especially off the east coast of America. The RAF, however, had increased its air strength over the Bay of Biscay and by March, all German submarines leaving and returning to their French bases had to transit the Bay submerged. This reduced, by days, the length of time the submarines could stay at sea.

In the air, the RAF had begun a series of night raids on Essen and other German centers of production in the Ruhr. The Luftwaffe was all but powerless to stop them.

One of Hitler's ongoing fears was that, with most of his forces engaged in the East, the Allies might try to invade western Europe. To meet this threat, Hitler authorized that the entire coast of occupied western Europe be strengthened. That would mean building a string of fortifications from the Spanish border to the Arctic. Such a project would be a giant undertaking that would further sap men and resources from the German economy. This was the inception of what became known as the "Atlantic Wall." It would consist of some 15,000 fortification and employ over 260,000 Germans, Frenchmen, North Africans, and others.

POLYGAMY – SMOKING – PRIVATE PROPERTY – BIG BUSINESS – LOTTERIES

At Hitler's dinner table on the evening of March 1, there was a discussion about the women of Germany and how, after the war, they would outnumber men. In this regard, Hitler made a comment indicating that he might support a program of polygamy. His words were, "Let's remember that after the Thirty Years' War polygamy was tolerated… (and) the nation recovered its strength." He went on to say that social mores had changed and that he would much rather see a woman with an illegitimate child than see her become an old maid. He said that every woman should have the opportunity to fulfill her destiny.

On the 11th, Hitler again denounced smoking. He said that it had been a mistake for the German High Command to give the soldiers a tobacco allowance. When peace returned, he said that he would abolish that ration and also instigate a program to prevent Germany's youth from smoking. He added that Germany could make better use of its foreign currency than squandering it on "imports of poison."

On March 24, Hitler spoke of private property, saying that he would "absolutely insist" on preserving it. He gave an example, suggesting that a factory that had gone into an estate should continue to run by the family and not pass to the government. "We must encourage private initiative," he said.

But, with regard to big business, Hitler had quite a different view. It was his opinion that profits from big businesses belonged to the state and not to the shareholders, and that the control of such enterprises should be transferred to the State.

Hitler also said at this dinner session that he liked the idea of national lotteries because they gave the lottery players hope, and hope was a positive force. It was his opinion that the lotteries should be "dragged out" for a year, if possible, so that the gambler would have time to nourish his illusions. Hitler said it was also a good idea to have a few casinos around because they too fostered hope, produced good taxes, brought in foreign currency and were beneficial to resort areas. He insisted, though, that lotteries and casinos should be monopolies of the State.

On the 27th, the subject at the table was art and artists. Hitler felt that there were too many art academies in Germany and that three should meet Germany's needs. He suggested they be established at Dussledorf, Munich and Vienna.

Then, on another of his favorite subjects — judges — Hitler said that the judicial system should be cleared of all judges who do not live up to the standards of National Socialism. He said that their numbers could be reduced to a tenth and that "the comedy of courts with a jury" must end. Hitler went on to explain that the judges of the future must consider the interests of the State over those of the individual.

On March 31, the topic was Turkey, where an unsuccessful assassination attempt had just been made on von Papen, Germany's Ambassador. In the discussion, the importance of Turkey becoming an ally of Germany was contemplated. Hitler said that he was ready to conclude treaties with Turkey that would supply her with arms and ammunition, guarantee her continued control of the Straits, and guarantee the integrity of her borders.

For the moment, however, the Turks were being very guarded with respect to their relationship with Germany. This was due to two things; Germany's poor military showing in the Soviet Union over the winter, and intense diplomatic pressures from the Allies.

TURKEY

Turkey had a precarious position in the politics of both Europe and the Middle East. On her European borders with Bulgaria and Greece, there were relatively strong Axis forces. On her southern border, there were British and Free French forces in Syria and British forces in Iraq. On her eastern border was the Caucasus, which might soon become a battleground. Also in the east was a short border with Iran, which was neutral, but which cooperated with the Allies.

Because of these conditions, the horrible prospect loomed in Ankara that Turkey could become a battleground from almost any direction. To prevent this from happening, the Turkish government was following a very delicate policy of neutrality.

Germany, however, throughout the 1930s, had made a strong effort to establish friendly ties with Ankara. This included the construction, through Turkey, of an important section of the Berlin-to-Baghdad Railroad. In early 1939, commercial air traffic had been established between Germany and Turkey, and the Germans committed themselves to aid in the construction of a new seaport at Golcuk, an undertaking very important to the Turks. Berlin Radio also began broadcasting to Turkey in the Turkish language. Furthermore, Berlin had sent Fritz von Papen, one of Germany's top political figures, to Turkey as its ambassador. Papen was a well-respected non-Nazi and very close to Hitler. Also, Berlin let it be known in Ankara that Germany's policy toward that Straits was one of hands-off.

While Germany was making inroads into Turkey, Italy was not. Rome's claims in the Middle East and her interference into Arab affairs did not sit well in Ankara.

During late 1940, German military planners had designs on Turkey. They saw the possibility of attacking Egypt from the east by an advance through Turkey, Syria, Lebanon and Palestine. The Turks, of course, were alert to this possibility and had announced that any invasion of Turkey would be vigorously opposed by military means. Unbeknownst to the Turks, Hitler vetoed the idea of marching through Turkey in early 1941 in order to maintain friendly relations with that country.

On June 18, 1941, with the invasion of the Soviet Union only four days away, Germany and Turkey signed a ten-year treaty of friendship in which both parties agreed to settle differences by negotiation. During the negotiations for the treaty, Germany asked the Turks to permit the transit of German forces through their territory, but the Turks steadfastly refused. The Germans backed down and a simplified treaty of friendship resulted. It was Berlin's thinking that a simplified treaty was better than no treaty at all. Furthermore, the Allies now had to concern themselves with the possibility that there might be secret clauses in the treaty permitting German transit.

When the Axis Powers invaded the Soviet Union, Turkey promptly proclaimed its neutrality, but also let Berlin know that it had concerns about the some twenty million ethnic Turks who lived in the southern Ukraine, the Crimea and the Caucasus.

Soon after the invasion, German-Turkish relations soured because the SS had labelled the Turkestanis of the Caucasus and Caspian Sea area an undesirable Asiatic race. Then, the Einsatzgruppen, in their zeal to racially cleanse the East, murdered a sizeable number of Turkestanis.

German-Turkish relations were further strained by reports of poor treatment of Turkestani POWs. Upon learning of these things, Ambassador Papen immediately appealed to Berlin to soften its stance against the ethnic Turks in the Soviet Union.

Hitler reacted by ordering Rosenberg's Ministry to create a committee to investigate the situation. Also, in October 1941, Hitler allowed two Turkish Generals and their aides to tour the Eastern front and later personally met with them.

In the meantime, a typhus epidemic broke out in some of the camps holding the Turkestani POWs and more ethnic Turks died. German-Turkish relations suffered again.

The problem of German mistreatment of the ethnic Turks did not go away, but some measures were taken by Berlin to eliminate the most grievous atrocities. Still, however, reports of German mistreatment of ethnic Turks continued to reach Ankara, forcing Papen to continually urge the German government to give the matter serious attention.

In late December 1941, the Americans offered the Turks Lend-Lease and Ankara accepted. Considering the needs of the German armed forces in the East, Berlin was unable to match this offer.

"CARPET BOMBING"

By the spring of 1942, the RAF had acquired enough planes to begin a new type of air bombardment called "Carpet Bombing." This consisted of large numbers of aircraft bombing a single city indiscriminately. Carpet Bombing hit the civilian population the hardest and was designed to weaken their morale.

The first such raid was carried out March 28, 1942, on the city of Lubeck. Three hundred and twenty civilians were killed and many more injured. The Luftwaffe soon realized what was happening and asked Hitler to release some German aircraft from the Eastern front in order to better protect the German cities. Hitler refused.

During a raid on Essen, the RAF introduced a new weapon, a two-ton bomb, the largest yet used in the war.

THE POSTWAR GERMAN GOVERNMENT

On March 31, 1942, Hitler informed his dinner companions as to the makeup of the German government after the war. He had given the matter considerable thought, he told them, and now his mind was made up.

He said that Germany would continue to be a republic with a Chief of State, a parliament (the Reichstag), a judicial system, and one political party — the National Socialist Party. The Chief of State would have absolute power and be elected, in secret session, by the senate of the Reichstag. This, of course, did not apply to Germany's current leadership. Hitler compared this type of election to that of the election of a pope in the Roman Catholic Church. Once a Head of State was elected the Party leaders, leaders of the armed forces and all important government officials must take an oath of allegiance to the new leader within three hours.

Hitler went on, saying that membership in the Reichstag would be by appointment of the Party and would not be permanent. The primary function of the Reichstag would be to advise the Chief of State. The Riechstag could debate and pass legislation, but the Chief of State would have veto power. Only the Chief of State would have the power to declare war, but the Reichstag would have the right "…to intervene in case of need." Hitler said that this system might last for eight or nine hundred years and cited the thousand year history of the Roman Catholic Church as an example.

BARBAROSSA RESUMES

On April 5, 1942, Jodl signed Directive #41, authorizing the advance in the East to resume. The advance was slow to get underway, however, due to continued strong Soviet resistance and the onset of the muddy season due to the annual spring thaw. The size of the Axis forces seemed impressive on paper, but it was now composed of some second-rate units and more allied units, some of which were poorly equipped and poorly motivated.

HITLER AT THE TABLE

On April 4, the Fuehrer discussed another matter for the future — that of inheritances. He said that he favored one child

in a family inheriting "everything" and that the other children should be given a good education and then "thrown out into life." This was to apply in both Germany and the colonial East.

The next day, the topic was patents once again. Hitler, and most Germans, had long been galled by the clause in the Versailles Treaty that required Germany to turn over to France all of its patents after World War I. Now, Hitler vowed that this would be reversed and Germany would exercise controls over French patents. And, as for the rest of the world, Hitler's solution was simple; German patents would be kept secret.

Then the conversation turned again to the East and Hitler told his listeners more of what they might expect there after the war. New armament factories would be built in the East using concentration camp labor. Also the marshes would be cultivated, by planting reeds which, in turn, will form a barrier against the extraordinary cold waves of the Russian winter.

Then, Hitler went on to say that there would be large nettle plantations in the East because the fiber from that plant was superior to cotton. And, he stated that a reforestation program must be carried out in the Ukraine in order to counterbalance the rains which are a real scourge in the area.

Turning to the northern front and Leningrad, Hitler said again that that city was "…doomed to decay," and that the Neva River would become the boundary between the Ostland and Finland. He said that the entire Baltic Sea would become a German "inland sea," and that the port cities in the Baltic states would be adequate to serve the maritime needs of the region. These projects, and others, Hitler predicted, would serve Germany's needs for several centuries.

The future of the Netherlands became a topic when Himmler, who was a dinner guest, stated that the Dutch would have no need for an army after the war because the defense of the North Sea and Channel coasts will be Germany's responsibility. Hitler agreed. Himmler went on to say that the

Dutch Frisians, who inhabited the northern part of Holland, had more of a kindred relationship with their fellow Frisians across the border in Germany than they did with the Dutch. He suggested that a new province be created to unite the Frisians. This, of course, would mean that Germany would annex the northern part of Holland. Both Hitler and Keitel agreed that this was a good idea. Himmler went on to say that, in Holland, three politically-oriented boarding schools, financed by the Party, should be established to train carefully selected Dutch men and women for future leadership roles in that country. Himmler added that such a plan was currently being considered for Norway. And again, Hitler approved of this idea.

The subject then turned to the General Government whose long-term future was, as yet, undecided. Hitler said that both he and Hans Frank, the Governor-General of the General Government, had agreed that, in time, the cities of Cracow and Lublin, and the surrounding agricultural lands in the central part of the General Government, should become exclusively German. This implied that those areas would be annexed to the Reich. The southernmost part of the General Government had already been promised to Hungary for her participation in the war. This left the northern part of the General Government, around Warsaw, as the remaining area for the Poles. Hitler added that care must be taken to see that Germans and Poles do not intermingle.

On April 7, the table talk was on the future German farms in the East. It had been agreed that young men who had completed twelve years of military service, and who would volunteer to settle in the East would be given farms free of charge. Hitler said that during their twelfth year of service, these men should be given specialized schooling on the types of farming they intended to pursue. And, he said again, that these men must not marry anyone except "country girls."

On the 9th, Hitler spoke of the future automobiles of Germany. He said that the proliferation of models, as had happened in the United States, must be avoided. Only about a dozen models would suffice and components, especially the engines and dashboards, must be "simplified." Hitler praised the twenty-eight-horsepower Volkswagen engine saying it can be used in autos as well as in many military vehicles such as field kitchens, reconnaissance cars, ambulances, small trucks and artillery tractors.

On the 11th, the subject at the table was once again religion. Here, Hitler put into simple terms how he would handle the religious questions after the war. He said that the people of each village must be allowed to evolve into their own independent sect, worshipping God as they saw fit. He added that if certain villages wanted to turn to "black magic," then they should be permitted to do so.

This conversation led to a discussion of who would keep the peace in the East after the war. Hitler said that there must be no native militia or native police lest they might, one day, turn on the German settlers. Keeping the peace would be strictly in the hands of the Germans and the settlers themselves who would be armed. Each settler must keep in contact with his local "strong point" and this policy should continue until the settlers far outnumber the local inhabitants.

Ironically, as Hitler spoke, tens of thousands of local inhabitants in the East were under arms fighting for the Germans.

On April 12, Hitler again addressed the expected imbalance between men and women after the war. He estimated that there would be two million women "condemned to celibacy," and that these women should be given special opportunities to become teachers and work, in other ways, with children in order to "...provide them with an outlet for their maternal instincts."

Hitler discussed, at length, the reforms he intended to impose on the German education system and concluded by saying that once these reforms were in place, the German educational system would surpass the British school system in every way.

TARTARS – A NEW ALLY

It was common knowledge in Germany that the Tartars of the southern Ukraine had long been opposed to communism. This belief was confirmed when, as German troops entered the Crimea, Tartars hailed them as liberators. As a result of this the decision was made in Berlin, in early April, to capitalize on the situation and welcome the Tartars as allies. This would have political advantages, too, since the Tartars had Turkish and Mongolian roots and were Muslims. This would provide a bridge between Germany and Turkey and the other Muslim nations on the one hand, and Germany and the peoples in Siberia, such as the Turkestanis, who might one day come under German control.

The program was to start with the Crimean Tartars who had a reputation of being diligent fighters. These people were to be given certain privileges over the other indigenous peoples and encouraged to join the German Army as auxiliaries. It was estimated that 20,000 would do so. There was further consideration being given in Berlin to offering the Tartars some form of autonomy after the war.

It was also agreed in April that Cossacks be recruited as both anti-Partisan fighters and front line troops. These things were already being done by commanders in the field, but now Hitler signed an order making it official.

FRANCE, BELGIUM AND BURGUNDY

The future of France was the topic of the dinner conversation on April 25, 1942. Hitler said that in formulating the future peace treaty with France, Germany's current needs must be emphasized and that historical precedents must also act as a guide: he emphasized that Germany must acquire and maintain military bases on the Atlantic coast of France. With regard to historical precedents, he said that Germany must not forget that "...the old Kingdom of Burgundy played a prominent role in German history..." Hitler was referring to the fact that Burgundy had been an effected buffer state

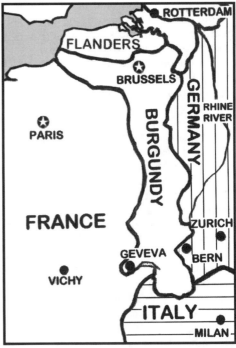

Germany's plan for the new state of Burgundy which would serve as a buffer state between Germany and France.

between Germany and France in the past and might serve that purpose once again. There were those in the Nazi leadership, and in the leadership of the French-speaking Walloon community of Belgium, who advocated the resurrection of the state of Burgundy. The creation of such a state would mean an end to the state of Belgium and the incorporation of territory from France and, perhaps, Switzerland.

LINZ VS BUDAPEST

Speer was a guest at the table on April 26 and the subject was the rebuilding of Linz. Hitler gave more details on what he was planning for his home town. It would become a Danubean city, he said, which would surpass Budapest for its beauty. The banks of the river at Linz will be built up in "a magnificent fashion," which will include a great hotel for the Strength-Through-Joy organization. There would be new municipal buildings, a Party House, an Army headquarters, an olympic stadium, and a new suspension bridge across the Danube.

On the other side of the Danube, Hitler said that he would build the great observatory of which he had often spoken. It would feature the "cosmological conceptions of... Ptolemy, of Copernicus and of Horbiger...," and it would serve to counter the pseudoscience of the Catholic Church." Hitler said that he would personally design the interior of the observatory in collaboration with Professor Paul Troost, Germany's renowned architect who had been credited with creating the National Socialist "new Style" of architecture. Then, Hitler made an interesting revelation, saying that he had recently made a mistake by inadvertently sending one of his sketches on the observatory's interior to Frau Troost instead of a birthday card "I'd done for her." Here, Hitler revealed that he still found time to dabble in art. It will be remembered that, as a struggling artist in Vienna before World War I, he supported himself, in part, by making and selling hand-painted postcards to tourists.

Hitler went on to tell how he would also beautify Vienna, which would "infuriate the Hungarians." This would be alright, he said, because it would be repayment for Germany's having to pull their "chestnuts out of the fire." This was a reference to the poor showing that the Hungarian Army was making in the East.

On April 30, Hitler's mind was on Linz again and on music. He said that he had given an order to the Director of the Munich Opera to recruit and train a troupe of artistes who would eventually become the resident artistes at the future Opera of Linz. Hitler stated he told the Director to take as much time as he liked, even two to five years if necessary, so that the performers could develop their special gifts to the maximum. He went on to say that it would be a good idea if other opera directors followed this example.

Continuing to speak of operas, Hitler said, "...the meretricious system of inviting 'guest artistes' for particular performances must cease." Hitler had a pension for learning and using new words. He said it would be better to develop the talents of the regular artistes rather than to rely on outsiders. Hitler added that he was already seeking an individual who could fill the post of Music Director at Linz.

"OPERATION BLUE"

On May 8, 1942, the Germans launched their spring offensive in the Ukraine — "Operation Blue." One of its first objectives was to advance into the northern Caucasus to secure the oil fields there. Another immediate objective was to capture the city of Kharkov on the northern flank of Blue and three hundred miles north of the Crimea.

By May 15, German troops had cleared the eastern end of the Crimea and attacks were underway at Kharkov against strong Soviet opposition. The city would not be secured until the end of June. Just before the launch of the new attacks, Hitler had received a report from the Army that it was short 625,000 men. To help make up this shortage, the draft age in Germany was lowered from eighteen to seventeen-and-a-half.

The Soviets still could not stop the German Blitzkrieg attacks but they had learned how to blunt them and make them more costly for the Germans. They also learned how to better extract their own troops so that they would not be surrounded by the Blitzkrieg maneuvers. Given the strong Soviet defense at Kharkov, and the new Soviet defensive tactics, it was reluctantly concluded at the Fuehrer's headquarters that the swift advances of 1941 would not likely be repeated.

LESS FOR POSTERITY

The records of Hitler's table conversations are noticeably fewer beginning on May 7, 1942. There are long gaps, up to seven days, between recorded sessions, and some records for a meal's conversation consist of only one paragraph. Obviously, other matters had become priority and/or the things being discussed at the table were not suitable for the historical record. But there were still some discussions about the future. A good example is the record of the midday meal on May 8, which is only one paragraph long. Here, Hitler gives his views on the future of the island of Crete in the Mediterranean. He said that Germany would not retain control of the island because it would require the presence of a German fleet in the Mediterranean which would be offensive to Turkey. He did not say who would control the former Greek island, but in all likelihood, it would be given to Italy.

The next recorded table conversations were made at the two meals on May 11 and consist of one paragraph each. At that time, Hitler expressed his interest in creating an exclusive national cemetery for Germany's great leaders. He said nothing, however, about his own final resting place.

Hitler also spoke of honey, saying that it was possible for German apiarists to increase their honey production "tenfold."

On the 12th, the recorded conversation is quite long compared to the days previous. Hitler, as usual, jumped from topic to topic. He lamented the decline of the whaling industry and said that, after the war, it should be revived. On the settling of the East, he said that only men under fifty should be sought out as settlers. Hitler also predicted that in ten years there would be some twenty million settlers in the East and that "bilingualism" would have been wiped out. Referring to the current Partisan menace in the East, Hitler predicted that by the second, or at the latest, the third of settlers, those regions would be completely pacified. But, he added, "…we shall not succeed except by the application of the most severe measures."

As for the people of Germany itself, it was generally agreed at the table that the physical appearance of certain Germans was not sufficiently Germanic. Hitler acknowledged this problem and said that he planned to station troops who were "ethnically healthy" in those areas in order to "…improve the blood-stock of the population."

On the 20th, Hitler praised the German miners, calling them the elite members of the German work force and men of stamina. When peace returns, Hitler said, "the amelioration of the standard of life of these men… .must be a matter for our particular concern."

Talking more on the future, Hitler said that Munich would acquire a great central railway station and that projects like that should be undertaken year-by-year at any cost.

A HOMELAND FOR THE JEWS

With the Jews of Europe being systematically exterminated in the Nazi death camps, and rumors of the exterminations reaching the Allies, it was most appropriate for the historical record that Hitler speak again of a Jewish homeland as part of the overall coverup that would have to be instigated after the war for these horrible deeds.

Heretofore, the location of a future Jewish homeland had not been decided. Ever since the invasion of the Soviet Union, Hitler had run hot and cold on the possibility of sending the Jews to Siberia. Now, on May 29, in a luncheon conversation with Goebbels, Hitler appeared to have made up his mind. He said that neither Siberia (and presumable Muscovy) nor Palestine could be future Jewish homelands. In Siberia, he said that the Jews might one day develop into a large and cohesive nationalistic group that might, again, threaten Europe. As for Palestine, that country was wanted by the Arabs. Hitler suggested now that somewhere in central Africa might be considered for the Jews and, of course, Madagascar was still an option.

This interchange between Hitler and Goebbels, who both knew of the death camps, is significant in that it appeared to be Hitler's plan to leave a relatively large number of Jews alive at the end of the war. This likelihood was supported by the fact that more and more Jews were being spared from the gas chambers because they were needed as workers. This portended that significant numbers of them would survive to the end of the war and, therefore, a decision had to be made as to what to do with them at that time.

MADAGASCAR INVADED BY THE BRITISH

On May 5, 1942, Madagascar was suddenly in the world's headlines. The British invaded the northern tip of the Vichy-controlled island and captured the port city of Diego Suarez which had one of the best harbors in the Indian Ocean. This was an effort to improve the position of the British Navy in that part of the world which had the task of protecting the Allies sea routes to Egypt, East Africa and the Middle East. The Vichy troops offered some opposition, but were quickly overcome.

Then, in September, the British invaded and conquered the remainder of the island, believing that the Vichy French were allowing Japanese submarines to use their harbors which, in fact, they were not. Again, the French offered some military resistance, but were eventually defeated. Later, the British turned control of the island over to the Fighting French.

As for Madagascar becoming a homeland for the Jews, that was no longer an option for the Axis Powers.

"SATURATION BOMBING"

On May 30, 1942, the British carried out their first thousand-plane raid on one city — Cologne. This ushered in a new phase of the air war over Europe which became known as "Saturation Bombing," an escalation of Carpet Bombing. And it was likely to continue because the Americans were rapidly building up their air strength in Britain. The raid, which took virtually every bomber in the British inventory, severely damaged Cologne, a major industrial city, and sent a clear message to the Nazi leaders that the air war had been escalated to a new level. Hitler was informed of the raid while it was still in progress and got the message loud and clear. He was noticeably angry and his reaction was to damn both the British and Goering.

At the time, he admitted to an aide that he saw no quick end to the air war.

Hitler's somber mood must have lingered on because no record of the dinner conversation was made for the night of May 30.

On June 2, the second thousand-plane raid was carried out on Essen, and from London came the announcement that the Allies would soon be capable of carrying out two-thousand and even four-thousand-plane raids.

MORE DECLARATIONS OF WAR AND THE ARRIVAL OF THE AAF

During the first two weeks of June 1942, the World War widened. Mexico and the Philippine Government-in-Exile in the United States declared war on Germany, while the United States declared war on Romania, Bulgaria and Hungary.

Then, on June 12, the first American Army Air Forces (AAAF) air raid was conducted over Europe. It came not from Britain, but from Egypt and targeted the oil facilities at Ploesti, Romania. The raids numbered only thirteen planes and did little damage, but the strategic significance was undeniable. This was an 800-mile raid carried by American's long-range B-24 bombers and demonstrated that Germany's main source for oil was within Allied bombing range. It also demonstrated that, if and when those bombers began flying out of Britain, they could reach every city in Germany and the northern half of Italy.

On top of these developments, reports were received in Berlin that the Japanese Navy had suffered a major defeat at the island of Midway in the Pacific and that the balance of naval power in the Pacific was now tilted toward the Americans.

"I SHALL NEVER GO TO SPAIN"

While the number of Allied nations was growing, Germany was losing one of its most promising potential allies, Spain. Spain had refused to grant German demands for bases in North Africa and the Canary Islands and now seemed, more than ever, determined to remain neutral. This became very obvious after the United States entered the war. Also, it must be remembered that the Spaniards had watched Italy lose her East African colonies to the Allies and realized it could also happen to them. Franco, though, still uttered public and private statements that the Axis Powers wanted to hear but, by now, no one in Berlin or Rome believed him. As an example, Franco told the Germans and Italians that if the Allies invaded northwest Africa, Spain would intercede. This was seen as something of a joke in Berlin and Rome because it was very unlikely that Franco would send his army to help defend French Morocco or French controlled Algeria. Furthermore, Franco's feeble army would be no match for the modern armies of the Allies. Germany's relations with Spain had become so strained that, at the Fuehrer's headquarters, no one dared mention Franco's name.

Furthermore, reports were being received of political turmoil in Madrid that led to street brawls. Then there was a most bizarre incident that finally got Hitler's goat. Word was received that Franco had promoted a long-dead saint to the rank of Field Marshal for a miracle that the saint had supposedly granted. From Hitler's point of view, this confirmed that Franco was a man of very poor judgement and a lackey of the Vatican.

The situation in Spain was discussed at the dinner table on June 5, 1942, and Hitler concluded by saying, "...I shall never go to Spain."

Ironically, the all-volunteer Spanish "Blue Division," fighting on the Eastern Front, was performing well. And not so ironically, Hitler saw its commander, General Munoz-Grande, as a possible alternative to Franco.

GOOD NEWS FROM NORTH AFRICA AND THE EASTERN FRONT

In North Africa, General Rommel had, once again, proven his worth and invaded Egypt for a second time. On June 21, Hitler awarded these efforts by promoting him to Field Marshal. By the end of the month, Rommel's forces had reached the coastal village of El Alamein, only eighty miles from the major British naval base at Alexandria which the British Navy was in the process of vacating. The conquest of Cairo and the Suez Canal seemed to be at hand.

In Cairo, Egyptian students took to the streets to cheer Rommel, and Egyptian Army leaders made preparations to welcome Rommel to Cairo. Others, however, fled to Palestine and the British diplomats at the embassy burned hundreds of pounds of documents so that they would not fall into German hands. Ashes fell all around the embassy area and the day became known as "Ash Wednesday."

Then on June 27, came the long-awaited news that the Soviet bastion of Sevastopol, in the Crimea, had finally been taken. Now all of the Crimea was in German hands and Army Group South had additional forces available that could be utilized in the invasion of the Caucasus and the advance to the Volga.

These events were reflected in the enthusiastic discussions that reappeared at Hitler's table on the 27th. Hitler spoke optimistically, once again, of building roads and railroads in the East, and that the time was near to start choosing sites in the East for the new German cities. On the 29th, he rehashed his plans to turn the Danube River into an all-German waterway and to the unification of all Europe under Germany's guidance. He predicted that future generations in Europe would "accept without comment" the unification of Europe under Germany.

On June 30, Hitler again discussed one of his favorite subjects — art. He condemned the current system whereby the "big-wigs" of the art academies dominated the art scene and frequently stifled the genius of young artists. (It must be remembered that Hitler had been rejected as a student at the Vienna Art Institute by the institute's big-wigs who claimed that his art was not good enough.) To solve this problem, Hitler said, the academies must be split up into a series of individual studios, on the lines of the State studio. This was a plan that insured that artistic talent, like his, would not be overlooked in the future.

THE FUTURE OF EGYPT

Up to now, the Axis Powers had paid little attention as to how they would administer Egypt after its conquest. Egypt was, technically, an independent and neutral country and it had been agreed that these conditions would be maintained when the Axis took over.

During the spring of 1942, negotiations were conducted in Berlin and Rome, and a workable plan for the future of Egypt emerged. Generally, the civil administration of Egypt would come under the guidance of the Italians in an arrangement that would become more-or-less permanent. The Germans would be responsible for the military occupation of the country for, at least, the duration of the war. With the Germans controlling the occupation, the presence of the Italian military in Egypt would be minimal and serve as a sign that the Italians had come as liberators and not as conquerors.

The Italians had already chosen their man for Egypt, Count Serafino Mazzolini, Italy's former ambassador to Cairo. Mazzolini was to acquire the title of "Delegato Politico" (Political Delegate) which was seen in Rome as a position considerably higher than that of ambassador. The government of King Farouk was to be preserved, with Mazzolini serving as the royal advisor and maintaining a low profile.

The Germans and Italians had also agreed that Italy should control the Suez Canal in similar fashion as the British had done in order to maintain a sea link with her colonies in East Africa, which would eventually be recovered. To guard the Suez Canal, Italian garrisons would be stationed permanently along the length of the canal.

The leaders in Cairo were aware of the Axis plan and that, in all likelihood, the Italians would simply replace the British. But the British had, by now, worn out their welcome in Egypt and the Egyptian leaders were willing to take their chances with the Italians. Besides, the prospect of playing Germany against Italy presented an opportunity that did not exist under the British.

The Italians, in keeping with their continuing effort to woo the Arab world, hoped to make Egypt into an idyllic Arab state — a state that others would emulate. Italy's two thousand years of friendly relations with Egypt would help in that respect.

In Berlin, the Germans had their doubts as to whether the Italians could pull it off. One major concern was food, which would be the responsibility of the Italians to provide. In this respect, prospects were not good. The Italians had demonstrated that they had not been able to provide enough food for the people of Greece and that famine conditions existed there. Furthermore, the Germans had let it be known that they could not be depended upon to furnish food for Egypt. Berlin also expressed concerns about Italy's ability to supply fuel and raw materials to Egypt. The Germans, though, were content to let matters take their course, because if the Italians proved incapable of managing the situation, they (the Germans) were in an advantageous position to intervene.

ADMINISTERING THE CAUCASUS

By the end of June, German plans for the administration of the soon-to-be-conquered Caucasus had been finalized. The region would be federated into one large political entity, under Rosenberg's Ministry, and be known as the "Reichskommissariat Kaukasien." It would be bounded on the north by the Don River, on the west by the Black Sea, on the east by the Caspian Sea, and on the south by Iran and Turkey. The Reichskommissariat would be subdivided into seven segments, three of which, Georgia, Azerbaijan and Armenia, would become independent states. The others would remain under German control for an undetermined period of time.

The all-important oil resources would be developed and exploited by a German-controlled cartel known as "Kontinentale Oel."

A native civil administration was currently being put together in Germany consisting primarily of pro-German emigres, most of whom had fled Russia during the Bolshevik revolution. The leaders of this body were to be given access to Caucasian POWs and could be allowed to select those who would be willing to work for them under the new arrangement. A propaganda campaign was planned to convince the people of the Caucasus that Germany was their friend, and vague comments were to be made that the Caucasus might, one day, become a united and independent entity.

OTHER EVENTS IN THE EAST

German advances in the East had reached the point whereby Army Group South had to be divided into two smaller components; Army Group A, which would advance into the Caucasus, and Army Group B, which would advance toward the Volga and eventually reach the river at Stalingrad. Once Stalingrad was secured, Army group B would turn south and take Astrakhan at the mouth of the river which had been planned as the southern anchor of the A-A Line frontier. By taking Astrakhan, the Soviet's oil supply from the Caucasus would also be cut off.

As Army Group B advanced toward Stalingrad, Germany's allies, Italy, Romania and Hungary, would guard Army Group B's left flank by positioning themselves along the southern bank of the Don River.

In the Crimea, civil changes were being implemented. Since it was to become an integral part of Germany, the roundup of Jews, Communists and Gypsies had begun. Determinations with regard to the other minorities would be made later.

CHAPTER 17

FROM HOPE TO DESPAIR

During the last half of July, the Axis advance in the Ukraine was progressing rapidly against light opposition. This gave rise to the hope, once again, that the Red Army was beaten. It was in this atmosphere that Hitler moved to an advanced Fuehrer headquarters built for him in the East at Vinnitsa, fifty-five miles southwest of Zhitomir and some 500 miles behind the front. Vinnitsa was also in the friendly Ukrainian district of Galicia.

TABLE CONVERSATIONS AT VINNITSA

Hitler's table conversations continued to be recorded at Vinnitsa and, once again, became frequent and lengthy. This reflected the fact that better news was now coming from the front.

As usual, part of Hitler's conversations dwelled on the future. On July 17, 1942, he spoke of the future of radio in the new German Empire. He lamented the fact that German radio had become wireless rather than wired. He explained what his table companions surely knew, that wired radio was a much better way to control the masses because wired radios could not pick up foreign broadcasts. Plus, he reminded his companions, atmospheric interference was not a problem with wired radio. As for the future of radio, Hitler said that all radios in the German Empire would be changed over to wired radio, and that the German people would not mind at all.

On the 18th, Hitler gave more insight into the construction of Autobahns that were to be built in the East. Instead of two lanes per side, he said that there would be three; slow-moving traffic will keep to right, normal traffic will be in the center, and swift-moving traffic will keep to the left. He added that such roads would be built throughout the East, all radiating out from Berlin.

On the 22nd, Hitler discussed the future of the Channel Islands, the only part of Great Britain that had been conquered. He said that after the war he would give them over to the Strength-Through-Joy organization and convert them into "marvelous health resort" because of their mild climate and the fact that the islands were already a vacation destination for the British and others.

Also on this day, Hitler lambasted lawyers again and added two more parts to his plans for the future of that profession. He said that it should be nationalized and that the lawyers would no longer be addressed as "Doctor."

July 22 was not a good day for Hitler. He complained of severe headaches, insomnia and impaired vision in his right eye. Doctor Morell diagnosed the problem as Arteriospasm and gave Hitler anticoagulant pills and had him bled again by leeches. All of this was in addition to the regular injections Hitler was now receiving. Hitler, believing that the bright sun was part of the problems with his eye, had a military cap made with an extra-large visor. With these measures taken, and with the help of nature, the Fuehrer slowly recovered.

On July 24, Hitler's table discussion addressed the problem of King Leopold of Belgium. Leopold had refused to flee into exile in Britain along with the Belgium government and thus considered himself a German prisoner of war. The Germans did not necessarily share this view. Nevertheless, Leopold remained in self-imposed isolation in his palace near Brussels. Unfortunately for the Germans, Leopold continued to be a rallying point for the Belgian people, both the Walloons and Flemings. Such a situation could cause problems in the future, especially if Belgium were to be dismantled. Hitler, though, had a solution. He said that he would pay him to go away by offering him a generous pension which would assure him a very comfortable exile.

ON THE FRONTS

July 23, 1942, was an eventful day. Word was received at Vinnitsa that the port city of Rostov, the gateway to the Caucasus, had been captured. The first of the Caucasus oil fields, at Maikop, lay only 150 miles to the south. Reports indicated, though, that Soviet forces south of Rostov were strong and that the Axis Powers would still have to fight for the oil.

To ease this burden, the ailing Fuehrer ordered that more Italian troops, which were now serving on the Eastern front in increased numbers, be used in the conquest of the Caucasus. This was a logical step, because once the Caucasus was taken, the next move would be into the Middle East, which was to become part of Italy's postwar domain.

Also ordered to the Caucasus was the Romanian Third Army, because Romania, which had a long coast line on the Black Sea, had a vested interest in seeing that as much of that coast line as possible was in friendly hands.

North of the Caucasus, at Stalingrad, reports came in, indicating that the Soviets intended to make a determined stand to hold that city. To address this situation, Hitler, on the 23rd, ordered that Leningrad, in the north, be taken by the beginning of September so that large numbers of German forces could be released to march on Moscow. This would force the Soviets to strengthen the Moscow defenses, hopefully at the expense of the Stalingrad front.

"FRIENDS"

To further facilitate the conquest of the Caucasus, Hitler ordered that the German armed forces treat the people of the Caucasus in a friendly manner. This order was in stark contrast to previous orders concerning the treatment of non-Germanic peoples of the East. It stated that the people of the Caucasus would be allowed to manage much of their own affairs and that places of worship would be allowed to reopen, private property would be respected, requisitioned goods would be paid for, and the local women would be respected. Each member of the German armed forces was ordered to do his best to "win the confidence of the people by model conduct."

The local people were also authorized to take over the collectives and do with them as they wished. One exception applied, however, with regard to the grain-producing collectives. They were to remain in operation under German supervision with their future to be decided later.

This proved to be an easy order for the Axis troops to carry out because, almost universally, the people of the Caucasus greeted the Axis troops as liberators. Two ethnic groups in the Caucasus, the Chechens and Karachai, were especially cooperative because they had been in armed revolt against the communists since the fall of 1941.

Living up to their word, the German Army allowed the various ethnic groups to form committees to manage local affairs and foster collaboration. Local men were also permitted to volunteer for service in the German Army.

As the SS followed in the wake of the Army, they imposed some restrictions on Caucasus Jews, such as the wearing of the yellow star, but there was no immediate on-the-spot executions or large-scale deportations to the concentration camps. The fate of the Caucasus Jews was to be decided later.

Because of this lenient treatment, the Germans expected that no strong Partisan forces would emerge in the Caucasus. But this was not to be. Partisan bands soon formed in the northern part of the Caucasus where Russian influence was the strongest.

Nonetheless, the Axis propagandists made certain that the people of the Middle East learned of the lenient treatment being extended to the people of the Caucasus and indicated that they, too, could expect lenient treatment when Axis forces appeared in their lands.

ON THE FRONTS AGAIN

From Egypt came reports stating that Rommel had attacked the British defense at El Alamein and that a breakthrough was expected soon.

During the last days of July, Axis forces in the East moved steadily forward toward Stalingrad and the Caucasus oil. From Egypt, however, came some disturbing news. Rommel's offensive at El Alamein had stalled and his forces were now badly depleted and on the defensive.

MORE DINNER CONVERSATION

At the midday meal on August 4, 1942, Hitler reminisced about his wartime experiences during the First World War. He went into some detail on how he was impressed by the beauty of the ancient Flemish town of Ypres. He said that Ypres was a city "out of fairyland," and that after the war, he would send the architects who were to undertake the task of rebuilding Lubeck to Ypres to study the city before they started work.

On the 5th, the Fuehrer predicted how the war would end. It would happen in two phases; in the East "it will be all over" once the Soviets' access to Caucasus oil was cut off, and when Murmansk (the main Lend-Lease port in the north) in the north was taken.

The second phase would come after the defeat of the Soviets when "even half of our forces" could be transferred to the Atlantic Wall. That would make it impossible for the Allies to conduct a successful invasion of western Europe and that the stalemate which followed would eventually bring about peace.

That evening, Hitler spoke of the recovery of Italian East Africa. He said that the Italians are "first-class colonizers" and given ten years of Italian rule, Addis Ababa (capital of Ethiopia) would have become a most beautiful city.

The topic turned to Norway and a problem there that had long vexed the German leadership: that being the inability of German forces to adequately defend the northernmost part of the country — the North Cape. The conversation centered on the single mountainous road connecting the North Cape with the rest of Norway. It was primitive, often closed by inclement weather, and totally inadequate for carrying heavy military traffic. A railroad was under construction out of the Trondheim area, but its construction would take time and Hitler was worried. He had to admit that Germany would not have complete control over the area until the railway reached Kirkenes (the largest city in the North Cape).

Hitler returned to the subject as to how the war might end. Speaking of the forthcoming invasion of the Middle East, he said that Axis forces need only capture the British-controlled oil fields around Mosul (in northern Iraq), cut the pipeline leading to the west, and the whole war would then end, because the British would have now only the port of Haifa (in Palestine) as their sole loading port for oil. This was certainly fuzzy thinking by the Fuehrer because Britain could continue getting oil from the Persian Gulf area and from the Western Hemisphere which had been sources of supply for them all along.

On the 6th, Hitler touted his vegetarian diet once again. He told his table companions that someone ought to write a book entitled, "The Ideal State of the Future — a Problem of Diet and Education." As Hitler saw it, a vegetarian diet was a sound way to control the masses because it increased "docility and amenity to discipline" among the people.

With this absurd statement and his previous reference to Haifa, one might conclude that the Fuehrer's judgement was becoming impaired.

The subject of conversation got around to the women of the Ukraine, many of whom were fair-haired, blue-eyed and beautiful. Hitler had received a steady stream of reports on this issue from observers in the field and from Rosenberg who had argued, all along, that the Ukrainian people had a high percentage of Germanic blood. In Hitler's mind, such attractive attributes proved that many of these people were, indeed, of Germanic origin. Casting aside his universal contempt for the untermenschen of the East, Hitler agreed that "the best among them" could gradually be assimilated into the Reich.

At the evening meal, Hitler offered his thoughts, again, on how to tax the peasants; that being, by accepting payment in farm products rather than money. He reminded his companions that this had been an acceptable method of tax payment in Germany in times past and that it was also beneficial to the peasants. For example, he explained that potatoes could be accepted at market value which would be advantageous to the peasants because he would otherwise sell the potatoes to a middle-man at a lower price and then use that lesser income to pay taxes.

In discussing the post-war problems associated with maintaining a vast colonial empire, Hitler said that the Germans should take their lead from the British. Then he made a rather curious comment for a teetotaler, saying, "They have convinced me on one point — you cannot exist in the colonies without Scotch whisky."

Hitler expected his colonial empire to produce prodigious amounts of grain. This being the case, the Fuehrer said that spaghetti factories should be built in the East as a cheap and expedient way to feed the local people.

Still speaking of food, Hitler said that one item the Eastern colonies would not be able to provide was coffee. But, he said, "we'll find a coffee-growing colony somewhere or other."

AT HOME AND IN THE CAUCASUS

On August 8, 1942, an article by Himmler appeared in the SS newspaper, Deutsche Arbeit, which read, in part, "It is not our task to Germanize the East...but to see to it that only people of German blood live there." If there were any vestiges of hope among the Eastern people that the Germans had come as liberators, this article dashed them. Such statements gave the Soviet propagandists very useful ammunition and only served to increase the willingness of the eastern people to resist the German onslaught.

The day after Himmler's article appeared, Axis troops took the Maikop oil fields. This was a time of rejoicing at Vinnitsa. The oil fields' processing equipment, though, had been removed or totally destroyed by the retreating Russians and it would be months before the oil fields could produce for Germany.

Following the capture of Maikop, Hitler ordered a rapid advance through the western foothills of the Caucasus Mountains to the Black Sea port of Taupse, 75 miles to the southwest. From Taupse there was a narrow coastal plain, containing roads and a railroad, running down the Black Sea coast to Batum and the Turkish border. From Batum, another major oil-producing area, Axis forces could then move eastward across the plains of the southern Caucasus to Baku on the coast of the Caspian Sea, yet another major oil-producing area. To aid in this operation, additional Axis forces would advance down the eastern coast of the Caspian Sea, around the eastern end of the Caucasus Mountains, and converge on Baku from the north. In this manner the remainder of the Caucasus would be conquered and the stage set for the invasion of the Middle East.

Once the Black Sea ports of the Caucasus were in Axis hands, the Russian Black Sea Fleet would be virtually eliminated as the threat. This being the case, men and supplies from Germany could then come by water down the Danube, across to Black Sea to ports such as Rostov. This would provide another major transportation route to the East, thereby lifting much of the burden now being carried by the land routes.

And finally, with Axis forces on the eastern border of Turkey, it could be expected that that country would become more cooperative.

DINING AT VINNITSA

On August 11, Speer was a guest again and the subject of conversation was the economy of postwar Germany. Hitler said that in the years following the war, the Reichsmark must become the world's most stable currency. He went on to say that in the East a new currency called the "Ostmark" would be used and have a value of five Ostmarks to the Reichsmark. However, Hitler stated that, tourists visiting the East would be given an exchange rate of only one for one with the difference being pocketed by the state. This would be justifiable because there would be plentiful bargains in the East for the tourists to enjoy.

Hitler continued, saying that the economy in the rest of Europe would be tightly controlled and beneficial to Germany so that Germany would be able to pay off the war debt within ten years. He further said that Germany could not count on receiving reparations from its former enemies. On the other hand, Hitler said, with all of Europe's economy under Germany's control, "The real profiteers of this war are ourselves, and out of it we shall come bursting with fat."

The Fuehrer told Speer that if Britain offered peace in the very near future on the basis that each party bears his own cost, he would most likely agree. He then added that the "greatest boon" to Germany would be peace as soon possible. With money matters on his mind, Hitler then launched into another tirade against the money-grabbing Jews and priests.

On the 12th, Hitler delved into the subject of soap. He complained that the soap of the prewar days, and the current wartime soap, cracked his hands. This was important to him because he said that he washed his hands frequently because of his dog (Blondi). Here, in Hitler's mind, was another problem that had to be addressed after the war.

WHO CAN SETTLE IN THE EAST

On August 20, an article appeared in the SS newspaper "Schwarz Korps" outlining who might be accepted for settlement in the East. The SS, it must be remembered, was in charge of race and resettlement issues in the East. According to the article, persons of pure Germanic blood would, of course, be accepted and preferred. But persons who were deemed to be "carriers of Germanic blood" would also be accepted. This opened the field for hundreds of thousands of people of mixed blood. Also acceptable as settlers, the paper continued, would be persons the SS had labelled as "renegades." These were people of Germanic blood who had completely lost their Germanism but would agree to submit to a program of re-Germanization. This category applied to Germanic people who had been living abroad for generations, such as the German-Americans.

This thinking was also supported by Reich Health Director, Dr. Leonardo Conti, who had proposed a program to introduce men and women to each other who were medically suitable for the rigors of settling in the East.

ALL MUST WORK

By now, the supply of foreign volunteers willing to work in Germany, or for Germany, was nearly exhausted. Various labor conscription programs had been imposed here and there, but such programs were uncoordinated and not standardized. This imbalance was remedied on August 22, 1942, by a decree making war-related work compulsory for men and women, aged eighteen through fifty-five, throughout German-occupied Europe.

A NEW ENEMY IN THE AIR

On August 17, 1942, a new enemy appeared over the skies of occupied Europe — the American Army Air Forces. On this day, the Americans carried out their first air attack from Britain, targeting an industrial complex in Rouen, France that was producing for the Germans. The next all-American raid came on the 20th and hit the marshalling yard at Amiens, France. On the 21st, the AAAF struck again in the Mediterranean with an attack on an Axis convoy near Crete. On the 23rd they attacked Axis shipping in the harbor at Tobruk, Libya, and on the 24th they hit Tobruk a second time. Also on that day, B-17 bombers from Britain bombed the ship-building complex at Le Trait, France.

This was the beginning of the American air campaign in Europe that would continue without letup. All of this was in addition to the regular RAF raids which continued as usual. Soon, the Germans were to learn that the British and Americans had divided the skies between themselves. The British bombed at night and the Americans bombed during the day.

SUCCESSES ON THE EASTERN FRONT

On August 23, German troops reached the Volga River north of Stalingrad. This effectively ended the Russian's use of the river as a means of transportation. The Luftwaffe and long-range artillery now began to bombard the city.

In the Caucasus, Axis troops had successfully repelled a major Soviet counterattack and were advancing south toward the oil center of Grozny, 300 miles east-south-east of Maikop in the northern foothills of the Caucasus Mountains. From Grozny, it was 100 miles to the coast of the Caspian Sea and then 200 miles along that coast to Baku. The conquest of the Caucasus was proceeding as planned.

A NEW ENEMY FROM SOUTH AMERICA

On August 22, 1942, Brazil declared war on Germany and Italy. This resulted from the indiscriminate sinking of Brazilian merchant ships by Axis submarines. With Brazil entering the war, the Axis Powers acquired a rather formidable enemy. Brazil was capable of putting several well-trained and well-armed army divisions in the field and its navy was capable of actively patrolling for, and sinking, submarines. The Brazilian Navy could also provide escort vessels for convoys.

HITLER GETS EVEN

On August 24, 1942, Hitler took a drastic step to reduce the powers of judges and lawyers. On that day, he appointed a Party loyalist, Otto Thierack, to the post of Minister of Justice. Hitler then decreed that Thierack had the power to set aside any written law. Thierack was now Germany's one-man supreme court.

"A PIMPLE ON THE FACE OF EUROPE" AND OTHER MATTERS

Hitler was still at Vinnitsa and the table conversation on the evening of August 26 turned to Germany's two neutral neighbors, Switzerland and Sweden. Switzerland was a state with a large German-speaking minority who, in Hitler's mind, should eventually be brought into the Reich. On this occasion, Hitler said of Switzerland that it was "nothing but a pimple on the face of Europe" and could not be allowed to continue in existence. A map of Gaus, Nazi Party political districts, had already been drawn up for Switzerland, as had war plans for conquering that nation.

As for Sweden, he called the Swedish people "vermin" that had to be "swept away." He did not elaborate on how this might be done.

On the 27th, Hitler spoke of moving some of Germany's industry to the East where it would be out of range of Allied bombers operating from either Britain or Egypt. The giant Soviet industrial complex located in the Donets Basis was now in German hands and Hitler had plans for using it. True, most of the machinery had been removed or destroyed, but it could be replaced — and Hitler wanted it done as fast as possible. One of the first requirements was electric power, and Hitler had already issued the necessary orders. He told his companions that during October, repairs to the huge power station at Zaporozhye (in the Donets Basin) would be completed and by the first of December would be in full working order. Hitler went on to say that the steel mills at Mariopol (also in the Donets Basin) were also to be repaired and once their steel became available, munitions would be made there. Here, it can be reasonably assumed, Hitler also foresaw a long-term need for munitions in the East to maintain the armed frontier and deal with the Partisan menace.

On the 28th, the dinner conversation touched on the rebuilding of Berlin, and Hitler again brought up one of the subjects that seemed to interest him — marshes. On the northern edge of Berlin was a low marsh-like area subject to occasional flooding. Hitler said that once they had gotten rid of this "hideous expanse of water" Berlin would have a parcel of real estate with a panoramic view stretching from the Sudbahnhof to the Triumphal Arch with the People's Palace in the distance.

That evening, Hitler talked in guarded terms about the air war, without acknowledging — on the historical record — the devastating effect it was having on Germany. He said that some German towns such as Weimar, Nuremberg, and Stuttgart must be protected at all costs. Factories can always be rebuilt, but these works of art were irreplaceable.

Then the Fuehrer indulged in a bit of wishful thinking — the bombing of New York City. He stated that that city's skyscrapers were especially vulnerable to bombing and if they were knocked down, it would be physically impossible to clear the mountains of rubble.

Alluding again to the air war, Hitler reminded his companions that some six thousand anti-aircraft guns were being produced per year and that every German village would soon have its own battery and searchlight section. The Fuehrer then offered a suggestion on a new and unique anti-aircraft weapon — mirrors. He said that by placing mirrors on the ground in a certain pattern light could be reflected into the eyes of the Allied pilots, temporarily blinding them.

At this dinner session, Hitler also delved into the field of anthropology. In discussing the many technical changes being brought about by the war, Hitler said that in a hundred years the number of people wearing spectacles, and the size of the human brain, would both increase considerably. He added that it was best not to try to imagine what they would look like.

DISTRESSING NEWS FROM THE EAST – MORE SOLDIERS NEEDED

At the end of August, reports reached Vinnitsa that the German offensive in the Caucasus was stalling due to heavy Soviet resistance, poor roads and rain.

Also, reports were received from German engineers in the Caucasus, stating that the recently captured Maikop oil fields could not be put into production in less than a year. This was longer than Hitler had anticipated.

At Stalingrad, very strong Soviet resistance was being experienced by the lead elements of the Axis columns approaching that city. The reports that the Soviets would make a determined stand at Stalingrad were being confirmed. On September 3, there was good news. Axis troops reached the Volga south of the city. Stalingrad was now besieged on three sides with the mile-wide, and bridgeless, Volga at its rear.

Another setback of sorts came when the Army High Command insisted that the existing Soviet three-year trade schools be reopened because of the lack of skilled laborers. Hitler, as commander-in-chief of the Army, was reluctant to permit this, but circumstances forced him to do so.

Then too, there was the on-going shortage of soldiers. This was solved, in part, by declaring the racially acceptable people of the newly annexed territories of Luxembourg and Alsace-Lorraine to be German citizens. This made the young men of these areas subject to the draft. Heretofore, those people had been classified as Volksdeutsch and military service was voluntary.

Another measure taken to acquire more men for the armed forces was to draft some 500,000 German factory workers, heretofore exempt from military service. To fill their jobs, the Germans recruited additional German women and brought in more workers from the East.

In yet another action taken to acquire soldiers, the German Navy was ordered to send several thousand sailors to the army, and the Luftwaffe was ordered to create twenty "Field Divisions" of Luftwaffe personnel for service with the Army.

During the first days of September, the Germans launched their offensive to capture Leningrad, but the results were disappointing. Soviet resistance was stronger than expected.

There was, however, some good news from the Leningrad front; that being that the first of the new "Tiger" tanks had gone into action there and had quickly proven to be better than any of the Soviet tanks. Production of the Tiger tanks was a high priority for Hitler and was being pursued with great effort.

PEERING INTO THE FUTURE

At the dinner table on September 2, Hitler offered another scenario as to how the war might end. He stated that the fall of Stalingrad might force Churchill to reconsider his position, especially if Germany offered peace. Hitler went on to say that the terms he would offer Britain would be generous and might well create an uproar throughout the Kingdom that might bring about Churchill's downfall. Hitler said that any number of things might happen. Churchill might well be seen as a puppet of Russia and be thrown out of office, and the people of Britain might begin to settle their accounts with the Jews. Furthermore, a revolution could break out in India at any time and the United States, seeing that the British Empire was disintegrating, might occupy Canada. Hitler then named the men he believed might take over in London. They would be Lord Beaverbrook and/or the media mogul Lord Rothermere. Both men, Hitler believed, were sympathetic toward Germany. Hitler recounted how Rothermere had approached him several years earlier and offered to use his newspaper empire to foster a rapprochement between Britain and Germany. Later in the conversation, Hitler said that they must remember that they are not waging war on the British people, but on the small clique who rule them.

On September 4, Hitler talked about circuses. He liked circuses, especially the clowns. Recently, however, he learned of a whole family of acrobats that had fallen to their deaths, and because of this, had ordered that, henceforth, all acrobatic acts have safety nets. It was his belief that such talented people should fall to their deaths through some tiny miscalculation.

Later in the meal, Hitler talked about the various house designs that should be built in particular parts of Germany after the war. He went into considerable detail saying that it would not be wise to build Swiss chalet type homes at Gruenwald even though broad pent-roofs were necessary to keep out the wind driven rain, which would run along the length of the planks and eventually rots the wood. In Erzgebirge it would be best to retain the dark-colored slates, while in the Rhineland, unfortunately, there was currently no uniformity.

On September 5, Hitler indicated that he might, one day, intrigue into the politics of Spain in order to remove Franco. As he had indicated in the past, his candidate as Franco's replacement would be General Munoz-Grande, commander of the Spanish Blue Division. Hitler said that on the first opportunity he would decorate Munoz-Grande with the Iron Cross with Oak Leaves and Diamonds. This will pay dividends, he said, and when the Spanish Legion prepares to return to Spain, we must re-equip it on a grand scale and give it a heap of booty and some captured Russian Generals as trophies. Then they will return to Madrid as heros, and Munoz-Grande's position would be militarily unassailable.

On the 6th, Hitler spoke of young women of the Netherlands and Flanders. Hitler said, "What a fine race the Dutch are! The girls are splendid and very much to my taste." Speaking then of his experiences in World War I, he said that the Flemish girls were very attractive also and that many of them would very likely have married Germans if Germany had been allowed to retain Flanders.

At the midday meal on September 7, 1942, Speer, Reichskommisar Koch of the Ukraine, and Field Marshal Milch of the Luftwaffe were guests. The table talk produced nothing of significance with regard to Germany's future. Rather, Hitler expounded, at length, on the very unpleasant experiences he had had in school as a child. He lambasted his teachers, calling them "mentally deranged...and lunatics." He was especially critical of the priest who tried to teach him religion.

Unbeknownst to anyone at the table, this would be the last meal at which Hitler's conversations would be recorded for almost a year.

Sometime during the day, word was received that the advance in the Caucasus had come to an unexpected halt, just twenty miles from the Caspian Sea. Hitler was furious, and saw in this what he believed was ineptitude in his Army commanders, and worse, possibly betrayal. Hitler came down hard on Keitel and Jodl and harsh words were exchanged. Hitler stomped out of the room and announced that he would no longer dine with them. From this moment on, Hitler took his meals alone.

The stenographic recordings of his dinner table ended and would not resume until June 1943.

WEIGHTY DECISIONS

As has been recounted, tens of thousands of eastern workers had been sent to Germany — most of them volunteers. By now, however, rumors and accounts had filtered back to the occupied areas on the difficulties those workers were experiencing as a result of long hours, low pay, shortages of food, air raids, general abuse by their employer and restrictions put on their social activities. Not surprisingly, volunteer workers in the East now became hard to find. The only alternative was conscription. This was decreed and eastern workers began to flow again to Germany in large numbers. Also, more individuals fled to the Partisans to avoid the conscription.

On September 4, Hitler gave some attention to the German civilian population which was suffering considerably from shortages and the air raids. On this date, he ordered that 400,000 to 500,000 young Ukrainian women, between the ages of fifteen and thirty-five, be sent to Germany to work as domestic servants. Blue-eyed blonds were eagerly sought for this program which, in its initial stage, was voluntary. Hitler further ordered that efforts should be made to Germanize these women so that they would remain in Germany permanently.

The program started off very slowly, however, due to the rumors and reports that were circulating with regard to the poor treatment eastern workers were receiving in Germany. There were also problems in getting the women to Germany due to the overloaded transportation system in the East. Yet, the program made some progress.

During the second week of September, Hitler learned that the Caucasus Mountains were more of a military obstacle than had been expected. At the eastern end of the mountains, where his strongest forces were now stalled, there were only four mule trails through the mountains and each of them was heavily guarded. This meant that carrying out flanking attacks against the enemy in this area would be impossible, and that the Axis forces would have to slug their way through the formidable defenses the Soviets were currently constructing along the narrow coastal plain bordering the Caspian Sea.

With his commitments at Stalingrad and Leningrad, Hitler had to conclude that any further advance into the Caucasus would have to wait until 1943. He also had to cancel the planned advance on Taupse on the Black Sea coast due to the lack of available forces. Therefore, the Axis juggernaut in the Caucasus remained stalled indefinitely on the northern side of the Caucasus Mountains. With this in mind, Hitler ordered that winter defensive positions be constructed there at strategic locations in case the Axis forces had to endure a second winter in the Caucasus.

This unwelcome delay in the East made Germany's western defenses more vulnerable because, with time, the western Allies steadily grew stronger. Because of this, he ordered a speed-up on the construction of the Atlantic Wall.

On September 9, Hitler fired Field Marshal Wilhelm List, commander of Army Group A, for failing to break through the Caucasus Mountains. Hitler took command of Army Group A himself. This meant that Hitler, as commander of Army Group A, answered to Hitler, as Commander-in-Chief of the Army, who answered to Keitel, Chief of OKW, who answered to Chancellor Hitler.

The atmosphere at Hitler's headquarters was now very tense and the situation conferences were brief and icy. All knew that Keitel's and Jodl's jobs were on the line. Hitler avoided being with them and spent much of his time alone with his dog.

On the 12th, there was some good news. The Soviet perimeter around Stalingrad had been reduced to thirty miles, meaning that the concentration of Axis forces around the city was increasing.

And, in the north, the attack on Leningrad was about to begin.

CHAPTER 18

FROM DESPAIR TO HOPE

LENINGRAD FALLS

On September 15, 1942, the German attack on Leningrad began. 🔊 On the 17th, the city fell and the next day, the Oranienbaum salient also fell. The fight was bloody but brief because the defenders, cutoff from supplies since the German-Finnish linkup at the Svir River in November 1941, simply ran out of ammunition, food, fuel and other necessities of war. Some of the defenders fled to the island-fortress of Kronstadt in the Gulf of Finland, and to the other Soviet-controlled islands scattered throughout the Gulf. Many more fled north to surrender to the Finns, knowing they would get better treatment as POWs from them than from the Germans. The Finns had not participated in the capture of Leningrad, refusing to go beyond what they considered their legitimate national boundary. The Germans captured a relatively small number of prisoners.

The fall of Leningrad was exceptionally good news at the Fuehrer's headquarters, because now Army Group North would be free to march on Moscow.

A few units of Army Group North were deployed to mop up the Leningrad area, while the bulk of Army Group North, which consisted of two powerful German armies, the 16th and 18th, turned about and began the march to the southeast. They were aided by the fact that ☑ all of the roads and railroads in the north converged on Moscow. 🔊 Progress was slow, however, because the advance was through heavily forested terrain and Soviet forces were still strong in many areas. A small German force was deployed to the north and crossed the Svir River into Finnish-controlled territory. There, they joined with a Finnish force, and together marched northward along a railroad that led to the coast of the White Sea; there it connected with the railroad from Murmansk. The objective was to cut the Murmansk railroad and stop the flow of Allied supplies entering Russia via that route. This would also isolate the Soviet forces north of the rail junction and in Murmansk if they did not withdraw to the south. This operation was of vital importance to the Finns, because the areas vacated were to go to Finland as her spoils of war. ☑

With the second winter in Russia approaching, the German troops in the north were much better supplied with warm clothing, and vehicles and weapons that could better withstand the cold. The soldiers of Army Group North would not suffer as much this winter as they had the last.

ELSEWHERE

On the Southern front, Axis troops were converging on Stalingrad from three sides against very strong Soviet opposition. Advance elements had entered the suburbs of the city and immediately became engaged in bitter house-to-house fighting. Also, a large part of the Luftwaffe had been committed to the battle of Stalingrad at the expense of other parts of the front.

In the Caucasus, the Axis advance remained stalled.

The Crimea, sufficiently pacified by now, was turned over to the civil administration of Erich Koch, Reichscommisar for the Ukraine, and the SS security units. This was a temporary measure until the Crimea could be annexed to Germany.

Over the summer, the transportation problems from Germany into Russia had eased a bit so more supplies were getting to the troops. Fall brought a better-than-expected harvest in Europe, which portended an easing of the critical food shortages there. Little in the way of food, however, could be expected from the occupied East due to the war conditions.

Design of a memorial pyramid to be built in the Dnieper River region of the Crimea honoring Germany's war dead.

Under Speer's direction, both German tank and aircraft production were up.

The construction of the Atlantic Wall was on schedule and German submarines were still causing considerable problems for Allied shipping, especially on the North Atlantic-Murmansk route. Because of the latter, the Soviet forces in the north were not as well supplied as they might have been.

In Norway, the country's 770 Jews had been removed with the cooperation of the Quisling government. By late November, the country was proclaimed Jew-free — one of the first in Europe to be so designated.

TROUBLES IN NORTH AFRICA

In North Africa, the Axis advance toward Cairo and the Suez Canal was still stalled at El Alamein by strong British opposition that was increasing by the day. One significant development on the Allied side was the introduction of the Hurricane IID fighter plane which mounted a tank-destroying 40 mm cannon under the fuselage. Armor-Piercing shells from this gun could penetrate the armor of any of the Axis tanks.

Most importantly, though, the British Navy, in combination with the RAF and the AAF, was gaining a dominant position at sea and in the air over the central Mediterranean, the shortest Axis supply route from Italy to North Africa. The Axis convoys, which consisted mostly of Italian merchantmen and Italian escort vessels, were experiencing increasing losses. The Italian Air Force was of some value in defending the convoys, but the main burden fell to the Luftwaffe which was hampered by shortages of planes and pilots. Under these conditions, the chances of Rommel taking the offensive once again in Egypt were very problematic.

Then too, rumors were rampant that the Allies would soon launch an invasion somewhere in the eastern or central Mediterranean. The Germans and Italians were well aware of the fact that the amphibious capabilities of the Allied forces were, by now, very capable of conducting a large-scale invasion.

On October 1, 1942, Rommel met with Hitler in the Berlin Chancellory to discuss the North African situation. Rommel asked for additional German armored forces, but Hitler could not comply. Virtually every German armored unit was committed elsewhere. Hitler did, however, promise Rommel forty new Tiger tanks, one of which was on display at the Chancellory for Rommel's inspection. Hitler also promised a generous supply of fuel. Both the tanks and fuel, of course, had to across the Mediterranean in the Italian convoys.

TROUBLES IN ITALY

The stress and strain of the war continued to plague the Italians. Italy had some 220,000 troops in Russia confronting, what many Italians now perceived to be, an unbeatable enemy. Then too, those troops were about to endure their second Russian winter. The military situation in North Africa was also of very great concern as were the rumors of an imminent Allied invasion somewhere in the Mediterranean.

Food was still in very short supply. All of the famed pigeons in St. Mark's Square in Venice had disappeared having been eaten by the local residents. The ration of bread in Italy was down to 150 grams per person per day. It was twice that in Germany. As fall approached, signs became evident that Italy would face its third bad wheat harvest in a row. The black market flourished and official corruption increased considerably.

Many Italians were losing weight due to the lack of food, and as the Italians tightened their belts, the last hole in the belt became known as the "Foro Mussolini" (Mussolini hole).

During the summer an old menace, supposedly suppressed by Mussolini and his Fascists in the 1920s, came to life again — communism. Communist cells had formed at the giant Fiat factory in Turin and in other factories in the north. These people, of course, were sympathetic to the Soviet Union and wanted to see Italy drop out of the war. The communist menace was dampened, somewhat, by the government transferring many factory workers to agricultural work due to a lack of fuel and raw materials for the factories.

In Rome and other big cities, Mussolini's former political opponents — the Social Democrats, Christian Democrats and others — began to surface again. They too, like the communist factory workers, wanted Italy to drop out of the war.

In Rome, there were demonstrations in the streets and the Italian Army had to be called out in several instances to keep order.

In an attempt to get the people's minds off their troubles, a steady stream of new building projects was announced; an olympic stadium, more canals, new bridges over the Tiber, a new observatory, public housing, a new prison, and a tunnel across the Strait of Messina between the toe of Italy and Sicily. The time and circumstances under which these projects would begin was, of course, vague.

Mussolini was suffering right along with his people. During October, he developed ulcers and was forced to live on fruits and liquids. He also had a yellow complexion and emotional highs and lows. By this time, he lost fifty pounds and had to make use of his own Foro Mussolini.

KILL THEM

On October 18, Hitler issued what became known as the "Extermination Order." The Partisan menace in the East had reached such proportions that something drastic had to be done. The Order stated that Partisans, whether not in uniform, were to be "...killed to the last man...or if captured, turned over to the SS."

By now, the forests of the East, especially in the north, had become the primary domain of the Partisans. One German report stated that the Partisans controlled about 75% of the forested areas behind the German lines, up from about 40% in April 1942. One of the areas most heavily infested with Partisans was the Pripet Marshes, the area Hitler hoped to turn into a future huge army maneuver area.

Many remote farms, dairies and cooperatives in the north were now controlled by, and operating for the benefit of, the Partisans. Lumbering had come to a standstill, and railroads running through forested areas had to be heavily guarded. Phone and power lines were often inoperative.

Conditions were similar in Romanian-controlled areas and to a lesser extent in Finnish areas.

In the broad, flat and relatively treeless steppes of the Ukraine, Partisan activities were much less. This was a significant benefit to the Germans because the major operations in the East were being conducted in the eastern Ukraine.

Partisan activities extended westward as far as the pre-war German border. In the areas annexed from Poland, all of the German male civilians were armed by governmental decree. Partisan activities were also extensive in the General Government.

Controlling the Partisans was now taking several hundred thousand men. The relatively small number of SS units originally assigned to anti-Partisan activities were far too few, so indigenous peoples, mostly anti-communists and re-educated POWs, were organized into anti-Partisan units and worked alongside the SS. German Army units also conducted anti-Partisan operations when they could be spared.

To add to these woes, Partisan activities in the occupied Balkan countries of Yugoslavia, Greece and Albania were considerable. The Germans were involved here, but not so heavily as in the East because these were problems that mostly affected Germany's allies, the Italians, Bulgarians, Romanians and the Croatians.

In addition to all of this, resistance organizations had sprung up in every occupied country in western Europe. There were no large Partisan-like organizations in western Europe, but rather, small bands of resistance fighters carried out acts of sabotage, espionage, reprisals and the rescue of downed Allied airmen.

MISERY AT STALINGRAD

At Stalingrad, heavy house-to-house fighting was now the norm. On October 21, it rained heavily. The next day it snowed. By November 3, the Volga River was clogged with ice — a benefit to the Germans because it slowed the delivery of supplies across the river to Stalingrad. Living conditions for the soldiers of both sides were miserable.

BRITISH ATTACK IN NORTH AFRICA

On October 23, 1942, the British forces at El Alamein launched a powerful attack against the German and Italian positions. The British had an overwhelming force of some 195,000 men, 800 planes, and over 1000 tanks including new American-made Sherman tanks that were more than a match for anything the Axis had. The British forces outnumbered the Axis forces two to one. To add to the dilemma for the Axis side, Rommel was sick and in Europe seeking medical attention. He hurried back to Egypt, but it was too late. The British broke through the Axis lines on the evening of the 24th. A battle royal ensued for the next few days, but on the night of November 3/4, the Axis forces were beaten and forced to withdraw to the west.

In Italy, there was a run on the banks, and the Italian government put part of the blame for the defeat at El Alamein on the Japanese Navy for failing to interdict the steady flow of Allied shipping through the western part of the Indian Ocean that had brought the supplies and reinforcements to the British in Egypt.

SPAIN OFFERS TO MEDIATE PEACE

While the deadly fighting was going on at both El Alamein and Stalingrad, an unexpected message arrived at Vinnitsa from Madrid on October 29. The Spanish government offered its services as a mediator to end hostilities. Hitler rejected the proposal out-of-hand. Franco was the last man he wanted to see assume the role of an international peace-maker.

Two days later, Hitler and his staff left Vinnitsa and returned to their headquarters near Rastenberg, East Prussia. Hitler was happy to leave because he hated Vinnitsa.

SOVIETS ABANDON MURMANSK

🔊 **In the far north of the Eastern front, the Axis forces won a major victory. The** joint German and Finnish force driving north from the Svir River was rapidly approaching the Murmansk railroad. Also, the Finns had launched attacks in the direction of the railroad at two places farther north from their eastern border. And finally, ☑ there was the joint German and Finnish force that had been operating along the Arctic coast, ever since the beginning of Barbarossa in the direction of Murmansk. 🔊 This force, too, was on the move.

The Soviets could see that if any one of these attacks was successful, Murmansk would be cut off. They therefore made the decision to abandon Murmansk and the western shore of the White Sea. Beginning on October 15 they withdrew down the rail line, taking with them as much of the Allied-supplied war material as possible, and destroyed the rest. They also destroyed long stretches of the railroad as they withdrew.

On the 18th, the German and Finnish force operating along the Arctic coast occupied Murmansk. Three days later, the Germans and Finns at Murmansk parted company. The Germans departed for the south while the Finns marched on to the east to secure the mineral-rich Kola Peninsula. Other Finnish forces followed in the wake of the German withdrawal and occupied the land between Finland's border and the White Sea. With the occupation of these lands, Finland's territorial war aims were completed. Finland was now about twice its pre-war size and was the largest of the Scandinavian countries.

The loss of Murmansk closed ☑ one of the five supply points from the West into the Soviet Union. 🔊 The other four still functioned, however. ☑ They were: 1) the White Sea port of Archangel, 380 miles to the southeast of Murmansk, 2) the supply route into southern Russia via Iran, 3) the supply route via the Pacific seaport of Vladivostok and the Trans-Siberian Railroad, and 4) the "Alsib" air route from Alaska, into Siberia. The port of Archangel, however, would be operative for only a few more weeks because its harbor freezes over during the winter months.

🔊 As the German forces coming down from Murmansk and the German and Finnish forces coming up from the Svir River linked up along the Murmansk railroad, they were only some two hundred miles east of Archangel. But the decision was made not to advance in that direction at this time since the port would be soon closing down. The capture of Archangel could wait, while the German troops were used elsewhere. ☑

THE MARCH ON MOSCOW FROM THE NORTH

🔊 During the last days of October, Army Group North's march from Leningrad was under way. The force divided into two components. One component followed the direct Leningrad-to-Moscow transportation corridor which consisted of a railroad and a good quality road system and led directly into Moscow. The other component followed another transportation corridor that emanated from Leningrad in a more easterly direction, but then turned south directly into the Moscow area. By following these two corridors, the Germans would approach Moscow from the northwest and the north.

Soviet resistance was strong, the terrain was forested and the weather turning cold. On the German flanks and in the rear areas, Partisans were very active. But the Germans had the superior forces and made steady progress toward Moscow. Advancing with the Germans were the Spanish Legion and Waffen SS units containing many Dutch, Flemish and Norwegian volunteers. ☑ Days later, the German Army Command elevated the status of the Spanish Legion to that of a "Grenadier" division. This was mainly a ceremonial gesture that gave the division, and its commander, General Munoz-Grande, more status.

🔊 The Soviet leadership then did exactly as the Germans had hoped. They began shifting some of their forces from the Stalingrad area to strengthen the defenses north of Moscow. ☑

INGERMANLAND

🔊 With hostilities moving south out of the Leningrad area, the Germans were, in effect, clearing an area of the Soviet Union known as Ingermanland. ☑

Ingermanland is an ancient land that stretches across a vast area, south of the Finnish border. It is bounded on the east by Lake Peipus in Estonia, and runs for some 350 miles in a northeasterly direction to the shores of Lake Onega. Its southern boundary with Russia is less well defined. Leningrad, since its inception as St. Petersburg, had always been a part of Ingermanland. This area was the ancestral homeland of the Inger people, a Scandinavian race ethnically related to the Finns. Throughout most of its history, however, Ingermanland had been controlled by the Russians, and Russian people had infiltrated into the area over the centuries until the Ingers were, at this point in time, a minority.

This was a productive land that the Germans planned to turn into one of the primary settlement areas in the East. It would be attached to Ostland and the Russians moved out and settlers moved in. The Ingers had the option to remain or relocate to Finland. An agreement to this effect had already been worked out between Berlin and Helsinki. An Autobahn was to be built from Estonia, through the Leningrad area, and on to the Finnish border. It was expected that the Finns would then continue the Autobahn on to Helsinki.

🔊 All of this, however, lay in the future because Ingermanland was a battleground and much of it was in the hands of the Partisans. ☑

INVASION — NORTH AFRICA

On November 8, 1942, American and British forces landed, en masse, on the Atlantic coast of French Morocco and the Mediterranean coast of Algeria. These areas were completely devoid of German and Italian troops and were defended only by French forces loyal to Vichy. The French forces offered resistance to the invaders during the first hours of the invasion, but soon capitulated.

The invasion was not all that much of a surprise at Hitler's headquarters. There was concern, though, that the Allies would advance swiftly across North Africa, through Tunisia and into Libya to trap Rommel's forces that were already in retreat from El Alamein.

There was also a measure of relief at the Fuehrer's headquarters that the attack had not come on the west or southern coasts of Europe. And too, with large numbers of Allied forces committed to North Africa, an invasion of Europe was much less likely. This would give the Germans more time to complete their Atlantic Wall and to withdraw some of the army units stationed in western Europe. These units numbered twenty-nine German Army divisions in Holland, Belgium and France.

On the down-side for the Germans, though, was the fact that most of French North Africa was now in Allied hands and Germany's prospects of marching down the west coast of Africa to attain her goals in Central Africa, and to establish bases on the Atlantic coast of Africa, were shattered. The route to Mittel Afrika was, however, still open via East Africa.

The invasion of French North Africa set in motion a rapid series of events. On November 9, the Germans began a massive airlift of paratroopers and other elite forces into Tunisia to defend that French protectorate against the Allies and to protect Rommel's rear. Italian forces entered Tunisia from Libya several days later. The Germans were forced to undertake the air lift because during October, 44% of the shipping tonnage across the Mediterranean had been lost. Hitler was not about to risk losing these elite troops at sea. The new German force gathering in Tunisia was labelled the 5th Panzer Army and under the command of General Hans-Jurgen von Arnim.

Days later, German tanks arrived after a safe crossing of the Mediterranean. Included in the shipment was a relatively large number of Tiger tanks that were, as had been proven in Russia, better than any of the enemy tanks — that is, when they worked. By now, certain mechanical difficulties had been experienced with the Tigers, such as engine and transmission problems and difficulties with the turret mechanisms. Because of these problems, the troops in the field often had to fall back on their old and reliable Panther tanks.

To the west, most of the Vichy French forces had changed sides and agreed to fight, once again, with the Allies. In Tunisia, the Germans disarmed as many French units as they could, but some were able to escape to the west.

On November 11, German and Italian forces invaded the unoccupied portion of France, while the Italians, alone, invaded and occupied the French island of Corsica. To carry out the invasion, the Italian Navy utilized requisitioned sail boats equipped with auxiliary motors. Such were the amphibious capabilities of the Italian Navy.

Also, by this date, Rommel had abandoned Egypt and was retreating into Libya.

With the German and Italian occupation of southern France, Switzerland was now completely surrounded by the Axis Powers.

On November 15, British and American troops entered Tunisia after a rapid advance across French Morocco and Algeria, and on the 16th Hitler went on the radio to tell the German people that Germany would, one day, reconquer the territory lost in North Africa. He said, "I assure you the hour will come when I will strike back with compound interest. They will get an answer which will knock them deaf and blind."

On November 17, the first clashes took place between Allied and German forces in Tunisia. Hard fighting then ensued and continued for weeks. In time, the former Vichy troops, now under Fighting French command, entered the fray.

By November 23, Rommel had established strong defensive positions at El Agheila in central Libya and stopped the British advance. In doing so, however, he had given up the eastern half of the Italian colony.

On the 27th, much of the French fleet, anchored at the huge naval base at Toulon,

France was scuttled by its own sailors to prevent it from falling into the hands of the Axis Powers.

ALL HELL BROKE LOOSE AT STALINGRAD

While the drama in North Africa was unfolding, all hell broke loose at Stalingrad. Early on the morning of November 19, the Soviets launched a massive attack against the northern flank of the Axis salient leading to Stalingrad. They chose a point seventy-five miles west of the city where the Romanian 3rd Army held the line. During the day, the Romanians held their own and, with the aid of German reserve units, launched a counterattack that temporarily stalled the attack.

The next day, a smaller, but still powerful Soviet force, struck the Axis's southern flank. Clearly it was a pincers movement designed to cut off the German 6th Army, commanded by General Friedrich von Paulus, fighting at Stalingrad.

On the 21st, the Soviets on the northern flank attacked again and overwhelmed the Romanian and German defenders. The Axis defenses then deteriorated rapidly and a link up between the northern and southern arms of the Soviet thrusts seem likely. Paulus asked Hitler for permission to withdraw from Stalingrad, but Hitler refused.

On November 22, the two Soviet attack columns met at the village of Kalach forty miles due west of Stalingrad. The German 6th Army and most of the Romanian 4th Army were trapped. Hitler's nephew, Leo Raubal, was one of those in the trap. On the 23rd, Soviet forces began attacking the 6th Army's rear areas. Hitler realized that a large-scale attack had to be made against the Soviet encirclement to relieve those forces trapped at Stalingrad. To lead this attack, Hitler called in one of his most capable commanders, Field Marshal Erich von Manstien, from Army Group North. Goering also came to the rescue and promised Hitler that the Luftwaffe could keep the 6th Army adequately supplied in the interim. Hitler took personal control of the relief attack which was given the name, "Operation Winter Storm." To man Winter Storm, the bulk of Army Group A, deep in the Caucasus, was ordered to disengage and march northward.

Taking advantage of the departure of most of Army Group A, the Soviet forces in the Caucasus launched a series of attacks that forced the remaining Axis defenders back to the Terek River.

With this, the Russians now had to make a decision. That was to continue the attack on the 6th Army, or to turn about to confront the incoming forces of Army Group A. Believing that Paulus's 6th Army could be beaten in a matter of days, they chose to continue the attack in the direction of Stalingrad.

On November 22, Hitler left the Berghof by train for Rastenberg. The next day, Doctor Morell noted in his records that Hitler was, "Getting scarcely any sleep because of huge responsibility and overwork."

During the next three weeks, hard fighting continued at Stalingrad and the forces of Army Group A were ready to launch Winter Storm. On December 12, the first attacks of Winter Storm were launched and some progress was made.

Then, on December 16, the Soviets struck again at the German's northern front again, this time hitting the Italian 8th Army and the Romanian 3rd Army. These forces quickly gave way and Manstien was forced to detach part of Army Group A to his left flank to stem this new attack.

At this point, the prospects of relieving Stalingrad were not good. Hitler was very worried.

At Stalingrad, there was fierce fighting inside the city and by the 23rd, lead elements of Winter Storm had inched their way to within thirty miles from Paulus's troops. At this point, Paulus asked Hitler if he could attempt a breakout toward the approaching Winter Storm forces. Hitler, still at the Berghof, refused. Manstien supported this view but Field Marshal Maximilian von Weichs, commander of Army Group B, and others supported Paulus. The German leadership

was divided, but a decision had to be made, and made quickly.

STALINGRAD RELIEVED

🔊 On the evening of December 23, the decision was made. Hitler recanted, and Paulus was authorized to attempt a breakout.

The breakout began on Christmas morning and on the 26th, Paulus's and Manstien's forces met. The encirclement of Stalingrad was broken. And by now, both side were exhausted and suffering shortages of all kinds. The Soviets, though, were the worse off having been weakened by the forces drawn from them to defend Moscow. Hitler, sensing this, ordered Manstien to charge forward with whatever forces he could muster, and advance to the Volga River south of Stalingrad. ☑ Hitler wanted desperately to hang on to his position on the Volga. 🔊 Reaching the Volga south of Stalingrad was preferable to reaching it north of the city. ☑

From Stalingrad, on south to Astrakhan, the Volga meanders through a broad flat valley and is very wide for most of its length. On both sides of the river are systems of rivulets that branched off from the main river, meandered on their own, sometimes sending off other rivulets, and then return to the main stream — only to branch off again further down stream. There is hardly a point along the Volga where a military force can cross the river valley without having to cross the Volga and two, three, four or more rivulets. There were no bridges across the Volga between Stalingrad and Astrakhan, and at that time of year the river and its rivulets were clogged with ice.

🔊 The Soviet forces south of Stalingrad now had a problem. With Axis forces on their northern and western flanks, and the difficult-to-cross Volga to the east, they were in danger of being trapped. Moscow saw this and ordered these forces to withdraw to Astrakhan and prepare strong defenses around that city. This was done with the Axis forces following closely behind, advancing down the west bank of the Volga. ☑

Astrakhan is on the east bank of the Volga with the broad mouth of the river to its west, and an extensive system of delta waterways to its north, east and south. Under these conditions, military attacks from any approach to the city would be very difficult to undertake. The only avenues of attack were from the west and across the mouth of the Volga, and directly into the city, or from the north along the roads and railroads leading to the city; these were built on embankments.

🔊 **The two highway bridges and a railroad bridge that crossed the Volga at Astrakhan were blown just before the Axis forces arrived. Because of these conditions, a relatively small Axis force was needed to besiege it. For the Axis, this neutralized the Astrakhan area and eliminated the threat of a Soviet counterattack from the east. Most of Army Group A was thereby free to return to the Caucasus safe in the knowledge that a Soviet attack from the rear was very unlikely. This, in turn, allowed the Axis leader to devote almost all of their strength toward the drive into the southern Caucasus.**

For the moment, the Volga became the southernmost segment of the A-A Line. The German planners, however, saw this as temporary and planned to move the armed frontier further to the east so that Germany could gain complete control of this vital river. ☑

THE MEDITERRANEAN AND NORTH AND WEST AFRICA

In the Mediterranean area, Italy was now being bombed more frequently by Allied planes from Britain. Most targets were seaports and industrial complexes in the north.

During the latter part of November, the U.S. Navy took over six French naval bases along the Mediterranean coast of Algeria and moved in large contingents of warships. This significantly tipped the balance of naval power in the Mediterranean toward the Allies.

The Americans also came to the aid of the Fighting French, via Lend-Lease, to help them rebuild their military strength in North Africa. Eight Fighting French Army divisions were equipped, along with nineteen French Air Force squadrons and elements of the French Navy.

Coming into Tunisia with the German Army was an 800-man Arab force that had been assembled and trained in Europe. This was the first commitment by the German Army of Arab volunteers to combat. Units of the Italian Army soon moved into Tunisia from Libya and promptly attempted to raise a local force of 20,000 Tunisians for military service. But, these hopes were dashed when it was realized that that many men could not be adequately armed due to the lack of war materials getting through from Italy.

The Italians also soon learned that the local Italian community in Tunisia had been relatively satisfied with its lot under French rule and was not very supportive of Fascism nor the prospects of an Italian political takeover. An attempt was made to create an all-Italian police force, but it failed for lack of volunteers.

On November 22, the German Navy took control of 158 of the 176 French merchant ships still operating in the Mediterranean. In an agreement with Vichy, the French were obligated to bear the costs of operating the ship as Vichy's commitment toward the struggle against the Allied takeover of French North Africa. The ships were then put into service transporting supplies and troops from Italy to North Africa. A number of them were sunk in the process.

On November 23, 1942, the colony of French West Africa, the largest French colony in Africa, announced for the Allies. This was expected in Berlin and it was further expected that other French colonies would soon follow suit.

Then on November 27 came the cruelest cut of all for Vichy. On that date, Hitler, by decree, dissolved what was left of Vichy's armed forces. The soldiers, sailors and airmen were discharged and their equipment confiscated. Vichy was now a government without arms and the German/French armistice of July 1940 became worthless. This action made good propaganda for the Fighting French recruiters throughout the French colonial empire, and many Frenchmen, heretofore loyal to Vichy, switched sides to the Fighting French.

In Tunisia, hard fighting continued well into December with neither side gaining an advantage.

Then, on December 17, 1942, British forces broke through Rommel's defenses at Al Agheila and the Germans began a fighting retreat toward Tripoli, Libya's capital and largest city. From Tripoli, it was only about 100 miles to the Tunisian border.

TUNISIA; WHO'S IN CHARGE?

With the influx of German troops into Tunisia, Hitler now experienced his first contact with the Arab world. Generally, the Germans were welcomed by the Tunisians, but this did not extend to the Italians.

With the dynamic changes taking place in Tunisia, the political climate there became very complex. The French colonial administrators were allowed to remain at their posts because they continued to profess their loyalty to Vichy, but there were other political currents at work in the country. Perhaps the most potent contenders were the Tunisian nationalists, who had been operating underground, but now saw opportunities for themselves to pursue their goal of establishing an independent Tunisia. They had a considerable following in the country.

Then there were the Italians who, after an Axis victory, were to take over the colony. But their prestige had plummeted and their popular support was almost nil.

Because of this struggle for power, the Germans, more or less by default, gained a favored position. With Berlin's long-term goal being to befriend the Arabs, the Germans took full advantage of the situation. Berlin, already well known in Arab lands for its anti-Jewish policy, promptly reminded the Tunisian people that they had come as liberators and not as conquerors. This was a

statement the Germans could make, but not the Italians. Then too, Berlin acknowledged that it would support the aspirations of the Arab nationalists in other Arab lands. This, of course, was a hint that they might also support Arab nationalism in Tunisia sometime in the future. For the moment, however, Berlin continued to officially support Italy's ambitions in Tunisia. This double-faced game put Germany in a win-win situation.

The Italians, in order to foster what favorable image they could, also acknowledged the Tunisian nationalists as a political force with whom they could work. With both the Germans and Italians paying homage to the nationalist, their prestige among the Tunisian population soared. The political control of Tunisia, therefore, became a four-way struggle between the French, Italians, Germans and Tunisian nationalists.

By agreement among the four parties, the nationalist's political party, the "Neo-Destour Party," was allowed to surface from underground, engage in political activities and print its own newspaper. Neo-Destour political prisoners were released from jail, including the Party's leader, Habib Bourguiba. Also, by agreement between the Germans and Italians, the French colonial administration was allowed to continue to function until such time when a decision would be made otherwise.

And there was yet another political factor in Tunisia, the Bey (Prince) of Tunis. As the country's political figurehead, he was allowed to continue his political activities so long as he did not criticize the Germans or Italians. This did little to stabilize the situation because it was well known that the Bey had, a few years earlier, favored the Allies and had not been supportive of either the Germans, nor the Italians, nor the Tunisian nationalists.

And finally, there was Amin el Husseini, the Grand Mufti of Jerusalem who claimed to speak for the entire Arab world. Husseini had been expelled from Palestine by the British and had become one of the most prominent pro-Axis leaders in the Arab society. The Mufti resided in Berlin and had Hitler's ear.

With regard to the situation in French North Africa, the Mufti introduced a new factor into the political equation. He suggested to Hitler that Germany support a massive Arab rebellion all across French North Africa with the goal being to gain independence for Tunisia, Algeria and Morocco from their colonial masters. The Mufti's argument was that these countries would then become permanent friends of Germany, permit the Germans to build the military bases in North Africa that Hitler had always wanted, as well as raise an Arab army to fight alongside the Axis Powers to liberate other Arab lands. Hitler politely rejected this idea because it was totally impractical for the conditions of the moment.

Overriding all of the political struggles in Tunisia was, of course, the war. The most devastating effect on the Tunisian people was that their cities were now being bombed for the first time in the war — a war between the Europeans. Many Tunisian civilians, therefore, fled to the countryside for safety. This created critical manpower shortages in the cities and all sorts of other problems.

These conditions remained in Tunisia throughout the war and, most importantly, portended the problems the Axis Powers would encounter when they marched into other Arab lands.

FUEHRER, YOU HAVE A HEART PROBLEM

On December 17, 1942, Hitler received some bad news from Dr. Morell. Hitler had coronary sclerosis, the restriction of blood vessels around the heart. Morell said he first suspected this in August 1941. Morell went on to tell the Fuehrer that he had been giving him iodine for the condition and that the condition was probably related to intense work and might only be temporary. Morell explained to the Fuehrer that he might experience chest pains and pains in the left arm because of the condition. To relieve the pain, if and when it occurred, Morell gave Hitler a supply of nitroglycerine tablets.

The next day, Morell saw Hitler again and recorded in his notes that Hitler's work load was as intense as ever. Morell wrote, "Very strenuous day! Ciano, Italian generals, Ribbentrop, Goering and the rest — at 10:30 p.m. blood pressure up to 144 mm." Hitler had good reason to be stressed, for it was at this time that Manstien's Winter Storm force was attempting to reach the trapped 6th Army at Stalingrad.

IN ROMANIA, THE JEWS NEXT DOOR, AND CODDLING THE RUSSIANS

During 1942, Romania deported a large number of its Jews to Transnistria, the easternmost part of its newly conquered area in the East. This was of concern to the Germans because this area bordered the Zhitomir area of the Ukraine, the first area of German settlement in the East. Hitler expressed annoyance at the situation, but did nothing about it. The Romanian position was that if the Germans were going to send their undesirables to Muscovy, on the eastern fringe of their colonial empire, then Romania could do likewise.

Another thing that galled the Germans was that the Romanians were favoring Russian collaborators in their areas more so than Ukrainians. This stemmed from a long-standing conflict over territory and other matters that had permanently soured Romanian-Ukrainian relations. The Romanians actively suppressed the Ukrainian culture and language in their new areas. They also let it be known in Berlin that they would not support any form of Ukrainian autonomy that might emerge after the war.

This being the case, the Romanians sought out the Russians in their area as collaborators. The Bucharest government even went so far as to allow their Russians to publish their own newspaper, establish their own theater, and use Russian, along with Romanian, as the official language in the annexed areas.

What is more, by showing such favoritism to the Russians, other Russian minorities in the Balkans were encouraged to look toward Romania as their protector. This, in turn, complicated internal affairs for some of the other regimes in the Balkans that were trying to keep their Russian minorities in check.

Here then, was a whole slate of additional, and difficult, issues that had to be dealt with after the war.

A SECOND RUSSIAN WINTER — SOVIETS OUT OF OIL

🔊 In southern Russia, the Axis forces dug in for their second winter in the East. However, for this winter, they were much better prepared than before to withstand the rigors of the fierce weather. Siege lines had been established at Astrakhan and around the southern portion of Stalingrad, and the Axis' eastern flank along the Volga was now well-protected.

By reaching the Caspian Sea at Astrakhan, the Germans had cut off much of the Russian's oil supply from the Caucasus which, heretofore, had amounted to 90% of their total. Only the oil from the southern Caucasus, and a few other smaller fields, was available to the Soviets. Furthermore, they had to truck most of the oil around the southern end of the Caspian Sea and through the desolate areas of Turkestan where the roads were few, of poor quality, and within range of German aircraft.

Army Group Center was holding its positions west of Moscow; and Army Group North, which did not dig in for the winter, continued inching its way toward Moscow.

The Soviets took advantage of the winter weather to launch counterattacks, as they had the year before, but the Germans were better prepared and gave up very little ground. ☑

Behind the lines, the Russian coal and iron mines were coming back on line and were now benefiting the Axis. The Russians, though, had ample supplies of these products in Siberia but, here again, transportation was a problem because of the few roads and railroads that existed in Siberia.

Also behind the lines, some important segments of Russian industry were being re-built by the hoard of German engineers and technicians who had flowed into the East in the wake of the army's advance. The Germans found many willing workers among the local peoples. Many of these people jumped at the chance to work at home rather than be conscripted for labor to Germany. The German armed forces got top priority with regard to the revitalized Soviet industrial services. Special attention was given to repair stations where tanks and aircraft could be repaired. Also, such things as horse-carts, sleighs, uniforms, boots and other items were being manufactured for the men at the front. Some manufacturing programs were actually moved from Germany to the East to get away from the bombings, to ease transportation problems, and to make use of the cheap and abundant labor.

By January 1943, the huge Dnepropetrovsk Dam, destroyed by the retreating Russians, was back in operation producing electric power for the recovering industry. Because of this huge source of energy now made available, the Germans were able to put several Russian steel mills back into production.

The Germans also revived the old Russian custom of "Kustar," the making of items at home. In this manner such things as bricks, pottery, lumber, peat, leather, etc. became available and did not have to be shipped in from the west. Kustar helped the German war economy but, because it was difficult to control, it also spawned an extensive black market.

🔊 And what about the future? Little-by-little, the German war economy was becoming more dependent on the labor of eastern workers, especially in the Ukraine. This, in turn, portended that the Nazi scheme to reduce the Ukrainian people to the level of semi-literate peasants was fading away. ☑

IN THE WEST

In the west, the Allied air war over occupied Europe intensified and in response to this, German industry continued its program of dispersal. Germany's small towns and villages were now crowded with refugees from the cities as well as workers, both German and foreign, who were needed for the newly-arrived industrial operations. Housing was scarce, city services became overloaded, and the quality of life declined for almost everyone.

And the situation was not likely to ease because German industrial leaders were still calling for more eastern workers. Since most of the foreign workers from the East were now conscripts and resentful of their lot, industrial sabotage became a big problem. This, in turn, put another burden on the SS because these workers had to be watched ever more closely.

The German Army and the SS, too, were recruiting more foreigners for their needs. By early 1943, the Army had nearly one million Hiwis, up from 200,000 in the spring of 1942.

Furthermore, many eastern women were brought to Germany to serve as prostitutes to help keep the workers in check. By 1943, there were thirty state-sponsored brothels for foreign workers in Germany and fifty more were being constructed or planned. Many of the ladies made more money than the workers.

Another victim of the war in Germany was the fashion industry for women's clothes. German women were instructed to wear what they had until the end of the war. A great number of them were wearing black.

The deterioration of German society affected Hitler personally. He gave up visiting heavily-bombed cities because he believed that photographs of him among the rubble were demoralizing to the public. He was probably right. When he travelled, he preferred to do so at night so that the devastation of Germany was not so obvious and because his train was safer from air attack. At his various headquarters, he and his staff lived under blackout conditions.

In the areas of eastern Germany annexed from Poland, the original plan had been to move the Poles out and move Volksdeutsch in. By 1943, however, this program was at a standstill. This was a heavily industrialized area and most of the Poles were employed in war work. Considering the war situation, it did not make sense to move these experienced workers out of the area and give their jobs to inexperienced newcomers. Therefore, the Poles remained and the area still had more Poles than Germans.

CHAPTER 19

THE WAR MOVES SOUTH

THE GERMAN SURFACE FLEET – A FAILURE

By the first week in January, 1943, Hitler had lost complete confidence in the German Navy's surface fleet and took out his wrath on Admiral Raeder during a stressful meeting on January 6. Raeder, humiliated, offered his resignation and Hitler accepted. During the encounter, Hitler threatened to scrap the Navy's capital ships, transfer their crews to smaller, more active ships, and strip the ships of their big guns and use them as coastal defense artillery.

Hitler later cooled down and did none of these things, but it was clear that he had lost all faith in Germany's ability to conduct warfare on the surface of the world's oceans. This meant that Germany would have absolutely no amphibious capabilities and could not carry out any large scale military campaigns across any sizeable body of water. Greater Germany would be a land-bound nation now and after the war.

The one remaining bright spot in the Navy was the submarine service commanded by Admiral Karl Doenitz whom Hitler selected as Raeder's replacement.

UNCONDITIONAL SURRENDER

On January 14, 1943, Roosevelt, Churchill and the leaders of the Fighting French met at Casablanca, French Morocco to discuss the future course of the war and to demonstrate that northwestern Africa was safely in Allied hands. The meeting resulted in a secret agreement that the western Allies would invade the western coast of Europe sometime in 1944. This was a front that the Soviets had long been demanding. It was also agreed secretly that the bombing of Germany and occupied Europe would be intensified, and, that after the Axis forces were defeated in North Africa, Sicily, and then Italy would be invaded.

At the end of the conference, Roosevelt made what appeared to be an offhand comment to the press, saying that nothing less than unconditional surrender would be acceptable from the Axis Powers. The other participants at the meeting, after some hesitation, supported this concept.

THE LAST WEEK IN JANUARY 1943

On January 23, the British 8th Army captured Tripoli, Libya and the Axis forces were in retreat to Tunisia.

In Tunisia, there was hard fighting, still with neither side gaining an advantage.

In the Mediterranean, the Allies continued to take a heavy toll on Axis shipping, but enough supplies were getting through to keep the Axis ground troops in Tunisia in fighting condition.

On the 27th, the U. S. 8th Air Force carried out its first raids on German territory by bombing Wilhelmshaven and Emden. This was only the beginning.

That same day, Hitler received intelligence reports that the Allies were about to invade Portugal. This gave him more to worry about.

On the 28th, Berlin decreed that men between age sixteen and sixty-five would be mobilized for military or other services, and women, between seventeen and forty-five would be subject to conscription for war work.

The next day, Rommel's forces crossed the border into Tunisia. Libya was lost.

On January 30, the tenth anniversary of the Nazi's rise to power, the RAF and AAF carried out two joint raids on Berlin. The first raid came during the afternoon when Goering was speaking on the radio in commemoration of the anniversary, and the second came at 7:30 p.m. when Goebbels was broadcasting his anniversary message. In addition to the Berlin raids, the RAF carried out a saturation bombing of Hamburg and the Americans bombed Messina, Sicily.

On the last day of the month, Hitler learned that twenty-two of the last fifty-one Italian merchant ships attempting to supply Tunisia had been lost.

BAD NEWS FROM THE PACIFIC

On February 9, 1943, word was received at Hitler's headquarters that the Japanese Army had withdrawn from the hotly-contested island of Guadalcanal in the South Pacific. This was a severe setback for Japan because it showed that the Japanese Army had been beaten by the American Army, and that the Japanese Navy could not save the situation. Hitler and his aides had to realize now that the quick and easy victory the Japanese had hoped for might not come about.

IN THE MEDITERRANEAN

During the first days of February 1943, reports continued to reach Hitler that the Allies might be preparing to invade the Iberian Peninsula. There were also reports that the Allies were massing troops on the Spanish Moroccan border and would invade that colony and then enter Spain from the south.

Hitler was so concerned that he moved a substantial German force to southern France with orders to invade Spain from the north if the Allies invaded from the south or the west.

From Tunisia came some good news. German forces scored a major victory over the Americans at the Kasserine Pass. The German penetration through the Americans' lines, however, was eventually stemmed by a combination of Allied forces, but it showed that the German forces in Tunisia could more than hold their own.

THE TREMBLING HAND

At the Fuehrer headquarters, Hitler was still keeping to himself, but changes in his mood and physical condition began to show for the worse. Most noticeably was the fact that his left hand now shook uncontrollably at times and, when he walked, he tended to drag his left foot and tip to the right. He also lost interest in music and movies and was quick to anger and less tolerant of mistakes. He complained again to some of his aides about bright lights hurting his eyes, and commented several times that he believed he was plagued with melancholia. He read medical books and frequently took his own pulse. This was in addition to his usual regimen of receiving injections from Dr. Morell and taking vitamins and pills for sleeping, digestion and colds. He sucked on eucalyptus candy, thinking it was good for him. Visitors who had not seen him in months commented on his deteriorated condition.

Rumors of Hitler's health leaked to the leaders of the armed forces and to the general public. Secretive comments were being exchanged that, perhaps, Hitler was no longer capable of ruling.

On March 1, Berlin suffered its most severe bombing yet. Considerable damage was done and many civilians were killed or injured. Such news as this did not help Hitler's condition and he became verbally abusive of Goering and the Luftwaffe leadership.

On the 3rd, Hamburg was hit hard, as was Essen on the 5th. In the days that followed, Allied planes began concentrating on attacking Germany's rail system.

THE DANISH ELECTIONS

On March 3, 1943, a very unique election took place in occupied Denmark. Since the Germans wanted to demonstrate to the world that Denmark was still an independent nation, they allowed the scheduled parliamentary elections to proceed without interference.

The small Danish Nazi Party, generously financed from Berlin, made a gigantic effort to gain seats in the Parliament to show that National Socialism was a political force on the rise. The election results, however, amounted to a devastating defeat for the Danish Nazis and an embarrassment for Berlin. Hitler and his entourage were, therefore, forced to secretly acknowledge that their plans to win over the Danes by political means had been a failure and that the future of Denmark had to be reevaluated. No immediate punitive actions were taken against the Danes, but Hitler decreed that this would be the last free election anywhere in occupied Europe.

ADVANCE ON MOSCOW FROM THE SOUTH BEGINS

During the first days of March, Hitler received a reliable report that the Soviets had begun drafting seventeen-year-olds. He took this as a sign that Stalin had reached the bottom of his manpower reserves.

🔊 Also at this time, Army Group B, now rested and resupplied, began its march to the north out of the Stalingrad area along the west bank of the Volga River. They had the river protecting their eastern flank, and their ultimate objective was to attack Moscow from both the south and east. ☑ This had been the German plan all along.

🔊 Siege lines had been established around Stalingrad and manned by a combined force of Germans and Romanians. Soviet resistance north of the city was strong, but was slowly overcome by superior German tactics, including the tried-and-true Blitzkrieg. The introduction of newly-arrived Tiger tanks gave the Axis forces a noticeable advantage. The first few days after the initial attack were encouraging. Soviet resistance gave way sooner than expected, and the Axis troops were able to advance up to sixty-five miles a day. ☑

MORE TROUBLE IN TUNISIA

Rommel's forces in southern Tunisia were experiencing serious setbacks at the hands of the British. Rommel pleaded with Hitler to send more men and arms. Despite the recent influx of Axis troops there were still less than a dozen Axis divisions in Tunisia. Rommel's argument had merit because there were over two-hundred Axis divisions in the East and some forty along the Atlantic Wall. Rommel thought that more of them could surely be sent to Tunisia. But Hitler was reluctant to grant Rommel's request because sending Axis troops to Tunisia was turning out to be a formula for disaster. So many men, and so much equipment, were being lost at sea. Out of desperation, the Germans and Italians began using destroyers and other small and fast warships to deliver men and supplies.

Unbeknownst to the Germans and Italians, the Allies had excellent intelligence on when, and from where, Axis ships and planes were leaving for Tunisia. This was due to the fact that the Ultra intercepts had reached a point whereby almost every Axis radio message in the Mediterranean area was being intercepted and read. On average, forty-one percent of the men and supplies being sent to Tunisia were lost at sea. The Italian sailors called it a "death run."

Hitler's response to the problems in Tunisia was to urge Rommel to hold on as best he could and that significant reinforcements would be sent at the earliest possible moment. Secretly, however, he told Jodl that he thought Tunisia might be lost.

NEGOTIATIONS WITH TURKEY

🎧 Hitler and his aides recognized that one way to save the situation in Tunisia was to launch an invasion into the Levant (Syria, Lebanon, Trans-Jordan, and Palestine) and threaten Egypt and the Suez Canal from the east. This would force the Allies to devote more of their strength to that area and, hopefully, away from Tunisia. ☑ An Axis invasion of the Levant had long been considered by the Axis planners.

But the key element here was neutral Turkey. To get forces into the Levant, the Axis would need transit rights through Turkey. This, they believed, was an attainable goal considering the fact that they had already gained transit rights through two other neutrals, Sweden and Switzerland. Furthermore, a precedent in this regard had already been made with Turkey during the uprising in Iraq in May/June 1941. At that time, the Turks permitted the transit of German aviation fuel and other supplies through their territory from Vichy-controlled Syria to Iraq along the section of the recently-completed Berlin-to-Baghdad railroad.

In addition, Turkey was militarily weak, and the Axis planners considered the fact that they could easily force their way trough Turkey if necessary.

🎧 Another factor that favored the Axis was the growing likelihood of an Axis victory in the Soviet Union and an eventual Axis move into the Middle East through the Caucasus. Such a move would put Axis troops on Turkey's western border and part of her southern border. It would also give the Axis Powers control of the Black Sea. If these things came about, Turkey would be partially surrounded by the Axis Powers.

Therefore, negotiations were begun in Ankara with the Turks at a considerable disadvantage.

Germany had the most to offer and took the lead in the negotiations. ☑ Germany already had a trade agreement with Turkey, written in June 1942, in which Germany would supply arms and munitions to Turkey in exchange for minerals and other raw materials. 🎧 Due to Germany's great needs, however, those arms and munitions had not been forthcoming. Now though, promises of faster delivery could be made along with other trade concessions, including easy access for Turkey to Caucasus oil, perhaps via a new pipeline which would run deep into Turkey. ☑

It was well known, too, that the Turks had hopes of recovering some of the territory they lost after World War I. 🎧 In this regard, Germany agreed to support Turkish efforts to recover the cities of Aleppo in Syria, Mosul in Iraq, and areas in the Caucasus lost to the communists during the Russian Revolution. ☑

A LITTLE VACATION

On March 22, Hitler retired to the Berghof for what he hoped would be an extended rest. He was exhausted and, once again, concerned about his health. He had recently suffered bouts of absentmindedness and had trouble making decisions. Two days after arriving at the Berghof, Hitler came down with severe headaches. He and Dr. Morell concluded that it might be the effects of the "Fohn", a warm southerly wind blowing down the mountain side locally believed to cause headaches, lassitude and insomnia. Morell recommended bed rest, a massage and egg yokes mixed with wine. Hitler did not improve so Morell gave him another metaflor cure to reduce the bacteria in his digestive tract. Hitler's recovery was slow, taking almost two weeks.

CONVERGING ON MOSCOW

🎧 In the East, Army Group North was steadily advancing on Moscow. The ancient Russian city of Novgorod was captured and from there the Germans gained access to the modern Novgorod-to-Moscow railroad and a good road system which facilitated their advance.

From the south, Army Group B, still following the Volga River and using the reliable Blitzkrieg, was advancing on the city of Kazan, 440 miles due east of Moscow. ☑ At

Kazan, the Volga turns to the west, providing an advantageous route of advance on Moscow from the east. Soviet troops had to be withdrawn from other locations to guard against this new threat to the capital.

🔊 The Soviets were also beginning to suffer from the lack of fuel after losing their oil supplies from the Caucasus. The Axis advance to the Caspian Sea at Astrakhan also cut the main Lend-Lease supply route into the southern part of the Soviet Union. Lend-Lease supplies coming from Iraq and Iran now had to travel through Turkestan, east of the Caspian Sea, where the roads and railroads were few and of poor quality.

During this time, Army Group Center launched a two-pronged attack against Moscow from the west. The northerly arm moved around the northern defenses of Moscow toward the city of Klin while the southerly arm advanced on Tula, south of Moscow. The encirclement of Moscow was beginning to take shape.

In the Caucasus, the Axis forces were on the defensive but holding their own against determined Soviet attacks. The Soviet forces there, however, were at an increasing disadvantage in that they were now cut off from their main supply link from the north. 📖 In preparations for the forthcoming drive into the Caucasus and Middle East Hitler ordered that a three-mile-long cable railroad bridge be built across the Strait of Kerch, the body of water separating the Crimea and the Caucasus mainland. This would shorten, by some four-hundred miles, the supply route into the Caucasus from the west. This bridge was a temporary structure that would allow loaded railroad cars to be towed from shore to shore by means of an overhead cable.

HOMELESS FOR THE FUEHRER

The Allied air war over Europe was continuing unabated. By the end of 1942, the Allies reported that they had bombed Cologne 103 times, Bremen 101 times, Hamburg 95 times, Kiel 71 times, and Berlin 53 times. In mid-March 1943, German radio admitted that there were over 120,000 people homeless in Germany. The actual count was almost certainly higher.

MOSCOW SURROUNDED

🔊 On March 24, 1943, units of Army Group North reached Klin, fifty miles northwest of Moscow. Three days later the northern arm of Army Group Center arrived. The Soviets abandoned Klin in face of this combined force, which was now the most powerful Axis force in the East. The Axis forces did not pursue the retreating Russians toward Moscow; rather they struck out to the east to complete the encirclement of Moscow.

South of Moscow, the southern arm of Army Group Center entered Tula, one hundred miles due south of Moscow. There they became engaged in deadly house-to-house fighting and their advance stalled.

To the southeast, Army Group B, still following the Volga, was nearing Kazan.

On March 28, the Soviet government began to flee Moscow for the safety of Gorky, 250 miles to the east. Stalin remained in the city to personally direct the defense of Moscow and bolster the morale of the troops.

During the last days of March, at Tula, the southern arm of Army Group Center went on the defensive and the main force bypassed the city and continued its advance to the east. Strong mobile forces struck out toward the Oka River, which ran in a northwesterly direction and then merged with the Moscow River, which flowed into the heart of Moscow.

Soviet troops south and east of Moscow began a massive evacuation to the east to avoid being trapped. Due to the lack of fuel, the Soviets destroyed many of their own tanks and other motorized vehicles and left behind much of their equipment. The Soviet Air Force also suffered from lack of fuel, allowing the Luftwaffe to slowly gain air supremacy on all of the fronts in the Moscow area.

The withdrawal of the Soviet forces substantially reduced the length of the Axis fronts which, in turn, allowed the Germans to concentrate more men and equipment to the forces gathering around Moscow.

North of Moscow, Army Group North, in conjunction with the northern arm of Army Group Center, continued its advance to the east. At the town of Zarajsk, forty miles northeast of Moscow, they turned to a southeasterly direction toward the advancing Army Group B.

South of Moscow, the southern Arm of Army Group Center reached the Oka River, crossed it and advanced in a northerly direction. On April 6, Army Group North and the southern arm of Army Group Center met at the village of Satura, seventy-five miles east of Moscow. Moscow was now surrounded. The day before, Stalin and his entourage secretly flew from Moscow to Gorky in a heavily-protected air convoy. With them went Lenin's preserved body.

In the Gorky area, Army Group B reached the outskirts of Kazan, 200 miles east of Gorky which was now in danger of being attacked from the south and the east.

Meanwhile, back at Moscow, strong siege lines were set up all around Moscow. It was not the intention of the Axis leaders to enter Moscow, but to starve the city into submission. Sieges had worked at Sevastopol and Leningrad and the Axis leaders had every reason to believe a siege would work here. This action freed a very large contingent of Axis tanks and other offensive and mobile units for action further east. After a few days of reorganizing, the new force, which now combined most of Army Groups North and Center and renamed "Army Group Urals," struck out in the direction of Gorky. This force was extremely powerful, but the Soviet forces retreating from Moscow made a determined fighting retreat. Within days, however, Soviet opposition diminished and the Army Group Urals' march on Gorky accelerated. Large numbers of Soviet prisoners — out of ammunition, out of food and demoralized — began surrendering by the thousands. But now, the muddy season had returned and the Axis advance toward the Urals slowed because of it. ☑

HOLD TUNISIA AT ALL COSTS

On April 7, 1943, Hitler and Mussolini met at Salzburg to discuss the situation in Tunisia. Both men could see that if all of North Africa were lost, the Mediterranean would also be lost and the entire southern coast of Europe, and especially Sicily and Italy, would be vulnerable to an Allied invasion. But, as long as the Allies were tied down in Tunisia, it was unlikely that they would invade either southern or western Europe.

However, there were monumental problems for the Axis leaders. The Axis forces in Tunisia had been driven into a condensed area in northern Tunisia and Hitler had received information that the German commanders in Tunisia were anticipating defeat.

Furthermore, increased Allied bombings of Italy, Sardinia and other places in the Mediterranean indicated that those areas were being softened up by the Allies for possible invasions. This demonstrated, too, that the Allies expected victory in Tunisia in the near future.

Hitler and Mussolini therefore agreed that Tunisia had to be saved at all costs, and proposals were put forward to accomplish this. In general, this decision meant that the Axis Powers would go on the defensive in Tunisia for the near future.

PREPARATIONS TO INVADE THE LEVANT

🔊 In Turkey, negotiations for the transit of Axis forces through that country were going well. Ambassador Papen was sending one encouraging report after the other to Berlin. He reported that many top Turkish political leaders, and even more military leaders, had indicated that they would welcome an Axis presence in the Middle East over that of the British and the Fighting French. The Turks, however, wanted to remain neutral — at least for now. The Italians enthusiastically supported Turkey's neutrality because, if Turkey entered the war, almost any military action the Turks would take would be directed toward Syria, Iraq and Iran — areas that were to be within Italy's sphere of influence after the war.

On April 9, Turkey and the Axis Powers reached an agreement. Axis forces would be allowed to travel through Turkey and assemble in southern Turkey for an invasion of the Levant. In return, the Axis Powers would guarantee Turkey's neutrality and territorial integrity, and recognized Turkey's claim to Cyprus, which had once been a part of the Ottoman Empire. The Axis also agreed to supply Turkey with a generous allotment of arms, and to aid Turkey in setting up an oil consortium to obtain a permanent supply of oil from the Caucasus once it was securely in Axis hands. Turkey was also to receive several German submarines in exchange for free access by German subs through the Straits to the Black Sea. Furthermore, ethnic Turk prisoners of war would gradually be released and allowed to return to their homes, or to Turkey, or to join the Axis armed forces as volunteers.

Within twenty-four hours of the signing of the agreement, German and Italian forces, which had gathered on the Bulgarian-Turkish border, began entering Turkey. Using the Berlin-to-Baghdad Railroad as one of their main routes, they moved to the southern border of Turkey and positioned themselves for the coming invasion of the Levant. With events winding down in the Soviet Union, the Axis leaders hoped to have a force in the Levant that outnumbered the Allies two-to-one.

Upon learning of the agreement, Britain, the United States and other Allied nations issued strong notes of protest to the Ankara government and recalled their ambassadors, leaving their diplomatic affairs in the hands of a charges d'affaires. Furthermore, the Americans ordered an immediate halt to Lend-Lease to Turkey which had been granted in December 1941. Britain and some of the other Allies also froze Turkish assets in their respective countries. ☑

SAVING TUNISIA

On April 8, 1943, British forces captured the Tunisian seaport of Sfax. This put the entire southern and central portions of Tunisia in Allied hands.

🔊 On this day, in accordance with the decision made with Mussolini to save Tunisia, Hitler ordered thirty German submarines from the Atlantic into the Mediterranean in an effort to stem the high losses being experienced in trying to supply Tunisia from Sicily and Italy.

Furthermore, contracts were let to Italian and Spanish ship yards to build more submarines and convoy escort vessels for operations in the Mediterranean.

German and Italian ground forces from all over Europe, and from some areas in the East, were scraped together and sent to ports of embarkation in Italy for transfer to Tunisia. These forces were equipped to serve primarily as defensive forces in keeping with Hitler's and Mussolini's decision to save Tunisia. This action weakened Germany's defenses along the Atlantic Wall and both Germany's and Italy's defenses along the southern coast of Europe. But it was a risk that Hitler and Mussolini were willing to take. ☑

As a show of support of the Axis Powers, Vichy authorized their administrators in Tunisia to impose mandatory labor service on all able-bodied Frenchmen there. Also, a small combat unit of some 200 French volunteers was raised to fight on the Axis side.

Getting the Axis troops to Tunisia was still very problematic. On April 18, 1943, an air battle over the Mediterranean highlighted this problem. On that day, some one hundred German transport planes flying to Tunisia in an air convoy were attacked by American fighter planes from the U.S. 9th Air Force. Over half of the German planes were shot down and many German soldiers were lost at sea. The Germans called it the "Palm Sunday Massacre."

🔊 Such was the price the Axis leaders would have to pay to save Tunisia. To meet this challenge, the Luftwaffe brought in additional fighter aircraft from the defense of western Europe and from the East, and merchant ships of all descriptions were requisitioned throughout the Mediterranean and Black Sea areas. Merchantmen were also purchased or leased from Turkey and Spain.

AND IN THE LEVANT

In Syria and Iraq, the British and the Fighting French rushed all of their available forces to the border with Turkey, while additional Fighting French, British, dominion and colonial troops were called in from many locations. The British-trained Jewish Brigade was also called in from Palestine to help defend Syria.

In Tunisia, General Montgomery was ordered to release two of his best armored divisions for service in the Levant. Three American divisions, including one armored division, were dispatched from Britain to Tunisia to replace the departing British divisions. With this, the war in Tunisia became Americanized. A short time later, Montgomery himself was sent to the Levant to take command there.

There would be no Americans, however, sent to the Levant. This was seen in Washington as contrary to America's long-standing anti-colonial foreign policy. Sending Americans to fight for other nation's colonies would not sit well with the American public and would be useful ammunition for Roosevelt's political opposition, especially in view of the fact that 1944 was a presidential election year.

There were many Americans already in Iraq and Iran, but they were primarily service personnel handling Lend-Lease and would not be expected to serve as combat troops. Furthermore, much of the Lend-Lease material in the pipeline destined for Russia was now diverted to the British and Fighting French. The Soviets protested this action, thus adding a strain to Soviet-American relations.

VICTORY IN THE EAST — FINALLY

🔊 On April 10, 1943, Stalin's government fled Gorky as Axis troops closed in on the city from two directions. Stalin and his entourage took up residence in the industrial city of Sverdlovsk on the eastern slope of the Ural Mountains in Siberia. Likewise, Soviet troops began streaming across the Urals to safety on the other side.

This was the news Hitler and the other Axis leaders had long hoped for. Hitler was

ecstatic. Now, victory was at hand in the East. Problems remained, however. Many Soviet forces had been bypassed and would have to be mopped up, the Partisans were still strong in the north, the new armed frontier would have to be established and, of course, Moscow, Stalingrad and Astrakhan had yet to be captured. Problems such as these, however, had been anticipated and ☑ the Barbarossa planners had estimated that sixty well-armed and winterized divisions would have to remain in the East to consolidate the conquests.

This would, however, leave over 140 other divisions for service elsewhere, such as the Middle East and North Africa. These divisions would be in addition to German troops, some one hundred divisions, operating in occupied Europe and Tunisia. In comparison, the U. S. Army, at the time, consisted of some ninety divisions with a large percentage of them in the Pacific. With regard to armored divisions, however, the tally was more equal. The Germans had twenty-one armored divisions at this time while the Americans had sixteen, but they were more organized. Combined with the British armored divisions, though, the Allies outnumbered the Axis Powers in this category. Furthermore, the Allied armored divisions were being trained in both carrying out, and stopping, the Blitzkrieg tactic.

🔊 On April 20, Hitler began the savory task of redeploying his 140 divisions now available from the East. To be sure, the Levant and North Africa were high on his list of priorities. The Allied leaders could easily surmise this.

News of the defeat of the Soviet forces west of the Urals had electrified the world. In the Axis countries, morale and hopes for an end to the war soared, while in the Allied countries there was dismay and grave concern. In some major Allied cities, small groups now began to form and speak out against the war. In the United States, the peace groups were led mostly by the long-silent isolationists.

Chances of ending the war were, however, a pipe dream. There was no stopping Hitler now. He had the world's largest army and he intended to use it.

REDEPLOYMENT

The redeployment of Axis forces in the East began in late April. One force, however, that had to remain in the East almost in its entirety, was the Luftwaffe's bomber command. The great industrial complexes in Siberia still made the Soviets a serious threat and it would be the task of the Luftwaffe bombers to keep that threat at a minimum by frequent and intensive air raids.

Most of the Luftwaffe's fighters, however, could be redeployed, but they would not be dispatched to Germany to counter the intense Allied bombing campaign of the German homeland because they were badly needed in the Mediterranean and the Levant. In the Mediterranean they would be used to help protect the Tunisia-bound convoys and in Tunisia itself, where the Allies had gained superiority in the air.

Hundreds more fighter aircraft would be sent to the Levant to support the coming invasion there.

As for the ground forces, those in need of rest and rehabilitation would be stationed along the Atlantic Wall to relieve the fresh and battle-ready there for use elsewhere. The largest contingent of troops would be sent to the Levant and some to Tunisia. Still more divisions would be sent to Army Group A, in the Caucasus, to help complete the conquest there and participate in the planned drive into Iran and Iraq.

All of the Italian divisions in the East would likewise, be redeployed to the Levant, Tunisia and the Caucasus. Some of the armored units of the Italian Army were now equipped with sizeable numbers of captured Soviet T-34 tanks, which made them more formidable on the battlefield. Furthermore, the Germans had given the Italians about thirty Tiger tanks.

Some of the Romanian and Hungarian units, as well as units of the other Axis allies, would remain in the East until the military situation was stable. Others would be redeployed to the Balkans to help eliminate the Partisan menace there.

Hitler and his aides now viewed the war from an entirely new prospective — a prospective that victory was in sight. And, in the Allied capitals, the leaders there had to accept the very unpleasant possibility that the war might be lost.

ON TO SUEZ — FROM THE EAST

On April 24, 1943, German and Italian forces invaded Syria from their staging areas in Turkey. The Fighting French and British defenders had prepared as best they could for the invasion, but the superiority in numbers of the Axis forces, the Blitzkrieg attacks, and the employment of dozens of Tiger tanks prevailed. For the moment, though, the Allies had air superiority and were able to inflict heavy damage on the Axis forces.

The main thrust of the Axis invasion occurred at two points north of Aleppo where a road and two railroads, leading from the Turkish border, converged on that city. The terrain was arid and relatively flat giving the Axis tanks the advantage on the ground. To their west was the coastal mountain range, and to the east, the desert. Both provided flank protection for the Axis advance. ◪ This was a route that invaders had used to invade the Levant since before the Crusades.

◖The Allied forces abandoned Aleppo and retreated, in good order, to Hama, eighty miles to the south. On the evening of the 25th, the Axis forces occupied Aleppo.

WE COME AS LIBERATORS

Just like the invasion of the Soviet Union twenty-two months earlier, the Axis forces invading the Levant proclaimed themselves the liberators of the people. This time, however, there was more truth to it. The Axis propagandists had long preached that Germany and Italy were friends of the Middle Eastern peoples and wanted to liberate them from their British and French oppressors. It must be remember that Mussolini was the

Protector of Islam and that Hitler had written in Mein Kampf of his hopes to befriend the Arab world.

As the Axis forces advanced, leaflets were dropped ahead of their advance telling the people that they would soon be liberated from their French and British masters. The Axis soldiers were given explicit instructions to respect the local people and their property. Fraternization with Muslim women was strictly forbidden and severe punishment was to be meted out to offenders.

Attached to both the German and Italian Armies were small units of Syrians, Lebanese, Palestinians and Jordanians. These people had been gleaned from Arab emigre communities in Europe, prisoner of war camps, European universities and other sources. They wore German and Italian uniforms and carried weapons, but their main value was that of propaganda. Whenever possible, they were thrust into the spotlight to be seen by, and to make contact with, the local people.

In addition to the Arab units, German and Italian information teams, which employed Arab civilian collaborators and Arab-speaking Germans and Italians, followed in the wake of the Axis advance to inform the locals of the Axis nation's intentions toward the Arab peoples. They handed out pamphlets and other documents telling of Germany's and Italy's friendly intentions and quoted statements made by well-known Arab collaborators such as the Mufti of Jerusalem and Rashid Ali Gailani of Iraq, who supported the Axis cause. Photographs of these people, Hitler, and Mussolini, suitable for hanging on the wall of a home or business, were generously distributed. ☑

Almost all of the Arab peoples in the Middle East and North Africa were aware of the Axis promises made to them over the years. This was that the sovereignty and independence of the Arab lands would be recognized and that the creation of a Jewish homeland in Palestine would be forbidden.

Then too, support came from Japan, calling for Arab independence and friendship. 🔊 This was in keeping with Japan's overall plans to "liberate" the European-controlled colonial territories of Southeast Asia and grant them independence.

The Axis leaders were soon to discover that their propaganda efforts had been very successful, because as German and Italian troops advanced into the Middle East, they were hailed, time and again, as friends and liberators.

Actually, though, the Germans were more welcome than the Italians. ☑ Many Arabs resented Italy's maltreatment of Arabs in Libya which dated back to Italy's acquisition of the colony from the Ottoman Empire in 1912. Also, many Arabs resented Italy's blatant invasion of Ethiopia in 1935.

Additionally, there was no great desire among the Lebanese and Syrians to adapt Fascism or National Socialism, nor to volunteer to fight in the Axis armies — especially the Italian Army.

🔊 But it was the dawn of a new era, and most Arabs were willing to accept the Axis' promises at face value over what they had experienced under the French and British. ☑

SYRIA AND LEBANON IN APRIL 1943

Syria was one of the most troubled lands of the Middle East and Lebanon was one of the most stable. France had been awarded mandates over both of these countries by the League of Nations following World War I, and the two countries took widely different political paths.

The Lebanese cooperated with the French, who gave them a republican constitution in 1926 with a promise of future independence, which was granted in 1941, albeit under trying circumstances. The French military stayed on in Lebanon because the Lebanese Army was small and weak. And, not surprisingly, the French continued to exercise considerable influence over political and economic matters.

The Syrians, unlike the Lebanese, deeply resented the French mandate and repeatedly resisted French authority, while at the same time, squabbling incessantly among themselves. There were also competing and strong pro-Axis factions in Syria that contributed to the boiling political pot. Then too, the Syrians had disputes with Turkey over territorial issues and were often at odds with neighboring Iraq.

When France went to war against Germany and Italy, the Syrians heavily favored the Axis Powers, and teams of militant extremists carried out sabotage against the British-owned oil pipeline running through their country from Iraq to the sea. When France surrendered, French influence in both Syria and Lebanon tumbled to a new low.

Following France's surrender, the two countries remained loyal to Vichy and became subject to the British blockade.

To add to the hardships of the Lebanese and Syrian people, Vichy allowed the Germans and Italians to generously requisition food and raw materials, but this had a mixed result. On the one hand, shortages of many items arose in Lebanon and Syria as did black markets, official corruption, and inflation. On the other hand, new industries were started, roads, railroads and airports were constructed, and there was full employment.

When the Fighting French took control of the countries during the summer of 1941, they allowed Lebanon to proclaim its independence in July 1941, and Syria in November 1941. Vichy, seeking not to be upstaged by the Fighting French, declared Syria and Lebanon independent a short time later.

This then, was the situation in Syria and Lebanon at the time of the Axis invasion.

A SECOND INVASION FROM TURKEY

🔲 On April 28, 1943, German and Italian forces launched a second invasion of Syria, this time advancing along the coast of the Mediterranean from the Antioch area of Turkey in the direction of the Syrian port city of Latakia. Allied resistance was light and the Axis advance was rapid.

On May 2, Latakia fell and the Axis drive continued down the coast. By May 4, they were sixty-five miles south of Latakia and reached a road junction which branched off

to the east and led to Hama. A sizeable Axis force was sent in that direction. Hama was then threatened from the north and the west. All the while, strong German reinforcements were arriving from the Eastern Front and the drive down the coast continued, forcing the British and Fighting French defenders into a steady retreat.

On May 6-7, after a fierce but brief fight, the Allies withdrew from Hama to new defenses at Homs, twenty-six miles to the south. The Axis forces followed closely on their heels.

Then followed a two-week lull in the fighting in the Levant as the Axis commanders consolidated their gains and brought in still more reinforcements and equipment. During this time, Montgomery's two armored divisions arrived from Tunisia, along with the 10th Indian Division from Iran and other units from Egypt, East Africa and South Africa.

AXIS STRENGTH IN TUNISIA BUILDS. BRITISH TROOPS TO THE MIDDLE EAST.

During May, the situation began to change in Tunisia. With the arrival of the German submarines and additional Luftwaffe units, more men and supplies were getting across the Mediterranean safely. By the end of May, losses at sea had come down from over 40% to 25%. Rommel's force had grown considerably and was now renamed the "Afrika Armee Group" (AAG).

The Allies, too, were bringing in more forces from both Britain and the United States, and they were still bombing Italian ports of embarkation and potential invasion sites in Sicily and Italy.

Furthermore, there was a great exodus of British troops from Britain to the Levant and Persian Gulf area. The latter was in preparation for a very likely Axis advance into Iran from the Caucasus.

Unbeknownst to the Axis leaders, the American and British leaders concurred that a cross-channel invasion in May 1944, as envisioned at the Casablanca Conference, was not feasible now because of the need for troops in Tunisia and the Middle East. Hitler and Mussolini had won a victory but did not know it.

The Allied leaders also agreed that the conflict in Tunisia would be, primarily, the responsibility of the Americans and the Fighting French, while that in the Middle East would be the responsibility of the British and Empire forces. This was a logical decision for the Americans because it was in America's interests that Axis forces be kept out of northwest Africa and, by all means, be prevented from establishing military bases on the Atlantic coast of Africa from which they could threaten the Western Hemisphere.

THE AXIS BUILDUP IN THE CAUCASUS, AND MOPPING UP IN THE EAST

With the muddy season ending in the East, strong Axis forces began to move into the Caucasus. Meanwhile, Moscow, Stalingrad and Astrakhan remained under siege enduring frequent shelling and aerial bombardments, while the defenders experienced ever diminishing reserves of food, munitions and other necessities of war.

A large part of the 60 Axis divisions remaining in the East were now mopping up isolated and bypassed pockets of Soviet forces and, at the same time, beginning to man the armed frontier. Establishing the armed frontier, however, became a low priority for the moment because of the weakened condition of Soviet forces. More pressing were the reduction of the besieged cities, the mopping up campaigns, and the suppression of the Partisans.

The capture of Archangel was now unimportant because there were no roads or railroads leading east out of that Arctic port to the Soviet strongholds behind the Urals.

In the Caucasus, the Soviet forces were holding their own along the Terek River, north of the Caucasus Mountains. They had plenty of fuel and were getting some supplies from Siberia and American Lend-Lease. Lend-Lease, however, did not include tanks, and this was likely to become the Achilles heel of the Soviet defensive effort. ☑

CHAPTER 20

FROM THE URALS TO PALESTINE

The beginning of good weather in the East was of considerable advantage to the Germans. The last pockets of Red Army resistance in the East, other than the Partisans of course, could be more easily eliminated and the military buildup in the Caucasus could be accomplished without major concerns for the weather. Likewise, good weather increased the efficiency of the German artillerymen and airmen besieging the cities of Moscow, Stalingrad and Astrakhan. Using the psychology of good weather to their advantage, the Germans intensified their propaganda directed toward the Soviet troops in the besieged cities to lay down their arms and accept the benevolent custody, food and care of the German Army.

In both the Ostland and the Ukraine, the local people and new settlers alike were encouraged to plant their crops in generous quantities. Promises were made of free seed, inexpensive fertilizer, assured markets and government help in obtaining farm equipment and farm animals.

VICTORY OVER THE JEWS PROGRESSING

In keeping with Nazi plans to make all of Europe Jew-free, the extensive campaign against the Jews continued.

In Warsaw, the Jews had revolted in an heroic, but unsuccessful, uprising. The superior German forces quelled the revolt and those Jews who were not killed were sent off to the labor camps or the extermination camps.

In the southern part of the General Government, the SS began to eliminate the sizeable Jewish ghetto at Lvov. Here too, the Jews were dispatched to labor camps or extermination camps. The Germans were approaching their goal of making all of the General Government Jew-free.

Between May 5–10, 1943, the last Jews were deported from Croatia. That Axis ally was then declared Jew-free.

In the East, the Einsatzgruppen continued their grizzly work eliminating Jews wherever they found them.

The purge of Jews extended to Spain. During May, the Spanish government enacted anti-Jewish legislation, closing all synagogues and Jewish communal offices and confiscating their property. Private Jewish homes were raided and many Jews imprisoned on trumped-up charges. A few were executed. Leaders of the Falange Party, Franco's surrogate Nazi-style party, announced that it was their goal to make Spain Jew-free along with the rest of Europe.

On May 23, 1943, Tsar Boris of Bulgaria, under strong German pressure, began a program to rid his country of Jews. He issued a decree expelling all Jews from Bulgaria's capital, Sofia, and handing them over to the Germans. This sparked an immediate public protest: Tsar Boris's control over his people was not nearly so complete as that of Hitler's over the German people. Crowds gathered at the royal palace to protest the edict, many political figures and intellectuals spoke out publicly against the action, and Exarch Stephen, head of the Bulgarian Orthodox Church, joined in the protest by giving sanctuary to the Chief rabbi of Sofia and other Jewish leaders.

In face of this opposition, Boris's edict was modified, calling for the distribution of Sofia's Jews to other locations throughout Bulgaria rather than handing them over to the Germans. For Hitler, this was a disappointment and another problem that would have to be addressed in the future.

Further to the south, the last Jews were deported from Salonica, Greece, Germany's permanent enclave on the Mediterranean, and from the Italian-controlled islands of Rhodes and Corfu. In Berlin, it was expected that Italy would, eventually, cooperate with Germany and expel the Jews from their occupied areas in southern Europe.

BAD NEWS AND CONSTIPATION

During the first days of May, much of the news received at Hitler's headquarters was negative. The Allied air campaign over Europe was intensifying, and the Allies had developed a new method of skipping bombs over water which was designed to destroy dams. Two dams in the Ruhr had already been destroyed. Germany was continuing to lose the air war.

Other reports were coming in from Admiral Doenitz's office that German submarine losses at sea were mounting.

Between May 15 — 17, Hitler suffered a severe bout of constipation and was attended to regularly by Dr. Morell.

Through it all, Morell continued giving Hitler daily injections and medications. Behind his back, some were calling Morell the "Reich Injection Master."

There was a spot of good news, however, from the Italians. They informed the German leadership that the prototype of a small submarine they had been developing had undergone its first successful test. This was a submarine designed to be carried by a mother submarine to a distant harbor, enter the harbor and sink enemy ships at their moorings. This was not the first mini-submarine developed by the Italians. Previous shorter range small underwater craft had been developed and used successfully in the Mediterranean. This new submarine, however, was designed to work at heretofore unreachable locations such as New York Harbor.

BLACK MAY

By the third week in May, the terrible news from Doenitz's headquarters was being confirmed. Germany's submarine fleet was in serious trouble. So far during the month, forty-one submarines had been sunk, which accounted for more than 1/3 of those at sea. This was a totally unacceptable situation. One of the submarines sunk, U-954, carried Doenitz's son to his death. The Germans came to call this period "Black May."

The source of this problem lay in the fact that the Allies had, by now, successfully developed and implemented three means of locating German submarines by electronic devices: radar, Sonar and High-Frequency Directional-Finding (Huff-Duff). The later was a radio tracking device that could accurately locate German submarines as they transmitted radio messages. Plus, there was the invaluable Ultra intercepts that were reading most of the German Navy's radio transmissions.

Another cause for the submarine losses was the fact that large numbers of Allied land-based aircraft were now employed in searching for submarines operating out of newly-acquired bases in the Western Hemisphere and western Africa.

But perhaps the most significant development of all was the Allied development of small aircraft carriers ("baby flattops").

These ships were fast and became the nuclei of small task forces, known as "Hunter-Killer" units, which were designed specifically to hunt and sink submarines. The baby flattops carried a compliment of small short-range aircraft capable of finding and sinking submarines. Baby flattops were also used to escort convoys. Experience soon showed that once a submarine was located by a Hunter-Killer force, it almost never escaped.

Another new weapon that the Allies had begun to use was the acoustic torpedo. This was a torpedo, usually dropped by an aircraft, that could seek out the sound of the electric motors of a submerged submarine, track it, and destroy it.

By May 1943, all of these tactics were being utilized by the Allies.

During the latter part of that month, Admiral Doenitz called off all submarine attacks in the Atlantic due to the high losses. Hitler approved this action and promised countermeasures, including an increase in submarine production from thirty submarines a month to forty, and the development of an acoustic torpedo of their own. Another development, already in production, was the new "snorkel" device which would allow a submarine to run its diesel engines while submerged. Up to this time, submarines could only run their diesels when on the surface of the water where they were most vulnerable.

Another development underway were larger submarines of a new design that would carry more anti-aircraft guns. This would allow the sub to stand and fight rather than dive and run.

Hitler called in Speer to address the submarine problem, but Germany's miracle worker was unable to come up with a solution.

Doenitz refitted his existing submarines with more anti-aircraft guns, radar detectors and radar. Then he released them again in early June. Losses for June dropped to seventeen, but rose again to thirty-eight in July. Survivability in the German submarine service had become a major concern.

Hitler could only conclude that his submarine force, while still a significant weapon, could not win the war for him. The hopes of 1940, that the submarines could starve Britain into submission, were dead. Now, the only armed service Hitler had left, capable of winning the war, was the army.

AXIS FORCES ADVANCE IN THE LEVANT

🔊 On May 26, 1943, Axis forces launched a major attack at Homs, Syria, using the Blitzkrieg tactic against the Allies' right flank where the terrain was flat and dry. Hard fighting ensued, but on the 28th, the Axis forces broke through. The Allies withdrew, in order, to new defenses at Damascus.

Along the coast, the Allied forces also withdrew to avoid being outflanked by the advance of the Axis forces inland.

To the north, a steady stream of Axis reinforcements were pouring into the Levant from Turkey. The Allies were also receiving reinforcements, but at a slower rate. The military balance in the Levant still favored the Axis.

Realizing this, and the fact that the British Army was stretched to its limit, the Americans agreed to send an armored division and a motorized infantry division to Palestine to help defend the Suez Canal which, as the American leaders told the American public, was of vital interest to the United States.

MOSCOW FALLS

By the last days of May, the Soviet defenders of Moscow were out of food and almost out of ammunition. Stalin had ordered them to fight to the last man, but without the means to do so, and with ever-sinking morale, small groups of soldiers began to abandon their posts and surrender to the Germans. As the mutiny spread, the Soviet Commander at Moscow ordered the NKVD to take drastic action to stop the defections. After several summary executions, the dam of resentment broke and the Red Army soldiers rose up en masse against their officers and commissars. As had been the case in 1917, when the Czar's soldiers turned against their leaders, so now the soldiers of the Red Army turned against theirs. A blood bath ensued as the revolution spread throughout Moscow. The city's defenses quickly collapsed and the Axis troops could have rushed in and occupied the city. But this did not happen. Orders had come down directly from Hitler not to interfere in the fighting. The Russians were to be allowed to go on killing each other as long as they wished.

The bloody infighting at Moscow eventually subsided and during the latter part of June, Axis forces occupied the city.

A section of the city was cordoned off to become a temporary prisoner of war camp to hold those who surrendered.

Most of those who did so were thoroughly emaciated and exhausted. Further orders came down from the Fuehrer's headquarters to withhold foods and other supplies so that large numbers of the POWs would die.

With the fall of Moscow, the new colony of Muscovy began.

The fall of Moscow released a large number of Axis forces for deployment elsewhere. It was the German's intent to use most of these troops in a march down the east bank of the Volga, which would finalize the sieges at Stalingrad and Astrakhan from the east and secure the southern section of the future armed frontier.

LULLS IN BOTH TUNISIA AND THE LEVANT

In both Tunisia and the Levant, there were extended lulls in the fighting as both sides brought up reinforcements and supplies.

In Tunisia, the Germans and Italians were able to build up a sizeable force of nine German and five Italian divisions despite the heavy losses being suffered at sea. This was about three times the force Rommel had commanded in 1942 when he was able to drive deep into Egypt.

Through Ultra, the Allies had good information on the Axis buildup in Tunisia and managed to keep ahead of the enemy by bringing in more troops from Britain as well as the United States. Also, the Allies sent in large numbers of aircraft, including tank-killing fighters, in anticipation of the time when the Germans would utilize the Blitzkrieg tactic, once again, to break out of their Tunisian redoubt.

In the Levant, the Allies did not have the advantage of Ultra, because fewer messages there were sent over the air waves. Here, the Axis buildup was much more extensive than in Tunisia because it was from this area that the main attempt would be made to capture the Suez Canal, Cairo, and eventually, most of North Africa. The British, having committed sizeable numbers of troops elsewhere, were hard pressed to find forces to serve in the Levant.

This was the military situation that existed throughout most of June. ☑

A MASTERFUL DECEPTION

During June 1943, the Allies undertook a world-wide operation designed to deceive the Germans into believing that a large American force was building up in Britain in preparation for an invasion somewhere on the western coast of the continent. This was part of the original planning for "Operation Overlord," the cross-channel invasion of France.

The deceptive operation, code named "Operation Bodyguard," consisted of phony troop movements; extensive, but meaningless, radio traffic; carefully planned news releases to the media; intentional intelligence leaks, and the like. It was the task of Bodyguard to convince the Germans that a major invasion might come at such points as the Pas de Calais, or Brittany, or Norway. The intent was, of course, to tie down German armed forces at several locations.

The Germans took the bait and devoted much time and effort tracking this imaginary invasion threat.

AT THE TABLE AGAIN

On June 13, 1943, after a long pause, Hitler's table talk was again recorded for posterity. The notes were taken by Bormann personally and, as earlier, were generally devoid of military talk. The transcripts of the conversations lasted only until June 24, then abruptly ended again.

At the evening meal on the 13th, Hitler spoke at length about the future museums he intended to build. He said it would be a mistake to congregate too many of them in Berlin and that they should be spread throughout Germany.

In the military museum he intended to build in Linz, he said he would devote one section on fortifications, covering those from ancient times to the Atlantic Wall. And, in the German Museum in Munich, there would be working models and displays that visitors could touch and operate.

He then went into a monologue on paintings and painters. Afterwards, he talked of opera houses saying that the new opera house that was to be built in Munich must surpass everything that had ever gone before it.

On the 19th, he talked about the German Navy, which he now saw as being of little value. Hitler said that formerly he had planned to construct the most powerful squadron of battleships in the world but had abandoned the idea. Hitler went on to say that they would be of little value in the postwar era and that the vessels of the future that would "carry on the fight" would be submarines and small, fast ships.

On the 24th, Hitler spoke of the fairness and equality that should prevail in Germany in the postwar era between cities and regions. He said that there should be no rivalry between Vienna and Berlin and that both should be treated equally. He added that if any city or province that tried to make unreasonable claims to their own individual advantage would put me "up in arms at once." A few minutes later, he contradicted himself by saying that he would make Berlin a great world capital and that he would take care to see that no town in the Reich became its rival.

In his dissertation on fairness, Hitler went on to say that Gauleiters should be treated equally and that no one Gauleiter would receive more support from him than was needed to carry out his duties.

Returning to the subject of Vienna, Hitler boasted that he had made the city Jew-free and said that after the war he would like to see the Czechs leave also. He also added that the slums had to be cleared.

Hitler's comments might well have been stimulated by the fact that, a few days earlier, Goebbels, as Gauleiter of Berlin, had announced that Berlin was Jew-free. It might also be possible that, since these records of Hitler's conversations were somewhat repetitive of those made earlier, Hitler concluded that he had said all he needed to say for posterity.

Thus ended Hitler's messages on the future. They would resume very briefly in March 1944 and, again, would be repetitive of what had been said earlier.

MUSCOVY

In the East, the time had come to establish the third and final Reichscommissariat — Muscovy. This was done by a decree issued by the Fuehrer on June 28, 1943. Berlin announced that Muscovy would be the homeland of the Russian people, and that Moscow would be its administrative capital. Nothing was said, of course, about Hitler's plan to eventually destroy the city or that the entire Reichscommissariat would be used as a dumping ground for the undesirables of Europe.

Muscovy was a huge area bordered on the south by the Ukraine, on the west by Ostland and Finland, on the north by the Arctic Ocean and on the east by the armed frontier.

Accompanying the announcement and the media coverage that followed, Muscovy was described as a happy place. Such promises were reminiscent of the propaganda the Germans put forth when the Soviet Union was invaded in June 1941, and of that which had currently been stated in the Levant. According to the media reports, the residents of Muscovy would be given land, homesteads, religious freedom, economic freedoms and

Muscovy was to be the homeland of the Russian people and Germany's penal colony.

incentives, markets for their products, guarantees with regard to the preservation of their Slavic culture, freedom from communism, protection by the Reich and, at some point in the future, autonomy.

Virtually all of these promises were lies. The people that were to be dispatched to Muscovy could not be told the truth of what awaited them.

Within weeks of the creation of the RK Muscovy, photographs appeared in the German media of smiling and healthy-looking Russian peasants arriving at their new homesteads in Muscovy. Some of the settlers were identified as Jews. Accompanying the photos were reports of the newcomers settling in, planting crops, building homes and working cheerfully with their German advisors. These photos and stories were all fakes because, in reality, virtually no Russian or Jewish settlers were being sent to Muscovy because it was a very dangerous place. Only about half of the land-mass of the colony was in German hands. The remainder was controlled by the Partisans and elements of the Red Army. Furthermore, it made no sense for the Germans to use precious resources at this time to relocate large numbers of people to the east.

Because of its isolation, the western world had no real knowledge of what was going on in Muscovy. Many people were duped by the German propaganda, but many too, were unconvinced. Reports on Muscovy were met with a great deal of skepticism, especially since the Germans denied access to every outsider including humanitarian agencies such as the Red Cross.

Next door, in Ostland, the SS began, in late July, a program of shutting down Jewish ghettos and announcing that the Jews were being sent to the East — presumably to Muscovy. But, as in the past, virtually all of the Jews went to the extermination camps or became slave laborers. ☑

During the first week in September, the last Jews were shipped out of Belgium. Here was another European country that was now Jew-free. Three weeks later, the last Jews were shipped out of Amsterdam. It was intended that Holland would soon be Jew-free.

REVELATIONS AT MOSCOW ON THE ATOM BOMB

🔊 Following the capture of Moscow, the Germans began evaluating some of the secret and confidential documents found in the Kremlin and elsewhere in Soviet Government offices. One discovery that was promptly sent to the Fuehrer's headquarters was an accumulation of reports by Soviet spies in the United States and Britain that indicated that those countries had a large-scale and super-secret project underway to development an atomic bomb. ☑ In comparison, Germany's atomic energy program was still in its infancy.

Hitler was aware that an extremely powerful bomb might possibly be made from uranium and that this element, in peacetime, might also be used as a great new source of commercial energy. But he did little to promote research and development in this field because he had been advised that such research would take years and that it would be very unlikely that a bomb could developed in time to be used in the war.

Germany, however, did have a small atomic energy program headed by Professor Werner Heisenberg, a highly-respected German scientist. The program operated under the army's "Heereswaffenamt" (the German Army's Ordnance Research Department — HMT) and had its own special building at the Kaiser Wilhelm Institute in Berlin. That facility was called the "Virus House." Research went slowly, though, because of the lack of funds and governmental support.

If the Germans knew little of what was going on in the Allied camp with regard to atomic energy, the Americans and British knew even less of what was happening in Germany. By late 1942, the two allies were seriously concerned that the Germans might be ahead of them in atomic research. This was not the case, but the fears in the West were so great that the Allies decided to take military action. On November 19, 1942, a British Commando raid was carried out on the Norsk-Hydro heavy water plant at Rjukan, Norway, the world's only commercial source for naturally-occurring heavy water. Heavy water was known to be the best neutron decellerant in the manufacture of plutonium and it was believed in the West that the Germans were using it. Pure carbon was the second-best decellerant and was the element the Americans were using. The raid on the Norsk-Hydro plant was unsuccessful, so a second raid was conducted on the night of February 27/28, 1943. This raid succeeded in putting the plant out of operation until August 1943. Unknown to the Allies, these raids were of little value because the Germans were not far enough along in their research to require large amounts of heavy water.

Months earlier, on April 24, 1942, the German atomic energy program had been taken away from the Army and placed under the direction of a government agency known

as the "Reich Research Council." With this development, the Army lost interest in the project and seldom mentioned it to Hitler. Thus, Hitler became even more remote from the project.

Goering, however, was one who continued to believe in the future of atomic weapons and became something of a mentor to Heisenberg and his colleagues. Goering and Heisenberg considered that it was too dangerous for the atomic research program to remain in Berlin because of the Allied air raids so, during the summer of 1943, it was removed, piece-meal, to an old textile factory in the small town of Heckingen. Heisenberg's precious, and only, reactor was set up in a nearby cave at the village of Haigerloch.

🔊 **Now, in July 1943, with the information gleaned from the Russian secret files, and with the fact that the recent British raids on the heavy-water facilities in Norway indicated the Allies' concern in the matter, Hitler had to conclude that Germany was in a race for the development of an atomic bomb and was, very likely, well behind.**

Hitler concluded that Germany's atomic energy program had to be accelerated. He authorized a quadrupling of Heisenberg's budget so that a cyclotron and a larger reactor could be built, and he authorized Heisenberg to acquire the services of any scientist he wished to work on the project. After consulting Goering, Hitler appointed Luftwaffe General Ludwig von Geholze, a highly respected and experienced engineer, to work with Heisenberg on the military aspect of the program. Geholze was given the authority to report directly to both Hitler and Goering. ✅

Germany had only one major source of uranium, a mine near Joachimsthal in the Sudetenland. 🔊 **Hitler ordered that it be modernized so that it could produce the amount of uranium needed for research and, eventually, the production of bombs.** ✅

The Germans also had access of a sizeable amount of uranium ore in Belgium which had come from the Shinkolobwe mine in the Belgian Congo. Uranium ore from this mine was the world's richest and the supply in Belgium was the property of a Belgian refining company that extracted the uranium metal from the ore. The refining company, though, had been shut down at the time of the invasion of Belgium. ♫ Hitler now ordered that this ore be requisitioned and held for Heisenberg's use. ☑

THE ALLIED AIR BLITZ CONTINUED

In the skies over western Europe, the Allied air forces continued to reign supreme.

One very deadly air raid occurred on the night of July 24, 1943 when an RAF raid devastated the city of Hamburg and killed and injured thousands of people. On the morning of the 25th, German radio admitted that, "All of Hamburg seems to be in flames."

Hours earlier, during daylight, the AAF bombed industrial targets at Heroya, Norway and naval installations at Trondheim.

On August 1, the AAF bombed the Ploesti oil fields of Romania again. Out of 177 bombers participating, 54 were lost. But, forty percent of the area's refining capacity was put out of action.

On the 8th, the RAF bombed Milan, Genoa and Turin, Italy. That same day, Berlin radio announced that one million women and children were being evacuated from Berlin because of the bombings. Also at this time, Hitler ordered several Luftwaffe fighter squadrons from the East to Germany to help defend German cities.

Throughout Germany and occupied western Europe, the Axis' war industry was now fragmented and dispersed. Hitler felt that this scattering of production facilities had to be coordinated under a centralized control so that it could produce as efficiently as possible. To head the project, Hitler appointed his most trusted and capable engineer, Albert Speer. With the assignment came a new title and a cabinet post; Minister of Armaments and War Production.

During August 1943, the Allies expanded the air war — this time over the Atlantic Ocean. In an agreement with Portugal, the British were allowed to base aircraft and ships in the Azores. This expanded Allied air and sea coverage over a critical part of the Atlantic Ocean that could not easily be covered from Britain or the Western Hemisphere. German submarines in the Atlantic were now more vulnerable. The acquisition of bases in the Azores by Britain was a set back for Hitler who had hoped that the islands might, one day, be utilized by the Axis Powers.

DAMASCUS FALLS

♫ In Syria, Axis forces attacked the British and Fighting French positions north of Damascus on July 24 and gained some ground, including the capture of a critical road junction at Adhra.

On the 30th, the Axis attacked the main Allied Damascus defenses and made a diversionary attack to the west toward Beirut, the capital of Lebanon. Then Axis tanks swept far out into the flat desert east of Damascus and managed to turn the Allies' right flank. For the next four days there was hard fighting at Damascus, but the Allies, with their lines of supply threatened, were forced to withdraw. On August 3, Axis troops made a triumphant entry into the city with the Italians in the lead.

The Allied forces withdrew to positions north of the strategic town of Dar'a. This strategic town is fifty miles south of Damascus, thirty miles east of the border with Palestine and five miles north of the border with Trans-Jordan.

The Axis' feint toward Beirut was successful in that the Allies withdrew their force from northern Lebanon and retreated to Beirut in order to protect that city from a possible assault from the east. Axis forces along the coast followed the retreating Allies who offered only light opposition.

To the east, at Damascus, the Axis forces split into three columns; one headed southwest along a road leading to the Golan Heights on the border with Palestine, one followed the Damascus-Dar'a road, and the third struck out in a southeastern direction along a road leading to the town of Ash-Shaykh, twenty-five miles east of Dar'a. Strong Axis forces were now on both flanks of the defenders at Dar'a and an invasion of Trans-Jordan appeared imminent.

Because of the Axis threat now to Palestine, the Allied forces abandoned Beirut and moved into northern Palestine to guard against an attack from the Golan Heights. Two days later, Axis forces entered Beirut in another triumphant parade, again, with the Italians in the lead.

On August 10, 1943, the main Axis force made contact again with the Allies at Dar'a, and on the 11th, their eastern column took Ash-Shaykh after a brief and weak defensive action by the Allies. The Allied positions at Dar'a were now threatened from the north and the east by superior forces. But the Allied commanders made the decision to stand and fight at Dar'a. The Axis commanders, however, had different ideas. The roads south of Dar'a led into Trans-Jordan and ultimately to the Gulf of Aqaba. This was not the route the Axis military planners wanted to follow. Their principle objective was the Suez Canal to the southwest, and the shortest distance to the Canal led through Palestine.

THE INVASION OF PALESTINE

Meanwhile, a portion of the Allied force that had retreated from Damascus put up a brief defense in the Golan Heights, but the Axis forces, following in close pursuit, attacked immediately and forced the Allies to withdraw into Palestine. The Allies then took up new positions at Safad, Palestine, just north of the Sea of Galilee. It was now mid-August.

The Allied defenses at Safad were very tenuous because they were on flat land at the base of the Golan Heights from which the enemy could view the defenders' every move. The Axis forces reached the western edge of the Golan Heights on August 22 and halted to gather their forces and survey the situation below. The Axis plan of attack was simple and predictable. It was to come down from the Golan Heights in Blitzkrieg formation, smash through the Allied lines, and then march on, due westward along a modern road to the port city of Acre, forty-five miles to the west. ☑ This city is only ten miles north of Haifa. ♫ By capturing Acre, the Axis forces could cutoff and destroy the Allied forces in Lebanon and then combine for the march through Palestine.

The Allies accurately deduced the Axis' plan of attack. But the Allies had one advantage. ☑ Just west of Safad, the road to Acre passed through a narrow pass in a low range of mountains. Immediately in front of the pass entrance is an expanse of flat land with sparse vegetation and few inhabitants. ♫ Here was where the Allies would make their stand as the enemy compressed his forces in order to advance through the pass and on to Acre.

The Allies went into action, putting as much artillery as possible on the high grounds on either side of the pass entrance in order to bombard the enemy as he approached the pass. In the pass, itself, they built multiple defensive positions comprising five parallel trench lines where infantry, equipped with every type of anti-tank weapons available, would attempt to stop those enemy forces that survived the artillery bombardment and entered the pass. The fighting trenches would be connected with a pattern of lateral trenches running to the rear so that those troops in the forward lines could retreat in relative safety if they were about to be overrun. They could then fight again in one of the other trench lines.

As a part of the Allied defenses, there would also be extensive mine fields, booby traps, tank traps, barbed wire, etc. The Allies' tanks would be stationed behind the trench lines, adding their fire power to the battle and ready to take on any Axis tanks that made it into the trench line defenses. Allied air units would also be generously employed at Safad, especially the aircraft equipped with tank-killing aerial cannons and air-to-ground rockets.

To accomplish all of the construction needed to build these defenses, the British conscripted thousands of civilian laborers throughout northern Palestine. Many of the

Palestinian Jews, too, came forward to volunteer their services.

The Axis commanders soon discovered the Allied plans and began to do all they could to delay construction of the defensive positions. They did this by initiating heavy air attacks and bombardments by their long-range artillery. Not only did the Allied troops become the targets of these attacks, but the conscripted workers as well.

The civilian population of Safad, seeing that their city was about to become a battle-ground, fled in large numbers to the south and west. Those fleeing to the west passed through the Allied defenses, clogging the roads and hindering the Allies' construction efforts.

THE BATTLE OF SAFAD

Fearful that the defenses at Safad would not hold, the Allies withdrew their coastal forces again to new positions along the Lebanon-Palestine border. From there they could quickly withdraw to help defend Acre if the Safad defenses failed.

The loss of Lebanon and most of Syria was a demoralizing blow to the Fighting French who were now withdrawn from combat due to their questionable value. They were sent deeper into Palestine for rest and rehabilitation. Newly-arrived British forces took their places in the line and the Americans were on their way.

Fearing that their homeland would now be overrun, thousands of Palestinian Jews offered their services to the Allies. Many were accepted to fill service positions and a few were given combat missions. At the same time, the Jewish underground military organizations, the Irgun, Haganah and the Stern Gang, which had been supplied arms and munitions by the Allies, began to bedevil the Axis invaders behind their lines in northern Palestine with daring and, at times, suicidal guerrilla attacks.

In a similar manner, Palestinian Arabs offered their services to the Axis Powers in large numbers. The great majority offered to serve the Germans rather than the Italians because

of the apprehension the Arab community had concerning their future overlords. To avoid an embarrassment for the Italians, the Germans turned away many of the Arab volunteers with the suggestion that they offer their services to the Italians. Few did.

Those Arabs that were accepted by the Germans and Italians were formed into anti-guerrilla organizations to counter the Jewish guerrillas.

The Axis commanders saw the great dangers that awaited them at the Safad pass and decided to abandon their plan to attack toward Acre. They soon developed an alternative plan which called for bypassing Acre with an advance southward to Tiberias, then southwest to the city of Hadera, ☑ twenty-seven miles south of Haifa and four miles from the sea. ♀ This route was over relatively flat land and there were no narrow passes such as that at Safad. The Axis commanders saw the possibility that, if they reached Hadera, the Allies might abandon both Acre and Haifa as they had abandoned other major cities in Lebanon and Syria.

The Allied commanders deduced that the Axis forces might now take this line of advance, and increased their defenses at Tiberias using some of the units withdrawn from Lebanon.

From Berlin and Rome came a deluge of propaganda, boasting of the liberation of Lebanon and Syria from their colonial oppressors. No mention was made, however, of the future status of those two countries. The Axis propagandists also condemned the Allies for having sacrificed the two nations in order to protect the Jews of Palestine.

AN INTENTIONAL STALEMATE IN TUNISIA

In Tunisia, a very unique military stalemate had evolved that served the purposes of both sides.

For the Axis, continuing to hold their Tunisian redoubt provided a future jumping-off place for a drive westward to French Morocco and the Atlantic coast of Africa — one of Hitler's great ambitions. It also provided a staging area for the reconquest of Libya, which appealed to the Italians, as well as justification for the Italians to claim Tunisia as their own after the war. Furthermore, to give up Tunisia would provide the Allies with a major propaganda victory and, perhaps, compromise the favorable relations the Axis Powers had with the Arab world. Therefore, the Axis leaders stood by their decision to hang on in Tunisia despite the high cost.

For the Allies, maintaining the stalemate in Tunisia had its advantages, too, in that it tied down sizeable numbers of Axis forces that might be used elsewhere, and it prolonged the high losses the Axis Powers were suffering at sea. Furthermore, since this was primarily an American undertaking, the Allied leaders agreed that it was better to utilize the American troops in Tunisia rather than having them waiting idly in Britain for a cross-channel invasion that might never come. ☑

OXYGEN AND NARCOTICS

In May 1943, Hitler had an oxygen-generating device installed in his sleeping quarters at the suggestion of Dr. Morell. Hitler thought it helped. Then, in mid-July, a few days before a scheduled meeting with Mussolini, Hitler suffered another bout of stomach pains, dizziness and a new development, the inability to close one eye.

Just prior to the meeting, Morell gave Hitler some narcotics that made him hyperactive and very talkative. As a result, the meeting, which was supposed to be an exchange of views between equals, turned out to be a one-sided lecture by Hitler.

TURNING HIGH-TECH

In the early morning hours of July 25, 1943, Hitler, just before going to bed, received a report that Hamburg was being bombed again and that, for some unknown reason, German radar had failed. This was the beginning of a week-long Allied air campaign that utterly destroyed Hamburg. The Allies called it "Operation Gomorrah." For the next seven days, the British bombed the city by night and the Americans bombed

by day. Huge, uncontrollable fire storms resulted and before the Allied airmen were done, 6,000 acres of the city had been gutted, 250,000 buildings destroyed and some 30,000 people killed.

All the while, German radar continued to fail. The reason, the Germans soon discovered, was that the Allied planes dropped thousands of aluminum foil strips as they passed over Hamburg which confused the German's radar signals.

While this was a very low-tech development, there were, at this time, numerous high-tech devices being developed by both sides. The Germans were developing new tanks; jet-powered aircraft; helicopters; guided and unguided missiles; radio-guided bombs; nerve gasses; a super cannon, called the "London Gun," which could bombard London from the Channel coast of France; acoustic torpedoes; long-range torpedoes that could pass through an entire convoy; a new submarine that ran on hydrogen peroxide; and at a special complex near Peenamunde on the coast of the Baltic Sea, long-range unmanned rockets. With regard to the latter, the Allies learned of this complex and it had become a regular target for Allied bombers. To solve this problem, an underground site was being sought in which to further develop and produce the rockets. Underground space was also being sought for the manufacture of other items such as tanks, vehicles, weapons, etc. In all, some ninety-three million square feet of underground floor space was planned.

The Allies were also developing new tanks, jet aircraft and other weapons, including, most importantly, atomic bombs.

In the fall of 1943, German propaganda began speaking of terrible new weapons that would kill thousands of people. The ploy worked and the British and Americans took this to mean that the Germans were well along in their development of an atomic bomb. This assumption, however, was very wrong. The Allies were much further along than the Germans, but no one in the West knew it.

WE NEED THE UKRAINIANS

As the war progressed, the Germans needed ever more manpower. Laborers all over Europe were now being conscripted, but one of the most sought-after groups of people were the Ukrainians. The Ukrainians were numerous, intelligent, and for the most part, cooperative. By mid-1943, one out of every forty Ukrainians was working in Germany.

Hitler was aware of this and his attitude was mellowing toward the Ukrainians. He realized that in order to retain their cooperation they had to be treated better than he had previously considered. This change of heart was supported by some of Hitler's advisors and, especially, by the German field commanders in the East who benefitted greatly from the Ukrainians' labor. Thus, on June 3, 1943, he allowed Rosenberg, who had long been the principle champion of the Ukrainians, to issue a decree granting full ownership of the land already assigned to Ukrainian peasants. The parcels of land in question were mainly homesteads and garden plots, but the decree was well-received by the people. This action was widely publicized throughout the Ukraine and a monthly publication came into being directed toward these "free tillers" in the East.

Other measures taken by the Nazi government included a decree ordering that Eastern workers in Germany would, henceforth, be treated as well as Western workers. Also, in the East, Partisans who voluntarily surrendered, and who showed genuine remorse, were allowed to go Germany as workers rather than be shot.

DENMARK, DENMARK

In Denmark, relations between the Danes and Germans had steadily deteriorated since the March elections. An active resistance movement had arisen and, correspondingly, German oppression had increased. To aggravate the situation further, the Germans had been requisitioning food from Denmark.

Tensions came to a head in late July and early August 1943, beginning with strikes, riots and sabotage. The sabotage was the most serious. On August 28, the Germans demanded that the Danish government instigate the death penalty for individuals convicted of sabotage. The government refused and, the next day, resigned en masse. The Germans responded by arresting many of the members of the government and placing the King under house arrest. They also disarmed the Danish Army and Navy. As for the Navy, the Danish sailors scuttled some of the ships and others escaped to Sweden.

A German-controlled civilian government was then established in Denmark under one Dr. Werner Best and, from then on, Denmark was ruled as an occupied country.

A NEGOTIATED PEACE AND A BUNKER

During August 1943, Hitler received reports indicating that both the British population and certain elements of the British military were showing signs of war weariness. This gave him hope that the time might be nearing for a negotiated peace settlement with the western Allies.

On the other hand, Hitler was forced to admit that that eventuality might be long in coming and in the meantime the Allied air offensive would continue in all its intensity. As such, the bombings had become a threat to his personal safety, especially when he was in Berlin. Therefore, on August 31, 1943, Hitler ordered that a large underground bunker be built at the chancellory building so that he and his staff would be safe from the Allied bombs when in Berlin.

CHAPTER 21

BUILDING THE AXIS EMPIRES

For the German leaders, the time had come to establish the southern sector of the armed frontier. German planners had decided that that frontier would be established just west of the Ural River which ran through the desert area of Turkestan 125 miles to the east of Astrakhan. The Ural River was wide and deep and ran from the Ural Mountains to the northern shore of the Caspian Sea. As such, it would be a formidable military barrier as was the case with the Ural Mountains themselves. The armed frontier would follow the contour of the river and be far enough to the west to be out of range of enemy artillery operating on the river's eastern bank — which would be considered enemy territory. The land between the river and the frontier would be a no-man's-land where no human life would be permitted to exist. That no-man's-land would be actively patrolled by mobile units of the German Army and by aircraft of the Luftwaffe. Highly mobile brigade and regiment sized German Army units would man the armed frontier and operate from strong points along its length. The strong points would also provide living accommodations for the officers, enlisted men and their families.

Located at strategic points behind the frontier would be sizeable, and highly mobile, reserve units ready to reinforce the frontier units at any time.

The Luftwaffe would operate from air fields directly behind the armed frontier and, like the Army, would have secure housing for the airmen and their families.

This arrangement would continue indefinitely as long as a hostile regime existed east of the Urals.

DOWN THE URAL RIVER TO GURIEV

But the land west of the Ural River area was not yet conquered. With this task in mind, strong German forces crossed the upper Volga River at Kubishev in late September 1943, and they began an advance overland in a southeasterly direction toward the Ural River city of Uralsk 150 miles distant. The terrain was flat and arid and ideal for mobile forces. Through Uralsk ran the only rail line supplying Stalingrad to the west on the Volga.

Little opposition was offered by the Red Army and the Germans advanced steadily southward. By the second week of October, as the Germans neared Uralsk, the Soviets began evacuating Stalingrad. During the next few days, German forces moved out of their siege lines and occupied the city.

The Soviets had established a defense line just north of Uralsk, and on October 17 a major battle erupted there that lasted for two days. The Soviet forces, however, were demoralized and low on ammunition, food and oil. German tanks, supported by strong Luftwaffe units, broke through the Soviet defenses on the morning of October 19 and the Soviets began a retreat down the western shore of the Ural River to the Caspian seaport of Guriev. German forces followed closely behind.

By mid-November, the Germans were approaching Guriev, at which time the Soviets began evacuating Astrakhan. The Soviet defenders at Guriev, now being reinforced by the withdrawing Astrakhan garrison, established a strong defense line north of Guriev hoping to save that city. Their supply situation was not so critical because the Soviet Navy still controlled the Caspian Sea and supplies were coming in, by boat, from the American Lend-Lease operations in Iran.

On November 18, the battle of Guriev began. It lasted for three days and, once again, the Germans prevailed. Guriev fell on November 22. The Soviet forces retreated to the east and German forces crossed the Ural River at Guriev to secure the city's environs and take control of the mouth of the river.

In the weeks that followed, German troops secured the land area between the Volga and Ural Rivers and, during December 1943, the Germans began constructing the first segments of the armed frontier. Towns and cities along the western bank of the Ural River, including Uralsk, were eventually levelled and their inhabitants — who had not already fled to the east — were used as conscripted laborers or deported to Muscovy.

This is the pattern that would be followed as other segments of the armed frontier were established. In the no-man's-land, there were to be no cities, no towns, no villages, and no structures of any kind. Even the debris would be levelled or removed so as not to provide cover and concealment for an approaching enemy. Likewise, forested areas and fields of tall vegetation would be cleared. The terrain in the no-man's-land would be made flat and serviceable for wheeled patrol vehicles.

With regard to this segment of the armed frontier, a road that already existed along the western bank of the river would be maintained to facilitate patrolling the western bank of the river.

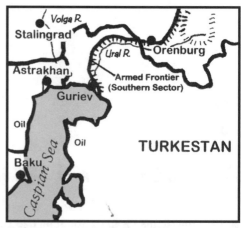

Turkestan was a target for future German expansion. It was rich in minerals and stretched all the way to the western border of China.

TURKESTAN – A FUTURE GERMAN SATELLITE

By establishing the southern part of the armed frontier along the Ural River, the Germans had entered Turkestan, which had become a Soviet republic in 1924. It was well-known, though, that the Muslim and independent-minded people of Turkestan had no love for communism nor for the Russians and were ruled from Moscow only by force and intimidation. Turkestan was rich in minerals and a sizeable new oil field was being developed on the eastern shore of the Caspian Sea. The Soviets had begun constructing a rail line to that oil field to carry the oil northward, but the rail line had not yet been completed.

It was the German plan to eventually detach Turkestan from the Soviet Union and establish it as an independent state friendly to Germany. Just how and when this would be done had not been determined. Turkestan was a huge area of mostly deserts and mountains, that stretched to the borders of Afghanistan and China.

As for the oil, theoretically it could reach the Soviets east of the Ural Mountains by being transported by tanker trucks over the few primitive roads and tracks in the area. It was unlikely, though, that any great quantity of oil could reach the Soviets by this method.

Nevertheless, the Germans planned to keep a close watch on the situation and, if necessary, mount a military operation down the eastern shore of the Caspian Sea to capture the oil field. ☑

With regard to Germany's political ambitions beyond the Urals, Himmler had advocated that after the fall of the Soviet regime, the land east of the Urals should be made into a free Siberian peasant state.

IN PALESTINE

🔲 In late September 1943, Axis forces in Palestine launched their attack on Tiberius on the Sea of Galilee. It was a well-coordinated frontal assault which soon overwhelmed the Allied defenders. The Allies then withdrew to the town of Afula, twenty miles to the southwest. Axis forces stayed in close pursuit while a small Italian force secured Tiberius unopposed.

As the Axis forces headed for Afula, a small detachment of Italian troops, accompanied by reporters and photographers, branched off to occupy the historic town of Nazareth. As the Italians prepared their victory ceremony in the town square, three bombs went off, set by the Irgun, killing five soldiers, wounding four others and destroying an armored car. Minutes later, snipers killed four more Italian soldiers and wounded two. The men of the Irgun were using British-made munitions and weapons given to them for just such purposes.

Additional Italian troops were detached from the main Axis force advancing on to Afula and rushed to Nazareth to restore order. In retaliation, the Italians rounded up fifteen Jewish men and boys and summarily executed them in the town square. News of the incident was suppressed in the Italian media.

AXIS INVASION OF TRANS-JORDAN

During the last week in September, the Axis forces at Dar'a, Syria, launched a Blitzkrieg attack against the extended Allied right flank, quickly broke through, then turned to the west to cut off the Allied retreat. A coura-

geous and determined British regiment held the Axis tanks at bay long enough for the main Allied force to withdraw from Dar'a. That force soon took up new positions that had been prepared at a strategic road junction, ten miles south of Dar'a in Trans-Jordan, and only forty miles north of the capital, Amman.

The Axis forces, following the retreating Allies, quickly attacked the new Allied defense with another Blitzkrieg attack around their right flank. The Axis tanks again broke through the Allied defenses and reached the village of Al-Buwardah cutting one of the two avenues of escape for the Allies. At the road junction, however, the Allies held firm.

With this, the battle subsided. It was not the intent of the Axis leaders to expend men and resources in the conquest of Trans-Jordan. The German and Italian planners had agreed that Trans-Jordan might capitulate peacefully after the British were driven from Palestine.

BACK IN PALESTINE

On October 5, 1943, Axis forces attacked the Allied positions at Afula. After an intensive artillery and air bombardment, the Axis tanks broke through the Allied center, splitting the Allied force in two. The Allies were forced, once again, to make a hasty retreat — this time to Hadera. Six miles beyond Afula is a road junction near the Tel Megiddo ruins, the site of a major battle of World War I, which leads northward into Haifa, eighteen miles distant. A sizeable Axis force, consisting mostly of Italians, sped up the road and established a siege line south of the city. They then marched westward the short distance to the sea to cut the coastal highway south out of Haifa. This action severed the ground supply and retreat route of the Allied forces between Haifa and the Lebanon border. Supplies and reinforcements now had to come by sea — but a sea dominated by the British Navy. It was not the intention of the Axis commanders to enter Haifa or attack any portion of the Allied redoubt at this time. The main objective remained the drive south, through Palestine, to the Suez Canal.

The remainder of the Axis force reached Hadera and halted opposite the Allied defenses.

On October 8, the Allies launched a surprise attack from Haifa, penetrated the siege line and moved down the Haifa-Tel Megiddo road into the rear of the Axis forces at Hadera. The Axis commanders, who were about to attack at Hadera, had to postpone that attack and send strong forces to the rear to stop this unexpected threat. For three days, tank, artillery and infantry battles took place along the Haifa-Tel Megiddo road. But the numerical superiority of the Axis prevailed and the Allies troops retreated to Haifa. The Axis commanders then strengthened the siege line around the city, but these actions had weakened the Axis forces to the point where an attack on Hadera had to be postponed until adequate reinforcements arrive. As a result, the fighting in Palestine went into a lull.

THE MUFTI ARRIVES

On October 10, the Grand Mufti of Jerusalem and his entourage arrived at Tiberius in northern Palestine. They had travelled from Damascus. In Tiberius they set up headquarters and announced, with Axis approval, their intentions of establishing a Palestinian political authority. Hours later, the Mufti called upon all Palestinian men to offer their services to the Axis in the liberation of Palestine. This appeal had a very dramatic effect. During the next few days, the Axis forces were deluged with young men answering the Mufti's call. Most offered to serve the Germans, but a significant number offered their services to the Italians so that, this time, the Italians were not embarrassed.

There were far too many volunteers for the Axis commanders to accept, so a screening process was established in which men with needed skills and/or military experience would be the first to be accepted. Those with military experience were formed into regiment-sized paramilitary units. These men were given Axis uniforms, arms and brief training. Then they were given security assignments to relieve Axis soldiers for combat duty. The armed Palestinians were given strict orders not to use their favored position to attack Jews. It was feared that such an action would spark a Jewish counter-action and that a mini civil war might erupt. ☑

MEANWHILE – BACK IN THE BOMB SHELTERS

On October 4, 1943, the Americans carried out a very heavy air raid on Frankfurt. No German fighter planes rose to challenge the attackers, and when Hitler heard of this he was furious. Goering took the brunt of Hitler's wrath, which went down the chain of command to the individual pilots.

By now, cracks in the morale of the German people due to the bombings were beginning to show. On October 7, Hitler called his Gauleiters together for a pep talk. He promised them that Germany would be victorious and that it was their job to keep the German people's will and determination on a wartime status. To reinforce this, a decree entitled, "Decree Respecting Preparations to Reconstruct Bomb-Damaged Cities" was issued and made public. Its intent was to keep up the morale of the German people with a positive glimpse of the future.

The decree did nothing to stop the Allied bombings, however. On October 14, the Americans bombed Schweinfurt, heavily damaging the ball bearing industry there.

On the night of the 22nd, the British bombed the city of Kassel and created fire storms that killed a reported 6,000 people.

And there was more devastation coming for the Germans. During October 1943, a second American Army Air Force, the 9th, became active in Britain. It would eventually double the bombing capacity of the Americans.

DENMARK JEW-FREE

During the last days of September, Denmark became Jew-Free although not in the manner the Germans had planned. The SS had prepared plans to strike by surprise during the first days of October and round up Denmark's 8,000 Jews. Word of this, however, was leaked to Danish authorities, and on the night of October 1/2 a most extraordinary event took place. Most of the Danish Jews were secretly spirited away by ordinary citizens in small boats across the Kattegat Strait to safety in Sweden. When the SS struck, they could find only about 450 Jews. Those few unfortunates were sent off to Germany's show-case concentration camp, Theresienstadt, in Bohemia-Moravia.

Another facet of Germany's Jew-free policy was more productive. The Italians, now more than ever, depended on Germany's military and industrial might and were in a position whereby they could not refuse requests from Berlin to help rid Europe of Jews. During October, 1,035 Jews were arrested by Italian authorities in Rome and handed over to the Germans. During November, Jews were rounded up in Genoa, Florence, Milan, Venice and Ferrara. Virtually all of them went to the death camps.

OLD SOLDIERS AND MULTIPLE WIVES ,

In early October, the German government raised the draft age for men from 49 to 60. Also, deferments given to sole-surviving sons of German families were canceled.

Not only the armed forces, but all of Germany needed people. At Hitler's headquarters serious consideration was given — again — to instigating a program of polygamy after the war in order to build up the German population. It was feared that Germany would not have enough people to fill the conquered East and that it might continue being the land of the Slavs.

Another sign of population problems was the fact that the German birth rate had fallen. This was believed to be the result of the recruitment of women for industry.

ANOTHER BLACK MONTH FOR THE GERMAN NAVY

October proved to be another bad month for the German Navy. Twenty-two submarines were lost during the month and the number of Allied ships sunk was minimal. Even the Brazilian Navy was having successes. During October 1943, that navy sank its eleventh U-boat.

Admiral Doenitz became desperate for solutions. He ordered submarines that had recently been equipped with more anti-aircraft guns to fight it out with attacking aircraft rather than dive and run. This had little positive effect. The high losses continued.

He also came to believe that the submarines operating in wolf packs were more vulnerable than before, so he ordered an end to that tactic.

The only bright spot for Doenitz was that German small craft were causing the Allies some damage in the English Channel. There, German patrol-torpedo boats sank the British cruiser "Charybdis" and a destroyer escort.

Doenitz was further disheartened, though, by intelligence reports that the American shipyards had replaced all of the Allied ship tonnage lost so far in the war, and that the capacity of those yards was steadily increasing. Hitler was informed of these facts, but could do nothing. The German Navy was now barely mentioned at his headquarters.

WE MUST KEEP OUR WORD

Heinrich Himmler, head of the SS, was certain that the Axis would win the war and was aware of the fact that the SS had to clean up its image for the coming of peace.

On October 4, 1943, Himmler instructed his subordinates that the SS must become a trusted and honorable organization. In a speech to his SS Generals in Posen, Himmler declared, "If we make a promise, it must be kept. We must acquire such a reputation for the keeping of contracts in the whole world...that we thereby gain for Germany advantages of the greatest value, namely, faith through confidence."

This would prove to be a very difficult undertaking for the men in black. One can only wonder to whom these promises would be directed because, a month earlier, Himmler told some of these same people that in the coming years some forty million people would have to be eliminated, and another seventy million deported to places like Siberia, Africa and Latin America. On that occasion, Himmler justified his numbers saying that by the year 2000, the German population would reach 400 to 500 million.

ATTACK AT HADERA

🔊 On October 11, 1943, the Axis forces at Hadera, Palestine, now reinforced, attacked the Allied defenses there. The lines of the attack followed two roads and a railroad that paralleled each other along the coast. The Allies held during the morning and launched a counterattack in the late afternoon, driving the Axis forces back several miles. During the night, the Axis commanders brought up their armored reserves and on the morning of the 12th attacked again, using virtually all their tanks and aircraft. The Allies gave some ground, but their line held again. That afternoon, the Axis forces attacked once again and this time penetrated the Allied line. The Axis tanks bypassed Hadera and headed down the coast toward Netanya, eight miles away.

Now, the Allies called up their reserves and additional reinforcements from Tel Aviv. Unfortunately for the Allies, the Axis tanks got to Netanya first, smashed through the ill-prepared Allied line and occupied the town. The Axis forces quickly passed through the town and exited its southern suburbs. There, they met the Allied reinforcements coming in from Tel Aviv and a deadly free-for-all battle ensued. The Axis forces, however, were exhausted and low on fuel and ammunition and withdrew back into the town. As darkness fell, the guns at Netanya fell silent.

ATTACK IN THE CAUCASUS

Military activity in the Caucasus had been relatively quiet since April, but by now, the Axis forces there had been heavily reinforced by utilizing veteran units pulled in from all over the East. All of them had been rested and re-equipped and were ready to fight again. Also, new units had arrived from Germany. The time had come to conquer the rest of the Caucasus and prepare the way for the invasion of the Middle East. Before them, however, lay a strong and viable segment of the Red Army and the mighty Caucasus Mountains that stretched, uninterrupted, from the Black Sea to the Caspian Sea. These mountains were a formidable military obstacle. There were a few passes through the mountains, but they were winding narrow deathtraps for long drawn-out columns of men and machines. The best way to traverse the mountains was along the coastal plains at either end of the mountain range where the land was relatively flat and the defenders would have the advantage of the high ground on only one flank.

But for the moment, however, the Axis forces were still on flat steppe land north of the Mountains — land ideal for tanks. And there was no shortage of fuel which was now close at hand. Several of the Caucasus oil wells in German hands had been brought on line, and two refineries had been rushed back into production.

On October 13, 1943, the Axis forces launched a three-pronged offensive along the Terek River in the eastern part of the Caucasus. They were able to commit some two thousand tanks to the undertaking. Nearly a thousand aircraft were also employed. All three prongs battled their way across the river and charged on in the direction of Grozny, the largest city in this part of the Caucasus and located at the foot of the mountains. Soviet defenses were inconsistent. Some units fought doggedly and others melted away as the battle intensified. The Soviets were fairly well-equipped, thanks to American Lend-Lease, which was still reaching them from Iran. But morale was low and the Axis forces took many prisoners.

Knowing that the Axis troops would attack along the coasts, the Soviets had prepared very strong defenses on both coasts. Having learned from the defenses in Palestine at the Safad Pass, the Soviets build a lattice-works of trenches and placed numerous artillery guns on the high ground. The Axis forces had little option but to force their way through these obstacles. For the advance around the mountains, the Axis commanders chose the Caspian Sea approach.

For the next five days, nearly constant fighting took place north of the mountains. Grozny was encircled and bypassed and the Axis forces reached the west coast of the Caspian Sea.

The Axis troops made first contact with the Soviet's coastal defenses on the afternoon of October 25. Incoming intelligence revealed, however, that the defenses were still incomplete and infested with civilians and soldiers working side-by-side. And, most surprisingly, the soldiers were not organized into a defensive posture. Furthermore, there were places where tanks could maneuver through the defenses encountering a minimum of obstacles. Based on this information, the Axis commanders ordered an immediate attack even though they knew their troops were fatigued and low on fuel, and ammunition. Army units and aircraft were hastily scraped together, as were cans of gasoline and boxes of bullets, and at 4:00 p.m. that afternoon the Axis troops charged into the defenses. The attack was a complete surprise. Civilians and soldiers alike fled in desperation to the rear. Little opposition was encountered and as darkness fell, the Axis lead elements exited the southern end of the defense onto open steppe land. The vaulted Caspian coast defenses had been breached. The very mobile Axis forces surged forward into the darkness, but lack of fuel and a second Soviet defense line, almost as formidable as the first, stopped them. This second line comprised the last defenses protecting Baku 110 miles away, and it too had not yet been completed. But the Axis troops could go no further. It now became a race against time — the revitalizing of the Axis forces against the Soviet's ability to complete the defenses. On the Axis side, a frantic effort was made to bring up fresh troops, fuel and other supplies in preparation for a renewed attack. On the Soviet side, the civilians and soldiers worked without letup and manned a defense line even as it was being constructed.

The Axis commanders soon discovered another development on the Soviet side. Large numbers of Soviet troops were moving northward out of Soviet-occupied Iran toward Baku. Stalin had ordered that the Soviet occupation of northern Iran be abandoned in an effort to save the southern Caucasus. British troops rushed into northern Iran to take the place of the departing Soviets. It was also soon learned that the British and Americans in Iran were facilitating the movement of the Soviet troops and that some British units had crossed the border into the Soviet Union and were also moving toward Baku. This would be the second time in the century that British troops moved into the Baku area. ◪ In 1918, they occupied Baku in order to secure its vital oil assets during the Russian Revolution.

🔖 In light of these new developments, the Axis commanders concluded that, this time, a hastily-put-together attack might be too risky. Furthermore, the Axis commanders were about to lose the services of the Romanian, Hungarian, Slovak and Croatian troops because their war aims in the East would be completed with the final conquest of the Caucasus. These Axis satellite forces were to be assigned to occupation and security duties and would not likely be used again as front-line troops. The Italian troops, however, would remain since they were expected to play a major role in the advance into the Middle East.

Considering all these factors, the Axis commanders decided to pause opposite the Soviet defense line north of Baku until additional reinforcements could be brought up.

AMERICANS ARRIVE IN PALESTINE

On October 14, 1943, the first contingents of the U.S. Army arrived in Tel Aviv. They consisted of one motorized infantry regiment and one armored regiment. They were dispatched, at once, to the Netanya front.

Back in the United States, however, there was a mounting outcry of anguish. The isolationists and political right-wingers, many of them southern Democrats from the President's own party, loudly complained about America's involvement in Palestine. Their claim was that Americans boys were now being used to protect Jews, Moham-medans (the word of the day for Muslims), and a British colony. Polls showed that there were many people in America who sympa-thized with this view. To counter this uproar, the U.S. government restated its claim that the American troops were there primarily to protect the Suez Canal which was of vital importance to the American war effort.

The issue went unresolved and when news of this problem reached the troops in Palestine, it had a demoralizing effect.

On the day the Americans arrived at Tel Aviv, the Axis forces launched a powerful Blitzkrieg attack at Netanya. Within hours they broke through the Allied lines and the defenders began to retreat toward Tel Aviv. As the Americans approached Netanya, they encountered their Allies in hasty retreat. With this surprise, and without a battle plan for such an eventuality, the Americans had no alternative but to join in the retreat. The fast Axis tanks smashed into the Americans before they could turn about and succeeded in capturing about 300 American soldiers. It was a bitter beginning for the green Ameri-can troops.

The Americans retreated to Tel Aviv and took over a segment of the defensive front. But the Americans would have no rest. Axis tanks, about 75 of them, reached the Tel Aviv defenses on the evening of October 16, and at once attacked the American segment of the line. The Americans fell back fighting and, together with the help of darkness and flanking attacks by British forces, were able to stop the penetration. But they regained no ground and suffered heavy casualties. The next morning the Allied front had a big bulge in it where the Americans had been. Hours later, back in the States, isolationist and anti-administration newspapers blared out the awful headlines.

Fortunately for the Americans and the Allies, the Axis drive was now spent and the attackers had to pause for supplies and rein-forcements.

As both sides regrouped, a mass exodus of civilians began to move southward out of Tel Aviv. They were mostly Jews and their numbers were swollen by large numbers of refugees who had already fled from points further north. These refugees, numbering in the tens of thousands, clogged the roads already overburdened with Allied supply columns and reinforcements moving north. Some of the refugees were able to leave by ship for the British-controlled island of Cyprus, 200 miles to the northwest and the only place in the eastern Mediterranean that would accept them.

There were many Jews, however, who refused to leave Palestine. Some of them simply wanted to take their chances under the Italians while others felt it was better to remain and fight than languish away in a refugee camp.

Along the roads south of Tel Aviv, the fleeing refugees passed through a number of local communities and stripped them clear of food, fuel and other necessities. Much of it was taken from Arabs and this caused con-frontations and fights. Back in Tel Aviv, there was looting. The Allies were forced to detach sizeable numbers of troops from their regular duties to keep order.

Into this mess, came the balance of the American forces arriving by ship at Tel Aviv.

From Berlin and Rome there was a chorus of propaganda, claiming that the poor show-ing by the Americans in Palestine proved that they were the weak link in the western Alliance. Photos of American soldiers sur-rendering were sent to all of the world's news services. The Axis propagandists also echoed the American political right, claiming that Roosevelt had given in to world Jewry and was sending American troops to protect the Jews of Palestine.

Behind the Axis lines in Palestine, how-ever, there were problems. The Irgun, Stern Gang and Haganah kept up a steady torrent of attacks on Axis troops and supply lines. In some of the bigger cities, order had broken down and Jews and Arabs were fighting each other, and there was looting. The Axis com-manders, however, had the advantage of mobilizing and employing thousands of Arab paramilitary volunteers to help restore order and did not have to commit large numbers of their soldiers for the tasks. Accordingly, the conflicts were generally resolved on Arab terms.

Having surrounded Tel Aviv on two sides, strong Axis forces were now detached and sent eastward along two roads that led to the towns of Lod and Ramla. Beyond there, the roads converged and led into Jerusalem.

The Allies had seen the possibility of such a move and had heavily mined the roads and put up a defense line in the Lod/Ramla area. The mines delayed the Axis advance, but the Allied defenses proved to be no match for the massed German tanks and heavy Luftwaffe air support. By the early afternoon of October 28, the attackers had breached the Lod/Ramla defenses and were fighting their way on to the town of Qiryat, ten miles to the southeast and only fifteen miles from Jerusalem. Allied reserve forces were rushed out from Jerusalem and managed to stop the Axis advance at the Qiryat defenses.

As the fighting raged in the Lod/Ramla area, an American armored column circled out of Tel Aviv and headed eastward to attack the Axis positions at Lod and Ramla from the rear. The Axis holding forces guarding the rear areas were quickly overcome and the commanders at Lod and Ramla were forced to halt the attacks at Qiryat and dispatch troops to the rear to meet the American threat.

As darkness fell, the Americans and Axis forces were facing each other just south of Ramla. For the Axis forces, it was an uncomfortable situation. They had the Americans facing them in the west, the British and their allies in the east, and north and south of their positions were high hills and rugged terrain. In a way, they were in a trap.

The Axis forces, however, had an ace in the hole. A second Axis column, having left Afula in northern Palestine, was moving southward down the Nabulus-Jerusalem road. This was a narrow and winding road, unpaved only in spots, and running through several mountainous passes. It was not a good road for tanks so the Axis force was comprised primarily of motorized mountain troops.

This northern force had left Afula on October 27 and made rapid progress down the road which was virtually undefended. The RAF attacked the approaching column and did some damage but did not stop the advance.

The Allies rushed a small delaying force to Nabulus and, at the same time, prepared a total of six ambush sites along the road between the towns of Nabulus and Ram Allah, the latter being nine miles north of Jerusalem.

The Allied delaying force, operating from high ground and supported by the RAF, was able to stop the Axis mountaineers at Nabulus on the afternoon of the 28th. During the night the British withdrew from Nabulus to reinforce the ambush sites. On the 29th, the Axis forces occupied Nabulus, but four miles out of town, they ran into the first British ambush. From then on, it was a battle between the Axis mountaineers making their way down the road to Jerusalem and British troops laying in ambush. Overhead, British and German fighter planes did battle with each other while, at the same time, doing what they could to support their respective troops on the ground.

SAVE THE HOLY SITES

As it became apparent that Jerusalem might become a battleground, outcries from religious leaders all across the globe were heard pleading with both the Axis and Allies to safeguard the city's religious shrines. Most called for Jerusalem to be declared an open city. The Axis governments announced that they would welcome and respect such a declaration while the Allied governments, upon orders from London, sidestepped the issue, stating only that every effort would be made to protect the holy sites.

The British planned to hold on to the city as long as possible, then withdraw to the west where the Axis forces were sandwiched between their forces and the Americans. It was hoped that that Axis force could be eliminated and that the Allied troops could go on to save Tel Aviv while, at the same time, save Jerusalem by destroying the Axis force coming in from the north.

If this plan failed, the Allies, at the last minute, would declare Jerusalem an open city. This would force the Axis troops in the north to immediately enter the city, thus neutralizing them for a brief period.

EXODUS FROM JERUSALEM

Not surprisingly, there was a surge of Jewish refugees fleeing Jerusalem as had been the case at Tel Aviv. The only route to safety was the southern road out of the city which led to Beer Sheva, fifty miles to the south. Here again, the refugees and the Allied supply column collided.

When the refugees reached Beer Sheva, most of them stopped. Soon, the city's services were overwhelmed and there were conflicts between the Jews and Arabs. The British were forced to fly in supplies, especially food, to meet the needs of the refugees as well as troops to maintain order. The International Red Cross and the Red Crescent (the Muslim world's equivalent to the Red Cross), sent food and administrators.

It was now obvious that the Allies had a major refugee problem on their hands. The field commanders sent urgent appeals to London to do something about it. After evaluating the problem and consulting other Allied governments and several of the neutral governments, a plan was approved. The refugees would be encouraged to head for the twin seaports of Elat in Palestine and Al Aqaba in Trans-Jordan at the headwaters of the Gulf of Aqaba. There they would be picked up by ships and taken to safety.

The question remained, however, where would those safe havens be? Appeals went out from London, Washington and other Allied capitals pleading for the world's governments to take some of the refugees. Most replies were negative, claiming that they had already taken as many refugees as they could. These claims had some merit because refugees had been flowing out of Europe since the late 1930s and some nations had to deal now with additional refugees from the Far East.

The British, therefore, were forced to consider a worst-case scenario and began building refugee camps in British-occupied Eritrea, British Somaliland, occupied Italian Somaliland, Kenya, Tanganyika, the island groups in the Indian Ocean and along the west coast of India.

General de Gaulle's headquarters in Algiers made it known quietly that refugees would not be welcome in Madagascar. The Fighting French wanted no foot-in-the-door arrangement that might lead to Madagascar becoming a Jewish homeland.

Similarly, South Africa, which had a long history of anti-semitism, refused to accept refugees.

JERUSALEM FALLS

By the first of November, it was apparent that the Axis force in the north could not be stopped, so on November 3, the Allies executed their plan to evacuate Jerusalem. The next day it was declared an open city. As the Allied troops departed to the west and east, Axis troops entered from the north. Departing with the Allies were virtually all of Jerusalem's Jewish policemen. The remaining Arab policemen were not able to maintain order, and looting and lawlessness soon became the norm. Now it was the turn of the Axis commanders to restore and maintain order. The troops of the northern Axis force would be engaged in the city for some time.

As planned, the main Allied forces moved westward out of the city while a small contingent of troops moved eastward into Trans-Jordan. Those troops halted just beyond its eastern edge of Jerusalem and turned about to guard against a possible, but unlikely, attack by Axis troops toward Amman.

The bulk of the Allied Jerusalem force reached Ramla in good order where they reinforced the Allied defenses. From Ramla, the Allied forces were able to circle about the Axis positions to the south and link up with the Americans. The Axis forces east of Tel Aviv were now confronted on three side.

On November 6, the Allies launched a strong attack at Ramla and a three-day battle ensued. The Allies were able to retake some ground but the Axis front remained intact and the Axis threat to Tel Aviv remained. The Allies though, having received two more divisions from India, a large contingent of The King's African Rifles from East Africa, and large quantities of Lend-Lease from America were now much stronger.

On the Axis side, with hostilities beginning in the Caucasus, and the need for reinforcements and supplies there, there was less for the forces in Palestine. For these reasons, the strength of the Axis forces at Tel Aviv increased slowly and those forces were forced to remain on the defensive.

THE ATLANTIC WALL

German defenses along the Atlantic Wall were rapidly being completed, plus there were now fifty of the German Army's 280 divisions stationed in France, Belgium and Holland, and another eighteen in Denmark and Norway.

A steady stream of reports reached German intelligence sources stating that the Allies were planning an invasion of Norway. These reports were false, but they kept the Germans on edge. Churchill, actually favored an invasion of Norway but the Joint Chiefs of Staff were cool to the idea. ☑

To maintain the supposed threat against Norway, American planes bombed targets in southern Norway on November 16. One of those targets was the heavy-water producing complex at Rjukan. The Allies were still concerned about Germany's atomic bomb program.

BOMBS – MISSILES – JETS

On the night of November 22/23, 1943, the British carried out the first of several devastating air raids on Berlin, concentrating on the government quarter. Damage was heavy to many of the buildings includ-

ing the chancellory. Before the British were through, the chancellory was virtually unusable. Hitler had ordered his underground bunker just in time.

The morale of the Berliners took a noticeable turn for the worst and there was bitter criticism against Luftwaffe commander, Hermann Goering. Hitler was also angry with Goering. Goering responded by admonishing his fighter pilots for not being able to stop the raids. Goering's star, however, dropped another notch and Hitler's image was also tarnished.

Hitler now feared for the safety of his close friend, Joseph Goebbels, Gauleiter of Berlin. For Christmas he gave Goebbels an armored car.

It was during November 1943 that Hitler planned to first use his new pilotless flying missile, the V1, against Britain. But that date was not met because of Allied air raids on the huge missile center at Peenamunde. The V1s would not be ready for deployment until June 1944. In the meantime, the manufacture of those new weapons would be moved into an underground industrial complex at Nordhausen.

On November 26, however, the Germans scored a major victory using a guided missile, the first action of its kind in the war. The guided missile was a bomb-laden He-177 bomber rigged to fly by remote control. This missile plane was flown into the British troopship "Rohna" in the Mediterranean. The ship sank quickly and 1,149 people were killed, about 1,000 of them American soldiers. The sinking of the Rohna was one of the greatest maritime disasters of the war. This secret weapon did not last long because the Allies began jamming the radio signals that controlled the plane, thereby sending it off course.

The next day was another positive day for Hitler. He travelled to Insterburg Air Base to witness the first flight of the eagerly awaited production model of the ME-262 jet fighter. He did not like what he saw, however. The plane performed well but it had been designed as a fighter — a defensive weapon. He wanted it to be a bomber — an offensive weapon. Since his word was law in Germany, he ordered the plane redesigned, setting back its deployment by months.

On December 3, the British bombed Leipzig. Some of the bombs hit the buildings of Leipzig University and destroyed a small laboratory used by Werner Heisenberg for his atomic research program.

MORE SETTLEMENTS IN THE EAST

Himmler was, as ever, touting the grandeur that would be Germany's new colonial empire in the East. At this time he told an assembly of his SS commanders, "A great task awaits us after the conclusion of peace. We shall colonize...In twenty to thirty years' time we shall be the ruling class of Europe; we must succeed in giving the German people the necessary living space and in controlling and ruling all the countries of Europe."

Hitler, too, saw great things in the East, and for himself — possibly sainthood. In a discussion with Bormann about allowing religion in the East, Hitler, in an upbeat mood, said, "I am going to become a religious figure. Soon I'll be the great chief of the Tartars. Already Arabs and Moroccans are mingling my name with their prayers. Amongst the Tartars I shall become Khan.

The only thing I shall be incapable of is to share the sheik's mutton with them. I'm a vegetarian."

During the latter part of 1943 numerous settlers arrived in the East. Thousands of Lithuanians and Volksdeutsch that had been transferred from the Soviet Union to Germany during the brief German-Soviet alliance of 1939-1941 were now returning. The Lithuanians returned to Lithuania, now a part of Ostland, while most of the Volksdeutsch, some 10,000, were settled together, according to German settlement plans in thirty-two new villages, in the Hegewald area, near the Pripet Marshes, also in Ostland. This was the second large-scale German settlement in the East, the first being at Zhitomir, Ukraine.

Plans were in the works to dispatch more settlers, most of whom would be settled in areas which were relatively free of Partisans; the Ostland, Galicia, Zhitomir, etc.

"...EVERY TRUMP CARD..."

The war at sea was still going very badly for the Germans. On November 12, 1943, Admiral Doenitz wrote in his diary, "The enemy holds every trump card, covering all areas with long-range air patrols and using locating methods against which we still have no warning...The enemy knows all our secrets and we know none of his."

CHAPTER 22

BAKU FALLS, TEL AVIV FALLS, CAIRO FALLS

On December 5, 1943, the Axis forces in the Caucasus launched a major assault on the Allied defenses north of Baku. Having learned from intelligence sources that there were tensions and a lack of coordination between the Soviets and British, the attack was directed at the area of the front where the two forces joined. Here, for a few meters, command and control was fuzzy. Within minutes, the massed Axis tanks broke through this weak link and quickly spread out to roll up the Allied lines. Within hours, the Allied front collapsed and both the Soviets and British retreated in confusion. Thousands of Soviet and British prisoners were captured.

Axis forces then entered Baku, and for the next few days there was deadly house-to-house fighting between Soviet diehards and the invaders. Eventually, however, the Axis forces secured the city. As the Soviet troops had departed they torched the area's oil producing facilities, but the Germans had expected this. Following closely behind the Axis troops were German and Romanian oil engineers and technicians who began, at once, to repair those facilities.

To the north, the besieged city of Grozny had capitulated during the battle for Baku.

In Berlin, Hitler authorized Rosenberg to proceed with forming the political structure of the Caucasus. The man selected to be Reichscommissar for the Caucasus had already been chosen. He was Arno Schickedanz, one of Rosenberg's closest associates.

Furthermore, a new homeland was to be staked out for the Cossacks in the Kuban area of the northwest Caucasus. This was one of Hitler's pet projects and was to be carried out by Rosenberg. The Cossack leader, Ataman T.I. Domanov, had been promised that his people would have their own autonomous settlement and a governmental structure, constructed along traditional lines. That government had already been organized and consisted of ministries of Education, Agriculture, Health Services and Police. The Cossacks were further authorized to practice their own religion and dismantle the Soviet collectives.

TEL AVIV FALLS

On December 8, the Axis forces, having been heavily reinforced, launched a massive attack against the Allied defenses at Tel Aviv. Taking advantage of their superior numbers, the Axis attack was opened with two diversionary attacks east of the city, followed a short time later by a main thrust aimed at the city's center.

House-to-house fighting occurred for the next two days with both sides taking heavy losses. Then on the 11th, a typical Blitzkrieg attack struck the Allied front east of the city at the point where it had been weakened by the earlier diversionary attacks. The Allied forces held during the day, but the next morning the attack was renewed and by 10:00 a.m. Axis tanks had broken into the rear areas of the Allied line. The tanks regrouped and struck out in a southwesterly direction toward the small port city of Ashdod, twenty miles south of Tel Aviv. If Ashdod fell, the Allied troops in Tel Aviv would be trapped.

Desperate for this not to happen, the Allied commanders rapidly withdrew their troops from Tel Aviv and threw everything they had into the path of the advancing Axis tanks. The tactic worked and the tanks of the American armored division were able to maneuver around the Axis force and attack their left flank. This action stopped the Axis thrust and the Allied forces in Tel Aviv were able to withdraw in an orderly manner. A temporary defensive perimeter was then thrown up around Ashdod by the Allies, but a much more substantial defense line was being built at Gaza City.

In all, the capture of Tel Aviv was a major victory of the Axis forces. Now, Axis forces were only sixty-five miles from the Egyptian border and less than 200 miles from the Suez Canal.

Tel Aviv, however, was still a very dangerous place for the Axis troops. The Jewish guerrilla organizations, having been generously supplied with Allied arms, now pulled out all the stops. A constant series of bold, and at times suicidal, attacks were carried out against the hated occupiers. The Germans were the favored target. In retaliation, both the Germans and Italians took revenge by summarily executing every guerrilla fighter who was captured and executing as hostages dozens of Jews who had not yet fled the city. They dared not to execute Arab hostages.

At Ashdod, both sides paused to build up their forces for the battle that was soon to come.

EXODUS

Tel Aviv was becoming an Arab city, but at a terrible cost.

Tel Aviv was the last Allied-controlled seaport in Palestine, which meant that supplies could no longer come in by sea. Also, this effectively cut off much of the flow of Jewish refugees to Cyprus.

The great flood of refugees to the south continued, however, passing through Beer Sheva and down the long desolate road to the Red Sea ports of Elat and Aqabah. There, Allied and some neutral ships had gathered to carry away the refugees. Axis propaganda was quick to claim that the British were dumping Jews into colonial lands and that the people of those lands should rise up against Britain.

To add to the exodus, refugees were now fleeing from Trans-Jordan, since it was now evident that that country would soon be overrun. Most of these refugees were Arabs who had supported the Allied cause — and they were numerous. ☑ Under pressures from London, Trans-Jordan had, early in the war, declared war on Germany and Italy. The Jordanians now feared that their country would be treated as an occupied enemy country and that its future as a separate state might be in jeopardy. Within Trans-Jordan there was a large minority of Palestinian Arabs and, within that community, there had long been undercurrents promoting the merger of Palestine and Trans-Jordan into a single state.

🎧 A large number of the Jordanian refugees were taken to locations in Allied-controlled Arab lands such as Egypt and Aden. Some fled into neutral Saudi Arabia, and still others fled eastward into Iraq, Iran and Kuwait.

ALLIES ABANDON THE EASTERN MEDITERRANEAN

Having lost Tel Aviv, and with the Suez Canal in danger, the Allied leaders made the painful decision, on December 19, to withdraw the British Navy from the Eastern Mediterranean. This doomed the Allied position at Haifa. Slowly and orderly, the Allied troops there were withdrawn and transferred to Egypt or to the Gaza area of Palestine. As the Allied troops departed from Haifa, they left behind substantial amounts of arms and munitions for the Jewish guerrillas.

The Axis troops at Haifa, mostly Italians, closely monitored the Allied pull-out and quickly occupied areas as they were abandoned. This unwritten understanding between the Allied and Axis forces prevented anarchy and looting which had been so prevalent elsewhere.

The majority of the withdrawn British warships were sent to the port city of Suez at the southern end of the Suez Canal, and to other ports in the Red Sea. A compliment of small, fast warships and submarines was left in the Eastern Mediterranean to harass the Italian Navy, to protect British-controlled Cyprus, to maintain a sea link with British-controlled Malta and, through Malta, to maintain connections with Gibraltar.

CYPRUS

With the withdrawal of the British from the eastern Mediterranean, the island of Cyprus was now in peril. On this issue, however, the Turks intervened. Ankara announced that they would supply and protect the people of the island, many of whom were Turks, with food and other necessities. This action was seen in various ways; as a humanitarian effort on Turkey's part, as a form of compensation to the Allies for Ankara's numerous concessions made to the Axis Powers, or as an opportunity for Turkey to become a dominant factor in the island's future. ☑ Gaining control of Cyprus, which was once a part of the Ottoman Empire, had long been a goal of the Turks.

🔒 London gave its less-than-enthusiastic approval of the scheme because of its humanitarian nature, but behind the scenes, the Britishers could clearly see Ankara's motives.

THE BATTLE OF GAZA

In early December the Allies abandoned Ashdod without a struggle and new battle lines were drawn at the city of Gaza.

On December 24, the Axis forces launched their first major attack on the Gaza defenses. It failed miserably with high losses. The Allies, strengthened by the forces from Haifa and reinforcements from all over the British Empire, and fearful of losing the Suez Canal, now fought with a renewed determination. Furthermore, the balance of forces had narrowed. Because of the needs of the Axis forces in the Caucasus, the forces in Palestine were now receiving less in the way of replacements and supplies. The Axis forces still had a numerical superiority in ground forces over the Allies, but the gap had lessened. Also, both the British and Americans had committed more aircraft to the defense of Gaza and now had a slight superiority in air power. A large number of the newly-arrived aircraft were tank-killers and a direct threat to the Axis tactic of Blitzkrieg.

A second and third Axis attack against the Gaza defenses, over the next two days, were beaten back, again with high losses to the attackers. These developments forced the Axis commanders to pause and reconsider their strategy. A spirited Allied counterattack on the third day also failed.

This would be the pattern of the battle of Gaza for several weeks to come. There would be attacks, counterattacks, pauses, and attacks again with neither side winning the advantage.

EXTENDING THE ARMED FRONTIER

With the creation of the southern sector of the armed frontier well under way, it was now time to work on the middle section — the heavily populated area east of Moscow.

The concept of this part of the armed frontier would be similar to that in the south. The frontier would be on relatively flat land and natural features of the terrain would be utilized to give the frontier defenders a military advantage. The frontier would be well back from the foothills of the Ural Mountains, and roads and railroads directly behind the frontier would be preserved and used as lines of supply and communication. A no-man's-land, sometimes up to twenty miles wide, would be maintained immediately east of the line. All cities, towns, villages and other entities in the no-man's-land useful to an enemy would be levelled to the ground and their population removed. Cities, towns and villages immediately behind the frontier would be vacated by their inhabitants and used to house the frontier troops until such time that well-planned communities could be constructed to serve as planned military strong points.

The recruitment of thousands of laborers needed to construct the frontier was begun, and care was taken not to employ those who would be likely to defect to the enemy. For this reason, Polish workers from the General Government, Balts from the Baltic states, Muslim workers from the Caucasus, etc., were to be used.

Movable assets of value in the no-man's-land, such as factories, bridges, lumber, railroad rails, etc., would be dismantled and moved to the west. As for immovable assets such as mines, dams, canals, irrigated areas and the like, the frontier would be adjusted, where possible, to utilize them. Otherwise, they would be destroyed.

This central section of the armed frontier would stretch some 700 miles from Uralsk, in the south, to the city of Berezniki 750 miles northeast of Moscow. ☑ Beyond Berezniki, the terrain, stretching to the Arctic Ocean, is heavily forested, sparsely-settled, and lacking in infrastructure and roads. ♫ And, for the moment, it was the domain of the Partisans.

It was planned in Berlin that this last section of the armed frontier would not be established until the Partisan menace was eliminated. Then the frontier would be built along one of two possible routes; from Berezniki to Archangel as originally planned, or from Berezniki to the town of Vorkuta, at the northern end of the Ural Mountains. ☑ From that town, it is 140 miles to the Arctic coast, and from Vorkuta, a modern railroad ran through the forested wilderness in the direction of Moscow. ♫ This rail line could provide a valuable communications corridor if the frontier were constructed along this route. ☑ The distance from Berezniki to the Arctic coast via Vorkuta is approximately 700 miles; to Archangel, it is about 650 miles. ♫ By utilizing the Berezniki-Vorkuta route, thousands of square miles of land would be added to RK Muscovy. It was as yet to be determined whether or not this would be an advantage — for its commercial value — or a detriment — because of the Partisan menace. That decision would be made in the future.

In the meantime, no significant military threat from the east was to be expected through this inhospitable terrain. ☑

THE PARTISANS

In May 1943, German estimates of Partisan strength in the north was 62,000 men in identified units and another 40,000 in unidentified units. This was the largest Partisan movement in history. The largest concentration of Partisans was in the area south of Minsk and in the eastern part of Belorussia. The Partisan menace in the Baltic states, the Ukraine, the Crimea and the Caucasus was considerably less.

Based on the history of colonization, the German planners had expected prolonged enemy resistance in certain areas of the East. Such resistance had been the case in virtually every part of the world where Europeans had established colonies. History also showed that that resistance had to be suppressed by force and that it would take years.

AN ARMY OF SHOULDER PATCHES

As history had also taught, in the process of colonization, local people were recruited, trained and trusted to help provide security in their own lands. The Germans were slow to recognize this, possibly due to the fact that this generation of Germans had had virtually no experience in creating colonies. But the Germans learned fast. As the need for manpower in the East skyrocketed, it became apparent that the Germans could not manage and control all of the conquered areas by themselves.

This had already led, in late 1942, to the utilization of tens of thousands of hiwis

An Arab soldier of the Lehr division wearing that unit's distinctive patch.

Here are but a few of the shoulder patches of osttruppen units that served in the German armed forces.

The osttruppen, for the most part, were organized into brigade- and regiment-sized units according to their ethnicity and commanded by German officers and non-commissioned officers (NCO) who spoke either their language or Russian. Some of the osttruppen who had military experience, or an education, were made officers and NCOs.

The volunteers were given a brief period of training and then sent into action. They wore German uniforms with distinctive shoulder patches showing their ethnic origin.

Both the German Army and the Waffen SS recruited easterners but, in the spring of 1944, this changed. It was decided in Berlin that the great majority of the eastern units would be incorporated into the Waffen SS since that organization was responsible for internal security. This meant that hundreds of thousands of non-Germans now became members of the SS. Gone forever were the days when only untarnished Aryans were accepted in the SS.

THE BALKANS

Russia was not the only place were there were large formations of Partisans. They existed in the former state of Yugoslavia, Albania, and in northern Greece. There were also well-organized non-communist guerrilla units operating in these areas.

Hitler showed considerable interest in the Balkans in that it was a source for much of Germany's raw materials: oil, chrome, bauxite, antimony and copper. Little interest, however, was shown in the politics of the Balkans because that area was the domain of Germany's allies: Italy, Bulgaria, Romanian, and Croatia. But, by early 1943, the Partisan

and osttruppen. Among those people most favored by the Germans were, not surprisingly, the well-respected Cossacks and other ethnic groups of this same ilk such as the Chechens, Tartars, Azerbaijanies, Armenians and the various Turkic communities scattered throughout the southern part of the Soviet Union.

As the Nazi leadership gained more experience in dealing with the eastern people, the doors were opened to others — even to Russians.

By early 1943, the osttruppen alone had become a wide mix of local peoples and numbered over 500,000, and was still growing. By comparison, the 60 German divisions committed to occupation duties in the East counted some 750,000 Germans. The army of occupation in the East was, therefore, approaching the point where it would become half German and half osttruppen.

menace had became so great that it soon became obvious that the situation could not be managed without German help. Therefore, German troops had gradually been committed to the Balkans to the point where, by early 1943, seven German Army infantry divisions were involved along with several units of the Waffen SS. These troops had a secondary mission, that of keeping Germany's Balkan allies from fighting each other. They were not always successful. In August 1942, there had been an ugly clash between Bulgarian and Italian troops in Macedonia. And it happened again the following October. Then too, Hungary and Romania were, at times, on the verge of war with each other because of their on-going dispute over Transylvania.

Furthermore, because the Partisans controlled so much territory, the Germans had a problem of maintaining communications between Germany and their permanent enclave on the Mediterranean at Salonica.

Here in the Balkans, the Germans followed a military policy similar to that in Russia. A large number of locals, both volunteers and conscripts, were organized into para-military units to fight Partisans and perform occupation duties.

The Balkan allies also recruited locals for military service, as did the puppet governments in occupied Serbia and Greece. Some of the units were comprised solely of Muslims. The result of all this resulted in a wide conglomerate of military units endeavoring to work together against the common enemy. This was not easy.

In addition to problems with the Partisans, there were also tens of thousands of people caught up in population transfers; Bulgarians were moving from Romania to Bulgaria, Romanians were moving from Bulgaria to Romania, Bulgarians were moving into Thrace (occupied Greece) and Macedonia (occupied Yugoslavia), Serbs were moving out of Croatia, Croatians were moving out of Serbia, Italians were moving into Slovenia and Dalmatia, Slovenians were moving into Croatia, Volksdeutsch were moving from Croatia to the General Government to become settlers, Macedonians were moving in several directions as the Bulgarians carried out a policy of Bulgarianizing their newly won territory. These transfers were often forced and had to be carried out by the armies of Germany's Balkan allies, thus sapping their military strength which could have been used more fruitfully against the Partisans.

Entwined within this multi-directional exodus were Jews and Balkan workers moving to the north — the Jews to concentration camps and the workers to German war plants.

Try as he might, Hitler could not ignore Balkan politics. Since he was the most powerful man in Europe, the various Balkan leaders sought his favor in a variety of ways and for a variety of reasons. Because of this, Hitler was drawn into almost all of the major Balkan disputes.

Hitler had to manage these problems very astutely in order to maintain harmony within his Axis family. Most agonizing of all for the Fuehrer was the fact that these problem were not likely to go away with the return of peace.

ALLIED AIR CAMPAIGN — SUCCESSES AND FAILURES

After dark, on New Year's Day, 1944, the British dropped another 1000 tons of bombs on Berlin. The next night they did the same. Happy New Year, Adolf!

Every day now, one or more cities in Axis-controlled Europe were being bombed. On the 11th, the Allied bombers began a campaign to hit factories building fighter planes for the Luftwaffe. On the 20th, Berlin was bombed again. On the night of January 28/29, Hitler was in Berlin and another air raid kept him awake all night in his bunker.

Surprisingly, though, German war production was on the rise. This was due to the fact that production had been dispersed to small communities, or had gone underground, or moved to the East. Munitions production for January 1944 showed an increase of 56% over January 1943, and during 1943, German industry produced 11,738 fighter aircraft compared to 5,213 in 1942. This of course, was a factor in the Allies targeting fighter production.

Not only were there more fighter planes produced during 1943, but production of bombers, transports and trainers increased.

In comparison, however, even these increases in production, impressive as they were, could not keep pace with the production of aircraft by the combined efforts of the Allies.

In early January, the Allied air forces began "Operation Carpet Bagger," the air-dropping of arms and ammunition to resistance fighters in France, Belgium and Holland.

THE "BABY BLITZ"

By January 1944, the Luftwaffe was able to assemble about 550 bombers to renew concentrated air attacks on Britain. It was not nearly as effective as the air blitz of the fall of 1940, but it was significant enough to be called "The Baby Blitz."

By 1944, Allied air defenses over Britain were much stronger, and took a heavy toll on the German formations. By March, the Luftwaffe could take no more and ended the Baby Blitz. The Baby Blitz had no effect on diminishing the Allied air offensive over Europe.

PALESTINE AND TRANS-JORDAN OCCUPIED

🔖 By mid-January, the fighting in the Gaza area of Palestine was coming to a successful conclusion for the Axis forces. The Allied forces had been pushed across the border into the Sinai Peninsula of Egypt and were now in defensive positions at the coastal town of Al-Arish, twenty-five miles inside Egypt, and at several points in the Sinai Desert.

In the last battles that had taken place in Palestine, the cities of Gaza and Khan Yunis had been decimated. Axis propagandists found ammunition in this and claimed that the Allies had been willing to sacrifice the cities in which there were heavy Arab populations, but had readily abandoned those with heavy Jewish populations.

To the east of Gaza, Axis forces took Beer Sheva and were marching southward on the seaports of Elat and Aqabah. The Allied resistance consisted only of delaying actions.

Once the Axis forces reached Aqabah, Trans-Jordan's only seaport, Trans-Jordan would be undefendable. Therefore, the Allies began to withdraw from all of Trans-Jordan. About half of the Allied forces retreated to Aqabah to board the waiting ships while the other half retreated eastward into British-controlled Iraq.

The Jordanian royal family and the British-backed Jordanian government fled into exile in Saudi Arabia. Many pro-Allied Arab leaders, who had taken refuge in Trans-Jordan, also fled.

During the first week of February, the Axis forces occupied Elat, and soon afterwards, Aqabah.

At this time, also, the last Allied forces left Haifa, and Rome announced that both Palestine and Trans-Jordan were under Italian occupation.

In London and New York, the stock markets fell sharply.

BREAKTHROUGH IN THE SINAI

During the last week of January 1944, the Axis forces in the Sinai went on the offensive once again. They attacked the Allied positions at Al-Arish and at two points to the south. After three days of hard fighting, the Allied positions at Al-Arish were overrun. This forced an evacuation all along the Allied front. Now, the Suez Canal was only seventy miles to the east.

Considering the geography of the canal, the most likely point of attack for the Axis forces would be at the city of Ismailia, located along the central portion of the canal. To the north, the canal passed through a wide area of marsh land, and in the south, there was an absence of east-west roads. The best east-west roads ran through Ismailia. The Allies had seen this possibility and concentrated their defenses east of Ismailia. By February 3, 1944, they had strong defensive positions along a ridge of hills fifteen miles east of Ismailia. ◼ It had been in this general area that the British stopped, and turned back, the Turks during World War I in their attempt to take the Suez Canal. 🔊 **It was the hope in London that that feat could be repeated.**

Having seen the threat to the canal, Washington ordered a sizeable contingent of AAF units from Britain to Egypt. But still the American government refused to send additional ground troops — it was an election year in the United States. The two American divisions fighting in Egypt would remain there.

During this time, the remainder of the British Naval units operating in the eastern Mediterranean withdrew into the Red Sea. Only the British submarines remained on station.

BAD OMENS FOR HITLER FROM THE FAR EAST

In the western Pacific, the American noose around Japan was tightening. During December 1943, American bombers from Alaska began bombing targets in the Kurile Islands, a long string of small islands north of Japan and considered, by the Japanese, as part of their home islands.

On January 31, 1944, the Americans invaded the Marshall Islands striking at the fortified island of Kwajalein. This was a 2,400 mile leap across the central Pacific from Hawaii. From Kwajalein, it was 2,600 miles to Tokyo.

By February 4, Kwajalein was in American hands, and all during the battle the Americans controlled the seas around, and the air above, the island. The Japanese Navy had proven incapable of saving one of its most important island outposts.

On February 19, the Americans invaded the Gilbert Islands, south of the Marshalls by landing on the island of Eniwetok. Within a few days that island was in American hands.

The invasion of the Gilbert Islands was an effort by the Americans to protect their southern flank. They were now free to move on to the next island group, the Marianas, 1500 miles southwest of Tokyo. With the new super-long-range B-29 bombers now in production in America, all of southern and central Japan would be within bombing range from the Marianas.

At Hitler's headquarters, these events were seen as bad omens of things to come in the Pacific.

HEAVY WATER AGAIN

On February 20, Norwegian saboteurs, assisted by British agents, sank a ferry boat loaded with heavy water bound for Germany. The Allies were still in a great state of anxiety about Germany's atomic bomb program. But the Allies were well ahead of the Germans. In Tennessee, a new uranium processing operation, known as the Clinton Engineer Works (Oak Ridge), had come into being and was successfully enriching uranium for use in a bomb. Also, a huge industrial complex was arising in the desert of Washington State to produce plutonium for a second type of atomic bomb.

THE GERMAN ATOMIC BOMB PROJECT GETS UNDERWAY

🔊 **Now, with ample funding and pressures from both Hitler and Goering, Germany's atomic bomb program, code named "The Sauerkraut Project," was underway with top priorities. Heisenberg had moved from his cave at Haiterloch to a newly-built laboratory in the small town of Stadtilm, seventy-five miles southwest of Leipzig. There he began building his first large reactor and worked on the problem of separating the uranium isotopes.**

The German scientist had come to the same conclusion as had the Americans, that ☑ **two giant facilities were needed, one to** separate the isotopes and one to make plutonium from the U-238 uranium isotope. 🔊 **It was also agreed that both facilities should be in the East away from the Allied bombings. Both facilities required** ☑ huge amounts of water and electric power to accomplish the processing of uranium and plutonium. 🔊 **The Germans further recognized that the plutonium facility should be in a remote and sparsely-populated area** ☑ because of the possibility of a nuclear accident.

🔊 **With these parameters, scientists and engineers began searching for locations.**

For the separation facility, the lower Dnieper River area, which was to be a part of the German Crimea, was of primary interest, and an area near the Volga and Don Rivers was being considered for the plutonium plant. Also, German geologists were travelling about searching for additional sources of natural uranium. They soon found them ☑ in the Ore Mountains in Germany, in France, and in the former Yugoslavia.

CLOSING THE CANAL

🔊 During the first week of February 1944, the Axis forces on the Ismailia front were able to advance a short distance toward the northern end of the Canal. There, from the edge of the great marsh, their long-range artillery was able to bombard ships plying the canal. This, in effect, closed the canal.

On February 9, the Axis forces attacked — Blitzkrieg style — at Ismailia. Four days of bitter fighting followed until, on the 13th, Axis tanks breached the Allied line. The Allies fell back to a secondary defense line five miles east of the canal, but on the 15th this line, too, was breached. On the 15th, Axis forces reached the eastern bank of the canal.

A powerful Axis force then struck out in a southerly direction along the eastern shore of Lake Timsah, a part of the canal system. They broke through the Allied defenses at the south end of the lake and crossed the canal there for the first time. They then marched up the western shore of the lake in an effort to attack Ismailia from the south. But this was not to be. A determined force of Highlanders, men of the Black Watch, three regiments of Indians and excellent air support from the RAF, the SAAF (South African Air Force), and newly arrived American air units, stopped the Axis drive in its tracks. It was now February 17 and the Axis forces were exhausted. They halted along the western shore of Lake Timsah to regroup and bring up supplies.

There were still enough fresh Axis forces available, however, to march south along the west bank of the canal to the north shore of the Great Bitter Lake, another integral part of the canal. Here, the Allies, recently reinforced

by troops from Palestine and Trans-Jordan, and with strong air support, managed to stop this Axis advance.

But the land between the lakes was in Axis hands and they were in a position now to march on Cairo, seventy miles to the west.

SECRET AGREEMENT IN LONDON

Unbeknownst to the Allied commanders in the field, the Allied Joint Chiefs of Staff had made the decision, two months earlier, that if the Suez Canal was lost, they would not expend men and resources to defend the remainder of northern Egypt. At the appropriate time, Cairo would be declared an open city and the Allied forces would set up defenses south of the city to prevent any attempt by the Axis forces from advancing southward through the Nile Valley and into East Africa.

Furthermore, with the loss of Cairo, no effort would be made to prevent an Axis advance westward into Libya as far as El Agheila. There, extensive defensive positions, built by the Axis forces, already existed. It was there that Rommel stopped the British advance into Libya in February 1941 and again in December 1941. Now the Allies would use the Axis-built defenses against them.

On February 20, the Allied commanders in Egypt were informed of the decision to systematically withdraw from Northern Egypt, now named "Operation Nefertiti."

Accordingly, the Allied troops then withdrew from Ismailia to a defense line fifteen miles west of the city. Axis forces rushed in to occupy Ismailia and then moved north to take control of the central portion of the canal up to the town of Balah, at the edge of the great marshes. The Allies still held Port Said at the northern end of the canal, and the city of Suez at the southern end, but these cities were also soon abandoned.

The Axis occupation of Ismailia, Port Said and Suez took time and a lull fell over the area as both sides regrouped.

Having captured the Suez Canal, the Axis had really gained very little of value because the British Navy still dominated the Red Sea. It was, therefore, unlikely that many Axis warships or commercial vessels would use the canal.

A SECRET AGREEMENT IN CAIRO

In Cairo, twenty-three year old King Farouk and his government (which had been forced upon him by the British) were unaware of the London decision but, from the military situation, could deduce that Cairo would very likely fall to the Axis invaders.

Therefore, Farouk and his government formulated a plan. For months, they had issued pleas to both the Allies and Axis leaders to declare Cairo an open city. ☑ During the summer of 1942, the Egyptian government had made similar pleas when Cairo was threatened by Rommel's forces at El Alamein.

🔊 Now, as had been the case earlier at Jerusalem and other cities, the Axis leaders responded that they would comply with an open city arrangement if the Allied leaders would do likewise. But the Allied leaders were noncommittal. The possibility existed, from Farouk's point of view, that Cairo could become a battleground.

To ingratiate himself with the Axis leaders, Farouk issued orders to the 40,000-man Egyptian Army not to oppose an Axis advance into Cairo, but to concentrate on maintaining order in areas undergoing transition. ☑ This was a repeat of the orders given to the Egyptian Army in the summer of 1942.

As for his own safety, as had also been the case in 1942, Farouk feared that he might be kidnapped by the British. To prevent this, he had decided that he and his family would go into hiding. The Germans had offered him sanctuary, but he refused, feeling that it was his duty to remain in Egypt.

Farouk's plan had to be kept absolutely secret from his own government ministers, some of whom were British informants.

NEW WEAPONS

By this time, some of Germany's new weapons were being deployed in combat. They included the small, remote-controlled "Goliath" tank designed to carry an explo-

sive charge into the enemy's line, a new self-propelled 88-mm anti-aircraft gun, and an improved version of the Panther tank. And, of course, Tiger tanks were steadily arriving from Germany.

Also under development were radio-guided missiles. This included the "Enzian" ground-to-air missile, the "Rheinbote" surface-to-surface missile with a range of 140 miles, the "Orkan" air-to-air missile, the Henschel "HS-294" submarine-launched missile, the Henschel "HS-295" twin-engine missile, the Henschel "HS-296" television-guided missile, and the Henschel "HS-298" air-to-air missiles. Overriding all of this, and nearing completion, were the V-1 and V-2 long-range ground-to-ground missiles. Werner von Braun and his engineers were also working on a submarine-launched V-2 missile for attacking the United States.

For the Luftwaffe, a wide range of new jets were in the design stages. They included swept-back-wing fighters and a six-engine jet bomber.

CAIRO FALLS

🔊 On March 3, 1944, the Allied forces east of Cairo began drawing back into the city. The next day, the Allies declared Cairo an open city and their force commenced a withdrawal to the south.

At this time, King Farouk went into hiding at the town of Mansura in the delta where a spacious underground suite had been built for him under a mosque. This was one of three such hideouts.

On March 6, Axis forces marched into the city with the Italians in the lead. Crowds lined the streets and greeted them as liberators and the next day the King came out of hiding and returned to the palace, dismissed his pro-British government and proclaimed that a new and enlightened era had begun for the Egyptian people. The King then formed a new government headed by ☑ Ali Maher-pasha, an ardent supporter of the Axis.

🔊 On March 8, after the city had been secured, Mussolini arrived to lead a grand

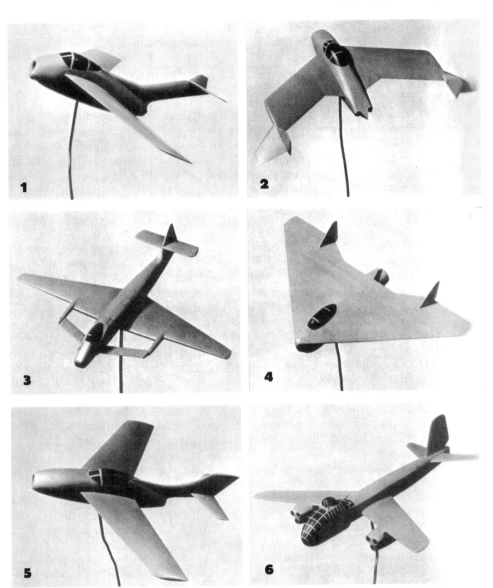

German jet aircraft under consideration: 1. The 600 mph Focke-Wulf Ta-183 fighter with four 30mm cannons. 2. Blohm & Voss P.215 bad-weather fighter. 3. Blohm & Voss P.192 ground-attack fighter-bomber with four cannons and a 1,100 lb bomb load. 4. Arado E.581.4 fighter with two cannons. 5. Focke-Wulf TA-183 all purpose fighter. 6. Junker JU-287 six-engine bomber with 550 mph top speed and 8,800 lb bomb capacity.

ceremonial parade into the city. Mussolini personally lead the parade mounted on a white horse and dressed in a marshal's uniform. The parade did not pass by the royal palace and Farouk was not invited to review the spectacle. This was an all-Italian affair.

With Mussolini came Count Serafino Mazzolini, Rome's appointed Delegato Politico to the Farouk government. Also in his entourage were representatives of the "Cassa Mediterranea di Credito par l'Egitto," a financial enterprise that was to become the new economic backbone of the country. It had long been planned that one of the first tasks of the Cassa Mediterranea would be to replace the British-supported Egyptian pound with Italian-supported Egyptian lire. Script would be issued in the interim at the exchange rate of 72.5 lire for the Egyptian pound. The script would be redeemable in Egyptian lire at some unspecified date in the future.

Mussolini's parade ended at Shepheard's Hotel in downtown Cairo, which had been the base of operation for the British for years. There, he made a rousing victory speech. It was a fitting example that change had come to Egypt. Mussolini and his entourage took up residence, however, at another hotel to avoid creating the image that they would be stepping into the shoes of the British.

For the next two days there were grand celebrations throughout the city and much speech-making. One of the most often mentioned themes in the speeches was that the conquest of Egypt portended the recovery of Italy's East African empire. By accomplishing this, the Italians also boasted that the Red Sea would become an Italian lake.

On March 11, Mussolini got down to business. He met with the King and assured him that, ✒ as Rome had previously promised, Egypt would remain independent, its governmental structure would remain in place and that it was Italy's intention to make Egypt into a happy and prosperous nation as a model that other Arab countries would want to emulate. 🔊 Il Duce also told Farouk that his government had prepared a number of treaties that he wished to negotiate and that Italy would take over full control of the Suez Canal.

The tone of the meeting was more of a lecture by Mussolini rather than a meeting of equals. Not surprisingly, the King and his entourage were mortified. It was a rude and sudden awakening for the Egyptian leaders to the fact that they had simply exchanged

one European master for another. It was a very bad beginning.

Fortunately for Farouk, his position as monarch was not in jeopardy because he was widely respected by the Egyptian people and his continued presence on the throne was a stabilizing influence throughout the country — which was something the Italians sorely needed during this period of change. Farouk realized this, but he had grave doubts about the future. ✒ Recent events had shown that after the Italian conquest of Ethiopia, the King of Italy had been proclaimed Emperor of Ethiopia, and after the conquest of Albania he became the King of Albania.

🔊 The fall of Cairo sparked a great outpouring of joy in Berlin. The German media heaped praise on their Italian ally and promised that Germany, too, would respect Egyptian independence. It was also stated repeatedly that the conquest of Egypt would provide a springboard from which the Germans could, along with the Italians, march south and recover their former German colonies of Tanganyika, Rwanda and Urundi. It was also announced in the German media, but with much less fanfare, that Germany hoped to restore the good trade relations she had with Egypt in the 1920s and 1930s. ✒

At the Fuehrer's headquarters, Hitler was having stomach problems again and was constipated.

🔊 In Rome, the people listened to the events in Cairo on radio — in their bomb shelters. The Allies bombed Rome three days in a row.

In London, there was gloom and anger and a rise in the heretofore almost invisible peace movement. In Parliament a vote of confidence was called for regarding Churchill's government. It passed in favor of his government by a narrow margin and Churchill remained in office.

In the United States there was also gloom, and the peace activists there, supported by a small covey of die-hard isolationists, began to speak of the unthinkable — ending the war in Europe.

CHAPTER 23

INTO THE MIDDLE EAST AND EAST AFRICA

AT HITLER'S TABLE AGAIN, AND VITAMULFIN-FORTE

After a long delay, Hitler's table conversations were recorded again on March 13 and 23, 1944. As usual, the record was devoid of war or politics. And again, Hitler spoke of the future, and of things that interested him. He spoke of how the image of the German film industry might be improved and he praised director Leni Riefenstahl. Then he spoke of art and again condemned art critics who, with their arbitrary judgements, could ruin the career of aspiring artists. Music critics received his venom, too.

On the 23rd, he reminisced about his experiences in World War I. He said he first saw the Rhineland in 1914 and was very impressed with its beauty and the kindness of its people. He said he hoped to visit the Rhineland at least once a year.

He commented, too, on how he enjoyed driving the long stretches of road through Germany's forests, "...far away from the throng," and how he longed to picnic by the roadside without being surrounded by people.

He spoke also, at some length, of all of the natural wonders in Germany, Austria and Bohemia-Moravia that were there for all to see. The record of this conversation concluded with Hitler saying, "To visit all the beauties of this country, a German today would require to take a holiday in a different district each year for the rest of his life."

Where these not the words of a man longing for retirement — or was it the Vitamulfin-forte — or both?

On March 14, Dr. Morell had recorded in Hitler's medical record that the Fuehrer had been "limp and tired" and that on this date, he gave "Patient A" his first shot of Vitamulfin-forte, a stimulant. Morell then recorded that the patient "...came to life at once... was noticeably fresher over lunch... kept up a very lively conversation... stayed awake a long time... slept well without sleeping tablets... Fuehrer very pleased." After that, Vitamulfin-forte shots became a regular part of Hitler's life.

ALLIES RETREAT FROM CAIRO

🔊 After giving up Cairo, the bulk of the Allied forces retreated south through the Nile Valley. This valley was the only practical way to traverse the mighty Sahara Desert, and trying to defend it was a military nightmare. On either side of the Valley were miles of flat, dry, uninhabited desert land — ideal for tanks. A defender would be required to extend his flanks out on either side as far as he could. And, if the attacker had the advantage of numbers, which had been the case ever since the invasion of the Levant, the attacker could simply maneuver around the ends of those flanks. But the Allies had to try. The Nile Valley would have to be defended from just below Cairo to the border of Ethiopia, a distance of 1,400 miles.

To the west of Cairo, the road to Libya was open and undefended. The Allies, however, were setting up a strong defense line at El Agheila, Libya, about midway between Cairo and Tunisia, to prevent the Axis forces from reaching, and reinforcing their compatriots in Tunisia.

The El Agheila line would be manned primarily by Americans and Fighting French forces. The British would have their hands full defending the Nile Valley.

Back in Cairo, the Axis forces were consolidating their hold on the city and the delta region. This took time, and the Allies were able to establish a defense line twenty-five miles south of Cairo at El Ayat. Their western flank extended to the dead lake of Birket Qaru and their eastern flank into the empty desert as far as their resources permitted. These resources were soon to be decreased by the withdrawal of the two American divisions that had retreated from Palestine with the rest of the Allied forces. The official reason given for the withdrawal was that the Americans had fought long and hard and now needed rest and rehabilitation. The real reason, however, was political. Roosevelt did not want to have American soldiers defending British colonies during an election year.

Roosevelt, however, did authorize increased use of the AAF in East Africa. He believed that the air war was less personal in the eyes of the American public than the ground war. Furthermore, the AAF had proven its worth and would almost certainly give the Allies superiority in the air.

CLEANING UP IN THE CAUCASUS

After the fall of Baku, Soviet resistance disintegrated in the southern Caucasus. Axis forces drove westward at a rapid pace capturing Tblisi, the capital of Georgia where, as a youth, Josif Stalin had studied for five years at the Tblisi Theological Seminary to become

a priest. From Tblisi, the Axis forces marched on to take Batum, the Soviets' last seaport on the Black Sea. Remnants of the Soviet forces fled into the Caucasus Mountains, into Iran, or into Turkey if they could get past the Turkish border guards.

As the Axis troops approached Batum, the last refuge for the Soviet Black Sea Fleet, the sailors scuttled their ships.

Along the Turkish border, the Germans established a military corridor, twenty-five to fifty-miles wide paralleling the entire length of the border which included the port of Batum. With this, the Germans now had military enclaves on both the eastern and western borders of Turkey, which served political as well as military purposes. The Turks could do little but take notice.

After the capture of Tblisi, Rashid Ali el-Gailani, the former premier of Iraq who had led the unsuccessful revolt against the British in May 1941, arrived and began making preparations for his return to Iraq. Similarly, pro-Axis Iranian leaders also arrived at Tblisi. Within days, and with Axis approval, the Iraqis proclaimed a provisional government with Gailani as its leader. It was hoped that this action would spark Arab uprisings against the Allied occupiers. With regard to Iran, the Iranian leaders were promised only that they would have important roles in the administration of an Axis-occupied Iran, but would not have, as yet, a provisional government. In Iran, the political situation was very complex.

BEGINNING THE MARCH SOUTH FROM CAIRO

On March 20, Axis forces attacked the Allied positions at El Ayat circling around their eastern flank. The Allies gave ground and then, after dark, withdrew to their next defense line at Bani Suwayf, twenty-seven miles to the south. The Allied plan was to conduct a fighting retreat all the way to the mountains of Ethiopia.

With each Allied withdrawal, however, the Axis commanders could expect the battlefields to be strewn with land mines, tank traps and booby traps. In the heavily urbanized valley itself, they could expect ambushes. They were also beginning to experience the combined strength of the RAF and AAF. The conquest of the Nile Valley was not going to be a cakewalk.

On March 27, the Axis attacked the Allied defense line at Bani Suwayf. Again they struck at the flanks, paid the price to gain ground, and then awoke the next morning to find the Allies gone; this time, digging in at the town of Al-Minya, sixty miles to the south.

On April 3, the Axis struck at the Al-Minya defenses. Here, they used a new tactic of dropping two German and one Italian parachute battalions behind the eastern part of the line in an effort to break up the Allies' orderly retreat. This tactic worked well and a sizeable number of Allied defenders, trapped between the paratroopers and the attacking force, were cut off and captured. But the Allied commanders learned fast. Using their air superiority, the Allied airmen now made a concentrated effort to destroy every Axis transport plane they could find capable of carrying paratroopers.

The Allied forces withdrew seventy miles to Asyut, but their forces were now weakened by the losses at Al-Minya, and they needed more time to recover. Since time meant distance, the Allies abandoned the Asyut defenses and withdrew to stronger defenses at Aswan, a further withdrawal of 210 miles. Allied delaying tactics and air attacks slowed the Axis followup. The air attacks were so effective that the Axis forces moved only at night. By the end of April, the Allies were firmly entrenched at Aswan and the enemy was still miles away.

BEGINNING THE MARCH WEST FROM CAIRO

To the west of Cairo, the nearest Allied force was 700 miles away in Libya at El Agheila. Closing this gap was assigned to the Italians since it was their colony that was being reconquered.

In late March, the Italian force set out from Cairo and made contact with the El Agheila defenses during the third week in April. There, they established defensive positions and awaited further developments.

THE GATHERING STORM IN THE MIDDLE EAST

Having conquered the Levant and the Caucasus, the Axis leaders now directed their attention to the Middle East — and to oil — oil for Italy.

Other pluses in the conquest of the Middle East would be that the primary supply route for American Lend-Lease going to the Soviet Union would be cut and, with Axis forces on the borders of India, Afghanistan and the Soviet Republic of Turkestan, Berlin and Rome would be in a position to influence events throughout the region.

The Axis military plan to conquer the Middle East called for a two-pronged offensive, a major thrust south from Turkey and a secondary thrust eastward from the eastern part of Trans-Jordan. The Axis troops would be very mobile and equipped for desert warfare. The Luftwaffe and Italian Air Force would also play major roles.

The countries to be conquered were Iraq, Iran and the British Protectorate of Kuwait. It was not within the Axis' plans to invade the desert kingdom of Saudi Arabia because such an undertaking would be very costly and have religious complications. Within the borders of Saudi-Arabia were the Muslim holy cities of Mecca and Medina, and a military conquest of these cities could be a major detriment to Germany's and Italy's relationships with the Arab world.

Therefore, it was the opinion in Berlin and Rome that a neutral Saudi-Arabia, on the southern border of the soon-to-be-conquered lands of the Middle East, would be an advantage rather than a detriment. This could change, of course, if the Allies entered Saudi-Arabia. In that case, Saudi-Arabia could then be drawn into the war.

The Allies, too, saw the advantage of keeping Saudi Arabia neutral, and it became a part of their overall planning for the region.

Realizing that the invasion of the Middle East was about to begin, strong Allied forces moved onto the island colony of Bahrain, a sheikdom, just off the coast of Saudi Arabia in the Persian Gulf. This was to be the primary staging area of future Allied operations in the region. ☑ In this respect, there was a precedent. During World War I British forces had staged on the island of Bahrain in the Persian Gulf before they invaded and conquered Turkish-controlled Mesopotamia (Iraq).

With the expectation that the British Navy would control the Persian Gulf, Bahrain would be unassailable. And, from Bahrain, Allied bombers could reach any part of the Middle East. Furthermore, an assault could be launched into Saudi Arabia if that nation became threatened.

Since the Americans had extensive oil interests in Saudi Arabia and a treaty obligation with that country, they too moved onto Bahrain. ☑ The treaty in question was written in 1939 and committed the United States to the defense of Saudi Arabia in return for oil concessions. Those oil concessions were located in the northeastern corner of Saudi Arabia, adjacent to Kuwait, and were being rapidly developed at this point in time. 🔊 If an Allied invasion of Saudi Arabia was to be undertaken, it would be an all-American affair. ☑ The Americans had already taken steps to strengthen Saudi Arabia by extending Lend-Lease to that nation in February 1943.

🔊 Another factor in selecting Bahrain was that it could be used as a base for B-29 bombers. When these bombers became available, all of the Middle East, the Levant, the Caucasus, most of the Crimea, and most of Turkey would be within bombing range. The latter country, it was surmised, would be strongly induced to remain neutral because of the presence of B-29s stationed on Bahrain.

To man their base at Bahrain, the Americans transferred the two divisions withdrawn from Egypt to the island. They were re-equipped and given training in amphibious assault operations, a fact that was made known to the enemy. In the following weeks, two more American divisions, one armored and one motorized infantry, arrived, as did two brigades of U.S. Marines, and two wings of the AAF. The U.S. Navy soon arrived in the form of four, then eight, then twelve, amphibious landing craft (LSTs and LSIs) to work with the British Navy.

The British were slower to move their forces into Bahrain because they were needed to defend Iraq and Iran.

Throughout April, the Axis built up their forces in eastern Turkey and in Trans-Jordan, and a target date for the invasion was set for the first week in May. The Allies also built up their forces in the region. More British troops arrived from Britain and two more Indian divisions were brought in. Both sides had volunteer Arab auxiliaries. ☑

EVENTS IN EUROPE

By April 1944, all of Axis-controlled Europe was on a permanent war-time footing. The people, especially the Germans, spent much of their time residing in bomb-shelters. Consumer goods had all but disappeared and food shortages continued.

Scattered throughout Germany were 7,000,000 foreign workers and millions more in the occupied countries. Women comprised 51% of the German work force. German citizens living in neutral countries were ordered by Berlin to return home in order to perform war work. The cumulative effect of these measures paid off. During 1943, production of armaments increased over 1942.

Over the years, the personal belongings of the Jews had been stored for future use except, of course, for the choicest items, which were picked over by the top Nazis. Now, the remaining material was released for distribution to those people in Germany who had lost their possessions in the bombings. Other measures were taken to lessen the burden of war on the German citizenry. Movie houses remained open and the annual Berlin flower show went on as usual.

Another measure taken to improve the morale of the soldiers was to provide them with female companions while on leave. This program was also intended to increase Germany's birth rate. Martin Bormann, a strong advocate for increasing Germany's population, and the father of ten children himself, prevailed upon Hitler to expand this program. Therefore, during April 1944, orders to the effect went out to Nazi Party headquarters throughout the Reich. It was suggested that dances, parties, sightseeing tours, factory tours, etc. be arranged for this purpose. It was further suggested that the young ladies should wear "attractive afternoon dresses or regional costumes."

FUEHRER IN BIFOCALS

For most of his life, Hitler had had trouble with his eyes, especially sensitivity to bright light. This was possibly related to the fact that, during World War I, he was temporarily blinded by poison gas.

In March 1944, his ophthalmologist prescribed bifocals. Hitler bought them but very seldom used them in private, and never in public. Instead, he used a magnifying glass, especially when reading maps. He also had special typewriters installed in his various headquarters that produced oversized type.

A JEW-FREE HUNGARY

During April 1944, the Nazi government prevailed upon its ally, Hungary, to rid itself of Jews. The SS would help. Within a few months some 470,000 Hungarian Jews were rounded up, of which approximately 140,000 were selected as laborers and the others were shipped off to the death camps.

ALLIES DRIVEN OUT OF EGYPT

🔊 On May 4, 1944, Axis forces attacked the Allied defenses at Aswan, Egypt. Again, it was an end run. Axis tanks attacked the extreme end of the Allied eastern flank, where it was the weakest, and charged into the rear of the Allied line. The Allied ground forces were able to slow the advance with determined resistance and near-mastery of the air, but the more powerful enemy prevailed on the ground.

On the 9th, the Allies gave up the Aswan defenses and withdrew to Wadu Halfa, 180 miles to the south and just inside the border of the Anglo-Egyptian Sudan. Egypt was lost.

Wadi Halfa was a very weak defensive position because ☑ at this point the Nile Valley

begins to flow in a slow "S" shaped formation. Across the top opening of the S, a road and railroad corridor existed that shortened the journey from Wadi Halfa to the center of the S to 300 miles compared to a 500-mile journey following the valley. Furthermore, this portion of the Nile Valley was less developed and there was only an unimproved road running through it and no rail lines. It was a stretch of the valley the Allies wanted to avoid.

🔊 And the 300 mile-long corridor was extremely vulnerable. The Axis forces could strike at it at almost any point, cutting it off as a supply route and escape route for the Allies. Therefore, it was decided by the Allied commanders to abandoned Wadi Halfa and retreat along the corridor to the town of Abu Hamad in the mid-section of the Nile Valley's S formation. With this, the northern part of the Sudan was relinquished to the Axis invaders.

ALLIES RETREAT FROM THE ANGLO-EGYPTIAN SUDAN

In London, a hard decision was made, that being to abandon the remainder of the Nile Valley in the central and southeastern part of the Anglo-Egyptian Sudan. This, in effect, meant giving up the capital, Khartoum, the center of the developed heart of the country. But, considering the strength of the enemy and the adverse terrain, the British leaders concluded that this region could not be defended. ☑

At Khartoum, the Nile Valley splits into the Blue Nile, which runs in a southeasterly direction into British-occupied Ethiopia, and the White Nile which continues south into a remote and primitive region of the country. 🔊 The British plan called for the Allied forces to make a fighting withdrawal to Khartoum and then down the Blue Nile Valley to the borders of Ethiopia and Eritrea, ☑ where the terrain is mountainous and more advantageous to the defender. 🔊 Small British detachments would be sent down the White Nile and into the desert areas west of Khartoum to secure provincial capitals, mining sites and others areas of importance.

Those forces would then be in contact with either the Fighting French in French Equatorial Africa or their own British forces in the British colony of Kenya.

At Wadi Halfa, the decision from London translated into a defense of very short duration. On May 13, as Axis forces gathered opposite the Allied lines, the Allies began to withdraw toward Khartoum. As the Allies withdrew, the Axis forces followed in their wake, usually at night to avoid the pesky Allied air attacks, but having to put up with delaying actions by small Allied forces, mine fields, tank traps and booby traps.

Meanwhile, 250 miles to the East, the British abandoned Port Sudan, the Sudan's only major seaport on the Red Sea. On May 28, an Italian force occupied the city to find its port facilities destroyed and the harbor's channels blocked with sunken ships and mines. The port would be of little value for months to come and, after that, would still be of little value as long as the British Navy controlled the Red Sea.

Then too, the port would have to be heavily defended, in the long term, for fear that the Allies might return, re-capture the port, and march westward to sever the all-important Axis supply and communications artery through the Nile Valley.

THE INVASION OF THE MIDDLE EAST

As the colonial war was raging in East Africa, the other colonial war began in the Middle East. During the first week of May, Axis troops invaded Iraq from two directions; from Trans-Jordan in the west, and from Turkey in the north. The strongest of the two forces, by far, was that in the north.

The Allies were aware of the Axis troop movements through Turkey and for weeks sharp diplomatic notes were received in Ankara from London, Washington and other Allied capitals, protesting Turkey's involvement in the coming invasion. The Turkish government was repeatedly warned that such actions were acts of war and could bring military reprisals against Turkey. Such reprisals would almost certainly come in the form of air attacks. Berlin and Rome hastened to Turkey's aid, promising that German and Italian air defenses would be sent to Turkey to guard against such attacks. This was of little comfort to the Turks, who were well aware of the inadequacies of those air defenses in defending their own territories. During April, the Germans and Italians sent several fighter squadrons and dozens of anti-aircraft batteries to Turkey to help allay Ankara's fears and, of course, to protect their own military activities there.

As for the other neutral nation in the region, Saudi Arabia, diplomatic notes were sent to Riyadh from Berlin and Rome, assuring the Saudis that there territory would not be violated or their political structure threatened.

The Axis plan of conquest in the Middle East was to march down the Tigres and Euphrates River Valleys, where the terrain is flat and desert-like and conducive to mobile warfare. Upon reaching the Persian Gulf, they would then occupy Kuwait and attack eastward into southern Iran to capture Iran's Persian Gulf ports, that nation's primary outlets to the sea. Here again, the terrain in southern Iran favors mobile operations. Beyond that, however, to the north and east, were mountains.

A relatively strong Axis force would be assembled in the southern Caucasus, along the border with Iran, and would make several incursions into northern Iran, forcing the Allies to maintain defensive forces in the area. Here, though, the terrain was mountainous and favored the defenders. No effort would be made by the forces in the Caucasus to penetrate deeply into northern Iran. The Axis planners believed that, as the Iranian ports on the Persian Gulf became threatened, the Allies would abandon northern and central Iran, lest they be cut off. At that point, the Axis forces in the Caucasus would invade Iran and march on the capital, Tehran. Under this plan virtually all of the actual fighting would be done in Iraq.

As the battles in the northern part of Iraq began, they were similar to those taking place in East Africa. The Axis forces, with their superiority in men and tanks, dominated the battle fields while in the air, the RAF and AAF had the advantage.

As was happening in East Africa, the Allied ground forces were steadily beaten back. By May 12, the Axis forces had traversed the 130-mile distance from the Turkish border to Mosul, Iraq's largest city in the north and an important oil center. The Allies put up a stiff fight for the city, but without success. By May 15, Mosul was in Axis hands. On that day, Allied aircraft bombed the Turkish city of Al-Qamishli, the point from which the Axis forces, and now their supplies, entered Iraq. The Turkish government took no action.

As the Allies withdrew from the Mosul area, they torched the oil wells, sending huge black oily clouds of smoke deep into Iran. They also destroyed oil in storage, refineries, pumping stations, and other oil facilities. The Axis leaders had anticipated this, so teams of engineers, technicians, fire-fighters and oil field workers followed closely behind the advancing Axis troops and began working to restore the damage as soon as possible.

In western Iraq, the Allied forces there were more successful. Having entered Iraq from Trans-Jordan on May 6, the Axis forces encountered their first Allied resistance at the road junction town of Al-Rahbah. Here, the Allies were dug in and well-prepared. They were the first to attack and drove the Axis forces back several miles. The Axis forces counterattacked, using their powerful Tiger tanks in the lead, and succeeded in driving the Allies back to their original defenses. For the moment, though, the Axis invasion from the west was stalled.

It was altogether different in the north. There, the Allies were in steady retreat from Mosul. Allied defenses failed at Ash-Sharqat and Tikrit, but held at Balad, fifty miles north of Baghdad, primarily because the Axis forces were exhausted and needed time to bring up reinforcements and supplies. It was now the 22nd of May, 1944.

Next door in Iran, Lend-Lease was still flowing to the Soviet forces east of the Urals, but had slowed considerably because of the difficulty of transporting it across the primitive roads of Turkestan. Also, much of the Lend-lease was now going to the Allies in Iraq and Iran and a trickle was being sent to Astrakhan, where Soviet forces were still holding out.

"OPERATION EASTER BUNNY"

In western North Africa, there was a new development in the war. The Allies had instigated a large-scale and masterful deception plan called "Operation Easter Bunny." It was designed to make the Axis leaders believe that preparations for a major amphibious operation was underway to strike at some undisclosed location in the western Mediterranean. To this end, large numbers of landing craft had been sent to the various Allied-controlled ports in Morocco and Algeria from both Britain and the United States. Allied warships and transports also gathered in sizeable numbers. A campaign of deliberate misinformation was instigated, indicating that the Allies were about to strike at one or more of the vulnerable Axis-held areas in the region. Sicily, Corsica, Sardinia, eastern Libya and southern France were frequently mentioned. Other measures taken to substantiate the deception consisted of conducting air reconnaissance over possible landing sites, the dropping of leaflets, warnings to the civilian populations, false documents deliberately placed where they would be found, etc.

In reality, the Allies had no plans for such an undertaking. The operation was designed solely to keep the Axis leaders off guard and obligate them to keep forces in the threatened areas.

Also in the western Mediterranean, the Allies were having another success. Ultra had reached the point whereby the people at Bletchley Park were reading every radio signal sent by the Italian Navy. This gave the Allies vital information on Axis convoys and on the success of Operation Easter Bunny.

TOWARD AN ATOMIC BOMB

By mid-May, the decision had been made by Heisenberg, and approved by Hitler, to build a huge uranium separation facility at a remote site twenty-five miles southeast of the Ukrainian city of Cherson on the Dnieper River. The site would be just inside the boundary of the mainland portion of the future German-owned Crimea. The facility, to be known as the "Eastern Engineering Facility," would be top secret, cordoned off from all outsiders, out of range of Allied bombers, and guarded by the SS. Available to the site would be large supplies of water and hydro-electric power from the Dnieper River.

With this decision made, construction of the facilities began in early June with the highest priorities and the greatest speed.

A location had also been chosen for the plutonium-producing facility. It would be located 700 miles to the northeast at a site forty miles south of the Volga River City of Saratov. This region had been part of the former Soviet-created Volga German Republic and the site of Soviet manufacturing facilities making poison gas. The facility, known as the "Spartan Works," was on a rail line and had access to water and hydro-electric power from the Volga River. In the event of a nuclear accident, which was always a concern because of the nature of this operation, any radioactive clouds created would drift on the prevailing winds into the desert areas of Turkestan.

Heisenberg also decided that some of the large reactors to be built at the site would use heavy water, while others would use carbon blocks. The heavy water reactors would be preferred as long as a supply of heavy water was available from Norway. ☑ Walter Gerlach, Goering's liaison officer with the Heisenberg group, had estimated that large reactors could not be put into operation until mid 1945. Gerlach had also told German naval commanders that it might be possible to power submarines with nuclear energy.

🔊 Like the Eastern Engineering Site, the Spartan Works would be top secret, inaccessible to outsiders, beyond Allied bomber range, and protected by the SS. Construction began in mid-June. ☑

Back in Germany, the Allies carried out several aerial photo reconnaissance flights over the Joachimstahl uranium mine. Some of the American aircraft were equipped with "scrubbers," a detection device that could sense xenon 133 gas in the air which was a by-product of uranium processing. The Allies were still very concerned about Germany's atomic bomb program and thought that the Germans might have a uranium processing facility near the mine. No such facility was detected.

Now that the war was dragging out, Hitler had come to believe that an atomic bomb might be possible before the end of hostilities. In early August, he told Antonescu of Romania that Germany would soon have a new weapon that would destroy all life in a two- to two-and-a-half mile radius.

In the United States, General George C. Marshall was informed by General Groves of the Manhattan Project that the first American atomic bomb would be ready by August 1, 1945. He had also been warned that the Germans might be capable of deploying bombs or rockets that could spread radiological agents over a wide area. In later years, this became known as a "dirty bomb."

DEVELOPMENTS IN THE AIR WAR

By the spring of 1944, both sides had made considerable technical progress in the air.

During April, the German Me-262 jet fighter-bomber was used for the first time in action. The targets were Allied reconnaissance planes. The Me-262 was still in development and there were problems with engine life, fuel consumption and the landing gear. The most pressing problem was engine life, which was only ten hours. Also during April, the Allies began using a more powerful bomb, the 5,000 ton "Tall Boy." This was the latest in the series of bombs the Allies called "blockbusters."

Available now to the Allies were long-range Mustang P-51 fighters that could accompany bombers deep into Axis territory.

And, most notable of all, was the ability of the Allies to produce aircraft in very large numbers. At this point in time, the Allies outnumbered the Luftwaffe ten to one in the skies over Europe.

At the Berghof, smoke-producing equipment was installed to protect Hitler's mountain home from Allied bombers.

In June, production began on the German AR-234 jet bomber.

On June 14, American B-29 bombers, flying from China, bombed Japan for the first time. Within a month, they would also be flying from the recently-conquered twin islands of Saipan and Tinian.

JAPANESE INVASION OF INDIA FAILS

On June 10, 1944, Japanese forces began to withdraw from eastern India into Burma. Their months-long attempt to invade that country had failed. And the sad state of the Japanese Army also became apparent. They had only three divisions available for the campaign.

The prospect of the Axis establishing a land route from the Middle East to Southeast Asia was now dead.

V-1

On June 12, 1944, the first un-manned, 400 mph, V-1 guided missile was launched against London from a launching pad near the English Channel. Nine more followed. This started a new phase of the war. On the 15th, a second batch of V-1s was launched and for the next twenty-four hours intermittent attacks were carried out. A total of 244 V-1s were launched from 55 sites during June 15-16. Because of the unique sound of the V-1s pulse-jet engine, the British quickly labelled them "Buzzbombs." There was high hope in Germany that the V-1s would hasten the end of the war.

In Britain, because of the Allied fear that the Germans might have atomic weapons, the craters and debris from the V-1s were checked for radiological agents. No traces of radioactivity were found.

By June 29, 2,000 V-1s had been launched, most of them against London.

The British defended themselves first with anti-aircraft guns, and then with souped-up fighter planes capable of overtaking the V-1s and shooting them down. Once a fighter plane got to within machinegun range, the V-1s were relatively easy to shoot down.

Then, in July, the first British jet fighter, the "Meteor," came on line. This aircraft was much faster than the modified propeller-driven aircraft, and its first assignment was to shoot down V-1s. The weapon that Hitler hoped would win the war for him became of little value.

A QUESTION OF EMPIRE

🔊 In the halls of the British Parliament, there was rising dissention toward the course of the war in which Britain was paying an ever higher price to hold on to its empire. Leading the charge were ☑ members of the Labour Party who had, for a decade or more, advocated fundamental changes within the British Empire. It was the opinion of the Labourite leaders that Britain should give up its role of being a colonial master, and take on the role of being a partner. This meant having fewer colonies and more Commonwealth members. And, the Labourites argued, let those people who wanted to leave the empire do so, but let them leave as friends. 🔊 With the war going badly in the Middle East and East Africa, this argument gained support.

Therefore, in this atmosphere of rising political dissention, Churchill and his aides decided to cut their losses. They would abandon the Middle East, ☑ a land where their presence had long been resented and whose maintenance had been a constant drain on the British treasury. 🔊 Those supporting this decision consoled each other by saying that it would be Britain's gain by turning the problems in Iraq and Iran over to the Italians. Furthermore, they lamented, the oil in Iraq and Iran was no longer a deciding factor, with the Axis Powers having conquered the Caucasus and the oil fields of Mosul. One of the most painful aspects of this decision was, however, that friendly Kuwait its oil, and its people would be thrown to the wolves. But, there would still be British oil in Bahrain and other parts of the Empire, and American oil in Saudi Arabia.

Therefore, top secret orders went down the line — abandon the Middle East!

IN IRAQ AND IRAN

In Iraq, the Allied forces began a fighting withdrawal toward Baghdad from both the north and west, and in Iran, the Allies began a gradual pullback from the Caucasus border. Delivery of the Lend-Lease in the pipeline to the Soviets was accelerated so that as much of it could reach the Soviets as possible before the supply routes were closed.

At the Iranian and Iraqi seaports, Allied ships began arriving empty instead of being loaded with Lend-Lease goods. The empty ships were soon loaded with evacuees and material assets that could be carted away.

The Axis leaders soon discovered what was happening and rightfully deduced that the British would abandon the Middle East. With this, there was elation in both Berlin and Rome — especially Rome. ▣

DE GAULLE MOVES UP

On June 3, 1944, the French Committee of National Liberation in Algiers announced that it now considered itself the Provisional Government of France. This move was viewed with apprehension in London and Washington — especially Washington.

WITHDRAWAL IN EAST AFRICA

🔊 On June 6, the Allies began their withdrawal from Khartoum. It was declared an open city and Axis forces quickly moved in, keeping looting and other mayhem to a minimum.

In Rome, Mussolini hoped to make another triumphal entry, but was talked out of it by his aides. They did not want to see Rome bombed again, and they feared for Il Duce's safety.

Having abandoned Khartoum, the bulk of the Allied force moved down the Blue Nile River Valley 120 miles to the Sudanese town of Wad Madani. A smaller force withdrew down the White Nile.

From Rome came the announcement that the Anglo-Egyptian Sudan, administered jointly between Britain and Egypt, would now become the Italian-Egyptian Sudan and be administered in a similar manner between Italy and Egypt. Rome also announced that when the three East African colonies of Eritrea, Ethiopia and Italian Somaliland were recovered, the Italian Empire in Africa would be one contiguous territory from Libya to Italian Somaliland.

BAGHDAD FALLS, TEHRAN THREATENED

During the last days of June 1944, the Allies abandoned Baghdad and continued their withdrawal down the Tigres and Euphrates River Valleys toward the Persian Gulf.

On July 1, Rashid Ali el-Gailani entered the city in triumph and proclaimed that he was, once again, Premier of Iraq. He also proclaimed that the state of war that had been declared against Britain in May 1941 was still in effect. Two days later the RAF bombed Baghdad, targeting the presidential palace and other government buildings. Additional air raids on Baghdad followed. The Iranian leaders in Tblisi and the Turkish leaders in Ankara took note.

In neighboring Iran, the Allied forces, accompanied by remnants of the Soviet forces from the Caucasus, withdrew to the city of Qazvin, 100 miles northwest of Tehran. There, they intended to hold the line while the last deliveries of Lend-Lease were dispatched to the Soviets.

In Kuwait, the government of Sheik Ahmad Ibn-Jabir as-Subah had been informed by the British of their decision to leave the country, and that Britain would do all in its power to aid those Kuwaitis who wished to leave. Places would be found for them in Bahrain, Oman, Aden and other parts of the British Empire. An agreement was reached with Saudi Arabia for Kuwaitis to go there if they wished.

The British abandonment of a friendly colony such as Kuwait had negative repercussions throughout the British Empire and in London. ▣ Earlier in the war the British had been accused of abandoning Hong Kong, Malaya, Burma and Borneo. Britain's — and Churchill's — colonial policy was deteriorating.

To add to these woes, the German Army had grown to 308 active divisions plus 41 replacement and reserve divisions. Unquestionably, it was the largest army in the world.

THE DJIBOUTI REDOUBT – THE DEFENSE OF KENYA

On July 3, the decision was made in London to give up most of Italian East Africa to the enemy and establish a strong and permanent defensive position around the colony of French Somaliland, often referred to as "Djibouti" after the name of its capital and principle seaport. The seaport of Djibouti is on the bab el-Mandeb Strait, the southern entrance to the Red Sea, and was the most important seaport in the region. With the fortified British-controlled island of Perim in the Strait, and the British colony of Aden on the eastern shore, the Allies would have total control of this entrance to the Red Sea and be able to keep the Italian Navy out of the Indian Ocean. Also, a permanent Allied military presence at Djibouti would be a continual threat to the adjoining Italian colonies.

There is a modern historical precedent for such a redoubt, for in the years 1874-1884, the Egyptians held out in this region in a war with the British.

The "Djibouti Redoubt," as it became known, would have a circular perimeter of about a 100-mile radius around the city of Djibouti. The perimeter began in the north on the shore of the Red Sea, just above the seaport of Assab, Eritrea, ran to the southwest to a series of lakes and marshes, which would become a part of the defenses, and then led off in a southeasterly direction, encompassing part of Ethiopia and cutting the vital Djibouti-to-Addis Ababa Railroad, Ethiopia's only outlet to the sea. From there, the redoubt perimeter would run to the town of Abdul Ghadir in British Somaliland, and then turn in a northeastwardly direction to the Gulf of Aden.

Another part of the British plan for East Africa was to use all available forces to de-

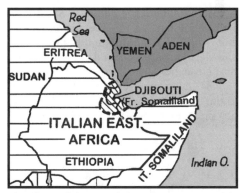

The Allies withdrew to a defensive position around the seaport of Djibouti in order to maintain a presence in the Italian East African region and to retain control of the southern entrance to the Red Sea. This became known as the Djibouti Redoubt.

fend the crown colony of Kenya bordering Italian East Africa on the south. Kenya was one of the jewels of the British Empire. Strongly defending it would also help to improve London's tarnished image with regard to defending its empire.

A third part of the plan was to provide arms, training and communications equipment to the Ethiopian guerrillas who could be expected to accumulate in Ethiopia's western mountains, as they had done following the Italian conquest of 1936. And in Italian Somaliland, there were a number of unruly and independent clans that could be recruited as Allies and supplied with arms and communications equipment. There was also an underground independence movement in Eritrea. It too, would be supported. By aiding these subversive elements, many Italian troops would be tied down in East Africa for a long time.

Throughout the remainder of July and into August, the Allies carried out these plans and, all the while, conducted a fighting retreat to the Kenya defense line. These tactics proved costly to the Axis forces because of the mountainous terrain of Ethiopia that gave the Allies the added advantage of conducting ambushes while the Axis forces could make little use of their armor.

By mid-August, the Djibouti Redoubt was well established, as was the Kenya defense line, which ran through southern Ethiopia and western Italian Somaliland just beyond the Kenyan border.

The Ethiopian government of Haile Selassie and its small army withdrew to Djibouti to participate in the defense of the Redoubt. ☑

HITLER'S LAST SPEECH IN PUBLIC

On July 4, 1944, Hitler made a speech to a select audience of military, party and industrial officials. His subject was winning the war, and he spoke at length of the blessings that would befall the German people after victory was won. No one knew it at the time, but this was to be his last public appearance. His deteriorating health was a major factor.

Hitler had aged rapidly during the last year and he undoubtedly knew it. His associates certainly knew it, and it was a frequent topic of conversation behind his back and he now walked, at times, with a cane.

FIRST ME-262 JET FIGHTERS GO INTO ACTION

On July 20, 1944, a new phase of the air war began — one that favored Germany. On this day, nine Me-262 jet fighters went into action against Allied bombers over Europe for the first time. These swift fighters had a big advantage of being able to swoop in on a group of Allied bombers, make their attacks, and escape without the Allied propeller-driven fighters being able to catch up with them. Furthermore, their great speed made it very difficult for the gunners on the bombers to track and fire at them.

The effectiveness of the Me-262s was somewhat slow to materialize, however. The first bomber was not downed until July 26. Although the Me-262 would go on to be an effective weapon, time, and the ever-increasing number of Allied aircraft, would soon reveal that its introduction would have little or no effect on the Allied air campaign over Europe.

On July 25, Allied planes again bombed Linz, Hitler's home town.

CHAPTER 24

ASIA, AFRICA AND SWITZERLAND

In the East, the Germans were following the traditional pattern that other colonial powers had followed in stabilizing their newly-won empires. And the natives were restless — very restless. The Partisans were still strong and the Germans had to recruit evermore easterners to contain them.

Along the armed frontier, hoards of laborers were at work building the necessary facilities and clearing the no-man's-land in front of it. The extension of the armed frontier beyond Berezniki had not yet been determined.

The Luftwaffe had its hands full trying to keep the Soviets in Siberia under control. Intelligence information reported that the Soviets were still capable of making substantial numbers of tanks, artillery pieces and may other weapons.

Romania acquired a large slice of Ukrainian territory known as Transnistria. It also included the important seaport of Odessa.

On August 17, 1944, the Germans and Romanians signed an agreement at Tighina, near Odessa, acknowledging that the land between the Bug and Dniester Rivers would be the new Romanian Province of Transnistria.

ALLIES WITHDRAW FROM THE MIDDLE EAST

In the Middle East, the Allies had given up Baghdad and Tehran. At Tehran the remnants of the Soviet forces from the Caucasus parted company with the British and withdrew eastward into Turkestan. The bulk of the Indian forces, and some of the British forces, withdrew into southeastern Iran. There they established a defense line to protect India 300 miles to the southeast. The defense line extended from the port of Bandar Abbas on the northern shore of the Strait of Hormuz, northeastward to Kerman, the largest city in southeastern Iran, and then eastward to the Afghan border. By defending this line, the Allies would retain control of about 20% of the country as well as the northern shore of the Strait of Hormuz, the narrow entrance into the Persian Gulf. This defense line was called the "Kerman Line."

The British also retained control of the large island of Jazireh Qeshm which parallels the northern shore of the Strait. The British already controlled the southern shore which was a part of the Arabian Peninsula.

This was not the first time the British had defended the Kerman Line. From 1907 to 1921, during a period in which Britain and Russia were contesting the control of Persia (Iran), the British manned this same line for the same purpose.

🔊 Leaving Tehran with the Allies were members of the Iranian government which fled to Bahrain. ☑ That government was headed by twenty-four year old Shah Muhammed Reza Pahlavi who, in September 1941, inherited the throne from his father, Reza Shah Pahlavi who was forced to abdicate by the Allies for his pro-Axis policies. Reza Shah was taken to the British-controlled island of Mauritius in the Indian Ocean where he was kept under close scrutiny. 🔊 He was still there, so the throne of Iran was vacant. Knowing this would happen, the Axis leaders had agreed that Iran would be run by an Italian military government until a suitable regent could be found and Iran's political future determined.

With the departure of the Allies from Tehran, the city's economy fell into sudden recession. ☑ Heretofore, it had been a boom town because of the Allied Lend-Lease activities. 🔊 Now the Italians had a large number of unemployed Iranians on their hands.

AFGHANISTAN

With the pull out of the Allies from northern Iran, Afghanistan was now threatened. ☑ Afghanistan was neutral, very poor, underdeveloped, and had an economy dependent, in many ways, on trade with India. 🔊 The Allies thought it very unlikely that the Axis Powers would invade Afghanistan, but felt the need to defend Afghanistan's western border as a security measure.

The Afghan government in Kabul agreed to this, so the British sent a small force to the Iran-Afghanistan border near the border town of Islam. ☑ There, the only modern road from Iran entered Afghanistan. The remainder of the 400-mile long Iranian/Afghan border was mountainous and primitive.

🔊 In their assumptions about Axis intentions, the Allies were right. ☑ The

Axis Powers had no intention of invading Afghanistan. Furthermore, Afghanistan fell within Japan's sphere of influence according to previous agreements.

"DUNKIRK MENTALITY"

🔊 As tens of thousands of people streamed out of Iran, Iraq and Kuwait to the waiting ships at Basra, Adaban and Khorramshar, the peace activists in London lamented the fact that Britain was undertaking yet another massive evacuation. Churchill's opponents increased their criticism of his government's policies and stated that the Prime Minister was now pursuing the war with a "Dunkirk mentality."

NEW BATTLE LINES IN EAST AFRICA

By early August, the new battle lines had been drawn in East Africa around the Djibouti Redoubt and along the Kenyan border.

With regard to the former, Hitler had informed Mussolini that it would be Italy's responsibility to contain and eventually eliminate the Redoubt. The German forces would be needed in the drive south to regain the lost German colonies.

Also, with the war winding down in the Middle East, the Germans now gave their forces in East Africa top priorities over the other fronts. As a result, thousands of German armored vehicles, including dozens of Tiger tanks, began rolling through the Nile Valley. These long winding convoys became prime targets for the Allied air forces which still dominated the East African skies. About 15% of those vehicles never made it to their destinations. The Germans were becoming painfully aware that maintaining far flung battle fields was a costly affair in the face of the Allies' superior air strength.

CONQUEST OF THE MIDDLE EAST COMPLETED — OR NEARLY SO

By the third week of August 1944, the massive evacuation of Allied forces from Iran, Iraq and Kuwait was nearing an end. As the Allies withdrew they torched the oil fields and destroyed rail lines, bridges, power stations, port facilities and many other things of value to the Axis. As the Axis forces entered the Persian Gulf ports, they found destruction in all directions, looting, anarchy, and large numbers of unemployed men. In the sky, the sun was blotted out by the black smoke coming from the oil fires.

In southeastern Iran, the Allies had established their defense line on either side of the city of Kerman, but the Axis troops had not followed. They were sorely needed to secure the Persian Gulf ports. Furthermore, Hitler had informed Mussolini that he could not count on German help to overcome the Kerman Line since Germany had no interests in India or Afghanistan. The Kerman Line would be Italy's responsibility.

Also, there was a problem with regard to Kuwait. The Iraqis had long laid claim to this oil-rich country and now had high hopes of attaining that goal. But the Italians were not about to relinquish such a valuable asset so easily. Kuwait had been a very profitable protectorate under the British and it could now be the same under the Italians. There was one big "if," however, that being if Kuwait could regain its world-wide oil market, the country's main source of revenue. With the Allies in control of the Persian Gulf, that trade avenue was closed and would remain so until peace returned. In the meantime, Kuwait became a nation in recession.

Having evacuated the northern shore of the Persian Gulf, another part of the Allied plan went into effect. Using their air superiority, these areas now became subject to constant air attacks. All military targets, including the service crews trying to extinguish the oil fires, became fair game for bombings and low-flying strafing attacks. It was the intent of the Allies to keep this area of the Middle East in turmoil for as long as possible. Furthermore, the Axis occupiers had to contend with the constant threat that the Allies, with their amphibious capabilities on Bahrain, might return at any time. The Axis leaders, especially the Italians, would have to keep large numbers of troops in the Persian Gulf region for a long time to come. Mussolini, the

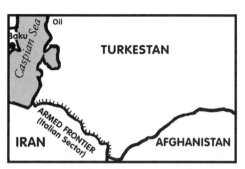

To protect the Middle East from a possible Soviet incursion, an extension of the armed frontier had to be established along the border between Italian-controlled Iran and Soviet-controlled Turkestan. Defending this sector of the armed frontier was the responsibility of the Italians.

Protector of Islam, would be called upon to live up to that title.

In northern Iran, the retreating Soviets crossed the mountainous Iran-Soviet border into Turkestan and the Axis forces pursuing them halted. The Axis leaders had no intention of invading Turkestan at this time. As a result, another section of the eastern armed frontier was created. It ran for some 400 miles between the Caspian Sea and the Afghan border and would be guarded by the Italians.

ONE IN SEVEN

By fall 1944, there were some ten million of Germany's nearly seventy million people in the country's armed forces — one in seven. If taken by gender, it meant one in every 3.5 German men. Clearly, Germany had reached the limits of its manpower. The workers in the factories were now mainly women, foreigners or slave laborers.

Of the ten million men in service, less than one million were in the Luftwaffe and German Navy. This showed the relative importance the German leaders put in their ground forces over their air and sea forces.

It was no wonder, then, that the German Army was racking up one victory after another while the Luftwaffe and German Navy were struggling to survive.

THE STRUGGLING GERMAN NAVY

Admiral Doenitz had very little to be happy about with regard to the German Navy. And he grasped at straws. He was now entering comments in his war diary to the effect that the German Navy was successfully tying down large numbers of Allied ships and planes. Gone were the days when he wrote of starving Britain into submission and keeping the Americans bottled up in North America.

Nevertheless, on the drawing board at the German Admiralty were designs of new submarines that could travel faster underwater. This was purely a defensive move so that the submarines could run faster from their pursuers. Something had to be done, however, because during August 1944, thirty-nine more submarines were lost. By now, all German submarines were equipped with snorkels, but the Allies had developed a short wave radar that could detect even the small head of the snorkel when in use. The German submarines were no longer invisible under water.

The German propagandists, though, were winning the war at sea. They told the German people that the Allies were suffering very heavy shipping losses and that they were finding it difficult to get crews for their merchant ships because the duty was so dangerous.

THE PEACE MOVEMENT ON THE AXIS SIDE

🔊 The Allies did not have a monopoly on peace movements. There were those in the Axis camps who also urged an end to hostilities. They were mainly the lesser Axis allies, most of whom had attained their war aims and now feared the ever-increasing strength of the Allies.

At Hitler's headquarters, these pleas fell on deaf ears. His thinking was that it was Germany who made it possible for the lesser allies to attain their goals, now it was their duty to stand by Germany while she attained hers.

There were also signs that the German people were weakening in their resolve, but no organized peace movements emerged under the watchful eyes of the SS. Hitler, however, knew what was happening. 🖋 He had written of World War I in Mein Kampf that after about a year-and-a-half, the people began to weaken. Specifically, he wrote of the winter of 1915–16 saying, "Horror took the place of the romance of fighting. Enthusiasm gradually cooled off and the glorious exuberance was drowned in the agony of death." 🔊 In this war, the year-and-a-half was almost four years ago.

THE BATTLE FOR KENYA

By late August 1944, the battle lines at Kenya were drawn. They stretched from Lake Rudolph, in northwest Kenya, to the Indian Ocean, a distance of some 700 miles. Long sections of the defense line crossed flat dry terrain ideal for armored warfare which, as always, favored the Germans.

Nevertheless, the Allies had staked everything on defending this line. There were troops from Britain, South Africa, Australia, New Zealand, India and numerous colonial troops. Militias had been formed of white settlers and Jewish refugees from the various refugee camps in East Africa. The Americans had sent in additional air support and the RAF and SAAF were at maximum strength. The great fear for the Allies was, as usual, the Blitzkrieg. They still had no effective way of stopping it. Multi-trench defenses were built at the most likely points of attack, but the line was so long that not all locations could be protected in this manner.

On the Axis side, the opposing forces now consisted mainly of Germans. The Italians were deeply engaged in containing the Djibouti Redoubt and in securing their recovered colonies. Their absence was made up, to a great degree, by reinforcements coming from Europe and from the East. Many of these men had suffered through the terrible Russian winters, and now they were expected to perform to their utmost in equatorial Africa.

On September 1, the Germans launched their attack. There were two diversionary attacks, one along the eastern shore of Lake Rudolph, and the other at the border town of Moyale ☑ where the only modern road crossed into Kenya from Ethiopia. 🔊 **The main thrust came a few hours later, seventy-five miles to the east at the village of Huwun, where the terrain is relatively hilly but still conducive to armored operations. And there were no anti-Blitzkrieg defenses at that location. The German thrust consisted of a heavy Blitzkrieg attack using some thirty Tiger tanks and most of the available Luftwaffe strength. It was unstoppable. The German forces broke through the British line and by dusk German tanks were driving westward, across open terrain, rolling up the British defense.**

The next day, September 2, those Axis forces did not resume the attack — much to the surprise of the British. Rather, the German force that had carried out the diversionary attack at Moyale launched a Blitzkrieg of its own and quickly captured the border town. The British defense of Kenya had failed. Now a race was on for Nairobi, 350 miles to the south. ☑ Nairobi is the capital of Kenya and in the temperate Kenyan highlands. It was the largest city in British East Africa, and the hub of all commercial and economic activities. 🔊 **If Nairobi fell, it would be very difficult for the British to defend the rest of Kenya and their colony of Uganda to the west. The door would also be open for a German drive into the former German colony of Tanganyika, which adjoined Kenya on the south.**

The withdrawal to Nairobi was typical of those through Egypt and the Sudan. Allied aircraft dominated the skies during the daylight hours, their ground troops carried out delaying tactics, and the Germans travelled at night. The Germans took their losses, but were gaining territory — their main objective.

The next Allied defense line was drawn north of Nairobi. ☑ All roads leading into the city pass through mountainous terrain in ascending the Kenyan highlands. 🔊 **It was along these roads that the British were preparing their defenses.** ☑

ENTER THE V-2

On September 8, 1944, the first German V-2 rockets fell on London. This was the culmination of years of efforts by Dr. Werner von Braun and his associates to produce giant, high altitude rockets, against which there was no defense. Unlike the V-1, which was launched from a ramp and flew like an airplane, the V-2 was fired vertically from almost any hard surface, reached a great height, flamed out and then fell to earth silently giving no warning. It carried a bomb load equal to seventeen B-17 bombers. V-2s had been in production at a huge underground facility near Nordhausen, Germany since January and by the end of August there were over 1,600 in inventory.

There were still a lot of technical flaws in the rocket, however. Many failed to launch properly, and their accuracy was poor. But Hitler gave the order to deploy them. Finally, he believed, he had a weapon that could bring the British to their knees. He awarded von Braun a high decoration and issued an order to increase production to 900 per month. By comparison, V-1 production was currently 3,400 per month. With both V-1s and V-2s striking Britain, Hitler hoped that Britain's will to fight on might crack.

AT NAIROBI

🔊 **At Nairobi, the British had established strong defenses on every road leading into the city. No matter from which direction the Germans attacked, they would have a tough fight on their hands.**

But Nairobi had an Achilles heel. That was the road coming in from Mombasa, Kenya's major sea port on the Indian Ocean. This was the main supply route for all of the British forces in East Africa. ☑ From Mombasa, a modern transportation corridor, consisting of a modern highway and a rail line, ran through the heart of British East Africa to Nairobi and on to Kampala, the capital of Uganda. 🔊 **If this route could be cut, Nairobi, the western part of Kenya, and all of Uganda would be in jeopardy.**

The British had seen this, of course, and extended their forces out from Nairobi to the east as far as possible, but it was not enough. Once again, numbers won the day. On Sep-

tember 10, the Axis forces made their move. It was not against Nairobi, but an advance eastward across the flat terrain of the Yatta Plateau which paralleled the transportation corridor on the north for some 200 miles. A small British force had tried to stop the advance, but was quickly pushed aside. The German tanks and motorized infantry units then charged along the plateau from which they could turn south and cut the corridor at any one of several locations. The point they chose was the village of Mtito Andei, about half the distance to Mombasa. The Axis forces paused, formed up into a Blitzkrieg formation and smashed into the British defenders. By September 14, they were across the corridor. Nairobi and points west were cut off. Thus began yet another British withdrawal, this time into Tanganyika.

The Germans occupied Nairobi without opposition as the British troops departed to the south. The road westward to Kampala, Uganda was left open because troops trapped in Uganda would have no way out. 🖾 Uganda is bordered on the south by Lake Victoria, on the west by the jungles of the Belgian Congo, and on the north by the Sahara Desert.

🕮 In the halls of Parliament, in London, there were cries of anguish once again. Some prominent members of the Labour Party were now saying the unthinkable; that being, to get out of the war and save what could be saved of the British Empire. An echo on the same theme was heard from some of the Commonwealth nations, especially from South Africa, which was now in the path of the advancing Germans.

AND A SURPRISE FOR THE AMERICANS

At this time, the German leadership took the opportunity to allow several carefully-placed news leaks to be released, stating that the German Navy was developing submarines that could launch V-1 rockets at sea with the prime targets being cities in the Western Hemisphere. 🖾 In reality, the Germans had been experimenting with launching V-1s, and even V-2s, from submarines for several years, but with little success.

"OVEREXCITED"

On the night of September 23-24, Hitler was suffering stomach spasms again. Dr. Morell diagnosed the problem as being "overexcited" and gave the Fuehrer a sedative.

On the 26th, Hitler was still ill and had a yellowish complexion. Morell became very secretive at this point, but others could see that the Fuehrer had jaundice. At one point he fainted. Hitler took to his bed and little was seen of him until October 2 when he resumed his normal schedule. Hitler remained weak, though, and napped whenever he had the opportunity. On top of all this, several of his teeth were giving him problems — again. All his adult life, Hitler had had trouble with his teeth. By now, he had only four upper teeth left and ten lower. The gaps were filled with bridges.

During his illness, the Fuehrer lost thirteen pounds and told several people that he believed he had only two or three more years to live.

TANGANYIKA AND A NATIONAL HOLIDAY

🕮 On October 5, the German forces moved out of Nairobi, Kenya, continuing their march to the south. British resistance again consisted of delaying actions and air strikes. On the 7th, lead elements of the German forces entered Tanganyika. This was a cause for great celebration in Germany. Hitler declared a national holiday and awarded decorations and cash bonuses to the commanders in the field. He also gave a brief address over German radio, saying that the recovery of Germany's colonial empire had begun. The German newspapers displayed photographs of German troops in Tanganyika with Mount Kilimanjaro in the background. 🖾 Mount Kilimanjaro had long been a symbol of Germany's colonial power because it was the empire's only permanently snow-capped mountain.

🕮 The German force that entered Tanganyika, though, was weaker than that which had entered Kenya. After capturing Nairobi, the German forces were split into three components; one being sent to the east to capture Mombasa, a second moved westward into Uganda, and the third force entered Tanganyika.

The British forces, too, were weaker because a portion of those forces went to defend Mombasa. It was now a weak German force against a weaker British force, but the Germans still had the superiority of numbers.

The British planned their next stand at the town of Dodoma, 250 miles south of the Kenyan border. Dodoma is a junction town where the only serviceable road leading south out of Kenya connects with Tanganyika's main east-west transportation corridor, which is similar to that in Kenya. This corridor runs from the colony's capital and major seaport of Dar es Salaam on the coast into the western interior of the colony. Along this route lived most of Tanganyika's white settlers, many of whom were Germans.

Using Dodoma as their center, the British spread their forces along the corridor to the east and west as they had done at Nairobi, but the terrain was flat and grassy at most locations and, once again, favored the Germans.

In London, there was some heated discussion on whether or not to defend Tanganyika at all. But the pressures to do so won out. These pressures came from South Africa, Washington, the Belgian government-in-exile in London who feared for their colony of the Belgian Congo, and from die-hards all over the Empire. The Americans and Belgians shared the same concern — retaining control of the Belgian Congo. If the Axis forces reached Tanganyika's eastern border with Northern Rhodesia, they would be within striking distance of the "Copper Belt" area of southern Belgian Congo and Northern Rhodesia. This was one of the richest mineral areas in the world. For the Belgians in London, it was their main power base in Africa and their main source of tax revenues. For the Americans, it was a major source of raw materials for their war effort, and for the war efforts of other Allied nations. Furthermore, at the northern end of the Copper Belt is the Shinkolobwe uranium mine, the main source for uranium ore for the Manhattan Project.

Another American concern was that if the Germans were able to capture the Copper Belt, they might then take all of the Belgian Congo, which had long been stated as one of their war aims. And, having acquired the Belgian Congo, the Germans would be in a position to establish military bases on the Atlantic coast of central Africa.

THE BATTLE FOR TANGANYIKA

On October 10, the advancing German forces made contact with the British defenses in central Tanganyika. The Germans were now in "friendly" territory. Some of the local German settlers came forward to divulge information on the British defenses, the terrain and other matters of military significance.

Armed with this information, the Germans launched their first attack on October 12 at the village of Manyoni, at the extreme western end of the British line, 110 miles west of Dodoma. The British reacted by sending a part of their mobile reserve force by train and truck to aid in the defense of Manyoni.

That evening, under the cover of darkness, the Germans launched a feint attack at the town of Kongwa, seventy-five miles east of Dodoma. The British reacted again by dispatching more of their reserves from Dodoma to Kongwa.

On the morning of the 13th, the Germans launched their main thrust directly at Dodoma. Such were the tactics that could be achieved by superior numbers.

The British defenses soon gave way and German troops spilled into Dodoma. The British commander and his staff barely escaped capture as their headquarters were overrun.

With their center broken, the British line collapsed and the troops began a wholesale retreat to the south over very primitive roads, trails and across open county.

The Germans did not give pursuit because their forces were spread out and short of supplies and reinforcements. Their supply lines now stretched some 2,000 miles back to Egypt and were under nearly frequent Allied air bombardment. Also, the Germans had to dispatch a force eastward to occupy Dar es

Salaam, which the British were in the process of abandoning.

The British withdrew 300 miles to the town of Makumbaku which is on the road to Northern Rhodesia, the route the Germans were most likely to take.

The Germans won the battle for Tanganyika, but they were soon to discover that they had yet another battle to win — the hearts and minds of the German settlers. These people had been less than sympathetic with National Socialism and had prospered under the free and open stewardship of the British. All that would now change.

AMERICANS TO NORTHERN RHODESIA, BRAZILIANS TO THE BELGIAN CONGO

In Washington the decision was made to send American troops to Northern Rhodesia to help stop the German advance into the Copper Belt and the Belgian Congo. The American public was told that this was an effort to keep the Copper Belt out of the hands of the Germans and to prevent them from reaching the Atlantic coast. Nothing was said about the Shinkolobwe uranium mine.

The Brazilians, who did not want to see German bases on the African Atlantic coast agreed to help. ☑ The Brazilians had several well-trained and well-equipped army divisions ready for deployment in the field. ☒ They were given the task of defending the eastern part of the Belgian Congo, north of the Americans, guarding against a German invasion from Uganda and western Tanganyika. In this area, the terrain consists of dense jungle and a German thrust to the west was unlikely but, nevertheless, it had to be defended. ☑

AMERICANS INVADE THE PHILIPPINES

On October 20, 1944, the Americans invaded the Philippine Islands, striking at the large island of Leyte immediately south of the main island of Luzon. A few days later came reports of a major naval battle in Leyte Gulf where, once again, the American Navy defeated the Japanese Navy. Accompanying the reports were accounts of the Japanese using suicide-piloted aircraft know as "Kamikazes."

This drastic measure was seen in Berlin and Rome as an indication that the Japanese war effort in the Far East was in serious trouble.

☒ News of these events were most disturbing to Hitler and his staff. They showed, beyond a doubt, how overpowering an American amphibious operation could be. This raised the question; what could the European Axis Powers do if faced with a similar situation? ☑

HITLER SICK AGAIN AND ANXIOUS

Hitler was sick again. This time he complained of upper respiratory problems and was concerned about his prostate. He was also very hoarse. For October 27, Dr. Morell recorded in Patient A's medical record, "In bad mood, Voice not good…could not talk to the German people even over a microphone."

Hitler was also very anxious — anxious to see any signs from Britain that the will of the British people was cracking under the bombardment of the V-2 rockets. The British were being hit with between twenty and thirty V-2s a day along with numerous V-1s. But Hitler learned little. The British government had decreed a strict blackout on news on the rocket attacks. Still Hitler was hopeful, convincing himself that the news blackout was Churchill's way of covering up very bad news.

Hitler's hoarseness persisted, and in early November he had an operation on his throat for another singer's node. Hitler had had this kind of operation before, and he would have it yet again. Shortly after this surgery, a second node was discovered which was removed on November 22.

AMERICANS AND BRAZILIANS LAND IN THE CONGO

☒ In early November, American and Brazilian troops landed in the Belgian Congo. As planned, the Americans travelled to the south and into Northern Rhodesia and took up positions along the Tanganyika border. With them, of course, came large compliments of tanks and aircraft both of which were being produced in very large numbers in the USA.

The Brazilians were stationed in the eastern part of the Congo manning a front north and south of Stanlyville.

ASTRAKHAN FALLS

In Russia, the Soviets finally abandoned Astrakhan on the northern shore of the Caspian Sea. The city had been under siege since October 1943. With the Axis conquest of Iran, Allied aid from the south had been cut off and made it impossible for the defenders to hold out. Most of the Soviet troops were evacuated by water to the eastern shore of the Sea which was still under Soviet control.

Since the Caspian Sea was to become a part of Germany's armed frontier, the Germans began building large gunboats at the shipyards scattered along the western and southern shores. Heretofore, the Soviet Navy had controlled the Sea, but that would change.

TIME TO RESTRUCTURE WESTERN EUROPE

For years the Nazi leaders had dreamed of this day — the day when they could restructure western Europe to their liking. The overall plan was extensive. The countries of Switzerland and Belgium must go, a new buffer state must be created between Germany and France, and the Netherlands must be restructured so that one day it would become a very close German ally or, perhaps, an integral part of Germany. Sweden, too, had to be brought into the new order, and the Danes — those stubborn Danes — had to be made to see that their future depended on full cooperation with Germany.

Hitler now had the wherewithal to accomplish these things. He had tens of thousands of experienced troops being freed from the East and the Middle East, and arms production was still good. In addition, the timing was good. These things are best done under the marshal atmosphere of war rather than under the more open conditions of peace time. ☑

FIRST SWITZERLAND

Both Hitler and Mussolini had long wanted to dismantle Switzerland — that tool of capitalism — that haven for spies and Jews — that pious champion of democracy.

One of Hitler's principle interests was that 2.9 million of Switzerland's 4.2 million people were Germans — Germans who should be returned to the Reich. There is a historical precedent for Germany controlling this part of Switzerland, because just before modern Switzerland emerged in the late 1400s, it was part of a Germanic state known as the Confederation of South Germany.

Like Hitler, Mussolini coveted the 200,000-plus Italians in Switzerland and wanted to annex their territory to Italy.

German and Italian leaders had spoken many times in private, and sometimes in public, in threatening terms with regard to Switzerland. On several occasions, Hitler spoke of Switzerland as "the rubbish heap" of Europe, and that Switzerland "...no longer had the right to exist." Goebbels publicly called Switzerland "that stinking little country."

In June 1940, after the defeat of France, the Nazis gave serious consideration to acquiring Switzerland; but then, Germany turned its venom on the Soviet Union in June 1941, and the Swiss were granted a reprieve.

🔊 Now though, Germany and Italy were the masters of all Europe and the question of Switzerland surfaced again. Hitler wanted the takeover of Switzerland to be a peaceful anschluss, as had been the case with Austria in 1938. After all, these future citizens of Germany had to be treated with respect.

But, in all likelihood, the Swiss would fight. The next best option, then, was to conquer the country militarily as fast and bloodlessly as possible.

Before military action was taken, though, diplomacy was tried. In early November, the Germans instigated a series of low-level discussions with the Swiss government, suggesting that Switzerland might one day willingly join in the new European order. The Germans offered to let the Swiss set their own conditions and time table.

This approach failed. The Swiss reply was a firm "no." Word of the talks reached the world press and it became obvious that Germany was about to make a move on Switzerland. This set off a run on the Swiss banks. Within a few days, every airliner flying into Switzerland was packed with individuals intent on retrieving their assets from their secret Swiss bank accounts. There was also a sudden exodus of people, and assets, fleeing Switzerland to the West. Also leaving the country were the leading officials of the League of Nations which was located at Geneva. The League of Nations officials made their way to Lisbon where they established a temporary headquarters.

With military action now a necessity, Hitler ordered the OKW staff to prepare an invasion of Switzerland for no later than November 15. Plans for such action had long been in OKW's files and the planning went rapidly. Soon, German and Italian troops were moving into position for the attack. The Swiss, who had long prepared for such a crisis, mobilized their army. Within two days, the Swiss had half a million men under arms. ◪ Every able-bodied man in Switzerland of military age was a reservist with his own uniform and rifle, and the Swiss plan of defense was no secret. The Swiss Army would fight as best it could on the low lands of the country, and then retreat to an extensive redoubt in the mountains that had been built up over the years. There, the Swiss would continue the struggle even though they were cut off from any hope of aid from the Allies.

♎ While the troops readied themselves, Hitler stopped the flow of assets out of Switzerland. He wanted everything in the country to be his when he made his move. He prevailed upon the Vichy French to close their border and the Spaniards, where many of the commercial flights to and from Switzerland terminated, to halt those flights. Franco and Petain promptly complied, although the French were very slow to act because it was to Vichy's advantage to have those assets flowing into France.

To quell the concerns of the world's financial markets, both the Germans and Italians announced that they would let the unique Swiss banking system continue as usual. Hardly anyone believed them. ◪

Of benefit to the Axis leaders was the fact that the morale of the Swiss people was at a low ebb. All during the war years they had endured shortages of food, fuel, rationing, loss of imports and exports, blackouts, several accidental bombings, and the burden of accommodating hoards of refugees.

Knowing these things, the Axis leaders believed they would find a large body of willing collaborators in the country. In anticipation of this, the Nazis had, several years earlier, formed two pro-German organizations out of Swiss emigres. They were the "National Sozialistische Schweizer Bund," headquartered in Vienna, and the "Bund der Schweizer im Gross-Deutschland," which operated out of Stuttgart. These organizations would be utilized at the time of the invasion. They had already been useful in Germany's propaganda operations and in recruiting Swiss emigres for service in the Waffen SS and other German organizations. In Italy, similar organizations existed and were tools of the Fascist government.

♎ On November 15, the Axis troops invaded Switzerland.

As expected, the Swiss Army put up a spirited, but futile, fight on the lowlands, and then withdrew, en masse, into the mountains. This meant that about one-third of the country's male population had suddenly disappeared.

During the first hours of the invasion, the Swiss were successful in destroying sections of the St. Gotthard and Simplon railroad tunnels, thus cutting off the main trade routes between Germany and Italy.

While the Axis troops came at the point of a gun, they also came waving the olive branch. There were no massive bombings of Swiss cities and other military attacks were carried out as sparingly as possible.

By November 20, two-thirds of the country was under Axis control. The remaining one-third consisted of the great redoubt. Sieges had worked well for the Axis before, and it was believed that this one would succeed also.

On the day Axis troops entered Switzerland, a small German force invaded the tiny principality of Liechtenstein on Switzerland's eastern border. There was no resistance. By noon, the Prince, his family and his government ministers were surrounded in the royal palace. Within a few days, the Prince was offered the opportunity to collaborate with Germany or accept a pension and retire. The Prince, however, delayed giving a response.

Liechtenstein, itself, was to be annexed to Austria and its population, virtually all ethnic Germans, prepared for Nazification and German citizenship. The country would also be made Jew-free.

As for the military situation in Switzerland, both the Germans and Italians wanted the siege to be as bloodless and non-destructive as possible. There would be no gallant charges up the mountain slopes with Germans killing Germans and Italians killing Italians. The Swiss would simply be waited out. Time favored the besiegers.

By December, the Swiss in their redoubt were being inundated with leaflets, loud speaker and radio messages urging them to give up their honorable, but hopeless, fight and acknowledge that the Germans and Italians had come as friends. The soldiers were urged to lay down their weapons — the word surrender was avoided — and promised that they would be treated humanely and quickly paroled if they gave assurances that they would cooperate with the new order. This offer was also made to the French Swiss soldiers, but with the stipulation that they must return to the French part of Switzerland. There were no promises made to the few Jewish Swiss soldiers.

As for the Jews in Switzerland, who were well-integrated into the society, no action was taken against them at this time because it would not be conducive to winning the hearts and minds of the Swiss people.

The Germans further promised the German Swiss soldiers that if their loyalty was confirmed, they could choose to join the German armed forces or become settlers in the East. The Italians made similar offers to the Italian Swiss with regard to settlement in the Middle East and Africa.

In the occupied areas of Switzerland, many collaborators came forth as had been expected. These people were given positions of importance in the military government and the economy. As a further show of cooperation toward the Swiss people, many current

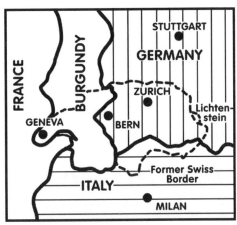

Switzerland was overrun by Axis forces and divided between Germany, Italy and Burgundy. Lichtenstein was taken by Germany.

government officials were allowed to retain their post so long as they cooperated with the occupiers.

The civilian population was given generous allotments of food, fuel, consumer goods, etc., and urged to report this fact to their family members in the mountains. Their letters were air-dropped into the redoubt.

Those who openly resisted the occupiers were, when captured, whisked out of the country to unknown locations. ✓

THE YEAR ENDING 1944

On December 11, 1944, Dr. Morell wrote in Hitler's medical records that the Fuehrer had a slight case of jaundice again and his urine was "beer brown." On the 30th he wrote, "...very strong tremors in left leg, obvious to others."

After a meeting with Hitler, naval Captain Heindrich Assman recorded in his diary, "He is a psychic wreck that moves slowly, slouching, step by step with a shaking head, bent over."

For the year of 1944, German industry had produced over 8,000 tanks. The Americans had produced over 50,000.

CHAPTER 25

EAST AFRICA AND THE LAST MONTHS OF HOSTILITIES IN EUROPE

The border between Tanganyika and Northern Rhodesia is a mountain range 200 miles long with large lakes at either end. 🔊 **It was here that the British and Americans decided to make their stand.** ☑ There is only one pass through the mountains where tank formations could maneuver. The shallow Momba River flows through the pass and at its center is the village of Nakonda.

🔊 **The Americans had sent three armored divisions, three motorized infantry divisions, two AAF wings and other units to the region. Together with the British forces, the manpower on each side was about equal but the Allies had more tanks and planes. For the first time in East Africa, the Allies had the advantage.**

Learning from past experiences, the Allies built five parallel lines of defensive trenches across the Nakonda Pass using the river as part of the defenses. They put numerous artillery pieces on the high ground on either side of the pass and planted large mine fields and other tank and infantry obstacles in the approaches.

By early January 1945, the Germans were assembling opposite these defenses preparing for an attack. But this was now more difficult for them than before because any significant assemblage of men and tanks was almost immediately attacked from the air. Furthermore, the Germans' 2,500-mile supply route from Egypt was still under repeated air attacks and supplies were coming in intermittently.

On January 12, the Germans attacked using their time-tested Blitzkrieg formation but from the beginning the attack was in trouble. The mine fields and aircraft took their tolls and then the artillery in the hills opened fire with all guns sighting on the Tiger tanks. Those tanks that got through this hail of steel were only able to penetrate to the second trench line. Losses were so horrendous that the tanks following turned and ran.

At this point, the Allied tanks, outnumbering the German tanks three to one, counterattacked. The counterattack was swift and penetrating. Two large German supply depots were captured near the towns of Mbalizi and Mbeya along with three field headquarters. For the first time in East Africa, the Germans were in full retreat. For the next three days, the Allied forces mopped up in the area east of the Nakonda Pass and then returned to the Pass with their large cache of prisoners and captured equipment. They then waited for a second attack. It did not come. Hitler turned the problem over to Keitel and the OKW staff and asked them to find a solution. ☑ This was Hitler's way of handling a problem for which he knew there was no solution.

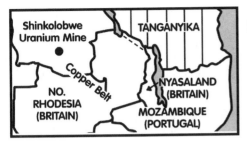

The German advance into Northern Rhodesia and toward the Belgian Congo was stopped at the mountainous border between Northern Rhodesia and Tanganyika.

🔊 Throughout Germany and occupied Europe, though, the defeat at Nakonda Pass was relegated to the inner pages of the newspapers because there was good news with which to make headlines. During this time, German forces were consolidating their hold on Uganda, 750 miles to the north, and had entered the two former German colonies of Rwanda and Urundi. From there, German troops penetrated several dozen miles into the inhospitable jungles of the Belgian Congo to strengthen their claim to that colony.

The German propagandists played these events to the hilt. Here, for the German people to savor, was the conquest of Uganda, the second largest British colony in East Africa, and the liberation of two more German colonies. By occupying Rwanda and Urundi, the Germans had recovered three of their six African colonies.

Those people in Europe, though, who listened secretly to the BBC and the Voice of America, knew that the mighty German Army had been stopped at the border of Northern Rhodesia and, before long, it was common knowledge.

BURGUNDY

Having eliminated Switzerland and acquired some 831,000 French Swiss, it was now logical to proceed with the next step in redrawing the map of western Europe. This would be the creation of a French-speaking, but German-controlled, buffer state between

Germany and France to be called Burgundy. ☑ The country of Burgundy had existed in this general area between the fifth and ninth centuries and served, at that time, as a buffer between the Germans and French. It also was the source of the famous wine that bears its name. The idea of a buffer state was not new. For decades both Germany and France had politically maneuvered for such a state. The French, of course, wanted it built on German soil while the Germans wanted it on French soil. Now the Germans would have their way.

🔊 The new state of Burgundy was assembled out of the Walloon (French speaking) part of Belgium, a slice of northern France, and the former French cantons of Switzerland. Burgundy would eventually have a National Socialist form of government with its capital at Brussels. In the meantime, in learning from the political disaster in Norway and Denmark, it would be a Reichscommissariat until a suitable local leader could be found. Also, the German Army was relieved of its occupation duties in Burgundy and, ☑ as previously planned, the SS took over.

🔊 As for the other part of Belgium, Flanders, it became a separate political entity with its future to be decided later. ☑ This idea, too, was not new. During World War I, the Germans had dismantled Belgium along these lines and considered creating a buffer state at that time. It was for this purpose that Belgium and the areas of northern France in question had remained under German military control ever since their conquest in 1940.

THE NETHERLANDS

🔊 The borders of the Netherlands also underwent a readjustment at this time. The northern province of Friesland was detached from The Netherlands and annexed to Germany. This was done to unite the Frisian people who lived on both sides of the border and were ethnic Germans rather than Hollanders. The Nazi propagandists proudly proclaimed that here was one more group of Germans who had come home to the Reich.

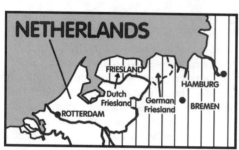

The northern part of the Netherlands was annexed by Germany to make the combined province of Friesland.

There was some consideration given to uniting Flanders and the Netherlands to compensate the Netherlands for the reduction in territory, but this idea was on hold for now.

Burgundy, the Netherlands and Flanders all became Reichscommissariats. ☑

V-1S FROM AIRCRAFT AND SUBMARINES, V-10S TO NEW YORK CITY

There was a mix of good news and bad news with regard to Germany's rocket program. The good news was that V-1s were now being launched successfully from aircraft. This reduced the need to launch them from ramps which were frequent targets of Allied aircraft. The bad news was that the RAF had become very proficient at shooting down the V-1s and less than half were getting through to their targets.

Also, the German Navy had had some success in launching V-1s from submarines, but there were problems. The main problem was that the submarine had to be on the surface of the water and, as a result, bobbed about. Because of this, the accuracy of the missile was poor. Also, submarines were most vulnerable to enemy attacks while on the surface.

No efforts were made to launch V-2s from submarines because they were too heavy and the launching procedure too complicated.

The most exciting news of all for Hitler was that the development of the super-long-range, two-stage, V-10 rockets were progressing well. This rocket was designed to reach North America from Europe. In fact, a target in the United States had already been selected. It was downtown Manhattan.

FEEBLE, BUT STILL FUEHRER

The routine at Hitler's headquarters continued as always. Decision after decision was made, but the man making them was now weak and feeble, and he was shrinking. Comments on this were made by several people who had not seen him in a while. Hitler had been five feet, nine inches, but now he was something less due to the onset of scoliosis. One of his doctors, Dr. Schenck, whom he saw on occasion, noted that Hitler might have Bechterev Syndrome, a slow bending of the spine.

Hitler's handwriting was now a barley legible scribble, and Goering commented

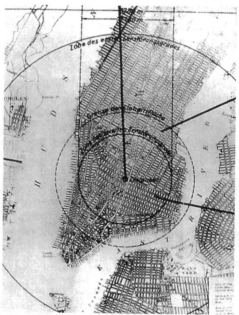

The German rocket scientists hoped that their new two-stage rockets would reach North America. A target had already been chosen; the vicinity of Delancy Street and the Bowery in New York City.

that the Fuehrer would spill food on his shirt and not notice.

Hitler said very little now about Japan and almost nothing about such far away places as Latin America, the Atlantic islands, India…

One topic still very much in his vocabulary, though, was his home town of Linz. He continued to make plans for the day when he would return and convert the city into a city of renown. He told an associate that he had already collected 5,350 objects for the grand museum he would build there.

GERMAN SKIES – STILL ALLIED TERRITORY

The introduction of the Luftwaffe's jets made little difference in the air war. There were simply too few jets and too many bombers. Besides, Allied aircraft were now stalking the airfields from which the jets operated, hoping to catch them when they were the most vulnerable; landing, taking off, taxiing and parked. Despite the deployment of the jets, the Allied planes kept coming in great numbers. On February 2, 1945, 1,200 RAF bombers hit Wiesbaden and Karlsruhr, and the next day another 3,000 tons of bombs were dropped on Berlin. Millions of man-hours were lost in Germany's war industry as workers huddled in shelters during raids. In March, the first Allied jets, the American P-80 "Shooting Star," was coming into service in small numbers, and the British "Vampire" jet was due to be deployed in June. At this time, the Luftwaffe had about 1,400 Me-262s in its inventory.

Also, about one-third of German gun production was now devoted to anti-aircraft guns at the expense of battlefield weapons.

Then there was the highly touted Amerika Bomber that was intended to bomb the USA. Its development had been slowed to a crawl because, with Allied air strength as strong as it was, there was little prospect that these planes could make it all the way across the Atlantic and back without suffering very high losses. Propaganda on the Amerika Bomber continued, though, as strong as ever.

On March 14, the British deployed the first of their latest Blockbuster, the ten-ton "Earthquake" bomb. It was intended to shake the ground so violently that buildings would be destroyed as though they were in an earthquake. Their first target was the viaduct at Bielfeld.

Goebbels recorded in his diary at this time, "The air war has now turned into a crazy orgy… the Reich will be turned into a complete desert."

NORWAY INVADED BY THE AMERICANS

🔊 The Axis invasion of Switzerland **spurred the Allies to action because Sweden could be next. And the Swedes feared this too. Therefore, a series of secret negotiations was instigated between Stockholm and the Allies on ways to protect Sweden. Since Sweden had no Atlantic or Arctic sea coast, it was decided that Norway would be invaded to acquire a route by which Allied aid could be sent to Sweden.** 📝 Several plans for the invasion of Norway had already been prepared by the Allies, and Churchill had long been an advocate of taking such action.

The Germans, too, had plans for Sweden. In 1940, Hitler had planned on invading Sweden along with Denmark and Norway, but Goering and others talked him out of it. Nevertheless, the conquest of Sweden was still on Hitler's agenda and several military plans existed.

The German military position in Norway had, from the time of the invasion in April 1940, been vulnerable. This came about because the Germans had no good supply route to Norway. Sea links across the North Sea became treacherous because that body of water had been heavily mined by both sides and was virtually useless to either. The only significant transportation route the Germans had to Norway was a land corridor that had been granted by the Swedes from Copenhagen, Denmark, along the Swedish west coast to the border with Norway — a distance of over 200 miles. Since the Swedes had said all along that they would fight if attacked, it was obvious that, if attacked, cutting this route would be one of their first objectives. If the Swedes were successful, supplies and reinforcement for the German forces in all of Norway would be cut off, except for those reinforcements and supplies that could reach northern Norway via Finland.

🔊 On February 25, the Allies struck. The naval and air assaults were carried out by both the British and Americans, but the ground operation was to be carried out solely by the Americans. This was because the invaders would eventually reach the border of northern Finland and ☑ the United States was not at war with Finland, but the British were. 🔊 It was thus hoped that Finland could be neutralized. The invasion came at three points in northern Norway where the highly-touted Atlantic Wall did not exist. The hub of the operation was the port city of Narvik ☑ which was the primary seaport for Swedish exports, including Sweden's high-grade iron ore, from northern Sweden. From Narvik, it is only twenty miles to the Swedish border and a modern railroad and highway ran from Narvik into northern Sweden. This was the route that Allied aid to Sweden would take if such aid became necessary.

🔊 The other points invaded were the coastal village of Fauske, ninety miles south of Narvik and Thomso, 100 miles north of Narvik.

Fauske is on the only road leading from the south into Narvik and points north. That road was unimproved and often closed in winter. It would be at Fauske that the Americans would defend against any German attempt to reach Narvik from the south. There were strong German forces in southern Norway, guarding against an invasion there, but they were of little value in defending northern Norway because of the poor overland connections.

Thomso is the capital and largest city in Finnmark, Norway's northernmost province. 🔊 From Thomso, the Americans soon moved east and south with the intention of occupying the entire province of Finnmark and reaching the northern border of Finland.

The American invasion came with overwhelming force and about all the Germans could do was to destroy Narvik's port facilities and retreat. This, though, was inconsequential to the Allies because infantry and tanks were offloaded in large numbers onto beaches and quays from LSIs and LSTs.

It was a terrible time of the year to conduct such operations because of the cold weather and short days, but the Allied and Swedish leaders agreed it had to be done. These hardships slowed the American's advance inland from the coast. On February 28, the Americans reached the Swedish border east of Narvik and were greeted warmly by Swedish civil and military authorities as well as the American military attache from the American embassy in Stockholm.

When the invasion of Norway began, Washington informed the government of Finland that they would not violate Finnish territory, but would not tolerate Finnish territory being used by the Germans in an attempt to defend Finnmark. The Finns, anxious not to cross swords with the Americans, complied.

American ground and air operation in Finnmark proceeded well and by the end of March the province was in American hands. The defending German forces fled into Finland.

For the Germans and Italians, the invasion of Norway demonstrated that virtually many parts of their respective empires were vulnerable to an Allied invasion. Also, in Berlin, any thought of military action against Sweden was now shelved.

American forces did not enter Sweden, but the Narvik area became a major American base of operations. Large numbers of well-equipped troops arrived in the area and new airfields were constructed. From those airfields, and airfields in Britain, all of Norway came within range of Allied aircraft. Furthermore, all of Finland and the Leningrad area of Ostland were now within range of American air power.

The Finns took note of these developments, and had one more reason to pressure Berlin for a quick end to hostilities.

In Oslo, the Quisling regime pleaded with Berlin to oust the Americans from northern Norway, but those pleas went unanswered. Now, what little support Quisling's regime had among the Norwegian people was all but gone.

THE CHANNEL ISLANDS

During the first week of March, while fighting was still going on in Norway, the British launched an amphibious assault on the Channel Islands, which consisted of the major islands of Guernsey, Jersey, Alderney and Sark. These islands, just off the southern coast of Brittany, are an integral part of England, and were occupied by the Germans in 1940. During the next few years, the Germans-built fortifications on the islands but they were not considered a part of the Atlantic Wall.

The British assault began on March 10, with three days of naval and aerial bombardment of the German defenses as well as attacks on military targets on the French mainland which could aid in the defense of the islands. The British Navy quickly gained control of the waters around the islands and the RAF and AAF dominated the skies.

Royal Marines then landed at two locations on Guernsey against strong German opposition. Four days of hard fighting ensued, but the Germans eventually capitulated. Next came Jersey. British Army units landed there at three locations and the Germans put up another spirited defense for five days before surrendering. The islands of Alderney and Sark, which were not strongly defended, were occupied soon afterwards. Hitler had lost another part of his empire.

AMPHIBIOUS OPERATIONS VS THE BLITZKRIEG

With the successful Allied invasions of Norway and the Channel Islands, a pattern had developed. The Allied had the advantage when it came to amphibious operations while the Germans still had the advantage in the ground war with their Blitzkrieg tactics and their huge army.

Furthermore, if and when the Japanese were defeated, the amphibious capabilities of the Allies would double or triple. Hitler and Mussolini were of the same mind — that hostilities in Europe had to end before that occurred.

WOULD SPAIN BE NEXT?

Given the Allied amphibious capabilities, there was concern among the Axis leaders that Spain might be their next target. From northern Spain, Allied troops could advance into southern France, thus skirting the Atlantic Wall. The northern coast of Spain and the Barcelona area, on the Mediterranean, were the most likely points for an invasion.

Indeed, the Allies had generated an ongoing stream of propaganda and misinformation that Spain, or some of the other soft targets in southern Europe, would be invaded. In response to this threat, the Germans had to keep strong mobile forces in southern France while the Italians had to keep forces on the islands of Sicily, Sardinia, Corsica, and on the mainland of Italy itself.

In Spain, the Franco government also had to prepare for such an eventuality. The Spanish plan for defense consisted of the Spanish armed forces offered initial resistance against an invader and then withdrawing to pre-determined defense lines in northern Spain to protect the interior of the county. It was the belief in Madrid that the Allies would not come to conquer all of Spain, but only to seek an avenue into southern France.

HOSTILITIES END IN EAST AFRICA

Because of the Allied amphibious threat, the Germans and Italians had to erect defenses along their now 2,000 mile coast line of East Africa. To do this, they had to use the forces already there because most of their other forces were committed elsewhere. For the Germans, this meant that an advance into Northern Rhodesia and the Belgian Congo had to be postponed indefinitely.

The Italians, like the Germans, now had to commit strong forces guarding their portion of the East African coast line. This made it very doubtful that they, even with the help of the Germans, could gather enough strength to attack and eliminate the Djibouti Redoubt.

These actions brought an end to hostilities in East Africa — except, of course, for the air war. In this regard, the British still controlled the large islands of Zanzibar and Pemba off the coast of Tanganyika. From these safe havens, and from Aden on the southern end of the Arabian Peninsula, Allied bombers could reach almost all of East Africa. Clearly, the Axis Powers were now on the defensive in East Africa. ☑

IT'S TIME TO QUIT

Hitler had aptly described in Mein Kampf how an army and a nation of people eventually wear out in time of war. ☊ That time was fast-approaching for his army and his people. Hitler discussed this with his top aides but, he insisted, there was one more goal that could be accomplished — the advance across North Africa to the Atlantic.

Hitler asked Mussolini to meet with him at the Brenner Pass to discuss these issues. They met on March 12 and Mussolini was in full agreement. Thus, it was decided. There would be one last major offensive to reach the Atlantic and, if all went well, an attempt might be made to advance down the west coast of Africa to take the important seaport of Dakar in French West Africa. Then, with these things done, they would, together, sue for peace.

But, before hostilities ended, there were several other important matters that had to be addressed.

IT DID NOT HAPPEN

"It" would soon have a name — "The Holocaust." ☑

The intention of the Nazi leaders, all along, had been that the deliberate extermination of Jews and other undesireables could not continue into peace time, and that a massive coverup scheme would have to be created to hide the truth. Considerable attention had been given to this by the Nazi leaders.

☊ Now it was time to implement those plans. Hitler ordered that all of the death camps be levelled so that no trace of them remained. ☑ Himmler had already ordered the destruction of one of the death camps in late 1944. The official reason given for the elimination of the camps was that they

had been nothing more than conventional concentration camps and were no longer needed because the majority of Europe's undesirables were now in the East. ☊ The land upon which the camps stood would be turned into agricultural land, industrial sites, parks, nature preserves, etc. A few would be retained as labor camps.

THEY KNOW TOO MUCH

A very special problem existed concerning those individuals who had carried out the mass exterminations. These people, a mix of Germans and foreigners, simply knew too much. They could not possibly be allowed to return to the general population. Instead, they would be transferred to Muscovy where they would continue to practice their unique profession. To encourage them to do this, they would be offered generous pay increases, bonuses, promotions, well-appointed living facilities with servants, and good pensions. Those who were reluctant to accept this offer would be gently coerced to do so. Those who refused altogether would simply disappear.

The Einsatzgruppen killing squads would be disbanded and their war records doctored to show that they had simply been an auxiliary police force. The men would be reorganized into elite anti-Partisan units and given all the perks normally associated with elite soldiers. As with the camp people, they could accept or disappear. There would also be a secret agreement among the Nazi leaders that these units would be used in the hottest spots where high casualties could be expected.

From now on, Jews still being rounded up in Europe would all be sent to conventional concentration camps and processed. Able-bodied individuals capable of working, and others of use to the Reich, were to be sorted out, and the others sent on to Muscovy.

Muscovy had, by now, become a closed area with no one being allowed to enter or leave without permission. In answer to inquiries about this, it would be claimed that the area was too dangerous because of the

Partisan menace, and that the civilian infrastructure of the colony was still in a state of flux. But, it would be maintained, that the general population was being well cared for. This policy would be continued for one or two generations.

Thus, the concentration camps in Europe would eventually be shut down and replaced by one huge camp in the East — Muscovy.

WHERE DID ALL THE JEWS GO?

The Nazis had answers for this question, too. They were numerous and it would be staunchly claimed that the German people would simply not do such things as the enemy propagandists had claimed. It would be stated that the vicious propaganda portraying the Germans as barbarians was an unjustifiable holdover from World War i ☑ when the Allies portrayed the Germans as Huns. ☋ Other excuses to be put forward were that: many Jews had escaped into neutral and Allied countries; many fled into the mountains and forests to hide or become resistance fighters; many were still in hiding; many eastern Jews escaped into Siberia with the Russians; many were killed in Allied air raids ☑ (Jews were not allowed in air raid shelters); ☋ disease and epidemics had claimed some; their birth rate had declined substantially; there was a very high suicide rate; some were killed resisting arrest or in riots and revolts; some died at the hands of other Jews in internal conflicts, power struggles, and fights over resources; some were killed in pogroms carried out by foreigners, especially people such as the Ukrainians, Russians and Belorussians, who had long histories of such behavior; and some were killed by the Partisans in Muscovy who did not want to see their Russian homeland overrun with Jews.

The Germans could also point to the fact that many Jews were still in Germany serving as laborers, and ☑ that the Jewish spouses of German citizens had, for the most part, been left alone, as had their half-Jewish children.

☋ When asked about individuals, the reply would be that little time and effort had been devoted to keeping detailed records.

When asked why the Red Cross and other humanitarian organizations had not been given access to the Jews, the reply would be that some of those services had been rendered. The ☑ show camp of Theresienstadt would be used as an example. ☋ A further explanation would be offered that the humanitarian needs of German civilians and service personnel — suffering greatly from the bombings — were given higher priorities. And on it would go; the lies that would never be believed.

ON TO THE ATLANTIC

The Germans and Italians made every effort to build up their forces in North Africa in preparation for the advance westward. With the Allies becoming stronger by the day, time was a factor. Axis forces were built up in eastern Libya, opposite the El Agheila defenses and in Tunisia. Of the two, the buildup in Tunisia was the more important.

General Rommel, ☑ who had been directing the construction of the Atlantic Wall, ☋ was sent back to Tunisia to direct the offensive.

The Allies soon learned of the buildup and responded in kind.

On March 28, Rommel made his move. In a powerful Blitzkrieg attack, one of the largest ever conducted in Africa, German forces struck southward out of their Tunisian stronghold hitting a segment of the Allied line held by the Fighting French. The Axis tanks broke through and headed due south. Their plan was to reach the Sahara Desert and thereby cut off the Allied troops at El Agheila.

Rommel's breakout of the Tunisian perimeter and the threat to the Allied position in Libya could not be denied. The troops at El Agheila were ordered to abandon their positions and head west as fast as possible to avoid the trap. Furthermore, the Americans pulled almost every available mobile unit out of their defenses in northern Tunisia and rushed them south to strike at the western flank of Rommel's salient in an effort to stop or slow his advance. This tactic worked for a while and a large number of Allied troops were able to escape to the west — but not all.

Rommel reached the desert, trapping many Allied troops in Libya. These forces withdrew to Tripoli where a hastily-assembled sea armada rescued most of them. This was a humiliating defeat for the Allies and the Axis propagandists called it another Dunkirk.

In Rome, Mussolini heaped praise on his armed forces and their commanders for recovering Libya. ☑ Actually though, not all of Libya had been reconquered. The Fighting French still controlled southern Libya and its oases.

🔊 Meanwhile, Rommel, taking advantage of the weakened Allied defenses in northern Tunisia, launched a second Blitzkrieg to the west from that location. This was a smaller attack than the first, but it was sufficient to win the day. Rommel's northern force broke through the American's line and began a rapid advance westward along the Mediterranean coast.

A war of maneuvers then began. The Americans, retreating from Libya were in Tunisia, and then Algeria, running south of Rommel's forces, trying to out pace them in order not to be trapped between those forces and the Sahara. But then Rommel's drive began to falter as he outran his supply lines which were under nearly constant Allied air attacks. The Axis forces reached the outskirts of Algiers, and stopped.

Meanwhile, the escaping Americans reached the coast at a point about 100 miles west of Algiers where they began to build a defense line. Now, sandwiched between the Americans and Germans were the Fighting French in Algiers. De Gaulle announced from his Algiers headquarters that his forces would defend the city to the last.

It was now late March 1945, and a prolonged lull in the fighting began.

Meanwhile, substantial numbers of American and some British troops were streaming into western Algeria and eastern French Morocco. With them came small numbers of the new U.S.-built Pershing and British-built Comet tanks, both of which were every bit a match for the Tigers. But the Germans had more Tigers than the Allies had Pershings and Comets. On the other hand, the Allies had more Sherman and British tanks than the Germans had Panthers. And the Allies continued to dominate in the air, and they had total control of the sea. The Luftwaffe, however, was receiving jets which would be used for the first time in ground support operations. The Allies had no jets in North Africa. The few that were operational were being used in Europe — some of them chasing V-1s.

Of importance to the Axis commanders now, was that they had a land route for supplies, although it was 3,000 miles long from the Balkans to Algeria. The costly process of sending convoys across the Mediterranean was abandoned, although air lifts continued. The end result was that the Axis forces were getting more in the way of reinforcements and supplies, but they were coming in more slowly.

THE TAWRIT GAP

The Allies could see that they might lose Algeria, but there was a place where the Axis advance could be stopped. It was the Tawrit Gap, just inside the border of French Morocco. ☑ Here is one of the world's best defensive positions. The Tawrit Gap, facing east, is like a funnel. The Gap is the neck of the funnel and there is high ground angling out on both sides of the neck forming the walls of the funnel. The approaches to the Gap consist of flat grassy plains where an advancing enemy force can be clearly seen from the high ground. Also, the enemy would become more and more condensed as it approached the Gap. Artillery pieces mounted on the slopes of the high ground would have a clear advantage.

And there is no easy way to bypass the Gap. To the south is the rugged Atlas Mountain range. North of the Gap is the Mediterranean Sea and the western end of Spanish Morocco which was politically inviolable. The reason for the latter was that if Axis troops entered Spanish Morocco, the Allies would almost certainly do likewise. They had had a plan, code named "Operation Backbone," in place for some time to do just this. The Allies could easily occupy all of western and central Spanish Morocco and march on to the southern shore of the Strait of Gibraltar. Furthermore, Spain might be dragged into the war 🔖 and, at this point, Hitler certainly did not want another weak ally to support.

In short, the only avenue to the west for Rommel's forces was through the Tawrit Gap.

Taking advantage of the Gap's favorable geography, the Americans began building very strong forces in the Gap and on its approaches. Using the experiences learned at other places in stopping the Blitzkrieg, a lattice work of ten trench lines was built in the Gap itself and hundreds of artillery pieces were hauled up to the high ground overlooking the approaches. On the flat terrain in front of the Gap, thousands of mines were planted and numerous tank traps and infantry obstacles were constructed, making it a field of death. German intelligence kept Rommel adequately informed as to what was taking place in the Tawrit Gap and he was worried. ☑

OTHER EVENTS

During March 1945, forty more German submarines were lost at sea, one of the largest monthly losses to date. On the plus side, the new fast, long-range "Walter" submarine was going into service. With twenty-four knots speed under water, it would be harder to track and sink.

🔖 In the Middle East and Egypt, the Italians had major problems on their hands providing food and jobs for their conquered masses. To help relieve the situation, thousands of Middle Easterners were recruited for work in Germany. As they streamed into Germany, the hard-core Nazis cringed. For years they had preached against the influx into Germany of large numbers of the "dark ones," but now, it was their own Nazi government that was bringing them in.

The food shortages continued and the Italians had to contend with food riots, work stoppages, hoarding, corruption and black markets everywhere. ☑

In Italy, visitors to Mussolini reported that he looked thin, pale and old. Like Hitler,

the long years of constant stress were taking their toll. Mussolini was sixty-two.

Goebbels' diary entries during this period give a picture of events inside Germany:

March 2; *"As a result... of the air war, some six million dwellings have so far been totally destroyed in the Reich... there is a shortage of nine million dwellings. After the war, therefore, we shall face a monumental task in this field:"*

on Speer; *"...Speer is the right man in the right place. He knows how to get to the root of enormously difficult problems:"* March 3; *"The population of the capital is gradually becoming habituated to the necessity of spending one or two hours every evening in the air raid shelter:"* March 4; *"This evening I had a long interview with the Fuehrer...I noticed with dismay that the nervous twitch in his left hand had greatly increased:"* March 6; *"Ribbentrop has been written off by the enemy...he is presumably no longer the appropriate person to make contact with London and Washington:"* March 7; *"Himmler is in Hohenlychen under medical care. He had had a bad attack of angina...He gives me a slightly frail impression..:"* March 9; *"At midday, received a large delegation of foreign workers...they expressed their readiness to collaborate...I outlined our future program for Europe based on a socialist reorganization of the continent:"* on Goering this date, whom Goebbels had come to hate; *"Almost all letters (received) describe Goering as the nigger in the woodpile responsible for Germany's set-backs..:"* March 11; *"He (Hitler) thinks that this (the removal of Goering) cannot be done in one fell swoop, but that...we must work slowly...and turn him into a figurehead:"* March 13; *"I am firmly determined...that when the war is over, not only shall I construct a new monumental ministry (building)...but restore the old ministry in all its old glory:"* March 15; *"The Fuehrer is determined...to reform the Wehrmacht and that it will emerge from the war fundamentally National Socialist in outlook and bearing:"* and: *"At midday we sat in our air raid shelter for three hours because Oranienburg and Zossen were being bombed:"* **March 21;** *"I then have a two-hour talk with the Fuehrer who makes a very weary and worn-out impression...His general attitude of mind, however, is still exemplary...One had the impression that he is only kept going by this iron will:"* and; *"The Fuehrer now places extraordinary hopes on these jet aircraft. He even refers to them as instruments of Germany's destiny... During the month 500 (jets) will be produced and next month 1,000:"* **March 30;** *"It is truly saddening to me to see the Fuehrer in such a bad physical state. He tells me that he is hardly sleeping at all, is continually plunged in his work and that he is totally worn down..."*

In the United States, people were saying similar things about Franklin Roosevelt's health.

APRIL 1945 – DYNAMIC EVENTS

On April 1, American troops landed on the island of Okinawa, a thousand miles southwest of Tokyo. Okinawa was considered by the Japanese as one of their home islands. In Tokyo, the government of General Kuniaki Kioso resigned, and a new government was then formed by Admiral Kantaro Suzuki. Goebbels noted in his diary, "Suzuki's new Japanese government is composed of fairly unknown people...one must treat (their) declarations (to fight on) with much suspicion."

On April 12, President Roosevelt died suddenly of a cerebral hemorrhage at his retreat at Warm Springs, Georgia. Vice-President Harry S Truman became the President of the United States. In Germany, Hitler drank a champaign toast to Truman's health.

Also that day, Hitler began a new treatment for Parkinson's Disease called the "Bulgarian Cure."

On April 21, Hitler suddenly dismissed Dr. Morell. Hitler had, for some time, been asking Morell to give him more medication. Yet, at other times, he complained that the medications he was receiving made him nervous and less alert. Morell was in an impossible position. On this date, Hitler demanded more medications and Morell told him they were not necessary. Hitler got angry and dismissed the good doctor.

On April 25, the RAF bombed the Berghof and the nearby villas of Goering and Bormann. All were made unlivable. The Fuehrer had lost his beloved mountain retreat, but he still had his apartment in Munich.

"THE SPEERS... WILL LONG BE WITH US"

During April the influential British newspaper, "The Observer," took note on how important Albert Speer had become to Germany. In one article, the newspaper stated, "The Hitlers and the Himmlers we may get rid of...but the Speers...will long be with us."

The argument can be made that Hitler had come to look upon Speer as his own alter ego. Speer was everything Hitler had ever hoped to be. Speer was tall, handsome, intelligent, well-educated, an architect, well-liked, polite, a skillful manager and fluent in several languages.

NEW YORK CITY – BOOM! -BOOM!

In early April, the British warned the Americans and Canadians that a group of six German submarines was on its way to North America and that they might be carrying V-1 or V-2 rockets. The operation was known to the Germans as "Operation Seewolf." This was of concern to the Americans who had previous reports that the Germans had successfully test-fired V-1s from submarines. Also, as early as January 1945, the Navy had announced to the American public that such attacks were possible.

The U.S. Navy reacted quickly and set up "Barrier Forces" to intercept the submarines. On April 15, the American ships made contact with the submarines and destroyed one of them and began tracking the others. The chase lasted until April 24 when the last submarine was sunk. Several German sailors were rescued and reported that none of the submarines carried missiles. The American leaders were greatly relieved.

🔊 But then, a month later, two large explosions rocked New York Harbor. The first came from an oil tanker anchored off Bayonne, New Jersey, waiting to offload its cargo to an oil refinery. The ship listed to one side, began to sink and spilled thousands of gallons of oil into the surrounding water that ultimately contaminated much of the eastern shore of Staten Island and parts of the Brooklyn water front.

An hour and ten minutes later, a second explosion rocked a baby flattop aircraft carrier, anchored at the Brooklyn Naval Yard. It, too, sank.

The Americans were mystified as to what caused the explosions, and it would be weeks before they would find out that it was the work of the Italians. ☑️

For two years, the Italians had been planning such an attack using their "Maiale" manned torpedoes which they had used successfully in the Mediterranean on several occasions. The Maiale was a torpedo with a saddle. The pilot rode atop the torpedo, with his head above water, operating a steering mechanism. He then maneuvered his craft to the side of an enemy ship, attached the front part of the torpedo, which was the explosive charge, to the side of the ship just under the water line. He then withdrew, and later, scuttled the remainder of the Maiale, and swam to shore. After deployment, the Italian sailor was authorized to surrender.

🔊 Two of these fascinating weapons were carried to the waters off New York Harbor by a giant unmarked CANT Z.511 Italian seaplane and released to find their way into the harbor. Thus, the two explosions.

As for surrendering, there was an alternative. The sailors wore civilian clothes under their military wet suits, carried three hundred dollars each in U.S. currency, had maps of New York City and fake identification papers including New York State drivers' licenses. After completing their missions, both sailors made their way to the "Little Italy" section of New York where they successfully blended in with the local residents.

The Maiale plot was uncovered when a fisherman discovered one of the abandoned rear portions of a Maiale in shallow water off East 14th Street in Manhattan. He alerted authorities, and the Americans then discovered the cause of the two attacks.

BATTLE ROYAL IN ALGERIA

The only major battle front now in the Euro-Africa theaters was in Algeria, and both sides were determined to win. Both were pouring in men and equipment.

Strong Allied units were sent to Algiers so that they could help the French defend Algiers which would then become a strong beachhead in Rommel's rear if and when he moved westward.

Knowing that they would have trouble stopping Rommel's powerful Blitzkrieg attacks in western Algeria, the Allied plan was to conduct a fighting withdrawal, wear down the Germans as much as possible, and buy time so that those constructing the defenses at the Tawrit Gap and at Tazah could complete their work. At Tawrit, and Tazah if necessary, the Allies planned to make all-out stands.

Rommel, noting the Allied build up in front of him, reported to Hitler that to capture Algiers would take a major effort and likely delay his advance to the west. He asked permission to bypass the city, and Hitler agreed.

Throughout the rest of May and into early June, the battle in western Algeria proceeded much as the Allies had planned. Algiers was bypassed and on June 12, German forces entered French Morocco. The Tawrit Gap was sixty-five miles to the west. ☑️

AROUND THE WORLD

On May 25, Churchill's coalition government came apart and he was forced, by law, to call for national elections — the first in ten years. The date was set for July 28.

In Washington, that same day, the Joint Chiefs of staff set the date for the invasion of Japan to be November 1.

In China, the Japanese were withdrawing forces and sending them to Japan. The Chinese Nationalist and Chinese Communists followed in their wake filling the voids and increasing their respective areas of control.

On June 3, the Japanese government sent peace-feelers to the Allies through the Soviet Embassy in Tokyo. They were rejected.

At Admiral Doenitz' office, records were showing that about 70% of the men sent out on submarines did not return.

By now, the Americans had some 4,000 B-29 bombers and were using them to bomb Japan every day.

INTO THE CALDRON

🔊 Thanks to the delaying tactics undertaken in Algeria, the Americans were well-prepared at the Tawrit Gap. Hundreds of guns looked down on the approaches to the Gap from the hills on either side. On the north side of the Gap is a small rounded mountain that the GIs had dubbed "Old Roundtop." South of the Gap is a ridge protruding out from the Atlas Mountains that was called "The Ridge." Behind the Ridge was a narrow valley called "Allen's Ally" after a popular American radio program. In Allen's Ally were stationed about fifty Sherman tanks. If the Germans succeeded in reaching the mid section of the trench maze, these tanks were in a position to smash into their left flank. If the German tanks made it trough the entire maze, they would run headlong into the bulk of the American armored forces that were dug in and waiting.

Running through the Tawrit Gap is the Muluya River, the largest in Morocco. All of its bridges had been destroyed and its fords dredged so that the Germans would have no easy way to cross it.

Rommel knew what he was up against and had pleaded, unsuccessfully, with Hitler to allow him to advance westward along the coastal plain through Spanish Morocco. But Hitler was firm iin his earlier decision that Spain should not be brought into the war. Rommel had to plunge into the caldron. And Rommel had other problems. Whenever his men and tanks tried to assemble in groups, they became instant targets from above. The Luftwaffe had proven to be totally inadequate and the few jets they had were withdrawn to Europe because they were too vulnerable on the ground. Even the magnificent Tiger tanks, with their long-range guns, were of reduced value because this battle would be fought at very close quarters.

On June 27, Rommel made his move. He sent his strong, tightly-packed armored force into the Tawrit Gap. It was a disaster. By noon, after reaching only the second line of trenches, the battle had been decided. One fourth of the German tanks had been knocked out and the motorized infantry units following them had been decimated. By nightfall, the approaches to the Gap were littered with broken machines and broken men. American losses were minimal.

From Germany, came an order to try again. Rommel dutifully sent his forces forward again, on the 29th, and it was another disaster. This time, the German tanks did not get past the first trench line. By 10:00 a.m., the Germans were in full retreat and Rommel knew he was beaten.

In Germany Hitler knew it too, and ordered a withdrawal to the east. As darkness fell on the 29th, Rommel's forces were in full retreat.

The next day, on the morning of June 30, the Germans received another nasty surprise. A powerful Allied armored force charged out of Algiers heading south. This force was 300 miles east of Rommel and was heading for the Sahara Desert to cut off Rommel's supply lines and lines of retreat.

Rommel's troops saw their desperate situation and the retreat turned into a rout. American tanks followed in hot pursuit and had constant air support. Then still another development — German troops began surrendering en masse — their will to fight shattered. Rommel's army was dying.

Hitler ordered that a strong defensive line be constructed in eastern Algeria from Philippeville on the coast, to Constantine, and then to Batna and points south. ☑ There, high hills and a series of marshes favored the defender. 🔊 On the afternoon of the 30th, Hitler phoned Mussolini and told him that it was time to end the war. Mussolini agreed. ☑

CHAPTER 26

SO MUCH TO DO
AND SO LITTLE TIME

itler once said, "You must understand that I always go as far as I dare and never further… It is vital to have a sixth sense which tells you broadly what you can and cannot do."

🔊 Now, it was time for Hitler to exercise that sixth sense. He had given much thought on how to end the war, and events had convinced him that a military solution was not attainable. The only other alternative, then, was a negotiated settlement. He had also concluded that it would be up to the Axis Powers to make the first move. To accomplish this, Hitler formulated a plan.

That plan called for Mussolini to act first. ✏ Before the war, Il Duce had a reputation as a peace-maker which came about at Munich in 1938 when he helped negotiate a successful solution to the Sudetenland crisis. 🔊 Hitler hoped that favorable image had survived enough to make it more agreeable for the Allies to reply to Mussolini than to himself.

On the morning of Tuesday, July 3, 1945, Rome radio began telling the people of Italy that an important announcement would be forthcoming from Mussolini at 2:00 p.m. that afternoon during the traditional Italian lunch break. Immediately, the news was flashed around the world and speculation was rampant that he would ask for peace. In some places, premature celebrations began. At the appointed time, Mussolini came on the air and soon confirmed that the rumors were right. He said that the war had gone on long enough and that the people of the world were weary and needed peace. Il Duce said that Italy had, after years of struggle, won its rightful place in the sun and could afford to be magnanimous toward its former enemies. He called upon the other world leaders to join him in ending hostilities. The speech was short and to the point.

During the next few hours, announcements of support were forthcoming from Finland, Romania, Hungary, Slovakia, and Bulgaria; Axis nations that had satisfied their war aims and truly wanted peace. Announcements also came from most of the neutral capitals of the world and from some of the Allied nations. All eyes, though, were now on Berlin. What would Hitler do?

The next morning, July 4, Berlin radio began announcing that the Fuehrer would speak to the German people at 4:00 that afternoon, the traditional time for important government announcements. Hope for peace rose in the hearts of millions.

At the appointed hour, an announcer came on Berlin radio and announced that Adolf Hitler would now address the German people. After a dramatic pause, the familiar voice of the Fuehrer was heard. He started speaking in low, somber tones, as was his style when beginning a speech. He told his listeners that Germany and her European allies had, over the last six years of struggle and suffering, righted the wrongs that had been done to them in the past decades. He reminded his listeners that in 1940 he had tried to prevent this catastrophic war from escalating by ☑ offering peace at that time, but it was rejected. 🔔 Now, he said, it was time to try again. He then paused, knowing that there would be some sort of vocal reaction from virtually every listener.

Hitler then announced that he would follow his good friend and ally, Benito Mussolini, in calling for an end to hostilities. He then heaped praise on Il Duce as the world's great peacemaker and promised that Germany and Italy would coordinate their efforts toward ending the war and bringing peace as stability to the world.

Hitler went on to say that it was his earnest hope that Germany's and Italy's enemies would cooperate in this great effort.

Hitler added that he had issued orders to military commanders in the field to cease fire, effective at noon the next day, July 5, and that the German forces were to stand down to a defensive posture and await developments. He then called upon the Allied leaders to reciprocate in kind and that arrangements be made for representatives of the belligerent nations to meet on some neutral ground to negotiate a cease fire and, eventually, an armistice.

As part of the cease fire, he called for an immediate release of prisoners of war and interned civilians by both sides, and the return to the freedom of the seas. He said that he wanted the British Empire, in general, to remain intact and prosperous. He added, for the benefit of the Americans, that their President Woodrow Wilson had called for "peace without victory" in 1917 at a time when the progress of World War I seemed to be at a stalemate.

He then said that if, and when, a formal cease fire agreement was reached he, personally, would step down from all of his political and military offices, except that as leader of the Party, and go into retirement. He said that the German government would be restructured according to the German constitution and in a form that could carry forth negotiations for an armistice and an eventual peace treaty.

Hitler warned, though, that if the Allies did not accept the cease fire proposals, German forces would respond aggressively to any attacks made against them.

As he ended his speech, his voice rose to an emotional level — another traditional mannerism in a Fuehrer speech — and said, with a slight quiver in his voice, that this terrible war must end — Germany wants peace — the world wants peace.

Upon hearing these words, instantaneous celebrations broke out all over the world. In Britain, election campaigning was under way and in the United States, it was the morning of July 4th, a national holiday. The timing for all this was not a coincidence.

In the hours that followed, the Italian government announced that it, too, had ordered Italian forces to cease fire at noon on July 5.

All of the leaders of the European Axis allies dutifully followed the announcements stating that they, too, would follow Germany's and Italy's lead and order their military forces to stand down at the appointed hour. Orders then went out from Berlin, Rome and other Axis capitals, radioed in the clear and repeatedly, to their respective commanders in the field, and ships at sea, to honor the cease fire.

TIMING

Hitler felt that the timing was right to sue for peace because the Allies were in a position to accept a cease fire and still be able to save face. They had just won a great battle in Algeria. Also, they had stopped the German advance toward the Belgian Congo, had had victories in Norway, the Channel Islands, the Far East and were winning the air war over Europe and the war at sea. With such successes, Hitler reasoned, the Allies would, hopefully, agree to end the war in Europe.

FIVE CAMPS

Almost immediately after the Axis cease fire announcements, the world was divided into five camps; the yeas, the nays, those who announced that they were studying the situation, those who proclaimed betrayal, and those who remained silent. Conspicuous in the last group were the British and the Americans. In Britain, both the Conservatives and Labourites temporarily halted their electioneering out of patriotic duty to the country. Churchill, however, spoke out warning that this might be a Nazi trick.

In the yeas group were all of the European Axis allies, the European puppet regimes, the neutrals, and some of the less-than-committed Allied nations. Gandhi, in India, announced his support for a cease fire, as did the International Red Cross. The Vatican made the statement that the return of peace would be a blessing to all mankind. Leaders of other religious organizations made similar pronouncements. Most of the world's labor leaders pledged their support, but most of the big industrialists remained silent.

Most of those supporting the cease fire were careful not to heap praise on Hitler, Mussolini or the other Axis leaders knowing that that would not set well in the West. Rather, they focused on the concept of the cease fire and its benefit to all.

In the nays group were the Soviets, who vowed to fight on until their homeland west of the Urals was recovered, and the Swiss announced from their Alpine Redoubt that they would fight on. The Zionists and other Jewish organizations, including the Jewish underground military organizations in Palestine, announced that an international cease fire would not alter their continuing struggle for a Jewish state. The governments-in-exile in London announced their opposition to the cease fire. Spokesmen for the Partisan organizations in Yugoslavia, Albania and Greece announced that they would continue their struggle. The Ethiopian guerrillas announced the same.

From the Far East, Japan and her satellites shouted "betrayal," and vowed to fight on. From Tokyo, urgent messages went out to all of the Japanese diplomatic missions in the European Axis capitals to terminate, immediately, all contact with their counterparts and await further instructions.

The nations that had announced that they were studying the situation consisted of the British Commonwealth nations and most of the other Allied nations. These governments, for the most part, were waiting to see the reactions from London and Washington.

THE IMMEDIATE AFTERMATH

In the hours and days following the cease fire announcements, a world-wide euphoria surfaced and celebrations continued. The stock markets rose in many nations except for those in Japan and their Far Eastern allies.

On the battle fronts there were no major operations launched by either side, but there were isolated incidents. In some cases, units in the field took this opportunity, especially in the hours before the deadline, to fire off all their remaining ammunition against the enemy.

The Italians, in a ploy to make the cease fire more palatable to the West, announced that if freedom of the seas came about, they would soon become major purchasers of food in the world markets and would offer payment in oil. Around the world, commodities markets rose while oil markets dropped.

Throughout Europe, the lights came on again in some, but not all, of the big cities.

In the United States the long-suffering isolationists were suddenly in the news again. They now had a powerful new slogan; "We told you so!"

NOON, JULY 5, 1945

At noon, July 5, Berlin time, an uneasy lull fell over the major battlefields in Europe, the Middle East and Africa. Everyone held their breath. As night fell, it was still holding. It appeared that the western world had a "de facto" cease fire.

JULY 6, 1945

As July 6 began, the cease fire was still holding, but there were several exceptions. A German submarine sank an American freighter off Nova Scotia and then ran for its life. In the Mediterranean, a British submarine sank an empty Italian tanker as it emerged from Tobruk harbor. These events were announced in both Allied and Axis media with explanations that ☑ submarines could not receive radio messages while submerged and, it was very likely, their commanders had not received word of the cease fire.

🔊 London and Washington continued their silence. Most of the yeas, nays and the others confirmed their stands. There was no word from Hitler or Mussolini.

Darkness fell on the 6th and the cease fire was still holding.

THE DAWN OF PEACE

For the next few days nothing much happened. London and Washington still made no pronouncements, but government spokesmen had to admit that the matter was being studied with intense interest.

From Portugal, Prime Minister Salazar offered the services of his government and the city of Lisbon as a site for formal negotiations on the cease fire and an armistice. A similar announcement came from Stockholm.

Skeptics and other impatient critics began calling this period of calm a "second phony war." ☑

On July 12, the Labour Party in Australia won control of the government in a nationwide election. This was a strong sign that the people of the British Commonwealth were moving away from the leaders that had brought them war and toward leaders who might bring them peace.

On July 26, the election was held in Britain with blockbuster results. Churchill was voted out of office by an overwhelming majority. Taking his place as Prime Minister was Clement Attlee, head of the Labour Party. The British people had turned sharply, and suddenly, away from the policies of Churchill. The world was stunned.

LISBON – SPEER – NEGOTIATIONS

🔊 On August 1, the Attlee government announced that it would be willing to discuss a formal cease fire with the Axis Powers and

that Lisbon would be an acceptable location for the talks. Announcements from the Commonwealth nations and the United State followed, as did announcements of acceptance from the Axis capitals.

Negotiations through third parties followed and it was agreed that the first talks would be held on August 9 in Lisbon.

On August 3, Hitler announced that he would keep his promise of July 4 to relinquish all of his governmental and military posts if a formal cease fire came about. Then he named those people who would take cantrol of the new German government. These men, Hitler believed, were individuals with whom the Allies could negotiate.

Goering was appointed President, a mainly ceremonial post; Speer became Chancellor; von Papen became Foreign Minister, and Rommel Minister of Defense. ☑

It appeared that Hitler had kept Papen in place for just this moment. Papen was not a Nazi. He had been a leader of the German Nationalist Party which was the Nazi's coalition partner in 1933 when Hitler became Chancellor. At that time, Papen served as Hitler's Vice Chancellor. Papen was well-educated, dapper, from a highly-respected family, had served as a former Chancellor, and was a practicing Catholic. He spoke English with a British accent, and had virtually no political enemies. After the demise of the Nationalist Party, Papen threw in his lot with the Nazis and had become something of a front man. He spent most of the war as Ambassador to Turkey and was, therefore, out of the decision-making process in Berlin.

Rommel, of course, was a very successful, professional army officer. He was highly-respected by the Allies and, like Papen, had no political enemies.

🔊 Hjalmar Horace Greeley Schacht was appointed to head the German negotiating team in Lisbon. ☑ Schacht had served as President of the Reichsbank, Minister of Economics and Cabinet Minister without portfolio on economic matters. He had been raised in the United States, spoke fluent American English, was well-versed on American politics and, before the war, had negotiated personally with President Roosevelt on the issue of German reparations from World War I.

🔊 The Americans appointed Joseph Kennedy, the former ambassador to England, to head their delegation. The British appointed Lord Beaverbrook.

At 4:30 p.m. that afternoon, August 3, Speer spoke on German radio, confirmed his appointment and said that the first objective of his administration would be to bring about peace.

PRESIDENT GOERING AND THE FUTURE GERMAN GOVERNMENTS

By appointing Goering the President of Germany, Hitler fulfilled his ☑ promise, made in the 1930s to Goering, that he would be his successor. 🔊 All knew, however, that this was just window dressing and that the real power lay with Speer and Hitler.

Nevertheless, Goering, the collector of titles, the lover of pomp and ceremony, and the one who craved being the center of attention, was satisfied. Furthermore, Hitler decreed that Goering's portrait would, henceforth, appear on German currency and postage stamps. ☑

It was Hitler's plan that the existing constitution would remain in place until his death. At that time, a new, and previously agreed-to, constitution would come into being that would comply with Nazi political ideology. The post of President would be eliminated and all power would be concentrated in the hands of the Chancellor who would be given the new title, "Head of State." Under the new constitution, successive Heads of State would be chosen by the members of the Reichstag's Senate, whose members would be appointed by the Party. Once a new Head of State was chosen, all Party members would be required to take an oath of allegiance to him within hours of the appointment. Hitler had often pointed out that this would be much on the order in which the Catholic Church functioned.

According to Hitler's plan, the other chamber of the Reichstag, which had not yet been given a name, would be elected by the people from lists of acceptable candidates provided by the Party. This chamber would be given, by the constitution, "emergency corrective powers" which could over-ride the Senate and take for itself the authority to remove a Head of State who was corrupt, incompetent or had otherwise lost the support of the people.

Until that time, however, it was Hitler's plan that the Chancellor would be the dominant member of the German government and would continue to use that title. His main legal authority would come from the Enabling Act of March 1933 which allowed the Chancellor, which at the time was Hitler, to deviate from the constitution.

Hitler hoped that by retiring, he would set an example for future Heads of State not to overstay their usefulness.

🔊 There was an understanding among many of the top Nazis that, with Hitler's passing, the title, Fuehrer, should be retired. Hitler had not approved, nor rejected, this concept, but all of his subordinates had agreed that the title of Fuehrer would be his alone until his death and through the ages. Germany would have only one Fuehrer. This was in keeping with the fact that ☑ Germany had only one Charlemagne, one Frederick the Great, and one Iron Chancellor (Bismarck).

🔊 There were those in the Nazi leadership that suggested the phrase, Third Reich, be eliminated because it insinuated a time limit. To replace it, the title "National Socialist Reich," was suggested. ☑

ATOMIC BOMB

On the morning of August 6, an atomic bomb obliterated the city of Hiroshima, Japan killing tens of thousands of people. The world was electrified. The atomic age had begun.

🔊 In the early morning hours of the 7th, European time, Berlin radio announced the attack and that Germany, too, had atomic weapons but, out of concern for humanity, had chosen not to use them. This latter statement was a bold-faced lie except for the fact that the Germans could have, at this stage, produced one or two dirty bombs. The announcement from Berlin, however, fed into the Allied fears that Germany did, indeed, have atomic weapons because the Allies had reports that the Germans were building, or had already built, a uranium separation facility and a plutonium producing facility somewhere in the East.

Actually, the Allied leaders had been duped. Germany was still several years away from producing atomic weapons of the type used at Hiroshima.

Following the news of the atomic bomb, Berlin radio began broadcasting almost continuously, stated that a cease fire agreement, as well as an armistice and peace settlement, were now imperative because the continuation of the war with atomic weapons would be unthinkable. There were few who disagreed. ☑

On August 8, came the announcement that the Soviet Union had declared war on Japan. 🔊 Soviet forces in the Far East were weak, but the Japanese forces in northern Japan and northern China were weaker. ☑

The Russians had several goals to achieve in the Far East. They wanted to recover the southern half of Sakalin Island and the Kurile islands, both of which were taken from Tsarist Russia in previous conflicts with Japan. Over the centuries, Russia had fought both China and Japan for control of Manchuria and Korea. Now, they had the upper hand in this matter. And lastly, the Russians wanted to make contact with Mao Tse-tung and his large Chinese Communist organization.

🔊 Over the next several weeks, the Russians accomplished these goals and demonstrated, for all the world, that despite the claims from Berlin and Rome, communism was not dead. ☑

In the early morning hours of August 9, the news arrived in Europe that the Americans had dropped a second atomic bomb on Japan obliterating the city of Nagasaki. 🔊 A few hours later the Allied and Axis delegates met for the opening session of the cease fire talks in Lisbon. The atmosphere

was intense. Both sides were motivated to reach a quick agreement. ☑

On August 10, the Japanese announced that they would accept America's terms for unconditional surrender provided the Emperor could retain his position. On August 14, after several days of negotiations, and more conventional bombings of Japan by B-29s, the Americans accepted the Japanese offer. World War II was over.

CEASE FIRE AGREEMENT REACHED

🔊 In Lisbon, a cease fire agreement was reached on August 17. It was agreed that the release of prisoners of war and interned civilians would begin immediately and that the battle lines that currently existed would remain static. The principle of freedom of the seas was accepted by all parties and it was stipulated that civilian trade could resume as market forces dictated.

It was also agreed that telephone, telegraph and postal communications would be re-established.

Within a few days, the first signs of the freedom of the seas appeared as ships set sail for distant ports and markets that had long been inaccessible. All over the world, prisoners of war and internees from both sides were told to make ready to return home.

Before the delegates in Lisbon departed, they agreed that talks on an armistice would begin, in Lisbon, on Monday, September 17. ☑

On September 2, Japan formally surrendered.

🔊 In most of the major nations, however, the development of weapons of war was still being pursued. German rocket scientists and engineers were in the final stages of developing the V-10 rocket that could reach North America, and Heisenberg's people were working frantically on the atomic bomb. ☑ In the United States, the Americans had the atomic bomb and were working on rockets.

AND NOW AN ARMISTICE

🔊 On September 17, 1945, the delegates resumed their talks in Lisbon. They all knew that arranging the cease fire had been relatively easy compared to what lie ahead. There were many issues to be discussed and neither party had the power to force their will on the other. Agreements on every issue would have to be by mutual consent. It was recognized that some issues could not be resolved at this time, but would have to be passed on to the eventual peace conference.

Topics on the agenda included atomic weapons, general disarmament, Norway, Poland, Africa, reparations, international trade and communications, and many other matters.

With regard to atomic weapons, both sides agreed that there should be some sort of international controls, but discussions could go no further. Neither side wanted to introduce third parties into their respective nuclear programs nor grant inspections. Both had too many secrets to protect.

With regard to general disarmament, here again, both sides agreed that this should happen, but mutual suspicions prevented any meaningful progress on the issue.

On Norway, there was a faint glimmer of hope that a settlement might be reached. With the country occupied in the North by the Americans, in the south by the Germans, and with the Quisling government totally discredited, Sweden made a proposal that had merit. It was that all foreign troops in Norway be withdrawn. This proposal had a recent historical precedent because ☑ agreement had been reached in 1939 between the warring parties in Spain for the removal of all foreign troops.

☐ The Swedish proposal went on to state that as the foreign troops withdrew from Norway, Swedish troops would enter the country to keep the peace until a plebescite could be taken to determine Norway's future. Accompanying the Swedes would be several ☑ Norwegian paramilitary forces comprised of Norwegian refugees that the Swedes had already trained and equipped for just such a purpose. ☐ Furthermore, guarantees would be given by all parties involved that Norway would become a neutral nation ☑ as had been the case during World War I. ☐ Also,

the Swedes proposed the revival of ☑ the Scandinavian Neutrality Bloc which had existed between Sweden and Norway before World War II.

☐ Another argument the Allies put forth with regard to both Norway and Denmark was that in 1940, when Germany invaded these countries, Berlin announced that they were doing so to protect those countries from the British. With that threat now gone, the Allies argued that Germany had no justification for remaining in either country.

Finland, Germany's ally, was very supportive of the Swedish proposal because it would remove American forces from Finland's northern border as well as the threat of American air power that currently threatened all of Finland.

The Germans knew that their hold on Norway was tenuous because the two countries had no common border. Land transit rights between Germany and Norway had been granted by Sweden in 1941, but this arrangement could not last indefinitely. Already, Stockholm was pressuring the Germans to give up those rights, and all along the transit route armed Swedish soldiers could be seen, as well as numerous signs reading, "Germans, go Home!"

Here then, with the prospect of foreign troops leaving Norway, and possibly Denmark, were bargaining chips that the Germans might use in other negotiations. Hitler, of course, would lose his cherished base at Trondheim, but he would also rid himself of the embarrassment of Quisling and those pesky Danes. Furthermore, Berlin could bring home the ☑ 350,000 German troops currently stationed in Norway.

☐ Poland was a more difficult question. ☑ After Germany's defeat of Poland in 1939, Hitler offered to reconstruct a Polish state. And, it must be remembered that, in 1916, Germany had resurrected Poland after years of its being partitioned between Germany, Russia and Austria-Hungary. ☐ On the issue of Poland, however, the Germans offered only platitudes and side-stepped the issue as much as possible.

Africa was very complex. The British, who were majority share-holders in the Suez Canal Corporation, insisted that control of the canal be returned to them. This argument went nowhere as the Italians refused to even discuss this issue.

With regard to other issues; the Fighting French wanted the Germans and Italians to withdraw from Tunisia and eastern Algeria, the Italians wanted the Fighting French to withdraw from southern Libya and the Djibouti Redoubt, the Allies wanted the Germans and Italians to withdraw from Turkey, and the Germans and Italians wanted the Allies to withdraw from the Azores. On most of these issues, here again, there was an impasse.

The British demanded the return of Uganda and Kenya while the Germans countered with their long-standing demands that all of the former colonies be returned to them.

The Germans demanded control of the Belgian Congo by right of conquest of Belgium. The Allies countered by demanding the reconstitution of Belgium and the elimination of the artificial state of Burgundy.

Reparations was a subject no one wanted to discuss. It was on the agenda, but neither side wanted to bring it up for discussion.

International trade, on the other hand, was an issue that could, in all likelihood, be resolved because it benefitted all parties. A joint committee was formed to make recommendations to the delegates on this issue. And, the Germans insisted that consideration be given to revising the whaling industry, a pet project of the Fuehrer.

HITLER'S FAREWELL ADDRESS

On Sunday, September 30, 1945, Hitler addressed the German people one last time. He said that his task of creating the Third Reich had been completed and that he intended to devote the rest of his days overseeing the many, and wondrous, plans that had been prepared for the German people. He also said he would rest and pursue his personal loves of art, architecture and mu-

sic. And too, he would remove his military uniform. This was in reference to a statement he made in September 1939 before the Reichstag in which he stated that he had donned a military uniform to become Germany's first soldier and that he would not take if off until "after victory." Now, he said, his mission had been completed and he would remove his beloved uniform and send it to the Linz Museum.

The Fuehrer ended his talk by telling the people that it would be a long time before they heard from him again and that they should now direct their loyalties to the new governmental leaders. What he did not say was that his health was failing and he dreaded being seen in public and especially on television, which was rapidly being developed throughout Germany. Hitler also avoided the movie camera, and any photograph of him had to be closely edited before publication.

A PRIVATE WEDDING

On October 6, Hitler married his long-time mistress, Eva Braun, in a private ceremony in his Munich apartment. Only his closest associates were in attendance. That evening, the marriage was announced to the German people. Here was another of his life's aims. He had told many people that he would like to have a family, but would not marry until his duty to the nation was completed.

Hitler and Eva journeyed to Florence, Italy for a honeymoon where a very special wedding gift awaited them. Hitler had told Mussolini and others that, when he had the time, he would love to tour Florence. As a wedding gift to his comrade-in-arms, Mussolini arranged an agenda for the couple's eight-day stay. It called for the museums, and other sites of interest that Eva and Hitler wanted to see, to be closed to the public during the time they were there. Mussolini, himself, acted as the tour guide on several occasions, and on two evenings Adolf, Eva, Benito and his wife, Rachele, dined together.

SO MUCH TO DO –

Hitler and Eva returned to their apartment in Munich where Hitler emersed himself in the many projects he had planned. Matters of state, such as bringing about peace, building of the East, etc., would be left to Speer. Hitler planned now to enjoy himself by picking only those projects he wanted to pursue. He also ordered a whole new wardrobe which included his beloved lederhausen (Bavarian bibbed leather shorts).

Hitler had dismissed his military and political advisors and began gathering about him men of culture. They would advise him on their respective specialties in carrying out the details of the many projects he planned.

High on his agenda was the rebuilding on the Berghof, which was underway. The rebuilding of Goering's and Bormann's villas at Birchtesgaden was also under way, but at a slower pace. It would not do for their villas to be completed before Hitler's.

Hitler brought Dr. Morell back into his graces and continued to rely heavily upon him for his health problems.

– AND SO LITTLE TIME

Hitler began his new work with a sense of urgency. He was ever mindful that his father had died suddenly at age 63. Hitler was 56. He also knew that he was the most hated man on earth and that assassination attempts might be made on his life. Several such attempts had been made through the years. It would now be Hitler's lot to live constantly surrounded by body guards and bulletproof glass.

HITLER'S PERSONAL PROJECTS

ART: Hitler began, once again, to paint. He would do very little serious work but would concentrate on hand-painted greeting cards which he sent to friends and associates. Hitler had done this a few times during the war, and it will be remembered that, as a young man in Vienna, he partially supported himself by painting and selling hand-painted post cards to tourists.

Hitler's early art works would be tracked down, purchased and displayed in a special room in the Linz Art Museum. The new Linz art museum would be bigger than the one in Vienna to intentionally steal away some of the luster of that city and transfer it to Linz.

Planning for that museum had begun and Hitler edited every blueprint. Once completed, it would exhibit most of his personal art collection along with paintings owned by others and by the state. Goering was expected to be one of the major contributor because he had an art collection estimated to be worth $200 million.

Hitler planned, to take a hand in the construction of the other art museums that were to be built across Germany. And he would oversee the creation of the new government-operated art academies to be built across Germany. He would take much personal delight in this by bringing down the influence of the art world's "big wigs," as he had called them.

ARCHITECTURE: The overall rebuilding of Germany would be left to others, but Hitler intended to take an active part in the architectural designs of important new buildings and monuments. He had insisted that new buildings should not all look alike, but should reflect the culture and traditions of the local communities in which they were to be built.

MUSIC: Here was one of the Fuehrer's great loves. He planned to devote considerable time to the architectural design and construction of new opera houses, especially the one to be built in Munich.

Another of his goals was to end the practice of having guest artists so that each community could better develop its own opera company.

Hitler loved the music of Wagner, Grieg and Bruckner. He planned to start a music festival at Linz which highlighted the music of Austrian composer Anton Bruckner. The festival would be similar to the Bayreuth Music Festival which highlighted Wagner's

Wooden model of Hitler's fortress-like retirement home at Linz.

the celebration of Easter and, instead, celebrate the Fuehrer's birthday. Both occurred in April.

And finally, Hitler wanted it preached in the Christian churches of Europe that Jesus was not a Jew, but rather the offspring of a Roman soldier and an Arab woman.

It was foreseen that such radical changes with regard to religions would provoke a negative world-wide reaction among almost all peoples of faith. At Speer's suggestion, Hitler agreed that the program should proceed very slowly.

music and which Hitler had attended many times. He planned to have a grand concert hall, named after Bruckner, built at Linz.

Hitler intended to devote many hours attending operas and music festivals. But herein lay a problem. A way had to be found to shield from public view his uncontrollable shaking and his haggard appearance.

RELIGION: Here, was serious business. Hitler had long intended to break down the power of organized religion because he saw the churches as political threats to National Socialism. He had said on several occasions that he had a Big Book in which he was keeping ideas and ammunition to bring down church rule.

Now, it was time to open the Big Book.

Hitler had no intention of eliminating religion. "It's impossible to escape the problem of God..." he once said. Rather, each community would be allowed to maintain its own religious institutions, but there would be no bishops, arch-bishops, monsignors, cardinals or popes. He said that the churchgoers could follow their own beliefs and even practice Black Magic if they wished. In fact, diversification, he had said, would be encouraged because it would make it very difficult for the churches to, once again, unite under a central leadership.

Others had suggested, and Hitler had supported, another step in reducing the influence of religion on the people. That would be to drop

ANOTHER BOOK: Hitler planned to write another book to be titled, "The Ideal State of the Future." In it, he intended to stress the importance of education and diet, especially a vegetarian diet. He also hoped to write his memoirs.

LINZ, HITLER'S HOME TOWN: Hitler intended to spend much of his time rebuilding and beautifying Linz. He said he wanted the city to rival the beauty of Budapest and Paris.

In addition to a world-class art museum, the city would have an olympic stadium, a suspension bridge across the Danube, an opera house, a magnificent twenty-story Strength-Through-Joy hotel overlooking the Danube, several tourist hotels, an attractive waterfront complex, a Party House, an Army headquarters, a new city hall, a European banking center, several new parks, a provincial theater, a large cinema, a library, a municipal auditorium, a giant statue of Siegfried atop the Freinberg heights, a monument to Bismarck, and an observatory which would have nationalistic and spiritual overtones. The existing historical museum in Linz would be greatly expanded and a permanent exhibit would be created on fortifications from ancient times to the Atlantic Wall. The city's famous Renaissance castle would be restored and the central railroad depot moved to the edge of town with the tracks put underground. Running from the new depot into the center of town would be a wide ceremonial boulevard named "Zu den Lauben," along which visiting dignitaries would travel when they arrived in Linz.

An effort would be made to encourage the start up of numerous small businesses in Linz, including pastry shops. Hitler loved the rich Austrian pastries and the pastry chefs of Linz could rise to the heights of their profession competing for Hitler's business.

In time, the Adolf Hitler Technical University would arise at Linz as would a vocational school. ☑

Hitler had long planned to build a magnificent, fortress-like home for himself near the outskirts of town. 🔔 He would then spend most of his time between this home, the Berghof and his Munich apartment. His trips to Berlin would be infrequent.

Linz would also be Hitler's final resting place. A magnificent bell tower would be built for that purpose and would also contain the remains of his parents. The bell tower would play passages from Bruckner's Fourth Symphony. ☑

If Hitler loved Linz, the citizens of Linz loved Hitler. Of all the cities in Austria, Linz had been one of the most supportive of National Socialism. There were no significant socialist or communist influences in the city and the SS had cleared it of Jews as early as 1939. The citizens of Linz seemed to even support the Nazi's plan to increase the German population because the birth rate in Linz was about twice that of the nation.

Unfortunately, the citizens of Linz paid a high price for this loyalty. Being a highly industrialized city and Hitler's home town, the Allies bombed it repeatedly. By May 1945, the Allies had dropped 800,000 tons of bombs on the city, killed 1,679 civilians, destroyed 602 city blocks, 2,940 living units, and made another 5,264 barely habitable.

THE EIGHT-YEAR PLAN

🔔 On December 1, 1945, the Speer government announced the Eight-Year Plan which was to be the primary program for rebuilding Germany and the occupied areas. In that time, it was predicted, the war damage would be removed and virtually all of the new construction slated for Germany's future would be completed or well under way.

The Plan would be a massive undertaking that would require hundreds of thousands of laborer. Because of this, the foreign workers in Germany would not likely be returning home anytime soon. These workers would continue to be strictly segregated from German society, but well treated. They would have an eight-hour day, decent housing, adequate food, medical care, trips home and state-controlled brothels.

One of the first projects to be carried out under the Plan would be the completion of the autobahn system including the long-planned Berlin-Nuremberg-Munich-Linz "Party Road."

Many Strength-Through-Joy projects would be undertaken, including the two-and-a-half mile long summer resort to be built on Rugen Island in the Baltic. This project had been announced at the 1937 Paris World Fair.

Other projects would be the modernization of the rail systems throughout the German empire, the resumption of the production of the Volkswagen, the dispersal of heavy industry from the over-industrialized Ruhr, and the construction of an extensive canal and river system across Europe from the English Channel to the Dnieper River. This latter project would include the Adolf Hitler Canal that would link the Oder, Elbe and Danube Rivers. A standardized European electrical grid would come into being with care given to preserve the beautify of the landscape. A system of secret patents would be worked out to protect Germany's most valuable industrial secrets. The civic centers of many German cities, heavily damaged by bombing, would be totally reconstructed. Special care would be given to Vienna to clear up the slums, beautify the city and, eventually, remove the Czechs.

As for Berlin, much of the city would be completely rebuilt. It would have a magnificent civic center dominated by a huge assembly hall, sixteen times the volume of St. Peter's in Rome, and capable of holding 180,000 people. There would be a triumphal arch (that which Hitler had first conceived in the 1920s) that would be 400 feet high and dwarf the Arc d'Triomphe in Paris. These and other magnificent buildings would be built along a new avenue called the "Prachtallee" (Avenue of Splendor). It would be twice the width, and three times the length, of the Champs Elysees. The city would also have sky-scrapers, larger than those in America. The Chancellory building, which was new in 1939 but was now heavily damaged, would be rebuilt and greatly enlarged to become the largest structure of its kind in all of Europe.

At Nuremberg, a huge Party complex would be built which would include a large congress hall, parade grounds, a Zeppelin landing field, and a magnificent 400,000-seat sports stadium which would become the permanent home of the Olympics.

Standardization programs of all kinds would be implemented throughout Germany and the occupied lands in the fields of banking, the monetary system, taxation, the legal system, meteorology, building codes, housing components, industrial equipment, medical care, and agricultural policies.

The East would become Germany's granary. Grain of all kinds would be grown there by the settlers and by minimally-educated local people who would be deemed suitable for that purpose. The latter would be paid in scarves, glass beads and other items that colonial peoples like. It would be national policy to keep money out of their hands as much as possible.

Windmills would be erected to grind and produce flour on the spot. Spaghetti factories would be built nearby to provide cheap, grain-based food for the local people. Meat and vegetable production would be greatly expanded and such items as citrus fruit, cotton, nettle and rubber would be grown in the Crimea on large plantations. The Black Sea would become Germany's inexhaustible source of sea food. The marshes would be cultivated by planting reeds and used as military training grounds. Honey production would be increased ten fold. In Germany, itself, the production of soy beans and tobacco would be encouraged.

With regard to meteorology, Hitler wanted the reporting of weather conditions taken from the army and put into the hands of a civilian organization that would rely, to a high degree, on the weather-reading skills of Germany's peasant farmers. He had said that these people had a sixth sense in this regard, and could read the weather from the conditions of the sky, the winds, and the flights of midges and swallows.

In the occupied areas, Germany would continue to rule until the future of each area was determined. The on-going effort to Germanize the Czechs would continue, and there, and in certain other areas, racially healthy people would be moved in to help accelerate the process of Germanization. In Holland and Norway, Party schools would be established to train future leaders. In the General Government, the cities of Lublin and Cracow would become German cities and given Germanic names. The Polish population would be compressed into a small area around Warsaw and become a source of laborers for Germany.

In the East, the Crimea and Ingermanland would be settled first. German names would replace the slavic names. Soldiers would be encouraged to become settlers and marry country women of good blood, and group marriages would be encouraged. People of good blood from all over the world would be invited to settle in the East. Even ethnically contaminated Volksdeutsch, and those people considered political renegades, but of good blood, would be accepted as settlers. For the foreseeable future, the settlers, who would be greatly outnumbered by the natives, would be armed for their own protection and strong points would be established to be used as fortresses if necessary. No native militia would be permitted and native police organizations strictly controlled. The goal was to have twenty million settlers in the East in ten years with German the common language for all. The Cyrillic alphabet would be abandoned.

The rail system in the East would be made compatible with that of Germany and specially designed locomotives would be built to withstand the harsh winters. The existing rail lines and roads useful to the Germans would be maintained. The remainder would be allowed to deteriorate to the point where they met only the needs of the local traffic.

The heavily industrialized Donitz Basin in the Ukraine would become one of Germany's main sources for munitions with German-owned factories using local labor.

A program of reforestation would be undertaken for areas of the Ukraine.

In the Caucasus, native administrations would be permitted so long as they were faithful to Germany. The Kontinental Oel Company would be the dominant industrial enterprise in that region.

Muscovy would continue, indefinitely, to be Germany's penal colony for undesirables and would be closed to outsiders. The people of Muscovy would be used as laborers in the area's forests, mines, farms, light industry, etc.

The armed frontier would be moved further to the east whenever possible. Since the agreement with Japan was now null and void, there lacked a reason why the German empire could not expand to the Pacific coast.

Agreements had to be reached with other European nations on such things as telephone and telegraph services, a postal system, passports and visas, air service, customs, the status of Volksdeutsch, and of course, a well-coordinated foreign policy and racial policy. Additional agreements had to be made with the countries bordering the Danube River so that it could become a dependable German waterway to the East.

The German government would have to insist that the governments of the other European nations would be compatible with National Socialism, and that the German language would be the accepted language of business and politics.

All around Germany's borders, monuments would be built at border crossings to inform visitors that they were entering the German Reich.

As for the German family, large families would continue to be encouraged and rewarded with recognition, tax incentives and social benefits. Increasing the population of Greater Germany would remain a top priority for years to come. Several schemes to do this would be employed. Young Ukrainian women of good blood would be made available as domestic servants and encouraged to eventually marry a German man. Similarly, Flemish and Dutch women would be favored as spouses for Germans. German embassies and consulates abroad would be "stuffed" with young unmarried men whose mission would be to find and marry a woman of good blood and bring her back to Germany.

The Liebensborn program would be expanded and made available to the two million surplus German single women of child-bearing age who wanted to have children. Some of the homes would eventually be expanded into villages.

The practice of securing — some said kidnapping — foreign children of good blood and raising them in foster homes or Liebensborn childrens' homes would continue.

In addition, the practice would continue in which the blond and blue-eyed women of the north would be transferred to homes in southern Germany so that their genes would mix with the black-haired, brown-eyed genes of the southern Germans. In Norway, nine Liebensborn homes were already operating.

In Denmark, there were no Liebensborn homes at present, but several were planned for that country when conditions were right. Several homes existed, however, in Holland, Belgium, and France. In France, only children fathered by Germans were accepted in the Liebensborn program. In the General Government, there were no homes, but there were reception centers where kidnapped children from all over the East were assembled and sent on to Liebensborn childrens' homes or adaptive German parents.

Special academies were to be established for selected young German women where they would be trained in Nazi ideology and prepared to be the wives of Nazi leaders and other men of stature. These women would be known as "Exalted Women." ☑

Polygamy was occasionally discussed among the Nazi leaders. One of the strongest proponents of polygamy was Martin Bormann, Hitler's Party Secretary. Bormann had ten children and a mistress that his wife approved of, and who would, most likely, become his second wife if polygamy was adopted. An action of this sort by the Party Secretary would set an example for other Nazi leaders to follow.

🔊 Inheritance laws would be created to insure that the oldest male child would receive the total family inheritance. The others, as Hitler had said, "…would be thrown out into life."

The German educational system, which was already highly Nazified, would continue to be revised. Gifted children would be advanced with the help of the state and such subjects as world history would be rewritten from a racial point of view.

German society would be swept clean of habitual criminals, male homosexuals and other sexual deviants. This would be accomplished by giving out long prison terms, imposing exile to the East or the African colonies, and executions. Female homosexuals would remain free because they were capable of bearing children.

The law profession and judicial system would be nationalized. In this way, the government would have an interest in both sides of any legal question.

The Euthanasia program for the mentally and physically incurable, begun in 1939, would be continued in both Germany and the occupied areas.

Groups of people who proved to be troublesome or politically unreliable, but of good blood, were to be uprooted and dispersed throughout society. If they continued to be a problem, they would be sent to Muscovy or to a concentration camp.

A national cemetery was to be created for Germany's national heros and greatest people.

Radios and television sets throughout Germany and the occupied areas would be wired instead of wireless so that the people would not receive foreign broadcasts.

The German government would be streamlined and the number of bureaucrats greatly reduced. There would be only four taxes; an income tax, a corporate tax, a tax on luxury goods and a stamp tax.

A program would be created to allow peasants to pay their taxes in kind.

Governmental ceremonies would be glamorized and become ceremonies for the public to watch. Here, the Germans would emulate what the British had done in this respect.

Hitler had predicted that Germany's war debt would be paid off in ten years' time. This would be another goal of the Eight-Year plan. ☑

AN INTERCONTINENTAL WAR

On November 19/20, 1945, an American B-29 bomber flew 8,198 miles nonstop from Guam to Washington, DC after having been refueled in the air. This demonstrated that, now, any target in the world could, with air refuelling, be attacked by planes that were capable of carrying atomic bombs. 🔊 This new development gave the Allied representatives in Lisbon a new advantage in their negotiations with the other side.

That advantage did not last long. The development of Germany's two-stage intercontinental rocket was progressing. ☑ It had been scheduled to be operational in November 1945. 🔊 On December 3, the German rocket engineers successfully launched one of these test rockets from Peenamunde, Germany to the Ogaden Desert area on the Ethiopia/Italian Somaliland border, a distance of 3,800 miles. This meant that such rockets launched from Norway could reach the northeastern part of North America. ☑

CHAPTER 27

1946

Compared to the last seven years, 1946 was a welcome year of peace. But peace is relative. There were still many conflicts in the world. Most notably were the Partisans in Russia and the Balkans who were still very much at war with the Axis occupiers. The armed frontier in the East was still a war zone and likely to be so for years. The Swiss were holding out in their mountains and there was active and passive resistance throughout occupied Europe. But these things did not halt the progress of international diplomacy.

Not much progress was being made by the negotiators in Lisbon and it looked as though those negotiations would go on for a very long time.

Both sides remained heavily armed and continued to develop new and more destructive weapons. In this arena, atomic weapons were the most frightening. The Americans were stockpiling atomic weapons and were preparing to conduct a series of atomic bomb tests. The Germans were racing to catch up. East of the Urals, the Communists, too, were pursuing an atomic energy program. ☑

In China, the Nationalists and Communists signed a truce that few people thought would hold. Elsewhere in the Far East there were wars of liberation, many of them communist-led, and there were nationalist movements surfacing throughout the colonial world.

IN GERMANY, RECONSTRUCTION AND A MELLOWING

Germany was a beehive of activity. Rebuilding the bomb-damaged cities and the country's badly damaged infrastructure were top priorities.

In Berlin, Chancellor Speer's influence was beginning to be felt. He added a new position to his cabinet, the Ministry of Colonies, to manage the affairs of Germany's newly-acquired overseas colonies. Rosenberg's Eastern Ministry remained and dealt exclusively with matters in the East. And Rosenberg, himself, was becoming more influential as Nazi attitudes toward their conquered subjects began to show signs of mellowing. The Speer government recognized that there was no more need for harsh rhetoric of the past that had kindled the fires of war. The war had been won; Germany's enemies had been vanquished; it was time to move ahead; and Speer had Hitler's support. ☑

Hitler had foreseen this moment. In June 1943, he told his associates, "One cannot rule by force alone. True force is decisive, but it is equally important to have this psychological something which the animal trainer also needs to be master of his beast." And, in Mein Kampf, Hitler had written, "For in the long run, government systems are not maintained by the pressure of violence, but by faith in their soundness and in the truthfulness with which they represent and advance the interests of the people."

MELLOWING IN THE EAST

🔊 The political and economic future for the East had, for the most part, already been decided. Now, it was time to win the support of the people. Those people who cooperated would be rewarded, those who remained in opposition would be punished. And large numbers of people would be relocated to serve the needs of the new colonial empire, but it appeared that this process would be long and drawn out.

The displacement of people would be more rapid in the Crimea, however, because this territory was to be annexed by Germany in the very near future. ☑

Steps had already been taken to soften the official attitude toward easterners. In 1944, certain easterners working in Germany, such as the Crimean Tartars, were reclassified as "western workers" which increased both their living conditions and wages. Also in 1944, several Soviet communal farms had been converted into cooperatives in which the members could keep their profits and rewarded for exceeding their quotas. This program had met with considerable success.

The wartime experience had shown that the people of Ostland, many of whom were racially acceptable Balts, had been cooperative. 🔊 This Reichscommissariat would be given a high priority in the near future in the doling out of perks and privileges. This had already begun. ☑ By the end of hostilities about 20% of the land confiscated by the Soviets had been returned to private ownership.

🔊 Similar things would be done in the Ukraine, especially the western Ukraine (Galicia).

The people of the Caucasus would, as planned, be allowed to pursue their own destinies within the limitations imposed upon them from Berlin.

In Muscovy, and along the armed frontier, wartime conditions continued. There were those in the Speer administration, however, who saw this as a lengthy and expensive burden on the German economy and suggested ways to reduce it. It was suggested that an amnesty program be instigated for those Partisans and Soviet soldiers who wished to surrender. ☑ A step in this direction had already been taken when, in May 1944, an order was issued that captured Partisans would, henceforth, be treated as prisoners of war. Heretofore, they had been executed upon capture.

Furthermore, amnesty programs had been offered, on occasions, to the Partisans in Yugoslavia with some success.

🔊 There were those in the Speer government who questioned the whole dumping process in Muscovy on the grounds that it simply created more Partisans and was an embarrassment to the German government. Other ways to deal with undesirables were being considered.

Service in Muscovy was very unpopular with the German soldiers and Waffen SS men who referred to themselves as "prison guards." Much to the dismay of the government, these people brought home very unpleasant stories of what was happening there. Not surprisingly, these stories made their way into foreign circles.

As for improving relations with the West, several of Speer's advisors suggested that cultural exchanges be started in sports and the theater. With regard to the latter, it was suggested that certain foreigners, influential in the field of music, be invited to the annual Bayreuth Music Festival, and the Bruckner Music Festival in Linz when it came into being. Another suggestion was that German opera companies be sent on tour in the west and that musical groups, such as the Glen Miller Orchestra, be invited to tour Germany. ☑ Miller's music had become quite popular with the German soldiers during the war.

🔊 Then there was the matter of the Olympics ☑ which were last held in Germany in 1936, and were scheduled to be held in Helsinki, Finland in 1940. The Finns had built a stadium for the event, but the onset of war forced the cancellation of the Olympics. 🔊 Speer entertained suggestions that Germany, by virtue of having been the last Olympic host, take the initiative in planning the next one. Since it was Germany's hope that future Olympics would be held permanently in Germany, a friendly action now would cast Germany into a leading role with regard to the Olympic program's future. Another suggestion put forth was that ☑ Sonja Heine, the pretty Norwegian girl who had won the gold medal in figure skating in 1936 and was now a famous movie star in America, be invited back to Norway and be encouraged to tour Europe with her ice show.

These suggestions on cultural exchanges and the Olympics were put to Hitler ☑ who had often attended such functions in the past. 🔊 But now, the Fuehrer made it clear that his attendance could not be counted upon because of his health problems, and that Speer and Goering should assume that role. He added that Goering would love it. ☑

LENINGRAD

Hitler had said on many occasions in his evil and hateful manner that, after the war, he would level both Moscow and Leningrad. The question remained as to whether or not he really meant it, or that it might have been another of his hate-inspired outbursts against the communists.

🔊 In any case, both schemes were impractical. Hitler had come to realize that in the case of Moscow. That city would have to be utilized as an administrative center for Muscovy and a stronghold against the Partisans. The administrative center for all Muscovy was centered in the ancient fortress to the Kremlin, and to many Russians, whoever ruled in the Kremlin, ruled in Russia.

Leningrad, though, was different. The Germans did not need it for administrative or military purposes and there were discussions on razing the city. Speer, however, saw the folly in this and prepared a plan to save the city. ☑

Previously, the Leningrad area had been offered to the Finns, but they declined the offer on the grounds that the area had never been a part of Finland and that its acquisition by Finland would only cause another negative situation with the Russians. Then too, the Finns had no interest in acquiring a vast field of rubble.

🔊 Thus, Speer had to address the problem head on. His plan began with the premise that certain elements of the city would had to be preserved under any circumstances. Mainly, because of its location at the mouth of the Neva River, it would have to continue to function as some sort of a commercial and transportation center. Then too, it was illogical to destroy the city's utilities, especially its power plants, which provided electrical power to most of the region.

Speer did agree, however, that the city was much too large for Germany's needs and that it could be reduced in size to match its usefulness.

Speer further suggested that the city could become an interesting tourist destination, especially for the Strength-Through-Joy program. This was calculated to attract the Fuehrer's attention because ☑ he had long been interested in tourism and believed that Germany's tourist industry was lopsided because of, as he had put it, "...the lure of the south." Here was an opportunity to lure tourists to the north.

🔊 Speer's plan suggested that the city's important structures, such as the Hermitage (the Tsar's imperial palace), be preserved and opened to the public. Speaking as an architect, Speer added that a historical connection could be made between the city and Germany because many of the city's most important buildings had been designed and built by Germans. This was a not-too-subtle appeal to Hitler's interests in architecture. This point was driven home further by the suggestion that the city could become a destination for German architectural students on how to design and build major buildings for northern climates.

There was another historical connection between the city and Germany that could be made. It could be emphasized, Speer suggested, that Catherine the Great, a German by birth, be given a positive Germanic image. ☑ Catherine had spent much of her life in the city and had ruled all of Russia from there. This would fit in with what Hitler had written in Mein Kampf; "...the organization of the Russian state...was not the result of the political abilities of the Slavs… but only a wonderful example of the state-forming efficacy of the German element in an inferior race."

🔊 And finally, Speer's plan offered a suggestion designed solely to stroke the Fuehrer's ego. It suggested that the city be renamed "Hitlerhafen" to serve as a perpetual memorial to the fact that it was Hitler's philosophy and will that had eventually triumphed over the city's founder, Peter the Great, and the city's usurper, Lenin.

The plan concluded with the suggestion that, in order to keep the city functioning as a historic memorial, it be detached from the Ostland and become a "Hauptbezirk," (a district directly under the control of the German government).

Speer circulated this plan among the top Nazi leaders and found considerable support. Goering, Goebbels, Papen, Rosenberg, Ley (head of the Strength-Through-Joy program) and others approved. Himmler and Bormann opposed it.

Speer then presented the plan to Hitler personally along with a verbal explanation. Hitler studied the plan for several days and finally gave his approval. Leningrad would become Hitlerhafen.

ITALY

Mussolini had no intentions of retiring. He intended to stay on as long as possible to direct Italy's new destiny and her new empire. That empire, however, was fraught with problems. In the Balkans, the Partisans were as strong as ever and there were still territorial disputes with Bulgaria. In the new states of Croatia and Serbia, the rulers there continued to maintain their strong ties with Germany ☑ which had been the case all through the war. 🔊 The task of replacing that influence with Italian influence would be difficult.

In the Middle East, there were problems in every country. Much of this had been brought about by Rome's own doing. ☑ In July 1940, Rome had promised independence to the countries of the region, and now, Rome was under pressure to make good that promise.

The city of Leningrad was renamed Hitlerhafen, reduced in size to became a regional commercial and transportation center and a tourist destination. The surrounding area was put under the direct control of the German government in Berlin.

🔊 Pressure was particularly strong from Syria and Lebanon. ☑ These countries had been granted independence by the French although that independence had not been fully implemented. 🔊 The leaders of those countries now pressed Rome to confirm their French-granted independence and abide by Italy's promise of July 1940 which, in their opinions, confirmed that independence. ☑

Trans-Jordan, too, had been promised independence by the British, 🔊 and the leaders in Amman besieged Rome for answers with regard to their political status.

In Palestine, the arrival of the Mufti, and the establishment of a Palestinian Authority under his leadership, had united most, but not all, of the various Arab factions because there were those Arabs in Palestine who continued to follow their local leaders. Also, there were the Jewish nationalist who had vowed to fight on. A solution for the problems in Palestine were nowhere in sight. The Italians had gained a country, but had inherited a big problem. In the meantime, the Italian Army had to plan on a commitment of an unknown duration to keep the peace in Palestine.

The prospect of ridding Palestine of its Jewish population was not an option. There was no place to send them. The Italians had never preached, as had the Germans, that their Jews would be sent to the East. Italy's "East" were the Muslim states of Iraq and Iran. Nor could the Palestinian Jews be sent off to Germany, ☑ as had been done with Italian Jews on several occasions during the war. ♟ The Germans did not want them now, even in Muscovy, and, of course, the death camps, according to Berlin, had never existed. ☑

In Iraq, the Italians had previously acknowledged the independence of the Gailani government during the war. ♟ But the country was still very much under Italian military control. The reason given was that the Italian Army had to remain in the country to guard against a possible Allied attack from Bahrain where the Allied military strength remained strong. This angered the Iraqis along with the fact that they had not been given Kuwait. But Kuwait was too valuable a colony to give away. There, the Italians were running the country and its oil industry to suit, and enrich, themselves.

Another problem in Iraq was that the country had lost its world oil market and its only major customer now was Italy. And it was Rome, not Baghdad, that was dictating oil production limits and prices.

Next door in Iran, that country was still under military occupation and without its own government, and the Italians were doing as they pleased with the country's oil. Rome had acknowledged that Iran would, once again, be an independent country, but little progress was being made to bring this about. The Italians claimed that Iranian independence could not be guaranteed until the British were expelled from the southeastern part of the country. The prospect of this happening any time soon was remote. It was further pointed out by the Italians that if a new and friendly government was established in Tehran, the British might set up a rival government in their area. It was made known by the British that plans for this were being made and that the new state would be called "Free Iran."

Then too, the Italians insisted, some sort of Italian military presence would have to remain in Iran permanently to guard Italy's section of the armed frontier with the Soviet Union. All of these things made the Iranians a very unhappy lot.

In Italy's newly-won North African empire, Tunisia and the eastern part of Algeria were still under Axis military control which was strongly dependent on a continuing German presence. Southern Libya was in the hands of the Fighting French and the Egyptians were not at all happy with the situation in their country.

In East Africa, the Djibouti Redoubt remained a major military threat and the Ethiopian guerrillas continued to cause problems in that country's western mountains. Ethiopian Emperor Haile Selassie had reestablished his government in the Ethiopian city of Harawa, just inside the Djibouti Redoubt, and many Ethiopians remained loyal to him and were openly resentful of the Italians.

On the positive side, the Germans were helping the Italians build new and improve existing roads, railroads and communications throughout East Africa because the Germans badly needed them to maintain communications with their newly liberated colonies of Rwanda, Urundi and Tanganyika, and their newly conquered British colonies of Kenya and Uganda.

Another positive development in East Africa was that both the Germans and Italians were preparing sites to grow rubber, coffee, cocoa and other products of the tropics. These projects provided employment for many Africans, as well as the prospects for continued employment once these resources were developed. Therefore, there was no great problem with unemployment in East Africa as there was in other parts of the Italian empire. Nevertheless, the rebellious spirit of nationalism was growing in East Africa and there was an undercurrent of rebellion.

And rebellion was on the rise all around the world. It was becoming clear that colonialism was on the decline and that Italy and Germany were going against that trend.

In the Mediterranean, the Allies still ruled the waters of the western Mediterranean and Spain was now a friend of the Axis in name only. Strong Italian forces were being maintained in Sicily, Corsica, Sardinia and Italy itself to guard against possible Allied attacks if the Lisbon talks should fail.

Then there were concerns with regard to the three important islands in the eastern Mediterranean, Malta, Crete and Cyprus. ☑

Malta, just south of Sicily and in one of the most sensitive parts of the Mediterranean, had been a bastion of the British strength throughout the war and its people had suffered heavily under the onslaught of Axis air attacks. As a result, there was anger in Malta toward the Italians. Furthermore, the British had promised the island its independence after the war and were following through with that promise. This was in conflict with Italy who had long-standing claims to the island.

♙ It was very likely that Malta would gain its independence, look upon Britain as a friend and Italy as an adversary. It was likely, too, that the island would remain a way station on Britain's sea route to the Far East, and continue to have a strong British military presence. Furthermore, by granting Malta its independence, Britain was setting a precedent that could only complicate Italy's relationships with their subject countries in the region. ☑

Crete, a part of Greece, had been occupied by the Germans and Italians since its conquest in 1941. An arrangement had been worked out whereby the Italians occupied the eastern fourth of the island and the Germans occupied the remainder. Italy had long claimed the island but knew that they would have to grant major concessions to the Germans to fulfill that claim.

♙ The Italians would have the added problem of gaining the loyalty of the Greek-speaking islanders.

As a result of all this, Crete remained occupied. ☑

The situation on Cyprus, as has been mentioned, was a four-way struggle between the Greek-speaking majority; the Turkish-speaking minority; the British colonial overlords; and the former overlords of the island, Turkey. Cast into this dilemma were the thousands of Palestinian Jews living in refugee camps on the island.

♙ The future for Cyprus was ambiguous, at best.

FRANCE

France was exactly where Hitler and Mussolini wanted it to be — weak, divided, and no longer a threat.

The Petain government remained in Vichy, but most of the French governmental offices had moved back to Paris. ☑ This process began in April 1944. France, for all intents and purposes, was now a vassal state with no army and no empire.

♙ In Algiers, de Gaulle's Provisional Government of France controlled all of France's empire and had a large army. The latter, however, was primarily made up of colonial troops and was dependent on American Lend Lease for its war supplies. ☑ As for the French empire, there were growing signs of nationalism in many places, and in French Indo China (Viet Nam) there already was open revolt.

A THREE WAY COLD WAR

♙ With a diplomatic solution to the war beginning to appear ever more remote, and with both the Axis and Allies still heavily armed and rapidly developing new and more powerful weapons, the threat of war still remained. In some circles, this grey area between war and peace was now being called a "cold war." And, with the Soviet Union and world-wide communism still showing signs of resilience, the cold war was being viewed as a three-sided struggle between the Allies, the Axis, and the communists. ☑

A GESTURE OF COOPERATION

During March 1946, outright civil war erupted in China. This was a war between the Chinese Nationalist regime of Chiang Kai-shek, a regime that had many fascist-like features, and the communists under Mao Tse-tung. The Soviets openly supported the communists while the western powers, especially the United States, supported the Nationalists.

Into this melee stepped the Germans who made an offer to send aid to the Nationalists. This offer had a precedent because in the 1930s, prior to China's going to war with Japan, the Germans had sent some military aid to the Nationalists. In yet a more recent precedent, the Allied military government in Japan delayed the withdrawal of the Japanese occupation forces in China and allowed them to cooperate with the Nationalists against the communists.

Germany's offer of aid was declined, but it was significant in that Berlin had made a gesture of cooperation with the Allies against the communists.

Could it be that this was an indication of what was to come?

THE OLD GUARD

With Hitler now in retirement and new people running the government in Berlin, the members of Hitler's old guard had to face, anew, their respective futures. Since Speer had been Hitler's hand-picked successor, they were expected to now transfer their loyalties to the new Chancellor. This they did, but at the same time they looked toward new horizons for themselves.

Goering was satisfied with his exalted position as President of the Reich and that his millions were safely stashed away. He now had the glory, but not the grief, of government, and he was not too displeased with the name that the German people were calling him behind his back; "Kaiser Hermann I."

Goebbels, as he had done all through his political career, emulated his Fuehrer. He turned the reigns of his Ministry of Propaganda over to his trusted aid, Hans Fritzche, and went into semi-retirement. He retained for himself two positions. The first was that of Gauleiter of Berlin so that he could oversee the rebuilding of the city, and the second was that of being the Tsar of Germany's entertainment industry. Goebbels had long had a fascination with movies and the theater and liked to be in the company of show business people — especially young starlets. It was widely rumored that he was highly proficient at couch-casting and, in the late 1930, it was well known that he had a beautiful Czech actress as a mistress. That relationship ended, though, when Goebbels' wife, Magda, threatened to divorce him. At that point Hitler intervened and ordered the amorous doctor to give up the mistress. Goebbels did as his leader ordered, but then began to avail himself of the industry's starlets and the unique opportunities available to him.

Ribbentrop, whose place at the Foreign Ministry was taken by Papen, retired to the country. He was having some health problems and had told several people that when his days in politics were over he would like to become a country gentleman.

Field Marshal Keitel, Hitler's yes-man, was sent off to retirement. Hitler had no more need of him — nor did Speer.

General Jodl, who had served Hitler faithfully throughout the war, became the chief liaison officer between Hitler and Speer. Jodl totally ignored Goering whom he disliked.

Then there was Himmler with whom Speer had clashed on several occasions during the war. Himmler was a relatively young man — forty-six, and he had no interests in retiring. Because of his highly unsavory image, though, Hitler ordered him to fade into the background while negotiations with the Allies were in progress. He was allowed, however, to retained full control of his powerful SS organization. Himmler did as his Fuehrer ordered. He withdrew quietly to his confiscated castle in Bohemia-Moravia, where the SS security apparatus held sway and the protectorate had become Himmler's own personal fiefdom.

Himmler, not surprisingly, was an outsider in the Speer administration and, in addition to this, had become a person to be feared. If there was anyone in Nazi Germany who could force his way to power it was Himmler. And, it must be remembered that ☑ his predecessor, Ernst Roehm had threatened to do just that and that Himmler had eliminated Roehm with his own hand.

🔊 Himmler would not make the mistakes that Roehm had made. At every turn, he professed absolute loyalty to both Hitler and Speer. But Speer and the others could see the danger. As a result, a silent conspiracy began to form around Speer with the aim of reducing Himmler's power. The conversion of the SS into police units was a good start, but even as policemen, these people were still under Himmler's command.

From Speer's perspective, the only force in Germany that was able to counter the strength of Himmler's SS was the army. But herein lay a problem. ☑ Hitler had ordered the Nazification of the armed forces after the war which would make it subordinate to the Party rather than to the government. 🔊 If this happened, and with the SS already under the control of the Party, Himmler and his close friend, Party Secretary Martin Bormann, would propel themselves into an unassailable position of power.

Speer and his associates could not let this happen under any circumstances. It was imperative that the government retain control of the armed forces and, at the same time, work to reduce the strength of the SS. Therefore, the invisible battle lines were drawn within the Nazi leadership.

Speer, in cooperation with Papen, Rommel and others, took steps to delay the Nazification of the armed forces. First and foremost was the retention in the armed forces of high-ranking professional officers who were opposed to a takeover by the Party. Fortunately for Speer, they were numerous. Some of those retained were Field Marshals Ewald von Kleist, Gunther von Kluge, Wilhelm List, Erhard Milch, Walther Model, Friedrich von Paulus, and Generals Ludwig Beck, Dietrich von Choltitz, Heinz Guderian, Franz Halder, and Colonel Claus von Stauffenberg. Grand Admiral Doenitz had demonstrated his loyalty to Speer and was retained as commander of the Navy. Goering was not included in the silent conspiracy, but it was presumed that, in a show down, he would side with Speer because a take-over by Himmler would threaten his exalted position. ☑ Furthermore, Goering did not like Himmler.

🔊 Professional officers known, or suspected of being pro-Nazi, were retired. These included Field Marshals Albert Kesselring, Erich von Manstein, Gurd von Runstedt, and Generals Otto Skorzeny and Walther Warlimont.

Undoubtedly, Hitler could see the potential schism within the Nazi leadership, but he did not take sides. His actions, however, indicated that he supported Speer. After all, it was Speer that he had chosen to lead Germany and not Himmler.

Hitler's favoritism toward Speer was demonstrated when he approved of Speer's suggestion that the size of the Waffen SS be reduced and that some of its military roles be assigned to the regular Army. Justification for this was based on the fact that ☑ a large number of the Waffen SS troops were foreigners and many were non-Aryans. Under Nazi racial theory, these non-Aryans would be more acceptable within the German army than within the SS which was an arm of the Nazi Party and which, by its very nature, sought to maintain racial purity within its ranks.

🔊 In addition, Hitler approved Speer's suggestion that Waffen SS operations against the Partisans in the East be reduced and turned over to the Army. In the Balkans, Hitler agreed to phase out the Waffen SS role there altogether and turn over the security of the region to the Italians. The German Army, however, would remain in the Balkan to insure the security of Germany's communications links between the homeland and the outposts at Salonica, Domotika and the Aegean islands.

Hitler did not commit himself on Speer's suggestion that the military role of the SS be gradually eliminated altogether. Hitler was firm in his belief that the Waffen SS should remain, albeit, in reduced strength. He tended to agree with Speer, though, that the organization might be renamed the "Armed State Police."

Another of Speer's suggestions that Hitler approved was that the word "Gestapo" be abandoned in favor of a more police-sounding name. He suggested "The State Bureau of Investigation."

This then, was the atmosphere in Berlin — one of polarization between the moderates and the hard-liners. In all likelihood, this would continue as long as Hitler was alive. But, when Hitler passed from the scene, there was a real danger that Himmler might make a bid for power. Himmler, who was in good health and eleven years younger than Hitler, would almost certainly outlive Hitler and still be a viable threat when Adolf Hitler passed on to his great reward.

This undercurrent of mistrust did not bode well for the future of Nazi Germany.

But then, ☑ such is the nature of police-state dictatorships.

🔊 *IN EARLY OCTOBER*

On May 2, 1946, the German news media announced that Eva Hitler and the Fuehrer were expecting a baby. The due date was early October. Eva was thirty-four. The father-to-be was fifty seven. ☑

THE END — FOR NOW

BIBLIOGRAPHY

ABBOTT, PETER, & NIGEL THOMAS, *Germany's Eastern Front Allies, 1941-45*, Osprey Pub., Ltd., London, 1982.

ALBERTINI, RUDOLF von, *Decolonization: The Administration and Future of the Colonies, 1919-1960*, Africana Pub. Co. NY 1982.

AMERY, L.S., MP, *The German Colonial Claims*, Longmans, Green & Co., NY 1940.

ANDENAES, O. RISTE, & M. SKODVIN, *Norway and the Second World War*, Tanum-Norge, Norway, 1983.

ANDERS, LT. GEN. WLADYSLOV, *Russian Volunteers in Hitler's Army 1941-45*, Axis Europa, NY 1957.

ATTANISIO, SALVATOR, Translated by, *Hitler's Secret Book*, Bramhall House, NY 1986.

BAILEY, RONALD H., ed. *Partisans & Guerrillas*, Time-Life Books, 1978.

BAUR, LT. GEN. HANS, *Hitler at My Side*, WW II Books & Video, Montecello, IL 1986.

BELOW, NICOLAS VON, *At Hitler's Side*, Greenhill Books, London 2000.

BENGSTON, ROBERT, PhD., *Nazi War Aims: The Plans for the Thousand Year Reich*, Augustana College, Lib. Rock Island, IL 1962.

BOYD, BARBARA, *Hitler's Route to Baghdad*, Books for Libraries Press, Freemont, NY, 1971.

BROGAN, PATRICK, *The Fighting Never Stopped*, Random House, NY 1990.

BUKEY, EVAN BURR, *Hitler's Home Town: Linz, Austria*, Indiana Univ. Press, Bloomington, 1986.

BUTLER, RUPERT, *The Black Angels — A History of the Waffen SS*, St. Martin's Press, NY 1979.

CAMERON, NORMAN, & R. H. STEVENS, Translated by, *Hitler's Table Talk*, 1941-1944, Enigma Books, NY, 2000.

CHAMBERLAIN, PETER, & HILARY DOYLE, *Encyclopedia of German Tanks of World War II*, Arms & Armour, London, 1999.

CHURCHILL, WINSTON, AND THE EDITORS OF LIFE, *The Second World War*, Golden Press, NY 1960.

COLLIER, RICHARD, *Duce: The Life and Death of a Dictator*, Viking Press 1971.

COHEN, MICHAEL J., & MARTIN KOLINSKY, ED., *Demise of the British Empire in the Middle East: Britain's Response to Nationalist Movements 1943-45*, Frank Cass Pub., London 1998.

COHEN, STAN, *The Games of '36: A Pictorial History of the 1936 Olympics in Germany*, Pictorial Histories Pub., Missoula, MT 1996.

CONOT, ROBERT. E., *Justice at Nuremberg*, Carroll & Graf, Pub. Co., 1984.

CONWAY, MARTIN, *Collaborators in Belgium: Leon Degrelle and the Rexist Movement 1940-44*, Yale Univ. Press, New Haven, and London 1993.

DALLEN, ALEXANDER, *German Rule in Russia, 1941-45: A Study in Occupation Policies*, Westview, Press, Boulder, CO 1981.

De GAULLE, CHARLES, *The Call to Honor, 1940-42; War Memories*, Viking Press, NY 1955.

DELMER, SEFTON, *Weimar Germany: Democracy on Trial*, Lib. of 20th Century, London, 1972.

DeJONG, LOUIS, *The Netherlands and Nazi Germany*, Harvard Univ. Press, Cambridge, MA, 1990.

DEUTSCH, HAROLD, & DENNIS SHOWALTER, *What If? Alternative Strategies to World War II*, Emperor's Press, Chicago, 1997.

DEZEL, CHARLES F., *Mediterranean Fascism 1919-1945*, Walker & Co., NY 1970.

DOWNING, DAVID, *The Devil's Virtuoso: German General at War 1940-45*, St. Martin Press, NY 1977.

DUIGNAN, PETER, & L.H. GANN, *World War II: Causes, Course & Consequences*, Stanford, Univ. Press 1984.

ELLIS, JOHN, *From the Barrel of a Gun*, Stackpole Books, PA 1995.

ENGELMANN, JOACHIM, *V2: Dawn of the Rocket Age*, Schiffler Pub., West Chester, PA 1990.

ETHELL, JEFFREY, & ALFRED PRICE, *The German Jets in Combat*, Jane's NY 1979.

FEST, JOACHIM C., *Hitler*, Harcourt Brale Jovanovich, NY 1973.

FRANKLIN, DR. NOBLE, *Encyclopedia of Twentieth Century Warfare*, Mitchell Beazley Pub., NY 1989.

FRIHEDSMUSEETS VENNER MUSEUM, *Danmark 1940-1945*, Kopenhavn, 1984.

FURLONG, PATRICK J., *Between Crown & Swastika: The Impact of the Radical Right on the Afrikaner National Movement in the Fascist Era*, Wesleyan University Press, Hanover 1991.

GALLO, MAX, *Mussolini's Italy: 20 years of the Fascist Era*, MacMillan Pub. Co., NY 1973.

GODA, NORMAN J. W., *Tomorrow the World: Northwest Africa and the Path Toward America*, Texas A & M Press, College Station, TX 1998.

GOSLING, F.G., *The Manhattan Project: Making of the Atomic Bomb*, History Div. of Depart. of Energy, 1994.

GREENFIELD, RICHARD, *Ethiopia: A New Political History*, Fredrich A. Praeger Pub., NY 1965.

HALBROOK, STEPHEN P., *Target Switzerland, Swiss Armed Neutrality in World War II*, Sarpedon, Rockville Ctr., NY 1998.

HALL, LUELLA, *The United States and Morocco*, Scarecrow Press, Metuchen, NJ 1971.

HAYS, JR., OTIS, *The Alaska-Siberia Connections: The WW II Air Route*, Texas A & M Press, 1996.

HAYWOOD, JOHN, *Historical Atlas of the Twentieth Century*, Barnes & Noble Books, NY 2000.

HECK, ALFONS, *A Child of Hitler: Germany in the Days When God Wore a Swastika*, Renaissance House, Frederich, CO 1985.

HENSHALL, PHILIP, *Vengeance — Hitler's Nuclear Weapon: Fact or Fiction*, Alan Sutton Pub, Ltd. London 1995.

HESS, WILLIAM H., *German Jets Versus the U.S. Air Force*, Specialty Press, North Branch, MN 1996.

HEVESI, EUGENE, "Hitler's Plan for Madagascar", article in *Contemporary Jewish Record* V4, N4, Aug. 1941.

HIGGINS, TRUBULL, *Soft Underbelly*, MacMillan, Co. NY 1968.

HILDEBRAND, KLAUS, *The Foreign Policy of the Third Reich*, Univ. of Calif. Press, Berkeley, CA 1970.

HIRSZLOWICZ, LUKASZ, *The Third Reich and the Arab East*, London Univ. of Toronto Press, 1966.

HITLER, ADOLF, *Mein Kampf*, The Houghton Miffin Co., 1971.

HOWELL, EDGAR M., *The Soviet Partisan Movement 1941-44*, Dept. of Army Pamphlet No. 20-244, Aug. 1956.

IRVING, DAVID, *The Secret Diaries of Hitler's Doctor*, MacMillan Pub. Co., NY 1983.

JACKEL, EBERHARD, *Hitler's World View: A Blueprint for Power*, Harvard Univ, Press, 1981.

JURADO, CARLOS CABALLERO, *Foreign Volunteers in the Wehrmacht 1941-45*, Osprey Pub. Ltd., London 1983.

KIRBY, D.C., *Finland in the Twentieth Century*, C. Hurst & Co. London, 1979.

KOCKLER, ANTHONY, *Haile Selassie's War — The Italian-Ethiopian Campaign, 1935-41*, Random House, NY 1984.

LAFFIN, JOHN, *Hitler Warned Us: The Nazis' Master Plan for the Master Race*, Brassey's, London, Washington, 1970.

LANG, SERGE, & ERNST von SCHENCK, *Memoirs of Alfred Rosenberg*, Ziff Davis Pub. 1949.

LATTIMER, JOHN K. MD., *Hitler's Fatal Sickness and Other Secrets of the Nazi Leadership*, Hippocrene Books, NY 1999.

LEMKIN, RAPHAEL, *Axis Rule In Occupied Europe: Laws of Occupation, Analysis of Government, Proposals for Redress*, Carnegie Foundation, Washington, DC 1944.

LITTLEJOHN, DAVID, *Foreign Legions of the Third Reich: Vol. 3., Albania, Czechoslovakia, Greece, Hungary, Yugoslavia*, R. James Bender pub., San Jose, CO 1985.

— *The Patriotic Traitors: The History of Collaboration in German-occupied Europe 1940-45*.

LOCHNER, LOUIS P., EDITED & TRANSLATED *The Goebbels Diaries*, Doubleday & Co., 1971.

MALLET, ROBERT, *The Italian Navy and Fascist Expansion 1935-1940*, Frank Cass Pub., London & Portland, OR., 1998.

MARRUS, MICHAEL R., *The Unwanted: European Refugees in the Twentieth Century*, Oxford Univ. Press, Oxford, ny 1985.

MESKILL, JOHANNA MENZEL, *Hitler & Japan: The Hollow Alliance*, Atherton Press, NY 1966.

MILLER, MARSHALL LEE, *Bulgaria During the Second World War*, Stanford University, 1975.

MORISON, SAMUEL ELIOT, *The Battle of the Atlantic Sept. 1939-May 1943*, Little Brown & Co., Boston, 1966.

— *Operations in North African Waters October 1942-June 1943*, Little, Brown & Co., Boston, 1947.

MUGGERIDGE, MALCOLM, ED., TRANSLATED BY STUART HOOD, *Ciano's Diplomatic Papers*, Odham Press, Ltd. London 1948.

MULLALLY, FREDERIC, *Hitler Has Won* (a novel), Simon & Schuster, NY 1975.

MUNOZ, ANTONIO J., *Lions of the Desert: Arab Volunteers in the German Army 1941-45*, Axis Europa, Bayside, NY.

NEKRICH, ALEKSANDR M., *The Punished People*, W.W. Norton, NY 1975.

OSBORNE, RICHARD E., *World War II in Colonial Africa*, Riebel-Roque Pub. Co., Indianapolis, IN 2001.

OVERY, RICHARD, *The Penguin Historical Atlas of the Third Reich*, Penguin Books, NY 1996.

PACKARD, JERROLD M., *Neither Friend Nor Foe: The European Neutrals in WW II*, Chas. Scribners' Sons, NY 1992.

PAGE, MALCOMB, *A History of the King's African Rifles and East African Forces*, Leo Cooper, London 1998.

PANHURST, SYLVIA, *Ex-Italian Somaliland*, Greenwood Press, NY 1951.

PAXTON, ROBERT. O., *Vichy France: Old Guards & New Order 1942-44*, Alfred A. Knopf, NY 1972.

PIMLOTT, JOHN, *Historical Atlas of World War II*, Henry Holt Reference Books, NY 1995.

PINE, LISA, *Nazi Family Policy 1933-1945*, Oxford Univ. Press, Oxford & NY 1997.

POCOCK, ROWLAND F., *German Guided Missiles of the Second World War*, AMSE Arco Pub. Co. NY 1967.

POTEN, EDWARD von der, *The Germany Navy in WW II*, Ballantine Books, NY 1974.

POWERS, THOMAS, *Heisenberg's War: The Secret History of the German Bomb*, Little, Brown & Co., NY 1993.

READY, J. LEE, *World War II Nation by Nation*, Arms & Armour Press, London, 1995.

REDLICH, FRITZ, MD., *Hitler: Diagnosis of a Destructive Prophet*, Oxford Univ. Press, NY and Oxford, 1999.

RICH, NORMAN, *Hitler's War Aims*, W. Norton & Co., NY 1973.

ROHWER, JURGEN, *Axis Submarine Successes 1939-1945*, Naval Institute Press, Annapolis, 1983.

SALMAGG, CESARE, & ALFREDO PALLAVISINI, *2194 Days of War: An Illustrated Chronology of the Second World War*, Gallery Books, NY 1977.

SCHECHTMAN, JOSEPH B., *European Population Transfers 1939-1945*, Oxford Univ. Press, NY 1946.

SCHENCK, DR. ERNEST GUNTHER, *Hitler's Final Days Recalled*, American Medical News (Newsletter), 1985.

SHIRER, WILLIAM L., *The Collapse of the Third Republic*, Simon & Schuster, NY 1969.

SHORES, CHRISTOPHER, *Dust Clouds in the Middle East: The Air War for East Africa, Iraq, Syria, Iran and Madagascar 1940-42*. Grub Street, London 1996.

SMITH, DENIS MACH, *Mussolini's Roman Empire*, Penguin Books, NY 1977.

SPEER, ALBERT, *Inside the Third Reich*, Avon Books, Div. of. Hearst Corp., NY 1971.

SUTHERLAND, DOUGLAS, *The Great Betrayal: The Definitive Story of Blunt, Philby, Burgess and Maclean*, Times Books, NY 1980.

TIERE, WILHELM, *The Caucasus and the Oil: The German-Soviet War in the Caucasus 1842/43*, J.J. Fedorowitz Publishing Co., Winnipeg, Canada, 1995.

TOYNBEE, ARNOLD & VERONICA, *Hitler's Europe*, Oxford Univ. Press London & Toronto, 1954.

— *The Realignment of Europe*, Oxford Univ. Press, London, Toronto & NY 1955.

— *The War and the Neutrals*, Oxford Univ. Press, London,, Toronto, NY 1956.

TREVOR-ROPER, H.R., *Blitzkrieg to Defeat: Hitler's War Directives, 1939-1945*, Holt, Rinehart & Winston, NY 1964.

— *Final Entries 1945: The Diaries of Joseph Goebbels*, Avon Pub., NY 1979.

TURNER, HENRY ASHBY, *German Big Business and the Rise of Hitler*, Oxford Univ. Press, 1985.

UNESCO, *Africa and the Second World War*, Imprimerie des Presses Universtaires de France, Verdome 1985.

VAJDO, FERENC A., AND PETER DANCEY, *German Aircraft Industry and Production 1933-1945*, SAE Intl., Warrendale, PA 1998.

VERE-HODGE, EDWARD REGINALD, *Turkish Foreign Policy 1918-48*, Impreimerie Franco-Suisse, 1950.

WAITE, ROBERT. G. L., *The Psychopathic God: Adolf Hitler*, DaCape Press, NY 1993.

WEINBERG, GERHARD L., *The Foreign Policy of Hitler's Germany*, Univ. of Chicago, Press 1970.

WEINBERG, ROBERT, *Stalin's Forgotten Zion*, Univ. of Calif. Press 1998.

WEINSTEIN, ALLEN & ALEXANDER VASSILIEV, *The Haunted Wood: Soviet Espionage in America*, Modern Library, NY 1999.

WIEDNER, DONALD L., *A History of Africa South of the Sahara*, Random House, NY 1962.

INDEX